iPhone® Application Development

ALL-IN-ONE

FOR

DUMMIES®

iPhone® Application Development

ALL-IN-ONE

FOR DUMMIES®

by Neal Goldstein and Tony Bove

WILEY

Wiley Publishing, Inc.

iPhone® Application Development All-in-One For Dummies®

Published by
Wiley Publishing, Inc.
111 River Street
Hoboken, NJ 07030-5774

www.wiley.com

Copyright © 2010 by Wiley Publishing, Inc., Indianapolis, Indiana

Published by Wiley Publishing, Inc., Indianapolis, Indiana

Published simultaneously in Canada

For general information on our other products and services, please contact our Customer Care Department within the U.S. at 877-762-2974, outside the U.S. at 317-572-3993, or fax 317-572-4002.

For technical support, please visit www.wiley.com/techsupport.

Wiley also publishes its books in a variety of electronic formats. Some content that appears in print may not be available in electronic books.

Library of Congress Control Number: 2010924562

ISBN: 978-0-470-54293-4

Manufactured in the United States of America

10 9 8 7 6 5 4 3 2 1

WILEY

About the Authors

Neal Goldstein is a recognized leader in making state-of-the-art and cutting-edge technologies practical for commercial and enterprise development. He was one of the first technologists to work with commercial developers at firms such as Apple Computer, Lucasfilm, and Microsoft to develop commercial applications using object-based programming technologies. He was a pioneer in moving that approach into the corporate world for developers at Liberty Mutual Insurance, USWest (now Verizon), National Car Rental, EDS, and Continental Airlines, showing them how object-oriented programming could solve enterprise-wide problems. His book (with Jeff Alger) on object-oriented development, *Developing Object-Oriented Software for the Macintosh* (Addison Wesley, 1992), introduced the idea of scenarios and patterns to developers. He was an early advocate of the Microsoft .NET framework, and successfully introduced it into many enterprises, including Charles Schwab. He was one of the earliest developers of Service Oriented Architecture (SOA), and as Senior Vice President of Advanced Technology and the Chief Architect at Charles Schwab, he built an integrated SOA solution that spanned the enterprise, from desktop PCs to servers to complex network mainframes. (He holds three patents as a result.) As one of IBM's largest customers, he introduced them to SOA at the enterprise level and encouraged them to head in that direction. He is currently leading an iPhone startup that is developing an application that will radically change how people can use iPhones to manage information.

Tony Bove is crazy about the iPhone, and not only provides free tips on his Web site (www.tonybove.com) but also took the plunge to develop an iPhone application (*Tony's Tips for iPhone Users*). Tony has written more than two dozen books on computing, desktop publishing, and multimedia, including *iPod and iTunes For Dummies* (Wiley), *Just Say No to Microsoft* (No Starch Press), *The Art of Desktop Publishing* (Bantam), and a series of books about Macromedia Director, Adobe Illustrator, and PageMaker. Tony founded *Desktop Publishing/Publish* magazine and the *Inside Report on New Media* newsletter, and wrote the weekly Macintosh column for *Computer Currents* for a decade, as well as articles for *NeXTWORLD,* the *Chicago Tribune* Sunday Technology Section, and *NewMedia*. Tracing the personal computer revolution back to the 1960s counterculture, Tony produced a CD-ROM interactive documentary in 1996, *Haight-Ashbury in the Sixties* (featuring music from the Grateful Dead, Janis Joplin, and Jefferson Airplane). He also developed the Rockument music site, www.rockument.com, with commentary and podcasts focused on rock music history. As a founding member of the Flying Other Brothers, which toured professionally and released three commercial CDs, Tony performed with Hall of Fame rock musicians. Tony has also worked as a director of enterprise marketing for leading-edge software companies, as a marketing messaging consultant, and as a communications director and technical publications manager.

Dedication

Neil Goldstein: To my wife, Linda. Without her, I never would have been able to write four books in the last year. She deserves special recognition for her support, patience, and maintaining her (and my) sense of humor. I've got to be the luckiest guy in the world. Thank you.

Tony Bove: Tony dedicates this book to his sons, nieces, nephews, their cousins, and all their children . . . the iPhone generation.

Authors' Acknowledgments

Neil Goldstein: Thanks to my friend Jeff Elias for the San Francisco photographs used in the RoadTrip application. Also thanks to my business partners, Jeff Elias and Jeff Enderwick, for their support and picking up the slack while I was engaged in finishing this book. Carole Jelen, agent extraordinaire, helped keep things together during some interesting challenges.

Senior Acquisitions Editor Katie Feltman was a delight to work with, as always. Her management skills and in-depth understanding of our readers' needs really helped focus this book. Paul Levesque has got to be the best Project Editor of all times, both because of his skills and his continued willingness to put up with me. Copy Editor Virginia Sanders did a great job in helping me make things clearer. Technical reviewer Glenda Adams, yet again, added a great second pair of eyes.

Tony Bove: Tony owes thanks and a happy hour or two to Carole Jelen at Waterside for agenting, to Maggie Canon for putting the authors together, and to Kathy Pennington for support.

Publisher's Acknowledgments

We're proud of this book; please send us your comments at http://dummies.custhelp.com. For other comments, please contact our Customer Care Department within the U.S. at 877-762-2974, outside the U.S. at 317-572-3993, or fax 317-572-4002.

Some of the people who helped bring this book to market include the following:

Acquisitions, Editorial, and Media Development

Senior Project Editor: Paul Levesque

Acquisitions Editor: Katie Feltman

Copy Editor: Virginia Sanders

Technical Editor: Glenda Adams

Editorial Manager: Leah Cameron

Media Development Project Manager: Laura Moss-Hollister

Media Development Assistant Project Manager: Jenny Swisher

Media Development Associate Producers: Josh Frank, Marilyn Hummel, Douglas Kuhn, and Shawn Patrick

Editorial Assistant: Amanda Graham

Sr. Editorial Assistant: Cherie Case

Cartoons: Rich Tennant (www.the5thwave.com)

Composition Services

Project Coordinator: Katherine Crocker

Layout and Graphics: Amy Hassos, Joyce Haughey, Christine Williams

Proofreaders: Laura Albert, Evelyn C. Gibson

Indexer: Rebecca R. Plunkett

Publishing and Editorial for Technology Dummies

Richard Swadley, Vice President and Executive Group Publisher

Andy Cummings, Vice President and Publisher

Mary Bednarek, Executive Acquisitions Director

Mary C. Corder, Editorial Director

Publishing for Consumer Dummies

Diane Graves Steele, Vice President and Publisher

Composition Services

Debbie Stailey, Director of Composition Services

Contents at a Glance

Table of Contents

Introduction

When Apple introduced the iPhone Software Development Kit (SDK) in 2008, the iPhone and iPod touch suddenly became the handheld computers they were meant to be. Interest in the SDK exceeded Apple's expectations — in fact, Apple's servers supplying the beta for the first SDK download were overwhelmed.

Since then, the App Store has grown to become the repository of over 140,000 applications, which collectively are driving innovation beyond the reach of other mobile devices. The success of the App Store — over *three billion downloads* — has turned the iPhone into the premier mobile device for publishing software. All the leading mobile applications typically appear on the iPhone first, and as a reader of this book, you may be creating the next one.

As I continue to explore the iPhone as a new platform, I keep finding more possibilities for applications that never existed before. The iPhone or iPod touch is a mobile computer, but not like a mobile desktop. Its hardware and software make it possible to wander the world, or your own neighborhood, and stay connected to whomever and whatever you want to. It enables a new class of here-and-now applications that give you access to content-rich services and let you view information about what's going on around you and where you are, and interact with those services or with others on the Internet.

One of the hallmarks of a great iPhone application is that it leverages the iPhone's unique hardware, especially its ability to know where the user is. The iPhone SDK includes tools such as MapKit, which makes it much easier to use the location-based features of the iPhone in an application. MapKit makes it possible for even a beginning developer to take full advantage of the location hardware, and I've included the code for an example app (called RoadTrip) to show you how. And the frameworks supplied in the SDK are especially rich and mature. All you really have to do is add your application's user interface and functionality to the framework, and then "poof" . . . an instant application.

If you're familiar with the first version of the SDK, you're in for a pleasant surprise: The latest version of the SDK, which includes Xcode 3.2.2, is a lot, lot better and easier to use. What's really hard, after you've learned your way around the SDK and its various framework, is figuring out how to create a structure for the iPhone application's data and models for the logic of how the application should work. Although there are lots of resources, the problem is exactly that: There are *lots* of resources — as in *thousands* of pages of documentation! You may get through a small fraction of the documentation before you just can't take it anymore and plunge right into coding. Naturally enough, there will be a few false starts and blind alleys until you find your way, but I predict that after reading this book, it will be (pretty much) smooth sailing.

That's why, when the *For Dummies* folks asked me to combine all the knowledge and wisdom I could muster to write these minibooks on developing software for the iPhone, I jumped at the chance. Here's the definitive tome that I wish I had for a reference myself when I started developing iPhone software.

Editor's note: Both authors (Tony and Neal) have published applications for the iPhone — you can find several of Neal's apps, including *ReturnMeTo,* in the App Store, along with Tony's app, *Tony's Tips for iPhone Users.*

About This Book

iPhone Application Development All-in-One For Dummies is more than just a beginner's guide to developing iPhone applications — it's also a concise reference work on programming with Objective-C. And not only do you *not* need any iPhone development experience to get started, you don't need any Macintosh development experience either. I expect you to come as a blank slate, ready to be filled with useful information and new ways to do things.

Because of the nature of the iPhone, you can create small, bite-sized applications that can be really powerful. And because you can start small and create real applications that do something important for a user, it's relatively easy to transform yourself from "I know nothing" into a developer who, though not (yet) a superstar, can still crank out quite a respectable application.

But the iPhone can be home to some pretty fancy software as well — so I take you on a journey through building an industrial-strength application and show you the ropes for developing one on your own.

This book distills the hundreds (or even thousands) of pages of Apple documentation, not to mention our own development experiences, into only what's necessary to start you developing real applications. But this is no recipe book that leaves it up to you to put it all together; rather, it takes you through the frameworks and iPhone architecture in a way that gives you a solid foundation in how applications really work on the iPhone — and acts as a roadmap to expand your knowledge as you need to.

It's a multicourse banquet, intended to make you feel satisfied (and really full) at the end.

Conventions Used in This Book

This book guides you through the process of building iPhone applications. Throughout, you use the provided iPhone framework classes (and create new ones, of course) and code them with the Objective-C programming language.

Code examples in this book appear in a monospaced font so they stand out a bit better. That means the code looks like this:

```
#import <UIKit/ UIKit.h>
```

In addition, code that you need to enter is set in bold, and code you need to delete is set in regular type with a strikethrough, as follows:

```
#import <UIKit/ UIKit.h> // Add this line to your code
```

```
#import <UIKit/ UIKit.h> // Delete this line to your code
```

Objective-C is based on C, which (I want to remind you) *is* case-sensitive, so please enter the code that appears in this book *exactly* as it appears in the text. This book also uses the standard Objective-C naming conventions — for example, class names always start with a capital letter, and the names of methods and instance variables always start with a lowercase letter.

All URLs in this book appear in a monospaced font as well:

```
www.nealgoldstein.com
www.tonybove.com
```

If you're ever uncertain about anything in the code, you can always look at the source code on Neal's Web site at `www.nealgoldstein.com`. From time to time, he provides updates for the code there, and posts other things you might find useful. (You can find a mirror image of Neal's site at `www.dummies.com/go/iphoneappdevaio`, if you happen to be strolling through the `dummies. com` site.) Tony offers tips about everything from developing to marketing apps at `www.tonybove.com`.

Foolish Assumptions

To begin programming your iPhone applications, you need an Intel-based Macintosh computer with the latest version of the Mac OS on it. (No, you can't program iPhone applications on the iPhone.) You'll also need to download the iPhone Software Development Kit (SDK) — which is free — but you do have to become a registered iPhone developer before you can do that. (Don't worry; I show you how in Chapter 3 of Book I.) And, oh yeah, you'll need an iPhone. You won't start running your application on it right away — you'll use the Simulator that Apple provides with the iPhone SDK during the initial stages of development — but at some point, you'll want to test your application on a real, live iPhone (and possibly also an iPod touch).

This book assumes that you have some programming knowledge and that you have at least a passing acquaintance with object-oriented programming, using some variant of the C language (such as C++, C#, or maybe even Objective-C). If not, we point out some resources that can help you get up to speed. The examples in this book are focused on the frameworks that come with the SDK; the code is pretty simple (usually) and straightforward. (I don't use this book as a platform to dazzle you with fancy coding techniques.)

This book also assumes that you're familiar with the iPhone itself and that you've at least explored Apple's included applications to get a good working sense of the iPhone look and feel. It would also help if you browse the App Store to see the kinds of applications available there, and maybe even download a few free ones (as if I could stop you).

How This All-in-One Book Is Organized

iPhone Application Development All-in-One For Dummies has seven minibooks.

Book 1: Creating the Killer App

Book I introduces you to the iPhone world and gives you the fundamental background that you need to develop iPhone applications. You find out what makes a great iPhone application, and how an iPhone application is structured. You also find out how to become an "official" iPhone developer and what you need to do in order to be able to distribute your applications through Apple's App Store. You find out how to download the Software Development Kit (SDK) — and then you unpack all the goodies contained therein, including Xcode (Apple's development environment for the OS X operating system) and Interface Builder. (You'll soon discover that the latter is more than your run-of-the-mill program for building graphical user interfaces.) I show how everything works together, which should give you a real feel for how an iPhone application works.

Book II: Objective-C and iPhone Technologies

Book II gives you a rundown on everything you need to know about Objective-C to write iPhone applications. Its focus is on the right way to structure your application — what's known as the *program architecture*. Having the right architecture results in an application that not only works but also can be extended to add new functionality (relatively) easily. And not only that, it enables you to easily track down and fix those pesky bugs that make their home in everyone's apps. I also show you how to deal with the mundane, but necessary, plumbing issues such as memory management and object initialization. You even find out some of the tricks that programmers use to extend frameworks to offer highly specific functionality.

Book III: Building a Utility App — DeepThoughts

With Objective-C basics behind you and a good understanding of the iPhone application architecture under your belt, it's finally time to have some fun doing something useful. In this minibook, I show you how to create an application that is simple enough to understand and yet demonstrates enough of the building blocks for creating a sophisticated app. I show you how an app fits into the user SDK-supplied frameworks that do all of the user interface heavy lifting on the iPhone. And because you design the app the right way from the start, you can plug it into the user interface with minimal effort by creating the interface in the Interface Builder (part of the SDK) and adding a few lines of code. No sweat, no bother. Putting this handy little app together will give you some practice at creating a useful utility application that allows your application's users to add preferences and settings. It's a great application to learn about iPhone development — it has enough features to be useful as an example, but simple enough not to make your head explode.

Book IV: Debugging and Tuning Your Application

Bugs can show up in your application in different forms and wreak different kinds of havoc with your programming efforts. As the nearly immortal Mr. Spock (the one from the planet Vulcan) once said, "Logic is the beginning of wisdom, not the end." And if Spock ever heard about Murphy's Law (that anything that *could* go wrong *will* go wrong), he'd probably reply, "Fascinating!" And yet, debugging is not considered fascinating — often it's something to put off until later, after the warnings and error messages pile up. (Perhaps you recall the classic *Star Trek* episode, "The Trouble with Tribbles.") This book sets you on the illuminated path of self-debugging. You find out how to recognize bugs in the Xcode editor and, most importantly, what to do about them. You get all the details about how to use the Debugger to track bugs, how to set breakpoints in your code to stop execution and examine the gory details, how to detect memory leaks, and how to fine-tune your app with the Instruments application.

Book V: Building an Industrial Strength Application — RoadTrip!

Book V introduces you to an iPhone application that contains lots and lots of functionality you can borrow for your app. I show you how to design an application with lots of data, views, and access to the Web. I don't go slogging through every detail, but I demonstrate almost all the technology you need to master if you're going to create a compelling application like this on your own. I also touch on a few advanced topics, such as creating self-config-uring objects so you don't find your classes multiplying like rabbits.

Book VI: Storing and Accessing Data

Book VI shows you how to deal with data using property lists, the URL Loading System, and Core Data. You learn how to download data for your app from a Web server, so you can update the data at any time and add new infor-mation. You also get an in-depth look at using dictionaries to hold property list objects and application objects. This minibook also takes you on a march through an array using a new language feature of Objective-C 2.0 called *fast enumeration* — starting at the first data element and returning each element for processing — which is an essential function of many applications.

Book VII: Extending the App to the Realm of Ultracool

Book VII takes the RoadTrip app out to the ever-expanding galaxy of iPhone functionality. You find out how to use data from the Contacts app in your app, display the standard e-mail view inside your app to manage editing and sending e-mails, and Core Location to find out exactly where the iPhone is located. At the end of this minibook, you should be ready to go out and con-quer the world with your app.

Because the application I develop in Books V–VII has lots of functionality, I won't be able to show you of all of the code in each of the books. But have no fear, because the listings for each minibook are available at www. dummies.com/go/iphoneappdevaio as well as on Neal's Web site at www.nealgoldstein.com.

Icons Used in This Book

This icon indicates a useful pointer that you shouldn't skip.

This icon represents a friendly reminder. It describes a vital point that you should keep in mind while proceeding through a particular section of the chapter.

This icon signifies that the accompanying explanation may be informative (dare I say, interesting?), but it isn't essential to understanding iPhone appli-cation development. Feel free to skip past these tidbits if you'd like (though skipping while leaning may be tricky).

This icon alerts you to potential problems that you may encounter along the way. Read and obey these blurbs to avoid trouble.

Where to Go from Here

Feel free to begin reading this book anywhere or skip particular minibooks or chapters (or go really wild and start on page 1 and continue reading to the Index). If you want to know how to tackle a particular task, look it up in the Index or Table of Contents and flip to the page you need. This is your book; dive right in.

Book I

Creating the Killer App

The 5th Wave   By Rich Tennant

"It's like any other pacemaker, but it comes with an internal iPhone docking accessory."

Contents at a Glance

Chapter 1: What Makes a Killer iPhone App

In This Chapter

✔ Figuring out what makes an insanely great iPhone application

✔ Discovering the features of the iPhone that can inspire you

✔ Facing the limitations you have to live with

✔ Understanding Apple's expectations for iPhone applications

✔ Making a plan for developing iPhone software

Faced with the complexity and the utter hopelessness of the situation, John Belushi in *Animal House* bellowed "Road trip!" In that movie, their plans were a no-brainer — just grab the beer and go — but for most people, preparation would be a bit more complicated. You'd need to gather all the maps, the hotel and campground brochures, the flyers and postcards that describe the places you want to visit, the most recent weather report for the areas you are traveling through, the schedule of appointments you need to keep, and your car's service records and vehicle ID, and throw all this stuff in the front seat . . .

Or just take your iPhone and the RoadTrip application (also known as the *app*) that this All-in-One book shows you how to create. To give you insight to the iPhone application-development process, this book describes how to develop and publish two apps: the simple and straightforward DeepThoughts, which is a meditative app that co-author Neal wrote in a frenzy one afternoon (too much caffeine that day?), and the more industrial-strength RoadTrip, which Neal developed in response to his daughter's 7,000 mile road trip.

The advantages you have with an iPhone app are more than just the difference between fumbling with papers and maps versus using an electronic device that stores everything. With an iPhone, an app can present information that is *relevant at that moment* — relevant to where you are, what time it is, and what your next activity might be. Because the iPhone platform offers a strong foundation for these functions, the app already knows your current location, the hotels or campgrounds you are going to stay at, and the sites you are planning to visit. Rather than pulling off the road and searching maps and brochures, you can know at a glance where you are, how to get to your destination, and what the weather's like so that you know what to wear (as shown in Figure 1-1).

Figure 1-1:
The RoadTrip app (see Book V) can present info that's relevant to where you are at any moment of your trip.

The iTunes App Store is loaded with travel apps, so you know already that finding apps like this one is not a fantasy. You may think it a fantasy that you could develop such an app in less than two months, starting from where you are now, with no iPhone programming experience. But you can — the only question is whether you can make a *great* app, or even a *killer* app. To do that, you need to look at what it takes for an iPhone app to be truly great.

Figuring Out What Makes a Great iPhone Application

In the App Store, you can find over 140,000 apps that take you far beyond the Stocks, Maps, Weather, Contacts, Calendar, YouTube, and other apps preinstalled by Apple on the iPhone. Popular social networks such as Facebook and MySpace offer apps to connect you with your friends on those services. Google offers an array of services through the Google Mobile app, including the ability to edit documents and spreadsheets, use the Gmail service, and share calendars and photos. Twitterific lets you post tweets on Twitter, and WhosHere and SKOUT can connect you directly to other iPhone users for chatting. Newspapers, book readers, shopping helpers, streaming music players, fitness calculators . . . the list goes on and on.

Most apps are designed to take advantage of the iPhone's multitouch display; accelerometer (which detects acceleration, rotation, motion gestures, and tilt); or GPS for detecting its physical location — or all three. Motion X Poker is actually a dice game that uses the accelerometer to let you roll the dice by shaking the iPhone. The Flick Fishing app senses motion so you can cast a fishing line with a flick of the wrist. Location is very important:

Showtimes uses your iPhone's location to show the closest movie theaters; Eventful uses it to display local events and venues; and Lethal can tell you the dangers that might surround you, such as the hostile animals, the likelihood of crimes, the prevalence of disease, and the potential accidents and disasters.

These apps fall along a continuum, which at one end might be called the *mobile desktop,* and at the other end a *mobile here-and-now experience.* The mobile desktop apps are ones you might use if you wanted to do the kinds of things you normally do with your computer but didn't have it handy — applications you could *port to* (rewrite for) the iPhone. For example, you might already have Weather, Stocks, Twitter apps, and book reader apps on your MacBook Pro, and it doesn't take any major imaginative leap to see how one can do these things on an iPhone. Although I can't write this book on an iPhone, it's still handy for note taking, searching, blogging, social networking, and stock-trading.

At the other end of this continuum are apps that serve a need that a desktop (or even a laptop) can't handle well, either because you don't want to carry the hardware around with you or because, even if you did, using it that way would be way too inconvenient. Imagine being at Heathrow Airport, dead tired, taking out your laptop in the middle of a crowded terminal, powering it up, launching the application, and then navigating through it with the touchpad to get the information you need — which you can now get while holding the iPhone in one hand. You want that kind of information quickly and conveniently; you don't want to have to dig your way to it through menus or layers of screens (or even going through the hassle of finding a wireless Internet connection). Seconds count. By the time any road warrior tied to a laptop did this at Heathrow, you should already be on the Heathrow Express.

With *here-and-now* apps, you want to do a specific task with up-to-date information, which the iPhone can access over the Internet through a cell network or Wi-Fi connection. You may even want the information or tasks tailored to where you are, which the iPhone can determine with its location hardware.

Somewhere in the middle of this continuum, most likely closer to the mobile desktop side, are apps that best-selling author Seth Godin would call *meatball sundaes* — "the unfortunate result of mixing two good ideas," according to his book *Meatball Sundae: Is Your Marketing out of Sync?* (Portfolio Hardcover). If the meatballs are the things I need, the commodities that so many businesses are built on, then the sundae toppings are the new marketing techniques, social networks, blogs, and fancy stuff that make people excited. But slapping them together doesn't make a good sandwich or a dessert. It doesn't work to take an old product, apply it to a new medium, and expect success.

With all that in mind, there are at least two things that you need to consider — besides functionality, of course — when it comes to creating a great iPhone app:

✦ Exploiting the platform

✦ Creating a compelling user experience

The rest of this chapter and Chapter 2 of this minibook dig more into this Two-Part Rule of Great iPhone Applications.

Exploiting the Platform

The iPhone's unique combination of software and hardware gives you the power to create an app that lets users do something that may not be practical (or even possible) with a laptop computer. Although the iPhone is a smaller, mobile personal computer, it isn't a replacement for one. It isn't intended to produce formatted documents or well-crafted spreadsheets (although some apps work with documents and spreadsheets). The iPhone has the capability to be an extension of the user, seamlessly integrated into his or her everyday life. With it, you can accomplish a singly focused task or step in a series of tasks, in real time, based on where you are.

Device-guided design

Although the enormous capabilities of the iPhone make it possible to deliver a necessarily compelling user experience, you must take into account the limitations of the device as well. Keeping the two in balance is *device-guided design.* The next two sections describe both the features and limitations of the iPhone — and how to take them into account as you plan and develop an app. But understanding these constraints can also inspire you to create some really innovative apps. After a closer look at device-guided design, I come back to what makes a compelling user experience.

Exploiting the features

One of the keys to creating a great app is taking advantage of what the device offers. In the case of a new platform with new possibilities, such as the iPhone, this is especially important. Think about the possibilities that open up to you when your app can easily do the following:

✦ Access the Internet.

✦ Know the location of the user.

✦ Track orientation and motion.

✦ Track the action of the user's fingers on the screen.

+ Play audio and video.

+ Access the user's contacts.

+ Access the user's pictures and camera.

Accessing the Internet

The ability to access Web sites and servers on the Internet gives you the ability to create apps that can provide real-time information. An app can tell a user, for example, that the next tour at the Tate Modern in London is at 3 p.m. This kind of access also allows you, as the developer, to go beyond the limited memory and processing power of the device and access large amounts of data stored on servers, or even offload the processing. You don't need all the information for every city in the world stored on your iPhone, and you don't need to strain the poor CPU to compute the best way to get someplace on the Tube. You can send the request to a server and have it do all that work.

This is *client-server computing* — a well-established software architecture where the client provides a way to make requests to a server on a network that's just waiting for the opportunity to do something. A Web browser is an example of a client accessing information from other Web sites that act as servers.

Knowing the location of the user

The iPhone operating system (OS) and hardware lets you create an app that can determine the device's current location or even be notified when that location changes. As people move, it may make sense for your app to tailor itself to where the user is, moment by moment.

Many iPhone apps use location information to tell you where the nearest coffee house is or even where your friends are. The RoadTrip application uses this information to tell you where *you* are and give you directions to your hotel.

When you know the user's location, you can even put it on a map, along with other places he or she may be interested in. In Chapter 3 of Book V, I show you how easy that really is.

Tracking orientation and motion

The iPhone contains three *accelerometers* — devices that detect changes in movement. Each device measures change along one of the primary axes in three-dimensional space. An app can, for example, know when the user has turned the device from vertical to horizontal, and it can change the view from portrait to landscape if doing so makes for a better user experience.

You can also determine other types of motion such as a sudden start or stop in movement (think of a car accident or fall) or the user shaking the device back and forth. (What's Shakin' uses this feature to give you a percussion instrument.) It makes some way-cool features easy to implement — for example, the Etch-A-Sketch metaphor of shaking a device to reset it, and controlling a game by moving the iPhone like a controller.

Tracking the action of the user's fingers on the screen

People use their fingers, rather than a mouse, to select and manipulate objects on the iPhone screen. The moves that do the work, called *gestures,* give the user a heightened sense of control and intimacy with the device. Several standard gestures — taps, pinch-close and pinch-open, flicks, and drags — are used in the applications supplied with the iPhone.

I suggest strongly that you use *only* the standard gestures in your app. Even so, the iPhone's multitouch hardware and software allow you to go beyond standard gestures when appropriate. Because you can monitor the movement of each finger to detect gestures, you can create your own, but use that capability sparingly — only when it's undoubtedly the right thing to do in your application.

Playing audio and video

The iPhone OS makes it easy to play and include audio and video in your app. You can play sound effects or take advantage of the multichannel audio and mixing capabilities available to you. You can also play back many standard movie file formats, configure the aspect ratio, and specify whether controls are displayed. This means your app not only can use the iPhone as a media player, but can also use and control prerendered content. Let the games begin!

Accessing the user's contacts

Your app can access the user's contacts on the iPhone and display that information in a different way or use it as information in your application. As a user of the RoadTrip application, for example, you can enter the name and address of your hotel, and the application files it in your Contacts database. That way, you have ready access to the hotel address, not only from RoadTrip, but also from Phone and other applications. Then, when you finally arrive in San Francisco, the application can retrieve the address from Contacts and display directions for you.

Accessing the user's pictures and camera

As with Contacts, your app can also access the pictures stored on the user's phone, not only to display them, but also to use or even modify them. For example, the Photos app supplied with your iPhone lets you add a photo to a contact, and several applications enable you to edit your photos on the iPhone itself. You can also incorporate the standard system interface to actually use the camera as well.

Embracing the iPhone's Limitations

Along with all those features, however, the iPhone has some limitations. The key to successful app development — and to not making yourself too crazy — is to understand those limitations, live and program within them, and even learn to love them. (It can be done. Honest.) These constraints help you understand the kinds of applications that are right for this device.

Often, it's likely that if you *can't* do something (easily, anyway) because of the iPhone's limitations, then maybe you shouldn't.

So learn to live with and embrace some facts of iPhone life:

✦ The small screen

✦ Users with fat fingers

✦ Limited computer power, memory, and battery life

The next sections can help get you closer to this state of enlightenment.

Living with the small screen

Although the iPhone's screen size and resolution allow you to deliver some amazing apps, it's still pretty small. Yet while the small screen limits what you can display on a single page, all you need to perform is some mental jujitsu to really think of it as a feature.

When your user interface is simple and direct, the user can understand it more easily. With fewer items in a small display, users can find what they want more quickly. A small screen forces you to ruthlessly eliminate clutter and keep your text concise and to the point (the way you like your books, right?).

Designing for fingers

Although the multitouch interface is an iPhone feature, it brings with it limitations as well. First of all, fingers aren't as precise as a mouse pointer, which makes some operations difficult (text selection, for example). User-interface elements need to be large enough (Apple recommends that anything a user has to select or manipulate with a finger be a minimum of 44 x 44 pixels in size) and spaced far enough apart so that users' fingers can find their way around the interface comfortably.

You also can do only so much using fingers. You definitely have a lot fewer options using fingers than you do using the combination of multibutton mouse and keyboard.

Because it's so much easier to make a mistake using just fingers, you also need to ensure that you implement a robust — yet unobtrusive — Undo mechanism. You don't want to have your users confirm every action (it makes using the app tedious), but on the other hand, you don't want your app to let anybody mistakenly delete a page without asking, "Are you *sure* this is what you *really* want to do?" Lost work is worse than tedious.

Another issue around fingers is that the keyboard isn't that finger-friendly. Using the keyboard is not up there on the list of things I really like about iPhones. So instead of requiring the user to type some information, Apple suggests that you have a user select an item from a list. But on the other hand, the items in the list must be large enough to be easily selectable, which gets back to the first problem.

But again, like the small screen, this limitation can inspire (okay, may force) you to create a better app. To create a complete list of choices, for example, the developer is forced to completely understand the context of what the user is trying to accomplish. Having that depth of understanding then makes it possible to focus the app on what's essential, eliminating anything that's unnecessary or distracting. It also serves to focus the user on the task at hand.

Balancing limited computer power, memory, and battery life

As an app designer for the iPhone, you have several balancing acts to keep in mind:

✦ Although significant by the original Macintosh's standards, the computer power and amount of memory on the iPhone are limited.

✦ Although access to the Internet can mitigate the power and memory limitations by storing data and (sometimes) offloading processing to a server, those Internet operations eat up the battery faster.

✦ Although the power-management system in the iPhone OS conserves power by shutting down any hardware features that are not currently being used, a developer must manage the trade-off between all those busy features and shorter battery life. Any app that takes advantage of Internet access using Wi-Fi or the 3G network, core location, and a couple of accelerometers is going to eat up the batteries.

The iPhone OS is particularly unforgiving when it comes to memory usage. If you run out of memory, it will simply shut down your app. This just goes to show that not *all* limitations can be exploited as "features."

Why Develop iPhone Applications?

Because you can. Because it's fun. And because the time has come (today!). Developing iPhone apps can be the most fun you've had in years, with very little investment of time and money (compared with developing for platforms like Windows). Here's why:

✦ **iPhone apps are usually bite-sized, which means they're small enough to get your head around.** A single developer — or one with a partner and maybe some graphics support — can do them. You don't need a 20-person project with endless procedures and processes and meetings to create something valuable.

✦ **The apps are crisp and clean, focusing on what the user wants to do at a particular time and/or place.** They're simple but not simplistic. This makes application design (and subsequent implementation) much easier and faster.

✦ **The free iPhone Software Development Kit (SDK) makes development as easy as possible.** This All-in-One book reveals the SDK in all its splendor and glory. If you can't stand waiting, you *could* go on to Chapter 1 of Book III, register as an iPhone developer, and download the SDK . . . but (fair warning) jumping the gun leads to extra hassle. It's worth getting a handle on the ins and outs of iPhone app development beforehand.

The iPhone has three other advantages that are important to you as a developer:

✦ **The App Store.** Apple will list your app in the App Store in the category you specify, and it will take care of credit-card processing, hosting, downloading, notifying users of updates, and all those things that most developers hate doing. Developers name their own prices for their creations; Apple gets 30 percent of the sales price, with the developer getting the rest.

✦ **Apple has an iPhone developer program.** To get your app into the store, you have to pay $99 to join the program. (An enterprise pays $299.) But that's it. There are none of the infamous hidden charges that you often encounter, especially when dealing with credit-card companies. Go to the Apple iPhone Developer site (`http://developer.apple.com/iphone/ program`) and click the Enroll Now button. Chapter 5 of this minibook describes how to work with the App Store to get your apps published.

✦ **It's a business tool.** The iPhone has become an acceptable business tool, in part because it has tight security as well as support for Microsoft Exchange and Office. This happy state of affairs expands the possible audience for your application.

Developing with Apple's Expectations in Mind

Just as the iPhone can extend the reach of the user, the device possibilities and the development environment can extend your reach as a developer. It helps to understand Apple's perspective on what iPhone apps should be — the company clearly has done some serious thinking about it far longer than anybody else out there, having taken years to bring the iPhone to market under a veil of secrecy.

So what does Apple think? Spokespeople often talk about three different application styles:

✦ **Productivity applications use and manipulate information.** The RoadTrip app is an example, and so are Travel Kit, Bento, Dropbox, Documents To Go, and Print n Share. Common to all these apps is the use and manipulation of multiple types of information. (I'm not talking about the Productivity category in the App Store — that's a marketing designation.)

✦ **Utility applications perform simple, highly defined tasks.** The preinstalled Weather app is an example — it deals only with the weather data — and so is RedLaser, which scans barcodes. The DeepThoughts app is considered a utility, as it performs a simple, highly defined task. (Again, I'm not talking about the Utilities category in the App Store, although many of those apps are considered utility apps because they perform simple, highly defined tasks.)

✦ **Immersive applications are focused on delivering — and having the user interact with — content in a visually rich environment.** A game is a typical example of an immersive application.

Although these categories help you understand how Apple thinks about iPhone apps (at least publicly), don't let them get in the way of your creativity. You've probably heard *ad nauseam* about stepping outside the box. But hold on to your lunch; the iPhone "box" isn't even a box yet. So here's a more extreme metaphor: Try diving into the abyss and coming up with something really new.

An Overview of the Development Cycle

To keep from drowning in that abyss, you need a plan to guide you through it. Socrates anticipated software development when he said that there's nothing stable in human affairs. Tacitus, with more data in hand 450 years later, saw that in all things there is a law of cycles. By the late 1960s, the Jefferson Airplane were singing, "go with the natural flow, like water off a spinning ball."

In plain words, your software development plan is a cycle; perhaps a vicious cycle, but it can be a cycle through the park. You may repeat procedures within the cycle iteratively until you get it right, but the key to understanding the cycle is the recognition that once you spin off version 1 of your app, you start all over again to develop an update.

In general terms, the software development cycle is the process of creating or altering a software product or service. Theorists have created models and methodologies for defining this cycle. Although there are at least half a dozen models (Neal's a recovering software development methodologist), the one I go through here is pretty simple and is well suited for the iPhone to boot. Here goes:

1. Defining the problems

2. Designing the user experience

    a. Understanding the real-world context

    b. Understanding the device context

    c. Categorizing the problems and defining the solutions

3. Creating the program architecture

    a. A main view

    b. Content views

    c. View controllers

    d. Models

4. Writing the code

5. Doing it until you get it right

Of course, the actual analysis, design, and programming (not to mention testing) process has a bit more to it than this — and the specification and design definitely involve more than what you see in this book. But from a process perspective, it's pretty close to the real thing. It does give you an idea of the questions you need to ask — and have answered — in order to develop an effective iPhone application.

A word of caution, though. Even though iPhone apps are smaller and much easier to get your head around than, say, a full-blown enterprise service-oriented architecture, they come equipped with a unique set of challenges. Between the iPhone platform limitations and the high expectation of iPhone users, you'll have your hands full.

The Sample Applications

It's hard enough to understand how to develop an app, and even harder if the first example you turn to is too complex to get your head around. The first sample app, DeepThoughts (shown in Figure 1-2), is simple enough to understand, and yet it demonstrates enough of the building blocks for creating a sophisticated app that you should have no trouble following along and building it. With a little more (although not much more) work, you can use the development environment to actually create something of value.

DeepThoughts displays whatever text you enter on the iPhone screen in a flowing animation supposedly suggesting a meditative state (as in "peace love groovy music"). It can also display a second page animated with whatever photo you select in the Photo library on your iPhone.

Figure 1-2: This book will provoke Deep-Thoughts.

After you know a bit more about the application design cycle and what makes a good user interface, and even more (actually quite a bit more) about the iPhone technologies that work behind the screen — such as frameworks, windows, views, and view controllers — and then just a few more details about getting your app ready for the App Store and the public, you're ready to plunge into Objective C, and do some coding — the DeepThoughts app.

After that, you find out about the design of the RoadTrip app, starting in Book V. You find out how to use table views (like the ones you see in the Contacts, iPod, Mail, and Settings apps that come with the iPhone); access data on the Web; go out to (and return from) Web sites while staying in your app; store data in files; include data with your app; allow users to set preferences; and even how to resume your app where the user last left off. The book even covers localization and self-configuring controllers and models. (Don't worry; by the time you get there, you'll know exactly what they mean.) And Book V shows you how easy it is to create a map (in RoadTrip) that is tailored to the needs of the users based on what they are doing and where they are.

What's Next

You must be raring to go now and just can't wait to download the Software Development Kit (SDK) from the iPhone Developers Web site. That's exactly what many new developers do — and later are sorry that they didn't spend more time upfront understanding the iPhone user experience, how applications work in the iPhone environment, and the guidelines that Apple enforces for apps to be approved for the App Store.

So be patient. The following chapters of Book I cover all the aspects of development you need to know before you spend time coding. Then, I promise, it's off to the races.

Chapter 2: Creating a Compelling User Experience

In This Chapter

↙ **Understanding what makes an iPhone app different**

↙ **Making an app that's worth the cost**

↙ **Avoiding the pitfalls that get apps rejected**

↙ **Designing for the best user experience**

*W*hen you have a handle on the possibilities and limitations of the iPhone, your imagination is free to soar to create a compelling user experience. But what is a "compelling user experience," really?

For openers, a compelling user experience has to result from the interaction of several factors:

✦ Interesting, useful, plentiful content

✦ Powerful, fast, versatile functionality

✦ An intuitive, well-designed user interface

The iPhone allows an immediacy and intimacy as it blends mobility and the power of the desktop to create a new kind of freedom. I like to use the term *user experience* because it implies more than a pretty user interface and nice graphics. A *compelling* user experience enables users to do what they need to do with a minimum of fuss and bother. But more than that, it forces you as a developer to think past a clean interface and even beyond basic convenience (such as not having to scroll through menus to do something simple). It includes meeting the expectations of the user based on the *context* — all the stuff going on around a user — in which they're using the app.

A guidebook app may have a great user interface, for example, but it may not give me the most up-to-date information or let me know that a tour of the Houses of Parliament is leaving in five minutes from the main entrance. Without those added touches, I don't consider an app compelling.

This chapter gently urges you to think about what those added touches should be for your app, from the perspective of the content you provide, the app's functionality, and its user interface. But first, you need to envision the totality of what your app's user experience should be.

Deep Thoughts on the User Experience

Pun intended — creating DeepThoughts, the star of Book III, is a fast way to get familiar with iPhone software development. Apple considers DeepThoughts to be a utility app — like the Weather app, but with a single view.

Utility applications can provide real value to the user and are also fun and easy to write — not a bad combination. The way the Weather application flips its view, for example, may seem a total mystery. But Apple goes out of its way to provide samples for many of the neater tricks and features out there, all in hopes of demystifying how they work. With the DeepThoughts application under your belt, you'll have a much easier time understanding and using all the resources Apple provides to help you develop iPhone apps.

What Apple doesn't show you (and where there's a real opportunity to develop a killer app) is how to design and develop more complex applications. Now, "more complex" doesn't necessarily — and shouldn't — mean "more complex *to the user.*" The real challenge and opportunity are in creating complex applications that are as easy to use as simple ones.

Because of its ease of use and convenience, its awareness of your location, and its ability to connect seamlessly to the Internet from most places, the iPhone lets you develop a totally new kind of application — one that integrates seamlessly with what the user is doing when he or she is living in the real world (what a concept). It frees the user to take advantage of technology away from the tether of the desk or coffee shop, and skips the hunt for a place to spread out the hardware. I refer to such applications as *here-and-now* — apps that take advantage of technology to help you do a specific task with up-to-date information, wherever you are and whenever you'd like.

All these features inherent in iPhone apps enable you to add a depth to the user's experience that you usually don't find in laptop- or desktop-based applications — in effect, a third dimension. Not only does the use of the app on the iPhone become embedded in where the user is and what the user is doing, the reverse is also happening: *Where the user is and what the user is doing can be embedded in the app itself.* This mutual embedding further blurs the boundaries between technology and user, as well as between user and task. Finally, developers can achieve a goal that's been elusive for years: the seamless integration of technology into everyday life.

The why-bother-since-I-have-my-laptop crowd still has to wrestle with this level of technology, especially those folks who haven't grown up with it. They still look at an iPhone as a poor substitute for a laptop or desktop — well, okay, for certain tasks, that's true. But an iPhone app trumps the laptop or desktop big-time in two ways:

✦ The iPhone's compact portability lets you do stuff not easily done on a laptop or desktop — on site and right now — as with the RoadTrip app you're about to find out how to build.

✦ The iPhone is integrated into the activity itself, creating a transparency that makes it as unobtrusive and un-distracting as possible. This advantage — even more important than portability — is the result of *context-driven design.*

The key to designing a killer iPhone application is to understand that the iPhone is *not* a small, more portable version of a laptop computer. It's another animal altogether and is therefore used entirely differently. So don't go out and design (say) the ultimate word-processing program for an iPhone. (Given the device's limitations, most people would rather use a laptop.) But for point-in-time, 30-second tasks that may provide valuable information — and in doing so make someone's life much easier — the iPhone can't be beat.

Creating Compelling Content

What most of the really good iPhone apps have in common is *focus:* They address a well-defined task that can be done within a time span that is appropriate for that task. If you need to look something up, you want it right now! If you're playing a game while waiting in line, you want it to be of short duration or broken up into a series of short and entertaining steps.

The content itself then, especially for here-and-now apps, must be stream-lined and focused on the fundamental pieces of the task. Although you *can* provide a near-infinity of detail just to get a single task done, here's a word to the wise: Don't. You need to extract the essence of each task; focus on the details that really make a difference.

Focusing on the task at hand

Suppose you want to offer a restaurant-finding app that's better than the apps now available. Imagine that your potential user is standing with some friends inside the lobby of a movie theater, trying to decide where to go to grab some dinner. They all have iPhones, and they're all using their favorite restaurant-finders, but none of them are providing what your user really needs — restaurants ranked by distance and type, with reviews and directions.

One of the apps is particularly frustrating because it lets the user select a restaurant by distance and cuisine. After selecting the distance, it gives back a list of cuisines. So far, so good. But the cuisine list is not context-based; when the user taps *Ethiopian,* all that comes back is a blank screen. Very annoying! So the user decides to stop using it then and there — nobody wants an app that makes you work only to receive nothing in return.

When you're using a good app, every piece of the app is not merely important to the task, but also important to *where you are in the task*. For example, if you're trying to decide how to get to central London from Heathrow, the app shouldn't offer detailed information about the Tube until you need it. The Maps app is another example — if you start searching by the name of a business or type of business *after* searching for your own location, as shown in Figure 2-1, Maps is smart enough to assume you mean a business or service nearby and thus locates the closest ones. Multiple pins appear on the map, showing the location of each one, and with a tap you can start getting directions to or from any of the pins.

Figure 2-1: From your location in Maps, type the name of a popular business (left) to see its nearest locations (right).

That doesn't mean your app shouldn't make connections that ought to be made. One aspect of a compelling user experience is that all the pieces of an application work together to tell a story. If the tasks in your app are completely unconnected, perhaps they should be separate apps.

Limiting the focus to a single task also enables you to leave behind some iPhone constraints, and the limitations of the iPhone can guide you to a better app design.

Maintaining consistency with the user's world

Great apps are based on the way people — users — think and work. When you make your app a natural extension of the user's world, it makes the app much easier and more pleasant to use and to learn.

Your users already have a mental model that describes the task your software is enabling. The users also have their own mental models of how the device works. At the levels of both content and user interface, your app must be consistent with these models if you want to create a superb user experience (which in turn creates loyalty to your app).

The user interface in RoadTrip was based on how people divide the experience of traveling by car. Here are some broad categories of the kinds of things folks tend to want to do when on the road:

✦ Use a map that shows your current location and lets you pin other locations on it so you can find them quickly.

✦ List the places you want to visit and browse information about them.

✦ Look up your hotels or campgrounds and read information about each; add new hotels and campgrounds to your list.

✦ Check the current weather and the forecast for where you are and where you're going.

✦ Keep your car's service record, vehicle identification, and other information handy.

This is only a partial list, of course. Chapter 1 of Book V gets into the RoadTrip application design in more detail.

There are other ways to divide up the tasks, but anything much different would be ignoring the user's mental model, which would mean the app would not meet some of the user's expectations. It would be less pleasant to use because it would impose an unfamiliar way of looking at things instead of building on the knowledge and experiences those users already have.

Modeling actions on the real world

When possible, model your application's objects and actions on objects and actions in the real world. For example, the Settings app displays on-off switches you can slide to turn things on or off. Many e-book readers let you flick the screen to view the next page as if you were turning a paper page.

These examples are based on physical counterparts in the real world, as are the apps shown in Figure 2-2: VoiceMemos and Cleartune. VoiceMemos starts immediately with the microphone image placed exactly where it should be for optimal voice recording, and an obvious red Record button. Cleartune displays what looks like a chromatic tuner for tuning acoustic instruments or vocals — which is what it is. Both are simple and elegant for those who already know something about recording or tuning an instrument.

Figure 2-2: Voice-Memos (left) and Cleartune (right) model real-world actions of recording vocals and tuning instruments.

Your application's text should be based on the target user. For example, if your user isn't steeped in technical jargon, avoid it in the user interface.

This doesn't mean that you have to "dumb down" the app. Here are some guidelines:

✦ If you're targeting your app toward people who already use (and expect) a certain kind of specialized language, then sure, use the jargon in your app. Just do your homework first and make sure you use those terms *correctly*.

For example, if your app is targeted at high-powered foreign-exchange traders, it might use *pip* (price interest point — the smallest amount that a price can move, as when a stock price advances by one cent). In fact, a foreign-exchange trader expects to see price movement in pips, and not only *can* you, but you *should* use that term in your user interface.

✦ If your app requires that the user have a certain amount of specialized knowledge about a task in order to use your application, identify what that knowledge is upfront.

✦ If the user is an ordinary person with generalized knowledge, use ordinary language.

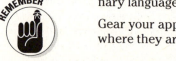

Gear your app to your user's knowledge base. In effect, meet your users where they are; don't expect them to come to you.

Designing the User Interface — Form Follows Function

Basing your app on how the user interacts and thinks about the world makes designing a great user interface easier.

Don't underestimate the effect of the user interface on the people who are trying to use it. A bad user interface can make even a great app painful to use. If users can't quickly figure out how to use your app or if the user interface is cluttered or obscure, they're likely to move on and probably complain loudly about the app to anyone who will listen.

Simplicity and ease of use are fundamental principles for all types of software, but in iPhone apps, they're critical. Why? One word: multitasking. iPhone users are probably doing other things simultaneously while they use your app.

The iPhone hardware and software are outstanding examples of form following function; the user interfaces of great applications follow that principle as well. In fact, even the iPhone's limitations (except for battery life) are a result of form following from the functional requirements of a mobile device user. Just think about how the iPhone fulfills the following mobile device user wish list:

✦ Small footprint

✦ Thin

✦ Lightweight

✦ Self-contained — no need for an external keyboard or mouse

✦ Task-oriented

It's a pretty safe bet that part of the appeal of the iPhone to many people — especially to non-technical users — is aesthetic: The device is sleek, compact, and fun to use. But the aesthetics of an iPhone app aren't just about how beautiful your app is onscreen. Eye candy is all well and good, but how well does your user interface match its function — that is, do its job?

Consistency across apps is a good thing

As with the Macintosh, users have a general sense of how applications work on the iPhone. (The Windows OS has always been a bit less user-friendly, if you ask a typical Mac user.) One of the early appeals of the Macintosh was how similarly all the applications worked. So the folks at Apple (no fools they) carried over this similarity into the iPhone as well. The resulting success story suggests the following word to the wise . . .

A compelling iPhone user experience usually requires familiar iPhone interface components offering standard functionality, such as searching and navigating hierarchical sets of data. Use the iPhone standard behavior, gestures, and metaphors in standard ways. For example, users tap a button to make a selection and flick or drag to scroll a long list. iPhone users understand these gestures because the built-in applications utilize them *consistently*.

Consistency is also important in functionality. Although you could design a page-reading app to add or delete a bookmark a different way, Safari already does it a certain way (see Figure 2-3), which is why co-author Tony's app, Tony's Tips for iPhone Users, provides the same methods for adding and deleting a bookmark.

Figure 2-3: Safari provides a model for adding or deleting a bookmark (left), so why not follow it, as Tony did with Tony's Tips for iPhone Users (right).

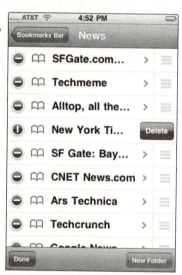

Fortunately, staying consistent is easy to do on the iPhone; the frameworks at your disposal have that behavior built in. This is not to say that you should never extend the interface, especially if you're blazing new trails or creating a new game. For example, if you're creating a roulette wheel for the iPhone, why not use a circular gesture to spin the wheel, even if it isn't a standard gesture?

Making it obvious

Although simplicity is a definite design principle, great apps are *also* easily understandable to the target user. If you're designing a travel app, it has to be simple enough for even an inexperienced traveler to use. But if you're designing an app for foreign exchange trading, you don't have to make it simple enough for someone with no trading experience to understand.

Keep these points in mind as you plan and create your app:

✦ The main function of a good application is immediately apparent and accessible to the users it's intended for.

✦ The standard interface components also give cues to the users. Users know, for example, to touch buttons and select items from table views (as in the Contacts app).

✦ You can't assume that users are so excited about your app that they're willing to invest lots of time in figuring it out.

Early Macintosh developers were aware of these principles. They knew that users expected that they could rip off the shrink-wrap, put a floppy disk in the machine (these were *really* early Macintosh developers), and do at least something productive immediately. The technology has changed since then; user attitudes, by and large, haven't.

Engaging the user

While I'm on the subject of users, here are two more important aspects of a compelling application: direct manipulation and immediate feedback. Here's what's so great about them:

✦ **Direct manipulation makes people feel more in control.** On the desktop, it meant a keyboard and mouse; on the iPhone, the multi-touch interface serves the same purpose. In fact, using fingers gives a user a more immediate sense of control; there's no intermediary (such as a mouse) between the user and the object onscreen. To make this effect happen in your app, one way is to keep your onscreen objects visible while the user manipulates them.

✦ **Immediate feedback keeps the users engaged.** Great apps respond to every user action with some visible feedback — such as highlighting list items briefly when users tap them.

Because of the limitations imposed by using fingers, apps need to be very forgiving. For example, although the iPhone doesn't pester the user to confirm every action, it also won't let the user perform potentially destructive, non-recoverable actions (such as deleting all contacts or restarting a game) without asking, "Are you sure?" Your app should also allow the user to easily stop a task that's taking too long to complete.

Notice how the iPhone uses animation to provide feedback. (For example, the flipping transition when you touch the Info button in the Weather app is very cool.) But keep it simple; excessive or pointless animation interferes with the application flow, reduces performance, and can really annoy the user.

Designing the User Experience

It's rare (except with sample apps) for an app's user experience to be simply a combination of some of the iPhone's basic experiences. But DeepThoughts, which you build in Book III, is simplicity itself. It displays whatever text the user enters, and the mechanism for changing the text works like most other iPhone apps — touch the *i* (information) button, and touch the text field to use the onscreen keyboard. As you build DeepThoughts, you discover how to use the basic building blocks of the iPhone user experience.

The RoadTrip app, starting in Book V, presents a more complex set of problems. To meet the needs of a Kerouac-style *On the Road* trip, the traveler doesn't need a lot of information at any one time. In fact, the user wants as little info as possible (just the facts ma'am) but also as current as possible. It doesn't help to have last year's train schedule.

To get the design ball of your application rolling, start thinking about what you want from the application; not necessarily the features, but what the experience of using the application should be like.

Understanding the real-world context

You can reach the goal of seamlessness and transparency by following some very simple principles when you design the user experience — especially with respect to the user interface.

Become the champion of relevance

There are two aspects to this directive:

✦ Search and destroy anything that is not relevant to what the user is doing while he or she is using a particular part of your application.

✦ Include — and make easily accessible — everything a user needs when doing something supported by a particular part of your application.

You want to avoid distracting the user from what he or she is doing. The application should be integrated into the task, a natural part of the flow, and not something that causes a detour. Your goal is to supply the user with only the information that's applicable to the task at hand. If your user just wants to get from an airport into a city, he or she couldn't care less that the city has a world-renowned underground or subway system if it doesn't come out to the airport.

Seconds count

At first, the "seconds count" admonition may appear to fall into the "blinding flash of the obvious" category — of *course* a user wants to accomplish a task as quickly as possible. If the user has to scroll through lots of menus or figure out how the application works, the app's value drops off exponentially with the amount of time it takes to get to where the user needs to be.

But there are also some subtleties to this issue. If the user can do things as quickly as possible, he or she is a lot less distracted from the task at hand — and *both* results are desirable. For example, RedLaser, shown in Figure 2-4, uses the iPhone camera to scan a product's barcode so you can check online prices; it's designed to be used right in the store aisle while walking by products. Rather than force the user to hold the iPhone steady and at the same time tap a button to take a picture, RedLaser immediately captures the barcode image as soon as it can recognize it in the viewfinder — so you can quickly scan with one hand while pushing your shopping cart with the other. As with relevance, this goal requires a seamless and transparent application.

Figure 2-4: RedLaser recognizes the barcode and captures it so that you don't have to touch a button while holding the iPhone steady.

Combine these ideas and you get the principle of *simply connect:* You want to be able to connect easily whether that connection is to a network, to the information you need, or to the task you want to do. For example, a friend of mine was telling me he uses his iPhone when watching TV so he can look up things in an online dictionary or Wikipedia. (He must watch a lot of Public TV.)

Doing it better on the iPhone

What you get by using the application has to have more value than alternative ways of doing the same thing.

The quality of information has to be better than the alternative

You can find airport transportation in a guidebook, but it's not up-to-date. You can get foreign exchange information from a *bureau de change,* but unless you know the bank rate, you don't know whether you're being ripped off. You can get restaurant information from a newspaper, but you don't know whether the restaurant has subsequently changed hours or is closed for vacation. If the app can consistently provide better, more up-to-date information, it's the kind of app that's tailor-made for a context-driven design.

The app has to be worth the real cost

By *real cost,* I don't mean just the amount you actually pay out — you need to include the time and effort of using the app. The real cost includes both the cost of the application and any costs you might incur by *using* the application. This can be a real issue for an application such as Tony's Tips for iPhone, because international roaming charges can be exorbitant for accessing the Internet for new pages. That's why the app must have the designed-in capability to download the information it provides and then to update the info when you find a wireless connection — Tony's Tips lets you save pages and update them later for that very reason.

Keep things localized

With the world growing even flatter (from a communications perspective, anyway) and the iPhone available in more than 80 countries, the potential market for an app is considerably larger than just the folks who happen to speak English. But having to use an app in a language you may not be comfortable with doesn't make for transparency. This means that applications have to be *localized* — that is, all the information, the content, and even the text in dialogs need to be in the user's language of choice.

Playing to the iPhone Strengths

Key to creating applications that go beyond the desktop and that take advantage of context-based design are four hardware features of the iPhone: knowing the location of the device, accessing the Internet, recording and playing content, and tracking orientation and motion.

There are others, of course, but you can expect to find one or more of these features in a context-based application.

Knowing the location of the device

Knowing the device's location (and hence, the user's) enables you to further refine the context by including the actual physical location and adding that to the relevance filter. If you are in Rome, the application can ask the user whether he or she wants to use Rome as a filter for relevant information (so that when in Rome . . .).

Because the iPhone knows where it is, apps can make use of this information to present content that is closer to them. The feature isn't just for travel — apps that have nothing to do with travel may still use location to improve the user experience. NPR Addict, for example, is not categorized as a travel app, but gives you the standard location button so that you can quickly find NPR stations near you, and you can also listen to NPR stations in other cities from home or work. (See Figure 2-5.)

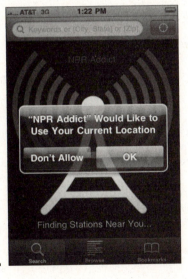

Figure 2-5: NPR Addict takes advantage of location to quickly find NPR stations near you.

Accessing the Internet

Accessing the Internet allows you to provide real-time, up-to-date information. In addition, it enables you to transcend the CPU and memory limitations of the iPhone by offloading processing and data storage out to a server in the clouds.

For example, Tony's Tips for iPhone uses the Internet for all its pages so that the pages can be updated at any time without affecting the app, thereby reducing the app's size and speeding up search (which takes place on the site across all pages), while also offering consistently updated info.

Recording and playing content

The iPhone evolved from the iPod, in which content is king. Not only can your app play music and videos, but it can also record voice-quality (actually telephone-quality) sound with its built-in microphone, or higher quality through external microphones. A number of audio-mixing apps have already made their debut in the App Store. And don't forget the iPhone's camera, which can take photos (and which RedLaser and others use to scan barcodes), and the iPhone 3GS video camera. All iPhones can send and receive images and video clips by e-mail and share multimedia content through the MobileMe service.

Tracking orientation and motion

When you rotate the iPhone from a vertical view (portrait) to a horizontal view (landscape), the accelerometer detects the movement and changes the display accordingly. In Safari and Mail, your display changes to show the text better.

The iPhone can also sense motion using its built-in accelerometer. Even in its simplest form, motion is useful: When entering text or using the copy and paste functions, you can just shake the iPhone to undo the action.

Motion detection happens so quickly that you can control a game with these movements. Pass the Pigs, for example, is a dice game in which you shake three times to roll your pigs to gain points. In Labyrinth, you tilt your iPhone to roll a ball through a wooden maze without falling through the holes. And you can shake, rattle, and roll your way around the world in Yahtzee Adventures as you rack up high scores, or tilt your iPhone to fly around tanks and bazooka-wielding madmen in Chopper. Even infants can join the fun: Silver Rattle shows a screen that changes color and rattles with every shake. (Big Joe Turner would be proud.)

Although the accelerometer is used extensively in games, it has other uses, such as enabling a user to erase a picture or make a random song selection by shaking the device (not to mention undoing the recent action).

Incorporating the Device Context

Not only do you have to take into account the user context, but you also need to take into account the device context.

After all, the device is also a context for the user. He or she, based on individual experience, expects applications to behave in a certain way. As I explain in Chapter 1, this expectation provides another perspective on why staying consistent with the user interface guidelines is so important.

In addition to the device being a context from a user perspective, it's also one from the developer's perspective. If you want to maximize the user experience, you have to take the following into account:

✦ **Limited screen real estate:** Although scrolling is built into an iPhone and is relatively easy to do, you should require as little scrolling as possible, especially on navigation pages, and especially on the main page.

✦ **Limitations of a touch-based interface:** Although the multitouch interface is an iPhone feature, it comes with limitations as well. Fingers aren't as precise as a mouse pointer, and user interface elements need to be large enough and spaced far enough apart so that the user's fingers can find their way around the interface comfortably. You also can do only so much with fingers. There are fewer options when using fingers than when using the combination of multibutton mouse and keyboard.

✦ **Limited computer power, memory, and battery life:** As an application designer for the iPhone, you have to keep these issues in mind. The iPhone OS is particularly unforgiving when it comes to memory usage. If you run out of memory, the iPhone OS will simply shut down your app.

✦ **Connection limitations:** There's always a possibility that the user may be out of range, or on a plane, or has decided not to pay exorbitant roaming fees, or is using an iPod touch, which offers only Wi-Fi capabilities for connecting to the Internet. You need to account for that possibility in your application and preserve as much functionality as possible. This usually means allowing the user to download and use the current real-time information, where applicable.

Some of these goals overlap, of course, and that's where the real challenges are.

Avoiding Practices that Get Apps Rejected

Apple exerts control over the app-development and App Store ecosystem, and if you want to play ball in Apple's ballpark, you have to, well, play ball. No matter how many developers complain about Apple's rejection policies, there will always be more developers willing to follow the guidelines. All you need to do is read the documentation, steer away from the Apple trademarks and images, and stay away from content that's questionable in any legal sense. By keeping those things in mind, you can make design decisions about your app now, before developing the app, that can save you time and money later.

Some people believe Apple has not only a right, but also an obligation, to police the App Store and reject questionable apps, if only to build trust with consumers. Anacharsis, one of Greek mythology's Seven Wise Men, warned people that the market is "the place set apart where men may deceive each other." Given the way the iPhone can be integrated into your everyday life and communications, a malicious app could do considerably more damage than a similar one on a desktop computer.

But Apple also wants the user experience to be a rewarding one, as well as one that's consistent with the way Apple designed its own apps and OS. And that makes perfect sense for a company that wants to expand its ecosystem and users so that it can continue to invest in research and keep innovation on the front burner.

So what kinds of things will get your app bounced before it ever has a chance to shine in the App Store? Here are just a few:

✦ **Playing good vibrations:** You can't use continuous vibration in your apps — short bursts, as warnings, are all that are allowed. Don't bother trying to set up a timer to keep the vibration going. (They know that trick.)

✦ **Linking to private frameworks:** Apple rejects apps that call external frameworks or libraries that contain non-Apple code. In addition, you can't download interpreted code to use in an app except for code that is interpreted and run by Apple's published APIs and built-in interpreters. Private frameworks and interpreted code may hide functions that Apple would want to know about. Some private frameworks have been found to mine personal information from iPhone users without their knowledge. Apple already knows about most of the private frameworks, so don't bother with them.

✦ **Straying too far from Apple's guidelines:** When co-author Tony submitted his app (Tony's Tips for iPhone Users), it was initially rejected because the app used highlighting in a menu in a way that did not conform to Apple's guidelines. If you let a user highlight a row in order to select something or initiate an action, you'd better make darn sure that the row is *deselected* by the time it's displayed again — not still selected (as if you're reminding the user what was last selected). Tony resubmitted the app after fixing this problem, and the app was approved.

✦ **Improper handling of editing in table view cells:** If you enable table cell editing, you have to manually specify which cells should respond to editing controls and which should not. I describe working with table views in Book V.

✦ **Copying existing functionality:** Although you should use the functionality provided for developers, you should not simply copy something that Apple already does. Mini Web browsers — apps that essentially show Web pages and do little else — are particularly vulnerable. For example, a simple app that duplicated the functionality of Safari's bookmark button was rejected.

✦ **Using an inappropriate keyboard type:** If your app needs a phone number or other numeral-only input, and it presents a keyboard that also includes the possibility of entering standard alphanumeric input, it will most likely be rejected.

✦ **Being oblivious about whether your user lost connection:** The iPhone is all about using the Internet. If your app uses a network connection, it is *your app's responsibility* to tell the user if and when his or her iPhone loses its network connection while using your app. For example, Tony's app (Tony's Tips for iPhone Users) didn't warn the user if the user switched to Airplane mode or otherwise lost the connection, so Tony had to add that warning, as shown in Figure 2-6.

Figure 2-6:
Tony's Tips
for iPhone
Users warns
the user
about a lost
connection.

Now that you have some idea what Apple expects of you — in terms of designing and developing your app — it's time for you to find out what to expect of Apple in terms of supporting your development efforts. The Apple Developer Program is rich with informative content, useful downloads, and no-nonsense guidelines. You simply have to become a registered developer to create apps for the App Store. So, onward to the next chapter, where you become a registered Apple software developer.

Chapter 3: Enlisting in the Developer Corps

In This Chapter

✔ **Registering as a developer**

✔ **Exploring the iPhone Dev Center**

✔ **Installing the Software Development Kit (SDK)**

✔ **Looking at the whys and hows of joining the Developer Program**

Benjamin Franklin's famous *Join, or Die* political cartoon of the 1760s could well be applied to Apple's role in today's mobile software industry. You can't gain independence on your own; you need the powerful movement of a large group. Apple needs developers, and developers need Apple.

For sure, you can develop your applications independently, and for other platforms (which is the topic of other books), but many of those platforms offer immature Software Development Kits and little or no support. What's more, you could develop for a number of platforms and then watch your product die in a diffused marketplace.

Apple is clearly on a mission with the iPhone and the App Store ecosystem to change the user experience, and you *have* to join (or die). No, you won't automatically turn into an Apple fanboy (but it doesn't hurt to be one, either). You *will* be supported with a robust Software Development Kit, comprehensive information, and reliable support.

Most importantly, you *must* join if you want to develop apps for the iPhone. You have to follow Apple's policies and procedures. Although the iPhone Software Development Kit (SDK) is free, you have to register as an iPhone developer first. Registering also gives you access to all the documentation and other resources found on the iPhone Developer Web site. This whole ritual transforms you into a *Registered iPhone Developer*.

Becoming a registered developer is free, as well as the SDK, but there's a catch: If you actually want to run your application on a real iPhone as opposed to only on the Simulator that comes with the SDK, you have to join the iPhone developer program. Fortunately, an individual membership costs only $99 as of this writing. This is called *Joining the iPhone Developer Program*. (I should mention as well that an individual membership is required of anyone who wants to distribute his or her app using the App Store.)

In this chapter, you go through the process of becoming a registered iPhone developer, signing on to and then exploring the iPhone Dev Center Web site, downloading the SDK so you can start using it, and then (finally) joining the iPhone Developer Program.

What you see when you go through this process yourself may be slightly different from what you see here. Don't panic. It's because Apple changes the site from time to time.

Becoming a Registered iPhone Developer

Although just having to register is annoying to some people, it doesn't help that the process itself can be a bit confusing. Fear not! Follow the steps, and you can safely reach the end of the road. (If you've already registered, skip to the next section, where you find out what the iPhone Dev Center offers and how to download the SDK.)

1. **Point your browser to `http://developer.apple.com/iphone`.**

   Doing so brings you to a page similar to the one shown in Figure 3-1. Apple does change this site occasionally, so when you get there, it may be a little different. You may be tempted by some of the links, but they get you only so far until you log in as a registered developer.

2. **Click the Register link in the top-right corner of the screen. (Refer to Figure 3-1.)**

   You see a page explaining why you should become a registered iPhone developer.

3. **Click Continue.**

   A page appears, asking whether you want to create a new Apple ID or use an existing one.

   You can use your current Apple ID (the same one you use for iTunes, MobileMe, or the Apple Store) or create a new Apple ID and then log in.

   • *If you don't have an Apple ID,* select Create an Apple ID and click Continue. You find yourself at the page shown in Figure 3-2.

   • *If you already have an Apple ID,* select the Use an Existing Apple ID option and then click Continue. You're taken to a screen where you can log in with your Apple ID and password. That takes you to the page shown in Figure 3-2, with some of your information already filled out.

4. **Continue filling out the personal profile form and then click Continue.**

   If you have an Apple ID, most of the form is already filled out.

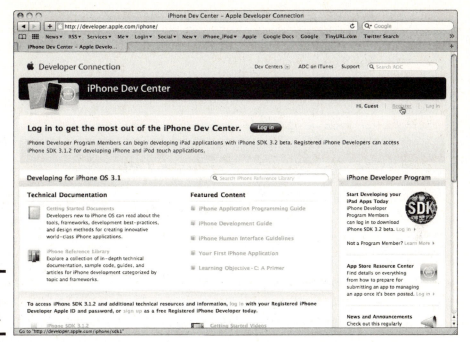

Figure 3-1:
The iPhone
Dev Center.

You must fill in the country code in the phone number field. If you're
living in the United States, the country code is 1.

5. **Complete the next part of the form to finish your professional profile.**

   You're asked some basic business questions. After you've filled everything in and clicked the Continue button, you're taken to a new page,
   which asks you to agree to the Registered iPhone Developer Agreement.

6. **Click I Agree.**

   Don't forget to select the confirmation check box that you have read and
   agree to be bound by the agreement and that you're of legal age.

   If you just created your Apple ID, you're asked for the verification code
   sent to the e-mail address you supplied when you created your Apple ID.
   If you used your existing Apple ID, you'll be taken to Step 8.

7. **Open the e-mail from Apple, enter the verification code, and click
   Continue.**

   Clicking Continue takes you to a thank-you page.

8. **On the thank-you page, click the Visit Phone Development Center
   button, and you're automatically logged in to the iPhone Dev center,
   which I describe in the section "Exploring the iPhone Dev Center" in
   this chapter.**

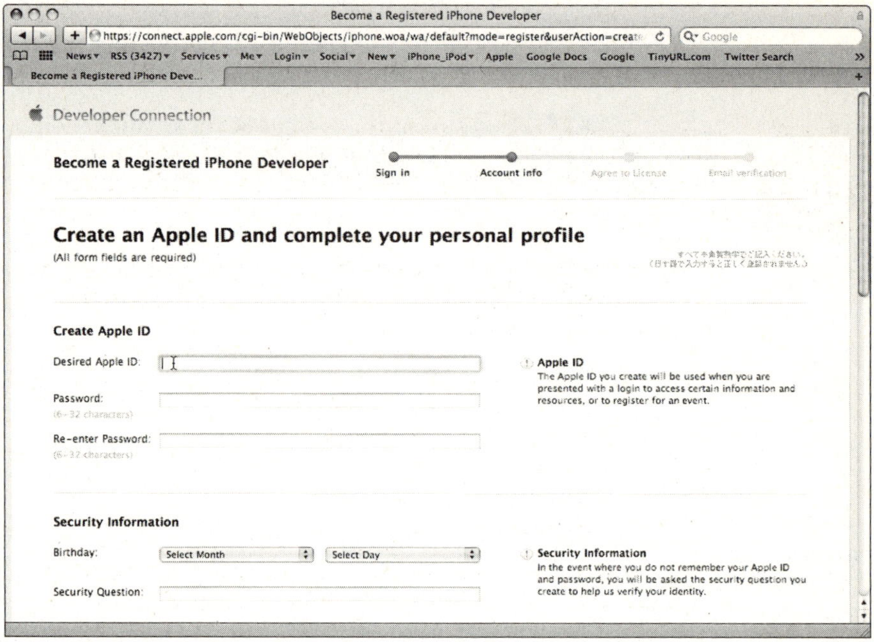

Figure 3-2:
Creating
an Apple
ID and
personal
profile.

So, you're now an officially registered iPhone developer, which enables you to explore the iPhone Dev Center and download the SDK (as I show in the section "Exploring the iPhone Dev Center" in this chapter — and you can jump to that section if you're not ready to join the iPhone Developer Program).

However, simply registering as a developer doesn't give you the status you need to actually run your app on your own (or anyone else's) iPhone or to distribute your app through the App Store. The next section shows you how to get with the program — the iPhone Developer Program.

Joining the iPhone Developer Program

The Simulator application for the Mac that comes standard with the iPhone SDK is a great tool for learning to program, but it does have some limitations. It doesn't support some hardware-dependent features, and when it comes to testing, it can't really emulate such everyday iPhone realities as CPU speed or memory throughput.

"Minor annoyances," you might say, and you might be right. But the real issue is that *just registering* as a developer doesn't get you two very important things: the ability to actually run your app on your own iPhone, and the ability to distribute your app through the App Store. (Remember that the App Store is the only way for commercial developers to distribute their apps — even free apps — to more than a few people.)

To run your app on a real iPhone or get a chance to profile your app in the App Store, you have to enroll in either the Standard or Enterprise version of the iPhone Developer Program.

It used to be that that the approval process could take a while, and although the process does seem quicker these days, it's still true that you can't run your apps on your iPhone until you're approved. You should enroll as early as possible.

If you go back to the iPhone Dev Center page, you see a section in the right column that says iPhone Developer Program. (Refer to Figure 3-1.) Here's how you deal with that section:

1. **Click the Learn More link next to the question "Not a Program Member?" (Refer to Figure 3-1.)**

The iPhone Developer Program page appears, as shown in Figure 3-3.

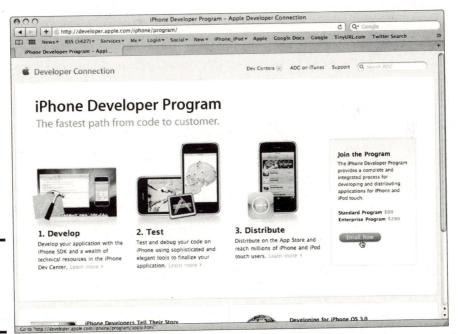

Figure 3-3:
The iPhone
Developer
Program
overview.

2. **On the right side of the screen, click the Enroll Now button.**

A new page appears, telling you to choose your program and outlining the details of each developer program, as shown in Figure 3-4.

The Standard program costs $99. The Enterprise program costs $299 and is designed for companies developing proprietary in-house apps for iPhone and iPod touch. To be sure you're selecting the option that meets your needs, give the program details a once-over.

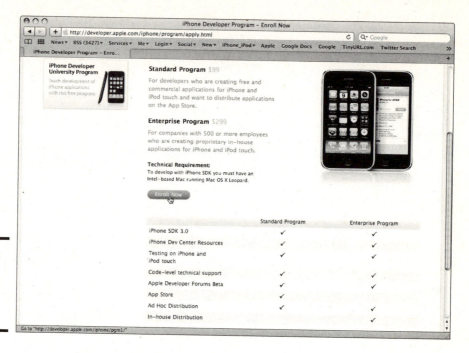

Figure 3-4:
You can
check out
program
details.

3. Click the Enroll Now button.

You don't actually get to choose Standard or Enterprise yet. But you do get an overview of the process and a chance to log in again with your Apple ID and password. Click Continue.

4. Do the logging-in stuff.

After logging in, you get a chance to go with either a Standard Individual, Standard Company, or Enterprise program. Figure 3-5 shows you the differences between the three options.

5. Make your choice and then click Select.

This step takes you to a page that gives you more information on the option you've selected.

6. Click Continue.

Depending on the option you selected, you're either given the opportunity to pay (if you selected Standard Individual) or you're asked for some more company or enterprise information and then given the ability to pay.

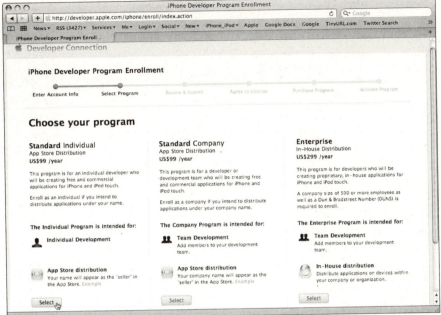

Figure 3-5:
Choose your
program.

Although joining as an individual is easier than joining as a company, there are clearly some advantages to enrolling as a company. For example, you can add team members (which I discuss in connection with the developer portal in Chapter 6 of this minibook), and your company name appears in your listing in the App Store.

When you join as an individual, your real name shows up when the user buys (or downloads for free) your app in the App Store. If you're concerned about privacy, or if you want to seem "bigger," the extra work invoked in signing up as a company may be worthwhile for you.

7. **Continue through the process, and eventually you will be accepted in the Developer Program of your choice.**

After acceptance, you can log in to the iPhone Dev Center as an Official iPhone Developer and see the page shown in Figure 3-6.

If you click the iPhone Developer Program Portal link in the right column, you see all sorts of things you can do as a developer, as shown in Figure 3-7.

You shouldn't linger too long at the iPhone Developer Program Portal page, simply because it can be really confusing unless you understand the process. I explain this portal — which lets you provision your device, run your application on it, and prepare your creation for distribution to the App Store — in Chapter 6 of this minibook.

Figure 3-6:
The iPhone
Dev Center
with
resources
and
downloads.

Figure 3-7:
The iPhone
Developer
Program
Portal.

Exploring the iPhone Dev Center

You can find more of the resources available to you in the iPhone Dev Center later in the section "Resources in the iPhone Dev Center," but for the moment, I want you to focus on what you're *really* after. I'm talking about the iPhone SDK.

The SDK offers tools for developing your iPhone app. Here's a handy list of what's inside:

✦ **Xcode:** This refers to Apple's complete development environment, which integrates all the SDK's features: the code editor, the build system, the graphical debugger, and project management. (I introduce you to the code editor's features in more detail in Chapter 4 of this minibook.)

✦ **Frameworks:** The iPhone's multiple frameworks help make it easy to develop apps. Creating an app can be thought of as simply adding your application-specific behavior to a framework. The framework does all the rest. For example, the UIKit framework provides fundamental code for building your app: the required application behavior, classes for windows, views (including those that display text and Web content), controls, and view controllers. (I cover all these things in Chapter 5 of this minibook.) The UIKit framework also provides standard interfaces to core location data, the user's contacts and photo library, accelerometer data, and the iPhone's built-in camera.

✦ **Interface Builder:** You find out about Interface Builder in Chapter 4 of this minibook, and use it to build the user interface for the DeepThoughts application in Book III. But Interface Builder is more than your run-of-the-mill program that builds graphical user interfaces. In Chapter 2 of Book III, you see how Xcode and Interface Builder work together to give you ways to build (and automatically create at runtime) the user interface — as well as helping to create objects that provide the infrastructure for your application.

✦ **iPhone Simulator:** The simulator enables you to debug your app and do some other testing on your Mac by simulating the iPhone. The Simulator runs most iPhone apps, but it doesn't support some hardware-dependent features. I give you a rundown on the Simulator in Chapter 4 of this minibook.

✦ **Instruments:** The Instruments application lets you measure your iPhone app while it's running on an iPhone. It gives you a number of performance metrics, including those for testing memory and network use. It also works (in a limited way) on the iPhone Simulator, and you can test some aspects of your design there.

The iPhone Simulator doesn't emulate such real-life iPhone characteristics as CPU speed or memory throughput. If you want to understand how your app performs on the iPhone from a user's perspective, you have to use the actual iPhone and the Instruments application.

Looking forward to using the SDK

The tools in the SDK support a development process that most people find comfortable. They allow you to rapidly get a user interface up and running to see what it actually looks like. You can add code a little at a time and then run it after each new addition to see how it works. I take you through this incremental process as you develop the DeepThoughts app; for now, here's a bird's-eye view of iPhone app development, one step at a time:

1. **Start with Xcode.**

    Xcode provides several project templates that you can use to get off to a fast start. (In Chapter 4 of this minibook, you do just that, and then you add code and more interface objects in Book III.)

2. **Design and create the user interface.**

    Interface Builder has graphic-design tools you can use to create your app's user interface. This saves a great deal of time and effort. It also reduces the amount of code you have to write by creating resource files that your app can then upload automatically.

    If you don't want to use Interface Builder, you can always build your user interface from scratch, creating each individual piece and linking them all together within your app. Sometimes Interface Builder is the best way to create onscreen elements; sometimes the hands-on approach works better.

3. **Write the code.**

    The Xcode editor provides several features that help you write code. You can find out more about these features in Chapter 3 of Book III.

4. **Build and run your app.**

    You build your app on your computer and run it in the iPhone Simulator application or (provided you've joined the Development Program) on your iPhone.

5. **Test your app.**

    You'll want to test the functionality of your app as well as response time.

6. **Measure and tune your app's performance.**

    After you have a running app, make sure that it makes optimal use of resources such as memory and CPU cycles.

7. **Do it all again until you're done.**

Resources in the iPhone Dev Center

You're not left on your own when it comes to the Seven-Step Plan for Creating Great iPhone Apps in the previous section. After all, you have this book to help you on the way — as well as a heap of information squirreled away in various corners of the iPhone Dev Center (refer to Figure 3-6). I've found the following resources to be especially helpful:

✦ **Getting Started Videos:** These are relatively light on content.

✦ **Getting Started Documents:** Think of them as an introduction to the materials in the iPhone Reference Library. These give you an overview of iPhone development and best practices. Included is "Learning Objective-C: A Primer," an overview of Objective-C that also includes links to "Object-Oriented Programming with Objective-C" and "The Objective-C 2.0 Programming Language" (the definitive guide).

If you have some experience with Objective-C or object-oriented programming, you're ready for Book II. If you've never programmed in the Objective-C language, you should check out the basic information in the iPhone Reference Library. If you want to get a handle on Objective-C as quickly (and painlessly) as possible, go get yourself a copy of *Objective-C For Dummies* by co-author Neal. (Neal does a great job explaining everything you need to know in order to program in Objective-C, and he assumes you have little or no knowledge of programming.)

✦ **The iPhone Reference Library:** This library includes all the documentation you could ever want (except, of course, the answer to that one question you really need answered at 3 a.m., but that's the way it goes). To be honest, most of this stuff only turns out to be really useful *after* you have a good handle on what you're doing. As you go through this book, however, an easier way to access some of this documentation will be through the Xcode Documentation window, described in Chapter 3 of Book III.

✦ **Coding How-To's:** These tend to be a lot more valuable when you already have something of a knowledge base.

✦ **Sample Code:** On the one hand, sample code of any kind is always valuable. Most good developers look over sample apps before they get started building their own. They'll take something that closely approximates what they want to do, and they modify it until it does exactly what they want it to do. When I started iPhone development, there were no books like this one; so much of what I learned came from looking at the samples and then making some changes to see how things worked. On the other hand, perusing the sample apps can give you hours of (misguided) pleasure and can be quite the time waster and task avoider.

✦ **Apple Developer Forums Beta:** I'm not the first to say that developer forums can be very helpful, and I'm also not the first to admit that they're a great way to procrastinate. As you scroll through the questions people have, be careful about some of the answers you see. No one is validating the information people are giving out. But take heart: Pretty soon you'll be able to answer some of those questions better yourself.

Downloading the SDK

Enough prep work. Time to do some downloading.

As of this writing, Apple offers version 3.1.2 of the SDK and a prerelease beta version 3.2 (which includes iPad development tools). You can use version 3.1.2, which is stable, to develop applications for iPhone and iPod touch, which run on iPhone OS 3.1.2 as of this writing. You can switch at any point to the beta or released 3.2 version to develop iPhone and iPod touch apps for iPhone OS 3.2 (when it becomes widely available), and for the new iPad, which runs iPhone OS 3.2.

Version 3.1.2 requires an Intel-based Mac running Mac OS X 10.5 (Leopard) or Mac OS X 10.6.2 (Snow Leopard) or a newer version. Version 3.2 beta requires an Intel-based Mac running Mac OS X Snow Leopard version 10.6.2 or a newer version.

By the time you read this book, it may no longer be version 3.2. You should download the latest SDK. That way you will get the most recent version to start with.

To install version 3.1.2 of the SDK, scroll to the bottom part of the iPhone Dev Center page, as shown in Figure 3-8.

Figure 3-8: Download the iPhone SDK version 3.1.2.

Underneath the download link there is another link to a Read Me file (iPhone SDK 3.1.2 with Xcode 3.2.1 Read Me). It is a PDF, "About Xcode and the iPhone SDK," that tells you everything you need to know (and more) about this version of the SDK. Peruse it at your leisure, but don't get too hung up on it if there are things you have no clue about. You can find details in Chapter 4 of this minibook.

After perusing "About Xcode and the iPhone SDK," click the iPhone SDK you want to download.

To install version 3.2 of the SDK, click the iPhone SDK 3.2 beta link above the left column of the iPhone Dev Center page (refer to Figure 3-6), which displays the iPhone Dev Center page for version 3.2. Scroll this page, as shown in Figure 3-9, to see the links for downloading the SDK. Underneath the download link there is another link to a Read Me file (Xcode 3.2.2 Read Me). Click this link to read "About Xcode and the iPhone SDK," which describes what Xcode can do (most of which I explain in Chapter 4 of this minibook). After perusing "About Xcode and the iPhone SDK," click the iPhone SDK 3.2 beta with Xcode 3.2.2 (Snow Leopard) link (refer to Figure 3-9) to download it.

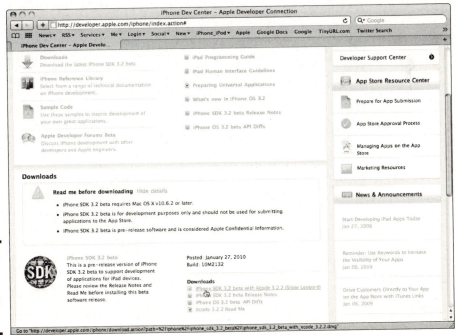

Figure 3-9: Download the iPhone SDK version 3.2 beta.

You can watch the download in Safari's download window (which is only a little better than watching paint dry).

When it's done downloading, the iPhone SDK window appears onscreen, complete with an installer and various packages tied to the install process. All you then have to do is double-click the iPhone SDK installer and follow the (really simple) installation instructions. After you do all that, you have your very own iPhone Software Development Kit on your hard drive.

Getting Yourself Ready for the SDK

Don't despair. The preceding process was tedious, but as the song goes, "It's all over now." Going through the process of registering and joining the program is probably the *second* most annoying part of your journey toward developing software for the iPhone. The *most* annoying part is figuring out what Apple calls "provisioning" your iPhone — the hoops you have to jump through to actually run your app on a real, tangible, existing iPhone. You go through the provisioning process in Chapter 6 of this minibook, and frankly, getting *that* process explained is worth the price of this book.

In the next chapter, you get started using the SDK you just downloaded, and you become intimately acquainted with the iPhone SDK during the course of your project. I assume that you have some programming knowledge and that you also have some acquaintance with object-oriented programming, with some variant of C, such as C++, C#, and maybe even with Objective-C. If those assumptions miss the mark, help us out, okay? Take another look at the "Resources in the iPhone Dev Center" section, earlier in this chapter, for an overview of some of the resources that can help you get up to speed on some programming basics. Or, better yet, get yourself a copy of *Objective-C For Dummies*.

I also assume that you're familiar with the iPhone itself, and that you've explored at least Apple's preinstalled apps to become familiar with the iPhone's look and feel.

Chapter 4: Getting to Know the SDK

In This Chapter

✓ **Getting a handle on the Xcode project**

✓ **Compiling an iPhone app**

✓ **Peeking inside the iPhone Simulator**

✓ **Checking out the Interface Builder**

✓ **Demystifying nib files**

Arthur C. Clarke's Third Law is that any sufficiently advanced technology is indistinguishable from magic. The collection of tools known as the iPhone Software Development Kit (SDK) is the crucible for the alchemy of creating an iPhone app. You pick a template for the type of app; stir in the content, behavior, and user interface; and grind it all up with magical code. The SDK builds your final product. Sounds easy, and to be truthful, it's *relatively* easy.

In this chapter, I introduce you to the SDK. It's going to be a low-key, get-acquainted kind of affair. You get into the real nuts-and-bolts stuff in Book III and Book V, when you actually develop the two sample applications.

Developing Using the SDK

The Software Development Kit (SDK) gives you the opportunity to develop your apps without tying your brain up in knots. You can rapidly get a user interface up and running to see what it looks like. The idea here is to add your code incrementally — step by step — so that you can always step back and see how what you just did affects the Big Picture.

Your general steps in development should look something like this:

1. Start with Xcode, Apple's development environment for the OS X operating system.

2. Design the user interface.

3. Write the code.

4. Build and run your app.

5. Test your app.

6. Measure and tune your app's performance.

7. Do it all again (or at least Steps 3–6) until you're done.

In this chapter, you start at the very beginning, with the very first step, which is Xcode. (Starting with Step 1? What a concept!) And the first step of the first step is to create your first project.

Creating Your Xcode Project

To develop an iPhone app, you work in what's called an *Xcode project.* So, time to fire one up. Here's how it's done:

1. **Launch Xcode.**

After you've downloaded the SDK (as described in Chapter 3 of this minibook), it's a snap to launch Xcode. By default, it's downloaded to /Developer/Applications, where you can track it down to launch it.

Here are a couple of hints to make Xcode handier and more efficient:

• Drag the icon for the Xcode application all the way down to the Dock, so you can launch it from there. You'll be using it a lot, so it wouldn't hurt to be able to launch it from the Dock.

• When you first launch Xcode, you see the Welcome screen shown in Figure 4-1. It's chock-full of links to the Apple Developer Connection and Xcode documentation. You may want to leave this screen up to make it easier to get to those links, but I usually close it. If you don't want to be bothered with the Welcome screen in the future, deselect the Show This Window When Xcode Launches check box.

Close the Welcome screen for now; you won't be using it.

Figure 4-1:
The Xcode welcome screen.

2. **Choose File⇨New Project from the main menu to create a new project.**

   You can also just press Shift+⌘+N.

   No matter what you do to start a new project, you're greeted by the New Project window, as shown in Figure 4-2.

   The New Project window is where you get to choose the template you want for your new project. Note that the leftmost pane has two sections: one for the iPhone OS and the other for Mac OS X.

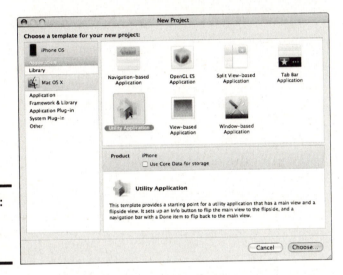

Figure 4-2:
The New
Project
window.

3. **In the upper-left corner of the New Project window, click Application under the iPhone OS heading.**

   After clicking Application, the main pane of the New Project window refreshes, revealing several choices. (Refer to Figure 4-2.) Each of these choices is actually a template that, when chosen, generates some code to get you started.

4. **Select Utility Application from the template choices displayed and then click Choose.**

   I'm selecting Utility Application to start the DeepThoughts app, the first sample app, which you develop in Book III. After selecting a template, the Save As dialog appears.

   Note that when you select a template, a brief description of the template is displayed underneath the main pane. (Again, refer to Figure 4-2 to see a description of the Utility Application template. In fact, click some of the other template choices just to see how they're described as well. Just be sure to click the Utility Application template again to follow along with developing the DeepThoughts app.)

5. **Enter a name for your new project in the Save As field, choose a Save location (the Desktop or any folder works just fine) and then click Save.**

I named the first sample app project DeepThoughts. (You should do the same if you're following along with developing DeepThoughts.)

After you click Save, Xcode creates the project and opens the Project window — which should look like what you see in Figure 4-3.

Overview menu   Toolbar   Breakpoints   Info button   Detail view

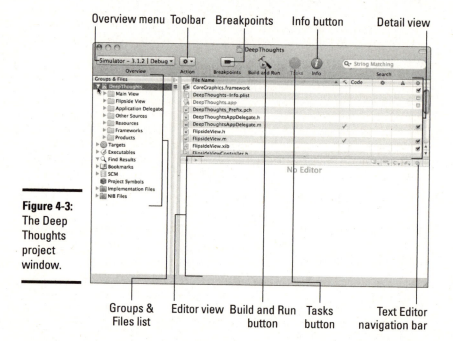

Figure 4-3:
The Deep
Thoughts
project
window.

Groups &   Editor view   Build and Run   Tasks   Text Editor
Files list   button   button   navigation bar

Exploring Your Project

To develop an iPhone app, you have to work within the context of an Xcode project. It turns out that you do most of your work on projects using a Project window very much like the one in Figure 4-3. If you have a nice, large monitor, expand the Project window so you can see everything in it as big as life. This is, in effect, Command Central for developing your iPhone app; it displays and organizes your source files and the other resources needed to build your app.

If you take another peek at Figure 4-3, you see the following:

✦ **The Groups & Files list:** An outline view of everything in your project, the Groups & Files list contains all of your project's files — source code, frameworks, and graphics, as well as some settings files. You can move files and folders around and add new folders. If you select an item in the Groups & Files list, the contents of the item are displayed in the topmost-pane to the right — otherwise known as the Detail view.

You may notice that some of the items in the Groups & Files list are folders, whereas others are just icons. Most have a little triangle (the disclosure triangle) next to them. Clicking the little triangle to the left of a folder expands the folder to show what's in it. Click the triangle again to hide what it contains.

✦ **The Detail view:** Here you get detailed information about the item you selected in the Groups & Files list.

✦ **The Toolbar:** Here you can find quick access to the most common Xcode commands. You can customize the toolbar to your heart's content by right-clicking it and selecting Customize Toolbar from the contextual menu that appears. You can also choose View⇨Customize Toolbar.

  • Pressing the Build and Run button compiles, links, and launches your app.

  • The Breakpoints button turns breakpoints on and off and toggles the Build and Run button to Build and Debug. (I explain breakpoints in Book IV.)

  • The Tasks button allows you to stop the execution of the app that you've built.

  • The Info button opens a window that displays information and settings for your project.

✦ **The status bar:** Look here for messages about your project. (There are none yet in Figure 4-3; for a peek at a status message, see Figure 4-6.) For example, when you're building your project, Xcode updates the status bar to show where you are in the process — and whether or not the process completed successfully.

✦ **The favorites bar:** Works like other favorites bars you're certainly familiar with; so you can bookmark places in your project. This bar isn't displayed by default (nor is it shown in Figure 4-3); to put it onscreen, choose View⇨Layout⇨Show Favorites Bar from the main menu.

✦ **The Text Editor navigation bar:** This navigation bar contains a number of shortcuts. These are shown in Figure 4-4. I explain more about them as you use them.

- *Bookmarks menu:* You create a bookmark by choosing Edit⇨Add to Bookmarks.

- *Breakpoints menu:* Lists the breakpoints in the current file — I cover breakpoints in Book IV.

- *Class Hierarchy menu:* The superclass of this class, the superclass of that superclass (if any), and so on.

- *Included Files menu:* Lists both the files included by the current file, as well as the files that include the current file.

- *Counterpart button:* This allows you to switch between header (or interface) file, such as `FlipsideView.h`, and the implementation file, such as `FlipsideView.m`. The header files define the class's interface by specifying the class declaration (and what it inherits from); instance variables (a variable defined in a class — at runtime all objects have their own copy); and methods. The implementation file, on the other hand, contains the code for each method.

- *Lock button:* Indicates whether the selected file is unlocked for editing or locked (preventing changes). If it's locked, you can click the button to unlock the file (if you have permission).

Included Files menu

Breakpoints menu   Lock button

Figure 4-4:
The Text
Editor
navigation
bar.

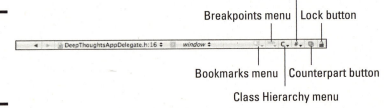

Bookmarks menu   Counterpart button

Class Hierarchy menu

✦ **The Editor view:** Displays a file you've selected, in either the Groups & Files list or Detail view. You can also edit your files here — after all, that's what you'd expect from the Editor view — although some folks prefer to double-click a file in Groups & Files list or Detail view to open the file in a separate window.

To see how the Editor view works, check out Figure 4-5, where I've clicked the Main View folder in the Groups & Files list, and the `MainView.h` class in the Detail view. You can see the code for the class in the Editor view.

Right under the Lock button (refer to Figure 4-5) is a tiny windowshade icon that lets you split the Editor view. Click it to look at the interface and implementation files at the same time, or even the code for two different methods in the same or different classes.

TIP

If you have any questions about what something does, just position the mouse pointer above the icon, and a tooltip explains it.

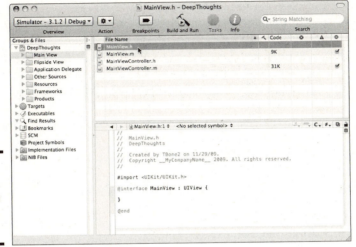

Figure 4-5:
The
MainView.h
file in the
Editor view.

The first item in the Groups & Files view, as you can see in Figure 4-5, is labeled DeepThoughts. This is the container that contains all the source elements for the project, including source code, resource files, graphics, and a number of other pieces that will remain unmentioned for now (but I get into those in due course). You can see that this project container has seven distinct groups — Main view, Flipside view, Application Delegate, Other Sources, Resources, Frameworks, and Products. Here's what gets tossed into each group:

✦ **Main view** is the group in which you place all of your code for the Main view of your utility app, although you are not obliged to. The Main View group has four distinct source-code files (which you can see in Figure 4-5):

- `MainView.h`

- `MainView.m`

- `MainViewController.h`

- `MainViewController.m`

✦ **Flipside view** is the group in which you place all of your code for the flipside view of your utility app — the view that appears when the user taps the *i* (information) button in the Main view (although again, you are not obliged to).

✦ **Application Delegate** is the group in which you place the code for app-specific behavior to customize the behavior of a framework object without having to subclass it (as I describe in Chapter 5 of this minibook). A behavior-rich framework object (used as is) would delegate the task of implementing one of its responsibilities to an object in this group for a very specific behavior. The delegation pattern of adding behaviors to objects is described in more detail in Chapter 5 as well.

✦ **Other Sources** is the group in which you typically would find the pre-compiled headers of the frameworks you will be using — stuff like `DeepThoughts_Prefix.pch` as well as `main.m`, your application's main function.

✦ The **Resources** group contains, well, resources, such as `.xib` files, property lists (which you will encounter in Book V), images, other media files, and even some data files.

Whenever you choose the Utility Application template (refer to Figure 4-2), Xcode creates the following files for you:

- `YourProject-Info.plist`

- `FlipsideView.xib`

- `MainView.xib`

- `MainWindow.xib`

I explain `.xib` files in excruciating detail in this chapter and in Book III and Book V. Soon you'll love the `.xib` files as much as I do.

✦ **Frameworks** are code libraries that act a lot like prefab building blocks for your code edifice. (I talk lots about frameworks in Chapter 5 of this minibook.) By choosing the Utility Application template, you let Xcode know that it should add the `UIKit framework`, `Foundation.framework`, and `CoreGraphics.framework` to your project, because it expects that you'll need them in a Utility Application.

I limit ourselves to just these three frameworks in developing the DeepThoughts app. But I show you how to add additional frameworks in Chapter 4 of Book V.

✦ The **Products** group is a bit different from the previous three items in this list: It's not a source for your app, but rather *the compiled app itself.* In it, you find `DeepThoughts.app`. At the moment, this file is listed in red because the file can't be found (which makes sense because you haven't built the app yet).

A file's name appearing in red lets you know that Xcode can't find the underlying physical file.

If you happen to open the `DeepThoughts` folder on your Mac, you won't see the "folders" that appear in the Xcode window. That's because those folders are simply groupings that help organize and find what you're looking for; this list of files can grow to be pretty large, even in a moderate-size project.

When you have a lot files, you'll have better luck finding things if you create subgroups within the Main View, Flipside View, and/or Resources groups, or even whole new groups. You create subgroups (or even new groups) in the Groups & Files list by choosing New Project⇨New Group. You then can select a file and drag it to a new group or subgroup.

Building and Running Your Application

It's really a blast to see what you get when you build and run a project that you yourself created using a template from the Project window. Doing that is relatively simple:

1. **Choose Simulator - 3.1 | Debug from the Overview drop-down menu in the top-left corner of the project window to set the active SDK and Active Build Configuration.**

It may be already chosen, as you can see in Figure 4-6. Here's what that means:

- When you download an SDK, you actually download *multiple* SDKs — a Simulator SDK and a device SDK for each of the current iPhone OS releases.

- Fortunately, for this book, I use the Simulator SDK and iPhone OS 3.1. Even more fortunately, in Chapter 6 of this minibook, I show you how to switch to the device SDK and download your app to a real-world iPhone. But before you do that, there's just one catch. . . .

- You have to be in the iPhone Developer Program to run your app on a device, even on your very own iPhone.

A *build configuration* tells Xcode the purpose of the built product. You can choose between Debug, which has features to help with debugging (there's a no-brainer for you); and Release, which results in smaller and faster binaries. I use Debug for most of this book, so I recommend you go with Debug for now.

2. **Choose Build⇨Build and Run from the main menu to build and run the application.**

You can also press ⌘+Return or click the Build and Run button in the Project Window toolbar. The status bar in the Project window tells you all about build progress, build errors such as compiler errors, or warnings — and (oh, yeah) whether the build was successful. Figure 4-6 shows that this was a successful build.

Because you selected Debug for the active build configuration, the Debugger Console may launch for you, as shown in Figure 4-7, depending on your Xcode preferences (more about them in a second). If you don't see the console, choose Run⇨Console to display it. (You find out more about debugging in Book IV.)

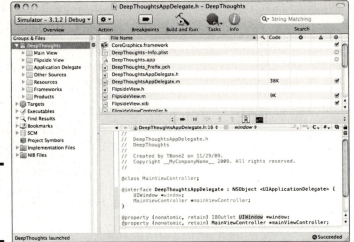

Figure 4-6:
A
successful
build.

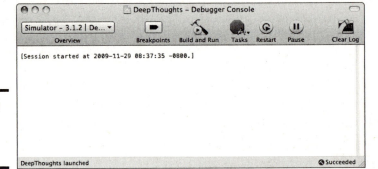

Figure 4-7:
The
Debugger
Console.

After it's launched in the Simulator, your first app looks a lot like what you see in Figure 4-8. You should see the status bar and a gray window with the *i* information button (the hallmark of an app built from the Utility template), but that's it. You can also see the Hardware menu in Figure 4-8, which I explain next.

Now click on the *i* information button to see the flipside view, as shown in Figure 4-9. Whoa! You now have a standard iPhone app flipside view, complete with a Done button. Click the Done button to go back to the Main view. (I know, big deal . . . but about half the work of designing the DeepThoughts app is already done, thanks to the Utility template, and you continue adding functionality in Book III.)

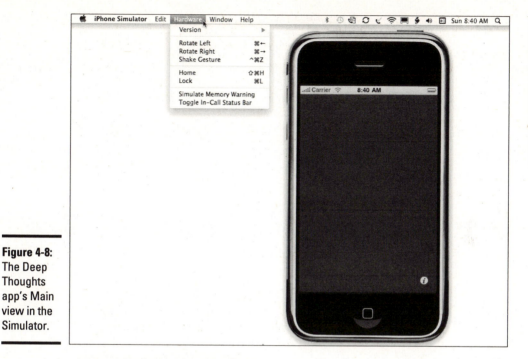

Figure 4-8:
The Deep Thoughts app's Main view in the Simulator.

Figure 4-9:
The Deep Thoughts app's flipside view in the Simulator.

The iPhone Simulator

When you run your app, Xcode installs it on the iPhone Simulator (or a real iPhone device if you specified the device as the active SDK) and launches it. Using the Hardware menu and your keyboard and mouse, the Simulator mimics most of what a user can do on a real iPhone, albeit with some limitations that I point out shortly.

Hardware interaction

You use the iPhone Simulator Hardware menu (refer to Figure 4-8) when you want your device to do the following:

✦ **Rotate left:** Choosing Hardware⇨Rotate Left rotates the Simulator to the left. This enables you to see the Simulator in Landscape mode.

✦ **Rotate right:** Choosing Hardware⇨Rotate Right rotates the Simulator to the right.

✦ **Use a shake gesture:** Choosing Hardware⇨Shake Gesture simulates shaking the iPhone.

✦ **Go to the Home screen:** Choosing Hardware⇨Home does the expected — you go to the home screen.

✦ **Lock the Simulator (device):** Choosing Hardware⇨Lock locks the simulator.

✦ **Send the running app low-memory warnings:** Choosing Hardware⇨Simulate Memory Warning fakes out your app by sending it a (fake) low-memory warning. I don't cover this, but it's a great feature for seeing how your app may function out there in the real world.

✦ **Toggle the status bar between its Normal state and its In Call state:** Choose Hardware⇨Toggle In-Call Status Bar to check out how your app functions when the iPhone is not answering a call (Normal state) and when it supposedly *is* answering a call (In Call state).

The status bar becomes taller when you're on a call than when you're not. Choosing In Call state here shows you how things look when your application is launched while the user is on the phone.

Gestures

On the real device, a gesture is something you do with your fingers to make something happen in the device, like a tap, or a drag, and so on. Table 4-1 shows you how to simulate gestures using your mouse and keyboard.

Table 4-1	Gestures in the Simulator
Gesture	*iPhone Action*
Tap	Click the mouse.
Touch and hold	Hold down the mouse button.
Double tap	Double-click the mouse.
Swipe	1. Click where you want to start and hold the mouse button down.
	2. Move the mouse slowly in the direction of the swipe and then release the mouse button.
Flick	1. Click where you want to start and hold the mouse button down.
	2. Move the mouse quickly in the direction of the flick and then release the mouse button.
Drag	1. Click where you want to start and hold the mouse button down.
	2. Move the mouse slowly in the drag direction.
Pinch	1. Move the mouse pointer over the place where you want to start.
	2. Hold down the Option key, which makes two circles appear that stand in for your fingers.
	3. Hold down the mouse button and move the circles in or out.

Uninstalling apps and resetting your device

You uninstall applications on the Simulator the same way you'd do it on the iPhone, except you use your mouse instead of your finger.

1. **On the Home screen, place the pointer over the icon of the app you want to uninstall and hold down the mouse button until all of the app icons start to wiggle.**

2. **Click the app icon's Close button — the little *x* that appears in the upper-left corner of the icon — to make the app disappear.**

3. **Click the Home button — the one with a little square in it, centered below the screen — to stop the other app icon's wiggling and finish the uninstallation.**

You can also move an app's icon around by clicking and dragging with the mouse.

To reset the Simulator to the original factory settings — which also removes all the apps you've installed — choose iPhone Simulator⇨Reset Content and Settings from the Hardware menu.

Limitations

Keep in mind that running apps in the iPhone Simulator is not the same thing as running them in the iPhone. Here's why:

✦ **Different frameworks:** The Simulator uses Mac OS X versions of the low-level system frameworks, instead of the actual frameworks that run on the device.

✦ **Different hardware and memory:** The Simulator uses the Mac hardware and memory. To really determine how your app is going to perform on an honest-to-goodness iPhone device, you're going to have to run it on a real iPhone device. (Lucky for you, I show you how to do that in Chapter 6 of this minibook.)

✦ **Different installation procedure:** Xcode installs your app in the iPhone Simulator automatically when you build the app using the iPhone Simulator SDK. (You can see that in Figure 4-8, earlier in this chapter, for example.) All fine and dandy, but there's no way to get Xcode to install apps from the App Store in the iPhone Simulator.

✦ **Lack of GPS:** You can't fake the iPhone Simulator into thinking it's lying on the beach at Waikiki. The location reported by the `CoreLocation` framework in the Simulator is fixed at

  • Latitude: 37.3317 North

  • Longitude: 122.0307 West

Which just so happens to be 1 Infinite Loop, Cupertino, CA 95014, and guess who "lives" there?

✦ **Two-finger limit:** You can simulate a maximum of two fingers. If your application's user interface can respond to touch events involving more than two fingers, you will need to test that on an actual device. The motion of the two fingers is limited in the Simulator — you can't do two-figure swipes or drags.

✦ **Accelerometer differences:** You can access your computer's accelerometer (if it has one) through the `UIKit` framework. Its reading, however, will differ from the accelerometer readings on an iPhone (for some technical reasons I don't get into).

✦ **Differences in rendering:** OpenGL ES (OpenGL for Embedded Systems), one of the 3D graphics libraries that works with the iPhone SDK, uses renderers on devices that are slightly different from those it uses in iPhone Simulator. As a result, a scene on the simulator and the same scene on a device may not be identical at the pixel level.

Customizing Xcode to Your Liking

Xcode gives you options galore; I'm guessing you won't change any of them until you have a bit more programming experience under your belt, but a few options are actually worth thinking about now.

1. **With Xcode open, choose Xcode⇨Preferences from the main menu.**

2. **Click Debugging in the toolbar to show the Debugging pane, as shown in Figure 4-10.**

   The Xcode Preferences window refreshes to show the Debugging pane.

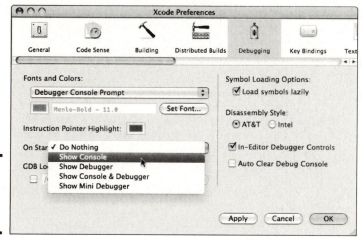

Figure 4-10:
Always
show the
console.

3. **Open the On Start drop-down menu and choose Show Console (as shown in Figure 4-10). Then click Apply.**

   This step automatically opens the Console after you build your app, so you won't have to take the extra step of opening the Console to see your app's output.

4. **Click the Building button in the toolbar to show the Building pane, as shown in Figure 4-11.**

5. **In the Build Results Window section of the Building pane, select the Open During Builds drop-down menu, and choose Always, as shown in Figure 4-11. Then click Apply.**

   The Always choice opens the Build Results window and keeps it open. You might not like this, but some people find having the Build Results window onscreen all the time makes it easier to find and fix errors.

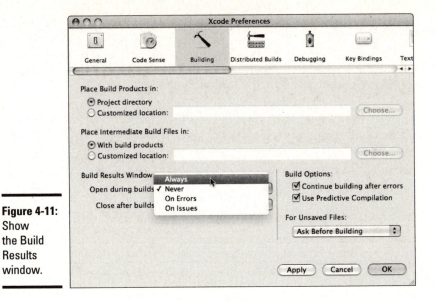

Figure 4-11:
Show
the Build
Results
window.

6. **Click the Documentation button in the toolbar, as shown in Figure 4-12. (You may have to scroll the toolbar horizontally to access it.)**

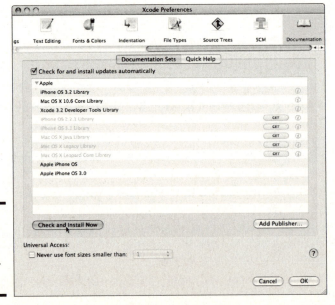

Figure 4-12:
Accessing
the
documenta-
tion.

7. **Select the Check for and Install Updates Automatically check box (shown in Figure 4-12) and then click the Check and Install Now button.**

   This step ensures that the documentation remains up-to-date and also allows you to load and access other documentation.

8. **Click OK to close the Xcode Preferences window.**

Set the tab width and other formatting options in the Indentation pane of the Preferences window.

You can also have the Editor show line numbers. If you click Text Editing in the Xcode Preferences toolbar to show the Text Editing pane, you can select the Show Line Numbers check box under Display Options. I don't take this step now, but having line numbers visible becomes very useful in Chapter 1 of Book IV.

Using Interface Builder

Interface Builder is a great tool for graphically laying out your user interface. You can use it to design your app's user interface and then save what you've done as a resource file, which is then loaded into your app at runtime. This resource file is then used to automatically create the single window, as well as all your views and controls, and some of your app's other objects — view controllers, for example. (For more on view controllers and other application objects, check out Chapter 5 in this minibook.)

If you don't want to use Interface Builder, you can also create your objects programmatically — creating views and view controllers and even things like buttons and labels using your very own application code. I show you how to do that as well. Often Interface Builder makes things easier, but sometimes just coding it is the best way.

Here's how Interface Builder works:

1. **In your Project window's Groups & Files list, expand the Resources group and select the `FlipsideView.xib` file.**

2. **Double-click the `FlipsideView.xib` file, which is shown in Figure 4-13.**

   You could have just double-clicked the file in the Groups & Files list as well.

   Note that `FlipsideViewController.m` is still in the Editor window; that's okay because I'm set to edit the `FlipsideView.xib` file in the Interface Builder, not in the Editor window. That's because double-clicking always opens a file in a new window — this time, the Interface Builder window.

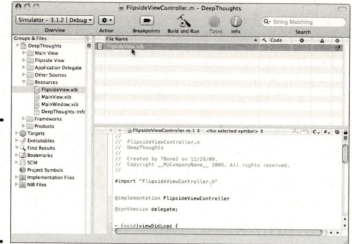

Figure 4-13:
Selecting
and double-
clicking the
Flipside
View.xib
file.

What you see after double-clicking are the windows as they were the
last time you left them. If this is the first time you've opened Interface
Builder, you see windows that look something like those in Figure 4-14.

Not surprisingly, the Flipside view window in Figure 4-14 shows the flipside view, which looks exactly as it did in the iPhone Simulator. (Refer to
Figure 4-9.)

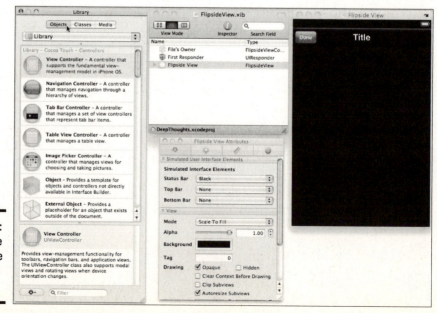

Figure 4-14:
The Flipside
View.xib file
in Interface
Builder.

Interface Builder supports two file types: an older format that uses the extension `.nib` and a newer format that utilizes the extension `.xib`. The iPhone project templates all use `.xib` files. Although the file extension is `.xib`, everyone still calls them *nib files*. The term *nib* and the corresponding file extension `.xib` are acronyms for NeXT Interface Builder. The Interface Builder application was originally developed at NeXT Computer, whose OPENSTEP operating system was used as the basis for creating Mac OS X.

The window labeled `FlipsideView.xib` (the top center window in Figure 4-14) is the nib's main window. It acts as a table of contents for the nib file. With the exception of the first two icons (File's Owner and First Responder), every icon in this window (in this case, there's only one, but you'll find more as you get into nib files) represents a single instance of an Objective-C class that will be created automatically for you when this nib file is loaded.

Interface Builder doesn't generate any code that you have to modify or even look at. Instead, it creates the ingredients for "instant" Objective-C objects that the nib loading code combines and turns into real objects at runtime.

If you were to take a closer look at the three objects in the `FlipsideView.xib` file window — and if you had a pal who knew the iPhone backwards and forwards — you'd find out the following about each object:

✦ **The File's Owner proxy object:** This is the controller object that's responsible for the contents of the nib file. In this case, the File's Owner object is actually the `FlipsideViewController` that was created by Xcode. The File's Owner object is not created from the nib file. It's created in one of two ways: either from another (previous) nib file or by a programmer who codes it manually.

✦ **First Responder proxy object:** This object is the first entry in an app's dynamically constructed responder chain (a term I explain in Chapter 1 of Book III) and is the object with which the user is currently interacting. If, for example, the user taps a text field to enter some data, the First Responder would then become the Text Field object.

Although you might use the First Responder mechanism quite a bit in your apps, there's actually nothing you have to do to manage it. It's automatically set and maintained by the `UIKit` framework.

✦ **View object:** The View icon represents an instance of the `UIView` class. A `UIView` object is an area (in this case, the Flipside view) that a user can see and interact with.

If you take another look at Figure 4-14, you notice two other windows open besides the main window. Look at the Flipside view window that has the word Title in the title bar. That window is the graphical representation of the View icon. If you close the Flipside view window and then double-click the View icon, this window opens again. This window is your canvas for creating your user interface: It's where you drag user-interface elements such as buttons and text fields. These objects come from the Library window (the leftmost window in Figure 4-14).

The Library window contains your palette — the stock Cocoa Touch objects that Interface Builder supports. Dragging an item from the Library to the Flipside view window adds an object of that type to the View (and remember, as subview).

If you happen to close the Library window, whether by accident or by design, you can get it to reappear by choosing Tools⇨Library.

It's Time to Explore

Finally, at what may seem at long last (although it's really been only a few pages), you're ready to look behind the screen and see exactly how an iPhone app works.

So take a break if you need to, but come back ready to explore.

Chapter 5: Looking Behind the Screen

In This Chapter

✔ Seeing how applications actually work

✔ Understanding how to use the fundamental design patterns

✔ Doing Windows (even if you say you don't)

✔ Exploring an app with a view

✔ Manipulating view controllers

✔ Listing the frameworks you can use

O ne thing that makes iPhone software development so appealing is the richness of the tools and frameworks provided in the Apple's iPhone Software Development Kit (SDK). The *frameworks* are especially important; each one is a distinct body of code that actually implements your application's generic functionality — gives the application its basic way of working, in other words. This is especially true of one framework in particular: the UIKit framework, which is the heart of the user interface.

In this chapter, you find out about most of the iPhone's user interface architecture, which is a mostly static view that explains what the various pieces are, what each does, and how they interact with each other. This chapter lays the groundwork for developing the DeepThoughts app's user interface, which you get a chance to tackle in Book III.

Using Frameworks

A *framework* offers common code providing generic functionality. The iPhone OS provides a set of frameworks for incorporating technologies, services, and features into your apps. For example, the UIKit framework gives you event-handling support, drawing support, windows, views, and controls you can use in your app.

A framework is designed to easily integrate your code that runs your game or delivers the information that your user wants. Frameworks are similar to software libraries, but with an added twist: They also *implement* a program's flow of control (unlike a software library whose components are arranged by the programmer into a flow of control). This means that, instead of the programmer deciding the order that things should happen — such as which messages are sent to which objects and in what order when an application launches, or when a user touches a button on the screen — the order is a part of the framework and doesn't need to be specified by the programmer.

When you use a framework, you provide your app with a ready-made set of basic functions; you've told it, "Here's how to act." With the framework in place, all you need to do is *add* the specific functionality that you want in the app — the content as well as the controls and views that enable the user to access and use that content — *to* the frameworks.

The frameworks and the iPhone OS provide some pretty complex functionality, such as

✦ Launching the app and displaying a window on the screen

✦ Displaying controls on the screen and responding to a user action — changing a toggle switch for example, or scrolling a view, like the list of your contacts

✦ Accessing sites on the Internet, not just through a browser, but from within your own program

✦ Managing user preferences

✦ Playing sounds and movies

✦ The list goes on — you get the picture

Some developers talk in terms of "using a framework" — but your app doesn't use frameworks so much as the frameworks use your app. Your app provides the functions that the framework accesses; the framework needs your code in order to become an app that does something other than start up, display a blank window, and then end. This perspective makes figuring out how to work with a framework much easier. (For one thing, it lets the programmer know where he or she is essential.)

If this seems too good to be true, well, okay, it is — all that complexity (and convenience) comes at a cost. It can be really difficult to absorb the whole thing and know exactly where (and how) to add your app's functionality to that supplied by the framework. That's where *design patterns* come in. Understanding the design patterns behind the frameworks gives you a way of thinking about a framework — especially `UIKit` — that doesn't make your head explode.

Using Design Patterns

A major theme of this chapter is the fact that, when it comes to iPhone app development, the `UIKit` framework does a lot of the heavy lifting for you.

That's all well and good, but it's a little more complicated than that: The framework is designed around certain programming paradigms, also known as *design patterns*. The design pattern is a model that your own code must be consistent with.

To understand how to take best advantage of the power of the framework — or (better put) how the framework objects want to use *your app* best — you need to understand design patterns. If you don't understand them or if you try to work around them because you're sure you have a "better" way of doing things, your job will actually be much more difficult. (Developing software can be hard enough, so making your job more difficult is definitely something you want to avoid.) Getting a handle on the basic design patterns used (and expected by) the framework helps you develop an app that makes the best use of the framework. This means the least amount of work in the shortest amount of time.

The iPhone design patterns can help you to understand not only how to structure your code, but also how the framework itself is structured. They describe relationships and interactions between classes or objects, as well as how responsibilities should be distributed amongst classes so the iPhone does what you want it to do.

The common definition of a design pattern is "a solution to a problem in a context." (Uh, guys, that's not too helpful.) At that level of abstraction, the concept gets fuzzy and ambiguous. So here's how I use the term throughout this All-in-One book:

> In programming terms, a *design pattern* is a commonly used template that gives you a consistent way to get a particular task done.

You need to be comfortable with these three basic design patterns:

✦ Model-View-Controller (MVC)

✦ Delegation

✦ Target-Action

Of these, the Model-View-Controller design pattern is the key to understanding how an iPhone app works. I defer the discussion of the last two until after you get the MVC under your belt.

The Model-View-Controller (MVC) pattern

The iPhone frameworks are *object-oriented*. The easiest way to understand what that really means is to think about a team. The work that needs to get done is divided and assigned to individual team members (objects). Every member of a team has a job and works with other team members to get things done. What's more, a good team doesn't butt in on what other members are doing — just like how an object in object-oriented programming spends its time taking care of business and not caring what the object in the virtual cubicle next door is doing.

Object-oriented programming was originally developed to make code more maintainable, reusable, extensible, and understandable (what a concept!) by tucking all the functionality behind well-defined interfaces. The actual details of how something works (as well as its data) are hidden, which makes modifying and extending an application much easier.

Great — so far — but a pesky question still plagues programmers:

Exactly how do you decide on the objects and what each one does?

Sometimes the answer to that question is pretty easy — just use the real world as a model. (Eureka!) In the RoadTrip app that serves as an example in Books V, VI, and VII, some of the classes of model objects are `Weather` and `CarInformation`. But when it comes to a generic program structure, how *do* you decide what the objects should be? That may not be so obvious.

The MVC pattern is a well-established way to group application functions into objects. Variations of it have been around at least since the early days of Smalltalk, one of the very first object-oriented languages. The MVC is a high-level pattern — it addresses the architecture of an application and classifies objects according to the general roles they play in an application.

The MVC pattern creates, in effect, a miniature universe for the application, populated with three kinds of objects. It also specifies roles and responsibilities for all three objects and specifies the way they're supposed to interact with each other. To make things more concrete (that is, to keep your head from exploding), imagine a big, beautiful, 60-inch flat screen TV. Here's the gist:

✦ **Model objects:** These objects together comprise the content "engine" of your app. They contain the app's data and logic — making your app more than just a pretty face. In the RoadTrip application, for example, the model maintains a list of hotels and information about each and allows you to add to that list. Chapter 1 of Book VII shows you how to create a `Hotel` model object to encapsulate that information.

You can think of the *model* (which may be one object or several that interact) as a particular television program, one that, quite frankly, does not give a hoot about what TV set it is being shown on.

In fact, the model shouldn't give a hoot. Even though it owns its data, it should have no connection at all to the user interface and should be blissfully ignorant about what is being done with its data.

✦ **View objects:** These objects display things on the screen and respond to user actions. Pretty much anything you can see is a kind of view object — the window and all the controls, for example. Your views know how to display information that it has gotten from the model object, and how to get any input from the user the model may need. But the view itself should know nothing about the model. It may handle a request to find a hotel, but it doesn't bother itself with what that request means. It may display the different ways to get to the hotel, although it doesn't care about the content options it displays for you.

You can think of the *view* as a television screen that doesn't care about what program it is showing or what channel you just selected.

The UIKit framework provides many different kinds of views, as you'll find out later on in this chapter.

If the view knows nothing about the model, and the model knows nothing about the view, how do you get data and other notifications to pass from one to the other? To get that conversation started (Model: "I've just updated my data." View: "Hey, give me something to display," for example), you need the third element in the MVC triumvirate, the controller.

✦ **Controller objects:** These objects connect the application's view objects to its model objects. They supply the view objects with what they need to display (getting it from the model), and also provide the model with user input from the view.

You can think of the *controller* as the circuitry that pulls the show off of the cable and then sends it to the screen or requests a particular pay-per-view show.

The MVC in action

Imagine that an iPhone user is in San Francisco, and he or she starts the handy RoadTrip app mentioned so often in these pages. The view will display his or her location as "San Francisco." The user may tap a button that requests the weather. The controller interprets that request and tells the model what it needs to do by sending a message to the appropriate method in the model object with the necessary parameters. The model accesses the www.weather.com Web site (or fails to access it, due to the lack of an Internet connection), and the controller then delivers that information to the view, which promptly displays the information — either the appropriate page from www.weather.com, or the Weather is not available offline message.

All this is illustrated in Figure 5-1.

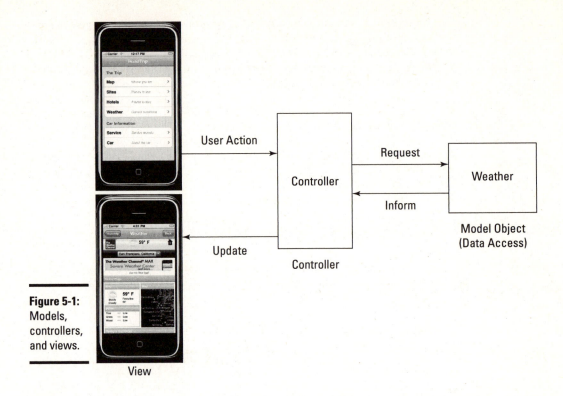

Figure 5-1:
Models,
controllers,
and views.

View

When you think about your application in terms of Model, View, and Controller objects, the `UIKit` framework starts to make sense. It also begins to lift the fog from where at least part of your application-specific behavior needs to go. Before I get more into that, however, you need to know a little more about the classes provided to you by the `UIKit` that implement the MVC design pattern — windows, views, and view controllers.

Working with Windows and Views

After an app is launched, it's going to be the only app running on the system — aside from the operating system software, of course. iPhone apps have only a single window, so you won't find separate document windows for displaying content. Instead, everything is displayed in that single window, and your application interface takes over the entire screen. When your application is running, it's all the user is doing with the iPhone.

Looking out the window

The single window you see displayed on the iPhone is an instance of the `UIWindow` class. This window is created at launch time, either programmatically by you or automatically by `UIKit` loading it from a *nib* file — a special file that contains instant objects that are reconstituted at runtime (You can find out more about nib files in Chapter 4 of this minibook). You then add views and controls to the window. In general, after you create the Window object (that is, if you create it instead of having it done for you), you never really have to think about it again.

A user can't directly close or manipulate an iPhone window. It is your app that programmatically manages the window.

Although your application never creates more than one window at a time, the iPhone OS does use additional windows on top of your window. The system status bar is one example. You can also display alerts on top of your window by using the supplied Alert views.

Figure 5-2 shows the window layout on the iPhone for the RoadTrip app.

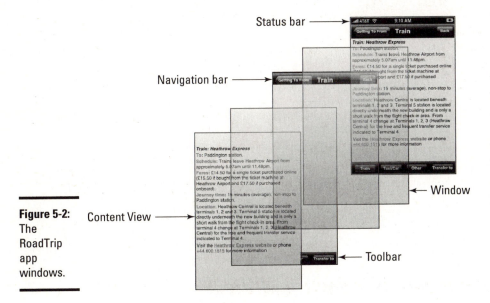

Figure 5-2: The RoadTrip app windows.

Admiring the view

In an iPhone app world, view objects are responsible for the view functionality in the Model-View-Controller architecture.

A view is a rectangular area on the screen (on top of a window). The *Content view* is that portion of data and controls that appear between the upper and lower bars shown in Figure 5-2.

In the `UIKit` framework, windows are really a special kind of view, but for purposes of this discussion, I'm talking about views that sit on top of the window.

What views do

Views are the main way for your app to interact with a user. This interaction happens in two ways:

✦ **Views display content.** For example, by making drawing and animation happen onscreen.

   In essence, the view object displays the data from the model object.

✦ **Views handle touch events.** They respond when the user touches a button, for example.

   Handling touch events is part of a *responder chain* (a special logical sequence detailed in Chapter 4 of Book III).

The view hierarchy

Views and subviews create a view hierarchy. There are two ways of looking at it (no pun intended this time): visually (how the user perceives it) and programmatically (how you create it). You must be clear about the differences, or you will find yourself in a state of confusion that resembles Times Square on New Year's Eve.

Looking at it visually, the window is at the base of this hierarchy with a *Content view* on top of it (a transparent view that fills the window's Content rectangle). The Content view displays information and also allows the user to interact with the application, using (preferably standard) user-interface items such as text fields, buttons, toolbars, and tables.

In your program, that relationship is different. The Content view is added to the window view as a *subview*.

✦ Views added to the Content view become *subviews* of it.

✦ Views added to the Content view become the *superviews* of any views added to them.

✦ A view can have one (and only one) superview and zero or more subviews.

It seems counterintuitive, but a subview is displayed *on top of* its parent view (that is, on top of its superview). Think about this relationship as containment: A superview *contains* its subviews. Figure 5-3 shows an example of a view hierarchy.

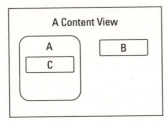

A Content View

A

C

B

The visual hierarchy
... translates to a structural one:

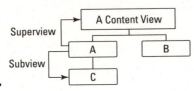

Superview

A Content View

A   B

Subview

C

Figure 5-3:
The view
hierarchy
is both
visual and
structural.

Controls — such as buttons, text fields, and the like — are really view sub-classes that become subviews. So are any other display areas you may specify. The view must manage its subviews, as well as resize itself with respect to its superviews. Fortunately, much of what the view must do is already coded for you. The UIKit framework supplies the code that defines view behavior.

The view hierarchy plays a key role in both drawing and event handling. When a window is sent a message to display itself, the window asks its subview to render itself first. If that view has a subview, it asks *its* subview to render itself first, going down the structural hierarchy (or up the visual structure) until the last subview is reached. It then renders itself and returns to its caller, which renders itself, and so on.

You create or modify a view hierarchy whenever you add a view to another view, either programmatically or with the help of the Interface Builder. The UIKit framework automatically handles all the relationships associated with the view hierarchy.

Developers typically gloss over this visual versus programmatic view hierarchy stuff when starting out — and without understanding this, it is really difficult to get a handle on what's going on.

The kinds of views you use

The UIView class defines the basic properties of a view, and you may be able to use it as is — like you do in the DeepThoughts app — by simply adding some controls.

The framework also provides you with a number of other views that are sub-classed from `UIView`. These views implement the kinds of things that you as a developer need to do on a regular basis.

It's important to use the view objects that are part of the `UIKit` framework. When you use an object such as a `UISlider` or `UIButton`, your slider or button behaves just like a slider or button in any other iPhone app. This enables the consistency in appearance and behavior across apps that users expect. (For more on how this kind of consistency is one of the characteristics of a great app, see Chapter 1 of this minibook.)

Container views

Container views are a technical (Apple) term for Content views that do more than just lie there on the screen and display your controls and other content.

The `UIScrollView` class, for example, adds scrolling without you having to do any work.

`UITableView` inherits this scrolling capability from `UIScrollView` and adds the ability to display lists and respond to the selections of an item in that list. Think of the Contacts application (and a host of others). `UITableView` is one of the primary navigation views on the iPhone; you'll work a lot with table views starting with Chapter 1 of Book VI.

Another container view, the `UIToolbar` class, contains button-like controls — and you find those everywhere on the iPhone. In Mail, for example, you touch an icon in the bottom toolbar to respond to an e-mail.

Controls

Controls are the fingertip-friendly graphics you see extensively used in a typical application's user interface. Controls are actually subclasses of the `UIControl` superclass, a subclass of the `UIView` class. They include touch-able items like buttons, sliders, and switches, as well as text fields in which you enter data.

Controls make heavy use of the Target-Action design pattern, which you get to see with the Done button in the Flipside view of the DeepThoughts app in Chapter 2 of Book III.

Display views

Think of display views as controls that look good, but don't really do anything except, well, look good. These include `UIImageView`, `UILabel` (which you use in the DeepThoughts app in Chapter 3 of Book III to display the area in which the falling words appear), `UIProgressView`, and `UIActivityIndicatorView`.

Text and Web views

Text and *Web views* provide a way to display formatted text in your application. The `UITextView` class supports the display and editing of multiple lines of text in a scrollable area. The `UIWebView` class provides a way to display HTML content. These views can be used as the Content view, or they can also be used in the same way as a display view above, as a subview of a Content view. Neal uses a `UIWebView` in the RoadTrip app in Chapter 4 of Book V to display car information and servicing views, as well as Weather views. `UIWebView` also is the primary way to include graphics and formatted text in text display views.

Alert views and action sheets

Alert views and *action sheets* present a message to the user, along with buttons that allow the user to respond to the message. Alert views and action sheets are similar in function but look and behave differently. For example, the `UIAlertView` class displays a blue alert box that pops up on the screen, and the `UIActionSheet` class displays a box that slides in from the bottom of the screen.

Navigation views

Tab bars and *navigation bars* work in conjunction with view controllers to provide tools for navigating in your app. Normally, you don't need to create a `UITabBar` or `UINavigationBar` directly — it's easier to use Interface Builder or configure these views through a tab bar or navigation bar controller.

The window

A *window* provides a surface for drawing content and is the root container for all other views.

Controlling View Controllers

View controllers implement the controller component of the Model-View-Controller design pattern. These Controller objects contain the code that connects the app's view objects to its model objects. They provide the data to the view. Whenever the view needs to display something, the view controller goes out and gets what the view needs from the model. Similarly, view controllers respond to controls in your Content view and may do things like tell the model to update its data (when the user adds or changes text in a text field, for example), or compute something (the current value of, say, your U.S. dollars in British pounds), or change the view being displayed (like when the user hits the Detail Disclosure button on the iPod application to learn more about a song).

As shown in "The Target-Action pattern" section later in this chapter, a view controller is often the (target) object that responds to the on-screen controls. The Target-Action mechanism is what enables the view controller to be aware of any changes in the view, which can then be transmitted to the model. For example, Figure 5-4 shows what happens when the user taps the Weather entry in the RoadTrip app to request the current weather conditions.

1. A message is sent to that view's view controller to handle the request.

2. The view controller's method interacts with the Weather model object.

3. The model object processes the request from the user for the current weather.

4. The model object sends the data back to the view controller.

5. The view controller creates a new view to present the information.

View controllers have other vital iPhone responsibilities as well, such as:

✦ Managing a set of views — including creating them, or flushing them from memory during low-memory situations.

✦ Responding to a change in the device's orientation — say, landscape to portrait — by resizing the managed views to match the new orientation.

✦ Creating a *modal* view, which is a child window that displays a dialog requiring the user to do something (touch the Yes button, for example) before returning to the application.

You would use a modal view to ensure that the user has paid attention to the implications of an action (for example, "Are you *sure* you want to delete all your contacts?").

View controllers are also typically the objects that serve as delegates and data sources for table views (more about those in Chapter 1 of Book VI).

In addition to the base `UIViewController` class, `UIKit` includes sub-classes such as `UITabBarController`, `UINavigationController`, `UITableViewController`, and `UIImagePickerController` to manage the tab bar, navigation bar, table views, and to access the camera and Photo library.

Even if you're developing a graphics-intensive app, you'll want to use a view controller just to manage a single view and auto-rotate it when the device's orientation changes.

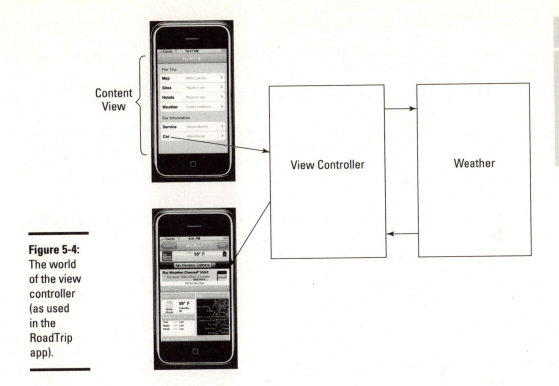

Figure 5-4:
The world
of the view
controller
(as used
in the
RoadTrip
app).

What About the Model?

As this chapter shows (and as you will continue to discover), a lot of the functionality you need is already in the frameworks.

But when it comes to the model objects, for the most part, you're pretty much on your own. You need to design and create model objects to hold the data and carry out the logic. In the RoadTrip app, for example, you create a `Weather` object that knows how to get the weather conditions for the iPhone's current location, and a `CarInformation` object that returns information about the car.

You may find classes in the framework that help you get the nuts and bolts of the model working. But the actual content and specific functionality is up to you. As for actually implementing model objects, you find out how to do that in Chapter 4 of Book V.

Using naming conventions

When creating your own classes, it's a good idea to follow a couple of standard framework-naming conventions.

✔ Class names (such as `View`) should start with a capital letter.

✔ The names of methods (such as `view DidLoad`) should start with a lowercase letter.

✔ The names of instance variables (such as `frame`) should start with a lowercase letter.

When you do it this way, it makes it easier to understand from the name what something actually is.

Adding Your Own Application's Behavior

Earlier in this chapter (by now it probably seems like a million years ago), I mention two other design patterns used in addition to the Model-View-Controller (MVC) pattern. If you have a photographic memory, you won't need us telling you that those two patterns are the Delegation pattern and the Target-Action pattern. These patterns, along with the MVC pattern and subclassing, provide the mechanisms for you to add your app-specific behavior to the `UIKit` (and any other) framework.

The first way to add behavior is through model objects in the MVC pattern. Model objects contain the data and logic that make, well, your application.

The second way, the way people traditionally think about adding behavior to an object-oriented program, is through *subclassing,* where you first create a new (sub) class that inherits behavior and instance variables from another (super) class and then add additional behavior, instance variables, and *properties* (I explain properties in Chapter 4 of Book II) to the mix until you come up with just what you want. The idea here is to start with something basic and then add to it — kind of like taking a deuce coupe (1932 Ford) and turning it into a hot rod. You'd subclass a view controller class, for example, to respond to controls.

The third way to add behavior involves using the Delegation pattern, which allows you to customize an object's behavior without subclassing by basically forcing another object to do the first object's work for it. For example, the Delegation design pattern is used at application startup to invoke a method `applicationDidFinishLaunching:` that gives you a place to do your own application-specific initialization. All you do is add your code to the method.

The final way to add behavior involves the Target-Action design pattern, which allows your application to respond to an event. When a user touches a button, for example, you specify what method should be invoked to respond to the button touch. What is interesting about this pattern is that it also requires subclassing — usually a view controller (refer to Figure 5-4) — in order to add the code to handle the event.

The next few sections go into a little more detail about Delegation patterns and Target-Action patterns.

The Delegation pattern

Delegation is a pattern used extensively in the iPhone frameworks, so much so that it's very important to clearly understand it. In fact, once you understand it, your life will be much easier.

Delegation, as I mention in the previous section, is a way of customizing the behavior of an object without subclassing it. Instead, one object (a Framework object) delegates the task of implementing one of its responsibilities to another object. You're using a behavior-rich object supplied by the framework *as is,* and putting the code for program-specific behavior in a separate (delegate) object. When a request is made of the Framework object, the method of the delegate that implements the program-specific behavior is automatically called.

For example, the `UIApplication` object handles most of the actual work needed to run the application. But, as you will see, it sends your application delegate the `applicationDidFinishLaunching:` message to give you an opportunity to restore the application's window and view to where it was when the user previously left off. You can also use this method to create objects that are unique to your app.

When a Framework object has been designed to use delegates to implement certain behaviors, the behaviors it requires (or gives you the option to implement) are defined in a *protocol.*

Protocols define an interface that the delegate object implements. On the iPhone, protocols can be formal or informal, although I concentrate solely on the former because it includes support for things like type checking and runtime checking to see if an object conforms to the protocol.

In a formal protocol, you usually don't have to implement all the methods; many are declared optional, meaning you only have to implement the ones relevant to your app. Before it attempts to send a message to its delegate, the host object determines whether the delegate implements the method (via a `respondsToSelector:` message) to avoid the embarrassment of branching into nowhere if the method is not implemented.

You can find out much more about delegation and the Delegation pattern when you develop the DeepThoughts app and especially the RoadTrip app in later minibooks.

The Target-Action pattern

You use the *Target-Action* pattern to let your app know that a user has done something. He or she may have tapped a button or entered some text, for example. The control — a button, say — sends a message (the Action message) that you specify to the target you have selected to handle that particular action. The receiving object, or the Target, is usually a view controller object.

If you wanted to develop an app that could start a car from an iPhone (not a bad idea for those who live in a place like Minneapolis in winter), you could display two buttons, Start and Heater. You could use Interface Builder to specify, when the user taps Start, that the target is the CarController object and that the method to invoke is ignition. Figure 5-5 shows the Target-Action mechanism in action. (If you're curious about IBAction and (id) sender, I explain what they are when I show you how to use the Target-Action pattern in your application.)

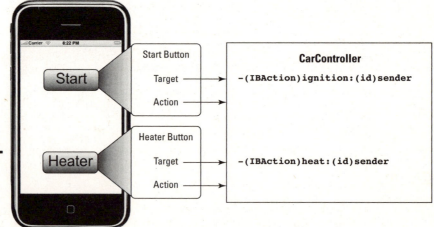

Figure 5-5:
The Target-Action mechanism.

The Target-Action mechanism enables you to create a control object and tell it not only what object you want handling the event, but also the message to send. For example, if the user touches a Ring Bell button onscreen, you want to send a Ring Bell message to the view controller. But if the Wave Flag button on the same screen is touched, you want to be able to send the Wave Flag message to the same view controller. If you couldn't specify the message, all buttons would have to send the same message. It would then make the coding more difficult and more complex because you would have to identify which button had sent the message and what to do in response.

It would also make changing the user interface more work and more error prone.

When creating your app, you can set a control's action and target through the Interface Builder. This setting allows you to specify what method in which object should respond to a control without having to write any code.

You can also change the target and action dynamically by sending the control or its cell `setTarget:` and `setAction:` messages.

For more on the Interface Builder, check out Chapter 2 of Book III.

Doing What When?

The `UIKit` framework provides a great deal of ready-made functionality, but the beauty of `UIKit` lies in the fact that — as this chapter explains — you can customize its behavior using three distinct mechanisms.

✦ Subclassing

✦ Target-Action

✦ Delegation

One of the challenges facing a new developer is to determine which of these mechanisms to use when. (That was certainly the case for me.) To ensure that you have an overall conceptual picture of the iPhone application architecture, check out the Cheat Sheet for Neal's other book, *iPhone Application Development For Dummies*, which offers a summary of which mechanisms are used when. You can find the Cheat Sheet at `www.dummies.com/cheatsheet/iphoneapplicationdevelopment`.

Whew!

Congratulations! You have just gone through the Classic Comics version of hundreds of pages of Apple documentation, reference manuals, and how-to guides.

Well, you still have quite a bit more to explore. But before you get started learning how to use Objective C with iPhone technologies (Book II), it helps to know more about the app publishing process, how to provision your app for development, and the App Store do's and don'ts (Chapter 6 of this minibook), as well as how to go beyond the App Store to market your apps (Chapter 7 of this minibook).

When you've had a stroll through those adventures, you'll know everything you need to know about provisioning your app for the App Store and designing an app that customers might actually want. (How's that for a plan?)

Chapter 6: Death, Taxes, and iPhone Provisioning

In This Chapter

✓ **Running your application on the iPhone**

✓ **Getting the app ready for distribution**

✓ **Taking the app to market — that is, the App Store**

Benjamin Franklin once said, "In this world nothing can be said to be certain, except death and taxes." Here's another certainty in this earthly vale of tears: Everybody has the same hoops to jump through to get an app onto an iPhone and then into the App Store — and nobody much likes jumping through hoops, but there they are.

So you're working on your app, running it in the Simulator, as happy as a virtual clam, and all of a sudden you get this urge to see what your creation will look like on the iPhone itself. Assuming that you've joined the requisite developer program (see Chapter 3 of this minibook), what do you have to do to get it to run on the iPhone?

For most developers, getting their apps to run on the iPhone during development can be one of the most frustrating things about developing software for the iPhone. The sticking point has to do with a technical concept called *code signing,* a rather complicated process designed to ensure the integrity of the code and positively identify the code's originator. Apple requires all iPhone apps to be digitally signed with a signing certificate — one issued by Apple to a registered iPhone developer — before the app can be run on a development system and before they're submitted to the App Store for distribution. This signature authenticates the identity of the developer of the app and ensures that there have been no changes to the app after it was signed.

As to why this is a big deal, here's the short and sweet (and, to our ears, convincing) answer: Code signing is your way of guaranteeing that no bad guys have done anything to your code that can harm the innocent user.

Okay, so nobody really likes the process, but it's doable, and it's certainly worth the trouble. In this chapter, I give you an overview of how it all works by jumping right to that point where you're getting your app ready to be uploaded to the App Store and then distributed. I'm starting at the end of the process, which for all practical purposes begins with getting your app to run on a device during development. I'm doing the overview in this order because the hoops you have to jump through to get an app to run on a single iPhone during development are a direct consequence of code signing, and of how Apple manages it through the App Store and on the device.

After the overview, which will give you some context for the whole process, I revert to the natural order of things and start with getting your app to run on your iPhone during development.

How the Process Works

It's very important to keep clear that you have to go through *two* processes: One for development, and one for distribution. Both produce different (but similarly named) certificates and profiles, and you'll need to pay attention to keep them straight. This section starts with the *distribution* process — how you get your app to run on *other people's* iPhones. Next up is the *development* process — how to get your app running on *your* iPhone during development.

The Distribution process

Before you can build a version of your app that will actually run on your users' iPhones, Apple insists that you have the following:

✦ **A Distribution Certificate:** An electronic document that associates a *digital identity* (which it creates) with other information that you have provided that identifies you, including a name, e-mail address, or business. The Distribution Certificate is placed on your *keychain* — that place on your Mac that securely stores passwords, keys, certificates, and notes for users.

✦ **A Distribution Provisioning Profile:** These profiles are code elements that Xcode builds into your application, creating a kind of "code fingerprint" that acts as a unique *digital signature*.

After you've built your app for distribution, you then send it to Apple for approval and distribution. Apple verifies the signature to be sure that the code came from a registered developer (you) and has not been corrupted. Apple then adds its own digital signature to your signed app. The iPhone OS runs only apps that have a digital signature. Doing it this way ensures iPhone owners that the apps they download from the App Store have been written by registered developers and have not been altered since they were created.

To install your distribution-ready app on a device, you can also create an *Ad Hoc Provisioning Profile,* which enables you to distribute your app on up to 100 devices.

Although the system for getting apps on other people's iPhones works pretty well, leaving aside the fact that Apple essentially has veto rights on every app that comes its way, there are some significant consequences for developers. In this system, there really is no mechanism for testing your app on the device it's going to run on:

✦ You can't run your app on an actual device until it's been code-signed by Apple, *but* Apple is hardly going to code-sign something that may not be working correctly.

✦ Even if Apple did sign an app that hadn't yet run on an iPhone, that would mean an additional hassle: Every time you recompiled, you'd have to upload the app to the App Store again — *and* have it code-signed again because you had changed it, *and* then download it to your device.

Bit of a Catch-22 here.

The Development process

To deal with this problem, Apple has developed a process for creating a *Development Certificate* (as opposed to the Distribution Certificate that I explain at the start of this section) and a *Development Provisioning Profile* (as opposed to the Distribution Provisioning Profile that I also explain at the start of this section). It's easy to get these confused — the key words are Distribution and Development. With these items in hand, you can run your application on a *specific* device.

This process is required only because of the code-signing requirements of the distribution process.

The Development Provisioning Profile is a collection of your App ID, Apple device UDID (a unique identifier for each iPhone), and iPhone Development Certificate (belonging to a specific developer). This Profile must be installed on each device on which you want to run your application code. (You see how that's done in "Creating your Development Provisioning Profile and Development Certificate" in this chapter.) Devices specified within the Development Provisioning Profile can be used for testing only by developers whose iPhone Development Certificates are included in the Provisioning Profile. A single device can contain multiple provisioning profiles.

It's important to realize that a development provisioning profile (as opposed to a distribution one) *is tied to a device and a developer*.

Even with your provisioning profile(s) in place, when you compile your program, Xcode will build and sign (create the required signature for) your app *only* if it finds one of those Development Certificates in your Keychain. Then, when you install a signed app on your provisioned device, the iPhone OS verifies the signature to make sure that *(a)* the app was signed and *(b)* the app has not been altered since it was signed. If the signature is not valid or if you didn't sign the code, the iPhone OS will not let the app run.

This means that each Development Provisioning Profile is also tied to a particular Development Certificate.

And to make sure the message has really gotten across:

> A Development Provisioning Profile is tied to a *specific device* and a *specific Development Certificate.*

> Your app, during development, must be tied to a specific *Development Provisioning Profile* (which is easily changeable).

The process you're about to go through is akin to filling out taxes: You have to follow the rules, or there can be some dire consequences. But if you do follow the rules, everything works out, and you don't have to worry about it again. (Until it's time to develop the next app, of course.)

Although this process is definitely not our favorite part of iPhone software development, I've made peace with it, and so should you. Now I can go back to the natural order of things and start by explaining the process of getting your device ready for development. Although Apple documents the steps very well, do keep in mind that you really have to carry them out in exactly the way Apple tells you. There are no shortcuts! But if you do it the way it prescribes, you'll be up and running on a real device very quickly.

With your app up and running, it's time for the next step: getting your creation ready for distribution. (This process is somewhat easier.) Finally, you definitely want to find out how to get your application into the App Store. After that, all you have to do is sit back and wait for fame and fortune to come your way — or read Chapter 7 in this minibook to discover why it hasn't yet.

What I describe on these pages is the way things looked when I wrote this book. What you see when you go through this process yourself may be slightly different from what you see here. Don't panic. It's because Apple changes things from time to time.

Provisioning Your Device for Development

Until just recently, getting your app to run on the iPhone during development was a really painful process. (In fact, co-author Neal had written a 30-page chapter on it, detailing step after painful step. Then, lo and behold, right when Neal had put the finishing touches on his *magnum opus,* Apple changed the process and actually made it much easier. Neal has mixed feelings about that, but they're mostly relief.)

In fact, the process is now so easy that there's no real need for us to linger over the details. Here's the drill:

1. **Go to the iPhone Dev Center Web site at**

   `http://developer.apple.com/iphone`

   The iPhone Dev Center appears, as shown in Figure 6-1. You can see the iPhone Developer Program Portal link, along with the iTunes Connect and the Developer Support Center links, in the iPhone Developer Program section on the right side of the Web page. (You can if you're a registered developer. You did take care of that, right? If not, look at Chapter 3 in this minibook for more on how to register.)

Figure 6-1: The gateway to the Program Portal.

2. **Click the iPhone Developer Program Portal link.**

   The iPhone Developer Program Portal screen appears, as shown in Figure 6-2.

3. **Assuming you're either a Team Admin or Team Agent or are enrolled in the Developer Program as an individual, use the Development Provisioning Assistant to create and install a Provisioning Profile and iPhone Development Certificate, as shown in the next section.**

   You need these to build and install applications on the iPhone. But you knew that.

You've already identified yourself to Apple as one of two types of developers:

✦ **If you're enrolled in the Developer Program as an individual,** you're considered a Team Agent with all the rights and responsibilities.

✦ **If you're part of a company,** you've set up a team already. If not, click the Setting Up a Team link on the right side of the iPhone Developer Program Portal page — right there under the Portal Resources heading — to get more info about setting up a team and who needs to do what when.

Figure 6-2: Behold the iPhone Developer Program Portal.

Creating Your Development Provisioning Profile and Development Certificate

When you've settled the matter of which kind of developer you are (for Apple's purposes), click the Launch Assistant button, and then you see the dialog in Figure 6-3.

As I mention earlier in the chapter, to run the app on the iPhone you must have a Provisioning Profile installed on the iPhone, as well as a Development Certificate on your Mac. The whole point of the Development Provisioning Assistant is to guide you through the steps to create and install your Development Provisioning Profile and iPhone Development Certificate.

Development and Distribution stay off each other's turf. The Development Provisioning Assistant creates a *Development* Provisioning Profile, not a *Distribution* Provisioning Profile. You have to use the Provisioning section of the Program Portal, described later in this chapter, to create the Distribution Provisioning Profile required to distribute the app to customers through the App Store.

Figure 6-3:
The Development Provisioning Assistant.

Here's what the Development Provisioning Assistant has you do:

1. **Choose an App ID.**

   An App ID is a unique identifier that is one part of your Development Provisioning Profile. iPhone OS uses it to allow your app to connect to the Apple Push Notification service (which I discuss momentarily), share keychain data between apps, and communicate with external hardware accessories that you want to pair your iPhone OS app with. But even if you don't want to do those things, you need to create an App ID anyway in order to install your app on an iPhone OS–based device.

   If you're creating a suite of apps that will share the same Keychain access (for example, sharing passwords between apps) or have no Keychain Access requirements, you can create a single App ID for your entire app suite by typing an asterisk as a wild-card character.

The App ID that the Assistant creates *can't be used* with the Apple Push Notification service. (This service lets your app keep its users up-to-date, offering the capability of sending a message that lets the user launch your app, or triggering audible alerts with your own custom sounds, or adding a numbered badge to your app icon — for details, see the App IDs section of the iPhone Developer Program Portal at `http://developer.apple.com/iphone/manage/bundles/index.action`). The App ID created by the Assistant *also can't be used* for In App Purchase. (See Chapter 7 for details on In App Purchase.) If you've previously created an App ID already that can be used with the Apple Push Notification service or for In App Purchase, you *can't* use the Assistant to create a Development Provisioning Profile. This isn't a big deal; you just have to follow the steps the Assistant follows on your own.

2. **Choose an Apple Device and connect your iPhone or iPod touch.**

   Development provisioning is also about the device, so you have to specify which particular device you're going to use, and connect it. You do that by providing the Assistant with the device's Unique Device Identifier (UDID), which the Assistant shows you how to locate using Xcode — with Xcode open, choose Window⇨Organizer after connecting your iPhone or iPod touch, and the 40-character string in the Identifier field is the device's UDID.

3. **Provide your Development Certificate.**

   Your existing Development Certificate appears in the Assistant, and all you need to do is click Continue. All apps must be signed with a valid certificate before they can run on an Apple device, so you have to create one at this point if you don't already have one. You can do so by visiting the Certificates section of the iPhone Developer Program Portal (click the Certificates link in the left column of the portal's home page), and following the instructions to request individual iPhone Development Certificates.

   For a Company (that is, a Team), each developer has to first create a Certificate Signing Request, which then has to be approved by your Program Admin or Team Agent. Visit the Certificates section of the iPhone Developer Program Portal for instructions.

4. **Name your Provisioning Profile.**

   You then give your Provisioning Profile a name and click Generate. The Provisioning Profile pulls together your App ID (Step 1), Apple device UDID (Step 2), and iPhone Development Certificate (Step 3). The Assistant then steps you through downloading the profile and handing it over to Xcode, which installs it on your device. You hand it over to Xcode by dragging it over the Xcode icon in the Mac OS X Dock or by dragging it directly to the Provisioning Profiles section of the Organizer window. (Choose Window⇨Organizer in Xcode to open the Organizer window.)

5. **Verify that the Provisioning Profile is installed.**

In Xcode, choose Window➪Organizer and click the device's name in the Devices section of the Projects and Sources pane of the Organizer window, as shown in Figure 6-4. The profile should appear in the Provisioning section of the Summary pane for the device.

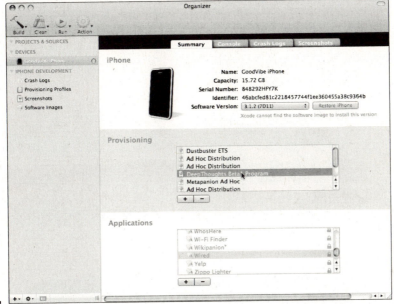

Figure 6-4:
The profile
is listed
in the
Provisioning
section as
installed in
the device.

At this point, you can choose iPhone Device 3.1 as the active SDK in the Project window, as shown in Figure 6-5. You can then build your app and have it installed on the provisioned device.

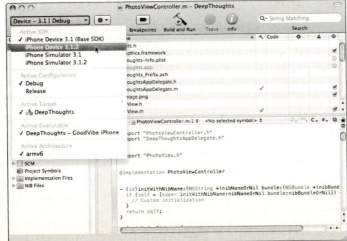

Figure 6-5:
Ready to run
your app on
the iPhone.

Provisioning Your Application for the App Store

Although there's no dedicated assistant to help you provision your application for the App Store, that process is actually a little easier — which may be why there's no assistant for it.

You start at the Developer Portal (refer to Figure 6-2), but this time you click the Distribution link on the menu on the left side of the page. Doing so takes you to the Prepare App page shown in Figure 6-6, where you can find an overview of the process, as well as links that take you where you need to go when you click them.

Figure 6-6: Getting your app ready for distribution: You are here.

You actually jump through some of the very same hoops you did when you provisioned your device for development — except that this time, you're going after a *Distribution* Certificate.

Here's the step-by-step account:

1. Obtain your iPhone Distribution Certificate.

   To distribute your iPhone app, you (as an Individual developer) or your Team Agent (as a development team) creates an iPhone Distribution Certificate. This works much like the Development Certificate, except that only the Team Agent (or whoever is enrolled as an Individual developer) can get one. Clicking the Obtaining Your iPhone Distribution

Certificate link on the Prepare App page (shown at the bottom of Figure 6-6) leads you through the process.

2. **Create your iPhone Distribution Provisioning Profile for App Store Distribution.**

   To build your app successfully with Xcode for distribution via the App Store, first you have to create and download an App Store Distribution Provisioning Profile, which is (lest we forget) *different* from the Development Provisioning Profiles described in the previous section.

    Apple will accept an app only after it's built with an App Store Distribution Provisioning Profile.

3. **Click the Create and Download Your iPhone Distribution Provisioning Profile for App Store Distribution link.**

   Scroll the Prepare App page (refer to Figure 6-6) to click the link, which leads you through this process.

4. **When you're done creating the Distribution Provisioning Profile, download it and drag it over the Xcode icon in the Mac OS X Dock.**

   That loads your Distribution Profile into Xcode, and you're ready to build an app you can distribute for use on actual iPhones.

5. **(Optional) You can also create and download a Distribution Provisioning Profile for Ad Hoc Distribution.**

   Going the Ad Hoc Distribution route enables you to distribute your application to up to 100 users without going through the App Store. Scroll the Prepare App page (refer to Figure 6-6) to click the Creating and Downloading a Distribution Provisioning Profile for Ad Hoc Distribution link, which leads you through the process. (Ad Hoc Distribution is beyond the scope of this book — the iPhone Developer Program Portal has more info about this option.)

6. **Build your app with Xcode for distribution.**

   After you download the distribution profile, you can build your app for distribution — rather than just building it for testing purposes, which is what you've been doing so far. It's a well-documented process that you start by scrolling the Prepare App page (refer to Figure 6-6) and clicking the Building Your Application with Xcode for Distribution link.

7. **Verify that it worked.**

   Scroll the Prepare App page (refer to Figure 6-6) and click the Verifying a Successful Distribution Build link to get the verification process started. In this case, there are some things missing in the heretofore well-explained step-by-step documentation — it tells you to open the Build Log detail view and confirm the presence of the `embedded.mobileprovision` file. In Chapter 4 of this minibook, I show you how to keep the Build Results window open in Xcode, but if you haven't been doing that, choose Build➪Build Results.

Depending on the way the way the Build Results window is configured, you may see a window only showing the end result of your build. To get the actual log of the process, you have to change Errors & Warnings Only in the drop-down menu in the scope bar to All Messages.

8. **At this point, do a couple of prudent checks:**

   • Verify that your app was signed by your iPhone Certificate. To do that, select the last line in the Build log — the one that starts with CodeSign. Then click the icon at the end of the line. You can see that it was signed by the iPhone Certificate. (Okay, you may need a magnifying glass, but trust me, it's there, and make sure yours is, too.)

   • Verify that the `embedded.mobileprovision` is there and is located in the Distribution build directory and is not located in a Debug or Release build directory. To do that, you can search for `embedded.mobileprovision` in the search field in the upper-right corner of the Build Results window.

When you've done this elaborate (but necessary) song and dance, you're ready to rock 'n' roll. You can go to iTunes Connect, which is your entryway to the App store. This is where the *real* fun starts.

Using iTunes Connect to Manage Apps in the App Store

iTunes Connect is a group of Web-based tools that enables developers to submit apps to the App Store and manage their apps in the store. It's actually the very same set of tools that the other content providers — the music and video types — use to get their content into iTunes.

In iTunes Connect, you can check on your contracts, manage users, and submit your app with all its supporting documentation — the *metadata,* as Apple calls it — to the App Store. iTunes Connect is also where you get financial reports and daily/weekly sales trend data, as I describe in Chapter 7 of this minibook.

Your first stopping point is the App Store, Logo Licensing, and Affiliate Program page (shown in Figure 6-7). To get there, select the App Store tab in the Distribution section of the Developer Portal, and then click the Learn More link right under the App Store heading.

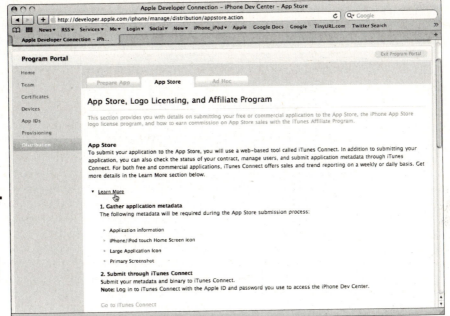

Figure 6-7:
The App
Store, Logo
Licensing,
and Affiliate
Program
page.

At this point, get your bearings and proceed:

✦ Whether you are a Team Agent or an Individual developer, you see the
Go to iTunes Connect link (after clicking the Learn More link). Click the
Go to iTunes Connect link to call up the login page of iTunes Connect.

✦ You need to use your Apple ID and password to log in.

✦ Before you can do anything, you're asked to review and accept the
iTunes Distribution Terms & Conditions. After taking care of that chore,
you land on the iTunes Connect page shown in Figure 6-8. You should
bookmark this page so that you don't have to go hunting for that Go to
iTunes Connect link.

At some point, you should also select To Become an Authorized
Licensee, which is a little farther down the App Store, Logo Licensing,
and Affiliate Program page you see back in Figure 6-7. This option allows
you to use the iPhone App Store artwork and iPhone images in your
advertising, Web sites, and other marketing materials.

When you want to add an application to the App Store or manage what you
already have there, the iTunes Connect main page is your control panel for
getting that done.

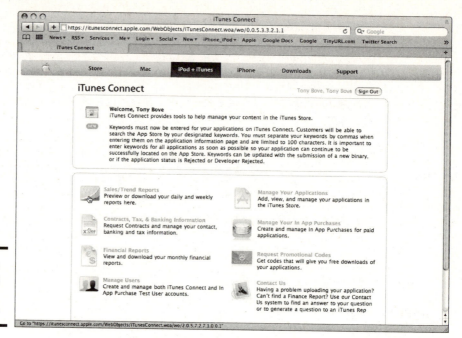

Figure 6-8:
The iTunes
Connect
main page.

Supplying the Information Required for the App Store

Apple is very strict about some things, and I speak from firsthand experiences.

The first time co-author Neal submitted the ReturnMeTo app from his other book, *iPhone Application Development For Dummies*, he received a polite, but firm, e-mail rejecting the application because the app's icon used an iPhone image. (You can see that icon and the rejection letters in the first edition of that book.) You may not think this is such a big deal, but it certainly is with Apple. The artwork you use for the app icon is just one of many pieces of information that must be submitted in advance and is subject to Apple's approval.

So how do you get your app into the App Store? To start with, there's a link on the iPhone Dev Center page, under News and Information, labeled Tips on Submitting Your App to the App Store. This page has information on keywords, assigning a rating for your app, and some other tips. Read it!

The Uploading Your Application to the App Store part is pretty easy. The hard part is collecting all the little bits of information you need to enter into all the text fields in the upload page.

Adding the metadata and artwork

Here's an overview of the kind of information you need (for more information, click the Prepare for App Submission link in the App Store Resource Center section of the iPhone Dev Center page shown earlier in Figure 6-1):

✦ **Metadata:** The ever-present data about data. Here's what Apple wants from you:

- *Application Name:* The name must conform to guidelines for using Apple trademarks and copyrights. Apple takes this very seriously, as evidenced by the company sending a cease-and-desist order to Neal's ISP when Neal tried (innocently) to use iPhoneDev411 as his domain name. (A word to the wise: Don't mess with Apple.)

- *Application Description:* When you go through the process of uploading your data, the field you have to paste this into will say you're limited to 4,000 characters. Apple suggests no more than 700.

   This description is what users will see when they click on your app in the App Store, so it's important that this description is well written and points out all your app's key features.

   Don't include HTML tags; they will be stripped out when the data is uploaded. Only line breaks are respected.

- *Device:* Basically, I'm talking iPhone and/or iPod touch as of this writing.

- *Primary Category:* A drop-down menu offers the primary category choices for your app — choose one. The App Store offers about 20 categories ranging from Reference to Games to Social Networking to Travel to Utility.

- *Secondary Category:* (Optional) You're offered the same categories that you see for the Primary Category.

- *Rating Information:* You're asked to provide additional information describing the content. This allows you to set your rating for your app for the purpose of parental controls on the App Store. You may see content types such as Cartoon or Fantasy Violence, Simulated Gambling, Mature/Suggestive Themes, and so on. For each type of content, you need to describe the level of frequency for that content — None, Infrequent/Mild, Frequent/Intense. Apple has strict rules stating that an app must not contain any obscene, pornographic, or offensive content. Oh and by the way, it's entirely up to Apple what is to be considered offensive or inappropriate.

- *Copyright:* Use a line such as:

   © Copyright *your name* 2010. All rights reserved.

   You can type the copyright symbol by pressing Option-G. If you have any questions about copyright registration, talk to your lawyer or check out www.copyright.gov.

- *Version Number:* People usually start with 1.0. Then, as you update the app to respond to suggestions and constructive criticism, you can move on to 1.1, and someday even version 2.0.

- *SKU Number:* The Stock Keeping Unit (SKU) number is any alphanumeric sequence of letters and numbers that uniquely identifies your app in the system. (Be warned — this is not editable after you submit it.)

- *Keywords:* Keywords describe your app. These are matched to App Store searches. Spend some time on this one. Keywords can be changed only when you submit a new binary, or if the app status is Rejected.

- *Support URL and Company URL:* You need a support URL, which appears on the app product page at the App store — this is the link users will click on if they need technical support from you or have a question about your app. You also need a company URL, which also appears on the app product page and enables potential customers to find out more about you. After you've assigned these URLs, you want to keep them the same as long as possible, even if you change the Web site's contents, because people bookmark them.

  If you don't have a Web site yet and don't know how to build one, try using iWeb with MobileMe (if you already have the service) or with your friendly ISP. MobileMe offers automatic Web publishing to a reasonably unique domain name that can serve well enough for your URLs — to find out more, see co-author Tony's book *iLife For Dummies*. If you use an ISP, obtain a domain name for your URLs that reflects your company or product name. You can also find out more about building a professional-looking site from David Crowder's book *Building a Web Site For Dummies,* 3rd Edition.

- *Support E-mail Address:* (For use by Apple only, not visible to end users of your app.) This address will likely be the one you used when you registered for the developer program.

- *Demo Account — Full Access:* This is a test account that the App Store *reviewers* can use to test your app. Include usernames, passwords, access codes, demo data, and so on. You should include any messages to the Apple app reviewers, in case they might incorrectly reject something — for example, lack of permission to use a piece of music in the app that it is in the public domain. Make sure the demo account works correctly. You'd hate to have your app rejected because you didn't pay attention to setting up a demo account correctly.

- *End User License Agreement:* (Optional) If you don't know what this is, don't worry. It's the legal document that spells out to your app's users what they're agreeing to do in order to use your app. Fortunately the iTunes Store has a standard agreement, which has been time-tested — but you should read it anyway before you use it.

- *Availability Date:* When your app will be available for download (for free apps) or purchase-and-download.

- *Application Price:* Free is easier, but later on I show you what you have to do if you want to get *paid* (what a concept) for all the work you did getting your app to the public.

- *Localization:* Additional languages (besides English) for your meta-data. You can have your text and images in Italian in all Italian-speaking stores, for example.

- *App Store Availability:* The territories in which you would like to make your app available (the default is all countries iTunes supports).

✦ **Artwork:** A picture is worth a thousand words, so the App store gives you the opportunity to dazzle your app's potential users with some nice imagery:

- *iPhone/iPod touch Home Screen Icon:* Your built app must have a 57×57-pixel icon included for it, following the procedure I describe in Chapter 5 of Book III. This icon is what will be displayed on the iPod touch or iPhone home screen.

- *Large Application Icon:* This icon will be used to display your app on your App Store page and other App Store pages. It needs to meet the following requirements, although the version you see in the App Store is resized by Apple:

    512 x 512 pixels (flattened, square image)

    72 dpi

    JPEG or TIFF format

- *Primary Screenshot:* This shot will be used on your application product page in the App Store.

    Apple doesn't want you to include the iPhone status bar in your screenshot. The shot itself needs to meet these requirements:

    320 x 460 portrait (without status bar) minimum

    480 x 300 landscape (without status bar) minimum

    320 x 480 portrait (full screen)

    Up to four additional optional screenshots can appear on the application product page. These may be resized to fit the space provided. Follow the same requirements from the preceding list.

To take a screenshot on an iPhone or iPod touch, quickly press and release the Sleep/Wake and Home buttons at the same time. The screen flashes (and if your volume is up, you can hear a shutter click). This indicates that the screen was saved in the Saved Images album (on an iPod touch) or the Camera Roll album — choose the album in the Photos app to see the image. You can take as many screen shots as you like. The next time you sync your iPhone or iPod touch, your photo application (such as iPhoto) launches to receive these new images.

You can also capture a screenshot using the Xcode Organizer window. Open Xcode and choose Window⇨Organizer. Plug in your iPhone and in a few seconds, it should appear in the list of devices on the left. Click the Screenshot tab at the top of the Organizer window, get the device to the point that you want a screenshot, and then click the Capture button. To make that screenshot your application's default image, click Save As Default Image. To get a PNG file of the screenshot, drag it to the desktop.

- *Additional Artwork:* (Optional) If you're really lucky — I mean *really* lucky (or that good) — you may be included on featured pages in the App Store. Apple will want "high-quality layered artwork with a title treatment for your application," which will then be used in small posters to feature your app in the App Store.

You're not done yet

If you're going to charge for your app, you have to provide even more information. Most of it is pretty straightforward, except for some of the banking information, which you *do* need to have available. To change this information after you've entered it, you have to e-mail iTunes technical support. It behooves you to get it right the first time.

Here's what I'm talking about:

- ✦ **Bank name**
- ✦ **Bank address**
- ✦ **Account number**
- ✦ **Branch/Branch ID**
- ✦ **ABA/Routing Transit Number:** Generally, this number is the first nine digits of that long number at the bottom of your checks that also contains the account number. If you aren't sure what the routing number is, contact your bank.
- ✦ **Your Bank SWIFT Code:** You will have to get that from your bank.

Take it from us; it's far easier if you have all bits and pieces together *before* you start the actual upload process, rather than having to scramble at 3 a.m. to find some obscure piece of information it wants. (The Bank SWIFT Code was the one that got co-author Neal.)

Uploading your information

At this point, you can start the app-upload process by clicking the Manage Your Applications link on the iTunes Connect main page. (Refer to Figure 6-8.) But hold it. Better to look before leaping: Check out the requisite Contracts, Tax & Banking Information.

Here's why: If you plan on selling your app, you need to have your paid commercial agreement in place and signed before your apps can be posted to the App Store.

If your app is free, you've already entered into the freeware distribution agreement by being accepted into the iPhone Developer Program. You may not want to charge for your app now, but just like with anything else at Apple, contract approval can take a while, so you should probably fill out the contract information just to get it out of the way.

Start by clicking the Contracts, Tax & Banking Information link on the iTunes Connect main page. The Manage Your Contracts page appears. You use this page to create a contract for your paid app. You can also see that you already have, by default, a contract in effect for free apps. To create a new contract, select the box under Request Contract in the Request New Contracts section, and you're taken though a series of pages that ask you to provide the information Apple needs, including the bank information I call your attention to earlier.

Uploading your app and its data

After you've set the wheels in motion, you can then go back to the iTunes Connect main page and upload your data. Click the Manage Your Applications link (refer to Figure 6-8) to call up the Manage Your Applications page, as shown in Figure 6-9. In that page, click the Add New Application button and go to town. Fill in all the blanks, using all that info I ask you to collect in the "Supplying the Information Required for the App Store" section earlier in the chapter. Along the way, you'll upload your metadata and the app itself to Apple.

Click the Download the Developer Guide link at the bottom of the Manage Your Applications page in iTunes Connect (refer to Figure 6-9) to obtain comprehensive information about submitting apps to the App Store.

Apple offers Application Loader, a Mac application that analyzes your iPhone app's zip file and verifies all the certificates and icons before uploading your app. Using the Application Loader minimizes your chances of app rejection. To download it, choose Manage Your Applications and scroll down to the bottom, and then click the Get Application Loader link. To use it, go ahead with the process of adding a new app to the App Store, but when iTunes Connect asks you to upload your app, select the Check Here to Upload Your Binary Later check box. Complete the rest of the information required for uploading an app. Then, to begin uploading, start Application Loader and choose File⇨New. You're asked to log in, and if all is well, you see a dialog with a drop-down menu of all the apps iTunes Connect recognizes that are waiting for a binary. Follow the instructions to upload.

Figure 6-9:
Add your
application.

Avoiding the App Store Rejection Slip

As of November 2009 (as quoted in *BusinessWeek*), about 90 percent of all submitted apps are accepted. Of the 10 percent rejected (mostly for bugs or for improper use of artwork or trademarks in the app), only a handful (less than 1 percent) fell into some gray area that Apple hadn't anticipated — for instance, apps intended to help people cheat at gambling in casinos. For guidelines on how to avoid rejection due to coding or user interface issues, see Chapter 2 in this minibook.

Before you upload your app and its data, make sure you haven't run afoul of any of Apple's rules about trademarks, copyrights, and artwork. Be sure to peruse Apple's posted Guidelines for Using Apple's Trademarks and Copyrights, which you can find here:

www.apple.com/legal/trademark/guidelinesfor3rdparties.html

Here are some tips:

✦ **Use the same icon for the app (the bundle icon) and the App Store page icon.** Make sure the 57-pixel bundle icon for your app is the same image as the 512-pixel version for your App Store page.

✦ **Icons must be different for *lite* and *pro* versions (such as free and paid versions).** Use a different icon image for app and page for a lite version than the one you use for the pro version. Using the same icon image for both sends your app straight to the rejection bin.

✦ **Don't use any part of an Apple image and certainly none of the company's trademark images or names.** Your app can't include any photos or illustrations of the iPhone, including icons that resemble the iPhone, or any other Apple products (including the Apple logo itself). I've heard of projects being rejected for using the Bonjour logo, as well as Apple's network icon (the little picture of the globe with all the glowing lines). Your app can't include the word *iPhone* in its title (although the app title Tony's Tips for iPhone Users is okay because the app's content is about the iPhone), and its use in the title or description of any components or features is very strict and probably not worth the trouble.

✦ **If you use any of Apple's user interface graphics, you must use them in the way they were intended.** For example, the blue + button should be used only to add an item to a list.

✦ **Don't infringe on other trademarks, either.** Your app's title, description, and content must not potentially infringe upon other non-Apple trademarks or product likenesses. I've heard of an app rejected for using an icon resembling Polaroid photos.

✦ **Keywords can get you in trouble.** Keyword terms must be related to your app's content. It should be obvious, but some developers do it: You can't use offensive terms. And it's a big no-no to refer to other apps, competitive or not.

✦ **Don't include pricing information in your app's description and release notes.** Your app's marketing text — the application description and release notes — should not include pricing information, mostly because it would cause confusion in other countries due to pricing differences.

✦ **Don't mention Steve.** Apple will reject any app that mentions Steve Jobs in any context, even as a clue in a puzzle — it does not matter how trivial the reference; just the name is enough.

✦ **Don't try to fool the ratings.** Apps are rated accordingly for the highest (meaning most adult) level of content that the user is able to access. If you hide it, they will find it, and if Apple's review indicates that the app's content is in any way inconsistent with the information you provided, out you go!

Now What?

You wait for your app's approval or rejection. The timeframe is, on average, about two weeks, though some developers have claimed much longer, and Tony can attest to it taking much shorter for his app.

So it varies, but if you follow our advice about submitting your app in the section "Avoiding the App Store Rejection Slip" in this chapter, and you take our advice in Chapter 2 of this minibook about development and user interface practices to avoid, it shouldn't take longer than a few weeks. Use the time wisely to set up your marketing campaigns, as I describe in the next chapter of this minibook — Chapter 7.

Chapter 7: The App Store Is Not Enough

In This Chapter

✔ **Reaching potential customers**

✔ **Measuring the success of marketing campaigns**

✔ **Analyzing customer activity**

✔ **Enabling in-app purchases**

✔ **Making a business out of software development**

*P*eter Drucker, known as the father of modern management, is also known for pointing out that business has only two functions: innovation and marketing. Because most of this book is about innovation, I need to spend at least one chapter explaining why so many developers don't make enough money from iPhone apps and what you can do to mitigate the complex issues surrounding the marketing of these apps.

Apple will list your application along with 100,000+ apps already listed in the App Store. Yes, it's wonderful that Apple takes only 30 percent of the sales price and takes care of hosting, downloading, credit card processing, and notifying users of updates. And if you remember the early days of developing for game machines, you may appreciate the fact that Apple lets you name your own price for your app. You can even distribute an app for free. What you can't do, and perhaps this is a good thing, is pay for preferential treatment. And as of this writing, Apple doesn't accept advertising within the store.

The App Store *does* offer lists of the top paid and free apps in each category and also lists the newest apps by release date, but unless your app is already successful and in the top paid or top free lists, your app's fleeting appearance in the list sorted by release date may provide only a short spike in sales — unless you prepare yourself to take advantage of it by applying some of the methods in this chapter.

The trouble with using any kind of technology to reach customers is the same, old or new: measuring the results. "Half the money I spend on advertising is wasted; the trouble is, I don't know which half," said John Wanamaker, founder of the first department store in Philadelphia (one of the first department stores in the United States) in 1861.

Why People Buy Apps from the App Store

If you think the reason people buy apps is "because it's there" (that is, the App Store is right in your iPhone), you're only partly right. According to AdMob, more than 90 percent of iPhone users browse and search for apps directly on their mobile device instead of their computer.

But that doesn't explain why people flocked to the iPhone in the first place and continue to do so. Besides the fact that Apple has created an ecosystem and a platform for true innovation, the company has wasted no time using traditional advertising to lure people into buying things they didn't know they needed, with the well-known tagline "There's an app for that."

A major factor in the App Store's appeal is its equal treatment of all customers. This equal treatment is a fact of life today in all but the most posh stores, but it was an innovation in John Wanamaker's store in 1861. Wanamaker created the price tag because he believed that if everyone was equal before God, then everyone should be equal before price. (He also invented the cash refund and guaranteed the quality of his merchandise in print.) Apple has also established trust with its customers by screening apps before listing them and enforcing among app developers guidelines for a "quality experience" for consumers. And, of course, the price tag is right up front.

Speaking of a quality experience, people are attracted to new technologies just for the experience. Wanamaker embraced innovation as early as possible to attract customers with a new experience — his was the first department store with electrical illumination (1878), the first with a telephone (1879), and the first to install pneumatic tubes to transport cash and documents (1880). Today, people are attracted to the App Store's use of technology, its ease of use, and this highly innovative form of shopping-on-demand right from your phone.

There is no substitute for combination of trust, equal treatment, and a high-quality experience. The App Store is *the* place to list your apps. Marketing them, however, is entirely up to you.

Finding out how to reach your potential customers

The App Store is right at your customers' fingertips. The Store screen appears with Featured, Categories, and Top 25 buttons along the bottom, ready to entice potential customers.

The Featured screen (shown in Figure 7-1, left side) includes the What's Hot list of the most popular apps based on downloads and the New list of apps sorted by release date. The Featured screen is where the action is for early adopter customers who are buying on impulse. Your app will make a brief appearance in the New list when you release it, only to be crowded out almost immediately by more new apps. There are, by my rough estimates, about nine iPhone apps born in the App Store every hour of every day.

Figure 7-1:
The App
Store's
Featured
apps (left),
Categories
(center),
and Social
Networking
category
(right).

But if you've properly categorized your app, it should appear in the list of apps on the screen devoted to that category — in the Release Date list as soon as you release it. Attaching your app to the appropriate category, as I describe in Chapter 6 of this minibook, is extremely important. Customers looking for a social networking app tap the Social Networking category to find the Top Paid, Top Free, and Release Date lists. Your new app may last a bit longer in the Release Date list of your category.

The Top 25 screen is for those customers who need to catch up to the early adopters and only have time to look at the most popular apps in the Top Paid, Top Free, and Top Grossing lists. Your app will not reach these lists unless you've engaged in a successful marketing strategy.

Some customers will take the time to tap the Search icon to search the store, and they tap the entry field to bring up the onscreen keyboard. As they type a keyword you assigned to your new app, or something close to its name, your app should pop up right away as a suggestion. It is therefore extremely important to use an appropriate name for your app (with terms that people might search for) and to assign appropriate keywords, as I describe in Chapter 6 of this minibook.

Many developers choose to develop a free, or *lite* version, of an app to draw attention to the paid version. Free apps are more likely to be downloaded because, well, they're free. And according to AdMob, Upgrading from the lite version was the top reason given when users were asked what drives them to purchase a paid app.

Note, however, that the free lite version of your paid app must be a fully functional app, and can't reference features that are not implemented or point users directly to the full paid version. What this means is that, although you can publish a free lite app with fewer features than the paid version, the free version must be a complete app in its own right, and you can't badger the free app's users with reminders to upgrade to the paid version, nor can you use placeholders in your app's interface for missing functionality that, when tapped, points users to the paid version. Tricks like these will get your free lite app rejected.

Developers also have the In App Purchase feature at their disposal to offer their app users the opportunity to buy other apps, merchandise, game levels, premium features, books, and so on. (See the "Deploying the In App Purchase Feature" section, later in this chapter, for more.) You may also want to consider offering your customers an incentive, such as free deals through the In App Purchase feature, if they tell their friends about your app. Anyone browsing the App Store can tap the Tell a Friend button at the bottom of the app's information screen to send the app information in an e-mail.

Besides getting your app listed in the App Store's lists, there's no way through Apple to reach potential customers. You need to consider all methods of reaching customers, and you need to price your app according to what your target customer expects, which is a primary topic of Marketing 101.

Marketing 101: Pricing your app

The literature about marketing could probably fill all the Trump Towers in the world, but if you want to learn about marketing quickly, there are at least two apps for that. Marketing Master and MarketingProfs, both free in the App Store, walk you through the basic concepts, and while you certainly could do better by enrolling at Wharton (where the first Marketing 101 course was taught in 1909), it's a place to start.

Marketing is setting up a strong bait attraction system that generates leads, sorts those leads into qualified prospects, and then turns those prospects into customers. Besides fishing for the right prospects, you have to convince them to buy your app — in other words, "ABC, *always be closing*" (as Alec Baldwin so succinctly put it in the movie *Glengarry Glen Ross*).

One of the biggest lessons of Marketing 101 is to determine your target audience for your product. Assemble as much information about your target customer as possible — demographics, education, income level, and so on — because this information will influence all your marketing decisions, from the text you write in your descriptions and ads to the channels you use to distribute your message.

Another big lesson is to determine the cost of acquiring new customers. The simple math here is to divide all the dollars you spend in marketing per month by all the new dollars you receive each month in sales. When you know this, it begs the question of how much you *should* be spending. To figure that out, you need to know how much your customers are worth to you — the lifetime value of your customer. The secret to increasing the lifetime value of your customer is to increase the quality of the customer experience, thereby encouraging repeat business. You're not in the iPhone app game to do just one app; you need to develop more apps and build a customer base that will be happy to buy them.

Keep in mind that iPhone users download approximately ten new apps a month, according to AdMob, and those who regularly download paid apps spend approximately $9 on an average of five paid downloads per month. You need to attract the right people, not just anyone — potential customers are those who will understand the value of your app (also known as the *value proposition,* otherwise known as "what's in it for me?").

But at what price? Much has been written about iPhone app pricing strategies. At the beginning of this gold rush, pricing an app at $0.99 helped to get the app into the Top 100. But now, with over 100,000 apps, that's no longer true. All good marketers know that price is never a good selling point; anyone can come along and be cheaper. A better approach is to determine the true value of the app. People will pay for quality — and as more business apps become available, their prices will likely reflect their value.

The best approach is to check out similar apps, especially competing ones (if any). Remember how costly it is to acquire customers. Starting at a higher price gives you some room to offer discounted prices at different times, such as the Black Friday and Cyber Monday that follow Thanksgiving, or the start of the annual Apple Developer Conference.

Knowing Your Customers

One of the biggest problems facing the iPhone app marketer is that the App Store doesn't tell you *who* your customers are. Sure, you know how many customers you have, and you also know from which countries, and how many of them have updated your app (if you provided an update). You even know how much they spent. What you don't know, however, can hurt you. How can you possibly build relationships with customers you don't know?

The vast majority of apps downloaded from the App Store are in use by less than 5 percent of users a month after downloading, according to Pinch Media. Just 20 percent of users return to run a free application one day after downloading. As time goes by, that decline in usage continues, eventually settling below 5 percent after one month and nearing 0 percent after three months.

Category matters, too — games are used for longer periods than any other genre. Pinch Media found the long-term audience for the average app is just one percent of the total number of downloads.

So customer loyalty is hard to build. It's difficult to determine whether a user's positive experience with your app will translate into sales of your next app or your more expensive desktop app. There are no guarantees. You need to get as much data about your customers as you can find.

You may want to add a link to a Web page that offers an optional customer registration process. You could then ask questions during this process to get more information about your customer. You probably need to offer some kind of incentive to get your customers to register, such as credit toward an in-app purchase, or an exclusive service — for example, in my app Tony's Tips for iPhone Users, I offer registered customers access to a support forum in which they can ask me specific questions about using the iPhone.

Tracking downloads

You use iTunes Connect, which I describe in Chapter 6 of this minibook, to submit apps to the App Store and manage apps in the store. Apple releases daily sales reports in iTunes Connect, which you can view online or download, with the name of the app, how many were sold and in which country, and your profit. You can import these reports into any spreadsheet program, like Excel or iWorks Numbers.

To find the reports, log into iTunes Connect (as I describe in Chapter 6 of this minibook), and click the Sales/Trend Reports link. Doing so gets you shunted to the Transaction Reports page, which should look a lot like what you see in Figure 7-2. Pick Summary in the Report Type pop-up menu and then click Daily or Weekly in the Report Period pop-up — you can't pick Monthly Free unless your app is free. After picking your report, click Download to download it or Preview to view it.

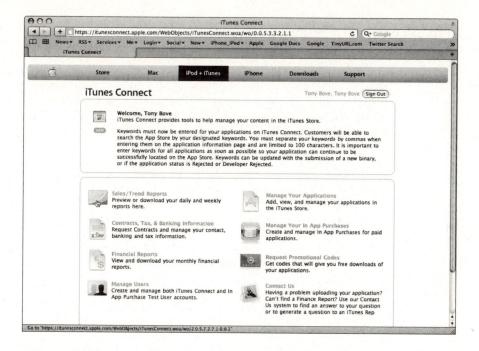

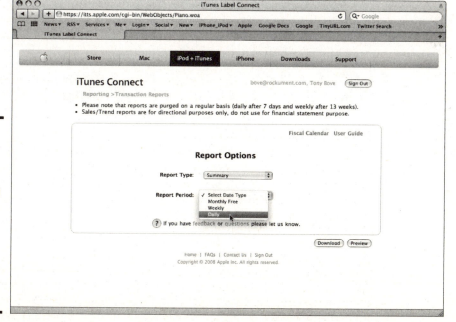

Figure 7-2:
Visit iTunes
Connect
and click
Sales/Trend
Reports
(top), and
then pick
the Daily
or Weekly
report
(bottom).

Some savvy developers out there have come up with a number of desktop applications that have been designed to download and graph the iTunes Connect sales data for you. For example, AppViz (`www.ideaswarm.com/products/appviz`) is a Mac application that can import the reports from the Web or from a downloaded file, and it display charts of your daily, weekly, and monthly sales. AppFigures (`www.appfigures.com`) is a Web-based solution for tracking app sales that can download and graph your reports from iTunes Connect.

Adding analytical code to your app

There are several analytics options for iPhone apps if you're willing to compile the necessary code into your app.

For example, Pinch Analytics from Pinch Media (`http://pinchmedia.com`), shown in Figure 7-3, is used in thousands of popular apps because it can track any action anywhere in your app. Armed with this information, you can fine-tune the user experience in your updates, and offer new features to try to catch usage drop-off as early as possible and retain more customers. You can also measure all types of revenue, from paid downloads and subscriptions to advertising and in-app purchases.

AdMob, recently acquired by Google, offers AdMob Analytics (`http://analytics.admob.com`), a service that works with your Web site to track customers that access pages on the site through your app. All you have to do is install a code snippet onto each page you want to analyze, and AdMob does the rest. When your app requests a page from your site, your server passes analytics-related data to AdMob, which processes your data and makes it available on `http://analytics.admob.com`. It can track the number of unique visitors and pages consumed on your site, and it can monitor user engagement metrics such as the length and depth of each visit.

Putting ads in your app

Free apps can still generate revenue — by *monetizing* the app with advertisements. In much the same way as adding Google AdSense ads to your Web pages, you can add AdMob (now part of Google) or Mobclix (`www.mobclix.com`) ads to your apps.

Both are ad exchanges (like Google AdSense, by the way) that act as online marketplaces for buying and selling advertising impressions. Developers can earn income by placing space in their apps (known as *inventory*) in an auction for advertisers, ad networks, and agencies. The latter can maximize their click-through rates by bidding on precisely targeted audience segments. Thus, the more you know about your own customers, the more ads you can get for your app that are precisely targeted for more clicks (and therefore, more income).

Figure 7-3:
Pinch
Analytics
tracks user
actions and
reports on a
wide variety
of metrics.

For details about advertising on these networks, see the "Buying advertising and publicity" section, later in this chapter.

Deploying the In App Purchase Feature

Apple offers the In App Purchase feature which developers can use in their apps. When incorporated, this feature enables the app users to purchase virtual items directly from inside the app. If you're developing a game app with multiple levels or environments, or virtual property, consider adding the In App Purchase feature to your app to sell more levels, environments, or property — the Eliminate app from ngmoco:) (yes, that's the developer's username) is a good example. If you're developing a book reader, use In App Purchase to sell books — Iceberg Reader 3.0 from ScrollMotion switched from selling books as separate apps to selling books through In App Purchase. Even if you're developing a productivity or travel app, you can deploy In App Purchase to sell additional premium features — Magellan RoadMate, for example, offers spoken street names and directions.

It's important to note that In App Purchase collects only payment. It doesn't download the book, add the game level, or hand over the virtual property. You need to provide the additional functionality, including unlocking built-in features or downloading content from your servers.

You put the In App Purchase store directly in your app using the Store Kit framework. (For more about frameworks, see Chapter 5 in this minibook.) The Store Kit framework connects to the App Store on your app's behalf to securely process the user's payments — see the model in Figure 7-4.

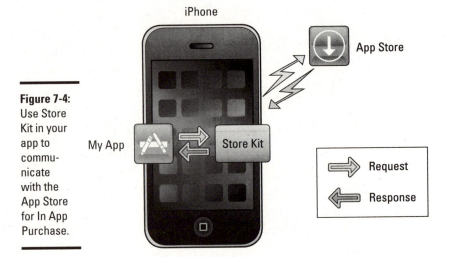

Figure 7-4: Use Store Kit in your app to communicate with the App Store for In App Purchase.

You use iTunes Connect to set up your products the same way you set up new apps. In App Purchase supports four types of products:

✦ **Content:** You can offer game levels, virtual property, and characters; digital books and magazines; photos and artwork; in short, any content that can be delivered within your app.

✦ **Functionality:** You can unlock or expand features you've already delivered in your app, such as a game that offers multiple smaller games for purchase.

✦ **Services:** You can charge users for a one-time service, such as voice transcription — each time the service is used, In App Purchase processes it as a separate purchase.

✦ **Subscriptions:** You can provide access to content or services on a subscription basis, such as a finance magazine or an online game portal. You're responsible for tracking subscription expirations and renewal billing — the App Store doesn't send out renewal notices for you.

Although the In App Purchase feature provides a general mechanism for creating products, everything else is up to you. You can't sell real-world goods and services, only digital content, functionality, services, or subscriptions that work within your app. No intermediary currency is allowed (such as a virtual world's currency), and you can't include real gambling (although simulated gambling is okay). And it goes without saying that pornography, hate speech, and defamation are not allowed.

In App Purchase divides the responsibilities of selling products between your app and the App Store, handling only the payment portion. Here's how it works (refer to Figure 7-5): Your app retrieves the list of product identifiers (set up with iTunes Connect) from its bundle, and the app sends a request to the App Store to localized information about the products. Your app displays this information so that users can purchase items. When a user elects to purchase an item, your app calls Store Kit to collect payment. Store Kit prompts the user to authorize the payment and then notifies your app to provide the items the user purchased.

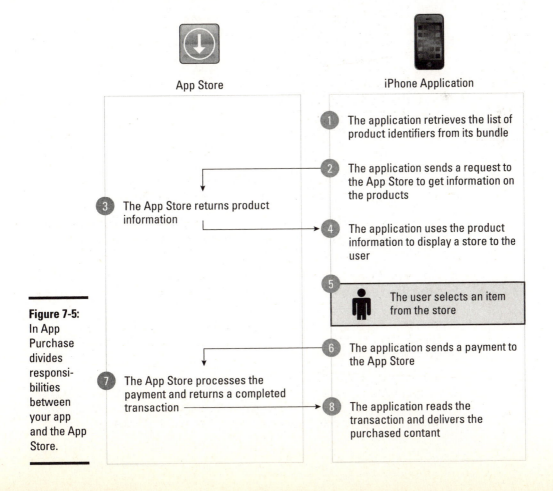

App Store

iPhone Application

1 The application retrieves the list of product identifiers from its bundle

2 The application sends a request to the App Store to get information on the products

3 The App Store returns product information

4 The application uses the product information to display a store to the user

5 The user selects an item from the store

6 The application sends a payment to the App Store

7 The App Store processes the payment and returns a completed transaction

8 The application reads the transaction and delivers the purchased contant

Figure 7-5:
In App Purchase divides responsibilities between your app and the App Store.

This process is spelled out (in more detail than I can go into here) in the In App Purchase Programming Guide, which you can find in the iPhone Dev Center.

Links Are Not Enough

It goes without saying that you have a Web page (or entire site) devoted to your app, and you've outfitted your site with keywords for search-engine optimization so that searches in Google result in your Web page appearing on or near the first search page. You also use Google Analytics to measure traffic. Reams have been written on this topic. (See *Web Analytics For Dummies* for one particularly good use of such paper reams.)

When promoting an app, use well-written copy, good screen shots, quotes from user reviews, and third-party recommendations. If you have the skills or the budget, develop a quick video, upload it to YouTube, and put that on your page.

Don't forget to display prominently on your Web page the Apple-legal App Store button that links visitors to the App Store on iTunes. You can find the link to this button in the iPhone Developer Program Portal under App Store Resources.

But Web page links are not enough. The ecosystem of iTunes, the App Store, and the iPhone offers more than a few methods of reaching potential customers, as discussed in the following sections.

Using iTunes affiliate links

Your App Store links should make you some spare change as well as tell you a few things about your customers. The iTunes affiliate program gives you links to put on your Web pages. When a visitor clicks this link and then buys something in the iTunes Store (including the App Store), you get 5 percent. Although that's not much, it doesn't hurt. You can add affiliate links to *any* apps (or songs or videos) in the store, not just your apps.

You can put an affiliate link on your blog, on your friends' Web pages, and even in the signature of your e-mails. Anywhere that you would normally link to your app in the App Store, replace it with your affiliate link.

Another good reason to do this is to obtain more data. You can find out how often visitors see your links, what percentage actually click on your links, and where they come from. Apple uses LinkShare (`www.linkshare.com`), a fairly popular affiliate manager. LinkShare also manages affiliate programs for AT&T, LEGO, Macys.com, TigerDirect.com, and hundreds of other companies.

Making use of user reviews

Users are your friends, even when they are bashing you in public.

The App Store customer review (see Figure 7-6) is one of the most valuable tools you have to convince potential customers to buy your app. Only people who have purchased your app can write a review. If you offer your users an optional registration on a Web site or by e-mail (using incentives such as insider news, discounts, or free stuff), you can use that opportunity to remind them to write a review of the app in the App Store.

Even harsh reviews can be helpful, pointing out bugs that you may have not previously uncovered, or offering ideas for additional features and functions you didn't think of. You should use this information to prioritize your development activities for future updates, and you can add information about fixed bugs in the app's description when you submit the update

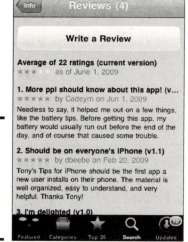

Figure 7-6:
Encourage user reviews, which can help boost sales.

Going social

Social networking spreads the buzz about your app. One of the most popular techniques is to publicize your app on dozens of forums including the iPhone Blog's Forum (http://forum.theiphoneblog.com), MacRumors Forums (http://forums.macrumors.com), or iPhone Fans (www.iphonefans.com).

It's a time-consuming job. Developers often turn to professional PR agencies that can put out press releases and work the blogs and forums for you. A good PR blast can drive thousands of sales within a few days. But beware: sales can fall off a cliff as new stories replace the old ones.

You should submit a press release about your app to the blogs and publications that directly serve your customers. You may not get attention for a paid app without also including a promotional code so that the reviewer can download the app for free. Apple gives you 50 promotional codes for each version of an app; use them wisely because there are far more than 50 general review blogs for iPhone apps, and there may be thousands of other blogs that serve your potential customers, such as travel blogs for customers of a travel app.

Remember that each promotional code you request expires four weeks after you requested it, so request only the number of codes you need at the moment. After you've submitted your app's information and promotional code to a few blogs, then go back and request more. These codes can be used only in the U.S. iTunes Store.

To get your promotional codes, visit iTunes Connect and click the Request Promotional Codes link. (Refer to Figure 7-2, top.) Then type the number of codes you need, as shown in Figure 7-7, and click Continue. iTunes Connect then provides the promotional codes to send in your e-mail or blog request. Reviewers already know how to enter promotional codes into the iTunes Store before buying an app.

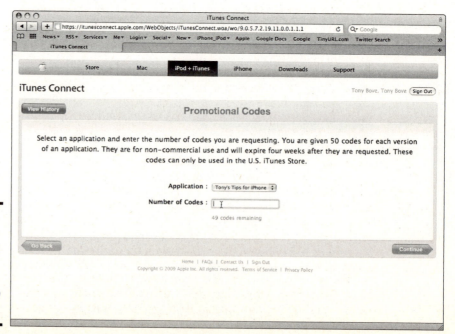

Figure 7-7: Request promotional codes to give your app away to reviewers.

Updating your app for attention

I dislike having to mention this cheap trick, but many developers are still trying to take advantage of it, even though Apple watches out for it. The Release Date lists in each App Store category lists updates — so if you release updates often, these updates will be on that list more often, reaching more eyeballs.

The problem with this trick is that customers might be irritated by frequent updates. And if you try to publish an "update" that's nothing more than a facelift, Apple will most likely reject it.

Buying advertising and publicity

Generating buzz through advertising is a time-honored tradition in marketing dating back to ancient times when Egyptians used papyrus to make sales messages and wall posters, and Roman emperors advertised military victories and public works on coins.

The coins are a good example: They were mobile, the image appeared often (at every transaction) to establish the "brand" of the emperor, and they cross-promoted other victories and public works.

Branding is a topic covered in grandiose detail in enough books to fill at least one Trump Tower. (Yup, there's even a *Branding For Dummies.*) Companies with very recognizable brands tend to make free iPhone apps to promote the brand. You may want to consider creating a version of your app that you could license or sell to a client company that then puts its recognizable brand on it. Such an arrangement is called a *white label* deal because the client company supplies the brand on the label.

If you are publishing more than one paid app, the first place to advertise your newest app is in your older apps — add links to cross-promote your other paid app. It costs nothing and helps to build customer loyalty, just because the customer can see that you've developed other apps.

Consider buying ads on other mobile networks that offer ads in iPhone apps. AdMob and Mobclix (described in "Putting ads in your app" earlier in this chapter) target iPhone apps and offer different ways to precisely target your ads. AdMob, for example, offers a video ad unit that runs a dedicated video player inside the app. The app's users can engage with interactive campaigns without leaving the video player. As the advertiser, you can also set up action buttons that let the app's users share video content with friends and connect to social networking sites — again, without ever leaving the video player. As an advertiser, you have a choice of auto-play or click-to-play: The former plays your video ads as soon as the app loads, whereas the latter requires the app's users to tap your banner in order to engage with the campaign.

Another popular choice is Google AdWords. You can reach anyone that searches on Google or on partner networks using any browser. There are close to a google of books available on this topic. (Well, almost 100; try *AdWords For Dummies* by Howie Jacobson.)

Publicity offers the biggest payoff in the short term, and the best way to get it is to pay an excellent PR firm. Good publicity can create a spike in sales that could be misleading, but if you've implemented other marketing campaigns to take advantage of it, sales could level out at a much higher rate than before the publicity hit. The best of the PR firms can help you with your entire marketing strategy.

But if you can't afford that . . . publicity stunts work well if received well by the public. Some of the world's most beloved annual events began their existence as cheap publicity stunts. In 1903, publisher Henri Desgrange started a bicycle road race as a publicity stunt to promote his newspaper, never imagining that the *Tour de France* would be going strong more than 100 years later. The Rose Bowl grew out of an 1890 stunt designed to promote Pasadena, California, the Miss America pageant began in 1921 as a publicity stunt to lure tourists to Atlantic City after Labor Day, and the Academy Awards began in 1929 as a cheap publicity stunt for the movie industry. As Lenny Bruce put it, "Publicity is stronger than sanity: given the right PR, armpit hair on female singers could become a national fetish." (It did, about 15 years later.)

If you can generate publicity, be sure to have a demo on hand — something to titillate people whether they have their iPhones in hand or not. Create a video on YouTube and link it to your press release. Offer a free lite version of your app and time its release to occur at the start of the publicity campaign. Leave no stone unturned in looking for promotional opportunities as part of the campaign. And make sure your demo works — a sacrifice to the demo gods can't hurt. Or just keep repeating the mantra from the patron prophet of demos, Demosthenes: "Small opportunities are often the beginning of great enterprises."

Book II

Objective-C and iPhone Technologies

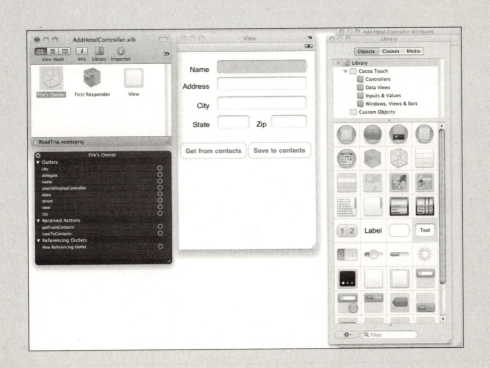

Contents at a Glance

Chapter 1: Using Objective-C's Extensions to C for iPhone Development

In This Chapter

↳ **Knowing how Objective-C works**

↳ **Understanding objects and classes**

↳ **Getting the naming conventions down pat**

↳ **Seeing how objects are created**

↳ **Checking out the standard way to do initialization**

↳ **Working with declared properties**

*O*bjective-C is an object-oriented programming language, which means that it was created to support a certain style of programming. Yes, there are many different styles, but unless you're a dyed-in-the-wool member of a particular camp, it's really unnecessary to get into that discussion now (or probably ever). Objective-C has its fans and its detractors, but my advice is to ignore both sides and get on with your development. There are some things I really like about the language, and others I don't, but in essence, it is what it is, and it is what you'll use.

You can pick up quite a bit about object-oriented programming in this book, but if you want a deeply intimate understanding of it, get Neal's *Objective-C For Dummies* (a shameless plug). After you read *that* book, you'll probably wonder why anyone would ever want to program in any other way.

As you might guess, object-oriented programs are built around *objects* — no surprise here. But a word to the wise: Keep your objects as ignorant as possible about the environment in which they work and the other objects they use. This is called *encapsulation* — an object hides all the details of how it works while allowing other objects to use its methods. Encapsulation makes it easier to enhance or extend an object's capabilities without disturbing how other objects use it (I explain why this is important in Chapter 2 of this minibook). Although there will always be some dependency whenever one object uses another, limit those dependencies to what other objects *do* rather than to *how* they do it, and limit the number of objects each one uses.

Similarly, avoid the compulsion to create `switch` statement control structures that determine the order in which objects get called and that dole out instructions to them. The best object-oriented programs have their objects work like a team, with everyone playing their roles and doing their part rather than submitting to the traditional hierarchical command and control structure where someone is in charge and tells everyone else what to do.

Sergeant Schultz of *Hogan's Heroes* captured the spirit of object-oriented programming with his trademark line:

"I hear nothing, I see nothing, I know nothing!"

What You Need to Know About Objective-C

You'll use Version 2.0 of the Objective-C language, which was released with Mac OS X 10.5, and yes, you should care. Version 2.0 has some new and very useful features — such as fast enumeration, which generates more efficient code, and a new syntax to declare instance variables as properties, with optional attributes to configure the generation of accessor methods (I describe declared properties in "Working with Declared Properties" in this chapter).

But it takes more than a language to write a program; it takes a village. So who lives in the Objective-C village? Most object-oriented development environments consist of several parts:

✦ An object-oriented programming language

✦ A runtime system

✦ A framework or library of objects and functions

✦ A suite of development tools

One of the defining features of Objective-C is its runtime system, which is linked to your program. It acts as a kind of operating system (like the Mac or iPhone OS) for an individual Objective-C program. This runtime system is responsible for making some of the very powerful features of Objective-C work.

The framework you use is called *Cocoa*. It came along with Objective-C when Apple acquired NeXT in 1996 (when it was called NextSTEP). Cocoa lets you write applications for Mac OS X and apps for the iPhone. If the operating system does the heavy lifting *vis-à-vis* the hardware, the framework provides all the stuff you need to make your program an application. It provides support for windows and other user-interface items as well as many of the other things that are needed in most applications. When you use Cocoa, developing your application is way easier because all you need to do is add the application's specific functionality — the content as well as the controls and views that enable the user to access and use that content — to the Cocoa framework. (I introduce frameworks in Chapter 5 of Book I.)

The Objective-C runtime environment also makes it possible to use tools like Interface Builder to create user interfaces with a minimum of work, (I show you how to use Interface Builder in Chapter 2 of Book III.) The two main development tools you use are the aforementioned Interface Builder and Xcode, both of which I introduce in Chapter 4 of Book I and show you how to use in Book III.

Introducing Objects and Classes

Book II
Chapter 1

Using Objective-C's
Extensions to
C for iPhone
Development

If you already know something about programming in C or C++, you are part of the way toward understanding Objective-C. For simplicity's sake, let's just say that the style of programming with C is *procedural* — a program is understood as a list of tasks (functions or subroutines) to perform on a separate *data structure* (which is a collection of variables under a single name).

The programming style with C++ is a mix of procedural and object-oriented: You can use objects that are defined by classes.

When I use the word *class,* I'm talking about code that you write, and when I use the word *object,* I'm talking about behavior at runtime. Whereas a *class* is a structure that represents an object's type, an *object* is something that exists in a computer's memory. An object is an *instantiation* (big computer science word here) of a class. In more down-to-earth terms, a class is a type, and an object is like a variable.

An object brings together the data structure and the methods that process the data in the structure. Each object is like an independent machine with a distinct role, and capable of receiving messages, processing data, and sending messages to other objects. C++ objects tend to be small and dependent on one another — each and every concept, no matter how small, gets its own class. Applications typically have hundreds if not thousands of classes, each one small, and all interconnected. C++ objects tend to come in groups — each time you want to include functionality from an object, you likely need to include an additional 10 to 20 objects.

The programming style of Objective C is to create objects that encapsulate the details of how they work. Classes are different between C++ and Objective C, especially in the declaration. In C++, each class is a structure, and variables and/or methods are included in that structure. In Objective-C, variables are in one section of the class, and methods in another. The methodology focuses on data rather than processes, with programs composed of self-sufficient objects, each containing all the information needed to manipulate its own data structure.

To understand the different programming styles, imagine a vacation budget app that keeps track of credit card transactions in a foreign currency and tells you how much each transaction is in U.S. dollars. It also keeps track of spending against a budget you can set at the beginning of a trip. (If you read Neal's *Objective-C For Dummies*, you can find out how to build this application step by step.)

In a procedural language, you might define a data structure and set of functions for a particular country and then modify them for other countries. But adding new functions for each country would be a lot of work, and it also seems like a waste because the functions all are basically the same — just operating on a different data structure. And, as you can imagine, adding more countries would require coding and testing new functions, and the project would quickly get out of hand.

But more importantly, if you ever wanted to change the data structure, you would have to go out and find all the functions that used it and change them also. If you wanted to have a different kind of budget for New Zealand, for example, one where you tracked your wool purchases, you would either have to add that to all the countries you visited, even though you didn't use it anywhere except New Zealand. Or you would have to create a special data structure for New Zealand and rewrite the functions to use the new data structure. If you then needed to go back to make a change to the original data structure for any reason, you would have to remember to change both, as well as all the functions that used them.

If you can't claim a photographic memory as one of your personal strengths, you've got a problem. Objects (and classes) provide the solution. An object packages together data with the particular operations that can use or affect that data.

A class definition is like a structure definition in that it defines the data elements (which are called *instance variables*) that become part of every instance. But a class expands the idea of a data structure — containing both data and functions instead of just data. Functions, however, become *methods* that both specify and implement the behavior of a class.

The class definition is a template for an object; it declares the instance variables that become part of every object of that class and the methods that all objects of the class can use.

Each object (an *instance* of a class) has memory allocated for its own set of instance variables, which store values particular to the instance.

When you create an object from a class, you're essentially establishing an area in memory land that will hold the object's instance variables. But while every object has its own instance variables, all objects of that class share a single set of methods.

One more thing — in Objective-C, classes have two parts:

✦ An *interface* that *declares* the methods and instance variables of the class and names its superclass (Don't worry. I explain all that.)

✦ An *implementation* that actually *defines* the class — the code that implements its methods

These two parts are almost always split between two files (although there can be more), but to make things easier, I postpone doing that until later, in "Spreading the wealth across files" later in this section.

Grasping objects and their classes

Once again, imagine the vacation budget app. You might create two functions, spendDollars: and chargeForeignCurrency:, that track your spending and foreign currency conversion charges against budgets for different countries. Rather than hard-coding the data for all the countries in one budget, you might use a different budget (such as europeBudget and englandBudget) for each country, and then use a pointer to a budget variable. A pointer's value is a memory address — it refers directly to (or "points to") another value stored elsewhere in memory. Using this pointer, the functions can access different budgets depending on where you were (Europe or England), and the function would operate on the data for that country.

The budget data structure definition would look like the following (I omitted the function implementations):

```
typedef struct {

   float exchangeRate;
   double budget;
   double exchangeTransaction;
} budget;

void spendDollars (budget *theBudget, double dollars);
void chargeForeignCurrency (budget *theBudget,
                                  double foreignCurrency);
```

The problem is that if you wanted to change the data structure struct, you would have to go out and find all the functions that used it and change them. Although in a program this small it would be simple (there are only two functions, after all), in a more complex program, there could be functions all over the place using the struct.

A class that provides the same functionality as the budget struct data structure and the functions that use it, spendDollars: and charge ForeignCurrency:, would look like this:

**Book II
Chapter 1**

**Using Objective-C's
Extensions to
C for iPhone
Development**

```
@interface

Budget : NSObject {

   float   exchangeRate;
   double budget;
   double exchangeTransaction;
}

- (void) spendDollars: (double) dollars ;
- (void) chargeForeignCurrency: (double) foreignCurrency;

@end
```

Data and functions are now both members of the object. You no longer need to track down all the functions that use a particular data structure and revise them. Object-oriented programming allows you to skate right by such headaches through *encapsulation*. You no longer use sets of global variables or data structures that you pass from one function to another as arguments. Instead, you use objects that have their own data *and* functions as members.

Operations (or functions) are known as the object's *methods*; the data they affect are its *instance variables*. In essence, an object bundles a data structure (instance variables) and a group of functions (methods) into a self-contained programming unit. You then ask an object to do something for you — such as subtract the amount you just spent from your budget — by sending it a *message*. When an object receives a message, it then executes the code in the appropriate method.

This encapsulation solves the problem of the widespread impact that changing a data structure may have. Only an object's methods that are packaged with the data can access or modify that data, although an object can — and often does — make its data available to other objects through its methods.

Scoping instance variables

Variables are not accessible from every nook and cranny in your program — they're accessible only within the function in which they are declared (that is, within the braces). This is also referred to as being *scoped* to the function. You could also have braces (which define a block) within a function, in which case variables are scoped within that code block.

A code block is a group of statements grouped together and enclosed in braces: { }.

Instance variables are scoped to (accessible within) the code block they're in. This can be a function, a code block within a function, or, in this case, a class. It is this built-in scoping mechanism that allows an object to hide its data by essentially limiting who (or what) has access to it. But to provide flexibility, when it comes to a class (here come the Objective-C extensions to C again), you can actually explicitly set the scope to three different levels through the use of a compiler directive:

✦ `@private`: The instance variable is accessible only within the class that declares it.

✦ `@protected`: The instance variable is accessible within the class that declares it and within classes that inherit it. This is the default if you don't specify anything.

✦ `@public`: The instance variable is accessible everywhere.

Don't use `@public`! If you do — go directly to jail, do not pass Go, and do not collect $200. If you have to ask why, reread the first part of this chapter.

Spreading the wealth across files

You may have started your coding in a single source file — perhaps `MyFirstProgram.m` and then moving on to `Budget.m` (for the vacation budget app) or `YourApp.m`. Although this works initially, it won't scale when you start to develop a real app. As your program gets larger, scrolling through a single file becomes more difficult. But there's a well-thought-out solution for that problem that just about everyone uses.

When I write even the simplest apps for the iPhone, I divide things into multiple files.

The source code for Objective-C classes is divided into two parts. One part is the interface, which provides the public view of the class. The `@interface` contains all the information necessary for someone to use the class. The other part of a class's source is the implementation. The `@implementation` contains the method definitions.

Because of the natural split in the definition of a class into interface and implementation, a class's code is often split into two files along the same lines. One part holds the interface components: the `@interface` directive for the class and any `enum`, `constants`, `#defines`, and so on. Because of Objective-C's C heritage, this typically goes into a *header* file, which has the same name as the class with an `.h` at the end. For example, the class `MainView` header file is called `MainView.h`. (You can see this file when you select the Utility Application template in Xcode, as I describe in Chapter 4 of Book I.)

All the implementation details, such as the `@implementation` directive for the class, definitions of global variables, the method definitions (implementations), and so on go into a file with the same name as the class and with an `.m` at the end. `MainView.m` would be the implementation file for the `MainView` class. (You can see this file when you select the Utility Application template in Xcode, as I describe in Chapter 4 of Book I.)

Knowing the naming conventions

It's helpful to have some idea about how to name things in order to avoid having the compiler scream at you. Here are some areas you need to pay attention to:

✦ The names of files that contain Objective-C source code have the .m extension. Files that declare class and category interfaces or that declare protocols have the .h extension typical of header files. (A category is used to extend a class; I explain that along with protocols in Chapter 5 of this minibook.)

✦ Class, category, and protocol names generally begin with an uppercase letter; the names of methods and instance variables typically begin with a lowercase letter. The names of variables that hold instances also typically begin with lowercase letters.

✦ In Objective-C, identical names that serve different purposes are allowed and are resolved at runtime. For example:

   • A class can declare methods with the same names as methods in other classes.

   • A class can declare instance variables with the same names as variables in other classes.

   • An instance method can have the same name as a class method.

   • A method can have the same name as an instance variable.

   • Method names beginning with _, a single underscore character, are reserved for use by Apple.

   • However, class names are in the same *name space* as global variables and defined types — the name space uniquely identifies a set of names so that there is no ambiguity when objects having different origins but the same names are mixed together. As a result, a program can't have a defined type with the same name as a class.

Objective-C is case-sensitive. Budget and budget are not the same thing — Budget is a class, and budget is a variable.

Using id and nil

As part of its extensions to C, Objective-C adds two built-in generic C types that you can use for objects.

id is a generic C type defined as a pointer to an object data structure, which you use to refer to any kind of object regardless of class. All objects, regardless of their instance variables or methods, are of type id. You use id when I explain protocols in Chapter 5 of this minibook. For now, just keep this in mind.

Similarly, `nil` is defined as a null object, an `id` with a value of 0.

`id`, `nil`, and the other basic types of Objective-C are defined in the `objc/objc.h` header file.

Declaring the Class Interface

The purpose of the class interface is to give users of a class the information they need to work with the class. The declaration of a class interface begins with the compiler directive `@interface` and ends with the directive `@end`. (All Objective-C compiler directives begin with `@`.)

```
@interface ClassName : ItsSuperclass {
  instance variable declarations
}
method declarations
@end
```

In the interface, you specify the following:

✦ **The class's name and superclass:**

```
@interface ClassName : ItsSuperclass {
```

A class can be based on another class called its *superclass,* and it inherits all the methods and instance variables of that class. I explain all about inheritance in Chapter 2 of this minibook.

✦ **The class's instance variables:** *Instance variables* correspond to the members (variable declarations) in a data structure (`struct`).

✦ **The class's methods:** *Methods* are a group of functions or operations specific to a particular class.

For example, here's the class interface for the `Budget` class shown in the section "Grasping objects and their classes" earlier in this chapter:

```
@interface Budget : NSObject   {

  float   exchangeRate;
  double  budget;
  double  exchangeTransaction;
}

- (void) createBudget: (double) aBudget
             withExchangeRate: (float) anExchangeRate;
- (void) spendDollars: (double) dollars ;
- (void) chargeForeignCurrency: (double) foreignCurrency;
@end
```

**Book II
Chapter 1**

Using Objective-C's
Extensions to
C for iPhone
Development

As you can see, the interface has four parts, which appear in this order:

1. The `@interface` compiler directive and first line
2. The instance variables
3. The methods
4. The `@end` compiler directive

By convention, class names begin with an uppercase letter (such as `Budget`); the names' instance variables and methods typically begin with a lowercase letter (such as `exchangeRate:` and `spendDollars:`).

The next few sections take a closer look at each one of the four parts.

The @interface compiler directive and first line

The `@interface` compiler directive tells the compiler that you're declaring a new class. It's the first line in the first example in the previous section:

```
@interface Budget : NSObject {
```

`Budget : NSObject` declares the new class name and links it to its superclass.

`: NSObject` on the `@interface` line tells the compiler that the `Budget` class is an extension of the `NSObject` class — `NSObject` is the `Budget` class's superclass, in other words. `Budget` will inherit all the methods and instance variables of `NSObject`. This means that, for all practical purposes, even though you don't see them in your class declaration, `Budget` includes all the instance variables and all the methods that are in `NSObject`.

NSObject is a root class that defines the basic framework for Objective-C objects and object interactions. It imparts to the classes and instances of classes that inherit from it the ability to behave as objects and cooperate with the runtime system. Because `Budget` inherits from `NSObject`, it has all the functionality an Objective-C object would need at runtime.

The instance variables

After starting to declare a new class, you tell the compiler about the various pieces of data you want to work with — the instance variables and methods.

In my (running) example, the following lines of code appear on the line after `@interface Budget : NSObject {`:

```
    float   exchangeRate;
    double  budget;
    double  exchangeTransaction;
}
```

exchangeRate, budget, and exchangeTransaction are the *instance variables* for objects of class Budget.

The reason they're called instance variables is that when you create an object of the Budget class, you're creating an *instance* of the class, which means that for each object you create, you allocate some amount of memory for its variables (just as you do for the data structure). The instance variables here correspond to the ones you would have used in the struct (data structure):

Book II
Chapter 1

Using Objective-C's
Extensions to
C for iPhone
Development

✦ exchangeRate is the current, well, exchange rate — the number of dollars it will cost you to get one euro or one pound, for example.

✦ budget holds the amount of dollars you have left to spend in a given country.

✦ exchangeTransaction is the amount in U.S. dollars of a foreign currency transaction.

Because budget, exchangeRate, and exchangeTransaction are declared in the class definition, every time a Budget object is created, it includes these three instance variables. So every object of class Budget has its own budget, exchangeRate, and exchangeTransaction. The closing brace tells the compiler you're done specifying the instance variables for Budget.

The methods

Keeping the focus on the running example, the following lines of code appear on the line after the brace (}):

```
- (void) createBudget: (double) aBudget
                withExchangeRate: (float) anExchangeRate;
- (void) spendDollars: (double) dollars ;
- (void) chargeForeignCurrency: (double) foreignCurrency;
```

In Objective-C, these lines of code are called *method declarations*. They make public the behavior that Budget has implemented — making it clear to the whole world that this is the kind of stuff any object of the Budget class can do.

Methods are like functions that return a value, and method declarations are like function prototypes in C or C++, (although they look different). A *function prototype* is a declaration of a function that omits the function body (its definition), but specifies its name so that you can start referring to the function in your code. Eventually you have to provide a function definition elsewhere in the program in order to actually use the function. The function prototype also specifies the data type (the kind of data, such as char, int, and float, to be stored in memory) of the function's arguments, and the data type of the value that the function returns.

Here is an example of a method declaration (from the preceding code):

```
- (void) spendDollars: (double) dollars;
```

The leading dash signals that this is the declaration for an Objective-C method. That's one way you can distinguish a method declaration from a function prototype, which has no leading dash.

Following the dash is the return type for the method, enclosed in parentheses — the value of what the method returns (similar to what a function returns). Methods can return the same types as functions, including standard types (`int`, `float`, and `char`), as well as references to other objects.

`spendDollars:` is a method that takes a single argument of type `double`. Notice that instead of the parentheses used in a function to indicate arguments, methods use a colon (`:`). Also notice that the colon is part of the method name.

Another difference between function prototypes and a method declaration is that in a method declaration, both the *return type* and the *argument type* are enclosed in parentheses. This is the standard syntax for *casting one type as another* — converting from one data type to another.

Although the `spendDollars` method I came up with doesn't return a value, I could add that functionality at a moment's notice by doing just what you'd do if you were dealing with a function prototype — adding the following:

```
return someValue;
```

For all practical purposes, `chargeForeignCurrency` works the same way as `spendDollars:`

```
- (void) chargeForeignCurrency: (double) foreignCurrency;
```

Finally, you've come to the mind-numbing part — `createBudget::`.

```
- (void) createBudget: (double) aBudget
        withExchangeRate: (float) anExchangeRate;
```

If a method takes an argument, it has one or more colons, corresponding to the number of arguments. If it takes no arguments, it has no colons. If you aren't going to specify the full name, you add the number of colons corresponding to the number of arguments to the name. For example, `createBudget::` indicates it takes two arguments.

The `createBudget::` method initializes the values — the `budget` and `exchangeRate` — for an object that is the budget for a particular country.

You might have coded this by assigning those values to the members in a `struct` data structure, as follows:

```
vacationBudgetEurope.exchangeRate = 1.2500;
vacationBudgetEurope.budget = 1000.00;
...
vacationBudgetEngland.exchangeRate = 1.5000;
vacationBudgetEngland.budget = 2000.00;
```

But because (as I explain in the earlier section "Scoping instance variables") you don't have access to the instance variables in a `Budget` object (say "encapsulation" three times and click your heels), you need to create a method to assign initial values to the instance variables. (Initialization is an important part of Objective-C, and I explain it in detail in Chapter 3 of this minibook.)

Book II
Chapter 1

Using Objective-C's Extensions to C for iPhone Development

Although you might be able to guess that the method takes two arguments, the syntax of the declaration is probably not something you're familiar with. (Talk about a classic understatement.) Here goes:

```
- (void) createBudget: (double) aBudget
            withExchangeRate: (float) anExchangeRate;
```

When there's more than one argument, the `aBudget` and `anExchangeRate` argument names are declared within the method name after the colon. The full method name is `createBudget:withExchangeRate:`.

Argument names make it easier to understand the messages in your code. `createBudget:withExchangeRate:` does have a nice ring to it. When you create your own methods, name them in the same way — make them closer to sentences. This way of naming methods makes it much easier to match arguments with what they're used for.

This does take some getting used to, but when you do, you'll like it a lot.

Because `createBudget::` won't be returning anything, I used `void` to indicate that there's no return value.

The @end compiler directive

The `@end` compiler directive does exactly what its name implies it's going to do: It tells the compiler that you've finished the interface declaration.

The complete interface for the `Budget` class is done. Now, anyone using this object knows that this class has three methods that can create a new budget, spend dollars, and charge something in a foreign currency: methods appropriately named `createBudget:`, `spendDollars:`, and `chargeForeignCurrency:`.

The Implementation — Coding the Methods

The `@interface`, described in the previous section, defines a class's public interface. This is the place where another developer (or even you) can go to understand the class's capabilities and behavior.

However, it's here in the implementation that the real work is described and done. Here are the steps:

1. Add the implementation compiler directive.

2. Define the methods.

3. Enter the `@end` compiler directive.

Sounds easy enough, right? The next sections give the play-by-play account.

The @implementation compiler directive

The implementation compiler directive — made instantly recognizable by its use of `@implementation` — tells the compiler that you're about to present the code that implements a class. For example,

```
@implementation Budget
```

lets the compiler know that `Budget` is coming down the pike. The name of the class appears after `@implementation`.

Here you code the definitions of the individual methods. When it comes to the implementation code, order is unimportant — the methods don't have to appear in the same order as they do in the `@interface`.

Defining the methods

After getting `@implementation Budget` in place, you would move on to define a method:

```
- (void) createBudget: (double) aBudget
          withExchangeRate: (float) anExchangeRate {
  exchangeRate = anExchangeRate;
  budget = aBudget;
}
```

The first line of the definition of `createBudget::` looks a lot like the declaration in the `@interface` section (one would hope), except that instead of a semicolon at the end, you find a brace. Notice that you have an argument named `aBudget` and an instance variable `budget`. If you had named that argument `budget`, the compiler would have needed to decide which one you meant when you tried to access the `budget` variable. You want to use a name like `aBudget` in the method declaration because it tells the reader exactly what the argument is for.

The body of the method contains these instructions:

```
exchangeRate = anExchangeRate;
budget = aBudget;
```

Adding the following lines of code after the `createBudget::` method would define two more methods:

```
- (void) spendDollars: (double) dollars {

  budget -= dollars;
  NSLog(@"Converting %.2f US dollars into foreign currency
                      leaves $%.2f", dollars, budget);
}

- (void) chargeForeignCurrency: (double)
                                     foreignCurrency {

  exchangeTransaction = foreignCurrency*exchangeRate;
  budget -= exchangeTransaction;
  NSLog(@"Charging %.2f in foreign currency leaves $%.2f",
                      foreignCurrency, budget);
}
```

Book II
Chapter 1

Using Objective-C's
Extensions to
C for iPhone
Development

The @end compiler directive

Once again, the last line of code — the `@end` compiler directive — tells the compiler that you have finished the task at hand — in this case, the implementation file.

Allocating Objects

It's all well and good to declare a new class with instance variables and methods, and to write the code for these methods (as you do in the previous sections). The next step is to give birth to an object based on the new class, which happens at runtime.

At runtime, a *class object* for each class is automatically created — one that knows how to build new objects belonging to the class. The class object is the compiled version of the class; the objects it builds are *instances* of the class. These instances are the objects that do the main work of your program.

Think of the class definition as really a prototype for a *kind* of object, not the object itself. The class definition declares the instance variables and defines a set of methods that all objects in the class can use. The objects you give birth to are instances of the class. To give birth to an object in Objective-C, you must do the following:

1. Dynamically allocate memory for the new object.
2. Initialize the newly allocated memory, as described in the upcoming "Initialization" section.

An object isn't fully functional until both steps have been completed. Each step is accomplished by a separate method but is typically carried out using a single line of code:

```
id anObject = [[Rectangle alloc] init];
```

Read on to find out what one simple line of code can do for you.

All objects are dynamic

Allocation (`alloc`) starts the process of creating a new object by getting the amount of memory it needs from the operating system to hold all of the object's instance variables. For example, in the RoadTrip app, the `Trip` model object is allocated (as shown in Chapter 4 of Book V) as follows:

```
trip = [[Trip alloc] initWithName:@"Road Trip"];
```

NSObject, which I explain in the section, "The @interface compiler directive and first line," earlier in this chapter, is a root class that defines the basic framework for all the Objective-C objects you use and their interactions. The `alloc` method is one of the principal methods of NSObject for allocating memory. This code sends the `alloc` message to the NSObject class. The `alloc` method in NSObject not only allocates the memory for the object, but also initializes all the memory it allocates to 0 — all the ints are 0; all the `floats` become 0.0; all the pointers are `nil`; and the object's isa instance variable points to the object's class. (This tells an object of what class it is an instance.)

The `alloc` method allocates enough memory to hold all the instance variables for an object belonging to the receiving class.

You can use the `new` method to combine `alloc` and `init` and instantiate an object using a line of code such as

```
Budget    *europeBudget = [Budget new];
```

This instantiates (creates) a new object and sends it a message. The `new` method is actually a holdover from Objective-C's earlier days when a two-phase initialization was not important. Separating allocation from initialization, as you do with `alloc` and `init`, gives you individual control over each step so that each can be modified independently of the other, but you can use the `new` method if you don't need to exert such control.

To create a new object, you send the new message to the class you're interested in. Here's the syntax of sending a message:

```
[receiver message : arguments];
```

The receiver of a message can be either an *object* or a *class*. One of the more interesting features of Objective-C is that you can send messages to a class. If you haven't done any object-oriented programming before, sending messages to a class probably doesn't strike you as that big of a deal. But if you're coming from something like C++, it's very interesting. By sending messages to a class, you can implement behavior that is not object-specific, but applicable to an entire class.

The methods defined for an object are called *instance* methods, and the ones defined for a class are called *class* methods. Although I mention class methods in this book, you don't use them. I only refer to them when it's important to distinguish them from instance methods or those (rare) situations where you really need to know about them — in Chapter 3 of this minibook, for example.

The following line,

```
Budget *europeBudget = [Budget new];
```

sends the new message to the Budget class. The new method (inherited from NSObject) does two things, in this order:

1. Allocates memory for the object to hold its instance variables.

2. Sends the new object an init message.

Initialization

The default init method will (more or less) initialize the instance variables to 0. Initialization, as boring as it sounds, is a very important part of working with objects. In many cases, you don't need to initialize all your instance variables. If you can live with all the instance variables initialized to 0 and nil, then there is nothing you need to do. But if your class (or your superclass) has instance variables that you need to initialize to anything other than 0 or nil, you're going to have to code some kind of initialization method. (Chapter 3 of this minibook goes into great detail about initialization and shows you how to write a proper init method for your objects.)

Objective-C, like other object-oriented programming languages, permits you to base a new class definition on a class already defined, so that the new class inherits the methods of the class it is based on. The base class is called a *superclass*; the new class is its subclass (I describe inheritance in detail in Chapter 2 of this book). The superclass's initialization method is always invoked before the subclass does any initialization. Your superclass is equally as respectful of its superclass and does the same thing.

When you invoke a superclass's initialization method, most of the time you get back the object you expect. Some of the framework classes such as NSString are really class clusters — a *class cluster* is an abstract base class (and a group of private, concrete subclasses) that hides implementation details so that their design can be modified later, without breaking your code (as long as you use the interface provided by the abstract class). When you create an object of one of these classes, its initialization method looks at the arguments you're passing and returns the object it thinks you need. If you're playing by the rules, it won't matter (as I show in Chapter 3 of this minibook).

It's possible to have more than one initializer per class. Once you have more than one initializer in a class, according to Cocoa convention, you're expected to set one up as the *designated initializer.* This designated initializer is usually the one that does the most initialization, and it is the one responsible for invoking the superclass's initializer. Because this initializer is the one that does the most work, again by convention, the other initializers are expected to invoke it with appropriate default values as needed. I explore this topic further in Chapter 3 of this minibook.

Sending Messages to Your Objects

To get an object to do something, you send it a message telling it to apply a method. In Objective-C, message expressions are enclosed in brackets, like this:

```
[receiver message]
```

The receiver is an object, and the message tells it what to do. In your code, the message is simply the name of a method and any arguments that are passed to it. When a message is sent, the runtime system selects the appropriate method from the receiver's repertoire and invokes it.

For example, you could use the following code after allocating the object Budget *europeBudget = [Budget new];:

```
[europeBudget createBudget:
              1000.00 withExchangeRate:1.2500];
[europeBudget spendDollars:numberDollarsInEuroland];
[europeBudget chargeForeignCurrency:numberEuros];
```

This code sends three messages to the europeBudget object just instantiated. Take a look at the first message:

```
[europeBudget  createBudget:1000.00
                 withExchangeRate:1.2500];
```

Using the `europeBudget` pointer to the object, you are sending it the `createBudget::` message with `1000.00` and `1.2500` as arguments. You use this to initialize the object with a budget and an exchange rate.

After initialization, the next message sent to the `europeBudget` object tells it how much was spent in dollars. (It has an argument `numberDollarsInEuroland` just like a function would).

```
[europeBudget spendDollars:numberDollarsInEuroland];
```

And the third message reports a credit card transaction.

```
[europeBudget chargeForeignCurrency:numberEuros];
```

**Book II
Chapter 1**

**Using Objective-C's
Extensions to
C for iPhone
Development**

The question that may occur to you at this point is how did the `europeBudget` method code (of which there is only a single copy) get to the object's instance variables, which are sitting some place in memory?

The answer is very clever. When you send a message in Objective-C, a hidden argument called `self`, a pointer to the object's instance variables, is passed to the receiving object. For example, in the code

```
[europeBudget spendDollars:numberDollarsInEuroland];
```

the method passes `europeBudget` as its `self` argument. Although the code in the method `chargeForeignCurrency:` looks like

```
NSLog(@"Converting %.2f US dollars into foreign currency
                     leaves $%.2f", dollars, budget);
```

what the compiler is really doing is modifying this code so that it conceptually looks like this:

```
NSLog(@"Converting %.2f US dollars into foreign currency
    leaves $%.2f", dollars, self->budget);
```

The `->` is the arrow operator. It's used only with pointers to objects. As you create objects, you get a new pointer for each one, and when you send a message to a particular object, the pointer associated with that object becomes the `self` argument.

Working with Declared Properties

If you need to have an instance variable accessible by other objects in your program, you'll need to create accessor methods for that particular instance variable. Accessor methods effectively get (using a *getter method*) and set (using a *setter method*) the values for an instance variable.

For many years, programmers had to code accessor methods themselves or buy add-on tools that would do it for them (usually advertised late at night on the Programmers Channel). The nice folks in charge of Objective-C came to our collective rescue when they released Objective-C 2.0 with its *declared properties* feature. Now, the compiler can write accessor methods for you, according to the direction you give it in the *property declaration*. It's kind of like getting the smartest kid in your class to do your homework while you hang out with your friends at the mall. As you'll soon discover, you're sure to use declared properties a lot in your application development work. (Most people just call them *properties*, by the way.)

Objective-C creates the getter and setter methods for you by using a `@property` declaration in the interface file, combined with the `@synthesize` declaration in the implementation file. The default names for the getter and setter methods associated with a property are *whateverTheProperty NameIs* for the getter (yes, the default getter method name is the same as the property's name) and `set`*WhateverThePropertyNameIs*`:` for the setter. (You replace what is in italics with the actual property name or identifier.) For example, the accessors that would be generated for the `exchangeRate` instance variable are `exchangeRate` as the getter and `setExchangeRate:` as the setter.

Adding properties

You need to do three things in your code in order for the compiler to create accessors for you:

1. Declare an instance variable in the interface file.

2. Add a `@property` declaration of that instance variable in the same interface file.

3. Add a `@synthesize` statement in the implementation file so that Objective-C generates the accessors for you.

In developing a vacation budget app as I describe in the previous sections, you might want to create a `Destination` class with methods that do the following:

✦ Create `Transaction` objects from the transaction amounts that will be sent from the user interface.

✦ Return whatever data the user interface needs to display.

To have your `Destination` class do all that, you'd have to add the following code to your class's `Destination.h` file; I explain the bold statements in more detail.

```
#import <Cocoa/Cocoa.h>
@class Budget;
```

```
@interface Destination : NSObject {

  NSString* country;
  double exchangeRate;
  NSMutableArray *transactions;
  Budget* theBudget;
}

- (id) initWithCountry: (NSString*) theCountry
           andBudget: (double) budgetAmount
           withExchangeRate: (double) theExchangeRate;
- (void) spendCash: (double) aTransaction;
- (void) chargeCreditCard: (double) aTransaction;
- (double) leftToSpend;

@property (nonatomic, retain) NSString* country;
@property (readwrite) double exchangeRate;
@end
```

Book II
Chapter 1

**Using Objective-C's
Extensions to
C for iPhone
Development**

Creating accessor methods is a two-step process that begins with the `@property` declaration, which tells the compiler that there are in fact accessor methods that it's going to have to deal with. The `@property` declarations for `country` and `exchangeRate` specify how the accessor methods are to behave.

The `@property` declaration specifies the name and type of the property and some *attributes* that provide the compiler with information about exactly how you want the accessor methods to be implemented.

For example, the declaration

```
@property (readwrite) double exchangeRate;
```

declares a property named `exchangeRate`, which is of the `double` type. The property attribute (`readwrite`) tells the compiler that this property can be both read and updated outside the object.

You also could have specified `readonly`, in which case, only a getter method is required in the `@implementation` — you don't need a setter method with a read-only property because you're not setting anything. Then, when you use `@synthesize` in the implementation block, only the getter method is synthesized. Moreover, if you attempt to assign a value using the accessor — "setting" a value, in other words — you get a compiler error.

Now take a look at the declaration right before the `exchangeRate` declaration:

```
@property (nonatomic, retain) NSString* country;
```

It declares a property named `country`, which is a pointer to a `NSString` object. Enclosed in parentheses are two attributes: `nonatomic` and `retain`.

`nonatomic` addresses an important technical consideration for multi-threaded systems, which is beyond the scope of this book. `nonatomic` works fine for applications like this one.

`retain` directs the compiler to create an accessor method that sends a `retain` message to any object that is assigned to this property. As I show in Chapter 3 of this minibook, properties can have some memory management implications — every object has its own reference count, or *retain count*. It's your responsibility to maintain that reference count by directly or indirectly increasing the retain count when you're using an object and then decreasing it when you're finished with it.

And, oh yes, `nonatomic` and `retain` apply only to pointers to objects.

But while the `@property` declaration tells the compiler that there are accessor methods coming — one if by land, two if by sea — the darn things still have to be created. In the good old days, you had to code these accessor methods yourself, which in a large program was very tedious.

Fortunately, Objective-C creates these accessor methods for you whenever you include a `@synthesize` statement for a property. To get this to work, you'd add the following code to the `Destination.m` file for the `Destination` class:

```
#import "Destination.h"
#import "CashTransaction.h"
#import "CreditCardTransaction.h"
#import "Budget.h"
#import "Transaction.h"

@implementation Destination

@synthesize exchangeRate, country;
```

The `@synthesize` statement — the bold line in the code — directs the compiler to create two accessor methods, one for each `@property` declaration.

The `@property` declaration only informs the compiler that there are accessors. It is the `@synthesize` statement that tells the compiler to create them for you. Using `@synthesize` results in four new methods:

```
exchangeRate
setExchangeRate:
country
setCountry:
```

If you didn't use @synthesize and you declared the properties, it would be up to you to implement the methods yourself, according to the attributes in the @property statement. So, if you were to write your own accessors, you would be responsible for sending a retain message to the exchangeRate when it's assigned to the instance variables. You may have to do that anyway, under certain circumstances, which I discuss in the later section, "Properly using properties."

Accessing the properties from within the class

After you've declared the properties, you can access them from other objects or from main. (main is the mother of all functions and is the place where all Objective-C programs start their execution — the instructions contained within main are always the first ones to be executed in Objective-C programs. All Objective-C programs have one.)

First, let me show you how you can access them within the class. If you want to take advantage of the retain message being sent automatically upon assignment, you have to access the instance variable directly, so you must invoke the accessor method, like this:

```
[self setCountry:theCountry];
```

You also can use the dot notation (something that refugees from other object-oriented languages might recognize).

```
self.country = theCountry;
```

When you use the setter method with a class to assign an object pointer, you don't need to send the object a retain message, like the one you had to send to the country object in the Destination's initWithCountry:: method, since the setter method does the retain for you.

```
[country retain];
```

Releasing the object assigned to a property

Using an accessor method automatically sends a retain message. But you still have to release it when you're done — properties are not automatically released for you.

Normally you send an object a release message:

```
[country release];
```

But if you use an accessor method, you have a new option:

```
self.country = nil;
```

Book II
Chapter 1

Using Objective-C's
Extensions to
C for iPhone
Development

That's because when you assign a new value to a property, the accessor sends a `release` message to the previous object. As you can see, accessors are good citizens here.

In your `dealloc` method, however, you need to send the object a `release` message.

Using accessor methods to get data from objects

The file corresponding to `Destination.h` for the `Destination` class (described earlier in the "Adding properties" section) is the `Destination.m` file:

```
#import "Destination.h"
#import "CashTransaction.h"
#import "CreditCardTransaction.h"
#import "Budget.h"
#import "Transaction.h"


@implementation Destination
@synthesize exchangeRate, country;
- (id) initWithCountry: (NSString*) theCountry andBudget:
   (double) budgetAmount withExchangeRate: (double)
   theExchangeRate{
  if (self = [super init]) {
    transactions = [[NSMutableArray alloc]
    initWithCapacity:10];

    theBudget = [[Budget alloc]
        initWithAmount:budgetAmount forDestination:self];
    self.exchangeRate = theExchangeRate;
    [self setCountry: theCountry];

    NSLog (@"I'm off to %@", theCountry);
  }
  return self;
}

- (void) spendCash: (double)amount{

  Transaction *aTransaction = [[CashTransaction alloc]
    initWithAmount: amount forBudget: theBudget];
  [transactions addObject:aTransaction];
  [aTransaction spend];
  [aTransaction release];

}

- (void) chargeCreditCard: (double) amount{
```

```
    Transaction *aTransaction = [[CreditCardTransaction alloc]
      initWithAmount: amount forBudget: theBudget];
    [transactions addObject:aTransaction];
    [aTransaction spend];
    [aTransaction release];
}

- (double) leftToSpend {

    return [theBudget returnBalance];
}

- (void) dealloc {

    [transactions release];
    [theBudget release];
    [country release];
    [super dealloc];
}

@end
```

**Book II
Chapter 1**

**Using Objective-C's
Extensions to
C for iPhone
Development**

The `Budget init` method (bolded in the preceding code) sends a message in order to get the `exchangeRate`:

```
theBudget = [[Budget alloc]
        initWithAmount:budgetAmount forDestination:self];
    self.exchangeRate = theExchangeRate;
    [self setCountry: theCountry];
```

An accessor method assigns the `theExchangeRate` argument in the `init-WithAmount::` method to the `exchangeRate` instance variable using dot notation:

```
    self.exchangeRate = theExchangeRate;
```

An accessor method also assigns the `theCountry` argument in the `initWithAmount:` method to the `country` instance variable using an Objective-C message.

```
    [self setCountry:theCountry];
```

Now that you've created these accessor methods, you can use them. First, in the `Budget.m` file, you use a pointer to the `Destination` object and include `#import "Destination.h"` to make the compiler happy when it sees a message to the `Destination` object. Here's what the `Budget.m` file would look like after you add the necessary code, which is in bold here, as you can see:

```
#import "Budget.h"
```

```
#import "Destination.h"


@implementation Budget
- (id) initWithAmount: (double) aBudget forDestination:
    (Destination*) aDestination {
  if (self = [super init]) {
    destination = aDestination;
    [destination retain];
    budget = aBudget;
  }
  return self;
}


- (void) spendDollars: (double) dollars {

  budget -= dollars;
}


- (void) chargeForeignCurrency: (double) foreignCurrency {
transaction = foreignCurrency*
                              [destination exchangeRate];
  budget -= transaction;
}


- (double) returnBalance {

  return budget;
}


- (void) dealloc {
  [destination release];
  [super dealloc];
}


@end
```

The code you added (see the preceding bolded code) uses a pointer to the
Destination object as an argument:

```
- (id) initWithAmount: (double) aBudget forDestination:
    (Destination*) aDestination {
  if (self = [super init]) {
    destination = aDestination;
    [destination retain];
    budget = aBudget;
  }
  return self;
}
```

It also stores the pointer to the Destination object in an instance variable destination. You send it a retain message to ensure that it won't be deallocated until you are done with it.

The chargeForeignCurrency: method uses the getter method exchange Rate to get the exchange rate from the Destination object.

Next, in the Budget.h file, you add a @class statement to make the compiler happy, as well as an instance variable, destination, and an init method declaration just like in the implementation:

```
#import <Cocoa/Cocoa.h>
@class Destination;

@interface Budget : NSObject {
  float        exchangeRate;
  double       budget;
  double       transaction;
  Destination* destination;
}
- (id) initWithAmount: (double) aBudget
              forDestination: (Destination*) aDestination;

- (void) spendDollars: (double) dollars ;
- (void) chargeForeignCurrency: (double) euros;
- (double) returnBalance;
@end
```

**Book II
Chapter 1**

**Using Objective-C's
Extensions to
C for iPhone
Development**

In main, you would use the Destination object's setExchangeRate: and country accessor methods to update the exchange rate and access the country name and display it:

```
[europe setExchangeRate:1.30];
[england setExchangeRate:1.40];
```

You would also send a setExchangeRate: message to both the europe and england objects, which updates the exchange rate for each, replacing the initialized value for exchangeRate. And being a good citizen about recycling memory for other uses, you also release the string returnedCountry:

```
NSString *returnedCountry = [england country];
NSLog (@"You have deleted the %@ part of your
  trip",returnedCountry);
[returnedCountry release];
[england release];
```

At the top of main, you would use the autorelease pool allocation to store objects in the autorelease pool, and at the bottom, pool drain to empty the autorelease pool as I describe in Chapter 3 of this minibook:

```
NSAutoreleasePool * pool = [[NSAutoreleasePool alloc] init];

...

[pool drain];
```

An autorelease pool contains objects that have received an `autorelease` message; when drained, it sends a `release` message to each of those objects. By sending `autorelease` instead of `release` to an object, you can extend the lifetime of the objects — at least until the pool itself is drained.

Properly using properties

There are times when accessor methods are the best way to do things:

✦ **Customizing user interface objects.** In a framework, the user interface object — a window or view, for example — really needs to have certain parameters set to make it function in the way the user needs. Instead of forcing the user to subclass it, properties allow it to be tailored to a particular user's (the developer's) needs. In this case, properties are being used to set parameters, like color, rather than to implement a class's responsibility to accept data.

✦ **Accessing instance variables.** Again, in a framework, the same argument applies to accessing the instance variables. The instance variables should become properties when they hold information about the state of the object — is the window opened or closed, where did the user just drag this object to on the screen, and so on.

Except for those and similar circumstances in your own classes, you're much better off avoiding using properties to implement an object's responsibility to accept data from (and supply data to) other objects. You should define methods that accept or supply data and not use a property that implies structural information about the data.

That being said, some features about properties also allow you to do some interesting things to mitigate the impact if you later decide to change an instance variable you've made available as a property. For example:

✦ **To deal with changes, you can implement the accessor method (instead of having it generated by the complier) to access the property.** For example, if you moved the exchange rate to an exchange rate object, you could implement your own `exchangeRate` method currently synthesized by the compiler. (It will only synthesize those methods if you have not implemented them in your implementation file.) The method you implemented would send a message to the new exchange rate object to get — and then return back — the exchange rate. (You probably wouldn't need a setter in this case.) If you do that though, be sure to implement the accessor in a way that's consistent with the property's attributes. Creating your own accessors for properties is another topic that is beyond the scope of this book.

✦ **The accessor doesn't have to be named the same as the instance variable.** For example, you can use

```
@property (readwrite, getter=returnTheExchangeRate)
                          double exchangeRate;
```

✦ **The property name must have the same name as an instance variable.** For example,

```
@property (readwrite ) double er;
...
@synthesize country, er = exchangeRate;
```

directs the complier to synthesize `getEr` and `setEr:` to get and set the instance variable `exchangeRate`. If you try this for yourself, you find that

```
[europe setEr:1.30];
[england setEr:1.40];
```

works just as well as `setExchangeRate:` does.

Extending the Program

As you discover earlier in this chapter, coding procedurally (as you would in C) using a data structure and set of functions for a vacation budget app to work in a particular country would require you to modify both the data structure and the set of functions for the other countries. Adding new functions for each country would be a lot of work, and changing the data structure would require changing all the functions that use it. This vulnerability you face — when all your functions have access to all the data and are dependent on that data's structure — is mostly solved by encapsulating the data in an object. The data becomes an internal implementation detail; the other objects that use this object's data know only the behavior they can expect from this object.

But what if another object needs to know the amount left in your budget for England, for example? To meet that need, you add a method that provides that information. Notice I say *information,* not the instance variable. It becomes the responsibility of an object to supply the budget information to any object that needs it. It doesn't mean, however, that there has to be an instance variable that holds that information. That makes it possible to change how you represent that data and also makes it possible to change what instance variables you choose for the object.

So, although its internal data structure is part of the class interface, in reality, an object's functionality should be defined only by its methods. As a user of a class, you shouldn't count on a one-to-one correspondence between a method that returns some data and an instance variable. Some methods might return information not stored in instance variables, and some instance variables might have data that will never see the light of day outside the object.

This setup allows your classes to evolve over time. As long as messages are the way you interact with a class, changes to the instance variables really don't affect its interface and also don't affect the other objects that use this class — and that's the point.

But what if you want a new kind of budget or want to tailor your Budget object to New Zealand to keep track of your wool purchases? Do you have to take the old object, copy and paste it, and add the new features — thus creating a new object that you have to maintain in parallel with the existing Budget object?

As you might expect, the answer is, "Of course not!" As you learn about an inheritance-based class structure, this greatly simplifies things, and you end up with a program that is a great deal easier to understand and extend. (The two actually go hand in hand.)

Inheritance

Objective-C, like other object-oriented programming languages, permits you to base a new class definition on a class already defined. The base class is called a *superclass*; the new class is its *subclass*. The subclass is defined only by its extension to its superclass; everything else remains the same. Each new class that you define *inherits* methods and instance variables of its superclass.

Inheritance allows you to do a number of things that make your programs more extensible. In a subclass, you can make three kinds of changes to the methods inherited from a superclass: add new methods and instance variables, refine or extend the behavior of a method, and change the behavior of an inherited method.

As a result, you can use a superclass's declaration (its list of methods) to define a modus operandi that all its subclasses must follow. When different classes implement similarly named methods, a program is better able to make use of *polymorphism*, which I describe in Chapter 2 of this minibook — adding new objects of the same type, and having your program handle them without making any changes to the code that uses them. You can also reuse code: If classes have some things in common, but also differ in key ways, the common functionality can be put in a superclass that all classes can inherit.

After you get into the rhythm of thinking this way, programming and making changes becomes more fun and less dreary. You introduce fewer bugs as you add functionality to your program, and your coding becomes completely focused on the new functionality instead of having to go back through everything you've done to see whether you're about to break something that now works just fine.

Delegation

Delegation is a pattern used extensively in the UIKit and AppKit frameworks to customize the behavior of an object without subclassing. Instead, one object (a framework object) delegates the task of implementing one of its responsibilities to another object. You're using a behavior-rich object supplied by the framework as is and putting the code for program-specific behavior in a separate (delegate) object. When a request is made of the framework object, the method of the delegate that implements the program-specific behavior is automatically called.

You're basically using delegation to get other objects to do the work for you, as I describe in Chapter 5 of this minibook. But first, you need to discover the real truth about object-oriented programming, find out how objects behave, and especially get to know all about encapsulation, polymorphism, and how inheritance really works — all that and more is in Chapter 2.

Book II
Chapter 1

Using Objective-C's
Extensions to
C for iPhone
Development

Chapter 2: The Real Truth about Object-Oriented Programming

In This Chapter

- ✔ Recognizing the importance of modules
- ✔ Getting a handle on objects
- ✔ Understanding inheritance
- ✔ Implementing inheritance
- ✔ Understanding the connection between inheritance and polymorphism
- ✔ Seeing encapsulation and polymorphism in action
- ✔ Understanding the Model-View-Controller pattern
- ✔ Refining the idea of "reusable code"

Albert Einstein once said that technological change is like an axe in the hands of a pathological criminal. Often a little change or bug-fix in one part of your program can have a disastrous impact on the rest of it. (Co-author Neal remembers a fellow programmer once lamenting, "but I only changed one line of code," after making changes to a program and then putting it into production without adequate testing — only to have it take down an entire mainframe complex.)

To minimize the side effects of "only changing one line of code," you need to divide your programs into *modules* so that a change you make in one module won't have an impact on the rest of your code. I refer to this Not-Rocking-the-Boat aspect of good code design as *transparency*.

A *module* is simply a self-contained, or independent, unit that can be combined with other units to get the job done. Modules are the solution to a rather knotty problem — even a simple program can run into hundreds of lines of instructions, and you need a way to break them into parts to make them understandable. But more importantly, you want to use modules because they make programs easier to modify.

Not All Modules Are Created Equal

The idea of dividing your program into modules is as old as programming itself, and you know how old that is. The programming style (or *paradigm*) of a particular programming language dictates the way you do that. You need to be concerned with two paradigms at this point, although with more experience you'll probably explore others.

Functions (or things like that) as well as groups of functions have historically been the basis of modularization. This way of dividing things into modules is used in the programming style or paradigm known as *procedural programming*. For example, in a vacation budget app that helps you track expenses in different currencies, you might write functions like *spend dollars* or *charge foreign currency,* which then operate on *transaction* and *budget data*.

In the last few years, however, the procedural paradigm has pretty much been supplanted, at least for commercial applications, by *object-oriented programming*. In Objective-C, objects (and, as you will see, their corresponding classes) are the way a program is divided up. In an object-oriented program, you find *transaction objects* and *budget objects*.

To give you some perspective, you can think of objects in an *object-oriented program* as working as a team necessary to reach a goal. Functions in a *procedural program* are more like the command and control structure of a large corporation (think GM) or the army. Which is more flexible?

For all practical purposes, the debate has been settled in favor of object-oriented programming for commercial applications (except for a few fanatics), and because you're learning Objective-C, which is an object-oriented language, it's time to get on with understanding objects.

Understanding How Objects Behave

An object-oriented program consists of a network of interconnected objects, essentially modules that call upon each other to solve a part of the puzzle. The objects work like a team. Each object has a specific role to play in the overall design of the program and is able to communicate with other objects. Objects communicate requests to other objects to do something using *messages*.

Object-oriented programmers think about objects as actors and talk about them that way. Objects have responsibilities. You *ask* them to do things, they *decide* what to do, and they *behave* in a certain way. You do this even with, for instance, a sandwich object or a shape object. You can, for example, tell a sandwich in an object-oriented program to go cut itself in half (ouch!), or tell a shape to draw itself.

This resemblance to real things gives objects much of their power and appeal. You can use them not only to represent things in the real world — a person, an airplane reservation, a credit card transaction — but also to represent things in a computer, such as a window, button, or slider.

But what gives object-oriented programming its power is that the way objects are defined and the way they interact with each other make it relatively easy to accomplish the goals of *extensibility* and *enhance-ability* — that is, achieve the transparency that is the hallmark of a good program. You can accomplish that by using two features that are the bedrock of object-oriented programming languages: *encapsulation* and *polymorphism*.

Okay, I know both terms sound either like bad sci-fi or advanced bioengineering, but they're actually not that complicated. Here's what they really mean:

**Book II
Chapter 2**

The Real Truth about Object-Oriented Programming

✦ **Encapsulation** is about keeping the details of how an object works hidden from the other objects that use it. Many people have no idea how a computer works but can effectively browse the Internet, create documents, and receive and send e-mail. Most people who can successfully drive cars have no idea of how the engine works. I refer to this as the I-Don't-Care-And-Please-Don't-Tell-Me approach.

Encapsulation makes possible the ability to change how an object carries out its responsibilities or behaves (enhance-ability) without having to disturb the existing code that uses the object. It also makes possible the ability to add new responsibilities to an object (extensibility) without disturbing the existing code. One of the primary things that objects encapsulate is their data, and another thing they do is transparently add new objects, as you see later in this chapter.

✦ **Polymorphism** is about cultivating more of the same. Your friend's refrigerator is not the same as yours, but you know how to open it and find the beer. Different refrigerator models offer different features, but they operate the same way. Your objects shouldn't have to care about how one object is different from another as long as the object does what the requesting object needs it to do. I refer to this as the More-Of-The-Same approach.

This feature in object-oriented languages makes it possible to add new objects of the same type, and have your program handle them without making any changes to the code that uses them. For example, you can create a program that processes cash and credit card transactions, and then sometime later you can add an ATM transaction and have the program process that new kind of transaction without having to make any changes to the processing logic.

With respect to all the new ideas you have to learn, this concept is usually the hardest one for most people to grasp right away (the name polymorphism doesn't help), although everyone gets it after seeing it in action. I give you a good example later in this chapter, and I promise you that after you use it in your program, you'll wonder why you thought it was so hard in the first place.

Seeing the Concepts in Action

To understand these concepts, you need some concrete examples from the real world. Imagine living in Minneapolis (where Neal lived briefly), where it can be not just cold, but *really* cold. You want a handheld device (something like Figure 2-1, which I call a "uPhone") that lets you start your car and turn on the heater before you leave the house in the morning.

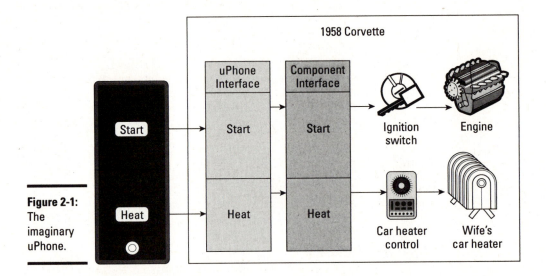

Figure 2-1: The imaginary uPhone.

Encapsulation

You may be happily using your uPhone until one day your mechanic finds a new heater that works better and is plug-compatible with your old heater — it has the same controls. And guess what? Adding this great new heater doesn't faze your (old) uPhone one bit. It just keeps on truckin'.

The reason is that the application (including the uPhone, uPhone Interface, and Component Interface — refer to Figure 2-1) knows nothing about heaters. All the application really cares about is the heater switch (car heater control). As long as that stays the same, everything works. If the uPhone had to interact directly with the heater components without these interfaces, it wouldn't work.

To make your programs enhance-able, you want to depend on the implementation details as little as possible. You'll remember that the programming term for this I-Don't-Care-And-Please-Don't-Tell-Me approach is *encapsulation*. What you're doing is hiding *how* things are being done from *what* is being done.

In a program, that means hiding the internal mechanisms and data structures of a software component behind a defined interface in such a way that users of the component (other pieces of software) only need to know what the component does and don't have to make themselves dependent on the details of how the component does what it promises to do. This means the following:

✦ The internal mechanisms of a module can be improved without having to make any changes in any of the modules that use it.

✦ The component is protected from user meddling (like trying to rewire a heater).

✦ Things are less complex because the interdependencies between modules have been reduced as much as possible.

This is the way modules, or objects, should work in an object-oriented program. You want the objects to limit their knowledge of other objects to what those objects can do — like turn on and off. That way, if you change something, you don't have to go digging through a zillion lines of code to figure out whether any code in your program is depending on something being done a particular way and then changing that dependent code to work with the new way it will be done. Ignorance is bliss . . . for the programmer that is.

Polymorphism

To carry the uPhone metaphor further, imagine that your spouse or friend wants one, but she or he has a different kind of car with a different heater control. All you have to do is change the Component Interface to the heater, keeping the uPhone Interface the same — which means no changes are required to the uPhone itself.

What you're looking for is a situation in which the requestor doesn't even care who receives the message, as long as it can get what it wants. So the uPhone doesn't care whether it's sending the message to a heater in a 1959 Cadillac, or a 1958 Corvette, or even an SSC Ultimate Aero TT, as long as the heater can respond to the message.

The capability of different objects to respond, each in its own way, to identical messages is called *polymorphism*.

Although encapsulation allows you to ignore how things are done, polymorphism allows you to escape the specific details of differences between objects that do the same thing in different ways. In the real world, if you can drive a Chevy, you can drive a Caddy or any other car, as long as the controls are more or less the same. It isn't that a 1959 Cadillac and a 1958 Corvette are the same; if they were, what would be the point? What's important is that they are different, but you can go about using them in the same way.

In a program, different objects might perform the same methods in different ways — if the user spends cash, a cash transaction object subtracts that amount from the user's budget. If the user uses a credit card, a credit card transaction will first have to convert the amount in foreign currency that the user charged to dollars and *then* subtract it from the budget.

How Inheritance Works

As I point out in "Understanding How Objects Behave" previously in this chapter, an object has responsibilities. Other objects ask it to do some action (such as draw a shape, or make a transaction), and it decides what to do and behaves in a certain way. The other objects don't meddle with the encapsulated details of how the action is accomplished, as long as the expected result occurs. They work as a team: Each object has a specific role to play in the overall design of the program and is able to communicate with other objects.

If an object needs to be modified, *encapsulation* ensures that the modifications don't interfere with existing code. Each object can also be replaced by a better, more functional object that does the same thing — *polymorphism* ensures that it's possible to add new objects of the same type, and have your program handle them without making any changes to the code that uses them.

What makes this scenario work is the fact that with object-oriented programming, you can essentially copy all the characteristics of an existing class to make a new class — the new class *inherits* the methods and data structure of the existing class. Inheritance is the reason why you can replace an old refrigerator with a new one that not only does the same thing, but does it better. The new refrigerator inherits all the best capabilities of the old one and improves them (at least you hope it does).

To show how inheritance works, I'm diving back into the vacation budget app from Chapter 1 of this minibook (you may want to take another look at declaring a class interface and defining class methods and instance variables). Let's say you want to create a transaction object that knows the difference between a cash transaction and a credit-card transaction (which includes an extra fee). First, look at the old-school way of programming the problem: You could take a C-like procedural approach to ensure that the transaction object sends the right message to the `Budget` object to record the credit-card or cash transaction properly. Consider how you might code this `Transaction` object and use a `switch` statement to manage more than one kind of transaction in a single array. The `Transaction.h` file would contain the code in Listing 2-1.

Book II
Chapter 2

The Real Truth about
Object-Oriented
Programming

Listing 2-1:   Transaction.h

```
#import <Cocoa/Cocoa.h>

typedef enum {cash, charge} transactionType;

@interface Transaction : NSObject {

  transactionType type;
  double amount;
}

- (void) createTransaction: (double) theAmount
                    ofType: (transactionType) aType;
- (double) returnAmount;
- (transactionType) returnType;
@end
```

This `Transaction` class stores both an amount and its type. To know what kind of transaction it is, the `typedef` creates a type, `transaction-Type`, and an instance variable `type` — cash for the dollar transaction and `charge` for the credit card ones. The instance variable `amount` is the value of the transaction. Three methods are also defined: The first method (`createTransaction`) simply initializes the object with a type and amount. The second (`returnAmount`) and third (`returnType`) methods return the amount of the transaction and type of transaction (cash or charge), respectively.

In the `Transaction.m` file you find the implementation code, shown in Listing 2-2.

Listing 2-2:   Transaction.m

```
#import "Transaction.h"

@implementation Transaction
- (void) createTransaction: (double) theAmount ofType:
    (transactionType) aType{

  type = aType;
  amount = theAmount;
}
```

(continued)

Listing 2-2 *(continued)*

```
- (double) returnAmount{

  return amount;
}

- (transactionType) returnType {

  return type;
};

@end
```

This implements the methods declared in the `Transaction.h` interface in Listing 2-1.

With a transaction object that has an amount and knows what kind of transaction it is, you can put both cash and charge transactions in the same array and use a `switch` statement to ensure that the right message is sent to the `Budget` object. A `switch` statement is a kind of *control statement* that allows the value of a variable or expression to control the flow of program execution. In this case, you would use `returnType` (the type of transaction) in a `switch` statement, as shown in Listing 2-3.

Listing 2-3:   The switch Statement

```
for (Transaction * aTransaction in transactions) {
switch ([aTransaction returnType]) {
     case cash:
       [europeBudget spendDollars:
                          [aTransaction returnAmount]];
       break;
     case charge:
       [europeBudget chargeForeignCurrency:
                          [aTransaction returnAmount]];
       break;
     default:
       break;
     }
  }
```

The problem with that approach is that the `switch` statements can rapidly get very complicated, and a program with `switch` statements scattered throughout becomes difficult to extend and enhance.

Quite frankly, this kind of complex control structure is characteristic of the procedural programming paradigm. Object-oriented programming and

Objective-C do not "improve" this control structure, but they let you avoid using it unless absolutely necessary. You can use one of Objective-C's extensions to C — *inheritance* — to take advantage of polymorphism. Inheritance greatly simplifies your code, and you end up with a program that's a great deal easier to understand and extend. (The two actually go hand in hand.)

Objective-C, like other object-oriented programming languages, permits you to base a new class definition on a class already defined. The base class is called a *superclass;* the new class is its *subclass.* The subclass is defined only by its extension to its superclass; everything else remains the same. For the vacation budget app, then all you need to do is create a Transaction Base superclass that encapsulates what is the same between a cash and credit card transaction, and then create Cash Transaction subclass and Credit Card Transaction subclass that implement the differences.

The terms *superclass* and *subclass* can be confusing. When most people think of *super,* they think of something with more functionality, not less. In some languages, the term used is *base class,* which I think does a better job of conveying what it all actually means. But it is what it is, so keep this in mind.

In Figure 2-2, you see an example of a *class diagram* used by programmers to describe their classes. The diagram uses the UML (*U*nified *M*odeling *L*anguage) notation. (The superclass and subclass arrows and terms are not part of the notation; they're there to illustrate the hierarchy of the Transaction classes in the program.) The name of the class is at the top of the box, the middle section describes the instance variables, and the bottom box shows you the methods of that (sub)class.

Figure 2-2 shows that both `CashTransaction` and `CreditCard Transaction` classes are subclasses of `Transaction`. Each subclass inherits all the methods and all the instance variables of its superclass. You therefore don't have to include references to re-implementing a method like `spend` in the interfaces for `CashTransaction` and `CreditCardTransaction`. All you have to do is implement `spend` in the `@implementation`.

Every class but `NSObject` (the root of all your classes) can thus be seen as another stop on the road to increasing specialization. As you add subclasses, you're adding to the cumulative total of what's inherited. The `CashTransaction` class defines only what's needed to turn a `Transaction` into a `CashTransaction`.

Incidentally, if you think about it, inheritance also implements a kind of encapsulation. You can extend the behavior of an existing object without impacting the existing code that already works — remember, it's all about enhance-ability and extensibility.

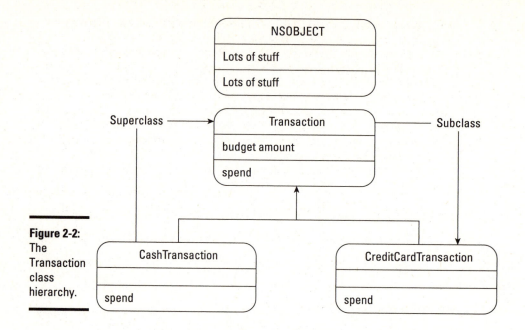

Figure 2-2:
The
Transaction
class
hierarchy.

In Objective-C, every class has only one superclass, but can have an unlimited number of subclasses. In some languages, however, a class can have multiple superclasses. This is known as *multiple inheritance*. Although Objective-C doesn't support multiple inheritance, it does provide some features not found in those languages that enable you to get many of the benefits of multiple inheritance, without the accompanying disadvantages. These features include categories and protocols, both of which are covered in Chapter 5 of this minibook.

Knowing what inheritance enables you to do

Inheritance allows you to do a number of things that make your programs more extensible and enhance-able. What kinds of things? Well, to be more specific, in a subclass you can make three kinds of changes to what you inherit from a superclass. (Think of this section as describing the mechanics of creating a subclass.)

✦ **You can add new methods and instance variables.** This is one of the most common reasons for defining a subclass in general.

✦ **You can refine or extend the behavior of a method.** You do this by adding a new version of the same method, while still continuing to use the code in the old method. To add a new version, you implement a new method with the same name as one that's inherited. The new version *overrides* the inherited version. In the body of the new method, you send a message to execute the inherited version. I illustrate this later in the "Deriving classes" section of this chapter.

✦ **You can change the behavior of a method you inherit.** You do this by replacing an existing method with a new version — by overriding the old method as described in the preceding bullet point. In this case, however, you *don't* send a message to execute the inherited version. The old implementation is still used for the class that defined it and other classes that inherit it, although classes that inherit from the new class use your implementation. Changing behavior is not unusual, although it does make your code harder to follow. If you find yourself frequently overriding a method to completely change its behavior, you should question your design.

Even though you may override a method in a class, subclasses of the class still do have access to the original. For obvious reasons, this is generally not a good idea, and again should have you questioning your design.

Although a subclass can override inherited methods, it can't override inherited instance variables. If you try to declare a new one with the same name as an inherited one, the compiler complains.

Using inheritance effectively

Given the preceding possibilities, here are some ways you can use inheritance in your programs:

✦ **Create a protocol.** The `Transaction` class is an example. A *protocol* in this sense is a list of method(s) that subclasses are expected to implement. The superclass might have skeletal versions of the methods with no real functionality (as `Transaction` does), or it might implement partially functional versions that you use in the subclass methods. In either case, the superclass's declaration (its list of methods) defines a protocol that all its subclasses must follow.

When different classes implement similarly named methods, a program is better able to make use of polymorphism.

✦ **Reuse code.** Reusing code has traditionally been a poster child for inheritance use. There are three approaches:

• *Increasing specialization:* If classes have some things in common, but also differ in key ways, the common functionality can be put in a superclass that all classes can inherit. `Transaction` is a good example of that.

• *Implementing generic functionality:* (This is often coupled with the protocol approach.) In the `AppKit` and `UIKit` frameworks, user interface objects have been created for your using pleasure. They implement as much generic functionality as they can, but it's up to you to add the specific functionality to make it so they do something useful in your application. For example, a view can display itself on the screen, scroll, and so on, but you need to implement methods that display what you want displayed.

• *Modifying a class that more or less does what you want it to do:* There may be a class that does most of what you want it to, but you need to change some things about how it works. You can make the changes in a subclass.

Implementing Inheritance in a Program

To realize how inheritance can work in a program, you can do what you did in the last section: Create an abstract superclass, `Transaction`, which creates a protocol for subsequent subclasses, then create two subclasses of `Transaction`, `CashTransaction` and `CreditCardTransaction`. They inherit all the methods and instance variables of the `Transaction` class, but each implements its own `spend:` method. (I just talked about creating `Transaction` in the last section; now you can actually get down to *doing* it.)

Deriving classes

To create the `Transaction` superclass, you need to change the `Transaction.h` and `Transaction.m` files from earlier in Listing 2-1 and Listing 2-2 so they look like what's shown in Listing 2-4 and Listing 2-5.

Listing 2-4: Transaction.h

```
#import <Cocoa/Cocoa.h>
@class Budget;

@interface Transaction : NSObject {

Budget *budget;
  double  amount;
}

- (void) createTransaction: (double) theAmount forBudget:
    (Budget*) aBudget;
- (void) spend;
- (void) trackSpending: (double) theAmount;
@end
```

Listing 2-5: Transaction.m

```
#import "Transaction.h"
#import "Budget.h"
@implementation Transaction
- (void) createTransaction: (double) theAmount forBudget:
    (Budget*) aBudget {
budget = aBudget;
  amount = theAmount;
```

```
}
- (void) spend {

// Fill in the method in subclasses
}

- (void) trackSpending: (double) theAmount {

  NSLog (@"You are about to spend another %.2f", theAmount);
}
@end
```

Go ahead and compare Listing 2-4 with Listing 2-1 (`Transaction.h`), and compare Listing 2-5 with Listing 2-2 (`Transaction.m`). You change the arguments used in `createTransaction::` by deleting aType, and using aBudget instead. Each transaction sends the right message to the `Budget` object. You also create a skeletal `spend` method as a placeholder, which will be implemented in the subclasses, and delete `returnAmount` and `returnType` because you won't need them any more — you only need that information if you decide to stick with the `switch` statement (shown earlier in Listing 2-3).

You also add a new method, `trackSpending:`, which tracks your spending and uses `NSLog` to display a message about it (and as an example, shows you how to send messages to inherited methods):

```
- (void) trackSpending: (double) theAmount;
```

Also included in the new `Transaction.h` file (Listing 2-4) is the `@class` statement coded here as `@class Budget`. The compiler needs to know certain things about the classes that you're using — such as what methods you defined and so on — and the `#import` statement in the implementation (the new `Transaction.m` file in Listing 2-5) solves that problem. But when you get into objects that point at other objects, you also need to provide that information in the interface (`Transaction.h` file), which can cause a problem if you end up with what are known as circular dependencies (which sounds cool but is beyond the scope of this book).

To solve that problem, Objective-C introduces the `@class` keyword as a way to tell the compiler that the `budget` instance variable, whose type `Budget` the compiler knows nothing about (yet), is a pointer to that class. Knowing that is enough for the compiler, at least in the interface files. However, you still have to do the `#import` in the implementation file when you refer to methods of that class.

Next, you can take advantage of what you just did and create two subclasses of `Transaction`, `CashTransaction` (`CashTransaction.h` in Listing 2-6, and `CashTransaction.m` in Listing 2-7), and `CreditCardTransaction` (`CreditCardTransaction.h` in Listing 2-8, and `CreditCardTransaction.m` in Listing 2-9). They inherit all the methods and instance variables of the `Transaction` class, but each implements its own `spend:` method. You can also have both methods send a message to their superclass's `trackSpending:` method, which shows how to send messages to a superclass.

Object-oriented programmers like to think of subclasses like `CashTransaction` as having an "is-a" relationship to their superclasses. For example, a cash transaction is-a transaction.

Listing 2-6:   CashTransaction.h

```
#import <Cocoa/Cocoa.h>
#import "Transaction.h"

@interface CashTransaction : Transaction {
}
@end
```

Listing 2-7:   CashTransaction.m

```
#import "CashTransaction.h"
#import "Budget.h"

@implementation CashTransaction
- (void) spend {

    [self trackSpending:amount];
    [budget spendDollars:amount];
}
@end
```

Listing 2-8:   CreditCardTransaction.h

```
#import <Cocoa/Cocoa.h>
#import "Transaction.h"

@interface CreditCardTransaction : Transaction {
}
@end
```

Listing 2-9:   CreditCardTransaction.m

```
#import "CreditCardTransaction.h"
#import "Budget.h"

@implementation CreditCardTransaction
- (void) spend {
```

```
    [super trackSpending:amount];
    [budget chargeForeignCurrency:amount];
}
@end
```

To add the two new subclasses, all you have to do is declare the unique behavior in each class. You use @interface statements to specify Transaction as the superclass:

```
@interface CreditCardTransaction : Transaction {
@interface CashTransaction : Transaction {
```

When you add a new class to a project, Xcode doesn't know what its subclass is, so it uses NSObject unless you specify a particular subclass — it's up to you to change the NSObject default to the right superclass.

Your new subclasses inherit all of the methods and instance variables of the Transaction class, which includes all the instance variables and methods it inherits from its superclass and so on up the inheritance hierarchy. (In this case, as you can see in Listing 2-4, the Transaction superclass is NSObject, so it ends there.) So you're cool when it comes to being able to behave like a good Objective-C object. And while you didn't do it here, you can also add instance variables to a subclass as well, and as many methods as you need.

You also need to import both interface files so the compiler can understand what Transaction and Budget are, so you add the #imports for the Transaction and Budget interface files because both are used by the methods in the CashTransaction and CreditCardTransaction classes.

The superclass's method trackSpending: displays that you're about to spend some money. You can have CashTransaction and CreditCardTransaction send a message to trackSpending:, in two different ways:

```
[self trackSpending:amount];
```

or

```
[super trackSpending:amount];
```

You'd use the first statement to send messages to methods that are part of your class, which includes those that you inherit. As you can see, even though trackSpending: is defined only in the Transaction superclass, your class inherited trackSpending: and the message to self works fine. Unless you have overridden the inherited trackSpending: method in your class, you should really use [super trackSpending: amount], because that makes sure that you are sending the message to the superclass method.

In this case `self` and `super` are interchangeable, but as you see when you initialize objects in Chapter 3 of this minibook, that isn't always the case.

You can now use that inheritance-based `Transaction` class design in your program. In Objective-C programs, the instructions contained within `main` (the mother of all functions and the place where all Objective-C programs start their execution) are always the first ones to be executed. The `main` function is in the `Vacation.m` file (named after the Xcode project Vacation), as shown in Listing 2-10. Note that it starts off with two `#import` statements: The second refers to the `Budget.h` header file, which I show in Chapter 1 of this minibook.

Listing 2-10:   Vacation.m

```
#import <Foundation/Foundation.h>
#import "Budget.h"

#import "Transaction.h"
#import "CashTransaction.h"
#import "CreditCardTransaction.h"

int main (int argc, const char * argv[]) {

    Budget *europeBudget = [Budget new];
    [europeBudget createBudget:1000.00
                                withExchangeRate:1.2500];
    Budget *englandBudget = [Budget new];
    [englandBudget createBudget:2000.00
                                withExchangeRate:1.5000];

NSMutableArray *transactions = [[NSMutableArray alloc]
    initWithCapacity:10];
    Transaction *aTransaction ;
    for (int n = 1; n < 2; n++) {
        aTransaction = [CashTransaction new];
        [aTransaction createTransaction:n*100
                                forBudget:europeBudget];
        [transactions addObject:aTransaction];
        aTransaction = [CashTransaction new];
        [aTransaction createTransaction:n*100
                                forBudget:englandBudget];
        [transactions addObject:aTransaction];
    }

    int n =1;
    while (n < 4) {
        aTransaction = [CreditCardTransaction new];
        [aTransaction createTransaction:n*100
                                forBudget:europeBudget];
        [transactions addObject:aTransaction];
```

```
    aTransaction = [CreditCardTransaction new];
    [aTransaction createTransaction:n*100
                            forBudget:englandBudget];
    [transactions addObject:aTransaction];
    n++;
  }

  for (Transaction* aTransaction in transactions) {
    [aTransaction spend];
  }

  return 0;
}
```

Stepping through all this code, you see that the first thing you need to do is add the necessary #import statements so the compiler knows what to do with the new classes.

```
#import "Transaction.h"
#import "CashTransaction.h"
#import "CreditCardTransaction.h"
```

Next, use Budget as an argument when you initialize the Transaction:

```
Budget *europeBudget = [Budget new];
[europeBudget createBudget:1000.00
                withExchangeRate:1.2500];

Budget  *englandBudget = [Budget new];
[englandBudget createBudget:2000.00
                withExchangeRate:1.5000];
```

The code that follows this sets up an array with NSMutableArray. As you find out in Chapter 4 of this minibook, NSMutableArray arrays are ordered collections that can contain any sort of object. The code creates the cash and credit card transactions for both Europe *and* England in both the for and while loops:

```
aTransaction = [CreditCardTransaction new];
[aTransaction createTransaction:n*100
                        forBudget:europeBudget];
[transactions addObject:aTransaction];
aTransaction = [CreditCardTransaction new];
[aTransaction createTransaction:n*100
                        forBudget:englandBudget];
[transactions addObject:aTransaction];
```

The code then sends the spend message to each Transaction object in the transactions array:

```
[aTransaction spend];
```

This is something you find in many applications — a set of instructions that send the same message to a list of objects. *This is what polymorphism is all about* — a program architecture that makes your program easier to extend. As long as your new transaction is a subclass of `Transaction`, it can be used immediately in your program without any changes to the rest of your program (except, of course, to create and implement the transaction itself)!

You can see how easy it is to add a new kind of transaction to the mix. All you have to do is create the new transaction type and add it to the array, and it makes itself at home with the rest of the transactions.

Keep in mind that the `for` and `while` loops are there only to generate transactions — think of them as simulating a user interface.

Replacing a control structure with polymorphism

Revisiting Listing 2-3, you have code that *iterates* through an array — accesses each array object in a `for` loop — and uses a `switch` statement to decide whether to send the `sendDollars:` or `chargeForeignCurrency:` message to a budget for that kind of transaction, passing the transaction as an argument.

In the object-oriented universe, you would set up your code to have two kinds of transaction objects — cash and credit card. Both kinds respond to a `spend` message, and every transaction has a pointer to the budget it is associated with. You iterate through the array and send the `spend` message to each transaction. If it is a cash transaction in Europe, for example, it has a reference to the `europeBudget` object and sends it the `spendDollars:` message. If it is a credit card transaction in England, it sends the `charge-ForeignCurrency:` message to `englandBudget`. No fuss, no bother, and no control structure. This means you have one array that holds every transaction for every country you visit — much better than managing multiple arrays for different countries and different transaction types. This enables you to change the entire `switch` structure in Listing 2-3 with the following:

```
for (Transaction*  aTransaction in transactions) {
  [aTransaction spend];
}
```

If you want a new transaction, all you need to do is code it up and add it to the array. And, if you wanted to visit a new country, all you'd have to do is create a budget for that country and attach it to the transactions that occurred in that country. You can see that illustrated in Figure 2-3.

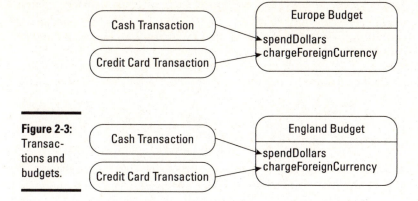

Figure 2-3:
Transac-
tions and
budgets.

Figure 2-3 gives you the bird's-eye view. To see how things actually work down on the ground, start with what a transaction object would look like. You'd need two instance variables:

```
Budget  *budget;
double  amount;
```

You'd also need two methods:

```
- (void) createTransaction: (double) theAmount
                           forBudget: (Budget*) aBudget;
- (void) spend;
```

As you can see, besides an initialization method, you have a method named spend. You also have an instance variable, budget, which enables the Transaction object to send a message to its budget; and another instance variable, amount, which holds the amount of this transaction. Because every type of transaction has a spend method, you can enumerate through the array and send each object a spend message, and each object, depending on its type, turns around and sends the right message to its budget.

So far, both cash and credit card transactions look the same; the only difference is in the implementation of spend. The cash transaction implements spend as:

```
- (void) spend {
[budget spendDollars:amount];
    }
```

The credit card transaction looks like this:

```
- (void) spend {
[budget chargeForeignCurrency:amount];
    }
```

Reusable code

When people talk about object-oriented programming, they tend to talk about two things. The first is all that cool encapsulation and polymorphism stuff, which makes it easy to modify programs. Then they talk about *reuse* — that you can create reusable objects that save time and money.

Will this book teach you how to write reusable code? Well, it depends on what you mean by *reusable.* When you enhance or extend your program, what you're doing is *reusing* the existing code to create essentially a new program. And in that respect, the answer is yes.

The best models for reusability are found in the frameworks you use to develop apps for the iPhone. You reuse the frameworks by adding your own app functionality to a framework that already includes the code for stuff like displaying windows and controls and menus — the whole kit and caboodle of the user interface, and then some.

I explain some of the things that the framework designers did to make reusing frameworks as easy as it is. You'll find that when you use those same principles and techniques in your programs, you will have taken a giant step forward in enabling the kind of reusability you need to make your programs enhance-able and extensible.

This ability for different objects to respond to the same message each in its own way is an example of polymorphism, and is one of the cornerstones of enhance-able and extensible programs.

The final word on polymorphism and inheritance

The preceding sections tell you how to use one of the Objective-C extensions to C — inheritance — to implement polymorphism (or More-Of-The-Same). Polymorphism is the ability of different object types to respond to the same message, each one in its own way. Because each object can have its own version of a method, a program becomes easier to extend and enhance because you don't have to change the message to add functionality. All you have to do is create a new subclass, and it responds to the same messages in its own way.

Polymorphism allows you to isolate code in the methods of different objects rather than gathering them in a single function that has to know all the possible cases as well as in control structures such as `if` and `switch` statements. When a new case comes along, you won't have to re-code all those `if` and `switch` statements — you need only add a new class with a new method, leaving well enough alone as far as the code that you've already written, tested, and debugged is concerned.

Using inheritance together with polymorphism is one of the extensions to C that is hard to implement without language support. For this to really work, the exact behavior can be determined only at runtime (this is called *late binding* or *dynamic binding*).

When a message is sent, the Objective-C runtime looks at the object you're sending the message to, finds the implementation of the method matching the name, and then invokes that method.

Encapsulating Objects

Book II
Chapter 2

As I point out at the beginning of this chapter, using encapsulation enables you to safely tuck data behind an object's walls. You can keep the data safe and reduce the dependencies of other parts of your program on what the data is and how it is structured.

Encapsulation is also useful when you apply it to application functionality. When you limit what your objects know about other objects in your application, changing objects or their functionality becomes much easier because it reduces the impact of those changes on the rest of your application.

The Real Truth about
Object-Oriented
Programming

Getting to know the Model-View-Controller (MVC) pattern

The Cocoa framework is designed around certain programming paradigms, known as *design patterns* — a commonly used template that gives you a consistent way to get a particular task done.

I talk about these design patterns in Chapter 5 of Book I. The Model-View-Controller (MVC) design pattern implements the kind of object encapsulation that reduces the impact of changes to an application. This design pattern is not unique to Cocoa; a version of it has been in use since the early days of Smalltalk — the programming language that Objective-C bases its extensions to the C language on. The MVC design pattern goes a long way back, and the fact that it is still being used tells you something about its value.

MVC divides your application into three groups of objects and encourages you to limit the interaction between objects to others in its own group as much as possible. It creates, in effect, a world for the application, placing objects in one of three categories — *model, view,* and *controller* (described in the following list) — and specifies roles and responsibilities for all three kinds of objects as well as the way they're supposed to interact with each other.

Here's that list I mentioned:

✦ **Model objects:** Model objects make up *the content engine* of your application. This is where all the objects are (as opposed to the code in the `main` function). In the examples in this chapter, they process transactions and compute what you have left in your budget. If you were to add things such as hotel objects, train objects, and the like, this is where they would belong. Model objects are very generous with what they can do and are happy to share what they know with the rest of your application. But not only do they not care about what other objects use them, or what these other objects do with the information they provide; being good objects, they really *don't want to know*.

Think of the experience of watching programs on TV. The *model* (which may be one object or several objects that interact) would be a particular program — one that does not give a hoot about what TV set it is being shown on.

✦ **View objects:** These objects display things on the screen and respond to user actions. This is what is generally thought of as the user interface, and pretty much anything you see on the screen is part of the View group of objects. View objects are pros at formatting and displaying data, as well as handling user interactions, such as allowing the user to enter a credit card transaction, make a new hotel reservation, and add a destination or even create a new trip. But they don't care about where that data comes from and are unaware of the model.

Back to watching TV: You can think of the *view* as a television screen that doesn't care about what program it's showing or what channel you just selected.

If you create an ideal world where the view knows nothing about the model and the model knows nothing about the view, you need to add one more set of objects. These objects connect the model and view — making requests for data from the model and sending that data back for the view to display. This is the collective responsibility of controller objects, described next.

✦ **Controller objects:** These objects connect the application's view objects to its model objects. They deliver to the view the data that needs to be displayed — getting it from the model. They deliver user requests to the model for current data (such as, how much money do you have left in your budget?), as well as new data (for instance, you just spent 300 euros).

Once again, think of watching TV: Picture the *controller* as the circuitry that pulls the show off the cable and sends it to the screen or that can request a particular pay-per-view show.

One of the advantages of using this application model is that it allows you to separate these three parts to your application and work on them separately. You just need to make sure each group has a well-defined interface. When the time is right, you just connect the parts — and you have an application.

A category of functionality that is not handled by the MVC pattern exists at the *application level,* or all the nuts and bolts and plumbing needed to run an application. These objects are responsible for startup, shut down, file management, event handling, and everything else that is not M, V, or C.

Implementing the MVC pattern

What makes the separation between models, views, and controllers possible is a well-defined interface. You can create an interface between the model and a sometime-in-the-future-to-be-developed controller by using a technique called *composition,* which is a useful way to create interfaces. Composition is another way to hide what's really going on behind the Wizard's curtains — it keeps the objects that use the composite object ignorant of the objects the composite object uses, and actually makes the components ignorant of each other, allowing you to switch components in and out at will.

You can create a composite object — call it `Destination` — that interfaces to `main` (which is used for the time being as a surrogate for both the views and controllers). Its design is really in the `@interface` for `Destination`. To act as an interface to be used by a controller, the `Destination` class needs to declare methods that do the following:

✦ Create `Transaction` objects from the transaction amounts that will be sent from the user interface.

✦ Return the data the user interface needs to display.

In Listing 2-11, you can see the `Destination` class interface that accomplishes both of these tasks.

Listing 2-11: Destination.h — the Destination Design

```
#import <Cocoa/Cocoa.h>
@class Budget;
@interface Destination : NSObject {

  NSString       *country;
  NSMutableArray *transactions;
  Budget         *theBudget;
}
```

(continued)

**Book II
Chapter 2**

The Real Truth about
Object-Oriented
Programming

Listing 2-11 *(continued)*

```
- (void) createWithCountry: (NSString*) theCountry andBudget:
    (double) budgetAmount withExchangeRate: (double)
    theExchangeRate;
- (void) spendCash: (double) aTransaction;
- (void) chargeCreditCard: (double) aTransaction;
- (double) leftToSpend;

@end
```

The `createWithCountry:::` method declaration's arguments let you initialize a new `Destination` with the country you are heading to, the amount you want to budget, and the current exchange rate.

You now have taken the creation of the `Budget` classes for each leg of your trip out of `main` (where they are placed in Chapter 1 of this minibook) and put them in `Destination`. You also have taken the creation and management of the `Transaction` array out of `main` and put that in `Destination` also. You enable `main` (the controller surrogate) to send transaction amounts to the `Destination` object (by sending the `spendCash:` and `chargeCreditCard:` messages). The `Destination` object can then, in turn, create and manage the appropriate `Transaction` objects and send them the `spend:` message.

You also enable the `main` method (by sending the `leftToSpend`) to ask the model for the information it needs to deliver to the surrogate user interface. This displays how much money remains in the budget.

Notice the instance variables that reference other objects — the `transactions` array and `theBudget`. This is a model for what makes a composite object and how it gets its work done — using other objects to distribute the work.

Object-oriented programmers like to think of composite objects like `Destination` as having a "has-a" relationship to their parts. The destination has-a budget, for example.

Listing 2-12 shows how you would implement these methods in the `Destination.m` file.

Listing 2-12:   Destination.m

```
#import "Destination.h"
#import "CashTransaction.h"
#import "CreditCardTransaction.h"
#import "Budget.h"
#import "Transaction.h"
```

```
@implementation Destination

- (void) createWithCountry: (NSString*) theCountry andBudget:
    (double) budgetAmount withExchangeRate: (double)
    theExchangeRate{

    transactions = [[NSMutableArray alloc]
                                    initWithCapacity:10];
    theBudget = [Budget new];
    [theBudget createBudget:budgetAmount
                        withExchangeRate:theExchangeRate];
    country = theCountry;
    NSLog (@"I'm off to %@", theCountry);
}


-(void) spendCash: (double) amount {

    Transaction *aTransaction = [CashTransaction new];
    [aTransaction createTransaction:amount
                                    forBudget:theBudget];
    [transactions addObject:aTransaction];
    [aTransaction spend];
}

-(void) chargeCreditCard: (double) amount {

    Transaction *aTransaction = [CreditCardTransaction new];
    [aTransaction createTransaction:amount
                                    forBudget:theBudget];
    [transactions addObject:aTransaction];
    [aTransaction spend];
}

- (double) leftToSpend {

    return [theBudget returnBalance];
}

@end
```

The method `leftToSpend` (near the very end of Listing 2-12) provides
the user interface with the data it needs to display. (It also requires adding
a new method to `Budget`, as you see next.) The `NSLog` statement (in the
middle of Listing 2-12) isn't intended to be part of the user interface —
you are just including it to trace program execution. It uses the `country`
instance variable.

Because the `Destination` object is responsible for reporting to the controller the amount left to spend, it needs to get the amount from the `Budget`
object, requiring you to code a method, `returnBalance`, in the `Budget`
class. The `Budget.h` interface is shown in Listing 2-13, and the `Budget.m`
implementation can be seen in Listing 2-14.

Listing 2-13:   Budget.h

```
#import <Cocoa/Cocoa.h>

@interface Budget : NSObject {

  float  exchangeRate;
  double budget;
  double transaction;
}

- (void) createBudget: (double) aBudget
             withExchangeRate: (float) anExchangeRate;



- (void) spendDollars: (double) dollars ;

- (void) chargeForeignCurrency: (double) euros;
- (double) returnBalance;
@end
```

Listing 2-14:   Budget.m

```
#import "Budget.h"

@implementation Budget

- (void) createBudget: (double) aBudget
             withExchangeRate: (float) anExchangeRate {

  exchangeRate = anExchangeRate;
  budget = aBudget;
}

- (void) spendDollars: (double) dollars {

  budget -= dollars;
}

- (void) chargeForeignCurrency: (double) foreignCurrency {

  transaction = foreignCurrency*exchangeRate;
  budget -= transaction;
}

- (double) returnBalance {

  return budget;
}

@end
```

Looking Ahead

Up until now, you've been doing initialization on an ad hoc basis, using initialization methods such as the one I rolled out back in Listing 2-1:

```
- (void) createTransaction: (double) theAmount
                      forBudget: (Budget*) aBudget;
```

Or this one in Listing 2-14:

```
- (void) createBudget: (double) aBudget
             withExchangeRate: (float) anExchangeRate;
exchangeRate = anExchangeRate;
  budget = aBudget;
}
```

There's a standard way to do initialization, however — one designed to work in a class hierarchy that ensures all the super- and subclasses are initialized properly. I show you how to implement these standard initialization methods in Chapter 3 of this minibook.

Chapter 3: Digging Deeper Into Objective-C

In This Chapter

✓ **Working through the standard way to do initialization**

✓ **Initializing superclasses and subclasses**

✓ **Managing memory**

C hapter 1 of this minibook explains that the birth of an object starts with `alloc` and `init`. It is `alloc` that sets aside some memory for the object and returns back a *pointer* to that memory. This fact is important to keep in mind, because after you create these new objects, you become responsible for *managing* them, as I show in this chapter. Managing the memory allocated for your objects can be one of the few real hassles in programming with Objective-C.

Memory management is not glamorous, but it trumps cool in an application. In fact, memory management is probably the single most vexing thing about iPhone programming. It has made countless programmers crazy, and I can't stress enough how important it is to build memory management into your code from the start. Retrofitting can be a nightmare. (Co-author Neal still has dreams in which hell is having to go back through an infinite number of lines of code and retrofit memory management code.)

The `init` method is named for initialization, which I introduce in Chapter 1 of this minibook. This chapter spells out some of your initialization options.

Initializing Objects

Initialization is the procedure that sets the instance variables of an object to a known initial state. Essentially, you need to initialize an object to assign initial values to these variables. Although initialization is not required — if you can live with all the instance variables initialized to `0` and `nil`, then there's nothing you need to do — you may have a class (or superclass) with instance variables that you need to initialize to something else, so you need some kind of initialization method.

An initialization method doesn't have to include an argument for every instance variable, because some will become relevant only during the course of your object's existence. You must make sure, however, that all the instance variables your object uses, including other objects it needs to do its work, are in a state that enables your object to respond to the messages it receives.

You may think the main job in initialization is to, well, initialize the variables in your objects (hence, the name), but more is involved when there's a superclass and a subclass chain.

To see what I mean, start by looking at the initializer I'm going to use for the CashTransaction class in Listing 3-1.

Listing 3-1:   The CashTransaction Initializer

```
- (id) initWithAmount: (double) theAmount forBudget:
   (Budget*) aBudget {

  if (self = [super initWithAmount:theAmount
                               forBudget:aBudget]) {

   name = @"Cash";
 }
  return self;
}
```

By convention, initialization methods begin with the abbreviation init. (This is true, however, only for *instance* — as opposed to *class* — methods.) If the method takes no arguments, the method name is just init. If it takes arguments, labels for the arguments follow the init prefix.

As you can see, the initializer in Listing 3-1 has a return type of id. You discover the reason for that later, in the section "Invoking the superclass's init method."

Initialization involves these three steps:

1. Invoke the superclass's init method.

2. Initialize instance variables.

3. Return self.

The following sections explain each step.

Invoking the superclass's init method

This is the type of statement you use to get the `init` method up and running:

```
(self = [super initWithAmount:theAmount
                               forBudget:aBudget])
```

In this part of the statement, you're invoking the superclass's `init` method:

```
[super initWithAmount:theAmount forBudget:aBudget]
```

The entire statement sets up `self` and `super` as equals so that you can then use `super`.

Chapter 2 of this minibook points out that this is the standard way of sending a message to your superclass.

Back in Chapter 2 of this minibook — in the section about deriving classes to implement inheritance in a program, to be precise — you also find out that you can use `self` to send a message to your superclass and that `self` and `super` are not always interchangeable. In this case, you need to be careful to use `super` because the method sending the message has the *same name* as the method you want to invoke in your superclass. If you were to use `self` here, you would just send a message to yourself — the `initWithAmount::` method in `CashTransaction` — which would turn around and send the same message to itself again, which would then send the same message to itself again, which would then . . . You get the picture. Fortunately, the OS will put up with this for only a limited amount of time before it gets really annoyed and terminates the program.

In this case, the superclass for the `CashTransaction` subclass is `Transaction`, and you invoke the `Transaction` superclass initialization method `initWithAmount::`. Your subclass should always invoke its superclass initialization method before doing any initialization. Your subclass's superclass is equally as respectful of its superclass and does the same thing; and up, up, and away you go from superclass to superclass until you reach the `NSObject` superclass `init` method. The `NSObject` superclass `init` method doesn't do anything; it just returns `self`. It's there to establish the naming convention, and all it does is return back to its invoker, which does its thing and then returns back to its invoker, until it gets back to you.

As you can see in Listing 3-2, `Transaction` invokes its superclass's `init` method as well. But in this case, it simply calls `init` (as per convention) because its superclass is `NSObject`.

Listing 3-2:   The Transaction Initializer

```
- (id) initWithAmount: (double) theAmount forBudget:
    (Budget*) aBudget {

 if (self = [super init]) {

    budget = aBudget;
    amount = theAmount;
    }
  return self;
}
```

Next, examine this unusual-looking statement:

```
if (self = [super initWithAmount:theAmount
    forBudget:aBudget]) {
```

Ignore the `if` for the moment. What you're doing is assigning what you got back from your superclass's `init` method to `self`. As you remember, `self` is the "hidden" variable accessible to methods in an object that points to its instance variables. (If you're unclear on this point, refer to the discussion in Chapter 1 of this minibook.) So it would seem that `self` should be whatever you got back from your allocation step. Well, yes and no. Most of the time, the answer is yes, but sometimes the answer is no, which may or may not be a big deal. So, check out the following bullet list and examine the possibilities.

When you invoke a superclass's initialization method, one of three things can happen:

✦ **You get back the object you expect.** Most of the time, this is precisely what happens, and you go on your merry way. This is true for the classes described in this part of the book (those where you have control over the entire hierarchy), such as the `Transaction` class.

✦ **You get back a different object type.** Getting back a different object type is something that can happen with some of the framework classes, but it's not an issue here. Even when it happens, if you're playing by the rules (a good idea if you're not the one who gets to make them), you don't even care.

Why a different object type, you might ask? Well, some of the framework classes such as `NSString` are really class clusters. When you create an object of one of these classes, its initialization method looks at the arguments you're passing and returns the object it thinks you need (big brotherish to say the least, but effective nonetheless). Anything more about getting back different object types is way beyond the scope of this book.

But, as I said, if you follow the rules, not only will you *not* notice getting back a different object type, you won't even care. In these cases, you can use the compound statement format — a sequence of statements surrounded by braces.

```
SomeClass *aPointerToSomeClass =
                        [[SomeClass alloc] init];
```

If you had done the following

```
SomeClass *aPointerToSomeClass = [SomeClass alloc]
[aPointerToSomeClass init];
```

`init` could return a different pointer, which you haven't assigned to `aPointerToSomeClass`. This is also why the return type for an initializer needs to be `id` (a pointer to an object) and not the specific class you're dealing with.

Book II
Chapter 3

Digging Deeper Into Objective-C

✦ **You get `nil` back.** One possibility, of course, is that you simply run out of memory or some catastrophe befalls the system, in which case, you're in deep trouble. Although there are some things you might be able to do, they aren't for the faint-hearted or beginners.

Getting back `nil` actually explains the statement that seems so puzzling.

```
if (self = [super initWithAmount:theAmount
    forBudget:aBudget]) {
```

When `nil` is returned, two things happen here: `self` is *assigned* to `nil`, which as a side effect causes the `if` statement to be evaluated as NO. As a result, the code block that contains the statements you would have used to initialize your subclass are never executed.

Initializing instance variables

Initializing instance variables, including creating the objects you need, is what you probably thought initialization is about. Notice that you're initializing your instance variable after your superclass's initialization, which you can see in Listings 3-1 and 3-2. Waiting until after your superclass does its initialization gives you the opportunity to actually change something your superclass may have in initialization, but more importantly, it allows you to perform initialization knowing that what you have inherited is initialized and ready to be used.

In the `CashTransaction initWithAmount::` initializer, all that's done is the initialization of the `name` instance variable of the superclass (`Transaction`) with the kind of transaction it is — cash, in this case.

```
name = @"Cash";
```

Returning self

In the section, "Invoking the superclass's init variable," the `self` = statement ensures that `self` is set to whatever object you get back from the superclass initializer. After the code block that initializes the variables, you put

```
return self;
```

Remember that if a method does not specify the type of its return value, the default is to return a pointer to an object (for example, something of `id` type). This means that, barring any other sensible thing to return, methods should always `return self`.

No matter what you get back from invoking the superclass initializer, in the initialization method you need to set `self` to that value and then return it to the invoking method. That could be a method that wants to instantiate the object or a subclass that invoked the `init` method (the `init` method being its superclass's `init` method).

When you're instantiating a new object, it behooves you to determine whether a return of `nil` is a nonfatal response to your request (and, if so, coding for it). In the examples in this book, the answer will always be no, and that will generally be the case with framework objects as well. In this example

```
theBudget = [[Budget alloc] initWithAmount:budgetAmount withE
    xchangeRate:theExchangeRate];
```

getting `nil` back would be more than your poor app could handle and would signal that you're in very deep trouble.

Listings 3-3 through 3-13 show how to implement initializers in the conventional way. You create the `init...` structure that enables you to more easily initialize any new instance variables you may add to existing classes, as well as ensure that you can do initialization correctly when you add any new superclasses or subclasses. (The lines in bold are changes to the code examples in Chapters 1 and 2 of this minibook.)

Listing 3-3:   Budget.h

```
#import <Cocoa/Cocoa.h>

@interface Budget : NSObject {

  float   exchangeRate;
  double  budget;
  double  transaction;
}
```

```
- (id) initWithAmount: (double) aBudget
               withExchangeRate: (double) anExchangeRate ;

- (void) spendDollars: (double) dollars ;

- (void) chargeForeignCurrency: (double) euros;
- (double) returnBalance;
@end
```

Listing 3-4: Budget.m

```
#import "Budget.h"

@implementation Budget

- (id) initWithAmount: (double) aBudget
               withExchangeRate: (double) anExchangeRate {

  if (self = [super init]) {
    exchangeRate = anExchangeRate;
    budget = aBudget;
  }
  return self;
}
- (void) spendDollars: (double) dollars {

  budget -= dollars;
}
- (void) chargeForeignCurrency: (double) foreignCurrency {

  transaction = foreignCurrency*exchangeRate;
  budget -= transaction;
}
- (double) returnBalance {

  return budget;
}
@end
```

Listing 3-5: Transaction.h

```
#import <Cocoa/Cocoa.h>
@class Budget;
@interface Transaction : NSObject {

  Budget *budget;
  double amount;
NSString *name;
}
```

(continued)

Listing 3-5 *(continued)*

```
- (id) initWithAmount: (double) theAmount
                              forBudget: (Budget*) aBudget;
- (void) spend;
@end
```

Listing 3-6:   Transaction.m

```
#import "Transaction.h"
#import "Budget.h"

@implementation Transaction

- (id) initWithAmount: (double) theAmount
                            forBudget: (Budget*) aBudget {
  if (self = [super init]) {
    budget = aBudget;
    amount = theAmount;
  }
  return self;
}
- (void) spend {
}
@end
```

Listing 3-7:   CashTransaction.h

```
#import <Cocoa/Cocoa.h>
#import "Transaction.h"

@interface CashTransaction : Transaction {

}

- (id) initWithAmount: (double) theAmount forBudget:
    (Budget*) aBudget ;
@end
```

Listing 3-8:   CashTransaction.m

```
#import "CashTransaction.h"
#import "Budget.h"

@implementation CashTransaction
```

```
- (id) initWithAmount: (double) theAmount forBudget:
    (Budget*) aBudget {

  if (self = [super initWithAmount:theAmount
    forBudget:aBudget]) {
    name = @"Cash";
  }
  return self;
}

- (void) spend {
  [budget spendDollars:amount];
}
@end
```

Book II
Chapter 3

Digging Deeper Into
Objective-C

Listing 3-9:   CreditCardTransaction.h

```
#import <Cocoa/Cocoa.h>
#import "Transaction.h"

@interface CreditCardTransaction : Transaction {

}
- (id) initWithAmount: (double) theAmount forBudget:
    (Budget*) aBudget ;
@end
```

Listing 3-10:   CreditCardTransaction.m

```
#import "CreditCardTransaction.h"
#import "Budget.h"

@implementation CreditCardTransaction

- (id) initWithAmount: (double) theAmount forBudget:
    (Budget*) aBudget {

  if (self = [super initWithAmount:theAmount
    forBudget:aBudget]) {
    name = @"Credit card";
  }
  return self;
}
- (void) spend {
  [budget chargeForeignCurrency:amount];
}
@end
```

The designated initializer

It's possible to have more than one initializer per class. When you have more than one initializer in a class, according to Cocoa convention, you're expected to designate one as the *designated initializer*. This designated initializer is usually the one that does the most initialization, and it *is the one responsible for invoking the superclass's initializer*. Because this initializer is the one that does the most work, again by convention, the other initializers are expected to invoke it with appropriate default values as needed.

Although at some point you may need to explore this topic further, it's really a framework and beyond the scope of this book.

Listing 3-11:   Destination.h

```
#import <Cocoa/Cocoa.h>
@class Budget;

@interface Destination : NSObject {

  NSString        *country;
  double           exchangeRate;
  NSMutableArray  *transactions;
  Budget          *theBudget;

}
- (id) initWithCountry: (NSString*) theCountry
        andBudget: (double) budgetAmount
        withExchangeRate:(double) theExchangeRate;
- (void) spendCash: (double) aTransaction;
- (void) chargeCreditCard:(double) aTransaction;
- (double) leftToSpend
@end
```

Listing 3-12:   Destination.m

```
#import "Destination.h"
#import "CashTransaction.h"
#import "CreditCardTransaction.h"
#import "Budget.h"
#import "Transaction.h"
@implementation Destination

- (id) initWithCountry: (NSString*) theCountry andBudget:
    (double) budgetAmount withExchangeRate: (double)
    theExchangeRate{
  if (self = [super init]) {
    transactions = [[NSMutableArray alloc]
    initWithCapacity:10];
```

```
      theBudget = [[Budget alloc] initWithAmount:budgetAmount
    withExchangeRate:theExchangeRate];
      country = theCountry;
      NSLog (@"I'm off to %@", theCountry);
   }

   return self;
}

-(void) spendCash:(double)amount{

Transaction *aTransaction = [[CashTransaction alloc]
    initWithAmount:amount forBudget:theBudget];
   [transactions addObject:aTransaction];
   [aTransaction spend];
}
-(void) chargeCreditCard: (double) amount{

Transaction *aTransaction =
         [[CreditCardTransaction alloc]
    initWithAmount:amount forBudget:theBudget];
   [transactions addObject:aTransaction];
   [aTransaction spend];
}
- (double ) leftToSpend {

   return [theBudget returnBalance];
}
@end
```

Listing 3-13:   main in Vacation.m

```
#import <Foundation/Foundation.h>
#import "Destination.h"

int main (int argc, const char * argv[]) {

  NSString* europeText = [[NSString alloc]
    initWithFormat:@"%@", @"Europe"];
  Destination* europe = [[Destination alloc]
    initWithCountry:europeText andBudget:1000.00
    withExchangeRate:1.25];

  NSString* englandText = [[NSString alloc]
                    initWithFormat:@"%@", @"England"];

  Destination* england = [[Destination alloc]
    initWithCountry:englandText andBudget:2000.00
    withExchangeRate:1.50];
```

(continued)

Book II
Chapter 3

Digging Deeper Into
Objective-C

Listing 3-13 *(continued)*

```
for (int n = 1; n < 2; n++) {
  double transaction = n*100.00;
  NSLog (@"Sending a %.2f cash transaction", transaction);
  [europe spendCash:transaction];
  NSLog(@"Remaining budget %.2f", [europe leftToSpend]);
  NSLog (@"Sending a %.2f cash transaction", transaction);
  [england spendCash:transaction];
  NSLog(@"Remaining budget %.2f", [england leftToSpend]);
}

int n = 1;
while (n < 4) {
  double transaction = n*100.00;
  NSLog(@"Sending a %.2f credit card transaction",
  transaction);
  [europe chargeCreditCard:transaction];
  NSLog(@"Remaining budget %.2f", [europe leftToSpend]);
  NSLog(@"Sending a %.2f credit card transaction",
  transaction);
  [england chargeCreditCard:transaction];
  NSLog(@"Remaining budget %.2f", [england leftToSpend]);
  n++;
}
return 0;
}
```

Raising and Terminating Responsible Objects

You have given birth to an object by allocating memory for it, and (to push the metaphor to its limits) you've raised it to maturity by initializing it — setting its instance variables to a known initial state. What about retirement (and dare I say it, termination)? As you give birth to more objects, you allocate more memory, until at some point (population explosion?) you run out of memory.

What with everything else going on in prepping your app for rollout, managing memory can be a real challenge not only to someone new to programming, but also to those people with many lines of code under their belts.

Allocating memory when you actually need it isn't that hard. It's realizing you don't need an object anymore and then releasing the memory back to the operating system that can be a challenge. If you don't do that, and your program runs long enough, eventually you run out of memory (see the upcoming sidebar, "The iPhone memory challenge") and your program comes crashing down. Long before that, you may even notice system performance approaching "molasses in February, outdoors in Hibbing, Minnesota" levels. Oh, and by the way, if you do free an object (memory) and that object is still being used, you'll have the "London Bridge Is Falling Down" effect as well.

The iPhone memory challenge

Although the iPhone OS and the Mac both use what's known as virtual memory, unlike the Mac, virtual memory in the iPhone is limited to the actual amount of physical memory. This is because when it begins to run low on memory, the iPhone OS frees up memory pages that contain read-only content (such as code), where all it has to do is load the "originals" back into memory when they're needed. It doesn't, like the Mac, temporarily store "changeable" memory (such as object data) to the disk to free up space and then read the data back later when it's needed. This state of affairs limits the amount of memory available.

If you've created a giant application and run out of memory while all the objects you created are being used, that's one issue (beyond the scope of this book). But if you run out of memory because you have all these objects floating around that no one is using, that's another thing, and it's known as a *memory leak*.

Keeping tabs of your app's memory needs — a process known as *memory management* — isn't really that hard if you understand how it all works, which also isn't that hard if you pay attention to it. In addition, Xcode can help you track down memory problems. I show you how to use Xcode's memory management features in the "Running the Static Analyzer" section, later in this chapter. The problem is that sometimes, in the rush to develop an application and see things happen on the screen, programmers ignore their memory management issues for the moment, telling themselves that they'll come back later to do it right. Trust me, this strategy does not lead to happy and healthy applications or application developers.

Understanding the object lifecycle

In Chapter 1 of this minibook, you found out how to allocate and initialize objects using a combination of `alloc` and `init`. Many objects you allocate stay around for the duration of your program, and for those objects, all you have to do is, well, nothing really. When your program terminates, they are de-allocated, and the memory is returned to the operating system.

But some objects you use for a while to get your money's worth out of them and then . . . you're done with them. When you're done with them, you should return the memory allocated to them back to the OS so it can allocate that memory for new objects. If you don't, you may cause problems.

Start by looking at how memory management works. In Objective-C 2.0 (as opposed to earlier versions), you can manage memory for iPhone apps by *reference counting* — keeping the system up to date on whether an object is currently being used. Read on to find out more.

Using reference counting

In many ways, Objective-C is like the coolest guy in your school, who now makes a seven-figure income bungee jumping and skateboarding during the summers, while snowboarding around the world in the winter.

In other ways, though, Objective-C is like the nerd in your class, who grew up to be an accountant and reads the *Financial Times* for fun. Memory management falls into this category.

In fact, memory management is simply an exercise in counting. To manage its memory, Objective-C (actually Cocoa) uses a technique known as *reference counting*. Every object has its own reference count, or *retain count*.

When an object is created via `alloc` or `new` — or through a `copy` message, which creates a copy of an object but has some subtleties beyond the scope of this book — the object's retain count is set to 1. As long as the retain count is greater than zero, the memory manager assumes that someone cares about that object and leaves it alone.

It's your responsibility to maintain that reference count by directly or indirectly increasing the retain count when you're using an object and then decreasing it when you're finished with it. When the retain count goes to zero, the runtime system (Cocoa) assumes that no one needs it anymore. Cocoa automatically sends the object a `dealloc` message, and after that, its memory is returned to the system to be reused.

Take a look at an example: In `Vacation.m`, you create a string object and then pass that as an argument into the `init` method when you create the `Destination` object, as shown here:

```
NSString* englandText = [[NSString alloc]
                    initWithFormat:@"%@", @"England"];
Destination* england = [[Destination alloc]
   initWithCountry:englandText andBudget:2000.00
   withExchangeRate:1.50];
```

The `Destination` object sticks around until the program is terminated. At that point, everything gets de-allocated, so there is really no problem and no real (although some potential) memory management issues.

But what happens if you decide sometime along the way on your trip not to go to England after all. You really have always wanted to go to Antarctica, and an opportunity to hitch a ride on a rock star's private jet presents itself, so bye-bye England, and hello Ushuaia, Tierra del Fuego, Argentina.

Before you take off, however, you want to do one thing — besides send for your long underwear. You need to delete England as a destination, freeing up that budget money, and create a new destination — Antarctica.

When you're doing memory management, it is *your responsibility* to keep the runtime system informed about your use of objects, so if you don't need an object any longer, you send it a release message.

```
[england release];
```

release does not de-allocate the object!

Let me say that again — release does not de-allocate the object!

All release does is decrement the retain count by 1. This is very important to keep in mind because while one method or object in your application may no longer need an object, it still may be needed by another method or object in your program. That's why you don't dealloc it yourself, and instead you need to trust the runtime system to manage the retain count for you. But it is *your job* to keep the runtime system informed of your object by using the release message.

Book II
Chapter 3

Digging Deeper Into Objective-C

Well that's cool, and being a good citizen, the england object wants to release all its objects in its dealloc method. No problem here, one would think. Destination has instance variables pointing to the objects it uses:

```
NSString* country;
double exchangeRate;
NSMutableArray *transactions;
Budget* theBudget;
```

So, in the dealloc method that is invoked before the Destination object is de-allocated by the OS, those other objects can be released.

```
- (void) dealloc {

    [transactions release];
    [country release];
    [theBudget release];
    [super dealloc];
}
```

Normally you don't send the dealloc message to the object directly; you send the object the release message and let the runtime system de-allocate it automatically. The exception is when you're invoking the superclass's implementation in a custom dealloc method (as in super dealloc) — you need to send your superclass a dealloc message after you release the objects that you need to release in the subclass.

Although you don't have to release the exchangeRate because it is not an object, do you really want to release all those other objects? What if other objects in your program still need to use those objects? Actually, taking that into account is very easy, as long as you follow the rules.

As I mention earlier, when you create an object using `alloc` or `new`, or through a `copy` message, the object's retain count is set to 1. So you're cool. In fact, whenever you create an object like that, your solemn responsibility is to release it when you are done. There is a flip side to this coin, however; if you're using an object, a pointer to it is sent to you as an argument in a message, as is the case for the `NSString` object in the following:

```
Destination* england = [[Destination alloc]
    initWithCountry:englandText andBudget:2000.00
    withExchangeRate:1.50];
```

Then it's also your responsibility to increment the retain count by sending it the `retain` message, as you can see in the bolded section of the implementation of the `initWithCountry:::` method:

```
- (id) initWithCountry: (NSString*) theCountry andBudget:
    (double) budgetAmount withExchangeRate: (double)
    theExchangeRate{
  if (self = [super init]) {
    transactions = [[NSMutableArray alloc]
                                   initWithCapacity:10];
    theBudget = [[Budget alloc]
                     initWithAmount:budgetAmount
                     withExchangeRate:theExchangeRate];
    exchangeRate = theExchangeRate;
    country = theCountry;
    [country retain];
  }
  return self;
}
```

In this method, the `Destination` object creates two objects on its own, `theBudget` and `transactions`. As a result, the retain count for each is set to 1. It also gets passed a pointer to an `NSString` object that was created at another time and place. If `Destination` plans to use that object, it needs to send it the `retain` message. That way, the retain count is increased by 1. If the creator of that object decides it no longer needs the object and sends it the `release` message, the retain count is decremented by 1. But because the `Destination` object sent it a `retain` message, the release count is still greater than 0 — the object lives!

In fact, that is exactly what happens. In `main`, after the object is created and sent as an argument to the `Destination` objects, the good little code releases the object because it really has no need for the object. When you do release an object in your code, you're counting on the fact that other objects are playing according to the rules, and the receiving object increases the retain count if it needs to continue to use an object you created. This frees the creator of an object from the responsibility of having to know anything about who's using an object it has created and worrying about when it has to free the object.

In the code in `main`, the string object sent in the `initWithCountry:::` message is released after the message is sent because the code in `main` has no further use for the string object it created. (Note the bolded code in the following block.)

```
NSString* englandText = [[NSString alloc]
    initWithFormat:@"%@", @"England"];
  Destination* england = [[Destination alloc]
    initWithCountry:englandText andBudget:2000.00
    withExchangeRate:1.50];
  [englandText release];
```

`europeText` is released as well. All's right with the world.

What really confuses some developers is the concept of `retain` and `release`. They worry that releasing an object will de-allocate that object. (Note that all `release` does is tell the memory manager that you're no longer interested in it. The memory manager is the one that makes the life-and-death decision.) New developers sometimes worry that, as a creator, they have to be concerned about others using their objects. In reality, it's your job to simply follow the memory management rules.

Here's the fundamental rule of memory management:

> You're responsible for releasing any object that you create using a method whose name begins with `alloc` or `new` or contains `copy`, or if you send it a `retain` message. In Applespeak, if you do any of these things, you're said to *own* the object. (Objects are allowed to have more than one owner — talk about how to use terminology to really make things confusing).You can release an object by sending it a `release` or `autorelease` message (which I explain shortly).

That's it, with corollaries of course.

> If you want to continue to use an object outside the method it was received in, save a pointer to it as an instance variable, as you did previously with the `NSString` object. Then you must send the object the `retain` message. In Applespeak, that means you are now an owner of the object.

In general, somewhere in your code there should be a `release` for every statement that creates an object using `alloc` or `new`, or contains `copy` or sends a `retain` message.

Running the Static Analyzer

Until the release of Xcode 3.2, you had to track down memory leaks by using the Instruments application (which I cover in Book IV).

But Xcode also has a new Build and Analyze feature (the Static Analyzer) that analyzes your code. It is especially good at detecting certain kinds of memory leaks — especially ones where you create an object and then pass it to another object, and then forget to release it.

When you run the Static Analyzer, the results show up like warnings and errors, with explanations of where (and what) the issue is. You can also see the flow of control of the (potential) problem. I say *potential* because the Static Analyzer can give you false positives. Here's how to put Static Analyzer through its paces:

1. **Choose Build⇨Build and Analyze.**

   The status bar in the Xcode Project window tells you all about build progress, build errors such as compiler errors, or warnings.

2. **Choose Build⇨Build Results.**

   The Build Results window appears. Line numbers appear in the text because I chose that option in the Editing pane of Xcode's Preferences window.

   You see four potential memory leaks in the Build Results window, as shown in Figure 3-1: two in `Vacation.m` and two in `Destination.m`.

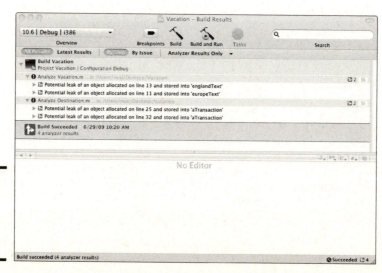

Figure 3-1: Build results for the Static Analyzer.

3. **Return to the Project Window, which shows the Static Analyzer Results in the Text Editor (as shown in Figure 3-2).**

   While you can work in either the Build Results window or the Text Editor, I prefer working in the Text Editor.

4. **Click the first error message (right after Line 13).**

   Figure 3-3 shows how you got into this predicament. The object you created on Line 11, europeText, is no longer referenced after Line 12, when you use it as an argument in initWithCountry::. It still has a retain count of 1, so even if all the other objects that use it do release it, it continues to take up precious memory, even though it isn't being used in main, for the simple reason that it hasn't been released.

5. **Open the Destination.m file.**

   When you look at Destination.m, you see the same sorry story. Figure 3-4 warns you of a potential leak.

6. **Click the error message on Line 28.**

   Figure 3-5 shows that the Transaction object you created on Line 25 is never referenced after you send it the spend: message and add it to the transactions array.

Figure 3-2: The Static Analyzer results in the Project Window.

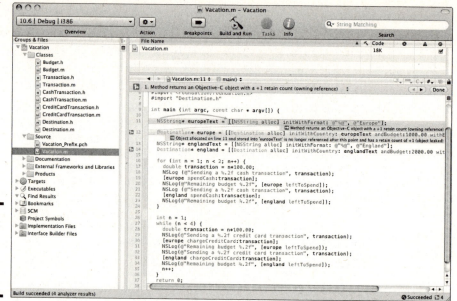

Figure 3-3:
The text objects are no longer referenced.

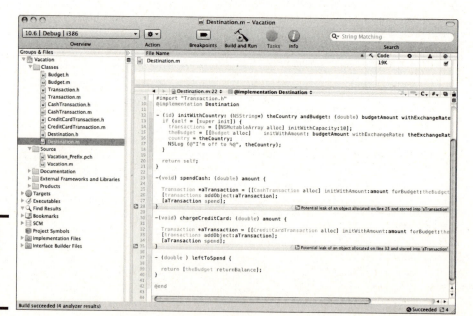

Figure 3-4:
A potential leak in Destination.m.

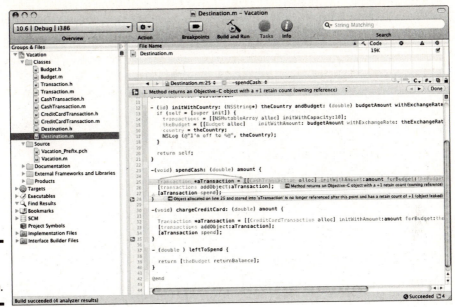

Book II
Chapter 3

Digging Deeper Into Objective-C

Figure 3-5:
A lonely
Transaction.

Plugging the Leaks

To plug the leaks Xcode's Static Analyzer has so kindly pointed out to you, add the code shown in bold in Listings 3-14 through 3-19 to Budget.m, Transaction.m, CashTransaction.m, CreditCardTransaction.m, Destination.m, and main in Vacation.m.

Listing 3-14: Budget.m

```
#import "Budget.h"

@implementation Budget

- (id) initWithAmount: (double) aBudget withExchangeRate:
    (double) anExchangeRate {

  if (self = [super init]) {
    exchangeRate = anExchangeRate;
    budget = aBudget;
  }
  return self;
}
- (void) spendDollars: (double) dollars {

  budget -= dollars;
}
```

(continued)

Listing 3-14 *(continued)*

```
- (void) chargeForeignCurrency: (double) foreignCurrency {
  transaction = foreignCurrency*exchangeRate;
  budget -= transaction;
}
- (double) returnBalance {

  return budget;
}

- (void) dealloc {

  [super dealloc];
}
@end
```

Listing 3-15:   Transaction.m

```
#import "Transaction.h"
#import "Budget.h"

@implementation Transaction

- (void) spend {
}

- (id) initWithAmount: (double) theAmount forBudget:
    (Budget*) aBudget {
  if (self = [super init]) {
    budget = aBudget;
    [budget retain];
    amount = theAmount;
  }
   return self;
}
- (void) dealloc {

  [budget release];
  [super dealloc];
}
@end
```

Listing 3-16:   CashTransaction.m

```
#import "CashTransaction.h"
#import "Budget.h"

@implementation CashTransaction
```

```
- (id) initWithAmount: (double) theAmount forBudget:
    (Budget*) aBudget  {

  if (self = [super initWithAmount:theAmount
    forBudget:aBudget]) {
    name = @"Cash";
  }
  return self;
}
- (void) spend {
  [budget spendDollars:amount];
}
- (void) dealloc {

  [super dealloc];
}
@end
```

Listing 3-17:   CreditCardTransaction.m

```
#import "CreditCardTransaction.h"
#import "Budget.h"

@implementation CreditCardTransaction

- (id) initWithAmount: (double) theAmount forBudget:
    (Budget*) aBudget {

  if (self = [super initWithAmount: theAmount forBudget:
    aBudget]) {
    name = @"Credit Card";
  }
    return self;
}
- (void) spend {

  [budget chargeForeignCurrency:amount];
}
- (void) dealloc {

  [super dealloc];
}
@end
```

Listing 3-18:   Destination.m

```
#import "Destination.h"
#import "CashTransaction.h"
#import "CreditCardTransaction.h"
#import "Budget.h"
```

(continued)

Listing 3-18 *(continued)*

```
#import "Transaction.h"

@implementation Destination

- (id) initWithCountry: (NSString*) theCountry andBudget:
    (double) budgetAmount withExchangeRate: (double)
    theExchangeRate{
  if (self = [super init]) {
    transactions = [[NSMutableArray alloc]
   initWithCapacity:10];
    theBudget = [[Budget alloc]  initWithAmount:budgetAmount
   withExchangeRate:theExchangeRate];
    exchangeRate = theExchangeRate;
    country = theCountry;
    [country retain];
    NSLog(@"I'm off to %@", theCountry);
  }
  return self;
}
- (void) updateExchangeRate: (double) newExchangeRate {

exchangeRate = newExchangeRate;
}
- (void) spendCash: (double)amount {

Transaction *aTransaction = [[CashTransaction alloc]
    initWithAmount:amount forBudget:theBudget ];
[transactions addObject:aTransaction];
[aTransaction spend];
[aTransaction release];
}
- (void) chargeCreditCard: (double) amount {

Transaction *aTransaction = [[CreditCardTransaction alloc]
    initWithAmount:amount forBudget:theBudget ];
[transactions addObject:aTransaction];
[aTransaction spend];
[aTransaction release];
}
- (double ) leftToSpend {

return  [theBudget returnBalance];
}
- (void) dealloc {

[transactions release];
[theBudget release];
[country release];
[super dealloc];
}
@end
```

Listing 3-19:   main in Vacation.m

```objc
#import <Foundation/Foundation.h>
#import "Destination.h"

int main (int argc, const char * argv[]) {

  NSString* europeText = [[NSString alloc]
    initWithFormat:@"%@", @"Europe"];
  Destination* europe = [[Destination alloc]
    initWithCountry:europeText andBudget:1000.00
    withExchangeRate:1.25];
  [europeText release];
  NSString* englandText = [[NSString alloc]
    initWithFormat:@"%@", @"England"];
  Destination* england = [[Destination alloc]
    initWithCountry:englandText andBudget:2000.00
    withExchangeRate:1.50];
  [englandText release];

  for (int n = 1; n <  2; n++) {
    double transaction = n*100.00;
    NSLog (@"Sending a %.2f cash transaction", transaction);
    [europe spendCash:transaction];

    NSLog(@"Remaining budget %.2f", [europe leftToSpend]);
    NSLog(@"Sending a %.2f cash transaction", transaction);
    [england spendCash:transaction];
    NSLog(@"Remaining budget %.2f", [england leftToSpend]);
  }

  int n = 1;
  while (n < 4) {
    double transaction = n*100.00;
    NSLog (@"Sending a %.2f credit card transaction",
  transaction);
    [europe chargeCreditCard:transaction];
    NSLog(@"Remaining budget %.2f", [europe leftToSpend]);
    NSLog (@"Sending a %.2f credit card transaction",
  transaction);
    [england chargeCreditCard:transaction];
    NSLog(@"Remaining budget %.2f", [england leftToSpend]);
    n++;
  }

  [england release];

  return 0;
  }
```

Book II
Chapter 3

Digging Deeper Into
Objective-C

To fix the problems discovered by the Static Analyzer, you need to release aTransaction in the spendCash: and chargeCreditCard: methods in

Destination.m (as shown earlier in Listing 3-18). You also need to release europeText and englandText in main (as shown in Listing 3-19).

Notice that in the Destination methods cashTransaction: and CreditCardTransaction:, you release the Transaction object when you're done with it. A bit later on in this chapter, the section "Considering objects in arrays" explains why that's safe, even though you've added it to the array.

Although the Static Analyzer is a giant step forward, it can't catch everything. You still need to be methodical about releasing objects for which you've increased the retain count in the Transaction and Destination objects' dealloc methods.

Two comments about the dealloc methods. First, as you can see, you need to send your superclass a dealloc message after you release the objects that you need to release in the subclass. Remember, the object that creates an object or retains the object needs to release it, so you may find yourself releasing the same object in both a subclass's and a superclass's dealloc method. That's fine, as long as the object was created or retained by the class that releases it.

You also add dealloc methods for those classes that (presently) do not have any objects they need to release when they are de-allocated. You do that to keep focused on how important it is to release objects. In fact, in the file templates that you use for iPhone classes, when you create a new class file that's derived from anything other than NSObject, the template has a default dealloc method that just invokes its superclass's dealloc method.

One final point: If you have a dealloc method that does release objects, when its superclass is NSObject, you really don't need to invoke it from dealloc. It is, however, not a bad habit to always invoke your superclass's dealloc method. This keeps you from getting into trouble when you *factor* your code — separate sections with different responsibilities into different objects. You may find yourself creating a new superclass for a class that previously was based on NSObject, and always invoking its superclass's dealloc method keeps you from having to remember to add the code to invoke it in your (now) subclass's dealloc method.

The program still functions the same way as it did before you made the changes, which underlies why it's so easy to postpone doing memory management until you need it. But while it doesn't seem to add any (observable) functionality early on, correctly managing memory saves you many hours of anguish later when your program expands to the point where memory becomes an issue, which (too) often happens much sooner than you might expect.

If you want to trace the de-allocation process, put an `NSLog` statement in your `dealloc` method to see when objects are being de-allocated. You can also send an object the `retainCount` message to find out its current retain count. (It returns an unsigned `int`.)

Attending to Memory Management Subtleties — Arrays and Autorelease

Although memory management is generally straightforward, there are a few subtleties that may not be so obvious — only a few mind you, but they're important. The following (two) subtleties deserve special attention:

Book II
Chapter 3

Digging Deeper Into Objective-C

✦ Objects in arrays

✦ Autorelease and the autorelease pool

Considering objects in arrays

Look at the `dealloc` method in `Destination.m`:

```
- (void) dealloc {

    [transactions release];
    [theBudget release];
    [country release];
    [super dealloc];
}
```

Notice you release the `transactions` array. What happens to all the objects you added to that particular array? As you might expect, the rules are that if you want to use an object, you must send it a `retain` message, and if you do, then at some point you must `release` it. The array follows those rules, and when you add an object to an array, the array object sends the object that was just added a `retain` message. When the array is de-allocated, it sends `release` messages to all its objects. If you want to use the object after the array is de-allocated, you need to send it a `retain` message before the array is de-allocated.

In addition, if you remove an object from a mutable array — which is the only kind that you can add and remove objects from (refer to Chapter 4 of this minibook for more on this topic) — the object that has been removed receives a `release` message. So, if an array is the only owner of an object, then (by standard rules of memory management) the object is de-allocated when it's removed. If you want to use the object after its removal, you need to send it a `retain` message *before* you remove it from the array.

Understanding autorelease

At the end of the discussion of using accessors to get data from objects in Chapter 1 of this minibook, you used the following code:

```
NSAutoreleasePool * pool = [[NSAutoreleasePool alloc] init];

  // insert code here...

[pool drain];
```

This code creates an autorelease pool that is a way to manage memory for objects when it is not possible for the object creator to easily release them.

The memory management rules require you to release objects when you're done with them, and often that's pretty easy, as shown in the following example:

```
NSString* englandText = [[NSString alloc]
    initWithFormat:@"%@", @"England"];

Destination* england = [[Destination alloc]
    initWithCountry:englandText andBudget:2000.00
    withExchangeRate:1.50];

  [englandText release];
```

In `main`, the string object is created and then used as an argument in the `Destination` object's `initWithCountry:::` method. After control is returned to `main`, you can safely release that object because, as far as you are concerned, you are done with it; if `Destination` needs it, well, it's the `Destination` object's responsibility to retain it. But what about those circumstances where the creator never gets control back? For example, what if you were to create a new method called `returnCountry` that created a copy of the `country` string and returned it back to the invoker?

```
- (NSString*) returnCountry {

  return [country copy];
}
```

You might want to do that if the receiver could possibly modify it. The problem here is that control is never returned back to `returnCountry`, so `returnCountry` never has a chance to release the copy it made.

To deal with the problem of control never being returned to a creator of an object so the creator can release it, Cocoa has the concept of an *autorelease pool,* and the statement

```
NSAutoreleasePool * pool =
                    [[NSAutoreleasePool alloc] init];
```

creates one of those pools to be used by `main`. The pool is nothing more than a collection of objects that will be released sometime in the future. When you send `autorelease` to an object, the object is added to an `NSAutoreleasePool`. When that pool is "cleared" (which happens on a regular basis), all the objects in the pool are sent a `release` message.

As glamorous as it sounds, the autorelease pool is just an array, and knowing what you know, you could write and manage one yourself, but why bother?

So, you can now write a `returnCountry` method that manages memory correctly.

**Book II
Chapter 3**

**Digging Deeper Into
Objective-C**

```
- (NSString*) returnCountry {

   return [[country copy] autorelease];
}
```

Now, memory management works just right because the `returnCountry` method creates a new string, autoreleases it, and returns it to the object that requested it. If that object wants to continue to use the string, that object has to send a `retain` message to the string because the string gets a `release` message in the future.

So when is that release message sent? If you're using an `AppKit` or `UIKit` application, the `release` message is sent in the main event loop that you return to after your program handles the current event, such as a mouse click or touch. With a Foundation Command Line Tool, the `release` message is sent when you destroy or drain the pool.

```
[pool drain];
```

That's as far as I'm going with how the autorelease pool works — anything else is beyond the scope of this book. Besides, I assume that you're using Cocoa (the runtime system) for your application, which automatically takes care of managing the autorelease pool for you — both creating the pool and releasing it periodically.

Using the autorelease pool

You want to avoid using the autorelease pool on the iPhone when possible. The memory allocated for an autoreleased object remains allocated for some period of time after you're done with it and can be an issue in more memory-intensive applications. But `autorelease` could be used "behind your back" at times.

For example, Objective-C has a concept called *class* methods. This method belongs to the class object (as opposed to an instance object of the class), and class methods used to create new instances are called *factory* or *convenience methods*. The objects it creates are autoreleased. The ones you probably will be most concerned with are in the `NSString` class (although there are more, even in the `NSMutableArray` class), such as the following:

```
stringWithContentsOfFile
stringWithContentsOfURL
stringWithCString
stringWithFormat:
stringWithString:
```

So, instead of using

```
NSString *newText = [NSString stringWithFormat:
@"Yo ", name];
```

You're using

```
NSString *newText = [[NSString alloc] initWithFormat:
@"Yo ", name];
```

and doing the `release` yourself.

Notice these methods are of the form `stringWith`, as opposed to `init`.... This naming convention is a handy way to differentiate a class method that uses autorelease from the `init` methods that use `alloc`.

If you do need to continue to use an autoreleased object, just like with any other object you receive, you need to send it a `retain` message. In doing so, you become responsible for managing that object, and you must send a `release` message at some point.

In iPhone programming, Apple recommends that you avoid using autorelease in your own code and that you also avoid class methods that return autoreleased objects. As I mention earlier, the memory allocated for an autoreleased object remains allocated for some period of time after you're done with it and can be an issue in more memory-intensive applications. This book doesn't cover these class methods, although you can find many examples of them being used.

These methods occur most commonly when creating an object using a class method, which saves you the trouble of doing an `alloc`, an `init`..., and then a `release` for the object. If you look in the documentation, as illustrated in Figure 3-6, these are under the heading Class Methods. They all have a + instead of a – before the return type, which designates them as a class method.

In Figure 3-6, you can see the `NSString` Class reference. In the Table of Contents, I expanded the disclosure triangle next to Class Methods and then clicked the `stringWithFormat:` class method, the counterpart to the `initWithFormat:` instance method. You can see the + in front of the method declaration.

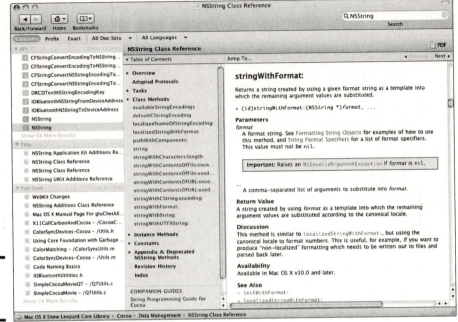

Figure 3-6:
Class
methods.

**Book II
Chapter 3**

**Digging Deeper Into
Objective-C**

Notice that for class methods like these, instead of having their names start with `init` (for example, `initWithFormat:` for an `NSString`), they start with a reference to the class name (`stringWithFormat:`, for example).

Some Basic Memory Management Rules You Shouldn't Forget

It all comes down to one simple rule:

> If you do anything to increase the retain count of an object, it's your responsibility to decrease the retain count by the same amount when you're no longer going to send messages to that object.

That's it. Of course, the wisdom lies in knowing when you've increased the retain count, and when you need to decrease it.

✦ You automatically increase the retain count whenever you create an object using `alloc` or `new` or any method that contains `copy`.

✦ You should decrease the retain count by sending an object a `release` message when you no longer need to send the object any messages.

✦ Assume that any object you receive whose creation you didn't personally witness dies as soon as you turn your back. It may have been passed
as an argument, for example, or perhaps you're using one of those class
convenience methods I spoke of earlier — you know, the ones you really
shouldn't use on the iPhone.

✦ As shown in the section on releasing an object assigned to a property in
Chapter 1 of this minibook, assigning an instance variable with a property attribute of `retain` is the moral equivalent of sending the object
the `retain` message yourself.

At the end of the day, the number of `alloc`, `new`, `copy`, and `retain`
messages should equal (not be close to, equal) the number of `release`
messages.

Do not make yourself crazy wondering about what is going on outside the
little world of your program. If you follow the rules in every object, things
work out correctly. This is one of the few times when everyone acting in his
or her best interest always works in the best interest of the whole.

Chapter 4: Leveraging the Foundation Framework in Your App

In This Chapter

✔ Seeing what the Foundation framework has to offer

✔ Working with mutable arrays

✔ Using each object in an array in a message

✔ Getting to know C arrays

✔ Creating and using property lists

✔ Discovering how dictionaries work

✔ Updating dictionaries and property lists

In *The Foundation Trilogy,* an epic science fiction series, Isaac Asimov and his editor John W. Campbell devised the concept of mathematical sociology (analogous to mathematical physics), in which the law of mass action can predict the future, but only on a large scale; it is error-prone on a small scale.

The Foundation framework has nothing to do with that, except that it too was devised to predict the future — what your app and many other apps may want to do — and it works on a large scale while remaining error-prone on a small scale (in the hands of inexperienced programmers). It provides a set of useful object classes in primitive form ready for you to flesh out, and introduces several paradigms that define functionality not covered by the Objective-C language. Think of it as providing the plumbing features such as data storage, text and strings, dates and times, object creation, disposal persistence, and common Internet protocols.

The Foundation framework is designed with these goals in mind:

✦ Provide a small set of basic utility classes.

✦ Make software development easier by introducing consistent conventions for things such as de-allocation.

✦ Support Unicode strings, object persistence, and object distribution.

✦ Provide a level of operating system independence, to enhance portability.

I describe how you can use the Foundation framework in this chapter, starting with useful utility classes for data storage, text and strings, dates and times, and object creation and disposal. I then cover other useful classes for arrays, dictionaries, and property lists.

Useful Utility Classes

The Foundation framework includes the root object class, collection classes for storing other objects, classes representing system information (stuff like dates), and classes representing communication ports. It also offers classes representing basic data types such as strings and byte arrays, along with utility classes for working with numbers, dates, arrays, dictionaries, files, and directories. You can see the entire list in "The Foundation Framework" in the iPhone OS Reference Library (`http://developer.apple.com/iphone/library/navigation`).

Many of the utility classes have closely related functionality:

+ **Data storage.** NSData and NSString provide object-oriented storage for arrays of bytes. NSValue and NSNumber provide object-oriented storage for simple C data values. NSArray, NSDictionary, and NSSet provide storage for Objective-C objects of any class.

+ **Text and strings.** NSCharacterSet represents various groupings of characters that are used by the NSString and NSScanner classes. The NSString classes represent text strings and provide methods for searching, combining, and comparing strings. An NSScanner object is used to scan numbers and words from an NSString object.

+ **Dates and times.** The NSDate, NSTimeZone, and NSCalendar classes store times and dates and represent calendar information. They offer methods for calculating date and time differences. Together with NSLocale, they provide methods for displaying dates and times in many formats, and for adjusting times and dates based on location in the world.

+ **Application coordination and timing.** NSNotification, NSNotificationCenter, and NSNotificationQueue provide systems that an object can use to notify all interested observers of changes that occur. You can use an NSTimer object to send a message to another object at specific intervals.

+ **Object creation and disposal.** NSAutoreleasePool is used to implement the delayed-release feature of the Foundation framework.

+ **Object distribution and persistence.** Persistence is the ability to store objects in and retrieve objects from a database, so that the objects exist from session to session. The data that an object contains can be represented in an architecture-independent way using

NSPropertyListSerialization. The NSCoder and its subclasses take this process a step further by allowing class information to be stored along with the data. The resulting representations are used for archiving and for object distribution.

✦ **Operating-system services.** Several classes are designed to insulate you from the operating system, so that subsequent changes to the system don't affect your code. NSFileManager provides a consistent interface for file operations (creating, renaming, deleting, and so on). NSThread and NSProcessInfo let you create multithreaded applications and query the environment in which an application runs.

✦ **URL loading system.** A set of classes and protocols provide access to common Internet protocols.

**Book II
Chapter 4**

Container Classes

In object-oriented programming, a *container* class is a class that is capable of storing other objects. In Cocoa, several kinds are available, and I explain the two most widely used, *dictionary* and *array,* in this chapter. You probably know what in general an array is: a number of items arranged in some specified way. In the more specific world of object-oriented programming, an array is a group of objects with the same attributes that can be addressed individually.

In the vacation budget examples of Chapters 1 through 3 of this minibook, you can see I use NSMutableArray, which allows you to add objects as needed — that is, the amount of memory allocated to the class is dynamically adjusted as you add more objects.

The following example explains why using a mutable array might be a good idea. You might want to code transactions with spendDollars: statements. For example, for every transaction where you spend dollars in Europe, you would need the following:

```
[europeBudget spendDollars:numberDollarsInEuroland];
```

But if you want to process 50 transactions, you need

```
[europeBudget spendDollars:numberDollarsInEuroland1];
```

all the way through

```
[europeBudget spendDollars:numberDollarsInEuroland50];
```

This is not a pretty picture. In most applications, you need a way to deal with large numbers of objects.

Often you may not even know how many transactions there are going to be. For example, you may be getting the transactions from a database or from a list of previously stored instructions, or user actions may determine how many transactions you're going to have — the user adds address book entries, for example, or enters transactions as they occur (bingo!).

But even if you did know how many transactions you were going to have, a long series of messages simply makes your program too confusing, prone to error, and hard to extend. Because this is a common problem, a widely available solution is available — container classes — and as I said before, the two most widely used are *dictionary* and *array*. I cover array first.

Taking Advantage of Array Objects

There are two kinds of arrays available to you in Cocoa. The first is an `NSMutableArray`, which (you'll remember) allows you to add objects to the area as needed. The second kind of array is an `NSArray`, which allows you to store a fixed number of objects — a number which is specified when you initialize the array.

`NSMutableArray` arrays are ordered collections that can contain any sort of object. In fact, the collection doesn't even have to be made up of the same objects. You can mix and match objects — `Budget` objects or `Xyz` objects — to your heart's content, as long as what you add to the mix are objects. One of the reasons for introducing you to `NSNumbers`, besides showing you how an object can use other objects, is that when you convert your transactions into `NSNumbers`, you make it possible to store them in an array.

I just said arrays can hold only objects. But sometimes you may, for example, want to put a placeholder in a mutable array and later replace it with the "real" object. You can use an `NSNull` object for this placeholder role.

The first step in being able to eliminate the prospect of a gazillion `spend-Dollar:` messages I mention in the previous section is to create an `NSMutableArray` of the `NSNumber` objects you'll be using in the `spend-Dollars:` message.

```
NSMutableArray *europeTransactions =
            [[NSMutableArray alloc] initWithCapacity:1];
```

This bit of code allocates and initializes the mutable array. When you create a mutable array, you have to estimate the maximum size, which helps optimization. This is just a formality, and whatever you put here does not limit the eventual size. I use 1 to illustrate that; even though I specify one, I can actually add two elements (or more) to the array.

After you create a mutable array, you can start to add objects to it. For example, you can create two `NSNumber` objects

```
NSNumber *europeDollarTransaction =
                [[NSNumber alloc] initWithDouble:100.00];
NSNumber *europeDollarTransaction2 =
                [[NSNumber alloc] initWithDouble:200.00];
```

and add both to the array:

```
[europeTransactions addObject:europeDollarTransaction];
[europeTransactions addObject:europeDollarTransaction2];
```

When you add an object to an Objective-C array, the object isn't copied, but rather receives a `retain` message before it's added to the array. When an array is de-allocated, each element is sent a `release` message. You can find more information about memory management and `retain` and `release` in Chapter 3 of this minibook.

Technically, what makes a collection an array is that you access its elements by using an index, and that index can be determined at runtime. You get an individual element from an array by sending the array the `objectAtIndex:` message, which returns the array element you requested. For example

```
[europeBudget spendDollars:
    [[europeTransactions objectAtIndex:0] doubleValue]];
```

returns the first element in the `europeTransactions` array (remember the first element is 0) as a `double`. (You send the `NSNumber` the `doubleValue` message so that you can continue to use the `spendDollars:` method as is — with the argument type of a `double`.)

In your program, the index you use is the relative position in the array, which starts at 0.

Depending on what you're doing with the array or how you're using it (arrays are very useful), `objectAtIndex:` will be one of the main array methods that you use. The other is `count`, which gives you the number of elements in the array.

Arrays have some other methods you might find useful — methods that sort the array, compare two arrays, and create a new array that contains the objects in an existing array, for example. In addition, mutable arrays have methods that include inserting an object at a particular index, replacing an object, and removing an object.

But one of the most powerful things you can do with an array is to use each of the elements in an array as an argument in a message — which means that you won't have to code a `spendDollars:` message for each transaction. You can even send messages to all the objects in the array.

Book II
Chapter 4

Leveraging the
Foundation
Framework in
Your App

Tiptoeing through an array

Objective-C 2.0 provides a language feature that allows you to *enumerate over* the contents of a collection — which means to process each element of the collection sequentially. This is called *fast enumeration,* and it became available in Mac OS X 10.5 (Leopard) with version 2.0 of Objective-C. (This book is based on using Mac OS 10.6 and OS 3.0 on the iPhone.) Enumeration uses the `for in` feature (a variation on a `for` loop).

What enumeration effectively does is sequentially march though an array, starting at the first element and returning each element for you to do "something with." The "something with" you will want to do in this case involves using that element as an argument in the `spendDollars:` message.

For example, this code marches through the array and sends the `spendDollars:` message using each element in the array (an `NSNumber` "transaction"), eliminating the need for a `spendDollars:` message statement for transaction.

```
for (NSNumber *aTransaction in europeTransactions) {
   [europeBudget spendDollars:[aTransaction doubleValue]];
}
```

Here's the way this works:

1. Take each entry (`for`) in the array (`in europeTransactions`) and copy it into the variable that you've declared (`NSNumber * aTransaction`).

2. You then get the value as a `double` (`[aTransaction doubleValue]`) and use `aTransaction` as an argument in the `spendDollars:` message (`[europeBudget spendDollars: aTransaction]`).

3. Continue until you run out of entries in the array.

The identifier `aTransaction` can be any name you choose. `NSNumber` is the type of the object in the array (or it can be `id`, as I show in Chapter 1 of this minibook).

You may also have noticed that `[europeBudget spendDollars: aTransaction]` is enclosed in braces. The braces signify a block. (Blocks are described with scoping instance variables in Chapter 1 of this minibook.)

To be more formal (put on a tie to read this), the construct you just used is called `for in`, and it looks like

```
for ( Type aVariable in expression ) { statements }
```

or

```
Type aVariable;
for ( aVariable in expression ) { statements }
```

where you fill in what's italicized. There is one catch, however: You are not permitted to change any of the elements during the iteration, which means you can go through the array more than once without worry.

What you have accomplished here is that no matter how many cash transactions you create for Europe, you'll only need one `spendDollars:` message. While that's pretty good, you can see, in Chapter 2 of this book, how to extend that so that you need only one `spend` message for every transaction (both cash and change and any other transaction you can come up with) statement for all the countries you visit.

Working with fixed arrays

Book II
Chapter 4

Leveraging the
Foundation
Framework in
Your App

Actually, `NSMutableArray` is a subclass of `NSArray`, which manages a static array — after you've created it, you can't add objects to it or remove objects from it. For example, if you create an array with a single `NSNumber` to represent a transaction, you can't later add another `NSNumber` object that represents another transaction to that array. While only allowing a single transaction may be good for your budget, it's not very flexible.

`NSArrays` give you less overhead at a cost of less flexibility. So if you don't need to be able to add and remove objects, `NSArrays` are the preferred choice. If you want to use an `NSArray`, you have to initialize it with the objects you want in it when you create it.

So instead of

```
NSMutableArray *europeTransactions =
            [[NSMutableArray alloc] initWithCapacity:1];
  [europeTransactions addObject:europeDollarTransaction];
```

you would do the following:

```
NSArray *europeTransactions =
            [[NSArray alloc] initWithObjects:
            [[NSNumber alloc] initWithDouble:100.00],
            nil];
```

Even though you added only one object to the fixed array, `initWithObjects:` allows you to initialize the array with as many objects as you want, separating them with commas and terminating the list with `nil` as you can see.

As with a mutable array, when you add an object to an `NSArray`, the object isn't copied, but rather receives a `retain` message before it is added to the array. When an array is de-allocated, each element is sent a `release` message.

Using C arrays

Arrays are also a part of the C language. Although you'll probably end up using array objects most of the time, you may also find uses for C arrays (and you can see them used in Apple's documentation and code samples).

Arrays in C store elements just as an NSArray does (although they must be of the same type), and you can think about them as an ordered list as well. That means, for example, that you can store five values of type int in an array without having to declare five different variables, each one with a different identifier.

To declare a C array, use

```
double europeTransactionsArray [2];
```

Now you have an array with enough room for two doubles, effectively similar to the NSMutableArray you created previously; but this one is of fixed size, just like an NSArray. It's really just like having a set of the same variable types, one right after another.

To access a specific element of the array, use

```
europeTransactionsArray[0] = 100.00;
```

This line places 100.00 in the first element in an array. (Again, element 1 is at index 0.)

You can also initialize arrays when you create them. For example

```
double europeTransactionsArray [2] = {100.00, 200.00};
```

creates a two-element array of doubles. You can access an element in the arrays as though it is a normal variable by doing the following:

```
transaction1 = europeTransactionsArray[0];
```

Expanding to multidimensional arrays

One useful aspect of arrays is the ability to use multidimensional arrays. For example

```
int twoDArray[3][3] = {{1,2,3}, {4,5,6}, {7,8,9}};
```

declares and initializes an array that has two dimensions, like a tic-tac-toe board. You can make three-dimensional arrays, and even arrays with more than three dimensions.

Although there are no multidimensional array objects in Objective-C per se, you could have an array of arrays that accomplish the same thing. Arrays of arrays are used extensively in Mac and iPhone programming, and you can find them used in some of the samples on their respective Dev Center sites.

The following code shows the previous example of a two-dimensional array in C, and the code it takes to simulate that two-dimensional array in Objective-C.

```
int main() {

    int twoDArray[3][3] = {{1,2,3}, {4,5,6}, {7,8,9}};
    NSLog (@"twoDArray[2][2] is %i", twoDArray[2][2]);

    NSArray *array1 = [[NSArray alloc] initWithObjects:
                       [[NSNumber alloc] initWithInt:1],
                       [[NSNumber alloc] initWithInt:2],
                       [[NSNumber alloc] initWithInt:3],
                       nil];
    NSArray *array2 = [[NSArray alloc] initWithObjects:
                       [[NSNumber alloc] initWithInt:4],
                       [[NSNumber alloc] initWithInt:5],
                       [[NSNumber alloc] initWithInt:6],
                       nil];

    NSArray *array3 = [[NSArray alloc] initWithObjects:
                       [[NSNumber alloc] initWithInt:7],
                       [[NSNumber alloc] initWithInt:8],
                       [[NSNumber alloc] initWithInt:9],
                       nil];

    NSArray *arrayOfArrays = [[NSArray alloc] initWithObjects:
                       array1, array2, array3, nil];
    NSLog (@"NSArray of NSArrays equivalent is %i",
      [[[arrayOfArrays objectAtIndex:2] objectAtIndex:2]
      intValue]);
}
```

Book II
Chapter 4

Leveraging the
Foundation
Framework in
Your App

The result is

```
twoDArray[2][2] is 9
NSArray of NSArrays equivalent is 9
```

Arrays can be passed as a parameter in C. To accept arrays as parameters, the only thing that you have to do when declaring the function is to specify that its argument is an array by using its identifier and a pair of void brackets []. For example, the function

```
void someFunction (int arg[])
```

accepts a parameter that is an array of `ints`.

Using Dictionaries

Dictionaries are cool. They are like the city cousins of arrays. Both do pretty much the same things, but dictionaries add a new level of sophistication. You can store an object in a list and assign a key that you can then use in the future to retrieve the data, eliminating the need to manually move through long lists of objects to find what you are looking for.

You can use them to hold both property list objects (which I describe in "Using Property Lists" in this chapter) as well as application objects — just as you did with the array that holds `Transaction` objects.

Understanding a dictionary's keys and values

So dictionaries are like arrays, in that they are simply a container for other objects. Dictionaries are made up of pairs of *keys* and *values,* and a key-value pair within a dictionary is called an *entry.* Both the key and the value must be *objects,* so each entry consists of one *object* that is the key (usually an `NSString`) and a second object that is that key's value (which can be anything, but in a property list must be a property list object). Within a dictionary, the keys are unique.

You use a key to look up the corresponding value. This works like your real-world dictionary, where the word is the key, and its definition is the value. (Do you suppose that's why this particular container class is called a dictionary?)

So, for example, if you have an `NSDictionary` that stores the currency symbol for each currency, you can ask that dictionary for the currency symbol (value) for the euro (key).

Although you can use any kind of object as a key in an `NSDictionary`, keys associated with *property list* objects in a dictionary have to be strings (I cover property list objects in "Using Property Lists" in this chapter). You can also have any kind of object for a value, but again if you're using them in a property list, they all have to be property list objects as well.

The same rules hold for arrays. You can use one to hold `Transaction` objects, but if you want to write and read an array as a property list file, the array can hold only property list objects.

`NSDictionary` has a couple of basic methods you'll surely be using regularly:

✦ `count:` — This method gives you the number of entries in the dictionary.

✦ `objectForKey:` — This method gives the value for a given key.

In addition, the methods `writeToFile:atomically:` and `initWith ContentsOfFile:` cause a dictionary to write a representation of itself to a file and to read itself in from a file, respectively.

If an array or dictionary contains objects that are not property list objects, you can't save and then restore them using the built-in methods for doing so.

Just as with an array, a dictionary can be *static* (`NSDictionary`) or *mutable* (`NSMutableDictionary`). `NSMutableDictionary` adds a couple of additional basic methods — `setObjectForKey:` and `removeObjectForKey:`, which enable you to add and remove entries, respectively.

Creating a dictionary

To create a dictionary — say, one that lets you look up the currency symbol for a given country — use the following:

```
NSDictionary *appDictionary = [[NSDictionary alloc]
    initWithObjectsAndKeys:
            @"€", @"Europe", @"£", @"England", nil];
```

This creates a dictionary with two keys, `Europe` and `England`. (To get the currency symbols, in Xcode select Edit➪Special Characters or press ⌘+option+T.)

`initWithObjectsAndKeys:` takes an alternating sequence of *objects* and keys, terminated by a `nil` value. (As you can probably guess, just as with an array, you can't store a `nil` value in an `NSDictionary`.)

The order is *objects* and keys. Developers often get that backward.

This step creates the dictionary that you see in Figure 4-1.

Book II
Chapter 4

Leveraging the
Foundation
Framework in
Your App

appDictionary	
Key	**Value**
Europe	€
England	£

Figure 4-1:
The app-
Dictionary.

To look up the value for a key in a dictionary, you send the `objectForKey:` message bolded in the following:

```
NSLog(@"The currency symbol for the euro is %@",
    [appDictionary objectForKey:@"Europe"]);
```

In this case, you use the key `Europe` to look up the currency symbol in the `appDictionary`. And lo and behold what you get is

```
The currency symbol for the euro is €
```

By the way, if there's no key — for Antarctica for example — `objectFor-Key:` returns `nil`, which gives you the opportunity to respond to the user or do whatever you might want to about it.

On Mac OS X v10.5 and later, `NSDictionary` supports fast enumeration just like its cousin `NSArray`. You can, for example, iterate through a dictionary by using the `for in` construct to go through the keys of a dictionary.

```
for (id key in appDictionary) {
  NSLog(@"key: %@, value: %@", key,
                       [appDictionary objectForKey:key]);
  }
```

These lines of code will go through every key in the dictionary, returning the key in the `key` variable, allowing you to look up that entry using the `objectForKey:` method.

```
key: Europe, value: €
key: England, value: £
```

Dictionaries can be used most effectively with property lists to create a "dictionary of dictionaries", as I show in the next section.

Using Property Lists

You may want your app to store information that will be needed at a later time, or when the app runs again (such as user preference settings). For situations where you need to store small amounts of persistent data — say less than a few hundred kilobytes — a *property list* offers a uniform and convenient means of organizing, storing, and accessing the data.

Property lists are used extensively by applications and other system software on Mac OS X and iPhone OS. For example, the Mac OS X Finder stores file and directory attributes in a property list, and the iPhone OS uses them for user defaults. You also get a property list editor with Xcode, which makes property list files (or *plists* as they're referred to) easy to create and maintain in your own programs.

Figure 4-2 shows a property list that enables you to add the euro and pound symbols to your application.

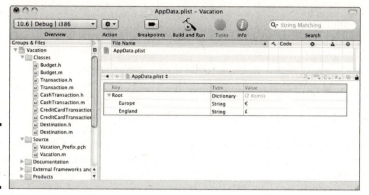

**Book II
Chapter 4**

Leveraging the
Foundation
Framework in
Your App

Figure 4-2:
AppData
property list.

When you know how to work with property lists, it's actually easy, but like most things, getting there is half the fun.

Working with property lists

Property lists are perfect for storing small amounts of data that consist primarily of strings and numbers (as you can see in the plist in Figure 4-2, the Europe and England currency symbols are strings). What adds to their appeal is the ability to easily read them into your programs, use or even modify the data, and then write them back out again. That's because Cocoa provides a small set of objects that have that behavior built in.

The technical term for such objects is *serializable*. A serializable object can convert itself into a stream of bytes so that it can be stored in a file and can then reconstitute itself into the object it once was when it is read back in — yes "beam me up, Scotty" does exist, at least on your computer.

These objects are called *property list objects*. There are two kinds of property list objects:

✦ **Primitives:** The term *primitives* is not a reflection on how civilized these property objects are, but describes the simplest kind of object. They are what they are. The primitive types are strings, numbers, binary data, dates, and Boolean values:

- `NSData` and `NSMutableData`

- `NSDate`

- `NSNumber`

- `NSString` and `NSMutableString`

✦ **Containers:** Containers are a bit more expansive, in that they can hold arrays and dictionaries (other containrs) as well as primitives.

- `NSArray` and `NSMutableArray`
- `NSDictionary` and `NSMutableDictionary`

One thing that differentiates property list object containers (`NSArray`, `NSDictionary`), besides their ability to hold other objects, is that they both have methods called `writeToFile::`, which write the property list to a file, and a corresponding `initWithContentsOfFile:`, which initializes the object with the content of a file. So, if you create an array or dictionary and fill it chock-full of objects of the property list type, all you have to do to save it to a file is tell it to go save itself or create an array or dictionary and then tell it to initialize itself from a file.

The containers can contain other containers as well as the primitive types. Thus, you might have an array of dictionaries, and each dictionary might contain other arrays and dictionaries as well as the primitive types.

Adding a property list to your project

Given the versatility of property lists, you're sure to turn to them time and again. For example, you can use a plist (property list) with the vacation budget app to store the currency symbol for each country in a file, so that you can later read the file into a mutable dictionary.

Here's how you'd incorporate a plist into your Xcode project:

1. **In the Groups & Files list (on the left in the Xcode Project window), select your project and choose File⇨New File from the main menu, or press ⌘+N.**

   The vacation budget app you've been working on in the example is called Vacation — select Vacation at the top of the Groups & Files list and then choose File⇨New File. The New File dialog appears.

2. **Choose Resource under the Mac OS X heading in the left pane and then select Property List from the upper pane on the right, as shown in Figure 4-3.**

3. **Click the Next button.**

4. **Enter a filename in the Name text field and then press Return (Enter) or click Finish.**

   (I went with `AppData.plist`, which is a nice generic name handy for any app.) If you went with my example, you now see a new item called `AppData.plist` under your project name (Vacation), in the Groups & Files list shown in Figure 4-4.

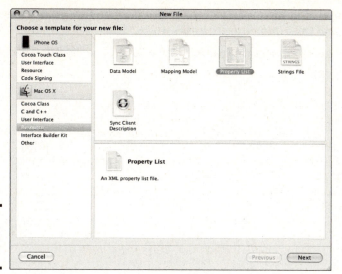

**Book II
Chapter 4**

Leveraging the
Foundation
Framework in
Your App

Figure 4-3:
Creating the
plist.

In the Editor pane, you can see Xcode's Property Plist editor with the
root entry selected. (In this case, it has defaulted to a Dictionary; the
other option is Array.)

5. Click the icon at the end of the entry, as shown in Figure 4-4.

Figure 4-4:
The new
plist file.

A new entry appears.

**6. For the new entry, select String from the Type pop-up menu, as shown
in Figure 4-5.**

It can be any type of property list object, but String, which is already
selected, is the one you want for this specific example.

TIP

7. **In the Key field, enter** Europe**, and then double-click (or tab to) the Value field and enter €, as shown in Figure 4-6.**

To get the currency symbols, select Edit➪Special Characters or press ⌘+option+T.

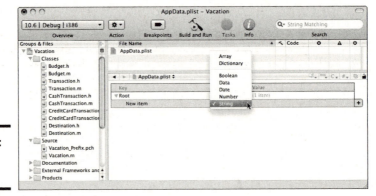

Figure 4-5:
Select
String.

Figure 4-6:
Enter
Europe
and €.

8. **Click the + icon at the end of the entry (row) you just added, and you will get a new entry. This time enter** England **and** £**.**

When you're done, your plist should look like the one you saw back in Figure 4-2.

Using plists

To see how you access the plist from your program, see the bold lines of code in Listing 4-1, which is a reworking of the `Vacation.m` implementation (from Chapter 3 of this minibook) that locates the plist and reads its contents into a mutable dictionary.

Listing 4-1:   Using plists

```
#import <Foundation/Foundation.h>
#import "Destination.h"

int main (int argc, const char * argv[]) {

  NSAutoreleasePool * pool = [[NSAutoreleasePool alloc]
    init];
  NSString* appDataPath  =
        @"/Users/neal/Desktop/Example 15A/AppData.plist";
  NSMutableDictionary *appDictionary = [[NSMutableDictionary
    alloc] initWithContentsOfFile:appDataPath];
  NSString* europeSymbol = [[NSString alloc]
    initWithFormat:@"%@",
          [appDictionary valueForKey:@"Europe"]];
  NSString* englandSymbol = [[NSString alloc]
    initWithFormat:@"%@",
          [appDictionary valueForKey:@"England"]];

  NSString* europeText = [[NSString alloc]
                          initWithFormat:@"%@", @"Europe"];
  Destination* europe = [[Destination alloc]
    initWithCountry:europeText andBudget:1000.00
    withExchangeRate:1.25];
  [europeText release];
  NSString* englandText = [[NSString alloc]
    initWithFormat:@"%@", @"England"];
  Destination* england = [[Destination alloc]
    initWithCountry:englandText andBudget:2000.00
    withExchangeRate:1.50];
  [englandText release];


  for (int n = 1; n < 2; n++) {
    double transaction = n*100.00;
    NSLog (@"Sending a $%.2f cash transaction",
    transaction);
    [europe spendCash:transaction];

    NSLog(@"Remaining budget $%.2f", [europe leftToSpend]);
  NSLog (@"Sending a $%.2f cash transaction", transaction);
    [england spendCash:transaction];
    NSLog(@"Remaining budget $%.2f", [england leftToSpend]);
  }

[europe setExchangeRate:1.30];
[england setExchangeRate:1.40];

  int n =1;
  while (n < 4) {
    double transaction = n*100.00;
```

(continued)

Book II
Chapter 4

Leveraging the
Foundation
Framework in
Your App

Listing 4-1 *(continued)*

```
    NSLog (@"Sending a %@%.2f credit card transaction",
    europeSymbol, transaction);
     [europe chargeCreditCard:transaction];
    NSLog(@"Remaining budget $%.2f", [europe leftToSpend]);
    NSLog (@"Sending a %@%.2f credit card transaction",
    englandSymbol , transaction);
     [england chargeCreditCard:transaction];
    NSLog(@"Remaining budget $%.2f", [england leftToSpend]);
     n++;
    }
    NSString *returnedCountry = [england country];
    NSLog (@"You have deleted the %@ part of your trip",
     returnedCountry);
    [returnedCountry release];
    [england release];

    [pool drain];
    return 0;
}
```

The first bold line of code in Listing 4-1 tells the file system where the
`AppData` file is.

```
NSString* appDataPath =
      @"/Users/neal/Desktop/Example 15A/AppData.plist";
```

The file is on the desktop (`/Users/neal/Desktop`) in a folder called
Example 15A (`/Example 15A`), and the name of the file is `AppData.plist`
(`/AppData.plist`), which is what you named it way back in Step 4 in
"Adding a property list to your project." This is known as a *path*. A path is
a string that contains the location and name of a file. Yours, of course, will
be in the folder in which your project is located. You have to change that
(unless your name is "neal") to reflect your unique configuration.

You need to change the path every time you change the location or name of
a folder your project is in.

When you start programming with the `UIKit` (for the iPhone), you won't
have to specify the path so precisely. You'll generally have your plist files
in either what's called a *bundle* or in your home directory. An application
bundle contains the application executable and any resources used by the
application. It includes, for example, the application icon, other images,
localized content, *and plist files.* You could also store your files in your home
directory, or some other place where you'll be able to find it using Cocoa
functionality available in your program — you won't have to hard code it. In
the case of a Foundation Command Line Tool, however, you need to specify
exactly where the plist file is.

Creating a mutable dictionary

Next, Listing 4-1 shows how to create a mutable dictionary and read the file into it using the `initWithContentsOfFile:` method (it needs to be mutable if you want to modify or update it). The next bit of boldness reads as follows:

```
NSMutableDictionary *appDictionary =
        [[NSMutableDictionary alloc]    initWithContentsOfFi
    le:appDataPath];
```

In the previous section, the code first specified where the file was located (`appDataPath`). Now it sends a message to the `NSMutableDictionary` to initialize itself with that file.

`NSDictionary`, `NSMutableDictionary`, `NSArray`, and `NSMutableArray` all have the methods `initWithContentsOfFile:` and `writeToFile::` that read themselves in from a file and write themselves out to a file, respectively. This is one of the things that makes property list objects so useful.

Property list containers — and *only* property list containers — can read themselves in from and write themselves out to a file. The other property list objects can only store themselves, without any effort on your part, as part of a file.

**Book II
Chapter 4**

**Leveraging the
Foundation
Framework in
Your App**

Creating, initializing, and using the symbol string

The next set of bold lines of code from Listing 4-1 access the key `Europe` and create and initialize a string `europeSymbol` with its value. I do the same thing for `England` and `englandSymbol`.

```
NSString* europeSymbol = [[NSString alloc] initWithFormat:
    @"%@", [appDictionary valueForKey:@"Europe"]];
NSString* englandSymbol = [[NSString alloc]
        initWithFormat:@"%@",
        [appDictionary valueForKey:@"England"]];
```

The `valueForKey:` method looks for the key you give it (`@"England"`). If it finds the key, the corresponding value is returned (in this case, £), if it can't find the key, it returns `nil`.

The rest of the bold lines of code in Listing 4-1 add the right currency symbol to the `NSLog` statements for the currency you are using — $ for your dollar-based transactions and the amount of your budget remaining, and `europeSymbol` (€) and `englandSymbol` (£) for credit card transactions in euros and pounds, respectively.

Dictionaries of Dictionaries

Although using a plist and dictionary this way is very clever (at least I think so), it just barely shows what you can do with dictionaries.

Follow these steps to delete all the entries in the plist and create a more interesting plist.

1. **Delete the Europe and England entries from your plist.**

   That takes you back to what's shown in Figure 4-4. You have no entries.

2. **In the Editor window, the root entry is selected. Click the icon at the end of the entry, as you did in Step 5 in "Adding a property list to your project." (Refer to Figure 4-4.)**

   A new entry appears.

3. **For the new entry, select Dictionary from the Type pop-up menu instead of String. (Refer to Figure 4-5.)**

4. **Type** Europe **as the key.**

5. **Click the triangle next to Europe and make sure it is pointing down, as shown in Figure 4-7. Then select the plus icon to the right of your new entry. (Make sure the triangle is pointing down; if it isn't, you won't be able to add a sub-item.)**

   A subitem is added below Europe.

These disclosure triangles work the same way as those in the Finder and the Xcode Editor. The Property List editor interprets what you want to add based on the triangle. So, if the items are revealed (that is, the triangle is pointing down), it assumes you want to add a subitem. If the subitems are not revealed (that is, the triangle is pointing sideways), it assumes you want to add another item at the same level. In this case, with the arrow pointing down, you'll be adding a new entry to the Europe dictionary. If the triangle were pointing sideways, you'd be entering a new entry under the root.

The icon at the end of the row also helps. A tiny icon of three lines, as you see under the pointer in Figure 4-7, indicates that you are able to add a new subitem of the entry (at a lower level) in that row. If it is a +, this tells you that you're able to add a new item at the same level.

6. **For the subitem entry, choose String from the Type pop-up menu, enter** Currency **as the Key and** euro **as the value, as shown in Figure 4-8.**

   This dictionary will have two entries. One is the name of the currency, in this case euro with the key of Currency, and the other is the currency symbol with the key of Symbol. (You won't actually need the currency name until you add more functionality, but you will have it here for future use.)

7. Repeat Step 5 to add the second `String` subitem entry to the Europe dictionary, this time with the key of `Symbol` and the value of €, as shown in Figure 4-9.

Figure 4-7:
Click to add a new entry to the Europe dictionary.

Book II
Chapter 4

Leveraging the
Foundation
Framework in
Your App

Figure 4-8:
Add an entry to the Europe dictionary.

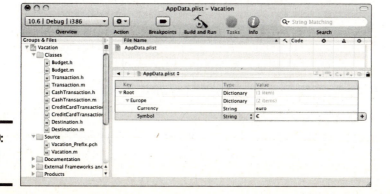

Figure 4-9:
One more entry.

8. **Click the disclosure triangle to hide the Europe dictionary entries, as shown in Figure 4-10.**

Figure 4-10:
Another
dictionary
entry.

9. **Click the + icon next to the Europe dictionary and add the England dictionary, as shown in Figure 4-11.**

Since the Europe dictionary subitems are hidden, clicking the + icon adds a new entry to the root.

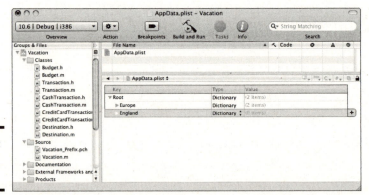

Figure 4-11:
Another
dictionary.

10. **Redo Steps 6 and 7 to create two new `String` subitem entries for the England dictionary. This time use the Key `Currency`, the Value `pound`, the Key `Symbol`, and the Value £.**

When you're done, it should look like Figure 4-12. (Make sure you click all the disclosure triangles to expand it all so you can see it all.)

Remember, the entries in a dictionary can be any property list object. What you have just done is create a dictionary of dictionaries. You have a dictionary for each country that enables you to find the currency (Currency) for each country you're visiting and its associated currency symbol (Symbol).

And because a picture is worth many hours of contemplation, Figure 4-13 shows how everything fits together.

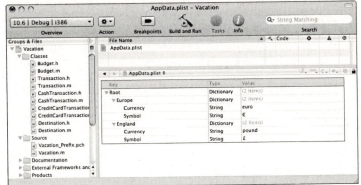

Figure 4-12:
A dictionary of dictionaries.

Book II
Chapter 4

Leveraging the
Foundation
Framework in
Your App

EuropeDictionary	
Key	**Value**
Currency	euro
Symbol	€

appDictionary	
Key	**Value**
Europe	EuropeDictionary
England	EnglandDictionary

EnglandDictionary	
Key	**Value**
Currency	pound
Symbol	£

Figure 4-13:
A dictionary of dictionaries.

Managing a dictionary of dictionaries

Using your new "dictionary of a dictionary" is a little more complex than using a simple dictionary. Admittedly, though, the first thing you make it do is read in the plist and create a dictionary, just as you did with the simple dictionary in the last version:

```
NSMutableDictionary* appDataDictionary=[[NSMutableDictionary
    alloc] initWithContentsOfFile:appDataPath];
```

This time, however, the Europe and England keys have a value of another dictionary instead of a currency symbol. So you treat them as NSDictionary objects. The following code takes the value for both the Europe and England keys and assigns it to pointers to those dictionaries.

```
NSDictionary* europeDictionary = [appDataDictionary
    valueForKey:@"Europe"];
NSDictionary* englandDictionary = [appDataDictionary
    valueForKey:@"England"];
```

Now, you can access the dictionary just as you did before using the key Symbol to get the currency symbol and store it in the variables europe-Symbol and englandSymbol.

```
NSString* europeSymbol = [[NSString alloc]
        initWithFormat:@"%@",
        [europeDictionary valueForKey:@"Symbol"]];
NSString* englandSymbol = [[NSString alloc]
        initWithFormat:@"%@",
        [englandDictionary valueForKey:@"Symbol"]];
```

The methods that add entries to dictionaries (as well as arrays) make *copies* of each key argument and add the copy to the dictionary. The value object, on the other hand, receives a retain message to ensure that it won't be deallocated before the dictionary is finished with it.

Modifying the Property List

One thing about property lists is that they can be modified. Although you don't want to directly modify the system-level files that you'll be using (like preferences — you should use the API provided instead), it's open season on your own files.

One of the limitations of the vacation budget application example is that each time you run it, you start with a clean budget. Although this is fun from a fantasy viewpoint, it doesn't help you manage your money. So, because all good things must come to an end, you need to start keeping track of the remaining budget. Each time you run the program, you start where you left off the last time.

You can do this a couple of ways. You can add a new entry to the existing container you created (`AppData`), or you can create a new file to store what remains in your budget. I show you both ways.

Start by adding a new entry to the `AppData` plist, a `Budgets` dictionary. This dictionary will have keys for Europe and England. The value for each key will be the amount of the remaining budget.

Of course, you could have used Xcode's Property List editor to add the new entry, but I want to show you how to do this kind of thing in your program.

Adding a new entry to the property list

To save the `budget` data, start by declaring two variables to hold the budget balances for `Europe` and `England`:

```
float europeBudget = 1000;
float englandBudget = 2000;
```

Checking to see if the dictionary is there

You have to initialize these variables because the first time you run the program, there will be no `Budgets` key and corresponding dictionary in the `AppData` plist. Initializing the variables gives you a place to start.

Just as you did with the value for the `Europe` and `England` keys, take the value of the `Budgets` key and assign it to a pointer to that dictionary.

```
NSMutableDictionary* budgetsDictionary = [appDataDictionary
    valueForKey:@"Budgets"];
```

This dictionary has to be mutable because you'll be updating the values later with the new balances.

Because the `Budgets` dictionary isn't in the plist, the first time you run the application you need to create it. You can determine whether it's already there by checking whether `valueForKey:` returns `nil` when you look up the `Budgets` key value.

```
if (budgetsDictionary) {
    ...
}
  else {
```

Creating the new entry if it's not there

If `valueForKey:` returns `nil`, you create the new dictionary with the default values and add it to the plist.

```
NSNumber* europeBalance = [[NSNumber alloc]
                          initWithFloat: europeBudget];
NSNumber* englandBalance = [[NSNumber alloc]
                          initWithFloat: englandBudget];
budgetsDictionary = [[NSMutableDictionary alloc] initWithO
   bjectsAndKeys:europeBalance, @"Europe", englandBalance,
   @"England", nil];
```

If you remember, this is similar to the code (in "Creating a dictionary" previously in this chapter) that you'd write to create a dictionary to hold currency symbols. In this case, you create a budgetsDictionary and initialize it with two objects and their keys: the europeBalance object (your old friend NSNumber) with its Europe key, and the englandBalance objects with its England key.

Because dictionaries require each entry to be an object, you need to create NSNumber objects for each of those balances.

Getting the data stored in the dictionary if it's there

If the dictionary is there, you look up the remaining balances for Europe and England using those keys, and you assign those values to the two variables you declared earlier.

```
if (budgetsDictionary) {
  europeBudget = [[budgetsDictionary valueForKey:@"Europe"]
   floatValue];
  englandBudget = [[budgetsDictionary valueForKey:@"England"]
   floatValue];
  }
```

Then, to keep everyone informed, you display the amount left to spend.

```
NSLog(@"You have $%.2f to spend in Europe",
      europeBudget);
NSLog(@"You have $%.2f to spend in England", englandBudget);
```

You also now use these balances when you create the destination objects.

```
Destination* europe = [[Destination alloc]
        initWithCountry: europeText
        andBudget:europeBudget withExchangeRate:1.25];
Destination* england = [[Destination alloc]
        initWithCountry:englandText
        andBudget:englandBudget withExchangeRate:1.50];
```

Updating the dictionary

Every time you run your program, you save what's left of your budget by
using `setObject:forKey:`. If you use `setObject:forKey:` on a key
that's already there, it replaces the old value with the new one. (If you want
to take a key out of a mutable dictionary, use the `removeObjectForKey:`
method.) Remember, these methods work only for `NSMutableDictionary`
objects.

First you create the `europeBalance` and `englandBalance` as objects.

```
NSNumber* europeBalance = [[NSNumber alloc]
        initWithFloat:[europe leftToSpend]];
NSNumber* englandBalance = [[NSNumber alloc]
        initWithFloat:[england leftToSpend]];
```

Now that you have `europeBalance` and `englandBalance` as objects, you
update the dictionary you created earlier when you read in the plist.

```
[budgetsDictionary setObject:europeBalance
                                forKey:@"Europe"];
[budgetsDictionary setObject:englandBalance
                                forKey:@"England"];
```

Now for the exciting part. After you update the `Budgets` dictionary, you
write the whole file back to the plist file using the path you defined earlier
(`appDataPath`).

```
[appDataDictionary writeToFile:appDataPath
                                atomically:YES];
```

Well, actually you don't write it; in fact, you don't do any work at all. `write-
ToFile::` is an `NSDictionary` method and does what it implies. You're
actually directing the dictionary to write itself to a file. The `atomically`
parameter tells it to first write the data to an auxiliary file and when that is
successful, rename it to the path you specified. This writing to an auxiliary
file procedure guarantees that the file won't be corrupted even if the system
crashes during the write operation.

Now that you've written it out, you can use the new updated dictionary
when you read it back in.

The bold lines of code in Listing 4-2 keep a running balance and save it in a
new dictionary in the plist.

Book II
Chapter 4

Leveraging the
Foundation
Framework in
Your App

Listing 4-2: Modifying the Dictionary and Plist

```objc
#import <Foundation/Foundation.h>
#import "Destination.h"

int main (int argc, const char * argv[]) {

  NSAutoreleasePool * pool = [[NSAutoreleasePool alloc]
    init];

NSString* appDataPath  = @"/Users/neal/Desktop/Example 15 C/
  AppData.plist";
  NSMutableDictionary* appDataDictionary=[[NSMutableDiction
    ary alloc]initWithContentsOfFile:appDataPath];
  NSDictionary* europeDictionary = [appDataDictionary
    valueForKey:@"Europe"];
  NSDictionary* englandDictionary = [appDataDictionary
    valueForKey:@"England"];
  NSString* europeSymbol = [[NSString alloc]
    initWithFormat:@"%@", [europeDictionary
    valueForKey:@"Symbol"]];
  NSString* englandSymbol = [[NSString alloc]
    initWithFormat:@"%@", [englandDictionary
    valueForKey:@"Symbol"]];

float europeBudget = 1000;
float englandBudget = 2000;
NSMutableDictionary* budgetsDictionary = [appDataDictionary
  valueForKey:@"Budgets"] ;
if (budgetsDictionary) {
  europeBudget = [[budgetsDictionary valueForKey:@"Europe"]
  floatValue];
  englandBudget = [[budgetsDictionary
  valueForKey:@"England"] floatValue];
}
else {
  NSNumber* europeBalance = [[NSNumber alloc]
  initWithFloat:  europeBudget];
  NSNumber* englandBalance = [[NSNumber alloc]
  initWithFloat:  englandBudget];
  budgetsDictionary = [[NSMutableDictionary alloc]
  initWithObjectsAndKeys:
        europeBalance,@"Europe",
        englandBalance,@"England", nil];
  [appDataDictionary setObject: budgetsDictionary
        forKey: @"Budgets"];
}
  NSLog(@"You have $%.2f to spend in Europe", europeBudget
  );
  NSLog(@"You have $%.2f to spend in England",
  englandBudget );
```

```
NSString* europeText = [[NSString alloc] initWithFormat:
  @"%@", @"Europe"];

Destination* europe = [[Destination alloc]
  initWithCountry:europeText andBudget:europeBudget
  withExchangeRate:1.25];
[europeText release];
NSString* englandText = [[NSString alloc]
  initWithFormat:@"%@", @"England"];

Destination* england = [[Destination alloc]
        initWithCountry:englandText
        andBudget:englandBudget withExchangeRate: 1.50];
[englandText release];

for (int n = 1; n <  2; n++) {
  double transaction = n*100.00;
  NSLog (@"Sending a $%.2f cash transaction", transaction);
  [europe spendCash:transaction];
  NSLog(@"Remaining budget $%.2f", [europe leftToSpend]);
  NSLog(@"Sending a $%.2f cash transaction", transaction);
  [england spendCash:transaction];
  NSLog(@"Remaining budget $%.2f", [england leftToSpend]);
}

[europe setExchangeRate:1.30];
[england setExchangeRate:1.40];

int n =1;
while (n < 4) {
double transaction = n*100.00;
NSLog (@"Sending a %@%.2f credit card transaction",
  europeSymbol, transaction);
[europe chargeCreditCard:transaction];
NSLog(@"Remaining budget $%.2f", [europe leftToSpend]);
NSLog (@"Sending a %@%.2f credit card transaction",
  englandSymbol, transaction);
[england chargeCreditCard:transaction];
NSLog(@"Remaining budget $%.2f", [england leftToSpend]);
n++;
}

NSNumber* europeBalance = [[NSNumber alloc]
  initWithFloat:[europe leftToSpend]];
NSNumber* englandBalance = [[NSNumber alloc]
  initWithFloat:[england leftToSpend]];
[budgetsDictionary setObject: europeBalance
  forKey:@"Europe"];
[budgetsDictionary setObject: englandBalance
  forKey:@"England"];
[appDataDictionary writeToFile:appDataPath atomically:YES];
```

(continued)

**Book II
Chapter 4**

**Leveraging the
Foundation
Framework in
Your App**

Listing 4-2 *(continued)*

```
NSString *returnedCountry = [england country];
NSLog (@"You have deleted the %@ part of your trip",
  returnedCountry);
[returnedCountry release];
[england release];
[pool drain];
return 0;
}
```

Of course, after you build and run this project a few times, you find yourself deeply in debt. If you close and then reopen the project, you'll actually see the new entry in the `AppData` plist. Delete it in the dictionary by using the Xcode Property List editor by selecting the `Budgets` dictionary entry and pressing Delete, and then choosing File⇨Save or pressing ⌘+S.

If you don't see the `Budgets` dictionary in the plist and you don't want to go to the trouble of closing and then opening the project, click in any Key or Value field in the `AppData` plist and add and then delete a space. (You really haven't changed anything, but that's the point.) Then choose File⇨Save or press ⌘+S. You get a message saying, "This document's file has been changed by another application since you opened or saved it"; click Save, and you go back to your original budget.

Chapter 5: Getting Other Objects to Do Your Work for You

In This Chapter

✔ Using delegation to implement a new transaction

✔ Defining formal and informal protocols

✔ Using categories to extend a class

In Chapter 2 of this minibook, you find out how to use inheritance to create subclasses such as `CashTransaction` and `CreditCardTransaction` to implement more specific functionality that was defined generically as a superclass — such as the spend functionality in the `Transaction` class. I also show back in Chapter 2 how you can use inheritance to add new functionality, new methods, and new instance variables to a subclass.

If you were to add ATM transactions (which require a transaction fee) to the mix, it would make sense to use inheritance to create a new subclass for an ATM transaction. If you did that it would also mean (thanks to the wonders of polymorphism, as described in Chapter 2 of this minibook) that the only changes you would have to make besides defining the new class would be to add a new method to `Destination` (in addition to the existing `spend-Cash:` and `chargeCreditCard:` methods): `useATM:` to create the new ATM transaction.

Frameworks provide a good model for how to create extensible and enhance-able applications. As you start to work with the `UIKit` and `AppKit` frameworks, you'll often use inheritance to extend the behavior of framework classes and to add your own unique application behavior. There are times, however, when inheritance is not an option due to technical or architectural reasons (which are beyond the scope of this book).

And yet, all is not lost. Objective-C allows you to accomplish virtually the same thing using *delegation* (which enables you to implement methods defined by other classes) and *categories* (which enable you to extend a behavior of a class without subclassing). In other words, rather than using inheritance and modifying the code in `Destination` (or creating a `Destination` subclass) to implement `useATM:`, you can accomplish the same thing by using delegation and categories.

I'm not necessarily suggesting you implement a new `Transaction` type this way. On the contrary, creating a new `Transaction` subclass is usually the best way to do that. But delegation and categories are used a lot in the frameworks. So, to make using the frameworks as transparent as possible, I explain delegation and categories in this chapter before you stumble across them on your own.

Understanding Delegation

Delegation is a design pattern used extensively in the `UIKit` and `AppKit` frameworks to customize the behavior of an object without subclassing. (I talk a lot about patterns in Chapter 5 of Book I.) Instead of having to bother with subclassing, one object (a framework object) delegates the task of implementing one of its methods to another object. You can use delegation to create a class that implements the `spend` method of the `Transaction` (the *delegator*) class, for example, one that will behave in the same way as subclass.

To implement a delegated method, you put the code for your application-specific behavior in a separate (*delegate*) object. When a request is made of the delegator, the delegate's method that implements the application-specific behavior is invoked by the delegator.

The methods that a class delegates are defined in a *protocol* — similar to the `spend:` protocol you define in the `Transaction` class in Chapter 2 of this minibook.

Using Protocols

The Objective-C language provides a way to formally declare a list of methods (including declared properties) as a protocol. When a framework object has been designed to use delegates to implement certain behaviors, the behaviors it requires (or gives you the option to implement) are defined in a protocol. Protocols declare methods that can be implemented by any class. They are useful for declaring methods that other delegate objects are expected to implement.

Objective-C lets you create *informal* protocols, which is a list of methods which a class can opt to implement (or not), and compiler-enforced *formal* protocols. With formal protocols, the compiler can check for types based on protocols, and objects can report whether they conform to a protocol. I start with formal protocols and cover informal ones later in this chapter.

Declaring a protocol

You declare formal protocols with the `@protocol` directive. If you want to create a Transaction Delegate protocol that requires that all its delegates implement a `spend` message (like its subclasses), you would code the following:

```
@protocol TransactionDelegate
@required

- (void) spend: (Transaction *) aTransaction;

@optional

- (void) transaction: (Transaction *) transaction spend:
    (double) amount;

@end
```

Methods can be optional or required. If you don't mark a method as optional, it is assumed to be required. For example, the preceding code declares the `TransactionDelegate` protocol with a required method (`spend:`) and an optional method (`transaction: spend:`).

The more formal representation is

```
@protocol ProtocolName

  method declarations
@end
```

The method `transaction: (Transaction*) transaction spend: (double) amount` may look a little weird. The method name is `transaction:spend:`, and in some of the framework protocols you can see examples of using a pointer to the delegating object as the first argument in the method.

As I describe in Chapter 3 of Book III, you can use Interface Builder to connect objects to their delegates; or you can set the connection programmatically through the delegating object's `setDelegate:` method or `delegate` property. In this chapter, I show you how to set the connection programmatically.

Generally, protocol declarations are in the file of the class that defines it. In this case, you would add the `TransactionDelegate` protocol declaration to the `Transaction.h` file.

Adopting a protocol

Adopting a protocol is similar in some ways to declaring a superclass. In both cases, you're adding methods to your class. When you use a superclass, you're adding inherited methods; when you use a protocol, you're adding methods declared in the protocol list. A class adopts a formal protocol by listing the protocol within angle brackets after the superclass name.

```
@interface ClassName : ItsSuperclass < protocol list >
```

A class can adopt more than one protocol, and if so, names in the protocol list are separated by commas.

```
@interface Translator : NSObject < English, Italian >
```

Just as with any other class, you can add instance variables, properties, and even nonprotocol methods to a class that adopts a protocol.

In this case, you're creating a new class, `ATMTransactionDelegate` that will adopt the `TransactionDelegate` protocol. To get this done, fire up Xcode and follow these steps:

1. **Select the Classes folder in the Groups & Files list and then choose File⇨New File from the main menu (or press ⌘+N) to get the New File dialog.**

   Selecting the Classes folder first tells Xcode to place the new file in the Classes folder.

2. **In the leftmost column of the dialog, first select Cocoa under Mac OS X; then select the Objective-C class template in the top-right pane. Make sure `NSObject` is selected in the Subclass of the drop-down menu.**

   You see a new screen asking for some more information.

3. **Enter ATMTransactionDelegate.m in the File Name field and make sure the check box to have Xcode create ATMTransactionDelegate.h is selected; then click Finish.**

   This is the new class that will process all ATM transactions.

4. **Add the code in bold to the `ATMTransactionDelegate.h` file.**

   ```
   #import <Cocoa/Cocoa.h>
   #import "Transaction.h"

   @interface ATMTransactionDelegate : NSObject
       <TransactionDelegate> {

   }

   @end
   ```

You add this code because you need to import the header file where the protocol is declared because the methods declared in the protocol you adopted are not declared anywhere else. In this case, you're declaring the protocol in the `Transaction.h` file.

5. **Add the `spend:` and `dealloc` methods to the `ATMTransactionDelegate.m` file.**

```
#import "ATMTransactionDelegate.h"
#import "Budget.h"

@implementation ATMTransactionDelegate

- (void) spend: (Transaction *) aTransaction {

  [aTransaction.budget spendDollars:
                       aTransaction.amount + 2.00];
}

- (void) dealloc {

  [super dealloc];
}

@end
```

When you adopt a protocol, you must implement all the required methods the protocol declares; otherwise, the compiler issues a warning. As you can see, the `ATMTransactionDelegate` class does define all the required methods declared in the `TransactionDelegate` protocol. (Remember, you can add instance variables, properties, and even nonprotocol methods to a class that adopts a protocol, although your `ATMTransactionDelegate` is a class that simply implements the required protocol methods.)

As you can see, this new transaction is at heart a dollar transaction that adds the $2.00 "convenience" fee charged by the ATM. (How convenient.)

Even though `ATMTransactionDelegate` implements a protocol that is used by the `Transaction` object, it doesn't automatically have access to the instance variables of the `Transaction` object. This means that you will have to make `amount` and `budget` `Transaction` class properties and pass them with a pointer to the `Transaction` object so `ATMTransactionDelegate` can access those instance variables.

Adding delegation to Transaction

So far, you've defined a protocol based on the `Transaction` class that requires `Transaction` class delegates to implement the `spend:` method. It now becomes the responsibility of the delegator, `Transaction`, to invoke the `spend:` method in its delegate. Here's how you do that in `Transaction`.

1. **Add the code in bold to the `Transaction.h` file.**

```
#import <Cocoa/Cocoa.h>
@class Budget;

@interface Transaction : NSObject {

  Budget *budget;
  double amount;
  NSString* name;
  id delegate;
}

- (id) initWithAmount: (double) theAmount forBudget:
    (Budget*) aBudget;
- (void) spend;
@property (nonatomic, retain) Budget *budget;
@property (nonatomic, retain) id delegate;
@property (readwrite) double amount;

@end

@protocol TransactionDelegate
@required

- (void) spend: (Transaction *) aTransaction;

@optional

- (void) transaction: (Transaction*) transaction spend:
    (double) amount;

@end
```

You added the `delegate` instance variable, which is the object that implements the behavior you specified in the protocol. An instance variable for an object that implements the behavior is generally declared to be a generic object (`id`) because the point here is that you won't necessarily know what class is implementing the delegate behavior (although you do here). You also added three properties: one to be able to set the delegate, and two others to allow the delegate access to the `amount` and `budget` instance variable. You also declared the `TransactionDelegate` protocol.

2. **Add the code in bold to the `Transaction.m` file.**

```
#import "Transaction.h"
#import "Budget.h"

@implementation Transaction
@synthesize budget, delegate , amount;
```

```
- (void) spend {
  if ([delegate respondsToSelector:
                        @selector(spend:)])
    [delegate spend:self];
}

- (id) initWithAmount: (double) theAmount forBudget:
    (Budget*) aBudget {
  if (self = [super init]) {
      self. budget = aBudget;
    amount = theAmount;
  }
   return self;
}

- (void) dealloc {

  [budget release];
  [super dealloc];
}

@end
```

Book II
Chapter 5

Getting Other
Objects to Do Your
Work for You

You added the @synthesize statement for delegate, amount, and budget to have the compiler generate the getters and setters (accessor methods) for you. When you need to have an instance variable accessible by other objects, you need to have the compiler create the getters and setter accessor methods, as I describe in Chapter 1 of this minibook).

Thus far, Destination has never created a Transaction object, and its spend: method has never been invoked. Using delegation, however, requires creating Transaction objects that invoke the delegate's spend: method in a Transaction object's spend: method.

Because this is a formal protocol, you can assume that since spend: is @required, the delegate object will have implemented it. If this were an informal protocol (which I show later in this chapter), you would need to determine whether spend is implemented. You can determine that by sending the delegate the following message, for example:

```
if ([delegate respondsToSelector:
                        @selector(spend:)])
```

respondsToSelector: is an NSObject method that tells you whether a method has been implemented. If the method has been implemented, you then send it the spend: message.

Categories

To complete the implementation of the ATM transaction you've been work-ing on in this chapter, you need to add a method to the `Destination` class to process an ATM transaction just as it does cash and credit cards (as I show in Chapter 2 of this minibook). The preferred approach is to add the new method to the `Destination` class or add a new method to a subclass — in fact, you'd *have* to add a subclass if you did have the source code, as is the case with a framework — but instead of going with the preferred approach, I want to show another Objective-C feature.

One of the features of the dynamic runtime dispatch mechanism employed by Objective-C is that you can add methods to existing classes without subclassing. Objective-C calls such new methods created in this fashion *cat-egories*. A *category* allows you to add methods to an existing class — even to one to which you don't have the source code. This is a powerful feature that allows you to extend the functionality of existing classes.

How would you use categories to add the `useATM:` method to your `Destination` class? You would start by creating a new category — ATM.

```
@interface Destination (ATM)
```

This line looks a lot like a class interface declaration — except the category name is listed within parentheses after the class name, and there is no superclass (or colon for that matter). Unlike protocols, categories *do* have access to all the instance variables and methods of a class. And I do mean *all,* even ones declared `@private`, but you'll need to import the interface file for the class it extends. You can also add as many categories as you want.

You can add methods to a class by declaring them in an interface file under a category name and defining them in an implementation file under the same name. What you can't do is add more instance variables.

The methods the category adds become honestly and truly part of the class type; they aren't treated as "step methods." The methods you add to `Destination` using the `ATM` category become part of the `Destination` class and are inherited by all the class's subclasses, just like other methods. The category methods can do anything that methods defined in the class proper can do. At runtime, there's no difference.

So, to add this new method, `useATM:`, to `Destination`, you create a cat-egory, as follows:

1. **Select the Classes folder in the Groups & Files list and then choose File⇨New File from the main menu (or press ⌘+N) to get the New File dialog.**

   Selecting the Classes folder first tells Xcode to place the new file in the Classes folder.

2. **In the leftmost column of the dialog, first select Cocoa under Mac OS X; then select the Objective-C class template in the top-right pane. Make sure `NSObject` is selected in the Subclass of the drop-down menu.**

   You see a new screen asking for some more information.

3. **Enter `DestinationCategory.m` in the File Name field and make sure the check box to have Xcode create `DestinationCategory.h`. is selected; then click Finish.**

4. **Be sure to change the `appDataPath` and `balanceDataPath` in main in `Vacation.m` (refer to Chapter 4 of this book for `Vacation.m`) to whatever your folder name is for this project.**

   I use the name Example 16, but use your own project name here.

   ```
   NSString* appDataPath = @"/Users/neal/Desktop/Example
       16/AppData.plist";
   NSString* balancePath = @"/Users/neal/Desktop/Example
       16/BalanceData.txt";
   ```

5. **Put this code in the `DestinationCategory.h` file.**

   ```
   #import <Cocoa/Cocoa.h>
   #import "Destination.h"

   @interface Destination (ATM)

     -(void) useATM: (double)amount;

   @end
   ```

6. **Put this code in the `DestinationCategory.m` file.**

   ```
   #import "DestinationCategory.h"
   #import "Transaction.h"
   #import "ATMTransactionDelegate.h"

   @implementation Destination (ATM)

   -(void) useATM: (double)amount {

     ATMTransactionDelegate *aTransactionDelegate =
       [[ATMTransactionDelegate alloc] init];

     Transaction *aTransaction = [[Transaction alloc]
       initWithAmount: amount forBudget: theBudget];
     aTransaction.delegate = aTransactionDelegate;
     [transactions addObject:aTransaction];
     [aTransaction spend];
     [aTransaction release];
   }

   @end
   ```

The new `useATM:` method is almost the same as the previous `Destination` methods; you even added the transaction to the `transactions` array. The differences here are that you're creating both a `Transaction` object and a delegate that will implement the `spend:` message and updating the transaction object with its delegate in the `useATM:` method.

Figure 5-1 shows the relationship between the `DestinationCategory`'s `useATM:` method, the `Transaction`'s `spend:` method, and the `ATMTransactionDelegate`'s `spend:` method.

Figure 5-1:
The relationship between UseATM: and the Transaction's spend: and ATMTransaction spend: methods.

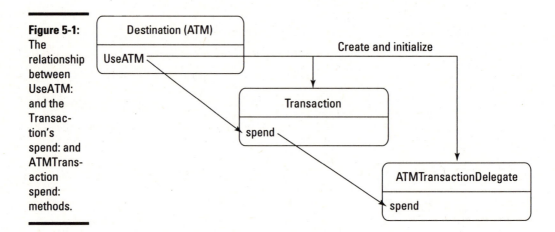

7. **Somewhere in the group of `#imports` in `main` in `Vacation.m`, add**

       #import "DestinationCategory.h"

8. **Scroll down and, after the `while` loop in `main` in `Vacation.m`, add the following line of code — this will be your only ATM transaction.**

       NSLog (@"Sending a $50.00 ATM transaction");
       [europe useATM: 50];
       NSLog(@"Remaining budget $%.2f",
                           [europe leftToSpend]);

9. **Delete the previous `balanceData.txt` file — which makes it easier to see that your updated application works correctly.**

10. **Select the Build and Run button in the Project Window toolbar to build and run the application.**

You now see the new ATM transaction among the other transactions.

Using categories

You can use categories the following ways:

✦ To extend classes defined by other implementers (instead of subclassing — this is what you just did for `Destination`).

✦ To declare informal protocols, described next.

Defining informal protocols

In addition to formal protocols, you can also define an informal protocol by grouping the methods in a category declaration:

```
@interface Transaction (TransactionDelegate)

- (void) spend;

@end
```

**Book II
Chapter 5**

**Getting Other
Objects to Do Your
Work for You**

In this case, you have only one method — `spend` — but if you need more methods for the informal protocol, you can declare them in the same way as `spend` in a list before the `@end`.

In fact, if you added the preceding code to the `Transaction.h` file and changed the `ATMTransactionDelegate.h` as follows:

```
@interface ATMTransactionDelegate : NSObject/*
    <TransactionDelegate> */
```

your program would work the same way.

Being informal, protocols declared in categories are not type-checked by the compiler, nor are they checked at runtime to see whether an object conforms to the protocol.

An informal protocol may be useful when *all* the methods are optional, such as for a delegate, but it's typically better to use a formal protocol that offers optional methods (if you need to provide optional methods). That way you get the benefit of the compiler's check on your code and the runtime system's check to make sure objects conform to the protocol.

Now that you understand the basics of getting other objects to do your work, you also understand the most popular and effective programming style for developing an iPhone app. As you'll see in the next minibook, frameworks help you create extensible and enhance-able applications — you'll be using inheritance to extend the behavior of framework classes and to add your own unique application behavior, delegation to implement methods defined by other classes, and categories to extend a behavior of a class without subclassing.

Book III

Building a Utility App — DeepThoughts

The 5th Wave   By Rich Tennant

"You ever notice how much more streaming media there is than there used to be?"

Contents at a Glance

Chapter 1: Understanding How an App Runs

In This Chapter

✔ **Watching how the template-based app works at runtime**

✔ **Following what goes on when the user launches your app**

✔ **Getting a handle on how nib files work**

✔ **Remembering memory management**

✔ **Knowing what else you should be aware of at runtime**

When you create an Xcode project and select a template, as shown in Chapter 4 of Book I, you get a considerable head start on the process of coding your very own iPhone app. Choosing the Utility Application template for the DeepThoughts app results in a working app that offers an information button to display the Flipside view, and a Done button on the Flipside view to get back to the main view.

As the wise sage (and wisecracking baseball player) Yogi Berra once said, "You can observe a lot just by watching." Before you add anything more to this skeleton of a utility app, it helps to look at *how* it does what it already does. By uncovering the mysteries of what this template does at runtime, you can learn a bit more about where to put *your* code.

As you find out in Chapter 5 of Book I, a *framework* offers common code providing generic functionality. The iPhone OS provides a set of frameworks for incorporating technologies, services, and features into your apps. The framework is designed to easily integrate your code; with the framework in place, all you need to do is *add* the specific functionality that you want in the app — the content as well as the controls and views that enable the user to access and use that content — *to* the frameworks.

App Anatomy 101 — The Lifecycle

The short-but-happy life of an iPhone app begins when a user launches it by tapping its icon on the Home screen. The system launches your app by calling its `main` function. Figure 1-1 shows the contents of the `main` function for the DeepThoughts app.

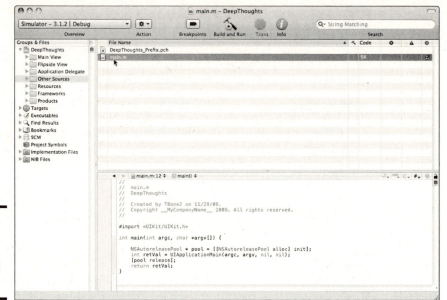

Figure 1-1:
The main
function is
where it all
begins.

The `main` function does only three things:

✦ Sets up an autorelease pool

✦ Calls the `UIApplicationMain` function

✦ At termination, releases the autorelease pool

To be honest, this whole `main` function thing isn't something you even need to think about. What's important is what happens *after* the `UIApplicationMain` function is called. Here's the play-by-play:

1. The main nib file is loaded.

A *nib file* is a resource file that contains the specifications for one or more objects. The main nib file usually contains a window object of some kind, the application delegate object, and any other key objects. When the file is loaded, the objects are reconstituted (think "instant application") in memory.

In the DeepThoughts app you just started (with a little help from the aforementioned Utility Application template), this is the moment of truth when the `DeepThoughtsAppDelegate`, `MainViewController`, `MainView`, and the main window are created, along with `FlipsideViewController` and `FlipsideView`.

For more on those objects and the roles they play in apps, see Chapter 5 of Book I.

2. **The `UIApplicationMain` sends the *application delegate* the `applicationDidFinishLaunching:` message.**

   You can see the `DeepThoughtsAppDelegate.m` file in Figure 1-2, as provided by the template — see how much code is already written for you!

   In this step, you initialize and set up your application. It's up to you whether to display your main application window as if the user were starting from scratch, or to go with the way the window looked when the user last exited the application. The application delegate object is a custom object that you code. It's responsible for some of the application-level behavior of your application. (Delegation is an extensively used design pattern that's introduced in Chapter 5 of Book I and explained more thoroughly in Chapter 5 of Book II.)

3. **The `UIKit` framework sets up the event loop.**

   The *event loop* is the code responsible for polling input sources — the screen, for example. Events, such as touches on the screen, are sent to the object — say, a controller — that you have specified to handle that kind of event, as shown in Figure 1-3. These handling objects contain the code that implements what you want your app to do in response to that particular event. A touch in a control may result in a change in what the user sees in a view, a switch to a new view, or even the playing of the song "Don't Touch Me."

Figure 1-2:
The code that helps initialize and set up the app, as provided by the template.

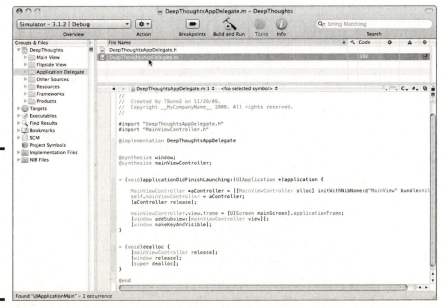

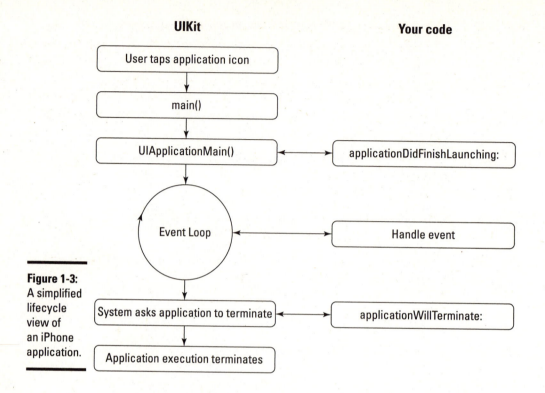

Figure 1-3:
A simplified
lifecycle
view of
an iPhone
application.

4. When the user performs an action that would cause your app to quit, UIKit notifies your app and begins the termination process.

Your app delegate is sent the `applicationWillTerminate:` message, and you have the opportunity to add code to do whatever you want to do before termination, including saving the state the user was in. Saving is important, because then, when the app is launched again (refer to Step 2) and the `UIApplicationMain` sends the app delegate the `applicationDidFinishLaunching` message, you can restore the app to the state the user left it (such as a certain view).

It all starts with the main nib file

When you create a new project using a template — quite the normal state of affairs, as shown in Chapter 4 of Book I — the basic application environment is included. That means when you launch your app, an application object is created and connected to the window object, the run loop is established, and so on — despite the fact that you haven't done a lick of coding.

Most of this work is done by the `UIApplicationMain` function, as illustrated back in Figure 1-3. Here's a blow-by-blow description of what the `UIApplicationMain` function actually does, and Figure 1-4 illustrates the process.

1. **An instance of `UIApplication` is created.**

2. **`UIApplication` looks in the `info.plist` file, trying to find the main nib file.**

It makes its way down the Key column until it finds the Main Nib File Base Name entry. Eureka! It peeks over at the Value column and sees that the value for the Main Nib File Base Name entry is `MainWindow`.

3. **`UIApplication` loads `MainWindow.xib`.**

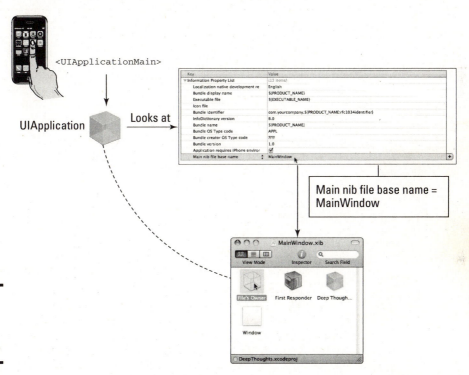

Book III
Chapter 1

Understanding
How an App Runs

Figure 1-4:
The
application
is launched.

The file `MainWindow.xib` is what causes your application's delegate, main window, flipside window, and view controller instances to get created at runtime. Remember, this file is provided as part of the project template. You don't need to change or do anything here. This is just a chance to see what's going on behind the scenes.

To take advantage of this once-in-a-lifetime opportunity, go back to your project window in Xcode, expand the Resources folder in the Groups & Files list on the left, and then double-click `MainWindow.xib`. (You do have a project already started, right? If not, check out Chapter 4 of Book I.) When Interface Builder opens, take a look at the nib file's main window — the one labeled `MainWindow.xib`, which should look like the `MainWindow.xib` you see at the bottom of Figure 1-4.

The `MainWindow.xib` window shows four icons, as follows:

✦ **File's Owner (proxy object):** The File's Owner — the object that's going to use (or *own*) this file — is of the class `UIApplication`. This object isn't created when the file is loaded, as are the window and views — it's already created by the `UIApplicationMain` object before the nib file is loaded.

`UIApplication` objects have a delegate object that implements the `UIApplicationDelegate` protocol. Specifying the delegate object can be done from Interface Builder by setting the `delegate` outlet of a `UIApplication` object. To see that this has already been done for you in the template, click File's Owner, and then click the Connections tab of the Inspector window (or choose Tools⇨Connections Inspector). The `delegate` outlet is set to Deep Thoughts App Delegate, as shown in Figure 1-5.

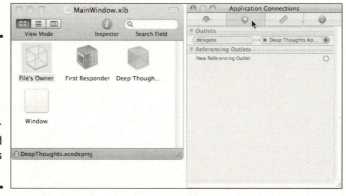

Figure 1-5: The Main-Window.xib in Interface Builder with File's Owner selected and Connections displayed.

✦ **First Responder (proxy object):** This object is the first entry in an application's responder chain, which is constantly updated while the application is running — usually to point to the object that the user is currently interacting with. If, for example, the user were to tap a text field to enter some data, the first responder would become the text field object.

✦ **An instance of `DeepThoughtsAppDelegate` set to be the application's delegate.**

✦ **Window:** The window has its background set to black and status bar set to gray, as shown in Figure 1-6, and is set to *not* be visible at launch. To see the window's attributes, click Window in the `MainWindow.xib` window, and click the Attributes tab in the Inspector window.

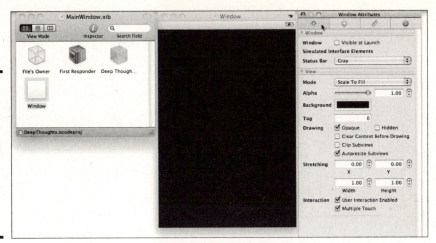

Figure 1-6:
The Main-Window.xib in Interface Builder with Window selected and Attributes displayed.

Initialization

`UIApplication` loads the parts of the `MainWindow.xib` as follows:

1. Creates **DeepThoughtsAppDelegate**.

2. Creates **Window**.

3. Sends the **DeepThoughtsAppDelegate** the **applicationDidFinish-Launching:** message.

4. The **applicationDidFinishLaunching:** method in **DeepThoughtsAppDelegate** initializes MainView.

Listings 1-1 and 1-2 show the header and implementation of `DeepThoughtsAppDelegate`. All this is done for you as part of the Xcode template.

Listing 1-1: DeepThoughtsAppDelegate.h

```
@class MainViewController;

@interface DeepThoughtsAppDelegate : NSObject
    <UIApplicationDelegate> {
    UIWindow *window;
    MainViewController *mainViewController;
}

@property (nonatomic, retain) IBOutlet UIWindow *window;
@property (nonatomic, retain) MainViewController
    *mainViewController;

@end
```

Listing 1-2:   DeepThoughtsAppDelegate.m

```objc
#import "DeepThoughtsAppDelegate.h"
#import "MainViewController.h"

@implementation DeepThoughtsAppDelegate


@synthesize window;
@synthesize mainViewController;


- (void)applicationDidFinishLaunching:(UIApplication *)
    application {

    MainViewController *aController = [[MainViewController
    alloc] initWithNibName:@"MainView" bundle:nil];
    self.mainViewController = aController;
    [aController release];

     mainViewController.view.frame = [UIScreen mainScreen].
    applicationFrame;
    [window addSubview:[mainViewController view]];
     [window makeKeyAndVisible];
}


- (void)dealloc {
    [mainViewController release];
    [window release];
    [super dealloc];
}

@end
```

In Listing 1-2, the MainView view controller is initialized with the
`initWithNibName:bundle:` method. You could use the `application-
DidFinishLaunching` method to do any other application initialization as
well — such as returning everything to what it was like when the user last
used the application.

If you look inside the `MainViewController.m` implementation file, as
shown in Listing 1-3, you can see that `showInfo` initializes the Flipside view
with the `initWithNibName:bundle:` method when the user touches the *i*
information button.

Listing 1-3:   showInfo in MainViewController.m

```
- (IBAction)showInfo {

    FlipsideViewController *controller
    = [[FlipsideViewController alloc]
    initWithNibName:@"FlipsideView" bundle:nil];
    controller.delegate = self;

    controller.modalTransitionStyle =
    UIModalTransitionStyleFlipHorizontal;
    [self presentModalViewController:controller animated:YES];

    [controller release];
}
```

Your goal during startup should be to present your application's user interface as quickly as possible — quick initialization = happy users. Don't load large data structures that your application won't use right away. If your application requires time to load data from the network (or perform other tasks that take noticeable time), get your interface up and running first and then launch the slow task on a background thread. Then you can display a progress indicator or other feedback to the user to indicate that your application is loading the necessary data or doing something important.

The application delegate object (refer to Listing 1-1) is usually derived from `NSObject`, the root class (the very base class from which all iPhone application objects are derived), although it can be an instance of any class you like, as long as it adopts the `UIApplicationDelegate` protocol. The methods of this protocol correspond to behaviors that are needed during the application lifecycle and are your way of implementing this custom behavior. Although you aren't required to implement all the methods of the `UIApplicationDelegate` protocol, every application should implement the following critical application tasks:

✦ Initialization, which I have just covered

✦ Handling events, which I cover in the next chapter

✦ Handling termination, which I cover next

✦ Responding to interruptions and low memory warnings, which I cover later in this chapter

Termination

When your app quits, you should save any unsaved data or *state* (where the user is in the app — the current view, options selected, and stuff like that) to a temporary cache file or to the preferences database. The next time the user launches your app, use that information to restore your app to its previous state.

Getting stuff to (safely) shut down is another application delegate responsibility. Although I don't do this in DeepThoughts, your app's delegate can implement the delegate method `applicationWillTerminate:` to save the current state and unsaved data to disk. (Yes, the disk in the iPhone is not *really* a disk — it's a solid state drive that Apple *calls* a disk.) You can also use this method to perform additional cleanup operations, such as deleting temporary files. I show you how to use the `applicationWillTerminate:` method to save and restore the RoadTrip app in Chapter 3 of Book V.

The state information you save should be as minimal as possible but still let you accurately restore your app to an appropriate point. You don't have to display the exact same screen used previously — for example, if a user edits a contact and then leaves the Phone app, upon returning, the Phone app displays the top-level list of contacts, rather than the editing screen for the contact.

Other Runtime Considerations

Launch, initialize, process, terminate, launch, initialize, process, terminate . . . it has a nice rhythm to it, doesn't it? And those *are* the four major stages of the application's lifecycle. But life isn't simple — and neither is runtime. To mix things up a bit, your application will also have to come to terms with interruptions and memory management.

Responding to interruptions

On an iPhone, various events besides termination can interrupt your app to allow the user to respond — for example, incoming phone calls, SMS messages, calendar alerts, or the user pressing the Sleep button. Such interruptions may only be temporary. If the user chooses to ignore an interruption, your app continues running as before. If the user decides to answer the phone or reply to an SMS message, however, your app will be terminated.

Figure 1-7 shows the sequence of events that occurs during the arrival of a phone call, SMS message, or calendar alert. Here's what that looks like step by step:

1. **The system detects an incoming phone call or SMS message, or a calendar event occurs.**

2. **The system sends your application delegate the `applicationWill-ResignActive:` message.**

Because these interruptions cause a temporary loss of control by your app — meaning that touch events are no longer sent to your app — it's up to you to prevent what's known in the trade as a "negative user experience." For example, if your app is a game, you should pause the game.

3. **The system displays an alert panel with information about the event.**

The user can choose to ignore the event or respond to it.

4. **If the user ignores the event, the system sends your application delegate the `applicationDidBecomeActive:` message and resumes the delivery of touch events to your app.**

   You can use this delegate method to restore the app to the state it was in before the interruption. What you do depends on your app. In some apps, it makes sense to resume normal processing. In others — if you've paused a game, for example — you could leave the game paused until the user decides to resume play.

5. **If the user responds to the event, instead of ignoring it, the system sends your application delegate the `applicationWillTerminate:` message.**

   Your app should do what it needs to do in order to terminate gracefully.

The way the Sleep/Wake button is handled is a little different. When the app enters or resumes from a sleep state, two messages are sent to the application delegate: `applicationWillResignActive:` and `applicationDidBecomeActive:`, respectively. In this case, your app always resumes, though the user might immediately launch a different app.

Book III
Chapter 1

Understanding
How an App Runs

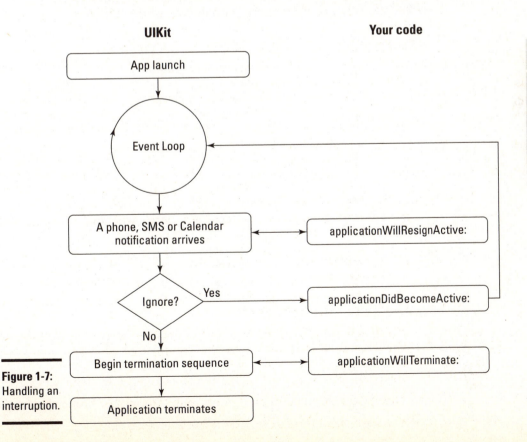

Figure 1-7:
Handling an
interruption.

Seeing how memory management works on the iPhone

One of the main responsibilities of all good little applications is to deal with low memory. So the first line of defense is (obviously) to understand how you as a programmer can help them *avoid* getting into that state.

In the iPhone OS, each program uses the virtual-memory mechanism found in all modern operating systems. But virtual memory is limited to the amount of physical memory available. This is because the iPhone OS doesn't store "changeable" memory (such as object data) on the disk to free up space, and then read it in later when it's needed. Instead, the iPhone OS tries to give the running application the memory it needs — freeing memory pages that contain read-only contents (such as code), where all it has to do is load the "originals" back into memory when they're needed. Of course, this may be only a temporary fix if those resources are needed again a short time later.

If memory continues to be limited, the system may also send notifications to the running application, asking it to free up additional memory. This is one of the critical events that all applications must respond to.

Observing low-memory warnings

When the system dispatches a low-memory notification to your application, it's something you must pay attention to. If you don't, it's a reliable recipe for disaster. (Think of your low-fuel light going on as you approach a sign that says "Next services 100 miles.") UIKit provides several ways of setting up your application so that you receive timely low-memory notifications:

✦ Implement the applicationDidReceiveMemoryWarning: method of your application delegate. Your application delegate could then release any data structure or objects it owns — or notify the objects to release memory they own.

✦ Override the didReceiveMemoryWarning: method in your custom UIViewController subclass. The view controller could then release views — or even other view controllers — that are off-screen. For example, in your new project (DeepThoughts) created with the Utility Application template, the template already supplies the following in both MainViewController.m and FlipsideViewController.m, ready for you to customize:

```
- (void)didReceiveMemoryWarning {
    // Releases the view if it doesn't have a superview.
    [super didReceiveMemoryWarning];
```

```
        // Release any cached data, images, etc that aren't
        in use.
    }

    - (void)viewDidUnload {
        // Release any retained subviews of the main view.
        // e.g. self.myOutlet = nil;
    }
```

✦ Register to receive the
   `UIApplicationDidReceiveMemoryWarningNotification:` notification. A model object could then release data structures or objects it
   owns that it doesn't need immediately and can re-create later.

Each of these strategies gives a different part of your application a chance
to free up the memory it no longer needs (or doesn't need right now). As for
how you actually get these strategies working for you, this is something that
is dependent on your application's architecture. That means you'll need to
explore it on your own.

Not freeing up enough memory will result in the iPhone's OS sending your
application the `applicationWillTerminate:` message and shutting you
down. For many apps, though, the best defense is a good offense, and you
need to manage your memory effectively and eliminate any memory leaks in
your code.

Avoiding the warnings

When you create an object — a window or button for example — memory is
allocated to hold that object's data. The more objects you create, the more
memory you use — and the less there is available for additional objects you
might need. Obviously, it's important to make available (that is, *de-allocate*)
the memory that an object was using when the object is no longer needed.
This is called *memory management*.

Objective-C uses reference counting to figure out when to release the
memory allocated to an object. It's your responsibility (as a programmer) to
keep the memory-management system informed when an object is no longer
needed.

Reference counting is a pretty simple concept. When you create the object,
it's given a reference count of 1. As other objects use this object, they use
methods to increase the reference count, and decrease it when they're done.
When the reference count reaches 0, the object is no longer needed, and the
memory is de-allocated. For details, see the section on raising and terminating responsible objects in Chapter 3 of Book II.

Some basic memory-management rules you shouldn't forget

For those who love "Do and Don't" lists, here are the fundamental rules when it comes to memory management:

✦ Any object you create using `alloc` or `new`, any method that contains `copy`, and any object you send a `retain` message to is *yours* — you own it. That means you're responsible for telling the memory-management system when you no longer need the object and that its memory can now be used elsewhere.

✦ Within a given block of code, the number of times you use `new`, `copy`, `alloc`, and `retain` should equal the number of times you use `release` and `autorelease`. You should think of memory management as consisting of pairs of messages. If you balance every `alloc` and every `retain` with a `release`, your object will eventually be freed up when you're done with it.

✦ When you assign an instance variable using an accessor with a property attribute of `retain`, `retain` is automatically invoked — that is, you now own the object. Implement a `dealloc` method to release the instance variables you own.

✦ Objects created any other way (through convenience constructors or other accessor methods) are not your problem.

If you have a solid background in Objective-C memory management (all three of you out there), this should be straightforward or even obvious. If you don't have that background, no sweat: See Chapter 3 of Book II for some background.

Reread this section!

Okay, there are some aspects of programming that you can skate right past without understanding what's really going on, and you can still create a decent iPhone app. But memory management is *not* one of them!

A direct correlation exists between the amount of free memory available and your application's performance. If the memory available to your application dwindles far enough, the system will be forced to terminate your application. To avoid such a fate, keep a few words of wisdom in mind:

✦ Minimize the amount of memory you use — make that a high priority of your implementation design.

✦ Be sure to use the memory-management functions.

✦ In other words, be sure to clean up after yourself, or the system will do it for you, and it won't be a pretty picture.

Whew!

Congratulations — you've just gone through the "Classic Comics" version of another several hundred pages of Apple documentation, reference manuals, and how-to guides.

Although there's a lot left unsaid (though less than you might suspect), what's in this chapter is enough to not only get you started but also to keep you going as you develop your own iPhone apps. It provides a frame of reference on which you can hang the concepts thrown around with abandon in upcoming chapters — as well as the groundwork for a deep enough understanding of the application lifecycle to give you a handle on the detailed documentation.

Time to move on to the really fun stuff: the user interface controls.

Chapter 2: Understanding the User Interface Controls

In This Chapter

✔ Using Interface Builder to see how controls work

✔ Inspecting an app with a view

✔ Examining how buttons connect to methods

✔ Understanding how events are processed

Steve Jobs said it best: "Design is not just what it looks like and feels like. Design is how it works." That's why you should know how an iPhone app works before trying to design a user interface for one.

For one thing, you need to consider the space and memory limitations of the iPhone display. That's why the Xcode templates are so useful — they take care of the display and memory management so that you can focus on what your app can do. After seeing how much the template provides, you may think the user interface for your app will be a piece of cake — and to some extent, it probably will be, thanks to Interface Builder.

The template you select for your Xcode project (as shown in Chapter 4 of Book I) provides the skeleton of a user interface. For example, the Utility Application template for the DeepThoughts app offers a Main view, a Flipside view, an information button on the Main view to display the Flipside view, and a Done button on the Flipside view to get back to the Main view. The flip graphical effect used for a transition between the Main view and Flipside view is also nicely done.

If you choose the Utility Application template, your app should work like a utility app — choose the appropriate template so that you don't have to reinvent the wheel. And before you start coding, examine how the template's interface works. That's what this chapter is all about.

Running the Utility Application Template

When you start a project based on the Utility Application template, you get the Main view that includes the *i* information button, and the Flipside view with a Title and Done button. The info button is a familiar symbol in iPhone utility-style apps that should always lead to a screen that supplies more information and may also enable the user to add or change information. (A good example is Weather, which offers an info button for adding or deleting cities.) The Done button is also familiar and used extensively to return to the previous screen.

After a user launches your app, the functionality provided in the `UIKit` framework manages most of the application's infrastructure. Part of the initialization process mentioned in Chapter 1 of this minibook involves setting up the main run loop and event handling code, which is the responsibility of the `UIApplication` object. When the application is onscreen, it's driven by external events — such as stubby fingers touching sleek buttons.

You can see this in action in the iPhone Simulator, even before writing any code — build and run the project after choosing the Utility Application template. Choose Build➪Build and Run from the Xcode main menu. (I show you how to build and run, and use the iPhone Simulator, in Chapter 4 of Book I.)

As you can see in Figure 2-1, when the user touches the info button (that is, when you click the button in the iPhone Simulator), the Flipside view appears with the Done button. When the user touches the Done button, the Main view reappears.

Figure 2-1:
Running the app in the iPhone Simulator to show how the Utility Application template's buttons work.

Inspecting the Main View

First things first: Start up Interface Builder from Xcode so that you can examine how the user interface works. To start it, click Resources in the Groups & Files list and then double-click the `MainView.xib` file to launch Interface Builder.

You can then click the Main View icon in the `MainView.xib` window and then click the Identity tab of the Inspector window (or choose Tools➪Identity Inspector) to see the identity of the Main view, as shown in Figure 2-2.

You can see that the Main view of this app belongs to the `MainView` class, and that user interaction has been enabled. You can also click the Attributes tab of the Inspector window (or choose Tools➪Attributes Inspector) to see the Main view's attributes — and you find that it includes a gray status bar and a gray background.

Click File's Owner in the `MainView.xib` window, and then click the Identity tab of the Inspector window (or choose Tools➪Identity Inspector) to see that the File's Owner — the object that is going to use ("own") this file — is of the class `MainViewController` (as shown in Figure 2-3).

How does this work? The Utility Application template set this all up for you, without you having to lift a finger. The next sections spell out in some detail all the heavy lifting the Utility Application template does for you.

Initializing the Main view

If you look back to Chapter 1 of this minibook, you can see that the Utility Application template supplies the following code in `DeepThoughtsApp Delegate.h`:

**Book III
Chapter 2**

**Understanding
the User Interface
Controls**

```
@class MainViewController;
@interface DeepThoughtsAppDelegate : NSObject
    <UIApplicationDelegate> {
    UIWindow *window;
    MainViewController *mainViewController;
}
```

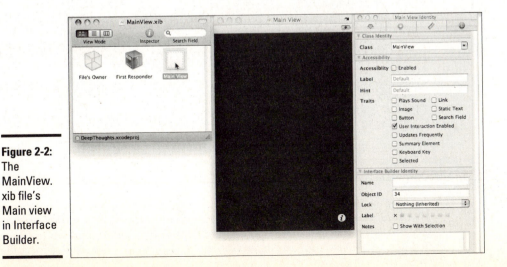

Figure 2-2:
The MainView. xib file's Main view in Interface Builder.

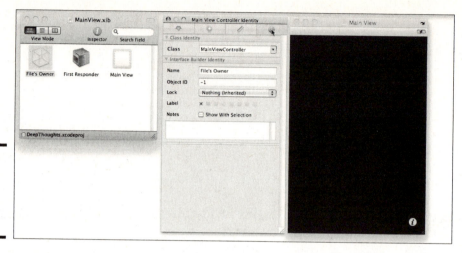

Figure 2-3:
The
MainView.
xib File's
Owner.

This sets up the UIApplicationDelegate protocol with window. The template also declares an accessor method for window and tags it with an IBOutlet so that Interface Builder can discover it, while also declaring an accessor method for mainViewController:

```
@property (nonatomic, retain) IBOutlet UIWindow *window;
@property (nonatomic, retain) MainViewController
    *mainViewController;
```

In the file DeepThoughtsAppDelegate.m, when the application has finished launching, the code implements the appropriate method from the UIApplicationDelegate protocol:

```
@implementation DeepThoughtsAppDelegate
@synthesize window;
@synthesize mainViewController;

- (void)applicationDidFinishLaunching:(UIApplication *)
    application {

    MainViewController *aController = [[MainViewController
    alloc] initWithNibName:@"MainView" bundle:nil];
    self.mainViewController = aController;
    [aController release];
      mainViewController.view.frame = [UIScreen mainScreen].
    applicationFrame;
    [window addSubview:[mainViewController view]];
[window makeKeyAndVisible];
}
```

The MainView view controller is initialized, and addSubView adds this view to window in order to display the Main view. Calling makeKeyAndVisible on window makes it visible as well as making it the first responder for events (touches).

Controller a subset of UIViewController

In `MainViewController.h`, you find this:

```
@interface MainViewController : UIViewController
    <FlipsideViewControllerDelegate> {
}
```

This tells you that `MainViewController` is a subclass of `UIView`
`Controller`. The `UIViewController` class provides the fundamental view-management model for iPhone apps. You use each instance of
`UIViewController` to manage a full-screen view. Because the amount of
available screen space is limited, user interfaces must be divided into one or
more screen's worth of information. The views used to present each distinct
screen are then managed by one of your `UIViewController` subclasses
(such as `MainViewController`).

In `MainViewController.m` near the top, you find the code that sets up
Main View initialization:

```
@implementation MainViewController
- (id)initWithNibName:(NSString *)nibNameOrNil
    bundle:(NSBundle *)nibBundleOrNil {
     if (self = [super initWithNibName:nibNameOrNil
    bundle:nibBundleOrNil]) {
         // Custom initialization
     }
     return self;
}
```

The `MainViewController` object is created by a nib file directly passed
on to `UIViewController` to handle the initialization. (You can add custom
initialization at the point where the `//` comment appears.)

Main view a subset of UIView

Now look in `MainView.h`, and you find the following statement:

```
@interface MainView : UIView {
}
```

This statement declares `MainView` to be a subclass of `UIView`, which is an
abstract superclass that provides concrete subclasses with a structure for
drawing and handling events. The `UIView` class provides common methods
you use to create all types of views and access their properties. For example,
unless a subclass has its own designated initializer, you use the `initWith-`
`Frame:` method to create a view. So, in `MainView.m`, you find this code:

```
@implementation MainView
- (id)initWithFrame:(CGRect)frame {
```

```
    if (self = [super initWithFrame:frame]) {
        // Initialization code
    }
    return self;
}
- (void)drawRect:(CGRect)rect {
    // Drawing code
}
```

The Main view is initialized by passing a CGRect — which defines a rectangular frame that sets the size of the view.

The return type is id because it returns the MainView object. The CGRect frame is then passed to UIView to be initialized. If the UIView initialization works, it returns a non-null pointer to an UIView in self.

As you see in Chapter 3 of this minibook, you can add code to MainViewController.h and MainViewController.m to control the Main view.

Inspecting the Flipside View

Click Resources in the Groups & Files list (if it's not already selected), and then double-click the FlipsideView.xib file to launch Interface Builder.

You can then click the Flipside View icon in the FlipsideView.xib window and click the Attributes tab of the Inspector window (or choose Tools➪Attributes Inspector) to see the Flipside View attributes, as shown in Figure 2-4. You can see that it includes a black status bar and a gray background.

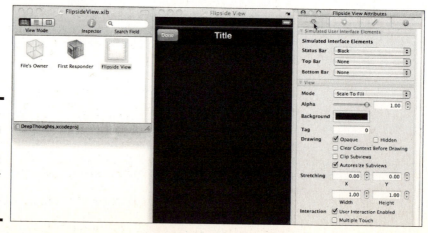

Figure 2-4:
The Flipside View attributes in the Flipside-View.xib file.

Click File's Owner in the `FlipsideView.xib` window, and then click the Identity tab of the Inspector window (or choose Tools⇨Identity Inspector) to see that the File's Owner — the object that is going to use (or *own*) this file — is of the class `FlipsideViewController` (as shown in Figure 2-5).

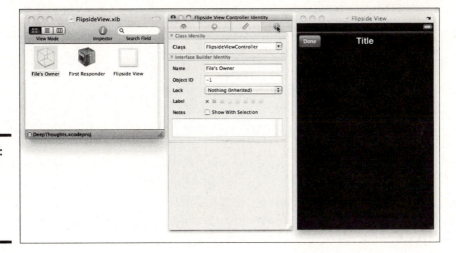

Figure 2-5:
The
Flipside-
View.
xib File's
Owner.

How does the Flipside view appear?

MainViewController initializes the Flipside view

As you may recall from Chapter 1 of this minibook, the `showInfo` method in `MainViewController.m` initializes the Flipside view with the `initWithNibName:bundle:` method when the user touches the *i* information button.

First, take another look at `MainViewController.h`:

```
@interface MainViewController : UIViewController
   <FlipsideViewControllerDelegate> {
}
- (IBAction)showInfo;
```

This tells you that MainViewController is adopting the `FlipsideView ControllerDelegate` formal protocol of `UIViewController` (put in angle brackets). What does it plan to do with it?

Take a look further down in `MainViewController.m`, and you find this:

```
- (void)flipsideViewControllerDidFinish:(FlipsideViewControl
   ler *)controller {
   [self dismissModalViewControllerAnimated:YES];
```

```
}
- (IBAction)showInfo {
    FlipsideViewController *controller
    = [[FlipsideViewController alloc]
    initWithNibName:@"FlipsideView" bundle:nil];
    controller.delegate = self;
    controller.modalTransitionStyle =
    UIModalTransitionStyleFlipHorizontal;
    [self presentModalViewController:controller animated:YES];
    [controller release];
}
```

This initializes the Flipside View nib file (`FlipsideView.xib`) when
`showInfo` is activated. While doing so, it also sets the `controller.`
`modalTransitionStyle` to `UIModalTransitionStyleFlipHorizontal`
for the slick animated flip transition when opening the Flipside view.

In `FlipSideViewController.h`, the `UIViewController` protocol
`FlipsideViewControllerDelegate` is used:

```
@protocol FlipsideViewControllerDelegate;
@interface FlipsideViewController : UIViewController {
    id <FlipsideViewControllerDelegate> delegate;
}
@property (nonatomic, assign) id
    <FlipsideViewControllerDelegate> delegate;
- (IBAction)done;
@end
@protocol FlipsideViewControllerDelegate
- (void)flipsideViewControllerDidFinish:(FlipsideViewControl
    ler *)controller;
@end
```

In `FlipSideViewController.m`, the class doesn't use an initialization
method like `MainViewController.m`. Instead, it uses a method called
`viewDidLoad`, which is most commonly used to perform additional initialization steps on views that are loaded from nib files:

```
@implementation FlipsideViewController
@synthesize delegate;
- (void)viewDidLoad {
    [super viewDidLoad];
    self.view.backgroundColor = [UIColor
    viewFlipsideBackgroundColor];
}
- (IBAction)done {
    [self.delegate flipsideViewControllerDidFinish:self];
}
```

This method is implemented in `UIViewController` — the code overrides it in order to change something after the view has been loaded from a nib (the background color).

Flipside view a subset of UIView

In `FlipsideView.h`, you find the following statement:

```
@interface FlipsideView: UIView {
}
```

This statement declares `FlipsideView` to be a subclass of `UIView`. And in `FlipsideView.m`, you find this code:

```
@implementation FlipsideView
- (id)initWithFrame:(CGRect)frame {
    if (self = [super initWithFrame:frame]) {
        // Initialization code
    }
    return self;
}
- (void)drawRect:(CGRect)rect {
    // Drawing code
}
```

The view is initialized the same way as the Main view — by passing a `CGRect` defining a rectangular frame. The return type is `id` since it returns the `FlipsideView` object.

As you see in Chapter 4 of this minibook, you can add code to `FlipsideViewController.h` and `FlipsideViewController.m` to control the Flipside view.

Unraveling the Info and Done Buttons

Now I show you how to take apart the Info and Done buttons supplied with the Utility Application template to see how they work — and, in the process, you find out a bit about how to connect user interface controls to your code.

Start with the Info button in the Main view: in Xcode, click Resources in the Groups & Files list, and then double-click the `MainView.xib` file to launch Interface Builder. In the Main View window, select the *i* (Info button) in the lower-right corner, and click the Attributes tab in the Inspector window (as shown in Figure 2-6) or choose Tools⇨Attributes Inspector.

**Book III
Chapter 2**

Understanding
the User Interface
Controls

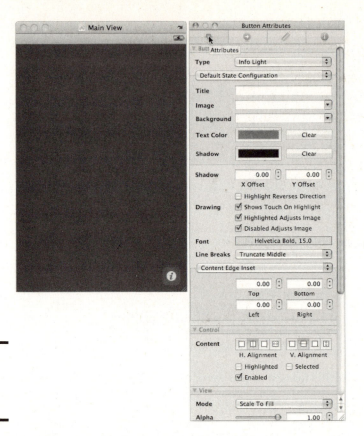

Figure 2-6:
The Info button's attributes.

As you can see in Figure 2-6, the Info button supplied with the Utility Application template is set to be a Light Info button in the Type pop-up menu in the Attributes Inspector. The iPhone SDK includes a specific button type for creating an Info button, in both dark background and light background versions, which enables the button to appear over most backgrounds. In Figure 2-6, you can see what the button looks like in its Default State Configuration; click the pop-up menu under the Type pop-up menu to choose other configurations, such as Highlighted State Configuration or Selected State Configuration, to see what the button looks like when highlighted or selected. You can also change the Text Color, Shadow, Background, and other attributes in the Attributes Inspector.

Info connects to showinfo

To find out more about the Info button in the Main view, Control-click (or right-click if you have a two-button pointing device) the Info button, as Figure 2-7 demonstrates, to see the button's possible events. The one highlighted is the button's actual event.

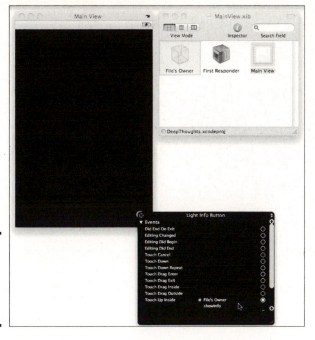

Figure 2-7:
The Info button's event is highlighted.

To see these events clearly, click the center View Mode button at the top of the `MainView.xib` window to show the window in hierarchical navigation view mode, and then click the triangle next to Main View to reveal its contents. You should see Light Info Button under Main View, as shown in Figure 2-8. Select Light Info Button to see the button attributes in the Inspector window, and click the Connections tab in the Inspector window (or choose Tools⇨Connections Inspector) to see the button's connections (refer to Figure 2-8).

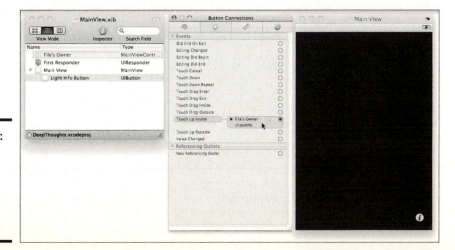

Figure 2-8:
The Info button reacts to a Touch Up Inside event.

The Info button reacts to a Touch Up Inside event — which occurs when the button is touched and then released, symbolizing a click. When that happens, it invokes showinfo in MainViewController — see Listing 2-1 and 2-2 (code for showinfo in bold).

Listing 2-1: MainViewController.h

```
#import "FlipsideViewController.h"
@interface MainViewController : UIViewController
    <FlipsideViewControllerDelegate> {
}
- (IBAction)showInfo;
@end
```

Listing 2-2: MainViewController.m

```
#import "MainViewController.h"
#import "MainView.h"

@implementation MainViewController
- (id)initWithNibName:(NSString *)nibNameOrNil
    bundle:(NSBundle *)nibBundleOrNil {
    if (self = [super initWithNibName:nibNameOrNil
    bundle:nibBundleOrNil]) {
        // Custom initialization
    }
    return self;
}
/*
 // Implement viewDidLoad to do additional setup after
    loading the view, typically from a nib.
 - (void)viewDidLoad {
 [super viewDidLoad];
 }
 */

/*
 // Override to allow orientations other than the default
    portrait orientation.
 - (BOOL)shouldAutorotateToInterfaceOrientation:(UIInterfaceO
   rientation)interfaceOrientation {
 // Return YES for supported orientations
 return (interfaceOrientation ==
   UIInterfaceOrientationPortrait);
 }
 */
- (void)flipsideViewControllerDidFinish:(FlipsideControl
   ler *)controller {

    [self dismissModalViewControllerAnimated:YES];
```

```
}
- (IBAction)showInfo {

    FlipsideViewController *controller
    = [[FlipsideViewController alloc]
    initWithNibName:@"FlipsideView" bundle:nil];
    controller.delegate = self;

    controller.modalTransitionStyle =
    UIModalTransitionStyleFlipHorizontal;
    [self presentModalViewController:controller animated:YES];

    [controller release];
}
/*
 // Override to allow orientations other than the default
    portrait orientation.
 - (BOOL)shouldAutorotateToInterfaceOrientation:(UIInterfaceO
    rientation)interfaceOrientation {
 // Return YES for supported orientations
 return (interfaceOrientation ==
    UIInterfaceOrientationPortrait);
 }
 */

- (void)didReceiveMemoryWarning {
    // Releases the view if it doesn't have a superview.
    [super didReceiveMemoryWarning];

    // Release any cached data, images, etc that aren't in
    use.
}
- (void)viewDidUnload {
    // Release any retained subviews of the main view.
    // e.g. self.myOutlet = nil;
}
- (void)dealloc {
    [super dealloc];
}
@end
```

Done sends an action to FlipsideViewController

To see how the Done button in the Flipside view works, double-click the
`FlipsideView.xib` file (in Resource) to launch Interface Builder. In the
Flipside View window, select the Done button in the upper-left corner
and then click the Attributes tab in the Inspector window or choose
Tools⇨Attributes Inspector to see its attributes. The button's class is
`UIBarButtonItem`, which encapsulates the properties and behaviors of
items added to `UIToolbar` and `UINavigationBar` objects — it inherits
basic button behavior from its parent class.

To see what's really going on, click the center View Mode button at the top of the `FlipsideView.xib` window to show it in hierarchical navigation view mode, and then click the triangle next to `FlipsideView` to reveal its contents. As shown in Figure 2-9, Navigation Bar appears first; click its triangle to reveal Navigation Item (Title), and click its triangle to reveal (finally!) the Bar Button Item (Done). The template has embedded the Bar Button Item (Done) object within the Navigation Item (title), which is embedded in the Navigation Bar.

The Navigation Bar's class is `UINavigationBar`, of course. The `UINavigationBar` class implements a control for navigating hierarchical content. It's a bar at the top of the screen that can offer buttons for navigating up and down a hierarchy. The primary properties are a left (back) button, a center title, and an optional right button. You use a navigation item (an instance of the `UINavigationItem` class) to specify what buttons or custom views you want displayed in the bar. A navigation bar manages a stack of `UINavigationItem` objects such as the Navigation Item (Title) (`UINavigationItem`) and the Bar Button Item (Done) (`UIBarButtonItem`).

Select Bar Button Item (Done) to see the button attributes in the Inspector window, and click the Connections tab in the Inspector window (or choose Tools➪Connections Inspector) to see the button's connections. (Refer to Figure 2-9.)

In Sent Actions, "done" is connected to the File's Owner (in this case, `FlipsideViewController`). You can see how this is set up in Listing 2-3 and 2-4.

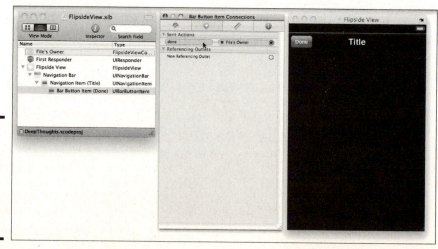

Figure 2-9: The Bar Button Item (Done) is connected to the File's Owner.

Listing 2-3: FlipsideViewController.h

```
@protocol FlipsideViewControllerDelegate;

@interface FlipsideViewController : UIViewController {
   id <FlipsideViewControllerDelegate> delegate;
}

@property (nonatomic, assign) id
    <FlipsideViewControllerDelegate> delegate;
- (IBAction)done;

@end

@protocol FlipsideViewControllerDelegate
- (void)flipsideViewControllerDidFinish:(FlipsideViewControl
    ler *)controller;
@end
```

Listing 2-4: FlipsideViewController.m

```
#import "FlipsideViewController.h"

@implementation FlipsideViewController
@synthesize delegate;

- (void)viewDidLoad {
    [super viewDidLoad];
    self.view.backgroundColor = [UIColor
    viewFlipsideBackgroundColor];
}
- (IBAction)done {
    [self.delegate flipsideViewControllerDidFinish:self];
}
/*
 // Override to allow orientations other than the default
    portrait orientation.
 - (BOOL)shouldAutorotateToInterfaceOrientation:(UIInterfaceO
    rientation)interfaceOrientation {
 // Return YES for supported orientations
 return (interfaceOrientation ==
    UIInterfaceOrientationPortrait);
 }
 */
- (void)didReceiveMemoryWarning {
    // Releases the view if it doesn't have a superview.
    [super didReceiveMemoryWarning];

    // Release any cached data, images, etc that aren't in
    use.
}
```

(continued)

Book III
Chapter 2

Understanding
the User Interface
Controls

Listing 2-4 *(continued)*

```
- (void)viewDidUnload {
    // Release any retained subviews of the main view.
    // e.g. self.myOutlet = nil;
}
- (void)dealloc {
    [super dealloc];
}
@end
```

The code in `FlipsideViewController.h` (Listing 2-3) declares the delegate for the `FlipsideViewController` and adds it as a property. The code in `FlipsideViewController.m` (Listing 2-4) uses the delegate object to intercept the "done" message.

Understanding Event Processing

What actually happens when the Info button reacts to a Touch Up Inside event? The event is processed. Here's a rundown of how such events drive a process inside the app (and you can see the process illustrated in Figure 2-10):

1. **You have an event — the user taps a button, for example.**

The touch of a finger (or lifting it from the screen) adds a touch event to the application's event queue, where it's *encapsulated* in — placed into, in other words — a `UIEvent` object. There is a `UITouch` object for each finger touching the screen, so you can track individual touches. As the user manipulates the screen with his or her fingers, the system reports the changes for each finger in the corresponding `UITouch` object.

2. **The run loop monitor dispatches the event.**

When there's something to process, the event-handling code of the `UIApplication` processes touch events by dispatching them to the appropriate *responder* object — the object that has signed up to take responsibility for doing something when an event happens (when the user touches the screen, for example). Responder objects can include instances of `UIApplication`, `UIWindow`, `UIView`, and its subclasses (all which inherit from `UIResponder`).

3. **A responder object decides how to handle the event.**

For example, a touch event occurring in a button (view) will be delivered to the button object. The button handles the event by sending an action message to another object — in this case, the `UIViewController` object. Setting it up this way enables you to use standard button objects without having to muck about in their innards — just tell the button what method you want invoked in your view controller, and you're basically set.

Processing the message may result in changes to a view, or a new view altogether, or some other kind of change in the user interface. When this happens, the view and graphics infrastructure takes over and processes the required drawing events.

4. **You're sent back to the event loop.**

   After an event is handled or discarded, control passes back to the run loop. The run loop then processes the next event or puts the thread to sleep if there's nothing more for it to do.

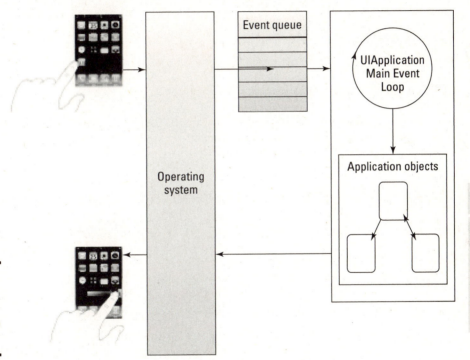

Figure 2-10: Processing events in the main run loop.

Book III
Chapter 2

Understanding
the User Interface
Controls

In putting together a great iPhone app, a big part of the process involves getting your app's user interface to work well. Interfaces are important — so important, in fact, that the templates try to enforce a user-friendly interface that adheres to Apple's standards. If you're putting out a utility app, Apple would really like you to use the Info and Done buttons and organize the app to have a Main view and a Flipside view. It's just the way it's done, so pick your template wisely.

But the user interface isn't the only important thing. Your iPhone app has to actually *do* something, and that's the subject of Chapter 3 of this minibook.

Chapter 3: Developing the Main View

In This Chapter

✔ **Using your friendly Xcode Text editor**

✔ **Adding your code to the Main view controller**

✔ **Creating animation in the Main view**

I wanted to keep this example iPhone utility app as simple as possible so that you can focus on how it works as an app in the iPhone OS — and you can then go off and design your complex app. The Utility Application template creates the skeleton for a fully functioning iPhone app (DeepThoughts) — and now you get to flesh it all out with some code that transforms it from an app that just sits there and looks pretty to an app that actually *does* something.

DeepThoughts is supposed to display "falling" words — text flowing down the Main view in different sizes, starting with the words "Peace Love Groovy Music" — at a specified time interval and at a speed the user can change. DeepThoughts should also allow the user to enter text in the Flipside view to substitute different words for "Peace Love Groovy Music" and, eventually, to select a photo from the iPhone's photo library to substitute for the words.

As you add the code to DeepThoughts, I also explain some of the features of the Xcode Text editor.

Using the Xcode Text Editor

The main tool you use to write code for an iPhone application is the Xcode Text editor. Apple has gone out of its way to make the Text editor as user-friendly as possible, as evidenced by the following list of (quite convenient) features:

✦ **Code Sense:** Code Sense is a feature of the editor that shows arguments, placeholders, and suggested code as you type statements. Code Sense can be really useful, especially if you're like me and forget exactly what the arguments for a function actually are. When Code Sense is active (it is by default), Xcode uses the text you typed, as well as the context within which you typed it, to provide suggestions for completing what it thinks you're *going to* type. You can accept suggestions by pressing Tab or Return. You may also display a list of completions by pressing the Escape key. You can set options for Code Sense by choosing Xcode⇨Preferences and clicking the Code Sense tab.

✦ **Code folding in the focus ribbon:** With code folding, you can collapse code that you're not working on and display only the code that requires your attention. You do this by clicking in the Focus Ribbon column to the left of the code you want to hide (right there between the gutter, which displays line numbers and breakpoints, and the editor) to show a disclosure triangle. Clicking the disclosure triangle hides or shows blocks of code.

✦ **Switching between header and implementation windows:** On the toolbar above the Text editor, you click the last icon before the lock to switch from the `.h` (header) file to the `.m` (implementation) file, and vice versa. While the header declares the class's instance variables and methods, the implementation holds the logic of your code. If you look inside the `MainView` and `FlipsideView` sections of the Groups & Files list in the Project window, you can see the separate `.h` and `.m` files for the Main and Flipside view classes.

✦ **Launching a file in a separate window:** Double-click the filename to launch the file in a new window. If you have a big monitor, or multiple monitors, this new window enables you to look at more than one file at a time. You can, for example, look at the method of one class *and* the method it invokes in the same class or even a different class.

Accessing Documentation

Like many developers, you may find yourself wanting to dig deeper when it comes to a particular bit of code. That's when you'll really appreciate Xcode's Quick Help, header file access, Documentation window, Help menu, and Find tools. With these tools, you can quickly access the documentation for a particular class, method, or property.

To see how this works, say you have the Project window open with the code displayed in Figure 3-1. What if you wanted to find out more about `UIApplicationDelegate`?

Quick Help

Quick Help is an unobtrusive window that provides the documentation for a single symbol. It pops up inline, although you can use Quick Help as a symbol inspector (which stays open) by moving the window after it opens. You can also customize the display in Documentation preferences in Xcode preferences.

To get Quick Help for a symbol, double-click to select the symbol in the Text editor (in this case UIApplicationDelegate; see Figure 3-1) and then choose Help⇨Quick Help.

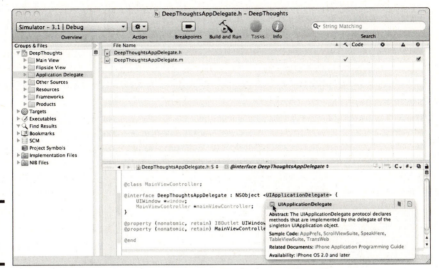

Book III
Chapter 3

Developing the
Main View

Figure 3-1:
Getting
Quick Help.

The header file for a symbol

Headers are a big deal in code because they're the place where you find the class declaration, which includes all of its instance variables and method declarations. To get the header file for a symbol, press ⌘ while double-clicking the symbol in the Text editor. For example, in Figure 3-2, I pressed ⌘ and then double-clicked UIApplicationDelegate.

This trick works for the classes you create as well.

Documentation window

The Documentation window lets you browse and search items that are part of the Apple Developer Connection Reference Library (a collection of developer documentation and tech notes) as well as any third-party documentation you have installed.

You access the documentation by pressing ⌘+Option while double-clicking a symbol. You get access to the Application Programming Interface (API) reference (among other things) that provides information about the symbol. This enables you to get the documentation about a method to find out more about it or the methods and properties in a framework class. In Figure 3-3, I pressed ⌘+Option while double-clicking UIApplicationDelegate.

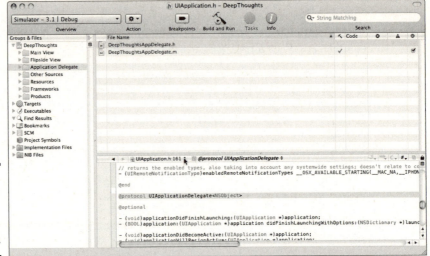

Figure 3-2:
The header file for UIApplicationDelegate.

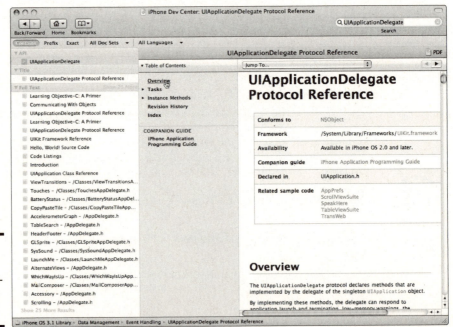

Figure 3-3:
The Documentation window.

Using the Documentation window, you can browse and search the developer documentation — the API references, guides, and article collections about particular tools or technologies — installed on your computer. It's the go-to place for getting documentation about a method or more info about the methods and properties in a framework class.

Help menu

The Help menu's search field also lets you search Xcode documentation as well as open the Documentation window and Quick Help.

You can also right-click on a symbol and get a pop-up menu that gives you similar options to what you see in the Help menu, including Quick Help (and other related functions).

Find

Xcode can also help you find things in your own project. The submenu that you access by choosing Edit⇨Find provides several options for finding text in your own project.

You'll find that, as your classes get bigger, sometimes you'll want to find a single symbol or all occurrences of a symbol in a file or class. You can easily do that by choosing Edit⇨Find⇨Find or pressing ⌘+F, which opens a Find toolbar to help you search the file in the editor window. In Figure 3-4, for example, I typed **viewDidLoad** in the Find toolbar, and Xcode found all the instances of viewDidLoad in that file and highlighted them.

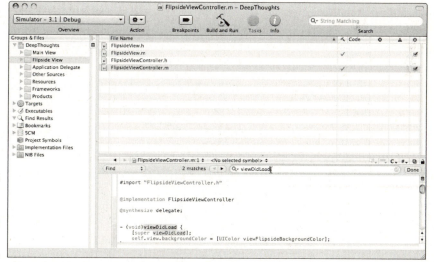

Figure 3-4:
Finding
viewDidLoad
in a file.

If you select an item in the top pane of the editor, as you can see in Figure 3-4, the file in which that instance occurs is opened in the bottom pane of the editor and the reference highlighted.

You can also use Find to go through your whole project by choosing Edit⇨Find⇨Find in Project or by pressing ⌘+Shift+F, which opens the window shown in Figure 3-5. You can type something like **MainViewController** in the

Find field, and then in the drop-down menu, choose In Project, or as I chose in Figure 3-5, In All Open Files. (A great feature for tracking down something in your code — you're sure to use it often.)

Your searches are saved in your project. Click the triangle next to Find Results in the Groups & Files list to reveal your searches, as shown in Figure 3-6. Select a search to see the search results.

Now that you have some idea of how to use the Xcode Text editor, it's time to write some code.

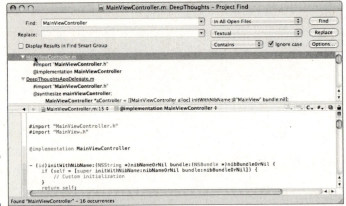

Figure 3-5:
Project Find.

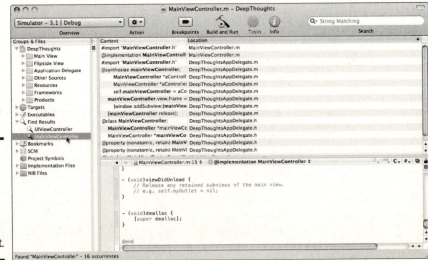

Figure 3-6:
Revisiting
your
searches,
which are
saved in
your project.

Where Does Your Code Go?

One of the biggest challenges facing a developer working with an unfamiliar framework and template is figuring out where in the *control flow* — the sequence in which messages are sent during execution — to put the code to get something done.

The delegate object

As you may recall from Chapter 1 of this minibook, `UIApplication` loads the parts of the `MainWindow.xib` to create `DeepThoughtsAppDelegate` and the window, and sends `DeepThoughtsAppDelegate` the `applicationDidFinishLaunching:` message. The `applicationDidFinishLaunching:` method in `DeepThoughtsAppDelegate` initializes `MainView`.

The `applicationDidFinishLaunching:` message is sent at the very beginning, before the user can even see anything on the screen. Here's where you'd insert your code to initialize your application — where you'd load data, for example, or restore the state of the application to where it was the last time the user exited.

The controller object

`MainViewController` is the controller responsible for managing `MainView`. If you look at the code in `MainViewController.m` (as shown in Chapter 2 of this minibook), you see the following commented-out code:

```
/*
// Implement viewDidLoad to do additional setup after
   loading the view, typically from a nib.
- (void)viewDidLoad {
[super viewDidLoad];
}
*/
```

The `viewDidLoad` message is sent right after the view has been loaded from the nib file — check out Chapter 1 of this minibook for a complete explanation of that loading process. This is the place where you insert your code for *view initialization*, which in this case means displaying the DeepThoughts' falling words.

Although I don't use it in this example, you could also make use of the `viewWillAppear` message, which is sent right before the view will appear. This would be the place to insert your code to do anything needed before the view becomes visible. Both `viewDidLoad` and `viewWillAppear` are methods declared in the `UIViewController` class and are invoked at the appropriate times by the framework.

Creating an Animated View

To add the code you need to display the falling words at speed that could be set by the user, first open `MainViewController.h` and insert the code in bold in Listing 3-1.

Listing 3-1: MainViewController.h

```
#import "FlipsideViewController.h"

@interface MainViewController : UIViewController
    <FlipsideViewControllerDelegate> {
  UIImage      *fallingImage;
  NSString     *fallingWords;
  double        speed;
}
- (IBAction)showInfo;
@end
```

This establishes the falling image itself (`fallingImage`), which will contain the text string in `fallingWords` and will flow down the display according to the `speed`.

Next, open `MainViewController.m` and insert the code in bold in Listing 3-2, which replaces the commented-out code described previously.

Listing 3-2: MainViewController.m

```
#import "MainViewController.h"
#import "MainView.h"

@implementation MainViewController

- (id)initWithNibName:(NSString *)nibNameOrNil
   bundle:(NSBundle *)nibBundleOrNil {
    if (self = [super initWithNibName:nibNameOrNil
    bundle:nibBundleOrNil]) {
        // Custom initialization
    }
    return self;
}

- (void)viewDidLoad {

  [super viewDidLoad];
  self.view.backgroundColor = [UIColor  colorWithRed:.5
    green:3 blue:.7 alpha:1];
```

```
  [NSTimer scheduledTimerWithTimeInterval:.5 target:self
    selector:@selector(onTimer) userInfo:nil repeats:YES];

  fallingWords = [[NSString alloc] initWithString:@"Peace
    Love Groovy Music"];
  speed = 10.0;
}

- (void)onTimer{

  UILabel *fallingImageView = [[UILabel alloc]
    initWithFrame:CGRectMake(0, 0, 100, 30)];
  fallingImageView.text = fallingWords;
  fallingImageView.textColor = [UIColor  purpleColor];
  fallingImageView.font = [UIFont systemFontOfSize:30];
  fallingImageView.backgroundColor = [UIColor
    colorWithRed:.5 green:3 blue:.7 alpha:1];
  fallingImageView.adjustsFontSizeToFitWidth = YES;

  int startX = round(random() % 80);
  int endX =   round(random() % 80);
  //speed of falling
  double randomSpeed = (1/round(random() % 100) +1) *speed;
  // image size;
  double scaleH = (1/round(random() % 100) +1) *30;
  double scaleW = (1/round(random() % 100) +1) *200;

  [self.view addSubview:fallingImageView];

  fallingImageView.frame = CGRectMake(startX, -100, scaleW,
    scaleH);

  fallingImageView.alpha = .75;

  [UIView beginAnimations:nil context:fallingImageView];
  [UIView setAnimationDuration:randomSpeed];
  [UIView setAnimationDelegate:self];
      [UIView
   setAnimationDidStopSelector:@selector(
   animationDone:finished:context:)];

  fallingImageView.frame = CGRectMake(endX, 500, scaleW,
    scaleH);

  [UIView commitAnimations];
}

-(void)animationDone:(NSString *)animationID
    finished:(NSNumber *)finished context:(id)context {
  UIImageView *fallingImageView = context;
  [fallingImageView removeFromSuperview];
  [fallingImageView release];
}
```

Book III
Chapter 3

Developing the
Main View

(continued)

Listing 3-2 *(continued)*

```
/*
// Override to allow orientations other than the default
   portrait orientation.
- (BOOL)shouldAutorotateToInterfaceOrientation:(
         UIInterfaceOrientation)interfaceOrientation {
// Return YES for supported orientations
return (interfaceOrientation ==
   UIInterfaceOrientationPortrait);
}
*/

- (void)flipsideViewControllerDidFinish:(FlipsideViewControl
   ler *)controller {

    [self dismissModalViewControllerAnimated:YES];
}

- (IBAction)showInfo {

    FlipsideViewController *controller
    = [[FlipsideViewController alloc]
    initWithNibName:@"FlipsideView" bundle:nil];
    controller.delegate = self;

    controller.modalTransitionStyle =
    UIModalTransitionStyleFlipHorizontal;
    [self presentModalViewController:controller animated:YES];

    [controller release];
}

/*
// Override to allow orientations other than the default
   portrait orientation.
- (BOOL)shouldAutorotateToInterfaceOrientation:(UIInterfaceO
   rientation)interfaceOrientation {
// Return YES for supported orientations
return (interfaceOrientation ==
   UIInterfaceOrientationPortrait);
}
*/

- (void)didReceiveMemoryWarning {
    // Releases the view if it doesn't have a superview.
    [super didReceiveMemoryWarning];

    // Release any cached data, images, etc that aren't in
    use.
}
```

```
- (void)viewDidUnload {
    // Release any retained subviews of the main view.
    // e.g. self.myOutlet = nil;
}

- (void)dealloc {
    [super dealloc];
}

@end
```

The viewDidLoad method

The first chunk of code to examine (in bold in Listing 3-2) changes the background color of the Main view and sets up a timer for the interval between each display of falling words or images:

```
- (void)viewDidLoad {

  [super viewDidLoad];
  self.view.backgroundColor = [UIColor  colorWithRed:.5
    green:3 blue:.7 alpha:1];
  [NSTimer scheduledTimerWithTimeInterval:.5 target:self
    selector:@selector(onTimer) userInfo:nil repeats:YES];

  fallingWords = [[NSString alloc] initWithString:@"Peace
    Love Groovy Music"];
  speed = 10.0;
}
```

The viewDidLoad method enables you to change the background color. A UIColor object represents color and sometimes opacity (alpha value). The colorWithRed:.5 green:3 blue:.7 alpha:1 creates and returns a color object using the specified opacity and RGB component values.

You use the NSTimer class to create timers. A timer waits until a certain time interval has elapsed and then fires, sending a specified message to a target object. I use the scheduledTimerWithTimeInterval:target :selector:userInfo:repeats: class method to create the timer and schedule it on the current run loop in the default mode. The interval is 0.5 seconds, the *target* is self, and the *selector* is the message to send to the target when the timer fires — in this case, onTimer. The *userInfo* is the user info for the timer (set to nil), and the timer is set to repeat — that is, it will repeatedly reschedule itself until invalidated.

An NSString object represents a character string. Representing strings as objects allows you to use strings wherever you use other objects. It also provides the benefits of encapsulation, so that string objects can use whatever encoding and storage are needed for efficiency while simply appearing as arrays of characters. In this case, `fallingWords` is initialized with the string `"Peace Love Groovy Music"`. The `speed` is initialized with the value `10`.

Drawing the view

Connecting the timer to the actual drawing of the display is the `onTimer` method. Take a good look at the code for this method (from the bold code in Listing 3-2):

```
- (void)onTimer{

  UILabel *fallingImageView = [[UILabel alloc]
    initWithFrame:CGRectMake(0, 0, 100, 30)];
  fallingImageView.text = fallingWords;
  fallingImageView.textColor = [UIColor  purpleColor];
  fallingImageView.font = [UIFont systemFontOfSize:30];
  fallingImageView.backgroundColor = [UIColor
    colorWithRed:.5 green:3 blue:.7 alpha:1];
  fallingImageView.adjustsFontSizeToFitWidth = YES;

  int startX = round(random() % 80);
  int endX =  round(random() % 80);
  //speed of falling
  double randomSpeed = (1/round(random() % 100) +1) *speed;
  // image size;
  double scaleH = (1/round(random() % 100) +1) *30;
  double scaleW = (1/round(random() % 100) +1) *200;

  [self.view addSubview:fallingImageView];

  fallingImageView.frame = CGRectMake(startX, -100, scaleW,
    scaleH);

  fallingImageView.alpha = .75;

  [UIView beginAnimations:nil context:fallingImageView];
  [UIView setAnimationDuration:randomSpeed];
  [UIView setAnimationDelegate:self];
      [UIView
    setAnimationDidStopSelector:@selector(
    animationDone:finished:context:)];

  fallingImageView.frame = CGRectMake(endX, 500, scaleW,
    scaleH);

  [UIView commitAnimations];
}
```

```
-(void)animationDone:(NSString *)animationID
    finished:(NSNumber *)finished context:(id)context {
  UIImageView *fallingImageView = context;
  [fallingImageView removeFromSuperview];
  [fallingImageView release];
}
```

The `UILabel` class implements a read-only text view. You can use this class to draw one or multiple lines of static text. In this case, the block of code uses the `initWithFrame` method with `CGRectMake` to create a rectangle, with the x-coordinate and y-coordinate of the rectangle's origin point at (0, 0) and a specified width and height (100, 30).

The code converts the `fallingWords` string to `fallingImageView` for display; sets up the text color, font, and background color; and adjusts the font size for the width. The `font` and `textColor` properties apply to the entire text string.

The next block of code uses the random function for the starting and ending points (`startX` and `endX`), for `speed`, and for width (`scaleW`) and height (`scaleH`) for `fallingImageView`. The `random` function uses a non-linear additive-feedback random number generator, with a default table of size 31 long integers, and returns successive pseudo-random numbers in the range from 0 to 2,147,483,647. Then, `addSubview` adds a view so that it's displayed above its siblings, and `frame` specifies the rectangle in the super-layer's coordinate space, using `startX`, `-100`, `scaleW`, and `scaleH`.

Book III
Chapter 3

Developing the
Main View

The animation block

The `UIView` class provides common methods you use to create all types of views. In this particular code, it's used for a block of animation. The `beginAnimations:context:` method starts the animation block, and the `commitAnimations` method ends the block. Inside the block, the code sets property values to make visual changes that comprise the animation. In this case, the code changes the rectangle's starting coordinates from `startX` to `endX`, and from `-100` to `500`:

```
fallingImageView.frame = CGRectMake(endX, 500, scaleW,
    scaleH);
```

The `setAnimationDuration` method sets the animation duration, and `setAnimationDidStopSelector` sets the message to send to the animation delegate when animation stops. The animation delegate is `animationDone`, uses `removeFromSuperview` (an instance method of the `UIView` class) to remove `fallingImageView` from its superview, its window, and from the responder chain; and then uses release (an instance method of the `NSAutoreleasePool` class) to release `fallingImageView`. Remember, you own any object you create with `alloc`, which means you're responsible for releasing it when you're done.

Testing the Main View

Save your Xcode project by choosing File➪Save. Then, to see the magic you've just wrought, click the Build and Run button. You should see the iPhone Simulator launch, run the app, and display the falling words, as shown in Figure 3-7.

Figure 3-7:
The Main view of the app in the iPhone Simulator.

The animation is quite impressive, but now is not the time to sit on your laurels. There's more work to be done — setting up the Flipside view controls so that users can change the text and speed, and saving the user's preferences. All that and more are covered in Chapter 4 of this minibook.

Chapter 4: Developing the Flipside Controls

In This Chapter

✔ **Loading and saving user preferences**

✔ **Adding a Constants.h file**

✔ **Connecting user preferences to the Settings app**

✔ **Adding a Settings bundle for user preferences**

✔ **Adding outlets to the view controller**

✔ **Connecting interface objects to your code in Interface Builder**

As you recall from Chapter 1 of Book I, Apple considers applications that perform simple, highly defined tasks as *utility* apps. The Weather app, for example, deals only with the weather data. One of the characteristics of utility apps is that the user can change aspects of it — in Weather, for example, the user can add and change the cities that Weather shows the weather data for.

The DeepThoughts app is considered a utility, as it performs a simple, highly defined task. With DeepThoughts, the idea is to enable the user to enter his or her own words for the falling words animation (which I show you in Chapter 3 of this minibook), as well as change the speed of the animation. For these functions to work, you need to enable the app to save data entered by a user for the next time he or she fires up the app. In this chapter, I tackle how to get your app to save data entered by the user, and then you set up the Flipside View controls for users to enter the data.

Respecting User Preferences

Most people these days have spent enough time around computers that they know what I mean when I throw the term *preferences* around. On your desktop, for example, you can set preferences at the system level for things like security, screen savers, printing, and file sharing — just to name a few. You can also set preferences for applications. For example, you can set all sorts of preferences in Xcode — not to mention all those preferences in your browser and word-processing programs.

The latter are application-specific settings used to configure the behavior or appearance of an application. On the iPhone, application preferences are supported as well, but the iPhone displays all application-level preferences through the Settings app. (Its icon looks like a bunch of gears.) Whatever separate settings feature you come up with has to function within the framework of iPhone's Settings app; in effect, the Settings app makes you color within the lines.

What guidelines does the iPhone impose for preferences? Here's a short summary:

✦ **If you have preference values that are typically configured once and then rarely changed:** Leave the task of setting preferences to the Settings app. On an iPhone, this would apply to things like enabling/disabling Wi-Fi access, setting wallpaper displays, setting up mail accounts, and any other preference you would set and then leave in place for a while.

✦ **If you have preference values that the user might want to change regularly:** In this situation, you should consider having users set the options themselves in your app.

The iPhone's Weather app is a good example: Suppose you have this thing for Dubrovnik — where it happens to be 48° F as I'm writing this — and you'd like to add it to your list of preferred cities that you want the Weather app to keep tabs on. To load Dubrovnik into the Weather app, all you would have to do is tap the Info button at the bottom of the screen; the view will flip around, and you can add it to your list of cities. That's a lot easier than going back to the Home screen, launching Settings, adding the new city, and then launching the Weather app again.

With DeepThoughts, I could go either way — set up preferences using the Settings app (assuming they are rarely changed by users) or set up preferences from inside the app (assuming they are changed frequently by users). To make DeepThoughts a better example, I show you how to do it both ways.

Setting Up User Preferences

To save and read preferences, you use a built-in, easy-to-use class that lets you read and set user preferences from your app — NSUserDefaults. The class is also used by the Settings app (which has graciously consented to let us peons use it).

You use NSUserDefaults to read and store preference data to a default database, using a key value — just as you would access keyed data from an NSDictionary. (For more on key-value pairs in general and NSDictionary in particular, see Chapter 4 in Book II.) The difference here is that NSUserDefaults data is stored in the file system rather than in an object in memory — objects, after all, go away when the application terminates.

By the way, don't ask why the language experts put `Defaults` in the name rather than something to do with preferences — fewer letters, maybe — but that's the way it is. Just don't let their naming idiosyncrasies confuse you.

Storing the data in the file system rather than in memory gives you an easy way to store application-specific information. With the help of `NSUserDefaults`, you can easily store the state the user was in when he or she quit the application — or store something simple like a text string — which just so happens to be precisely what you need for DeepThoughts.

Identifying preferences for NSUserDefaults

The first thing you need to decide is where you plan on gathering and then using the user's preferences. In this example, the preferences are a) the text for the falling words, and b) the speed of the animation. The obvious place to use the preferences data is `MainViewController.m`, where it sets `fallingWords` and `speed` (refer to the listing for `MainViewController.m` in Chapter 3 of this minibook):

```
fallingWords = [[NSString alloc] initWithString:@"Peace Love
    Groovy Music"];
speed = 10.0;
```

And the obvious place to gather the preferences data is in the Flipside view, where the user enters the replacement text for `fallingWords` and changes the `speed` — and this would be in `FlipsideViewController.m`, as you see in this chapter. (Don't forget: I also show you how to offer these preference settings through the Settings app.)

It's really easy to both access and update a preference — as long as you have `NSUserDefaults` by your side. The trick here is to use the `NSUserDefaults` class to read and update the replacement text and speed. `NSUserDefaults` is implemented as a *singleton,* meaning there's only one instance of `NSUserDefaults` running in your application. To get access to that one instance, you invoke the class method `standardUserDefaults`:

```
[NSUserDefaults  standardUserDefaults]
```

`standardUserDefaults` returns the `NSUserDefaults` object. As soon as you have access to the standard user defaults, you can store data there and then get it back when you need it. To store data, you simply give it a key and tell it to save the data using that key.

The way you tell it to save something is by using the `setObject;forKey:` method. In case your knowledge of Objective-C is a little rusty (or not there at all), that's the way any message that has two arguments is referred to.

The first argument, `setObject:`, is the object you want `NSUserDefaults` to save. This object must be `NSData`, `NSString`, `NSNumber`, `NSDate`, `NSArray`, or `NSDictionary`. In this case, `savedData` is an `NSString`, so you're in good shape.

The second argument is `forKey:`. In order to get the data back, and in order for `NSUserDefaults` to know where to save it, you have to be able to identify it to `NSUserDefaults`. You can, after all, have a number of preferences stored in the `NSUserDefaults` database, and the key tells `NSUserDefaults` which one you are interested in.

The particular keys you will use are `kWordsOfWisdom` for the falling words replacement text, `kSpeed` for the animation speed, and `kMaxSpeed` for the maximum speed possible. (Assuming you use a slider on the Flipside view to set the speed, the maximum speed is the far right point on the slider.)

Adding a Constants.h file

To use keys like `kWordsOfWisdom`, `kSpeed`, or `kMaxSpeed`, you need to define them in a `Constants.h` file. To implement the `Constants.h` file in your project, do the following:

1. **Select the project name (DeepThoughts) in the Groups & Files list and then choose File⇨New File from the Xcode main menu.**

2. **In the New File dialog that appears, choose Other from the listing on the left (under the Mac OS X heading) and then choose Empty File in the main pane, as shown in Figure 4-1.**

3. **In the new dialog that appears, name the file `Constants.h` (as shown in Figure 4-2) and then click Finish.**

   The new empty file is saved in your project, as shown in Figure 4-3.

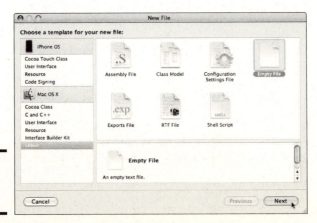

Figure 4-1:
Create an empty file.

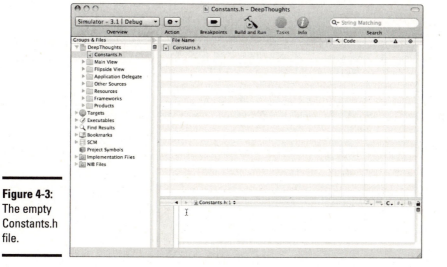

Figure 4-2:
Name the
new file.

Figure 4-3:
The empty
Constants.h
file.

With a new home for your constants all set up and waiting, all you have to
do is add the constants you need, as shown in Figure 4-4:

```
#define  kWordsOfWisdom    @"wordsOfWisdomPreference"
#define  kSpeed            @"speedPreference"
#define  kMaxSpeed         20.0
```

Having a `Constants.h` file in hand is great, but you have to let
`MainViewController.m` know that you plan to use it, as I show in the next
section.

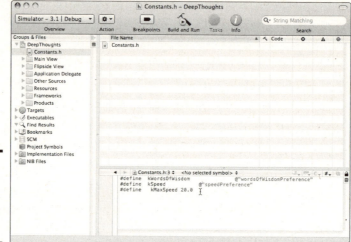

Figure 4-4:
Define the
keys in the
Constants.h
file.

Reading Preferences into the App

It may seem like starting at the end and working backwards, but it makes sense to show the code in DeepThoughts that uses these preferences first, and then show how you can enable the user to change and save these preferences in the Settings app, as well as from the Flipside view of the DeepThoughts app.

To put the preferences data to use in the app's view, you have to link it up with the view's controller — in this case, `MainViewController`. The best place to do that is `viewDidLoad`, which is invoked right after the view has been loaded from the nib file. `viewDidLoad` is found in the `MainViewController.m` file, so that's where you'd go to insert your code to use the preferences.

Edit the `MainViewController.m` file code where it sets `fallingWords` and `speed`. (Look in the first half of the code — refer to the listing for `MainViewController.m` in Chapter 3 of this minibook.) I've commented out the old code (which begins with `//`) and added the new code (shown in bold) in Listing 4-1.

Listing 4-1: Reading the Settings into the App in MainViewController.m

```
#import "MainViewController.h"
#import "MainView.h"
#import "Constants.h"

@implementation MainViewController
```

```
- (id)initWithNibName:(NSString *)nibNameOrNil
   bundle:(NSBundle *)nibBundleOrNil {
    if (self = [super initWithNibName:nibNameOrNil
   bundle:nibBundleOrNil]) {
        // Custom initialization
    }
    return self;
}

- (void)viewDidLoad {

   [super viewDidLoad];
   self.view.backgroundColor = [UIColor  colorWithRed:.5
   green:3 blue:.7 alpha:1];
   [NSTimer scheduledTimerWithTimeInterval:.5 target:self
   selector:@selector(onTimer) userInfo:nil repeats:YES];
// fallingWords = [[NSString alloc] initWithString:@"Peace
   Love Groovy Music"];
// speed = 10.0;
   if (![[NSUserDefaults standardUserDefaults]
   objectForKey:kWordsOfWisdom]) {
    [[NSUserDefaults standardUserDefaults]setObject:@"Peace
   Love Groovy Music"
            forKey:kWordsOfWisdom];
    fallingWords = @"Peace Love Groovy Music";
   }
   else {
    fallingWords = [[NSUserDefaults standardUserDefaults]
                    stringForKey:kWordsOfWisdom];
   }

   if (![[NSUserDefaults standardUserDefaults]
    objectForKey:kSpeed] ){
    [[NSUserDefaults standardUserDefaults]setDouble:10.0
   forKey:kSpeed];
    speed = kMaxSpeed-10.0;}
   else {
        speed = kMaxSpeed-[[NSUserDefaults
   standardUserDefaults] doubleForKey:kSpeed] ;
   }

}
- (void)onTimer{
```

(The rest of the code in `MainViewController.m` *stays the same; see Chapter 3 of this minibook for the full listing.)*

Here's what this code does for you:

1. Imports `Constants.h` into `MainViewController.m`.

   ```
   #import "Constants.h"
   ```

You can now use these keys with NSUserDefaults to save and retrieve the user preferences.

2. Checks to see whether the kWordsOfWisdom setting has been moved into NSUserDefaults.

```
if (![[NSUserDefaults standardUserDefaults]
    objectForKey:kWordsOfWisdom]) {
```

The Settings app or the Flipside view code moves the user's preferences into NSUserDefaults only *after* the application runs for the first time; Settings will, however, update preferences in NSUserDefaults if the user makes any changes.

3. If the settings have not been moved into NSUserDefaults yet, the code uses the initial preference value ("Peace Love Groovy Music") for fallingWords.

```
[[NSUserDefaults standardUserDefaults]setObject:@"Peace
    Love Groovy Music"
            forKey:kWordsOfWisdom];
        fallingWords = @"Peace Love Groovy Music";
```

4. If the settings *have* been moved into NSUserDefaults, the code reads them in and then sets fallingWords to whatever the user's preference is.

```
else {
    fallingWords = [[NSUserDefaults
    standardUserDefaults]
                stringForKey:kWordsOfWisdom];
    }
```

5. Repeats the procedures in Steps 2–4 with the speed setting.

```
if (![[NSUserDefaults standardUserDefaults]
    objectForKey:kSpeed] ){
    [[NSUserDefaults standardUserDefaults]
    setDouble:10.0 forKey:kSpeed];
    speed = kMaxSpeed-10.0;}
else {
        speed = kMaxSpeed-[[NSUserDefaults
    standardUserDefaults] doubleForKey:kSpeed] ;
    }
```

Your code is now ready to use the preference settings. Now, as I mentioned at the beginning of this chapter, one way to enable the user to change and save preferences is inside the Settings app — you set up the preferences in a Settings bundle that you add to your project. Another way to enable the user to change and save preferences is from inside your app (in this case, in the Flipside view). I'm going to tackle the Settings app first and deal with the Flipside view scenario later in this chapter.

Setting Up Preferences for the Settings App

The Settings app uses a property list, called `Root.plist`, found in the Settings bundle inside your application. The Settings app takes what you put in the property list and builds a Settings section for your application in its list of application settings as well as the views that display and enable the user to change those settings. The next sections spell out how to put that Settings section to work for your app.

Adding a Settings bundle to your project

For openers, you have to add a Settings bundle to your application. Here are the moves:

1. **In the Groups & Files list (at the left in the Xcode Project window), select DeepThoughts at the top and then choose File⇨New File from the main menu.**

The New File dialog appears.

2. **Choose Resource under the iPhone OS heading in the left pane and then select the Settings Bundle icon, as shown in Figure 4-5.**

Figure 4-5:
Creating the Settings bundle.

Book III
Chapter 4

Developing the
Flipside Controls

3. **Click the Next button.**

A new dialog appears, allowing you to change the name of the file.

4. **You don't have to change the default name of `Settings.bundle`, so just click Finish.**

You should now see a new item called `Settings.bundle` in the DeepThoughts project in the Groups & Files list.

5. **Click the triangle to expand the `Settings.bundle` subfolder in Groups & Files, as shown in Figure 4-6.**

   You should see the `Root.plist` file as well as an `en.lproj` folder — the latter is used for dealing with localization issues, as discussed in Chapter 2 of Book V.

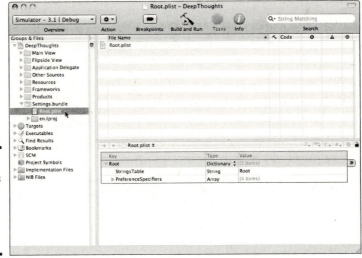

Figure 4-6: The Settings bundle appears in Groups & Files.

Setting up the property list

Property lists are widely used in iPhone apps because they provide an easy way to create structured data using named values for a number of object types.

Property lists all have a single root node — a dictionary, which means it stores items using a key-value pair, just as an `NSDictionary` does: All dictionary entries must have both a key and a value, as I describe in Chapter 4 of Book II. In this dictionary, there are two keys (refer to Figure 4-6):

✦ `StringsTable`

✦ `PreferenceSpecifiers`

The value for the first entry is a string — the name of a strings table used for localization, which I don't get into here. The second entry is an array of dictionaries — one dictionary for each preference. `PreferenceSpecifiers` is where you put the user preferences, which in this case are the text entered by the user for `fallingWords` and the animation speed selected on a slider by the user for `speed`. Here's how you'd get `PreferenceSpecifiers` to do that for you:

1. **In the Groups & Files list of the Project window, select the triangle next to the `Settings.bundle` file to reveal the `Root.plist` file, and then double-click the `Root.plist` file to open it in a separate window, as shown in Figure 4-7.**

Okay, you don't *really* have to do this, but you might find it easier to work with this file in its own window.

2. **In the `Root.plist` window you just opened (refer to Figure 4-7), click the triangle next to `PreferenceSpecifiers`, and click the triangle next to Item 0.**

`PreferenceSpecifiers` is an array designed to hold a set of dictionary nodes, each of which represents a single preference. For each item listed in the array, the first row under it has a key of `Type`; every property list node in the `PreferenceSpecifiers` array must have an entry with this key, which identifies what kind of entry this is. The `Type` value for Item 0 — `PSGroupSpecifier` — is used to indicate that a new group should be started. The value for this key actually acts like a section heading for a Table view.

3. **Double-click the value next to `Title` and delete the default `Group` (see Figure 4-7), and then type the title you want to appear in the Settings app.**

You will want to either delete the title's value of `Group` entirely or replace it with something like *Your App's* `Settings`. (I use `Deep Thoughts Settings`.)

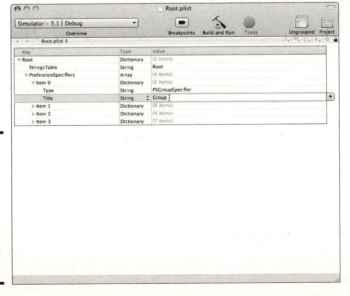

Figure 4-7:
Item 0 in the Root. plist file is the title of your app's screen in the Settings app.

4. **Click the triangle next to Item 1 to open it, as shown in Figure 4-8.**

The `Type` value for Item 1 is `PSTextFieldSpecifier`, which enables a text field that a user can type into. Its title is set to `Phrase` which is okay for your purposes.

5. **Double-click the value for Key in Item 1, and replace the default preference text with `wordsOfWisdomPreference`. (See Figure 4-8.)**

This is the user preference for the text for `fallingwords`, which the user can enter into a text field.

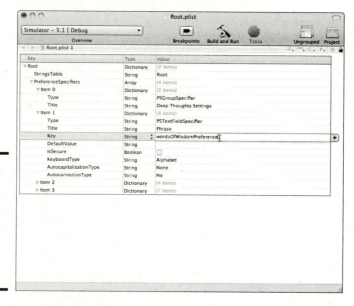

Figure 4-8:
Item 1 in the Root. plist file holds the phrase for the falling words.

6. **Select Item 2 and choose Edit⇨Cut or ⌘+click (right-click) and choose Cut, as shown in Figure 4-9.**

I opened Item 2 in Figure 4-9 to show its contents. Item 2 is defined as a toggle switch, which you can modify by changing the `Title` value and so on. However, because you're not using it, you need to remove it from the file.

The item numbers change as you delete them, so you need to be careful. Fortunately, Undo is supported here; if you make a mistake, press ⌘+Z to undo the delete.

Item 3 is now Item 2, as shown in Figure 4-10.

7. **Select Item 2 and change the `Key` to `speedPreference`, the `DefaultValue` to 10, and the `MaximumValue` to 20 (and keep the `MinimumValue` set to 0).**

The `Type` value is `PSSliderSpecifier`, which enables a slider that a user can slide to set the value. The `DefaultValue` is the middle of the slider (`10`), with the `MinimumValue` at the far left and the `MaximumValue` at the far right.

When you're done, the `Root.plist` window should look like Figure 4-10.

Figure 4-9:
Item 2 in the Root.plist file originally holds a toggle switch, which you don't need (so you can use Cut to remove it).

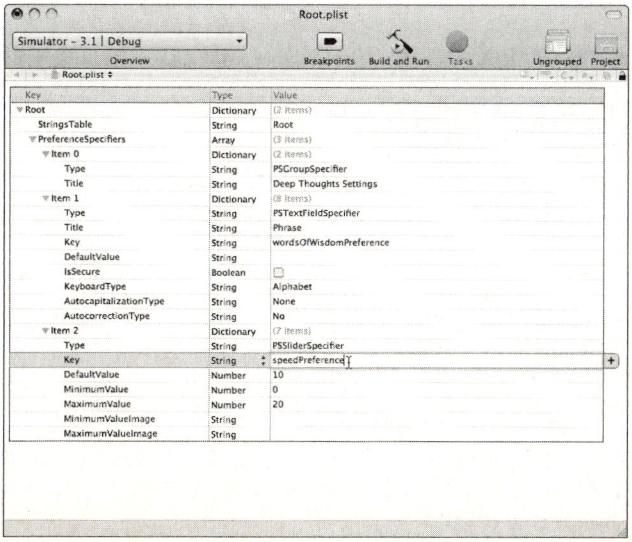

Figure 4-10:
Item 3 becomes Item 2 and now holds the speed slider preference.

8. **Save the property file by pressing ⌘+S (or choose File⇨Save).**

Testing your app with the Settings app

To see how your DeepThoughts app makes do with user preferences set within the Settings app, build and run your project as I describe in the last part of Chapter 3 of this minibook. When the iPhone Simulator appears and the app starts running, quit the app by clicking the Home button on the iPhone Simulator. Then drag to the right across the screen of the Simulator to go to the first Home screen, which contains the Settings app, as shown in Figure 4-11.

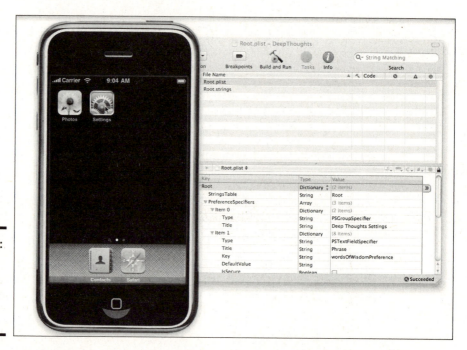

Figure 4-11: Run the Settings app in the iPhone Simulator.

Click the Settings icon to launch the Settings app, and you can then click DeepThoughts in the menu of app settings, as shown in Figure 4-12.

The settings now appear in the DeepThoughts settings screen. Click the Phrase entry field (to simulate a user touching the field), and the onscreen keyboard appears for typing the replacement text for `fallingWords`, as shown in Figure 4-13. You can also click and drag the slider (to simulate a user touching and sliding the slider) to set the value for `speed`.

Figure 4-12:
Choose Deep-Thoughts in the Settings app.

Figure 4-13:
Change the entry in the Phrase field with the keyboard and slide the slider for the speed.

Click Settings in the top-left corner to return to the Settings menu, and then click the Home button to quit Settings. Drag across the Home screen to the left to switch to the next screen, which contains the DeepThoughts app. Click DeepThoughts to run it again, and the changes made in Settings should change the text and speed, as shown in Figure 4-14.

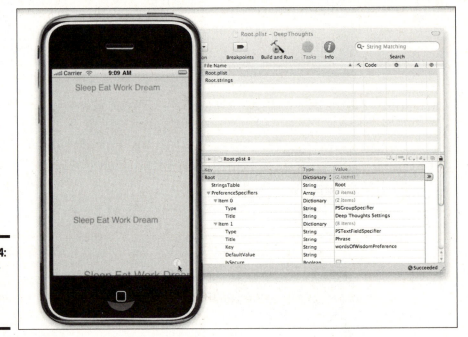

Figure 4-14: Run Deep-Thoughts to see the changes.

As you experiment with code and build and run your project, you need to delete the application and its data from the iPhone Simulator if you change anything of significance — before building and running again. The consequences of not doing so will become obvious when things don't work like you would expect them to. See Chapter 4 of Book I for details on deleting specific apps from the iPhone Simulator. For a fast reset of all apps and all data in the simulator, choose iPhone Simulator⇨Reset Contents and Settings, and then click Reset. Note that this removes *all* apps and data that you have installed in the simulator.

Setting Up Preferences in the Flipside View

As you may recall from Chapter 2 of this minibook, FlipsideView-Controller owns the Flipside view's FlipsideView.xib (which you can open in the Interface Builder). You can add the interface objects you need for DeepThoughts — the text entry field for the replacement text for fallingWords, and the speed slider for speed — using Interface Builder, but first you have to put *outlets* in the code that connect your methods to the Interface Builder interface objects.

The fact that a connection between an object and its outlets exists is actually stored in a nib file. When the nib file is loaded, each connection is reconstituted and reestablished, thus enabling you to send messages to the object. IBOutlet is the keyword that tags an instance-variable declaration so the Interface Builder application knows that a particular instance variable *is* an outlet — and can then enable the connection to it with Xcode.

In your code, it turns out that you need to create *two* outlets: one to point to the text entry field and one to point to the speed slider. To get this outlet business started, you need to *declare* each outlet, which you do with the help of the aforementioned IBOutlet keyword.

Add the bold lines of code in Listing 4-2 — the <UITextFieldDelegate> between UIViewController and the first curly brace, the code (including IBOutlet statements) after delegate; and before the last curly brace as well as all the @property statements before the @end.

Listing 4-2:   FlipsideViewController.h

```
@protocol FlipsideViewControllerDelegate;

@interface FlipsideViewController : UIViewController
   <UITextFieldDelegate> {

  id <FlipsideViewControllerDelegate> delegate;
            NSString*      wordsOfWisdom;
  IBOutlet UITextField *theTextField;
            float          sliderValue;
  IBOutlet UISlider      *slider;
}

// @property (nonatomic, assign) id
   <FlipsideViewControllerDelegate> delegate;
- (IBAction)done;

@property (nonatomic, assign) id
   <FlipsideViewControllerDelegate> delegate;
@property (nonatomic, assign) NSString* wordsOfWisdom;
@property (nonatomic, assign) UISlider* slider;

@end

@protocol FlipsideViewControllerDelegate
- (void)flipsideViewControllerDidFinish:(FlipsideView-
   Controller *)controller;
@end
```

The IBOutlet statements declare the outlets, which will automatically be initialized with a pointer to the UITextField (theTextField) and the UISlider (slider) when the application is launched. But while this will happen automatically, it won't *automatically* happen automatically. You have to help it out a bit.

Objective-C properties

In procedural programming — you know, all that Linux Kernel stuff — variables are generally fair game for all. But in object-oriented programming, a class's instance variables are tucked away inside an object and shouldn't be accessed directly. The only way for them to be initialized is for you to create what are called *accessor methods,* which allow the specific instance variable of an object to be read and (if you want) updated. Creating accessor methods is a two-step process that begins with a @property declaration, which tells the compiler that there are accessor methods. And that is what you did in the preceding section; you coded corresponding @property declarations for each IBOutlet declaration.

The methods that provide access to the instance variables of an object are called *accessor methods,* and they effectively get (using a *getter method*) and set (using a *setter method*) the values for an instance variable. Although you can code those methods yourself, it can be rather tedious. This is where properties come in. The Objective-C Declared Properties feature provides a simple way to declare and implement an object's accessor methods. The compiler can synthesize accessor methods according to the way you told it to in the property declaration. Objective-C creates the getter and setter methods for you by using an @property declaration in the interface file, combined with the @synthesize declaration in the implementation file.

All that being said, at the end of the day, you need to do three things in your code to have the compiler create accessors for you:

1. **Declare an instance variable in the interface file.**

2. **Add an @property declaration of that instance variable in the same interface file (usually with the nonatomic attribute).**

The declaration specifies the name and type of the property as well as some attributes that provide the compiler with information about how exactly you want the accessor methods to be implemented.

For example, the declaration

```
@property (nonatomic, assign) NSString* wordsOfWisdom;
```

declares a property named wordsOfWisdom, which is a pointer to an NSString object. As for the two attributes — nonatomic and assign — nonatomic tells the compiler to create an accessor to return the value directly, which is another way of saying that the accessors can be interrupted while in use. (This works fine for applications like this one.)

The second value, `assign`, tells the compiler to create an accessor method that sends an `assign` message to any object that is assigned to this property.

3. **Use `@synthesize` in the implementation file so that Objective-C generates the accessors for you.**

   The `@property` declaration only declares that there are accessors. It is the `@synthesize` statement that tells the compiler to create them for you. You add this statement in the next section, along with more code, to the `FlipsideViewController.m` implementation file. (Cue the next section!)

Adding methods for the interface objects

Okay, time to add the bold lines of code in Listing 4-3 to the `Flipside VrewController.m` implementation file.

Listing 4-3:   FlipsideViewController.m

```
#import "FlipsideViewController.h"
#import "MainViewController.h"
#import "Constants.h"

@implementation FlipsideViewController

@synthesize delegate , wordsOfWisdom, slider;

# pragma mark textField methods
- (BOOL)textFieldShouldBeginEditing:(UITextField *)textField
   {
   [textField setReturnKeyType:UIReturnKeyNext];
   return YES;
}

- (BOOL)textFieldShouldReturn:(UITextField *)textField {
   [textField resignFirstResponder];
    return YES;
}

- (void)textFieldDidEndEditing:(UITextField *)textField {
   wordsOfWisdom = textField.text;
}
# pragma mark view methods
- (void)viewDidLoad {

   [super viewDidLoad];
   self.view.backgroundColor = [UIColor
   viewFlipsideBackgroundColor];
```

Book III
Chapter 4

Developing the
Flipside Controls

(continued)

Listing 4-3 *(continued)*

```
NSLog(@"Slider value %f parent value %f" ,slider.value ,
  ((MainViewController*)(self.parentViewController)).speed);
slider.value = + kMaxSpeed - ((MainViewController*)(self.
  parentViewController)).speed; //added
NSLog(@"Slider value %f parent value %f" ,slider.value ,
  ((MainViewController*)(self.parentViewController)).speed);
}

- (IBAction)done {
  if(! [theTextField.text isEqualToString: @"" ])
  wordsOfWisdom = theTextField.text; // added
  [self.delegate flipsideViewControllerDidFinish:self];
}
/*
// Override to allow orientations other than the default
  portrait orientation.
- (BOOL)shouldAutorotateToInterfaceOrientation:(UIInterfaceO
  rientation)interfaceOrientation {
// Return YES for supported orientations
return (interfaceOrientation ==
  UIInterfaceOrientationPortrait);
}
*/
- (void)didReceiveMemoryWarning {
  // Releases the view if it doesn't have a superview.
   [super didReceiveMemoryWarning];

  // Release any cached data, images, etc that aren't in
  use.
}

- (void)viewDidUnload {
  // Release any retained subviews of the main view.
  // e.g. self.myOutlet = nil;
}

- (void)dealloc {
    [super dealloc];
}
@end
```

Although the @property declaration in the previous section tells the
compiler that there are accessor methods, they still have to be created.
Fortunately, Objective-C will create these accessor methods for you whenever you include an @synthesize statement for a property:

```
@synthesize delegate , wordsOfWisdom, slider;
```

The @synthesize statement tells the compiler to create accessor methods for you — one for each @property declaration.

Next, you add the text field methods to obtain the wordsOfWisdom:

```
# pragma mark textField methods
- (BOOL)textFieldShouldBeginEditing:(UITextField *)textField
   {
   [textField setReturnKeyType:UIReturnKeyNext];
   return YES;
}
- (BOOL)textFieldShouldReturn:(UITextField *)textField {
   [textField resignFirstResponder];
    return YES;
}
- (void)textFieldDidEndEditing:(UITextField *)textField {
   wordsOfWisdom = textField.text;
}
```

The UITextFieldDelegate protocol defines the messages sent to a text field delegate as part of the sequence of editing its text. When the user performs an action that would normally start an editing session, the text field calls the textFieldShouldBeginEditing: method first to see whether editing should actually proceed. In most circumstances, you would simply return YES from this method to allow editing to proceed.

The text field calls the textFieldShouldReturn: method whenever the user taps the Return button on the keyboard to find out whether it should process the Return — you can use this method to implement any custom behavior when the Return button is tapped, but for your purposes, you simply return YES (which is the default), although you could return NO to ignore the Return button.

After saying "yes" to this and that, the real action happens with the text-FieldDidEndEditing: method, which is called after the text field resigns its first responder status to tell the delegate that editing stopped for the specified text field, so that you now have the edited wordsOfWisdom.

The # pragma mark statement is simply a way to organize your methods in the Method list pop-up in the Xcode Text Editor Navigation bar (to the left of the Bookmarks menu). You use it with a label (such as textField methods or view methods) to add the label in bold to the Method list so that you can identify and keep separate the methods logically in the list.

Next, you modify the viewDidLoad method to obtain the speed from the slider (new code is in bold):

```
# pragma mark view methods
- (void)viewDidLoad {
```

```
    [super viewDidLoad];
    self.view.backgroundColor = [UIColor
     viewFlipsideBackgroundColor];

    NSLog(@"Slider value %f parent value %f" ,slider.value ,
     ((MainViewController*)(self.parentViewController)).speed);
    slider.value = + kMaxSpeed - ((MainViewController*)(self.
     parentViewController)).speed; //added
    NSLog(@"Slider value %f parent value %f" ,slider.value ,
     ((MainViewController*)(self.parentViewController)).speed);
}
- (IBAction)done {
    if(! [theTextField.text isEqualToString: @"" ])
     wordsOfWisdom = theTextField.text; // added
    [self.delegate flipsideViewControllerDidFinish:self];
}
```

You wrap the code in NSLog statements to report back a message to the
system log facility, but mostly this code assigns the slider.value to
speed in MainViewController (which, as you recall from Chapter 3 of
this minibook, uses speed to control the animated flowing text). Next, you
deal with the possibility of a blank text field in the IBAction method. The
code assigns the text field's text to wordsOfWisdom *only* if the field is *not*
theTextField.text isEqualToString: @"".

Fine, but there are still a few problems: How will MainViewController
know about the new speed assignment? How will the app save the
preferences? You have to modify the MainViewController.h and
MainViewController.m files by adding the code in bold, as I show in
Listing 4-4 and Listing 4-5, to cover your bases here.

Listing 4-4:   MainViewController.h

```
#import "FlipsideViewController.h"

@interface MainViewController : UIViewController
   <FlipsideViewControllerDelegate> {

  UIImage     *fallingImage;
  NSString    *fallingWords;
  double       speed;
}

- (IBAction)showInfo;
@property (readwrite)  double speed;

@end
```

Listing 4-5:   MainViewController.m

```
#import "MainViewController.h"
#import "MainView.h"
#import "Constants.h"

@implementation MainViewController
@synthesize speed;

- (id)initWithNibName:(NSString *)nibNameOrNil
  bundle:(NSBundle *)nibBundleOrNil {
    if (self = [super initWithNibName:nibNameOrNil
  bundle:nibBundleOrNil]) {
        // Custom initialization
    }
    return self;
}


- (void)viewDidLoad {

  [super viewDidLoad];
  self.view.backgroundColor = [UIColor  colorWithRed:.5
    green:3 blue:.7 alpha:1];
  [NSTimer scheduledTimerWithTimeInterval:.5 target:self
    selector:@selector(onTimer) userInfo:nil repeats:YES];

// fallingWords = [[NSString alloc] initWithString:@"Peace
    Love Groovy Music"];
// speed = 10.0;
  if (![[NSUserDefaults standardUserDefaults]
    objectForKey:kWordsOfWisdom]) {
    [[NSUserDefaults standardUserDefaults]setObject:@"Peace
    Love Groovy Music"

    forKey:kWordsOfWisdom];
    fallingWords = @"Peace Love Groovy Music";
  }
  else {
    fallingWords = [[NSUserDefaults standardUserDefaults]
                    stringForKey:kWordsOfWisdom];
  }

  if (![[NSUserDefaults standardUserDefaults]
    objectForKey:kSpeed] ){
    [[NSUserDefaults standardUserDefaults]setDouble:10.0
    forKey:kSpeed];
    speed = kMaxSpeed-10.0;}
  else {
       speed = kMaxSpeed-[[NSUserDefaults
    standardUserDefaults] doubleForKey:kSpeed] ;
  }
}
```

(continued)

Listing 4-5 *(continued)*

```objc
- (void)onTimer{

  UILabel *fallingImageView = [[UILabel alloc]
    initWithFrame:CGRectMake(0, 0, 100, 30)];
  fallingImageView.text = fallingWords;
  fallingImageView.textColor = [UIColor  purpleColor];
  fallingImageView.font = [UIFont systemFontOfSize:30];
  fallingImageView.backgroundColor = [UIColor
    colorWithRed:.5 green:3 blue:.7 alpha:1];  // Transparent
    instead?
  fallingImageView.adjustsFontSizeToFitWidth = YES;

  int startX = round(random() % 80);
  int endX =  round(random() % 80);
  //speed of falling
  double randomSpeed = (1/round(random() % 100) +1) *speed;
  // image size;
  double scaleH = (1/round(random() % 100) +1) *30;
  double scaleW = (1/round(random() % 100) +1) *200;

  [self.view addSubview:fallingImageView];

  fallingImageView.frame = CGRectMake(startX, -100, scaleW,
    scaleH);

  fallingImageView.alpha = .75;

  [UIView beginAnimations:nil context:fallingImageView];
  [UIView setAnimationDuration:randomSpeed];
  [UIView setAnimationDelegate:self];
  [UIView setAnimationDidStopSelector:@selector(animationDone
    :finished:context:)];

  fallingImageView.frame = CGRectMake(endX, 500, scaleW,
    scaleH);

  [UIView commitAnimations];
}

-(void)animationDone:(NSString *)animationID
    finished:(NSNumber *)finished context:(id)context {
  UIImageView *fallingImageView = context;
  [fallingImageView removeFromSuperview];
  [fallingImageView release];
}

/*
 // Override to allow orientations other than the default
    portrait orientation.
  - (BOOL)shouldAutorotateToInterfaceOrientation:(UIInterfaceO
    rientation)interfaceOrientation {
```

```objc
// Return YES for supported orientations
return (interfaceOrientation ==
  UIInterfaceOrientationPortrait);
}
*/

- (void)flipsideViewControllerDidFinish:(FlipsideViewControl
  ler *)controller {

  if (controller.wordsOfWisdom ) {
    fallingWords = controller.wordsOfWisdom;
    [[NSUserDefaults standardUserDefaults]
    setObject:fallingWords  forKey:kWordsOfWisdom];
    [fallingWords retain];
  }

  if (controller.slider.value) {
    speed = kMaxSpeed-controller.slider.value; // can access
    it directly or use an ivar as above
    [[NSUserDefaults standardUserDefaults]setDouble:
    controller.slider.value forKey:kSpeed];
  }

  [self dismissModalViewControllerAnimated:YES];
}
- (IBAction)showInfo {

  FlipsideViewController *controller
   = [[FlipsideViewController alloc]
   initWithNibName:@"FlipsideView" bundle:nil];
  controller.delegate = self;
  controller.modalTransitionStyle =
  UIModalTransitionStyleFlipHorizontal;
  [self presentModalViewController:controller
   animated:YES];
  [controller release];
}
```

(The rest of the code in MainViewController.m stays the same; see Chapter 3 of this minibook for the full listing.)

In Listing 4-4, you add the @property declaration for speed. Then in Listing 4-5, you add the @synthesize statement for the property.

Below the animation block in MainViewController.m (see Listing 4-5), you modify the flipsideViewControllerDidFinish: method to save the user preferences:

```objc
if (controller.wordsOfWisdom ) {
    fallingWords = controller.wordsOfWisdom;
    [[NSUserDefaults standardUserDefaults]
    setObject:fallingWords  forKey:kWordsOfWisdom];
```

```
    [fallingWords retain];
}

if (controller.slider.value) {
  speed = kMaxSpeed-controller.slider.value; // can access
 it directly or use an ivar as above
  [[NSUserDefaults standardUserDefaults]setDouble:
  controller.slider.value forKey:kSpeed];
}

  [self dismissModalViewControllerAnimated:YES];
```

As you'll recall from earlier in this chapter, you use `standardUser` `Defaults` (a `NSUserDefaults` class method) to gain access to the standard user defaults; you can store data there, and then get it back when you need it. To store data, you use the `setObject;forKey:` method. The first argument, `setObject:`, is the object you want `NSUserDefaults` to save (`fallingWords`); the second argument is `forKey:` (`kWordsOfWisdom`), which is how `NSUserDefaults` identifies it. For the slider value, `set` `Double: controller.slider.value forKey:` sets the value of the specified default key to the double value.

The `dismissModalViewControllerAnimated:` method animates the view as it's dismissed. You're sending the message to the view controller that invoked the `presentModalViewController` method — in this case, the `(IBAction)showInfo` method. (Take another peek at Listing 4-5 at the end.)

Don't forget to save your changes in Xcode; otherwise, Interface Builder won't be able to find the new code.

Connecting the Interface Objects in Interface Builder

You've created the outlets and their accessor methods in your code. Now you can create the connection in Interface Builder so that when the nib file is loaded, the nib loading code will create these connections automatically, using the accessors you had the compiler create for the `slider` and `the-TextField`.

Now that you have the code ready to connect to the interface objects you want to use in the Flipside view, you can open the view in Interface Builder. Click Resources in the Groups & Files list and then double-click the `FlipsideView.xib` file to launch Interface Builder, as I describe in Chapter 2 of this minibook.

You can then click the Flipside View icon in the `FlipsideView.xib` window of Interface Builder, so that you can add the objects to it. If the Library window isn't already open, choose Tools⇨Library. Then select Inputs & Values from the Library pop-up menu to see the input objects you can use. Information about each object appears in the lower portion of the Library window. The slider, for example, is of the `UISlider` class; it displays a horizontal bar representing a range of values.

Drag the slider, as shown in Figure 4-15, from the Library window over to the Flipside View window. Horizontal and vertical guides appear to help you place the slider where you want it.

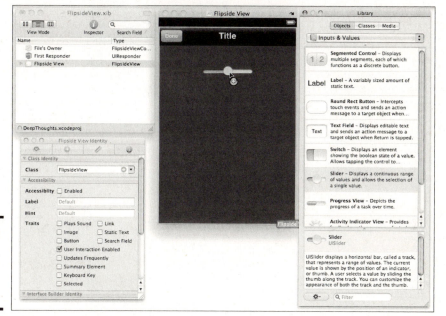

Figure 4-15: Drag a slider to the Flipside view.

You can select the horizontal slider in the Flipside View window and then drag its edges to make it longer. To set the slider's values, click the Attributes tab in the Inspector window (or choose Tools➪Attributes Inspector) and then change the Minimum, Maximum, and Initial values as shown in Figure 4-16.

To connect the horizontal slider to your code, first click the triangle next to the Flipside View icon in the `FlipsideView.xib` window to reveal its contents (which includes Horizontal Slider) and then select Horizontal Slider. Then click the Connections tab in the Inspector window (or choose Tools➪Connections Inspector) and scroll down to the Referencing Outlets section. Drag from the connection point for a new referencing outlet to File's Owner, as shown in Figure 4-17. Then choose `slider` from the pop-up menu to connect the object to your code's outlet (`slider`), as shown in Figure 4-18.

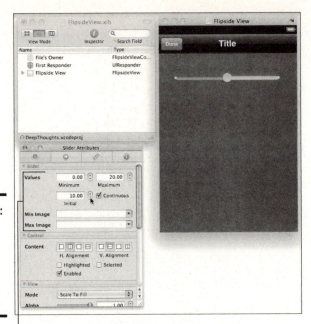

Figure 4-16:
Set the
slider's
Minimum,
Maximum,
and Initial
values.

Change Slider
Values here

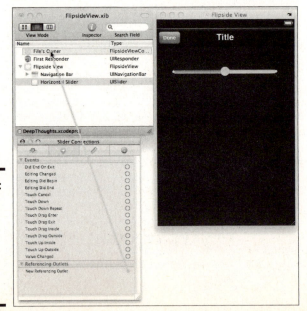

Figure 4-17:
Make a
connection
from the
Horizontal
Slider to
the File's
Owner.

Figure 4-18:
Connect the
Horizontal
Slider to
slider in
your code.

**Book III
Chapter 4**

**Developing the
Flipside Controls**

Now, perform the same procedure with the Text Field object in the Interface
Builder Library window. (If the Library window isn't already open, choose
Tools⇨Library.) Drag the Text Field for text entry, as shown in Figure 4-19,
from the Library window to the Flipside View window. Horizontal and vertical guides appear to help you place it where you want it.

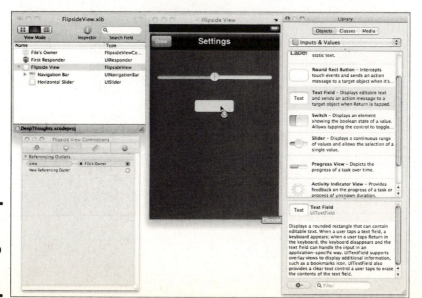

Figure 4-19:
Drag a text
entry field to
the Flipside
view.

You can select your new text field in the Flipside View window and then drag its edges to make it longer, and change its attributes by clicking the Attributes tab in the Inspector window (or choosing Tools⇨Attributes Inspector).

To connect the text field to your code, first select Round Style Text Field (which is now underneath Horizontal Slider) in the `FlipsideView.xib` window. Then click the Connections tab in the Inspector window (or choose Tools⇨Connections Inspector), and scroll down the Text Field Connections window to the Referencing Outlets section. Drag from the connection point for a new referencing outlet to File's Owner, as shown in Figure 4-20. Then choose `theTextField` from the pop-up menu to connect the object to your code's outlet (`theTextField`), as shown in Figure 4-21.

Finally, with Round Style Text Field still selected, drag from the connection point for `delegate` (at the top of the Text Field Connections window) to File's Owner, in order to hook up the text field's delegate connector to `FlipsideViewController`.

Figure 4-20:
Make a
connection
from the
Round Style
Text Field
to the File's
Owner.

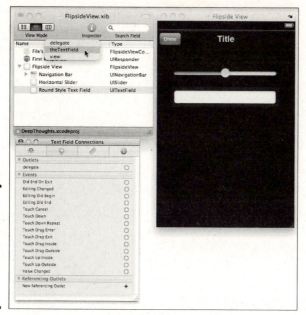

Figure 4-21:
Connect the Round Style Text Field to theTextField in your code.

So it looks like you now have all the pieces in place for the DeepThoughts application — build and run your project to see what you have. You can now enter a new phrase, speed up or slow down the animation, and save both preferences using either the Flipside view or the Settings app.

Ah, but there's more you can do with this little app, as you see in the next chapter.

Chapter 5: Extending Your App with a Photo View

In This Chapter

✔ **Using polymorphism to add a new Photo view**

✔ **Setting up horizontal scrolling between views**

✔ **Creating subclasses of UIView and UIViewController**

✔ **Animating the photo view**

✔ **Accessing photos and other media on the iPhone**

✔ **Adding an application icon**

*O*ne reason why it's easy to extend and enhance your iPhone app is the fact that the template sets you up to take advantage of *delegation* — you're using a behavior-rich object supplied by the framework *as is,* and you're putting the code for program-specific behavior in a separate (delegate) object. You're basically using delegation to get the framework objects to do the work for you.

Government and military leaders know all about delegation. Ronald Reagan could have been talking about extending the functionality of apps object-oriented programming when he said "Surround yourself with the best people you can find, delegate authority, and don't interfere." And General George S. Patton seemed to know all about combining delegation with encapsulation to enhance applications when he said, "Never tell people *how* to do things. Tell them *what* to do and they will surprise you with their ingenuity."

When you combine delegation, encapsulation, and inheritance, changing or enhancing objects or their functionality becomes much easier because it reduces the impact of those changes on the rest of your application. As I point out in Chapter 1 of Book II, inheritance allows you to do a number of things that make your programs more extensible — in a subclass, you can add new methods and instance variables to what is inherited from a super-class, refine or extend the behavior of an inherited method, and change the behavior of an inherited method. With encapsulation, you're hiding *how* things are being done from *what* is being done. Combining inheritance and encapsulation gives you *polymorphism* — using objects that do the same thing in different ways. (See Chapter 2 of Book II for background info on these programming patterns.)

In this chapter, you enhance your app to show photos or images from the Photo library on the user's iPhone. You use instances of the same object (the Main view controller) along with inherited methods of a superclass to implement a second view (a flowing image) next to the first view (flowing words) so that the user can horizontally scroll between them. Because you've encapsulated the details of how to set the falling words and falling image, how to save preferences, and how to show info from the main screen to select new preferences, it's a piece of cake to add the ability to select and display photos.

Adding a Second View

To use instances of the same controller to control other views, you need to first define the number of views, or "pages," as a key in the `Constants.h` file. Add the following to `Constants.h` (refer to Chapter 4 of this minibook for details on editing `Constants.h`):

```
#define kNumberOfPages  2
```

The game plan is to initialize two instances of `MainViewController` (`mainViewController1` and `mainViewController2`), and to set up the ability to scroll horizontally — swipe to the left or right — in order to switch views.

Initializing view controllers in the app delegate

In Chapter 1 of this minibook, I show how the Utility Application template provides the code you need for loading the parts of the `MainWindow.xib` to create both `DeepThoughtsAppDelegate` and the window and for sending `DeepThoughtsAppDelegate` the `applicationDidFinishLaunching:` message. The `applicationDidFinishLaunching:` method in `DeepThoughtsAppDelegate` initializes `MainView`.

The `applicationDidFinishLaunching:` message is sent at the very beginning, before the user can even see anything on the screen. Here's where you'd insert your code to initialize two instances of `MainView Controller`: the declarations go in the `DeepThoughtsAppDelegate.h` header file, as shown in Listing 5-1, and the implementation goes in the `DeepThoughtsAppDelegate.m` file, as shown in Listing 5-2. I've commented-out the old code (which begins with `//`) and added the new code (shown in bold) in both listings.

Listing 5-1:   DeepThoughtsAppDelegate.h

```
@class MainViewController;

@interface DeepThoughtsAppDelegate : NSObject
    <UIApplicationDelegate, UIScrollViewDelegate > {
```

```
    UIWindow *window;
    //  MainViewController *mainViewController;
    MainViewController *mainViewController1;
    MainViewController *mainViewController2;
    IBOutlet UIScrollView *scrollView;
}

@property (nonatomic, retain) IBOutlet UIWindow *window;
//@property (nonatomic, retain) MainViewController
    *mainViewController;
@property (nonatomic, retain) MainViewController
    *mainViewController1;
@property (nonatomic, retain) MainViewController
    *mainViewController2;
@property (nonatomic, retain) UIScrollView *scrollView;

@end
```

Listing 5-2:   DeepThoughtsAppDelegate.m

```
#import "DeepThoughtsAppDelegate.h"
#import "MainViewController.h"
#import "PhotoViewController.h"
#import "Constants.h"

@implementation DeepThoughtsAppDelegate

@synthesize window;
//@synthesize mainViewController;
@synthesize mainViewController1;
@synthesize mainViewController2;
@synthesize scrollView;

- (void)applicationDidFinishLaunching:(UIApplication *)
    application {

// MainViewController *aController = [[MainViewController
    alloc] initWithNibName:@"MainView" bundle:nil];
// self.mainViewController = aController;
// [aController release];
// mainViewController.view.frame = [UIScreen mainScreen].
    applicationFrame;
// [window addSubview:[mainViewController view]];
    scrollView.pagingEnabled = YES;
    scrollView.contentSize = CGSizeMake(scrollView.frame.size.
     width * kNumberOfPages, scrollView.frame.size.height);
    scrollView.showsHorizontalScrollIndicator = NO;
    scrollView.showsVerticalScrollIndicator = NO;
    scrollView.scrollsToTop = NO;
    scrollView.delegate = self;
```

(continued)

Listing 5-2 *(continued)*

```
MainViewController *aController = [[MainViewController
  alloc] initWithNibName:@"MainView" bundle:nil];
MainViewController *bController = [[PhotoViewController
  alloc] initWithNibName:@"PhotoView" bundle:nil];

self.mainViewController1 = aController;
self.mainViewController2 = bController;

[aController release];
[bController release];

// mainViewController1.view.frame = [UIScreen mainScreen].
  applicationFrame;
CGRect frame1 = scrollView.frame;
frame1.origin.x = frame1.size.width * 0;
frame1.origin.y = 0;
mainViewController1.view.frame = frame1;

CGRect frame2 = scrollView.frame;
frame2.origin.x = frame2.size.width * 1;
frame2.origin.y = 0;
mainViewController2.view.frame = frame2;
[scrollView addSubview:[mainViewController1 view]];
[scrollView addSubview:[mainViewController2 view]];
[window makeKeyAndVisible];
}

- (void)dealloc {
  //  [mainViewController release];
  [mainViewController1 release];
  [mainViewController2 release];

    [window release];
    [super dealloc];
}

@end
```

In Listing 5-1, you modify the template declarations in `DeepThoughts` `AppDelegate.h` so you can add the `UIScrollViewDelegate` protocol as well as declare `mainViewController1` and `mainViewController2`, while commenting out the declaration of `mainViewController`. You also add an `IBOutlet` so that Interface Builder can discover `UIScrollView`, then go on to add property declarations for `mainViewController1`, `mainView-Controller2`, and `scrollView`.

In Listing 5-2, you modify the template implementation code in `DeepThoughtsAppDelegate.m` to import the `Constants.h` file and the new `PhotoViewController.h` file to control the second view (the Photo view), which you create later in this chapter. You then synthesize `mainViewController1`, `mainViewController2`, and `scrollView` so that the compiler can synthesize these accessor methods according to the way you told it to in the property declaration. (See Chapter 1 of Book II for background info about accessor methods.) Further down in the code, you initialize with `aController` the `MainView` to be controlled by `mainView-Controller1`, and with `bController` the `PhotoView` to be controlled by `mainViewController2` (as instances of `MainViewController`). Finally, you implement the two views with horizontal scrolling.

Discovering how horizontal scrolling works

The `UIScrollView` class adds scrolling without you having to do any work, and in this case you use it for horizontal scrolling. The methods declared by the `UIScrollViewDelegate` protocol allow the adopting delegate to respond to messages from the `UIScrollView` class. The `UIScrollView` class provides support for displaying content that's larger than the size of the app's window — users can swipe to scroll within that content and zoom in and out from portions of the content by pinching and un-pinching.

A `UIScrollView` object (a Scroll view) is a view with an origin point that is adjustable over the Content view — it clips the content to its frame, which usually coincides with that of the app's main window. The Scroll view tracks the movements of fingers and adjusts the origin accordingly. The view that is showing its content "through" the Scroll view draws that portion of itself based on the new origin, which is pinned to an offset in the Content view. The Scroll view itself does no drawing — unless you include the displaying of vertical and horizontal Scroll indicators.

The Scroll view must know the size of the Content view so it knows when to stop scrolling; by default, it bounces back when scrolling exceeds the bounds of the content. Your code sets the `pagingEnabled` property for `scrollView` to `YES` so that paging is enabled — the Scroll view stops on multiples of the view bounds (pages) when the user scrolls. (The default value is `NO`.) You set the `contentSize` property (the size of the Content view) by using the scrolling frame size and `kNumberOfPages` (which is a constant now set to `2`). The code then shuts off the horizontal and vertical scroll indicators and scrolling to the top. Finally, you add `CGRect` (rectangle) structures to draw the Scroll view frames for the two views, and you add each view as a subview of the Scroll view.

Playing the memory management game

In Chapter 1 of this minibook, I spend some time nagging you about memory management. Back in Listing 5-2 — right there, at the bottom — you add `mainViewController1` and `mainViewController2` to the `dealloc` method supplied by the template. Here's why: You created those objects by sending a `retain` message in the `@property` declarations. (See Listing 5-1.) Now you have to *release* them. You're responsible for telling the memory-management system you're done with them.

TIP

Don't forget to save your Xcode project before going any further! Choose File➪Save. To use Interface Builder, your project must already be saved so that Interface Builder can identify the accessor methods.

Implementing the Photo View

Now comes the easy part: creating the Photo view that will display a flowing image in the same way that the Main view displays flowing words. You need not just a version of the `MainViewController` code, but also the Light Info button, which you may have encountered in Chapter 2 of this minibook.

Start by creating a new group for your project in the Groups & Files list in Xcode. Click DeepThoughts at the top of the pane so that the new group you create is placed outside any other group in the pane, and choose Project➪New Group. You can then select the new group and change its name to Photo View, as shown in Figure 5-1.

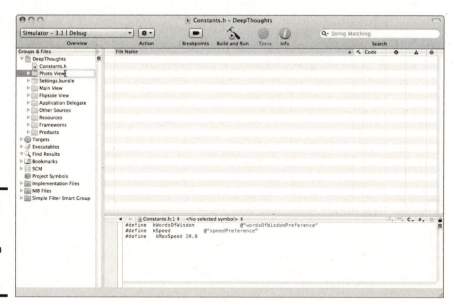

Figure 5-1: Create the new Photo View group in your project.

Creating subclasses of UIView and UIViewController

Next, create a new `UIView` subclass in your new group. Select the Photo View group and then choose File➪New File. In the New File dialog that appears, select Cocoa Touch Class in the left panel under iPhone OS, as shown in Figure 5-2, and then select Objective-C class from the top row of file types. In the Subclass Of pop-up menu, choose `UIView`, and then click Next.

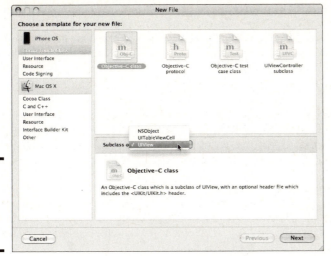

Figure 5-2:
Create
a new
subclass of
UIView.

In the next New File screen, enter the filename for the implementation file
(**PhotoView.m**), as shown in Figure 5-3. Be sure to also select the Also Create
`PhotoView.h` option. (The filename in the option depends on the name you
provide for the `.m` file.) Finally, click Finish.

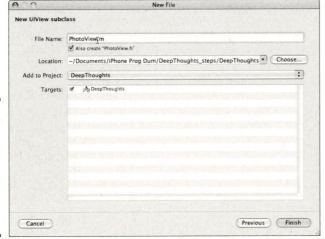

Figure 5-3:
Name the
subclass
PhotoView
(to create
PhotoView.m
and Photo
View.h).

Xcode creates `PhotoView.h` and `PhotoView.m` and stashes them in the
Photo View group (since that is the group you selected at first). You modify
these files later in this chapter.

The Photo view, just like the Main view, will be accessed by a subclass of `UIViewController`. Select the Photo View group (if it's not already selected) and then choose File⇨New File. In the New File dialog that appears, select Cocoa Touch Class again, as shown in Figure 5-4, but this time select `UIViewController` subclass and then click Next.

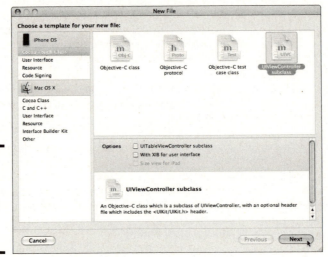

Figure 5-4: Create a new subclass of UIViewController.

In the next New File screen, enter the filename for the implementation file (`PhotoViewController.m`), as shown in Figure 5-5. Be sure to also select the Also Create "`PhotoViewController.h`" option. Finally, click Finish.

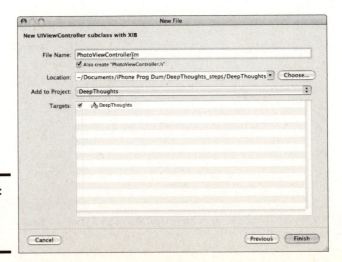

Figure 5-5: Here you name the subclass.

Xcode creates `PhotoViewController.h` and `PhotoViewController.m` in the Photo View group.

Creating a nib file for the Photo view

A *nib file,* as you may recall from Chapter 1 of this minibook, is a resource file that contains the specifications for one or more objects. The main nib file usually contains a window object of some kind, the application delegate object, and any other key objects. When the file is loaded, the objects are reconstituted (think "instant application") in memory. The single window you see displayed on the iPhone is an instance of the `UIWindow` class. This window is created at launch time automatically by `UIKit`, which loads it from the nib file. You can add views and controls to the window. The `UIView` class defines the basic properties of a view, and you can use it as is by simply adding some controls.

First, create a nib file for the view, being sure to specify that it be included in the Resources group in your Xcode project. Select the Resources group, and then choose File⇨New File. In the New File dialog that appears, select User Interface in the left panel under iPhone OS, as shown in Figure 5-6, select `View XIB` from the top row of file types, and then click Next.

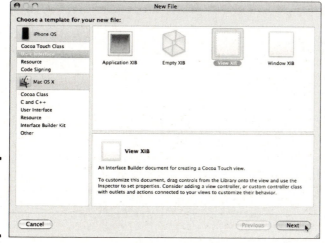

Figure 5-6:
Create a nib file for the Photo view.

In the next New File screen, enter the filename for the nib file (`PhotoView.xib`), as shown in Figure 5-7, and then click Finish.

Xcode creates `PhotoView.xib` in the Resources group in your project. Double-click `PhotoView.xib` to open it in Interface Builder.

To control the Photo view from the `PhotoViewController` subclass of `UIViewController`, select File's Owner in the `PhotoView.xib` window, click the Identity tab in the Inspector window (or choose Tools⇨Identity Inspector), and choose `PhotoViewController` from the Class pop-up menu in the Class Identity section, as shown in Figure 5-8. Then quit Interface Builder, saving the half-done `PhotoView.xib` file in the process.

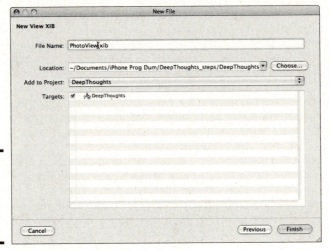

Figure 5-7:
Name the nib file PhotoView. xib.

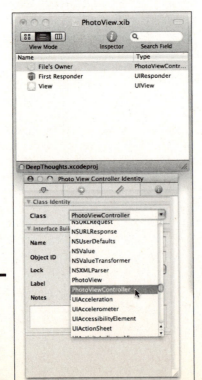

Figure 5-8:
Change the File's Owner to MainView-Controller.

Now you need some of the objects from the main view — the `MainView` object and its Light Info Button. It just so happens that you can simply copy them from one nib file to the other. Double-click `MainView.xib` in the Resources group to open it in Interface Builder, select Main View in the `MainView.xib` window, as shown in Figure 5-9, and then choose Edit⇨Copy.

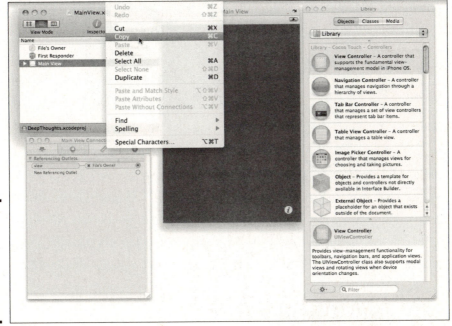

Figure 5-9: Copy Main View from MainView. xib to use in PhotoView. xib.

Book III
Chapter 5

Extending Your App
with a Photo View

Quit Interface Builder and then double-click `PhotoView.xib` in the Resources group to open it in Interface Builder. Select View in the `PhotoView.xib` window, choose Edit⇨Delete to delete the plain vanilla view, and then choose Edit⇨Paste to paste in the Main View from `MainView.xib`. As a result, you automatically get the Main view and its Light Info button, as shown in Figure 5-10.

Now all you need to do is connect the view and Info button to the appropriate methods.

To connect the view, select Main View in the `PhotoView.xib` window, click the Connections tab in the Inspector window (or choose Tools⇨Connections Inspector), and drag a New Referencing Outlet to the File's Owner to make a connection, as shown in Figure 5-11. The `view` method pops up so that you can select it for Main View, as shown in Figure 5-12.

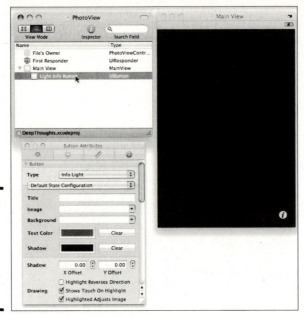

Figure 5-10:
After
pasting
Main
View into
PhotoView.
xib.

Figure 5-11:
Connect
Main View
to the File's
Owner for
PhotoView.
xib.

Figure 5-12:
Connect
Main View
to the `view`
method.

To connect the Info button to the appropriate method, click the triangle next to Main View in the `PhotoView.xib` window to open it, select Light Info Button underneath Main View, click the Connections tab in the Inspector window (or choose Tools⇨Connections Inspector), and drag the outlet for a Touch Inside Up event to the File's Owner to make a connection, as shown in Figure 5-13. The `showinfo` method pops up so that you can select it for the Info button, as shown in Figure 5-14.

Book III
Chapter 5

Extending Your App
with a Photo View

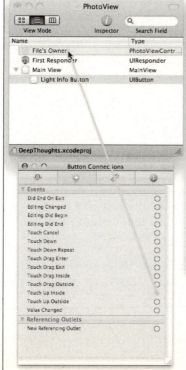

Figure 5-13:
Connect
Light Info
Button to
the File's
Owner for
PhotoView.
xib.

Figure 5-14:
Connect
Light Info
Button
to the
showinfo
method.

Modifying the window nib file for scrolling

Remember, you are (in a sense) combining two views into one for the purpose of horizontal scrolling — controlling the falling words (Main) view and the falling images (Photo) view through instances of `MainViewController`. What you need to do now is add a scrolling view (`UIScrollView`) to the window and connect that to the DeepThoughts application delegate and its `scrollView` method.

Double-click `MainWindow.xib` in the Resources group in your project to open it in Interface Builder. You can then click Window in the `MainWindow.xib` window of Interface Builder, so that you can add a Scroll View object to it, as shown in Figure 5-15. If the Library window is not already open, choose Tools➪Library. Then select Data Views from the Library pop-up menu to see the views you can use. Information about each object appears in the lower portion of the Library window. The Scroll View is of the `UIScrollView` class; it provides a way to display content that is larger than the window and enables users to scroll within that content.

Drag the `UIScrollView`, as shown in Figure 5-15, to the window. Horizontal and vertical guides appear to help you place it where you want, but for this app's purposes, you want it to fill the entire black portion of the window. As you drag, the `UIScrollView` snaps into position to cover the black portion of the window (unless you drag a side of it to resize it). Interface Builder creates the Scroll View object underneath the Window object in the `MainWindow.xib` window.

To connect the Scroll view to the appropriate method, first click the triangle next to Window in the `MainWindow.xib` window to open it and reveal Scroll View underneath Window. Select Deep Thoughts App Delegate, click the Connections tab in the Inspector window (or choose Tools➪Connections Inspector) and then drag the outlet for the `scrollView` method to connect it to Scroll View, as shown in Figure 5-16.

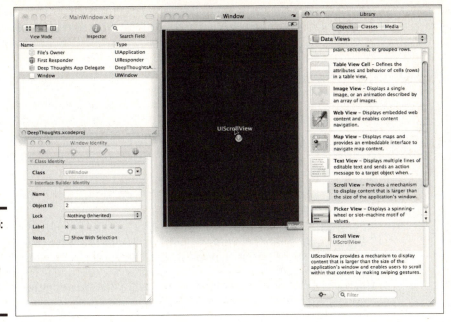

Figure 5-15:
Drag a
Scroll
View to the
Window
window.

**Book III
Chapter 5**

**Extending Your App
with a Photo View**

Figure 5-16:
Connect the
scrollView
method in
the Deep
Thoughts
App
Delegate to
Scroll View
in Main
Window.
xib.

You have now successfully implemented the Photo view and modified the window for horizontal scrolling between the Main and Photo views.

Animating the Photo View

In Chapter 3 of this minibook, you created the animated view for the falling words (the Main view) in `MainViewController.h` and `MainViewController.m`. You can now reuse most of that code to animate the Photo view.

Reusing MainViewController code for PhotoViewController

As you enter the `PhotoViewController` code in Listing 5-3 and Listing 5-4 (the code to add is in bold), compare it with the `MainViewController` code in Chapter 4 of this minibook. (The full `MainViewController` code is in Chapter 3, with changes made in Chapter 4 to include user preferences.) Much of it is identical; the difference is that you are animating `fallingImage` without having to convert a string of words first.

Listing 5-3: PhotoViewController.h

```
@interface PhotoViewController : UIViewController   {
  UIImage                 *fallingImage;
}

- (IBAction)showInfo;

@end
```

Listing 5-4: PhotoViewController.m

```
#import "PhotoViewController.h"
#import "PhotoView.h"

@implementation PhotoViewController

// The designated initializer... un-comment to use:
- (id)initWithNibName:(NSString *)nibNameOrNil
    bundle:(NSBundle *)nibBundleOrNil {
  if (self = [super initWithNibName:nibNameOrNil
    bundle:nibBundleOrNil]) {
    // Custom initialization
  }
  return self;
}

- (void)viewDidLoad {
```

```
  [super viewDidLoad];
  self.view.backgroundColor = [UIColor  colorWithRed:.9
    green:.3 blue:.9 alpha:1];
  fallingImage = [UIImage imageNamed:@"fallingImage.png"];
  [NSTimer scheduledTimerWithTimeInterval:.2 target:self
    selector:@selector(onTimer) userInfo:nil repeats:YES];
}
- (void)onTimer{
  UIImageView *fallingImageView = [[UIImageView alloc]
    initWithImage:fallingImage];
  int startX = round(random() % 420);
  int endX = round(random() % 420);
  //speed of falling
  double speed = (1/round(random() % 100) +1) *10;
  // size of the image
  double scale = (1/round(random() % 100) +1)* 100;

  [self.view addSubview:fallingImageView];

  fallingImageView.frame = CGRectMake(startX, -100, scale,
    scale);

  fallingImageView.alpha = .75;

  [UIView beginAnimations:nil context:fallingImageView];
  [UIView setAnimationDuration:speed];
  [UIView setAnimationDelegate:self];
  [UIView setAnimationDidStopSelector:@selector(animationDone:
      finished:context:)];

  fallingImageView.frame = CGRectMake(endX, 500, scale,
    scale);
  [UIView commitAnimations];
}
-(void)animationDone:(NSString *)animationID
    finished:(NSNumber *)finished context:(id)context {
  UIImageView *fallingImageView = context;
  [fallingImageView removeFromSuperview];
  [fallingImageView release];
}
/*
 // Implement viewDidLoad to do additional setup after
    loading the view, typically from a nib.
 - (void)viewDidLoad {
 [super viewDidLoad];
 }
 */
/*
 // Override to allow orientations other than the default
    portrait orientation.
 - (BOOL)shouldAutorotateToInterfaceOrientation:(UIInterfaceO
    rientation)interfaceOrientation {
```

(continued)

Listing 5-4 *(continued)*

```
// Return YES for supported orientations
return (interfaceOrientation ==
  UIInterfaceOrientationPortrait);
}
*/

- (IBAction)showInfo {
}

- (void)didReceiveMemoryWarning {
// Releases the view if it doesn't have a superview.
  [super didReceiveMemoryWarning];
// Release any cached data, images, etc that aren't in use.
}
- (void)viewDidUnload {
  // Release any retained subviews of the main view.
  // e.g. self.myOutlet = nil;
}
- (void)dealloc {
  [super dealloc];
}

@end
```

Adding a default image

Besides changing the background color with the `self.view.background-`
`Color` statement, and the time interval from `.5` to `.2`, the `PhotoView-`
`Controller` code (in Listing 5-4) differs from the `MainViewController`
code (in Chapter 4 of this minibook) by assigning a default image to
`fallingImage` rather than converting words to the falling image:

```
fallingImage = [UIImage imageNamed:@"fallingImage.png"];
```

You can copy any photo or graphic image file, convert it to the `.png` format
using an image editing program, rename it to `fallingImage.png` and then
add the file.

To add the file to your project in Xcode, select the Resources group in the
Groups & Files list to add the file to, and choose Project⇨Add to Project.
Navigate your folders and choose the file to add. Xcode displays a dialog,
shown in Figure 5-17, which lets you specify how the files are added to the
project. Be sure to check the Copy Items into Destination Group's Folder
option so that the file is copied into your Project folder and stored in the
appropriate subfolder.

If you build and run your project now, you can drag the Main view horizontally to simulate the swipe gesture and see the Photo view with the flowing
default image, as shown in Figure 5-18. (The default image is a dollar sign.)

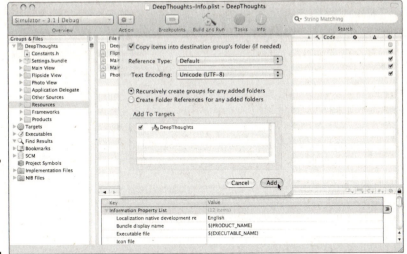

Figure 5-17:
Add the
default
image file to
the project.

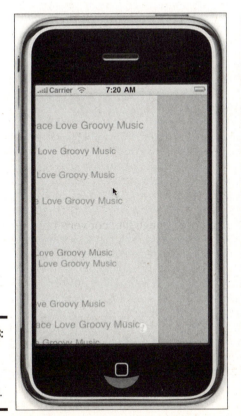

Figure 5-18:
Swipe the
main view
to see the
photo view.

Accessing Media on the iPhone

At this point, the Photo view's Info button, which connects to the `showInfo` method, leads to a blank screen (unlike the Main view's Info button, which leads to the Flipside view). To enable the user to pick a photo from the iPhone photo library (accessible from the Photos app), you can create an object of the `UIImagePickerController` class.

The `UIImagePickerController` class manages the system-supplied interfaces for choosing pictures (iPhone and iPod touch), taking pictures (iPhone), and capturing movies (iPhone 3GS). By default, the `UIImagePickerController` class handles all user interactions — all you have to do is tell it which user interface to display, present it, and then dismiss it from your associated delegate object when the user picks an image or movie or cancels the operation.

Because you're using this class to access saved or synced photos, which all iPhone and iPod touch models support, you don't need to verify that the device is capable of picking this content. However, if you're using this class to *capture* photos or videos, you need to verify that the device is capable of picking the content you want by calling the `isSourceTypeAvailable:` class method *before* presenting the interface. Also check which media types are available for the source type by calling the `availableMediaTypes-ForSourceType:` class method. This latter method allows you to distinguish between a camera that can be used for video recording and one that can be used only for still pictures.

To use this class, you provide a delegate that conforms to the `UIImagePickerControllerDelegate` protocol and the `UINavigationControllerDelegate` protocol by putting the code in Listing 5-5 (in bold) in the `PhotoViewController.h` file.

The `UIImagePickerControllerDelegate` protocol defines methods that your delegate object must implement to interact with the image picker interface. The methods of this protocol notify your delegate when the user either picks an image or movie, or cancels the picker operation. The `UINavigationControllerDelegate` protocol defines methods a navigation controller delegate can implement to manage the currently displayed view using the navigation stack. For example, a navigation controller delegate implements the `pushViewController:animated:` method to push a new view controller object onto the stack, which causes the view of that view controller to be displayed and the navigation controls to be updated to reflect the change. You can also pop a view controller (remove it from the stack) using the `popViewControllerAnimated:` method.

Listing 5-5:   PhotoViewController.h

```
@interface PhotoViewController : UIViewController
  <UIImagePickerControllerDelegate,
  UINavigationControllerDelegate>    {
 UIImagePickerController    *imagePickerController;
 UIImageView                *imageView;
 UIImage                    *fallingImage;
}

- (IBAction)showInfo;

@end
```

After the interface starts, this class notifies your delegate of the user's actions. Your delegate is then responsible for dismissing the picker and returning to your application's views. Enter the code in Listing 5-6 (in bold) in the PhotoViewController.m file.

Listing 5-6:   PhotoViewController.m

```
#import "PhotoViewController.h"
#import "DeepThoughtsAppDelegate.h"

#import "PhotoView.h"

@implementation PhotoViewController

// The designated initializer... un-comment to use:
- (id)initWithNibName:(NSString *)nibNameOrNil
   bundle:(NSBundle *)nibBundleOrNil {
  if (self = [super initWithNibName:nibNameOrNil
   bundle:nibBundleOrNil]) {
    // Custom initialization
  }
  return self;
}

- (void)viewDidLoad {
  [super viewDidLoad];
  self.view.backgroundColor = [UIColor  colorWithRed:.9
   green:.3 blue:.9 alpha:1];
  fallingImage = [UIImage imageNamed:@"fallingImage.png"];
  [NSTimer scheduledTimerWithTimeInterval:.2 target:self
   selector:@selector(onTimer) userInfo:nil repeats:YES];
}
- (void)onTimer{
  UIImageView *fallingImageView = [[UIImageView alloc]
   initWithImage:fallingImage];
  int startX = round(random() % 420);
```

(continued)

Listing 5-6 *(continued)*

```objc
int endX = round(random() % 420);
//speed of falling
double speed = (1/round(random() % 100) +1) *10;
// size of the image
double scale = (1/round(random() % 100) +1)* 100;

[self.view addSubview:fallingImageView];

fallingImageView.frame = CGRectMake(startX, -100, scale,
  scale);

fallingImageView.alpha = .75;

[UIView beginAnimations:nil context:fallingImageView];
[UIView setAnimationDuration:speed];
[UIView setAnimationDelegate:self];
[UIView setAnimationDidStopSelector:@selector(animationDone:
    finished:context:)];

fallingImageView.frame = CGRectMake(endX, 500, scale,
  scale);
[UIView commitAnimations];
}
-(void)animationDone:(NSString *)animationID
   finished:(NSNumber *)finished context:(id)context {
UIImageView *fallingImageView = context;
[fallingImageView removeFromSuperview];
[fallingImageView release];
}

- (void)imagePickerController:(UIImagePickerController *)
  picker
       didFinishPickingImage:(UIImage *)image
               editingInfo:(NSDictionary *)editingInfo
{
  // Dismiss the image selection, hide the picker and
  //show the image view with the picked image
  [picker dismissModalViewControllerAnimated:YES];
  fallingImage = image;
  [fallingImage retain];
}

// from PickImageAppDelegate.m
- (void)imagePickerControllerDidCancel:(UIImagePickerControl
  ler *)picker
{
  // Dismiss the image selection and close the program
  [picker dismissModalViewControllerAnimated:YES];
  //  exit(0);
}
```

```
/*
 // Implement viewDidLoad to do additional setup after
    loading the view, typically from a nib.
 - (void)viewDidLoad {
 [super viewDidLoad];
 }
 */
/*
 // Override to allow orientations other than the default
    portrait orientation.
 - (BOOL)shouldAutorotateToInterfaceOrientation:(UIInterfaceO
   rientation)interfaceOrientation {
 // Return YES for supported orientations
 return (interfaceOrientation ==
    UIInterfaceOrientationPortrait);
 }
 */

- (IBAction)showInfo {
   imagePickerController = [[UIImagePickerController alloc]
      init];
   imagePickerController.delegate = self;
   imagePickerController.sourceType =
      UIImagePickerControllerSourceTypePhotoLibrary;
   imagePickerController.delegate = self;
   // imagePickerController.view.frame = self.view.frame;

   // imageView = [[UIImageView alloc] initWithFrame:[window
      bounds]];

   imagePickerController.modalTransitionStyle =
      UIModalTransitionStyleCoverVertical;
   DeepThoughtsAppDelegate* appDelegate = (
      DeepThoughtsAppDelegate*)[[UIApplication
      sharedApplication] delegate];
   CGRect frame1 = appDelegate.scrollView.frame;
   frame1.origin.x = frame1.size.width * 0;
   frame1.origin.y = 0;

      [ self presentModalViewController:imagePickerController
      animated:YES];
   // [appDelegate.scrollView scrollRectToVisible:frame1
      animated:YES];

      [imagePickerController release];
}

- (void)didReceiveMemoryWarning {
// Releases the view if it doesn't have a superview.
   [super didReceiveMemoryWarning];
// Release any cached data, images, etc that aren't in use.
}
```

(continued)

Listing 5-6 *(continued)*

```
- (void)viewDidUnload {
    // Release any retained subviews of the main view.
    // e.g. self.myOutlet = nil;
}
- (void)dealloc {
    [super dealloc];
}

@end
```

The following code from Listing 5-6 tells the delegate that the user picked an image. It then dismisses the image selection, hides the image picker, and shows the photo view with the picked image:

```
- (void)imagePickerController:(UIImagePickerController *)
    picker
        didFinishPickingImage:(UIImage *)image
                    editingInfo:(NSDictionary *)editingInfo
{
    // Dismiss the image selection, hide the picker and
    //show the image view with the picked image
    [picker dismissModalViewControllerAnimated:YES];
    fallingImage = image;
    [fallingImage retain];
}
```

The `image` used with this instance method is the image that the user picked. (`editingInfo` is a dictionary containing any relevant editing information, but if editing is disabled, as it is in this app, this parameter is nil.)

The `imagePickerControllerDidCancel:` instance method tells the delegate that the user cancelled the pick operation. Your code then dismisses the image selection:

```
- (void)imagePickerControllerDidCancel:(UIImagePickerControl
    ler *)picker
{
    // Dismiss the image selection and close the program
    [picker dismissModalViewControllerAnimated:YES];
    //  exit(0);
}
```

The new code in Listing 5-6 between the angle brackets for the `(IBAction)` `showInfo` method uses the image picker interface for the view accessed by the Info button. The following statement sets the type of picker interface displayed by the controller to the Photo library:

```
imagePickerController.sourceType =
    UIImagePickerControllerSourceTypePhotoLibrary;
```

The next statement (after the commented-out code available for experimentation) sets the transition style to use when presenting the current view controller (it's set to the default, which is vertical):

```
imagePickerController.modalTransitionStyle =
    UIModalTransitionStyleCoverVertical;
```

At the end of the `(IBAction)showInfo` method, the code presents a modal view managed by the view controller and then releases `imagePicker Controller`:

```
[ self presentModalViewController:imagePickerController
    animated:YES];
[imagePickerController release];
```

That's it. If you build and run your project now, you can drag the Main view horizontally to see the Photo view with the flowing default image (the dollar sign), as shown in Figure 5-19 (left side). Click the Info button, and the image picker interface appears (right side). (You won't be able to actually browse for images from within the Simulator, but at least you get a chance to see how the process would work with a real device.)

Book III
Chapter 5

Extending Your App
with a Photo View

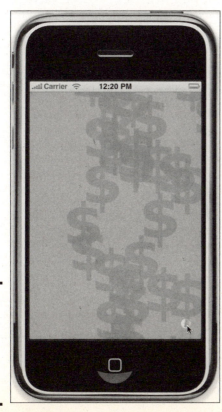

Figure 5-19: Click the Info button in the Photo view for the image picker.

Adding an Application Icon

With an app nearly ready for release, you shouldn't procrastinate about the selection and installation of a graphic image as the app's icon.

An application icon is simply a 57-x-57-pixel .png graphics file. Add the file in the same way you added the default image in the "Adding a default image" section, earlier in this chapter. Select the Resources group in the Groups & Files list and then choose Project⇨Add to Project. After you navigate your folders and choose the file to add, Xcode displays a dialog (refer to Figure 5-17), which lets you specify how the files are added to the project. Be sure to select the Copy Items into Destination Group's Folder option so that the file is copied into your Project folder and stored in the appropriate subfolder.

After you add the icon's graphics file, you also need to specify that this file is what you want used as the application's icon. You do that using one of those other mysterious files you see in the Resources folder. Here's how:

1. **In the Resources folder, click the `DeepThoughts-Info.plist` file, as shown in Figure 5-20.**

    The contents of the `info.plist` file are displayed in the Editor pane. You're treated to some information about the application, including an item in the Key column labeled Icon file.

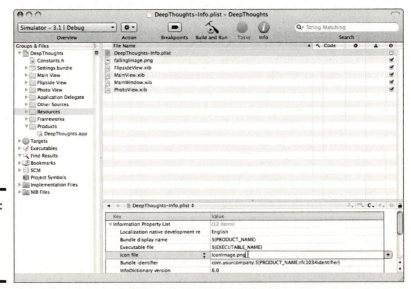

Figure 5-20: Adding the icon file in the info. plist.

2. **Double-click in the empty space in the Value column next to Icon file.**

3. **Type in the name of your .png graphics file and then build the project as you normally would.**

   You know, clicking the Build and Run button in the Project Window toolbar, choosing Build⇨Build and Go (Run) from the main menu, or pressing ⌘+Return. Building the project gives you the opportunity to save it.

Click the Home button in the iPhone Simulator after building and running the project, and you should be able to see your application icon.

A Lot Accomplished Very Quickly

So it looks like you have all the pieces in place for the DeepThoughts application. The user can now enter any phrase for the flowing words and any photo in the iPhone photo library for the flowing images. The user can switch back and forth by swiping the view.

Appearances can be deceiving, though.

Reality check: Some how-to books on software development should really be housed in the Fiction section of your local bookstore because all their examples work flawlessly. In the real world, everything does not always go as planned; occasionally your software program blows up on you. That's why an essential part of software development is the debugging phase — teasing as many flaws out of your app as possible so you can squash 'em. Book IV shows you how to work through the debugging phase of your project and introduces you to the SDK's very own debugging tool, something that's sure to make your software-development life a lot easier.

Book IV

Debugging and Tuning Your Application

Contents at a Glance

Chapter 1: Using the Xcode Debugger

In This Chapter

✔ Understanding the kinds of errors that may come up

✔ Using Xcode's Debugger

✔ Zeroing in on errors the Debugger can help you find

✔ Stamping out logic errors with the Debugger

✔ Using the Static Analyzer to analyze your code for memory leaks

*W*hen you're developing an application, sometimes things don't work out quite the way you planned — especially when you knock over a can of Jolt Cola on the keyboard and fry it out of existence.

Murphy was an optimist about computer programming with his law that there is always one more bug. It took Weinberg's Second Law to put debugging into perspective: If builders built buildings the way that programmers program programs, the first woodpecker to come along would destroy civilization.

As this experienced co-author learned the hard way (indeed, Tony wrote *Murphy's Computer Laws* in 1980 for Celestial Arts, only to violate most of them in his latest iPhone app project), debugging is not something to put off until later, after the warnings and error messages pile up. Keep in mind Bove's Theorem: The remaining work required to finish a project increases as the deadline approaches. It's best to tackle any errors and warnings you get immediately.

So, what does it take to tackle the inevitable errors that will find their way into your code? In a word, *debugging:* the process of analyzing your code line by line to view your program's state at a particular stage of execution. To debug a program, you run it under the control of a debugger, which lets you pause the program and examine its state. In this chapter, I show you how to use the Xcode Debugger to understand, locate, and fix bugs.

Understanding Bugs

"Stuff happens," in the immortal words of a famous ex-U.S. Secretary of Defense. When it comes to developing your own programs, that "stuff" comes in three categories:

✦ **Syntax errors:** Compilers — the Objective-C compiler in Xcode is a case in point — expect you to use a certain set of instructions in your code; those instructions make up the language it understands. When you type `If` instead of `if`, or the subtler `[view release}` (with a curly closing bracket) instead of `[view release]` (with a straight closing bracket), the compiler suddenly has no idea what you're talking about and generates a syntax error.

Syntax errors are the most obvious, simply because your program won't compile (and therefore won't run) until all of them are fixed. Generally, syntax errors spring from typographical errors. (And yes, the errors can be pretty penny-ante stuff — an *I* for an *i*, for goodness sake — but it doesn't take much to stump a compiler.)

In Figure 1-1, you can see an example of a syntax error — simply forgetting to put a semicolon at the end of the `CGRect frame2 = scrollView.frame` statement. This one is kindly pointed out by Xcode's friendly Debugger feature. After choosing Build⇨Build and Run to build and run the application (and saving all changes in the process), the build fails — a tiny hammer icon and Failed appears in the notification section (in the bottom-right corner of the Xcode window), and the compiler highlights the statement after the syntax error with three red exclamation marks — in the gutter to the left of the statement after the syntax error, in the strip of debugging information that appears around the statement after the syntax error, and in the notifications section of the Xcode window.

A syntax error in a different place in the code might not be detected by the compiler and might therefore wreak havoc with subsequent code, causing the build to fail. For example, in Figure 1-2, I forget to include a semicolon at the end of the `@synthesize speed` statement, and as a result, the compiler found a problem with subsequent code. Click the exclamation mark, and Xcode brings up the Build Results window, as shown in the upper part of Figure 1-3, with a long list of errors starting with `Expected ';' before '-' token`. The Build Results window shows a more detailed view of the consequences of an error.

It's generally better to ignore the subsequent errors after the first syntax error because they may be the result of that first error. In this case, because of the first error, that line and the next one were treated as a single instruction, causing an incomplete implementation of `MainViewController`.

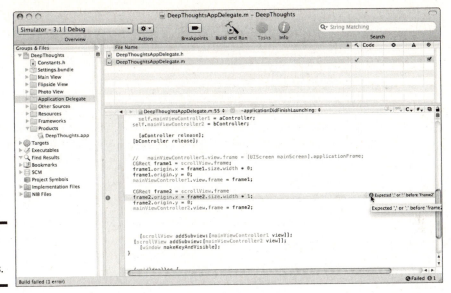

Figure 1-1:
A syntax
error. Oops.

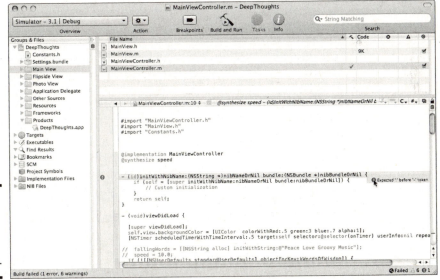

Figure 1-2:
A subtle
but more
damaging
syntax error.

✦ **Runtime errors:** *Runtime errors* cause your program to stop executing —
it *crashes,* in other words, as in "crash and burn to much wailing and
gnashing of teeth." Something might have come up in the data that you
hadn't expected (a division-by-zero error, for example), or the result of
a method dealt a nasty surprise to your logic, or you sent a message to

an object that doesn't have that message implemented. Sometimes you even get some build warnings for these errors; often the application simply stops working or *hangs* (stops and does nothing), or shuts down.

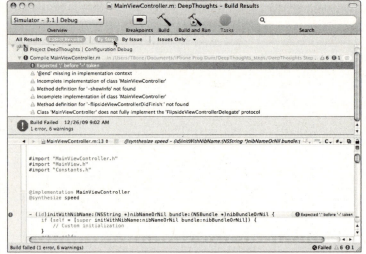

Figure 1-3:
The Build Results window lists the damage from this one error.

✦ **Logic errors:** Your literal-minded application does exactly what you tell it to, but sometimes you unintentionally tell it the wrong thing, and it coughs up a *logic error*. For example, in Figure 1-4, I deliberately created a logic error by dividing by zero. Xcode warns you about the divide-by-zero error but goes ahead anyway and builds and runs the app.

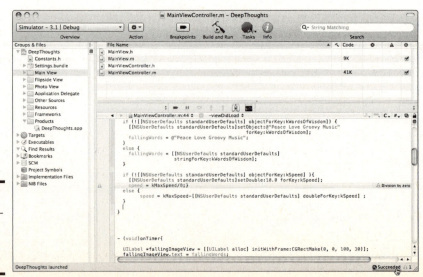

Figure 1-4:
Oh, great — it builds but doesn't work.

I typed the divide-by-zero error (`speed = kMaxSpeed/0`) to make the point that you may be able to build and run your app, but it may not work as intended. In this case, the app starts up but doesn't display the animated default words.

You can see in Figure 1-4 the yellow exclamation point, which is a warning (rather than a red one, which is an error), and the message `Division by zero`. Clicking the exclamation point brings up the Build Results window, as shown in Figure 1-5, with the `Division by zero` warning and the steps of compiling and building the app.

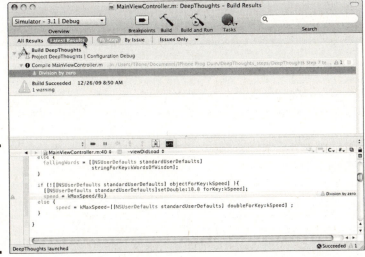

Figure 1-5:
The Build Results window shows what happened.

With a complex app, you might be pelted with compiler warnings that you don't have time to take care of because they have no impact on the execution of the program. One reason to set Xcode preferences to always open the Build Results window is to continually remind yourself about these warnings if you haven't fixed them. To set this preference, choose Xcode⇨Preferences⇨Building and choose Always from the Open During Builds pop-up menu.

Syntax errors, runtime errors, and logic errors can all be pains in the behind, but there's no need to think of them as insurmountable roadblocks. You're still on your way to a cool iPhone app.

Using the Debugger

The Debugger can be really useful when your program isn't doing what you expect. For the blatant errors, the Debugger can show you exactly what is going on when the error occurred. It provides you with a trail of how you got to where you are, highlights the problem instruction, and shows you your application's variables and their values at that point.

If you've been following the examples in Book III for developing the DeepThoughts app, you're ready to debug the app, and your configuration should still be set to Simulator-3.1 | Debug in the pop-up menu in the upper left corner of the Xcode Project window. If you've been developing a project with a different configuration, you must change it to the Debug build configuration. Before you can take advantage of the Debugger, the compiler must collect information for the Debugger, and the Debug build configuration generates the debugging symbols for that purpose.

You can tap the Debugger from the Xcode Text editor and set breakpoints that stop execution at any point and trace the messages sent up to that point (as I describe in "Using Breakpoints" in this chapter), so that you can step through the program's execution and view the contents of variables. The Debugger window offers even more control over the process and provides detailed information. You can also use the Mini Debugger — a floating window — that offers many of the functions of the Debugger window, as I show later in this chapter.

You can even use the Mac OS X Console utility application to view messages and interact with the GNU Source-Level Debugger with typed commands, as I explain in the "Using the Console" section in this chapter.

Debugging in the Text editor

You can set the Xcode Text editor to recognize breakpoints by clicking the Breakpoints button in the Project window toolbar — the Build and Run button changes to Build and Debug. (I talk more about breakpoints in the "Using Breakpoints" section, later in this chapter.) Click Build and Debug to build and run the program.

A red exclamation point, as shown in Figure 1-6, points to the instruction that caused the program to stop building — that's the Debugger pointing out the problem.

There's even some information about the error. The Debugger offers a strip of information called a *datatip,* which you can see in Figure 1-8 right underneath the offending line. The datatip says Can not use an object as parameter to a method and ends with a 2, which means another error or warning is there. In Figure 1-7 I click the 2, and it reveals a second warning, Conflicting types.

It turns out that the first message is all I need to know. The compiler thinks I'm trying to use an object (UIApplication) rather than a pointer to an object (UIApplication *) — and that's because I forgot to include an asterisk within the parentheses with UIApplication. The statement should be

```
- (void)applicationDidFinishLaunching:
                (UIApplication *)application {
```

Figure 1-6:
Xcode
highlights
an error and
displays a
datatip.

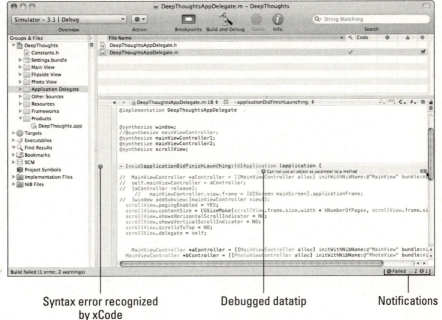

Syntax error recognized   Debugged datatip   Notifications
by xCode

**Book IV
Chapter 1**

**Using the
Xcode Debugger**

Figure 1-7:
The datatip
shows a
second
warning.

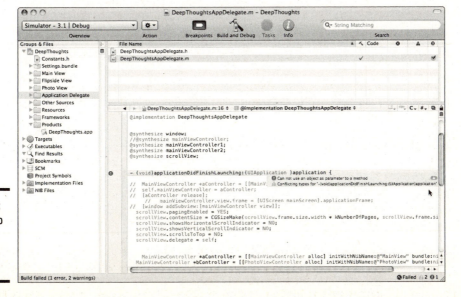

TIP

When you move your pointer over a variable in a datatip, its contents are revealed, and if more disclosure triangles appear, you can move your pointer over them to see even more information. You can also modify the contents of mutable variables.

Click the up and down arrows next to @implementation DeepThoughts AppDelegate (or whatever you have in your project) in the Debugger strip (refer to Figure 1-6), so that you can see the *stack* — a trace of the objects and methods that got you to where you are now, as shown in Figure 1-8.

Although the stack isn't really all that useful in this particular context, it *can* be very useful in a more complex application — it can help you understand the path that you took to get where you are. Seeing how one object sent a message to another object — which sent a message to a third object — can be really helpful, especially if you didn't expect the program flow to work that way.

Getting a look at the stack can also be useful if you're trying to understand how the framework does its job, and in what order messages are sent. As you'll see later in this chapter, using something called a *breakpoint* can stop the execution of your program at any point and trace the messages sent up to that point.

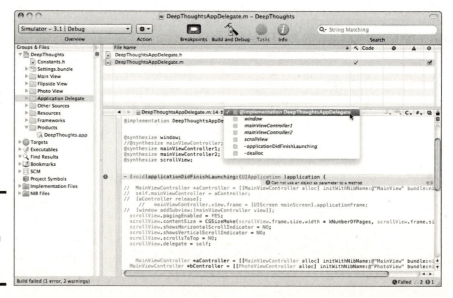

Figure 1-8:
Looking at the stack in the Editor view.

If your app manages to build and run (which can happen even with a warning, as you can see back in Figure 1-4), that means it has passed through the compiler without syntax errors. But you're not out of the woods yet — even if you don't see evidence of runtime errors that crash the app, you certainly haven't tried all the app's functions yet. You also don't know whether there are logic errors. But don't despair; you have options.

The Debugger strip appears just above the Text Editor pane, as shown in Figure 1-9, while the app is running in the iPhone Simulator.

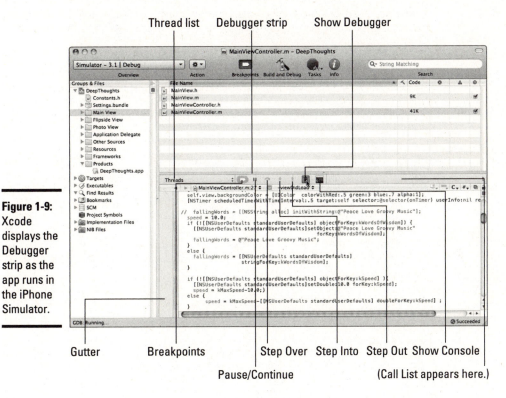

Figure 1-9:
Xcode displays the Debugger strip as the app runs in the iPhone Simulator.

The Debugger strip offers several buttons for your pushing pleasure:

✦ **Thread list:** Displays a list of the threads in your program. I explain this in the "Using the Debugger window" section, coming up next.

✦ **Breakpoints:** Activates or deactivates breakpoints, which I describe in the "Using Breakpoints" section later in this chapter.

✦ **Continue:** Continues execution of a paused process in your program.

✦ **Step Over:** Steps over the current line of code. The *process counter* (PC), which is identified by the red arrow in the gutter, moves to the next line of code to be executed in the current file.

**Book IV
Chapter 1**

**Using the
Xcode Debugger**

✦ **Step Into:** Steps into a function or method in the current line of code. If possible, the Text editor shows the source file with the called routine. The PC (red arrow) points to the line of code to be executed next.

✦ **Step Out:** Steps out of the current function or method. The Text editor shows the source file with the function's caller.

✦ **Show Debugger:** Opens the Debugger proper.

✦ **Show Console:** Opens the Mac OS X Console, which I describe in the "Using the Console" section in this chapter.

✦ **Call list:** Displays a list of the called functions or methods in the current call stack, which I explain in the "Using the Debugger window" section, coming up really, really soon.

You can play with your app in the iPhone Simulator and then switch back to launch the Debugger window from the Debugger strip.

Using the Debugger window

After clicking the Show Debugger button in the Debugger strip in the Project window, or choosing Run⇨Debugger (or pressing Shift+⌘+Y), the Debugger window appears. (Even though the Debugger is officially running, you have to open the Debugger window explicitly.) You can then click the Pause button along the top of the Debugger window to stop execution. (The Restart button replaces the Pause button after clicking Pause, as shown in Figure 1-10.)

Thread list   Variable list   Toolbar

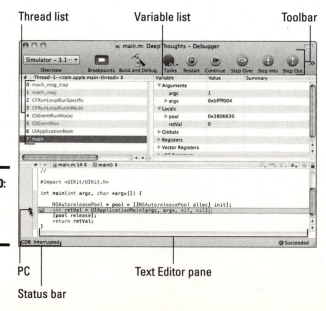

Figure 1-10:
The
Debugger
window.

PC

Status bar   Text Editor pane

The Debugger window has everything the Text Editor pane has, but you can also see your stack and the variables in scope at a glance. It also has some extra functionality I show you in the upcoming section "Using Breakpoints."

Here's what you see in the Debugger window:

✦ **Toolbar:** Offers buttons for controlling the program's execution, including Pause/Restart, Continue, Step Over, Step Into, and Step Out. (Restart starts execution from the beginning, whereas Continue continues execution from a breakpoint).

✦ **Thread list:** Shows the call stack of the current thread. For each function or method call that your program makes, the Debugger stores information about it in a stack frame. These stack frames are stored in the call stack. When you pause execution by clicking the Pause button in the Toolbar, Xcode displays the call stack for the currently running process in the Thread list and puts the most recent call at the top. The pop-up menu above this view lets you select different threads to view when debugging a multi-threaded application.

✦ **Variable list:** Shows information — such as name, type, and value — about the variables for the selected stack frame. To see the contents of a structured variable (including arrays and vectors) or an object, click the triangle next to the variable.

✦ **Text Editor pane:** Displays the source code you are debugging. When you pause execution by clicking the Pause button in the Toolbar, the Debugger highlights the line of source code where execution paused and displays the PC red arrow indicator.

✦ **Status bar:** Displays the current status of the debugging session. For example, in Figure 1-10, Xcode indicates that GDB (the GNU Source-Level Debugger) has just been interrupted.

Your window may not look exactly like Figure 1-10 — that's because Xcode gives you lots of different ways to customize the look of the Debugger window. You can, for example, choose Run➪Debugger Display from the main menu and then choose Horizontal Layout or Vertical Layout to change the window's layout.

TIP

You might want to choose Run➪Debugger Display➪Source and Disassembly if you have a hankering for checking both the source code *and* the assembly language (if you really care about assembly language); in that case, the Text Editor pane divides down the center into two panes, with the source code on the left and the assembly code in the right. The option I choose for Figure 1-10 is Source Only — so that only the source code appears in the Text Editor pane.

Using the Mini Debugger

The Mini Debugger is a floating window that provides debugging controls similar to those of the Xcode Text editor. It can make debugging a bit easier, because you don't have to switch back and forth between your running application and your Xcode Project window and Debugging window.

To show the Mini Debugger while running your program, choose Run⇨Mini Debugger. The Mini Debugger appears as shown in Figure 1-11 (left side) with buttons to stop or pause the program, open the Xcode project, or activate or deactivate breakpoints.

Figure 1-11:
Use the Mini Debugger to pause program execution and check out the code.

After pausing or stopping the program (or reaching a breakpoint), the Mini Debugger displays the same information you would see when debugging in the Text editor, as shown in Figure 1-11 (right side). As you can see in Figure 1-11 (right side), you can click the rightmost pop-up menu along the top of the window to see the call stack.

Using the Console

The Console utility application, supplied with Mac OS X, lets you watch error and status messages as they appear. If your computer appears to be stalled or is acting in an unusual manner, the Console might be producing information that can help debug the problem. While the Xcode Debugger provides a graphical interface for GDB (the GNU Source-Level Debugger), the Console lets you interact directly with GDB using a command line. You can type commands using the Console to perform simple debugging tasks, such as displaying the value of something.

For example, I use `NSLog` statements to log messages to the Console before and after the `slider.value` statement that tells me the information I need to know:

```
NSLog(@"Slider value %f parent value %f" ,slider.value ,
    ((MainViewController*)(self.parentViewController)).speed);
slider.value = + kMaxSpeed - ((MainViewController*)(self.
    parentViewController)).speed;
NSLog(@"Slider value %f parent value %f" ,slider.value ,
    ((MainViewController*)(self.parentViewController)).speed);
```

To open the Console window, choose Run⇨Console. After building and running the Xcode project, the messages appear in the Console in bold, as you can see in Figure 1-12. At the top are the Console messages before adding the slider.value statement, and at the bottom are the messages after adding the slider.value statement.

Figure 1-12: Use the Console to monitor messages sent from your code.

Book IV Chapter 1

Using the Xcode Debugger

You can use the Console window to see the commands that Xcode sends to GDB or the Java command-line debugger, to actually send commands directly to GDB or the Java command-line debugger, and to look at the debugger output for those commands. To enter commands, click in the Console window and type at the gdb or JavaBug prompt. To get help with GDB and Java debugging commands, type help. (To get the gdb or JavaBug prompt, the program you're debugging must be paused.)

Using Breakpoints

A *breakpoint* is an instruction to the Debugger to stop execution at that instruction and wait for further instructions (no pun intended). By setting breakpoints at various methods in your program, you can step through its execution — at the instruction level — to see exactly what it's doing. You can also examine the variables the program is setting and using. If you're stymied by a logic error, setting breakpoints is a great way to break that logjam.

To set a breakpoint in the Xcode Text editor, click inside the far-left column of the Editor pane. In Figure 1-13, I've set two breakpoints — one to stop execution right before the `(IBAction)done` statement and one to stop execution right after the statement.

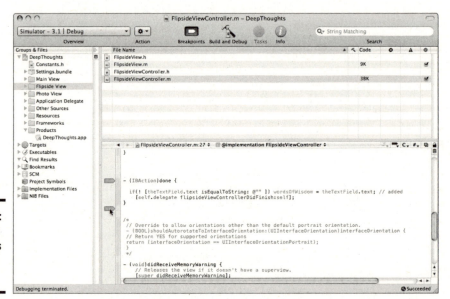

Figure 1-13: Setting two breakpoints in the Text editor.

To get rid of a breakpoint, simply drag it off to the side. You can also right-click the breakpoint and choose Remove Breakpoint from the pop-up menu that appears.

When you build and run the program, the Debugger strip appears in the Text editor as the program runs in the iPhone Simulator. The program stops executing at the first breakpoint. The process counter (PC) red arrow points to the line of code in the Text editor immediately following the breakpoint. You can then click the Show Debugger button in the Debugger strip (refer to Figure 1-9), or choose Run➪Debugger, to bring up the Debugger window.

In the Debugger window, as shown in Figure 1-14, you can move your pointer over an object or variable in the Text Editor pane to show its contents, and move your pointer over other disclosure triangles to see even more information.

For example, in Figure 1-14, I move the pointer over `self` to expand the view of `self` to show `FlipsideViewController`, and then expand the view of `FlipsideViewController` to see that `NSString` (`wordsOf Wisdom`) is `nil`, which it should be at this point. In Figure 1-15, I move the pointer over `delegate` in order to expand the view of `self.delegate` to show `MainViewController`, and then expand the view of `MainView Controller` to see that the value of `speed` is `10`. This is a powerful way to find out the value of variables at any given point during execution.

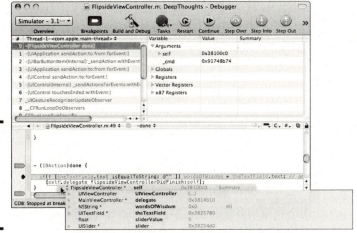

Figure 1-14: The Debugger window at the first breakpoint.

Figure 1-15: Expand the view of self. delegate to show MainView Controller.

You can click the Step Into button to go through your code instruction by instruction. The Debugger window also gives you other options for making your way through your program:

✦ **Step Over** gives you the opportunity to skip over an instruction.

✦ **Step Into** takes you step-by-step into a function or method in the current line of code.

✦ **Step Out** takes you out of the current method.

✦ **Continue** tells the program to keep on with its execution.

✦ **Restart** restarts the program. (You were hoping maybe if you tried it again it would work?)

Expanding the view of objects not only helps you check variables, but also checks messages sent to object reference instance variables. Objective-C, unlike some other languages, allows you to send a message to a `nil` object *without* generating a runtime error. If you do that, you should expect to subsequently see some sort of logic error because a message to a `nil` object simply does nothing. But it's possible that an object reference hasn't been set, and you're sending the message into the ether. If you look at an object reference instance variable and its value is `0x0`, any messages to that object are simply ignored. So when you get a logic error, the first thing you may want to check is whether any of the object references you're using have `0x0` as their values, informing you that the reference was never initialized.

As you can see, the Debugger can be really useful when your program isn't doing what you expect. For the blatant errors, the Debugger can show you exactly what is going on when the error occurred. It provides you with a trail of how you got to where you are, highlights the problem instruction, and shows you your application's variables and their values at that point.

What's just as valuable is how the Debugger can help you with logic errors. Sending a message to `nil` is not uncommon, especially when you're making changes to the user interface and forget to set up an outlet, for example. In such situations, the ability to look at the object references can really help.

Using the Static Analyzer

Xcode offers the Build and Analyze feature (the Static Analyzer) that analyzes your code for memory leaks. The results show up like warnings and errors, with explanations of where and what the issue is. You can also see the flow of control of the (potential) problem.

To show how this works, I deliberately created a memory leak in `Deep ThoughtsAppDelegate`. In the beginning of Chapter 5 of Book III, you commented out some code because you no longer needed it. I now bring it back just to prove a point.

To make my point, I uncommented the following lines of code in `DeepThoughtsAppDelegate.h`:

```
MainViewController *mainViewController;
```

And a few lines down, I did the same with

```
@property (nonatomic, retain) MainViewController
    *mainViewController;
```

Then, in `DeepThoughtsAppDelegate.m`, I added the following line of code after allocating the other view controllers:

```
MainViewController *cController = [MainViewController alloc];
```

Allocating a new object without doing anything with it is sure to cause a memory leak warning.

To run the Static Analyzer, choose Build⇨Build and Analyze. Sure enough, the change to the code I show above causes the warning in Figure 1-16. I get a warning (ignore the unused variable warning) with a little blue icon that says

```
Potential leak of an object allocated on line 35 and stored
    into 'cController'
```

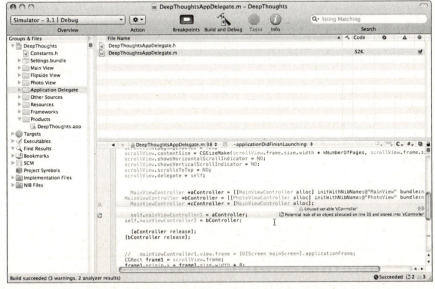

Figure 1-16: The Static Analyzer warns about a memory leak.

If you click on the little blue icon for the warning, you get a "trace" of what happened, as I show in Figure 1-17.

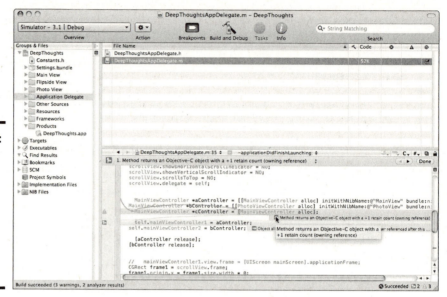

Figure 1-17:
The expanded Static Analyzer warning showing a trace of what happened.

First you get the following warning, which you can see by moving your pointer over the blue arrow icon in the trace (as shown in Figure 1-17):

```
Method returns an Objective-C object with a +1 retain
count (owning reference)
```

Then, in the next line, if you move your pointer over the blue arrow icon, you can see this:

```
Object allocated on line 35 and stored into 'cController' is
no longer referenced after this point and
has a retain count of +1 (object leaked)
```

Notice that the results refer to line numbers. That's why I made a point of explaining how to turn on line numbers in Xcode back in Chapter 4 of Book I.

As you know by now, memory management is a big deal on the iPhone.

Before you attempt to get your app into the App Store or even run it on anyone's iPhone, you need to make sure it's behaving properly. By that I mean not only delivering the promised functionality, but also avoiding the unintentional misuse of iPhone resources. Keep in mind that the iPhone, as cool as it may very well be, is nevertheless somewhat resource-constrained when it comes to memory usage and battery life. Such restraints can have a direct effect on what you can (and can't) do in your application.

Although the Static Analyzer can help you detect memory leaks, the real champ at doing that is Xcode's Instruments application, which also lets you know how your application uses iPhone resources such as the CPU, memory, network, and so on. Not sure what's up with the Instruments application? Then check out the next chapter of this minibook, devoted as it is to revealing its many mysteries.

Chapter 2: Tuning Your Code Using Xcode's Instruments Application

In This Chapter

✔ **Measuring application performance**

✔ **Finding memory leaks**

✔ **Keeping in mind that the Simulator is not the device**

✔ **Hunting down zombies**

Yogi Berra, in my humble opinion, is one of the great philosophers of all time. I'm sure he was talking about application development when he said, "It ain't over till it's over." So even if you've successfully compiled and launched your app and it seems to run (correctly), there's still work you need to do.

Before you attempt to get your application into the App Store or even run it on anyone's iPhone, you need to make sure it's behaving properly. By that I mean not only delivering the promised functionality, but also avoiding the unintentional misuse of iPhone resources. Keep in mind that the iPhone, as cool as it may very well be, is nevertheless somewhat resource-constrained when it comes to memory usage and battery life. Such restraints can have a direct effect on what you can (and can't) do in your application. Xcode's Instruments application lets you know how your application uses iPhone resources such as the CPU, memory, network, and so on.

The Instruments application allows you to observe the performance of your application while running it on the IPhone, and to a lesser extent, while running it on the Simulator. Here, *instrument* means a specialized feature of the Instruments application that zeroes in on a particular aspect of your app's performance (such as memory usage, system load, disk usage, and the like) and measures it. What's really neat, however, is the fact that you can look at these different aspects simultaneously along a timeline and then store data from multiple runs, so you get a picture of how your application's performance changes when you tune it.

The Instruments application is a very powerful piece of software. I have used it quite a bit in my own applications and there is no way, given the number of features Instruments has, and the amount of information it shows you, to include an in-depth discussion within the scope of this book.

to focus on how the Instruments application can help you deal
problems you will undoubtedly face:

is memory leaks. When a block of allocated memory is no
being referenced from any of the objects in your application, you
have a *memory leak*.

✦ The second is the memory leak's evil twin — trying to access a block of
memory (sending a message to an object for example) that has been prematurely (at least from your perspective) de-allocated. What makes this
a particular challenge is that the stack is often corrupted, meaning you
can't even see where you tried to access the object, much less how and
why the memory for it was de-allocated in the first place.

After you see how you can use the Instruments application to deal with
these two issues, you can explore other capabilities of the Instruments application at your leisure — something I suggest you do before circumstances
force you to do so, like the app is due tomorrow and it's still crashing
occasionally.

Getting Started with the Instruments Application

To use Instruments, you start with your compiled application — meaning
you've already done the Build stuff. Figure 2-1 shows you how to put your
application through the Instruments ringer launch by choosing Run⇨Start
With Performance Tool⇨Leaks from Xcode's main menu. (If you're curious,
the submenu way to the right shows the various tools you can use in the
Simulator — Object Allocations, Leaks, CPU Sampler, Leaks, and Activity
Monitor.)

When you start your application using Instruments — the performance tool
mentioned in the Run menu — your app starts either in the Simulator or in
the actual device (if you're running it on an iPhone). Where it starts depends
on the kind of SDK you've selected in Xcode. Check out Figure 2-1, paying
special attention to the drop-down menu in the upper-left corner of the
Project window; Figure 2-1 shows Simulator – 3.1.2 Debug selected. That's
fine for now. But when the time comes to test your app on a real device,
you'll have to let the Instruments application know that fact by choosing the
device from this drop-down menu.

Starting your application via the Instruments application *will* launch your
application, as you can see in Figure 2-2. This stands to reason; your app has
to be *running* in order for there to be data for Instruments to display. Wait
for your app to load fully and then keep your eye out for the Instruments
window, which should look something like Figure 2-3.

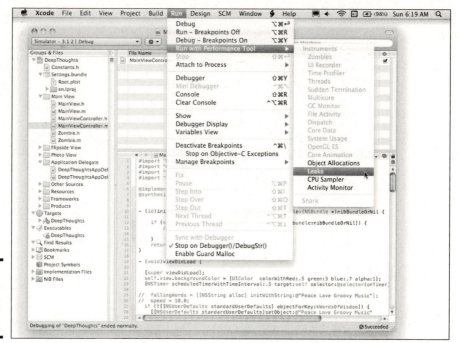

Figure 2-1:
Starting the
Instruments
application.

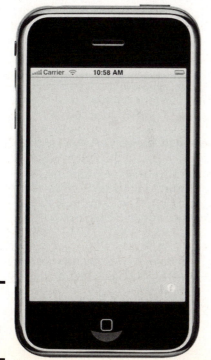

Figure 2-2:
Deep
Thoughts is
launched.

Book IV
Chapter 2

Tuning Your Code
Using Xcode's
Instruments
Application

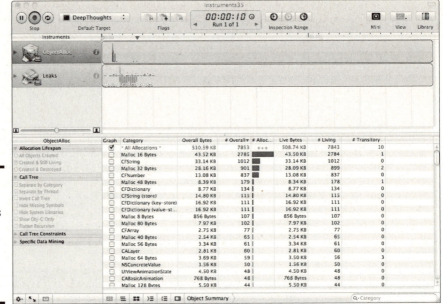

Figure 2-3:
The
Instruments
window
starts out
looking
pretty
boring.

The top pane of the Instruments window shows what particular instruments you're currently running. Figure 2-3 shows that, besides Leaks (which I chose from the menu), the ObjectAlloc instrument is also running. Next to each instrument listed you see a graphical summary of the data that the running instruments generate; each instrument has its own "track." (I guess that's why they call that part of the top pane the Track pane.) You can use the Time Scale slider — located right under the instrument listing in the top pane — to expand the tracks, letting you see the finer details of how each instrument is running. Similar to Interface Builder, the Library button allows you to drag more instruments into the Instruments pane.

The ObjectAlloc instrument — one of the many tools at Instrument's disposal — shows you how your application is using memory. It also shows you a trace of how you create and then release your objects. In a more complex application, it can be very useful to see whether you're actually releasing objects after you're done with them. The Track pane in Figure 2-3 graphs the net amount of memory that your app is currently using. I'll leave it up to you to explore the finer aspects.

Although the ObjectAlloc instrument is very useful, you're not going to find out how to use it in *this* book. (Hey, I have to prioritize.) Even though it's somewhat interesting to watch what's going on in an application like DeepThoughts (at least one level above watching paint dry), it can be extremely interesting (and also very useful) in more complex applications. In these applications, you can exercise your app and see whether memory is being allocated in the way you expect. You can also find out at what points you're at maximum memory usage, and then you can tune your app if necessary. Here again you should start with an idea of how your application works and the ObjectAlloc traces can confirm or call into question your understanding. You may have been mistaken, or your application may not be behaving in the way you intended. (Ah, yes, your old nemesis the logic error rears its ugly head.) In either case, you now have the information you need to do something about it.

A Leaks instrument preview

When a block of allocated memory is no longer being referenced from any of the objects in your application, you have a *memory leak.* The Leaks instrument shows you where to go to fix the leak. It works by recording all allocation events in your application and then scanning the application's writable memory, registers, and stack to see whether it can still find references to those particular blocks. If there's no way to either use or free those blocks in your application, the instrument reports them as memory leaks.

The problem is that memory leaks are just sitting there, taking up space until your application terminates. If your application needs to run for a long time or requires a lot of memory, leaks can seriously reduce its performance. That's especially important on the iPhone, which, as I often point out, isn't able to expand memory use beyond physical memory.

Memory is a precious iPhone resource. Too many leaks, and eventually your application may be reduced to a crawl, and it may even crash because it can't get the memory it needs to perform an operation.

Notice that in Figure 2-3, a memory leak does show up. That's the big spike you see in the Leaks track.

Now, let me show you something very interesting. This time I'm going to run the Instruments application on a real device, rather than the Simulator.

I've said it before, and I'll say it again: Running an app on the Simulator is not like running it on the device. The Simulator is not a true simulator; it is an API simulator. This means that even though it's using the same APIs, it still is using your Mac's CPU and memory. It's a marvelous piece of engineering but not a perfect replica of an iPhone, so I want to show you what happens when I test the same application when it's running on an iPhone. In Figure 2-4, you can see that I changed the target SDK to the device (in the upper-left corner), and then I compiled and ran the app and then chose Run⇨Start With Performance Tool⇨Leaks. (You'll notice that when the Instruments application runs your application on the device, there are more tools available to you than when it runs in the Simulator — System Usage, OpenGL ES, and Core Animation, to be precise; compare Figure 2-1.)

If you compare the ObjectAlloc track in Figure 2-5 with the one in Figure 2-3 — where I was running the application in the Simulator — you can see it has changed.

Book IV
Chapter 2

**Tuning Your Code
Using Xcode's
Instruments
Application**

More importantly, notice now that there are *no* leaks in the Detail pane!

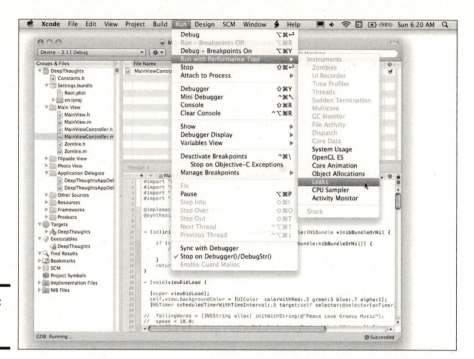

Figure 2-4:
Changing
the target.

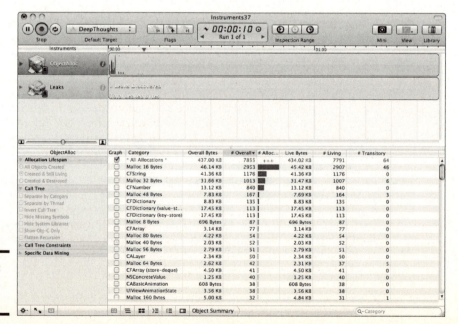

Figure 2-5:
Look, Ma!
No leaks!

Keeping this in mind, feel free to use the Simulator if accuracy just isn't your thing, but in this example I'm sticking with the iPhone.

You're ready to get started, then, with the Leaks instrument.

Actually using the Leaks instrument

To illustrate the Leaks instrument, as well as how to deal with prematurely de-allocated objects (which I'll do next), I've added a new class to DeepThoughts — Zombie.

Zombie is designed to do only two things: leak memory and be the vehicle for the later example of how to use Instruments to track down *zombies* — what I'll call those de-allocated objects that still stay around in memory.

You can see the inner being of Zombie in the Zombie.m file. Check out Listing 2-1.

Listing 2-1:   Zombie.m

```
#import "Zombie.h"

@implementation Zombie

- (void) zombieTester {

  NSLog(@" You've reached a zombie");
  NSString* testString = [[NSString alloc]
          initWithUTF8String: "A never released  object"];
}

@end
```

As you can see in Listing 2-1, I've allocated a string:

```
NSString* testString = [[NSString alloc]
          initWithUTF8String: "A never released  object"];
```

I never release it, however (how irresponsible of me). So after the zombie Tester method completes, this bit of memory is no longer accessible and becomes (horrors!) a leak.

In viewDidLoad in MainViewController.m, I need to instantiate and send the Zombie object the zombieTester message. You can see that in Listing 2-2. (To create a zombie, I release the object before I send it another message. You can see that in the next section.)

Book IV
Chapter 2

Tuning Your Code
Using Xcode's
Instruments
Application

Listing 2-2: Instantiating the Zombie and Sending It a Message

```
- (void)viewDidLoad {

    zombie = [[Zombie alloc]init];
    [zombie zombieTester];
```

I compile and run the app and then choose Run⇨Start With Performance Tool⇨Leaks. (Remember — you're running on the device.)

This time, as you can see in Figure 2-6, the leak appears in the Instruments' Track Pane as a noticeable blip. I select Stop; now, take a look at what this little blip tells you.

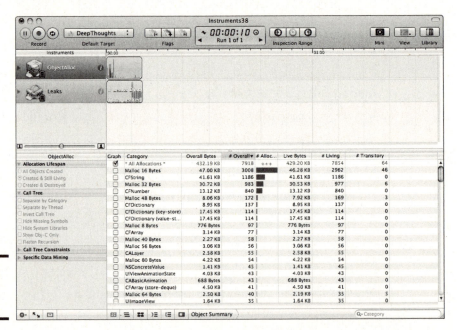

Figure 2-6: A real leak this time.

In Figure 2-7, you can see that I've selected the Leaks instrument in the Instruments Pane, which calls up a detailed view of the Leaks instrument in the lower pane of the Instruments window. In this detailed view, the leaked object is revealed to be a `NSCFString` object.

When I click the entry showing the culprit, as shown in Figure 2-8, a Follow Link button appears in the Address column.

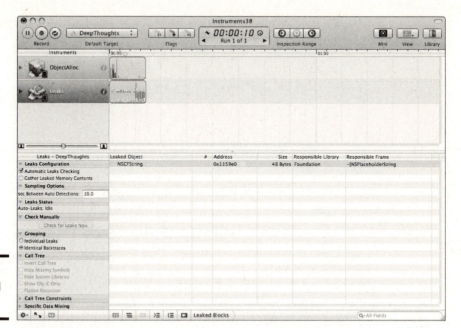

Figure 2-7:
The leaked
object.

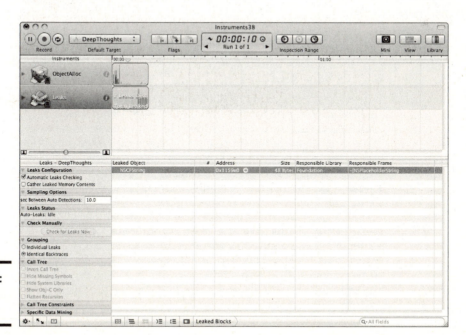

Figure 2-8:
The Leak
entry.

Book IV
Chapter 2

Tuning Your Code
Using Xcode's
Instruments
Application

Clicking the Follow Link button takes you to an allocation history (a listing of the allocations and de-allocations) for memory blocks at that address. You can see that history in Figure 2-9.

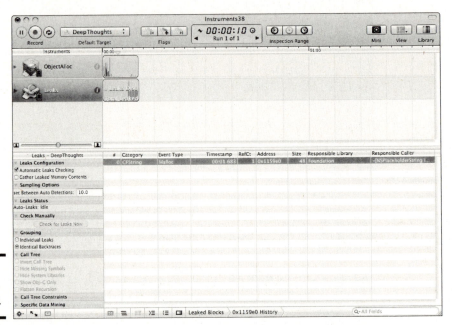

Figure 2-9:
Follow the
Follow Link.

In this view, I'm looking for an allocation (Malloc) without a matching de-allocation (Free) for that block. To refresh your memory, you create a memory leak when you allocate (Malloc) memory and don't de-allocate (Free) that block when there are no longer any objects referencing it.

In Figure 2-10, you can see that tracking down the source of the leak was pretty easy, since there was only one malloc, and no frees. (You should only be that lucky.)

Next, I want to look at all this in an Extended Detail view. To show the Extended Detail view, click the icon my mouse pointer is pointing to in Figure 2-11. (I could also get to this view by choosing View⇨Extended Detail or by pressing ⌘+E, or even by selecting the View Button on the right side of the top toolbar and selecting Extended Detail from the drop-down menu that appears.)

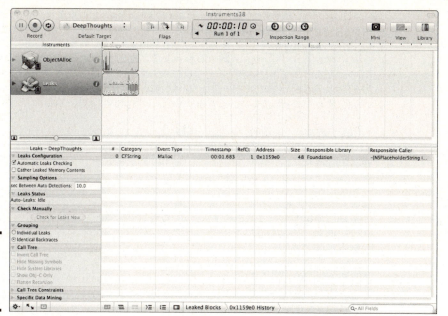

Figure 2-10:
You can
see the
allocations.

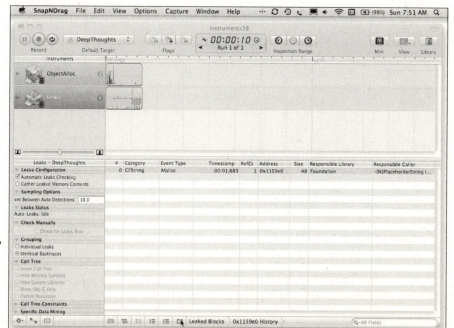

Figure 2-11:
Getting
to the
Extended
Detail view.

**Book IV
Chapter 2**

Tuning Your Code
Using Xcode's
Instruments
Application

When I'm in the Extended Detail view, I can see a stack trace (a trace of the objects and methods that got you to where you are now) in the Extended Detail pane on the right, as shown in Figure 2-12. When I select an allocation event in the Detail pane, the Extended Detail pane displays the stack trace for that event. This stack is organized starting with the oldest call at the top. In Figure 2-12, I've selected the allocation event in the Detail pane that allocated the 48 bytes that were leaked — displaying the stack at that point.

What you also see under General in the Extended Detail pane is a description of the allocation, including the Retain Count, which in this case is, not unsurprisingly, 1.

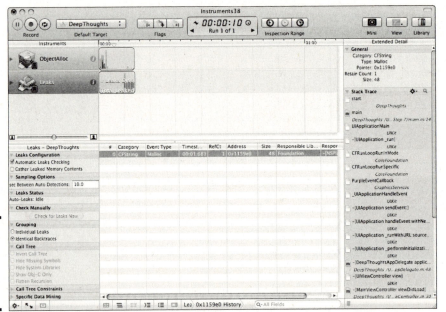

Figure 2-12:
Check
out the
Extended
Detail pane.

What I'm going to look for is one of my own application methods. If you right-click in the Extended Detail pane, you can see a contextual menu offering a number of options, including inverting the stack. As you can see in Figure 2-13, that's precisely what I've done.

This moves the offending method (or at least the one that did the allocation) to the top. In this case, you can see the last one of my methods was zombie Tester in the Zombie class — and that was where the memory allocation that resulted in the leak was done.

When I double-click the [Zombie zombieTester] stack entry, I'm shown the problem line of code, as you can see in Figure 2-14.

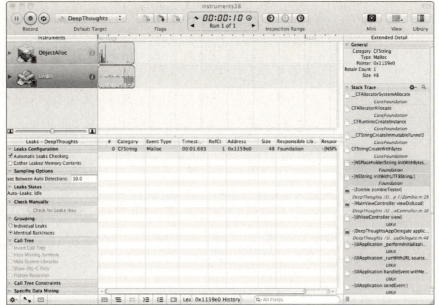

Figure 2-13:
Inverting the stack in the Expanded Detail pane.

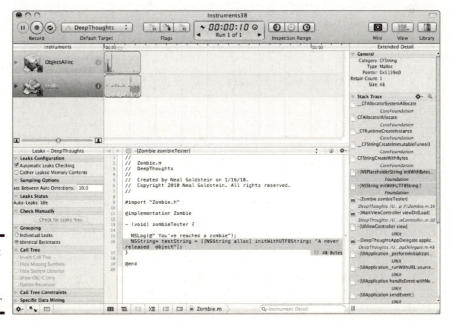

Figure 2-14:
The offending line of code.

Book IV
Chapter 2

Tuning Your Code
Using Xcode's
Instruments
Application

Very cool.

Yes Virginia, There Are Zombies Amongst Us

When you really get into development and your applications become more complex, you'll begin to run into a bug that can be very difficult and frustrating to track down.

It is in fact the evil twin of the memory leak, and it occurs when you send a message to an already de-allocated object. In the example I'm about to show you, you'll be able to see quite a bit of information in the debugger about the problem — like the offending instruction. Often however, the stack is completely obliterated and all you get is a cryptic message that the program has aborted.

In DeepThoughts I send the message [zombie zombieTester] twice: once in MainViewController.m in viewDidLoad and then later in showInfo, right before I instantiate and initialize a FlipsideViewController. This second time is shown in Listing 2-3.

Listing 2-3:   A Second zombieTester Message

```
- (IBAction) showInfo {

    [zombie zombieTester];

    FlipsideViewController *controller =
                [[FlipsideViewController alloc]
                initWithNibName:@"FlipsideView" bundle:nil];
    controller.delegate = self;
    controller.modalTransitionStyle =
                        UIModalTransitionStyleFlipHorizontal;
    [self presentModalViewController:controller
                                        animated:YES];

    [controller release];
}
```

If I compile and run DeepThoughts and then touch the Info button, what I will see in the Debugger Console is the following:

```
2010-01-17 08:36:55.594 DeepThoughts[10285:207]  You've
    reached a zombie
2010-01-17 08:37:04.411 DeepThoughts[10285:207]  You've
    reached a zombie
```

This makes sense, because I've sent two messages to the Zombie object.

Now, I'll make things a little more interesting. After I send the first zombie Tester message, I'll release the Zombie objects, as you can see (in bold) in Listing 2-4.

Listing 2-4: Asking for Trouble

```
- (void)viewDidLoad {

  zombie = [[Zombie alloc]init];
  [zombie zombieTester];
  [zombie release];
```

If I compile and run DeepThoughts now, and then touch the Info button, this time I see the following:

```
2010-01-17 08:41:04.777 DeepThoughts[10309:207]  You've
    reached a zombie
2010-01-17 08:41:15.955 DeepThoughts[10309:207] ***
    -[NSCFTimer zombieTester]: unrecognized selector sent to
    instance 0x11fea0
2010-01-17 08:41:15.958 DeepThoughts[10309:207]
    *** Terminating app due to uncaught exception
    'NSInvalidArgumentException', reason: '*** -[NSCFTimer
    zombieTester]: unrecognized selector sent to instance
    0x11fea0'
2010-01-17 08:41:15.961 DeepThoughts[10309:207] Stack: (
    844776241,
    843056877,
    844780055,
    844282517,
    844245696,
    15519,
    844537573,
    851058789,
    851058693,
    851058647,
    851057969,
    851060293,
    851056221,
    851054649,
    851040559,
    851039143,
    848378745,
    844528685,
    844526429,
    848374975,
    848375147,
    850798447,
    850793587,
    10193,
    10088
)
terminate called after throwing an instance of 'NSException'
Program received signal:  "SIGABRT".
```

Book IV
Chapter 2

Tuning Your Code
Using Xcode's
Instruments
Application

At first blush, this may not make any sense — I just *know* that `zombie Tester` is a method of `Zombie`. In fact, I just sent it the same message a few seconds before and it worked just fine.

But looking at it in more depth, you can see that it was not `Zombie` that was complaining,

```
-[NSCFTimer zombieTester]
```

It was an `NSCFTimer` object. What happened was that the memory had been de-allocated and then reallocated to a timer object. When I sent the message to where the `Zombie` object had been, it was sent to the `NSCFTimer` instead, because that was the object that was currently at that address.

That was perhaps a bad break — but better than being confronted by some obscure message and an unrecognizable stack.

There's a way to keep zombies around, however, which can be helpful.

`NSZombieEnabled` is an *environment* variable — a variable that tells Xcode how to set up the executable's environment before launching it — that tells the runtime to do something special when an object is de-allocated. When this variable is turned on, a de-allocated object is not de-allocated. Instead, its class is changed to `NSZombie`, and the memory region is not marked as free. Whenever that zombie object gets called, it throws an exception and logs the fact that it was called.

As I have said, on some occasions, the message and the stack trace can hold little information about what happened in your application. `NSZombie Enabled` does an end run around this unfortunate fact of life by instead logging a message and dying in a predictable fashion, thus stopping the stack right where you need it.

Follow along with me on how to enable it.

1. **In the Groups & Files list, double-click your application under Xcode's Executables heading, as I have in Figure 2-15.**

   You should find yourself in the Arguments section of the Executable DeepThoughts Info window. If not, click the Arguments tab at the top.

2. **Click the + tab in the bottom left of the window to add a new variable to the environment.**

3. **Fill in the values for the new variable, as shown in Figure 2-16.**

   Name the new variable `NSZombieEnabled`, and set its value to `YES`.

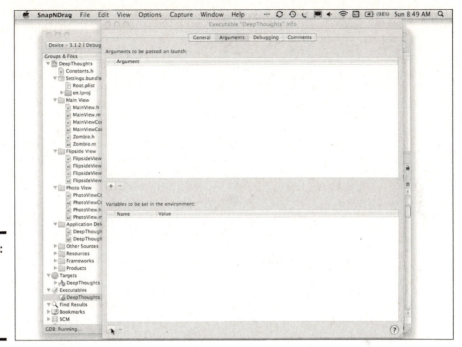

Figure 2-15:
Adding
a new
environ-
mental
variable.

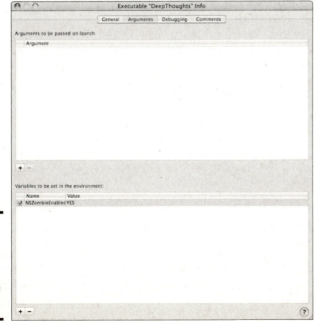

Figure 2-16:
Adding the
NSZombie
variable
with a value
of YES.

Book IV
Chapter 2

Tuning Your Code
Using Xcode's
Instruments
Application

Now, when your application crashes, the Run Log will explain what crashed, and the debugger will contain a useful stack.

So, if you were to build and run the application now, you'd see the following:

```
2010-01-17 08:58:17.748 DeepThoughts[10352:207]  You've
    reached a zombie
2010-01-17 08:58:41.520 DeepThoughts[10352:207] *** -[Zombie
    zombieTester]: message sent to deallocated instance
    0x126b40
```

You must be careful not to leave NSZombieEnabled in place permanently. Because objects are never truly de-allocated, you'll find yourself using prodigious amounts of memory.

Although this does get me closer to some kind of answer, it doesn't really help me find out what caused the problem in the first place. For that, you need to return to the Instruments application.

In this case, however, I'm going to have you launch Instruments directly. If you notice back in Figure 2-4, the Zombies selection is grayed out when you chose Run➪Start With Performance Tool. Missing out on the Zombies selection just comes with the Run➪Start With Performance Tool territory.

It turns out that launching Instruments directly gives you access to the Zombies selection. To get that launch going, you need to find the Instruments application, which most likely is hiding in *YourHardDriveName/* Developer/Applications. If for some reason it isn't there, you can search for it in Spotlight. (It's a Unix Executable file, but don't panic — it has a nice Mac interface on it.)

When you launch Instruments, the first screen you see asks you to Choose a Template for the Trace Document window. Select Zombies, as I have in Figure 2-17 and then click Choose. You then see the old familiar Instruments window.

This time, you'll have to choose the executable you want to trace. In Figure 2-18, I've selected Launch Executable➪DeepThoughts in the Instrument's window's toolbar. Notice that My Computer is selected as well. That tells the Instruments application to display what's in the Simulator and to launch the application there.

I then click the Record button in the toolbar. When the application is running, I touch the Info button, and lo and behold, what you see in Figure 2-19 should bring tears to your eyes — a message balloon telling you that the Zombie sent a message from the grave.

Figure 2-17:
Off to
zombie land.

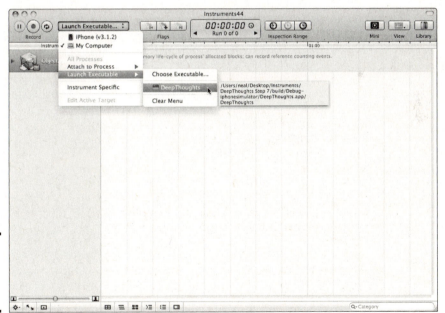

Figure 2-18:
Choosing
the
executable.

But wait! There's more! Lurking in the message balloon is a Forward Link
that you can click. If you were to do so, you'd see something similar to
Figure 2-20, which displays a list of the parties involved — some just innocent bystanders, but also the perpetrators themselves.

**Book IV
Chapter 2**

Tuning Your Code
Using Xcode's
Instruments
Application

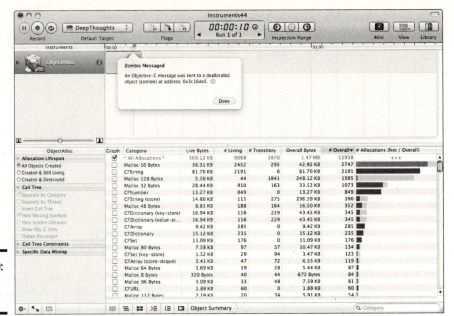

Figure 2-19:
A zombie
detected.

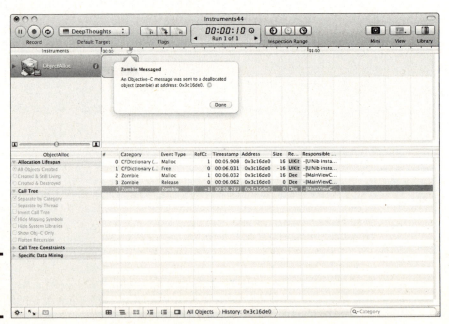

Figure 2-20:
Parties to
the crime.

I'm interested only in my code, so I start at the bottom and select the last method involved. The Ref Count is – 1 here, so this is where the crash occurred and I tried to send the message. (I actually could have gotten this information in the Debugger, but why bother when it's right here.)

I click the Extended Detail View icon in Figure 2-21, and you can see the stack trace that ends at this method — [MainViewController showInfo].

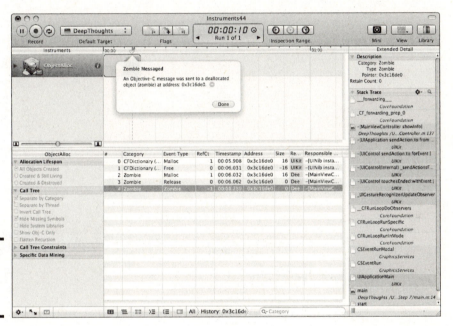

Figure 2-21:
The stack
trace at the
crash.

When I double-click on that entry, the listing for that method and where it crashed appears in the Detail pane, as shown in Figure 2-22.

Now, I need to figure out how this mess happened.

I go back to the message balloon and click the Foreword Link again to get me back to the Extended Detail view and the list of methods. This time I select the next to last method, as shown in Figure 2-23. You can see that this is the place the object was released (look in the Event Type column in Figure 2-23) and the place that the reference count was decremented to 0, resulting in the memory being de-allocated. This time, in the stack trace I double-click the [MainViewController viewDidLoad] method that did the release.

Figure 2-24 shows the dirty deed.

**Book IV
Chapter 2**

Tuning Your Code
Using Xcode's
Instruments
Application

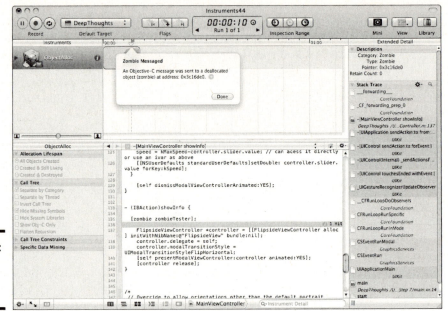

Figure 2-22:
[MainView
Controller
showInfo].

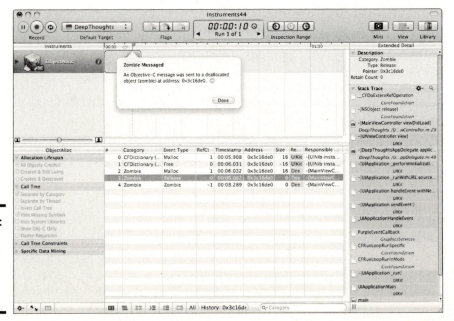

Figure 2-23:
Selecting
[MainView
Controller
viewDid
Load].

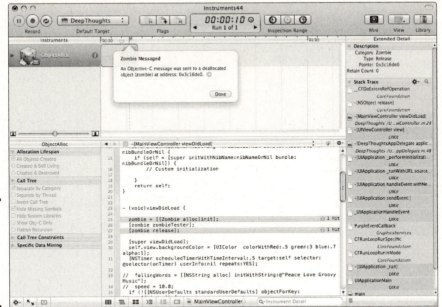

Figure 2-24:
[MainView Controller viewDid Load] is the guilty party.

I can't begin to tell you how valuable this feature in the Instruments application will be to you, especially at 3 a.m. on the day your application is due. Learning about how to use this feature alone is worth the price of this book and something you will thank me for.

There's a lot more in the Instruments application — and you're off to a good start. But I warn you, it will take a while to really get comfortable with Instruments, so start playing with it now.

Book V

Building an Industrial Strength Application — RoadTrip!

The 5th Wave   By Rich Tennant

"Stop working on the Priority Parking Spot Allocation program. They want to fast track the Coffee Pot/Cubicle Proximity program."

Contents at a Glance

Chapter 1: Designing Your Application

In This Chapter

✔ Asking "Where's the beef?" in your application

✔ Making sure your users don't hate you

✔ Designing for perpetuity

✔ Providing lots of functionality

*W*hile DeepThoughts is a fun little app, and debugging is well, debugging, it's time to move on to the more interesting stuff. In this chapter, I'll start you down the path to developing a more complex application. While I won't be dotting all the i's and crossing all the t's (I'll leave the memory management details for you to explore on your own, for example) I will be showing you how to use many of the technologies you need to know as you develop your own applications.

Defining the Problems

Necessity is the mother of invention, and the RoadTrip project was no exception. My daughter was about to leave on a 7,000 mile road trip around the U.S,, and, in anticipation of the Great Adventure, every square inch of surface area in her apartment was covered with maps, campground information, places to see, a schedule of who to visit where, and on and on.

"Please, Dad," she said, "you're so smart. Can't you figure out a way so that I can do all this on my iPhone." Being a sucker for the "Please, Dad" and the "you're so smart" combination, I started to give it some thought, and eventually the RoadTrip application idea was brought kicking and screaming into the world.

The purpose of the application would be to present information that's relevant to a) where you are, or b) where you plan to be. By concentrating on that kind of relevance, the app would reduce the amount of information you'd need to deal with at any one time. The application would be driven by maps and *core location* (the technologies that let you know where you are) and because of the need to save and manage what could be a significant amount of data, it would also use *core data* (the iPhone's preferred object/ data management technology) to store your objects and data.

Of course, like any other self-respecting iPhone app, it also goes out onto the Web to get the latest information as well as letting you update your information requests wherever you are. (Taos not doing anything for you? Then it's time to switch gears and plan that day-trip to Sedona.)

The ultimate RoadTrip application is far more complicated than I can cover here. Even though the stripped down version I explain isn't a killer app, it is useful, and it uses a lot of the technology you need to know when you *do* figure out that killer app. As you can see in Figure 1-1, it allows you to do the following:

Figure 1-1: The RoadTrip application.

✦ **Bring up a map based on your current location.** The map shows your current location, the sites you're planning to visit, and the hotels or campgrounds you're going to stay at. It also allows you to type in an address, and it will place a pin on the map.

You can see the pin business illustrated in Figure 1-2.

✦ **List the places you want to visit along the way and some information about each.** Figure 1-3 gives you an idea of what I mean here.

Figure 1-2:
Finding
your way
with literal
pinpoint
accuracy.

Figure 1-3:
RoadTrip
lists some
handy
places to
visit (left)
and even
provides
more details
about them
(right).

✦ **Display your hotels or campgrounds with information about each.**
This feature is pretty straightforward, but pretty cool as well.

Stick around, because I also show you how easy it is to add a new hotel and
have it appear on your map. Along the way, I even explain *core data,* the
iPhone's (and Mac's) handy technology for allowing you to store and then
reconstitute *objects* — those modules you create to carry out the work of
your program. A very handy piece of technology I might add. You can see
the list of hotels and the screen for adding a new hotel in Figure 1-4.

✦ **Get real-time weather access.** Snow in San Anselmo? Not likely, but you
never can tell. You can see real-time weather access at work in Figure 1-5.

✦ **Access your car's service records.** A handy thing to know because during
the course of 7,000 miles you'll probably need to get your car serviced.

✦ **Store essential data about your car.** Stuff like your car's make, model, year,
or vehicle identification number (VIN). This is something you may never
need, but if you do, you want it easily accessible, and not in the car itself.

You can see the Service Records and Essential Car info screens in
Figure 1-6. Admittedly, there's room here only for very basic information
about the car; in a commercial application, you'd want to include more
information of course, and some proper formatting, but in this case,
barebones screens make the point. As you can see, my daughter saved
all her babysitting money, and the proceeds from her lemonade stand,
and bought herself a nice car to go cruising with.

Figure 1-4:
You can
check the
hotels list
(left) and
add a new
hotel (right).

Figure 1-5:
The weather
in San
Francisco.

Figure 1-6:
The app
shows you
the car info
(left) and a
servicing
record
(right).

So, in this minibook and as well as in the following minibooks, I dive into how to actually implement the application. I cover the major components — user interface, mapping, core location, e-mail, core data — and everything in between. And the best place to start is to come to terms with what's at the heart of many of the iPhone applications that try to do the kinds of things RoadTrip does. And what, pray tell, is at the heart? Table views, my friend, table views. (Table views are so important that I'm devoting the entire next chapter — Chapter 2 — to their idiosyncrasies.)

Part of making the RoadTrip app easy to use involves giving users a way to set their preferences for how the app should work. I've included a setting for using stored data as an example of how an app can make use of preferences, but the stored data feature also lets me address an even more important issue: how to deal with limited or no connectivity. Working in *stored data mode* gives continuity to your app in those situations where you can't hop on the Web — basically, it lets you use previously stored data rather than the current real-time version that would require Internet access. The idea is to download the information your apps need before you venture into the Dead Zone where Internet access may be a problem. Figure 1-7 shows you what a Use Stored Data preference would look like.

Figure 1-7:
Use offline data.

Creating the Program Architecture

Given the user interface described in the previous section, the big question is how do you get there from here?

Keeping things at a basic level — a level that will be familiar to you if you worked through the DeepThoughts application in Book III — the RoadTrip application is made up of the following:

+ **Models:** Model objects encapsulate the logic and (data) content of the application. There was no model object in DeepThoughts. In RoadTrip, I show you how to design, implement, and use model objects.

+ **Views:** Views present the user experience; you have to decide what information to display and how to display it. You have several different *kinds* of views — different ways of displaying both information and navigation choices to the user. There will be a *Main* view, several *List* views, and several corresponding *Content* views. You'll be using some of the view classes available on the iPhone to do that.

+ **View controllers:** View controllers manage the user experience. They connect the views that present the user experience with the models that provide the necessary content. In addition (as you see in section appropriately entitled "View controllers"), view controllers also manage the way the user navigates the application.

No big surprises here — especially because the MVC model (Model-View-Controller) is pretty much the basis for all iPhone application development projects. The trick here is coming up with just the right views, view controllers, and model objects to get your project off the ground.

Models

Although you could write a book on model design (in fact, I've written a couple, not to mention an Apple video — but that's another story), I want to concentrate on a couple things now to keep you focused. I elaborate more in Chapter 4 of this minibook.

When you begin to think about all the models you'll need for the application, you may think you've opened up a very large can of worms.

To show you the proper (and far less work-intensive) way to think about it, I want to review what the model objects need to do.

The models own the data and the application logic. In the RoadTrip application, for example, the model maintains a list of hotels and information about each and allows you to add to that list. Here's where the real-world objects associated with object-oriented programming come into play. (In Book VI, I create a `Hotel` model object to encapsulate that information.)

Interestingly enough, the models that own the car information, car servicing information, the weather, and even information about a site, work a little differently than you might expect.

The model object doesn't have to *care* about the weather, for example; all it *really* needs to do is have the logic to go out and get the data from a file, database, or server. For my purposes, a model object that gets weather information and a model object that gets information about the car or even about the Golden Gate Bridge are pretty much the same. The logic for this object revolves around what the data is, how to access the data, and how this data may be connected to other data — the logic isn't about the *content* of the data. This means that I can create a single model class to handle all those requirements.

I won't be creating a single model class in this minibook, but in Book VI, I show you a couple ways to implement that yourself. All the model objects are of a subclass `NSObject` because `NSObject` provides the basic interface to the runtime system. (Interesting factoid: "NS" here illustrates that this was part of the Next Step framework that was the basis for the iPhone and Mac SDK's). `NSObject` already has methods for allocation; initialization; memory management; introspection ("what class am I?"); encoding and decoding (which make it quite easy to save objects as objects instead of just data); message dispatch; and a host of other equally obscure methods that I don't get into but are required for objects to be able to behave like they're expected to behave in an iPhone OS/Objective-C world.

In RoadTrip, the data will be found in one of a few places: a program resource, a Web server, a Web site, a local file, or a local object store.

In this minibook, I concentrate on showing you how to interact with both the file system to get your data and the outside world. For example, because the make, model, and VIN information about a car rarely changes, it gives me an opportunity to show you how to include a stable data set as a resource in your application.

Similarly, for car servicing information — refer to the right side of Figure 1-6 — my daughter has access to information about the last time the car was serviced and when the next service is due. Because this is the kind of information that changes regularly, I have this stored on my own Web site, where it will be easy to update. However, I do want to *cache* the information — that is, save the data on the iPhone as a backup — in case the Internet is not available.

Finally, because I don't have my own weather station, I use a Web site to get the weather. I show you how to download a Web site and display it in your application and even how to allow the user to navigate around that site (or even the Web) and then return to your application without ever leaving it.

Views

There are number of view classes you'll use to implement the three (main, list, and content) different *kinds of views* — ways to display both information and navigation choices to the user.

This one was a no-brainer. The *Main* view for RoadTrip is a `UITableView`, no question about it.

Table views are used a lot in iPhone applications to do two things:

✦ **Display hierarchal data:** Think of the iPod application, which gives you a list of albums, and if you select one, a list of songs.

✦ **Act as a table of contents (or for my purposes, contexts):** Now, think of the Settings application, which gives you a list of applications that you can set preferences for. When you select one of those applications from the list, it takes you to a view that lists what preferences you're able to set as well as a way to set them.

In RoadTrip, the *List* views — such as the ones shown earlier in Figure 1-3 (left) and both images in Figure 1-4 — are also table views. The views that display content — such as Figure 1-3 (right), Figure 1-5, and both views in Figure 1-6 — are all *Web* views, for some good practical reasons.

First and foremost, some of the views must be updated regularly. Web views, in that context, are the perfect solution; they make it easy to access data from a central repository on the Internet. (Client-server is alive and well!)

As for other benefits of Web views, keep in mind that real-time access isn't always necessary — sometimes it's perfectly fine to store some data on the iPhone. It turns out that Web views can easily display formatted data that's locally stored, which is very handy.

Finally, I use Web views for the simple reason that they can access Web sites. If users want more detailed weather information, they can get to the ten-day forecast by simply touching a link.

Models yet again

To implement table views such as the one that displays a list of sights, I need to have the data. I use *property lists* (XML files, in other words) to take care of that because they're well suited for the job and (more importantly) support for them is built in to the iPhone frameworks.

I also need a way to save and restore objects, especially if I'm going to be adding data. I use core data to manage the hotels. Core data is great at managing the storing and then retrieving of your objects and their data for you. Core data has been available on the Mac for some time and is now available on the iPhone as well. Although a bit daunting at first, you'll be surprised at how easy it is to use and how much power it has, especially when you're using table views.

I tell you more about property lists, the best way (asynchronously) to download lots of data, and core data in Book VI.

View controllers

View controllers are responsible not only for providing the data for a view to display, but also for responding to user input and navigation.

For the Web views you're going to focus on in this minibook, the view controllers all do pretty much the same thing. They send a message to the model to get some data and then they pass the data onto the view to display. With a bit of clever programming (and not even that clever), you can create a single view controller class that can manage each of the view classes you'll create to implement the User Content views — Weather, Car Information, and Car Servicing. (I go into great detail on all this in Chapter 4 of this minibook.) Keeping things to one view controller class really helps cut down the number of classes that you need and presents a straightforward way to think about how you need to display straight content (like an overview of the Golden Gate Bridge).

Stored data mode, saving state, and localization

Using the application design I describe in this chapter, adding stored data mode, saving state (or where the user was in the application when they last quit) and localization (enabling you to easily display your content in the user's choice of language) is easy; I explain them as I work through the implementation in Chapter 3 of this minibook. Although I don't dig too deeply into localization in this minibook, I show you how to build your application so that you can easily include that handy feature in your app.

Understanding the Iterative Nature of the Process

If there's one thing I can guarantee about development, it's that *nobody gets it right the first time.* Although object-oriented design and development are in themselves fun intellectual exercises (at least for some folks), they're also very valuable. An object-oriented program is relatively easier to modify and extend, not just during initial development, but also over time from version to version. (Actually, the initial development and the version updating are both the same; they differ only by a period of rest and vacation between them.)

The design of even this simple application evolved over time, as I figured out the capabilities and intricacies of the platform and the impact of my design decisions. What I'm doing in this chapter, and the ones following, is helping you avoid (at least most of) the blind alleys I stumbled down while developing my first application. So get ready for a stumble-free experience.

Chapter 2: Setting the Table

In This Chapter

✔ **Checking out the versatile table view**

✔ **Making the table look good**

✔ **Ensuring that your application is usable worldwide**

✔ **Making sure something happens after a user makes a selection**

*V*iews are the user's window into your application; they present the user experience on a silver platter, as it were. Their associated view controllers manage the user experience by providing the data displayed in the view, as well as by enabling user interaction.

In this chapter, you get a closer look at the RoadTrip *Main view* — the view you see when you launch the application — as well as the view controller that enables it. As part of your tour of the Main view, I show you how to use one of the most powerful features of the framework: table views. In the chapters that follow, I show you how to create the views that you set up to deliver the content of your application — how to add a hotel or campground, display places to visit, get directions from San Francisco to Big Sur, or even check on the weather in both places to see whether you really want to go.

In this and the following minibooks books, I get a chance to dive into how you would actually *implement* the application. I cover topics like the user interface, mapping, core location, e-mail, core data, and everything in between. But the best place to start — in my humble opinion — is right here with table views, which is why I'm giving the subject its own chapter right up front.

Understanding Table Views

Table views are front and center in several applications that come with the iPhone out of the box; they play a major role in many of the more complex applications you can download from the App Store. (Obvious examples: Almost all the views in the Mail, iPod, and Contacts applications are table views.) Table views take on such a significant role because, in addition to displaying data, they can also serve as a way to navigate a hierarchy.

If you take a look at an application such as Mail or iPod, you find that table views present a scrollable list of *items* (or *rows* or *entries* — I use all three terms interchangeably) that may be divided into *sections.* A row can display text or images. So, when you select a row, you may be presented with another table view or with some other view that may display a Web page or even some controls such as buttons and text fields. You can see an illustration of this diversity in Figure 2-1. Selecting Map on the left leads to a Content view displaying a map of San Francisco, which is very handy when you roll into town.

Figure 2-1:
A table and
map view.

A table view is an instance of the class UITableView, whereas each visible row of the table uses a UITableViewCell to draw its contents. Think of a *table view* as the object that creates and manages the table structure, and the *table view cell* as being responsible for displaying the content of a single row of the table.

Creating the Table View

Although powerful, table views are surprisingly easy to work with. To create a table, you need only to do four — count 'em, four — things, in the following order:

1. **Create and format the view itself.**

   This includes specifying the table style and a few other parameters, most of which is done in Interface Builder.

2. **Specify the table view configuration.**

   Not too complicated, actually. You let UITableView know how many sections you want, how many rows you want in each section, and what you want to call your section headers. You do that with the help of the numberOfSectionsInTableView: method, the tableView:numberO fRowsInSection: method, and the tableView:titleForHeaderIn Section: method, respectively.

3. **Supply the text (or graphic) for each row.**

   You return that from the implementation of the tableView:cellFor RowAtIndexPath: method. This message is sent for each visible row in the table view, and you return a table view cell to display the text or graphic.

4. **Respond to a user selection of the row.**

   You use the tableView:didSelectRowAtIndexPath: method to take care of this task. In this method, you create a view controller and a new view. For example, when the user selects Map in Figure 2-1, this method is called, and then a Map controller and a Map view are created and displayed.

A UITableView object must have a *data source* and a *delegate*. The data source supplies the content for the table view, and the delegate manages the appearance and behavior of the table view. The data source adopts the UITableViewDataSource protocol, and the delegate adopts the UITableViewDelegate protocol — no surprises there. Of the preceding methods, only tableView:didSelectRowAtIndexPath: is included in the UITableViewDelegate protocol. All the other methods I list earlier are included in the UITableViewDataSource protocol.

The data source and the delegate are often (but not necessarily) implemented in the same object — which is often a subclass of UITableViewController. (You'll be using the RootViewController for my RoadTrip app, by the way.)

Implementing these five (count 'em, five) methods is all you need to do to implement a table view. If you then take Interface Builder for a spin or two, along with the same kind of initialization methods and the standard memory-management methods you used in the DeepThoughts application back in Book III, you find yourself with a table view that can respond to a selection made in the table.

Not bad.

Creating and Formatting a Grouped Table View

Table views come in two basic styles:

✦ **Plain:** The default style is called *plain* and looks really unadorned — plain vanilla. It's a list: just one darn thing after another. You can index it, though, just as the table view in the Contacts application is indexed, so it can be a pretty powerful tool. Figure 2-2 shows a plain table view on the left.

A plain view can also have section titles (as I describe shortly) and footers.

✦ **Grouped:** The other style is the *grouped* table view; unsurprisingly, it allows you to clump entries into various categories. In Figure 2-2, you can see a grouped table view on the right.

Grouped tables cannot have an index.

When you configure a grouped table view, you can also have header, footer, and section titles. I show you how to do section titles shortly.

To see how table views work, you of course need a project you can use to show them off. With that in mind, fire up Xcode and officially launch the RoadTrip project. (If you need a refresher on how to set up a project in Xcode, take another look at Book I, Chapter 4.) For this project, you need to go with the Navigation-Based Application template, which I've selected in Figure 2-3.

You are not going to use core data yet, so leave the Use Core Data for Storage check box deselected.

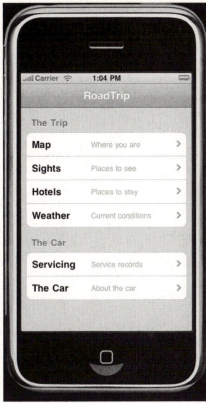

Figure 2-2:
A plain
table view
(left) and
a grouped
table view
(right),

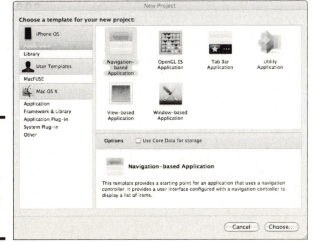

Figure 2-3:
Selecting
the
Navigation-
Based
Application
template.

Click Choose and then use the Save As dialog to save the project as RoadTrip in a folder on the desktop, as shown in Figure 2-4.

Figure 2-4:
Naming and saving the project.

To no one's surprise, your new project gets added to the Groups & Files list on the left side of the Xcode Project window. Next, take a look at what happens when you drill down in your project folder in the Groups & Files list until you end up selecting `RootViewController` (as shown in Figure 2-5). The main pane of the Xcode Project window reveals that `RootViewController` is derived from a `UITableViewController`.

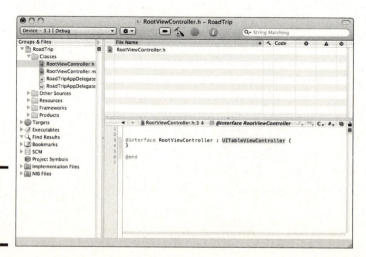

Figure 2-5:
The RootView-Controller.

Inquisitive type that you are, you look up `UITableViewController` in the Documentation reference by right-clicking its entry in the Project window and choosing Find Selected Text in Documentation from the pop-up menu that appears. The Class reference tells you that `UITableViewController` conforms to the `UITableViewDelegate` and `UITableViewDataSource` protocols (and a few others), which are the two protocols I said were necessary to implement table views. What luck. (Kidding. It's all intentional.)

Always on the lookout for more information, you continue down the Groups & Files list to open your project's Resources folder, where you double-click the `RootViewController.xib` file to launch Interface Builder. You are reassured to see a table view set up in front of you. Admittedly, it's a plain table view rather than the grouped table view you want, but it's a table view nonetheless. To get the final duck in a row, choose Grouped from the Style drop-down menu in Interface Builder's Attributes Inspector, as shown in Figure 2-6, to make the switch from plain to grouped. Be sure to save the file after you do this.

At this point, you can build and run this project; go for it. What you see in the Simulator is a table view. If you try to scroll it, you get a *bounce scroll,* where the view just bounces back up when you scroll it, but not much else. In fact, you don't even see it as a grouped view. What you do have is the basic framework, however, and now you can format it the way you'd like.

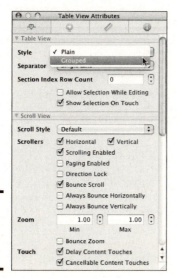

Figure 2-6:
Setting the
style of the
table view.

Making UITableViewController Work for You

The data source and the delegate for table views are often (but not necessarily) the same object — and that object is frequently a custom subclass of `UITableViewController`. For the RoadTrip project, the `RootViewController` created by the Navigation-Based Application template is a subclass of `UITableViewController`, and the `UITableViewController` has adopted the `UITableViewDelegate` and `UITableViewDataSource` protocols. So you're free to implement those handy methods I mention in the "Creating the table view" section, earlier in the chapter. (Just remember that you need to implement them in `RootViewController` to make your table usable.) Start with the methods that format the table the way you'd like.

Adding sections

In a grouped table view, each group is referred to as a *section*.

In an indexed table, each indexed grouping of data is also called a section. For example, in the iPod application, all the albums beginning with *A* would be one section, those beginning with *B* another section, and so on. Although the indexed grouping has the same name, this is not the same thing as sections in a grouped table (which doesn't have an index).

The two methods you need on hand to start things off are as follows:

```
numberOfSectionsInTableView:(UITableView *)tableView
tableView:(UITableView *)tableView
          numberOfRowsInSection:(NSInteger)section
```

Each of these methods returns an integer, and that integer tells the table view something — the number of sections and the number of rows in a given section, respectively.

In Listing 2-1, you can see the code you need in order to create a table view that has two sections with three rows in each section. These methods are already implemented for you by the Navigation-Based Application template in the `RootViewController.m` file. You just need to remove the existing code and replace it with what you see in Listing 2-1.

Listing 2-1: **Modify numberOfSectionsInTableView: and tableView:numberOfRowsInSection:**

```
- (NSInteger)numberOfSectionsInTableView:
                           (UITableView *)tableView {

    return 2;
}
```

```
- (NSInteger)tableView:(UITableView *)tableView
            numberOfRowsInSection:(NSInteger)section {

   NSInteger rows;
   switch (section) {
     case 0:
       rows = 4;
       break;
     case 1:
       rows = 2;
       break;
     default:
       break;
   }
   return rows;
}
```

You implement `tableView:numberOfRowsInSection:` by using a simple `switch` statement:

```
switch (section) {
```

Keep in mind that the first section is zero, as is the first row. This means, of course, that whenever you want to use an index to get to the first row or section, you'll need to use 0, not 1 — and an index of 1 for the second row and so on.

Although that's as easy as it gets, it's not really the best way to do it. Read on.

In the interests of showing you how to implement a robust application, I'm going to use constants to represent the number of sections *and* the number of rows in each section. I'll put those constants in a file, `Constants.h`, which will eventually contain other constants. I do this for purely defensive reasons: Both of these values — the number of sections *and* the number of rows in each section — will be used often in this application (I know that because hindsight is 20-20), and declaring them as constants makes changing the number of rows and sections easy, and it also helps avoid hard-to-detect typing mistakes.

Later I show you some techniques here that make life much, much easier. It means paying attention to some of the less-glamorous application nuts and bolts functionality — can you say "memory management"? — that may be annoying to implement along the way but that are *really* difficult to retrofit later. I want to head you away from the boulder-strewn paths that so many developers have gone down (me included), much to their later sorrow.

To implement the `Constants.h` file, do the following:

1. **Choose File⇨New File from the Xcode main menu.**

I recommend having the `Classes` folder selected in the Groups & Files list so the file will be placed in there.

2. **In the New File dialog that appears, select Other from the listing on the left (under the Mac OS X heading) and then select Empty File in the main pane, as shown in Figure 2-7.**

3. **In the new dialog that appears, name the file `Constants.h` (as shown in Figure 2-8) and then click Finish.**

   The new empty file is saved in the Classes folder, as you can see in Figure 2-9.

With a new home for your constants all set up and waiting, all you have to do is add the constants you need so far. (Listing 2-2 shows you the constants you need to add to the `Constants.h` file.)

Figure 2-7: Creating an empty file.

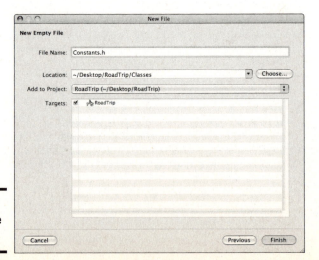

Figure 2-8: Naming the new file.

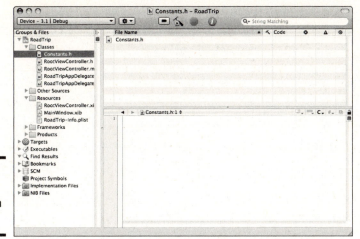

Figure 2-9:
The
Constants.h
file.

Now, using the Xcode Project window conveniently opened to the newly created Constants.h file (refer to Figure 2-9) — type in what you see in Listing 2-2.

Listing 2-2:   Adding to the Constants.h File

```
#define kSections       2
#define kSection1Rows   4
#define kSection2Rows   2
```

Having a Constants.h file in hand is great, but you have to let RootViewController.m know that you plan to use it. To include Constants.h in RootViewController.m, open RootViewController.m in Xcode and add the following statement:

```
#import "Constants.h"
```

You can then use these constants in all the various methods used to create your table view, as shown in Listing 2-3.

Listing 2-3:   Sections and Rows Done Better

```
- (NSInteger)numberOfSectionsInTableView:(UITableView *)
                                          tableView {

   return kSections;
}
```

(continued)

Listing 2-3 *(continued)*

```
- (NSInteger)tableView:(UITableView *)tableView
                   numberOfRowsInSection:(NSInteger)section {

  NSInteger rows;
  switch (section) {
    case 0:
      rows = kSection1Rows;
      break;
    case 1:
      rows = kSection2Rows;
      break;
    default:
      break;
  }
  return rows;
}
```

When you build and run this (provisional) app, you get what you see in Figure 2-10: two sections, the first with four rows and the second with two.

Although using constants and a `switch` statement does make your program more extensible, it does require you to change the `switch` statement if you want to add or change the layout. An even better solution is to create an array in `viewDidLoad` that looks like this.

```
- (void)viewDidLoad {
  [super viewDidLoad];
  sectionsArray = [[NSArray alloc] initWithObjects:
                    [[NSNumber alloc]initWithInt:4],
                    [[NSNumber alloc]initWithInt:2], nil];
}
```

Add the code in bold to the `viewDidLoad` method in the `RootViewController.m` file. The method is already there; all you have to do is uncomment it out.

Then you can use the array count `[sectionsArray count]` to return the number of sections, and then use the index path section as an index into the array for the number of rows in a section `[sectionsArray objectAtIndex:section]`. And in fact, that's what I'm doing. You can see that in Listing 2-4, where I replaced the `numberOfSectionsInTableView:` and `tableView:numberOfRowsInSection:` yet again (and for the last time).

Listing 2-4: Final Versions of numberOfSectionsInTableView: and tableView:numberOfRowsInSection:

```
- (NSInteger)numberOfSectionsInTableView:
                                 (UITableView *) tableView {

  return [sectionsArray count];
}

- (NSInteger)tableView:(UITableView *)tableView
            numberOfRowsInSection:(NSInteger)section {

  return [[sectionsArray objectAtIndex:section] intValue];
}
```

You also have to add the following to RootViewContoller.h

```
NSArray *sectionsArray;
```

Figure 2-10:
Now I have
sections.

Adding titles for the sections

With sections in place, you now need to title them so users know what the sections are for. Luckily for you, the UITableViewDataSource protocol has a handy method — titled, appropriately enough, the tableView:title ForHeaderInSection: method — that enables you to add a title for each section. Listing 2-5 shows how to implement the method.

Listing 2-5:   Add Section Titles

```
- (NSString *)tableView:(UITableView *)tableView
             titleForHeaderInSection:(NSInteger)section {

   NSString *title = nil;
   switch (section) {
     case 0:
       title = @"The Trip";
       break;
     case 1:
       title =  @"The Car";
       break;
     default:
       break;
   }
   return title;
}
```

This (again) is a simple switch statement. For case 0, or the first section, you want the title to be @"The Trip", and for case 1, or the second section, you want the title to be @"The Car".

Okay, this, too, was really easy, so you probably won't be surprised to find out that it's *not* the best way to tackle the whole titling business. It's another path not to take — in fact, a really *important* one not to take. Really Serious Application Developers insist on catering to the needs of an increasingly global audience, which means — paradoxically — that they have to *localize* their applications. In other words, an app must be created in such a way that it presents a different view to different, local audiences. The next section explains how to do that.

Localization

Localizing an application isn't difficult, just tedious. To localize your application, you create a folder in your application bundle (I get to that in a bit) for each language you want to support. Each folder has the application's translated resources.

In the Settings application for the RoadTrip app, you're going to set things up so the user can set the language — Spanish or Italian, for example — and the region format.

For example, if the user's language is Spanish, available regions range from Spain to Argentina to the United States and lots of places in between. When a localized application needs to load a resource (such as an image, a property list, or a nib file), the application checks the user's language and region and looks for a localization folder that corresponds to the selected language and region. If it finds one, it loads the localized version of the resource instead of the *base* version — the one you're working in.

Showing you all the ins and outs of localizing your application is a bit too Byzantine for this book. But I *do* show you what you must do to make your app localizable when you're ready to tackle the chore on your own.

What you have to get right — right from the start — are the strings you use in your application that get presented to the user. (If the user has chosen Spanish as his or her language of choice, what's expected in the Main view is now *Plano,* not *Map.*) You ensure that the users see what they're expecting by storing the strings you use in your application in a `strings` text file, which contains a list of string pairs, each identified by a comment. You would create one of these files for each language you support.

Here's an example of what an entry in a `strings` file might look like for this application:

```
/*Hotel choices */
"Hotels"  = "Hotels";
```

The values between the `/*` and the `*/` characters are just comments for the (human) translator you task with creating the right translation for the phrase — assuming, of course, that you're not fluent in the ten-or-so languages you'll probably want to include in your app, and therefore will need some translating help. You write such comments to provide some context and explain how that string is being used in the application.

Okay, this example has two strings: The one to the left of the equals sign is used as a key, and the one to the right of the equals sign is the one displayed. In the example, both strings are the same, but in the `strings` file used for a Spanish speaker, here's what you'd see:

```
/*Hotel choices */
 "Hotels"  = "Hoteles";
```

Looking up such values in the table is handled by the `NSLocalizedString` macro in your code.

To show you how to use the macro, I take one of the section headings as an example. Instead of

```
title = @"The Trip";
```

I code it as follows:

```
title = NSLocalizedString(@"The Trip",
                                    @"The trip by car");
```

As you can see, the macro has two inputs. The first is the string in your language, and the second is the general comment for the translator. At runtime, `NSLocalizedString` looks for a `strings` file named `localizable.strings` in the language that has been set, such as Spanish. (A user would have done that by going to Settings and choosing General⇨Internati onal⇨Language⇨Español). If `NSLocalizedString` finds the `strings` file, it searches the file for a line that matches the first parameter. In this case, it would return *hoteles,* and that is what would be displayed as the section header. If the macro doesn't find the file or a specified string, it returns its first parameter, and the string appears in the base language.

To create the `localizable.strings` file, you run a command-line program named `genstrings`, which searches your code files for the macro and places them all in a `localizable.strings file` (which it creates), making them ready for the (human) translator. The `genstrings` program is beyond the scope of this book, but it's well documented. When you're ready, I leave you to explore it on your own.

Okay, sure, it's really annoying to have to do this sort of thing as you write your code. (Yes, I know, *really, really* annoying.) But that's not nearly as annoying as having to go back and *find and replace all the strings you want to localize* after the application is almost done. Take my word for it!

Listing 2-6 shows how to use the `NSLocalizedString` macros to create local-izable section titles. Add this method to the `RootViewController.m` file.

Listing 2-6:   Add Localizable Section Titles

```
- (NSString *)tableView:(UITableView *)tableView
            titleForHeaderInSection:(NSInteger)section {

  NSString *title = nil;
  switch (section) {
    case 0:
      title = NSLocalizedString(@"The Trip",
                                  @"The trip by car");
      break;
    case 1:
      title = NSLocalizedString(@"The Car", @"Car detail,
                insurance, and servicing information ");
```

```
        break;
    default:
        break;
    }
  return title;
}
```

Creating the Row Model

As all good iPhone app developers know, the Model-View-Controller (MVC) design pattern is the basis for the design of the framework you use to develop your applications. In this design pattern, each element (model, view, or controller) concentrates on the task at hand; it doesn't much care what the other elements are doing. For table views, that means the method that draws the content doesn't know what the content is, and the method that decides what to do when a selection is made in a particular row is equally ignorant of what the selection is. The important thing is to have a model object — one for each row — to hold and provide that information.

In this kind of situation, you usually want to deal with the model-object business by creating an array of models, one for each row. In this case, the model object will be a dictionary that holds the following three items:

+ **The selection text:** Map, for example

+ **The description text:** Where you are, for example

+ **The view controller to be created when the user selects that row:** `MapController`, for example

You can see all three items illustrated in Figure 2-11.

In more complex applications, you could provide a dictionary *within* the dictionary and use it to provide the same kind of information for the next level in the hierarchy. The iPod application is an example: It presents you with a list of albums, and then when you select an album, it shows you a list of songs on that album.

The following code shows you how to create a single dictionary for a row. Later on, I show you how to create all the dictionaries and tell you where all this code needs to go.

```
menuList = [[NSMutableArray alloc] init];

[menuList addObject:[NSMutableDictionary
    dictionaryWithObjectsAndKeys:
    NSLocalizedString(@"Map", @"Map Section"),kSelectKey,
    NSLocalizedString(@"Where you are", @"Map Explain"),
                                            kDescriptKey,
    nil, kControllerKey, nil]];
```

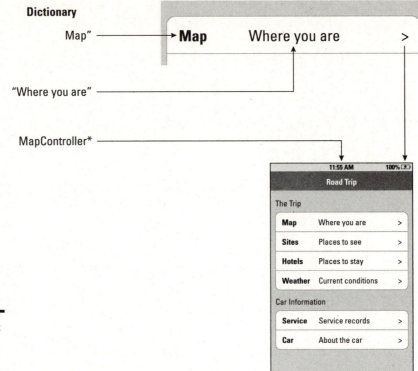

Dictionary

Map" ────────────▶ **Map**   Where you are   >

"Where you are" ──────────────

MapController* ──────────────

Figure 2-11:
The model
for a row.

Here's the blow-by-blow account:

1. **Create an array to hold the model for each row.**

An `NSMutableArray` is a good choice here because it allows
you to easily insert and delete objects. You need to add this to
`RootViewController.h`.

In such an array, the position of the dictionary corresponds to the row it
implements, that is, relative to row zero in the table and not taking into
account the section.

2. **Create an** `NSMutableDictionary` **with three entries and the following keys:**

- `kSelectKey`: The entry that corresponds to the main entry in the
  table view (`"Map"`, for example).

- `kDescriptKey`: The entry that corresponds to the description in the
  table view (`"Where you are"`, for example).

- `kControllerKey`: This entry contains a pointer to a view controller
  that will display the Map. You create an entry for the controller, but
  not just yet; you just use `nil` for now. The first time the user selects

a row, you create the view controller and save that value in here. That way, if the user selects that row again, the controller will simply be reused.

3. **Add the keys to the `Constants.h` file.**

```
#define kSelectKey      @"selection"
#define kDescriptKey    @"description"
#define kControllerKey  @"viewController"
```

The @ before each of the preceding strings tells the compiler that this is an NSString.

With all of this information, you are now in a position to get rid of these controllers if you were to ever get a low-memory warning. You'd simply go through each dictionary in the array and release every controller except the one that's currently active.

You'll want to create this array and all the dictionaries in an initialization method viewDidLoad, which you need to add to the RootViewController.m file. (You can see viewDidLoad in all its glory in Listing 2-7.) The viewDidLoad message is sent to the RootViewController after all the objects in the nib file have been loaded and the RootViewController's outlet instance variables have been set.

You could argue that you really should create a model class that creates this data-model array and get its data from a file or property list. For simplicity's sake, I add it in the viewDidLoad method for the RoadTrip app.

Listing 2-7:   viewDidLoad

```
- (void)viewDidLoad {
  [super viewDidLoad];
  sectionsArray = [[NSArray alloc] initWithObjects:
                    [[NSNumber alloc]initWithInt:4],
                    [[NSNumber alloc]initWithInt:2], nil];

  self.title = [[[NSBundle mainBundle] infoDictionary]
    objectForKey:@"CFBundleName"];
  menuList = [[NSMutableArray alloc] init];
  [menuList addObject:[NSMutableDictionary
    dictionaryWithObjectsAndKeys:
    NSLocalizedString(@"Map", @"Map Section"),kSelectKey,
    NSLocalizedString(@"Where you are", @"Map Explain"),
                                        kDescriptKey,
    nil, kControllerKey, nil]];
  [menuList addObject:[NSMutableDictionary
    dictionaryWithObjectsAndKeys:
    NSLocalizedString(@"Sights", @"Sights Section"),
```

(continued)

Listing 2-7 *(continued)*

```
                                                    kSelectKey,
        NSLocalizedString(@"Places to see",
                    @"Places to see Explain"), kDescriptKey,
        nil, kControllerKey, nil]];
[menuList addObject:[NSMutableDictionary
    dictionaryWithObjectsAndKeys:
    NSLocalizedString(@"Hotels", @"Hotels Section"),
                                                kSelectKey,
        NSLocalizedString(@"Places to stay",
                    @"Places to stay Explain"), kDescriptKey,
        nil, kControllerKey, nil]];
[menuList addObject:[NSMutableDictionary
    dictionaryWithObjectsAndKeys:
    NSLocalizedString(@"Weather", @"Weather Section"),
                                                kSelectKey,
        NSLocalizedString(@"Current conditions",
                    @"Weather  Explain"), kDescriptKey,
        nil, kControllerKey, nil]];
[menuList addObject:[NSMutableDictionary
    dictionaryWithObjectsAndKeys:
    NSLocalizedString(@"Servicing", @"Service Section"),
                                                kSelectKey,
        NSLocalizedString(@"Service records",
                    @"Service records Explain"), kDescriptKey,
        nil, kControllerKey, nil]];
[menuList addObject:[NSMutableDictionary
    dictionaryWithObjectsAndKeys:
    NSLocalizedString(@"The Car",
                    @"Car Information Section"), kSelectKey,
    NSLocalizedString(@"About the car",
                        @"About the car"), kDescriptKey,
        nil, kControllerKey, nil]];
}
```

You also have to add the following to `RootViewContoller.h`

```
NSMutableArray *menuList;
```

Going through the code in Listing 2-7, you can see that the first thing you do is get the application name from the bundle so you can use it as the Main view title.

```
self.title = [[[NSBundle mainBundle] infoDictionary]
                    objectForKey:@"CFBundleName"];
```

"What bundle?" you ask. Well, when you build your iPhone application, Xcode packages it as a bundle containing the following:

✦ The application's executable code

✦ Any resources that the app has to use (for instance, the application icon, other images, and localized content)

✦ The `info.plist`, also known as the information property list, which defines key values for the application, such as bundle ID, version number, and display name

`infoDictionary` returns a dictionary that's constructed from the bundle's `info.plist`. `CFBundleName` is the key to the entry that contains the (localizable) application name on the home page. The title is what will be displayed in the Navigation bar at the top of the screen.

As I mention earlier, I also create `sectionsArray`, which I can use to compute the offset in the menu. I save reference to that array in the instance variable.

Going through the rest of the code, you can see that for each entry in the Main view, you have to create a dictionary and put it in the `menuList` array. You put the dictionary in the `menuList` array so you can use it later when you need to provide the row's content or create a view controller when the user selects the row.

Seeing How Cells Work

I've been going steadily from macro to micro, so it makes sense that after setting up a model for each row, I get to talk about cells, the individual constituents of each row.

Cell objects are what draw the contents of a row in a table view. The method `tableView:cellForRowAtIndexPath:` is called for each visible row in the table view. It's expected that the method will configure and return a `UITableViewCell` object for each row. The `UITableView` object uses this cell to draw the row.

When providing cells for the table view, you have three general approaches you can take:

✦ Use vanilla (not subclassed) `UITableViewCell` cell objects.

✦ Add subviews to a `UITableViewCell` cell object's Content view.

✦ Use cell objects created from a custom subclass of `UITableViewCell`.

The next few sections take a look at these options, one by one.

Using vanilla cell objects

Using the `UITableViewCell` class directly, you can create cell objects with text and an optional image. (If a cell has no image, the text starts near the left edge of the cell.) You also have an area on the right of the cell for accessory views, such as disclosure indicators (the one shaped like a regular chevron), detail disclosure controls (the one that looks like a white chevron in a blue button), and even control objects such as sliders, switches, or custom views. The layout of a cell is shown in Figure 2-12. If you like, you can format the font, alignment, and color of the text, and you can even have a different format when the row is selected.

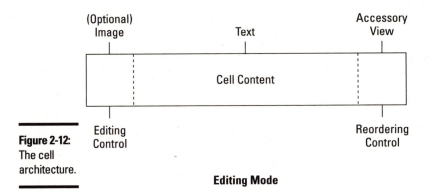

Figure 2-12: The cell architecture.

Adding subviews to a cell's Content view

Although you can specify the font, color, size, alignment, and other characteristics of the text in a cell using the `UITableViewCell` class directly, the formatting is applied to all of the text in the cell. To get the variation that I suspect you want between the selection and description text (and, it turns out, the alignment as well), you have to create subviews within the cell.

A cell that a table view uses for displaying a row is, in reality, a view in its own right. `UITableViewCell` inherits from `UIView`, and it has a Content view. With Content views, you can add one subview (containing, say, the selection text `"Weather"`) formatted the way you want and a second subview (holding, say, the description text `"Current conditions"`) formatted an entirely different way.

Creating a custom subclass *UITableViewCell*

Finally, you can create your very own custom cell subclass when your content requires it — usually when you need to change the default behavior of the cell.

Creating the Cell

As I mention in the previous section, you're going to use the `UITableViewCell` class to create the cells for your table views and then add the subviews you need in order to get the formatting you want. The place to create the cell is `tableView:cellForRowAtIndexPath:`. This method is called for each visible row in the table view, as shown in Listing 2-8. A code stub (a method with no — or only example — instructions) is already included in the `RootViewController.m` file, courtesy of the template. Replace the whole thing with Listing 2-8.

Listing 2-8:   Drawing the Text

```
- (UITableViewCell *)tableView:(UITableView *)tableView
        cellForRowAtIndexPath:(NSIndexPath *)indexPath {

  UITableViewCell *cell = [tableView
      dequeueReusableCellWithIdentifier:kCellIdentifier];
  if (cell == nil) {
    cell = [[[UITableViewCell alloc] initWithStyle:UITableVie
  wCellStyleDefault
            reuseIdentifier:kCellIdentifier] autorelease];

    cell.accessoryType =
    UITableViewCellAccessoryDisclosureIndicator;

    CGRect subViewFrame = cell.contentView.frame;
    subViewFrame.origin.x += kInset;
    subViewFrame.size.width = kInset+kSelectLabelWidth;

    UILabel *selectLabel = [[UILabel alloc]
                            initWithFrame:subViewFrame];
    selectLabel.textColor = [UIColor blackColor];
    selectLabel.highlightedTextColor =
                                [UIColor whiteColor];
    selectLabel.font = [UIFont boldSystemFontOfSize:18];
    selectLabel.backgroundColor = [UIColor clearColor];
    [cell.contentView addSubview:selectLabel];

    subViewFrame.origin.x += kInset+kSelectLabelWidth;
    subViewFrame.size.width = kDescriptLabelWidth;
```

(continued)

Listing 2-8 *(continued)*

```
    UILabel *descriptLabel = [[UILabel alloc]
                            initWithFrame:subViewFrame];
    descriptLabel.textColor = [UIColor grayColor];
    descriptLabel.highlightedTextColor =
                            [UIColor whiteColor];
    descriptLabel.font = [UIFont systemFontOfSize:14];
    descriptLabel.backgroundColor = [UIColor clearColor];
    [cell.contentView addSubview:descriptLabel];

    int menuOffset =
            [self menuOffsetForRowAtIndexPath:indexPath];


    NSDictionary *cellText =
                    [menuList objectAtIndex:menuOffset];
    selectLabel.text = [cellText objectForKey:kSelectKey];
    descriptLabel.text =
                    [cellText objectForKey:kDescriptKey];
    [selectLabel release];
    [descriptLabel release];
  }
  return cell;
}
```

Here's the logic behind all that code:

1. **Determine whether there are any cells lying around that you can use.**

   Although a table view can display only a few rows at a time on iPhone's small screen, the table itself can conceivably hold a lot more. A large table would chew up a lot of memory if you were to create cells for every row. Fortunately, table views are designed to *reuse* cells. As a table view's cells scroll off the screen, they're placed in a queue of cells available to be reused.

2. **Create a *cell identifier* that indicates what cell type you're using. Add this to the `Constants.h` file:**

   ```
   #define kCellIdentifier  @"Cell"
   ```

   Table views support multiple cell types, which makes the identifier necessary. In this case, you need only one cell type, but sometimes you may want more than one.

   If the system runs low on memory, the table view gets rid of the cells in the queue, but as long as it has some available memory for them, it will hold on to them in case you want to use them again.

   You can ask the table view for a specific reusable cell object by sending it a `dequeueReusableCellWithIdentifier:` message:

   ```
   UITableViewCell *cell = [tableView
       dequeueReusableCellWithIdentifier:kCellIdentifier];
   ```

This asks whether any cells of the type you want are available.

3. **If there aren't any cells lying around, you have to create a cell by using the cell identifier you just created.**

```
if (cell == nil) {
  cell = [[[UITableViewCell alloc]
        initWithStyle:UITableViewCellStyleDefault
        reuseIdentifier:kCellIdentifier] autorelease];
```

You now have a table view cell that you can return to the table view.

UITableViewCellStyleDefault gives you a simple cell with a text label (black and left-aligned) and an optional image view. There are also several other styles:

- UITableViewCellStyleValue1 gives you a cell with a left-aligned black text label on the left side of the cell and smaller blue text and right-aligned label on the right side. (The Settings application uses this style of cell.)

- UITableViewCellStyleValue2 gives you a cell with a right-aligned blue text label on the left side of the cell and a left-aligned black label on the right side of the cell.

- UITableViewCellStyleSubtitle gives you a cell with a left-aligned label across the top and a left-aligned label below it in smaller gray text. (The iPod application uses cells in this style.)

4. **Define the accessory type for the cell.**

```
cell.accessoryType =
        UITableViewCellAccessoryDisclosureIndicator;
```

As I mention earlier in the brief tour of a cell, its layout includes a place for an accessory — usually something like a disclosure indicator.

In this case, use UITableViewCellAccessoryDisclosureIndicator (the one shaped like a regular chevron). It lets the user know that tapping this entry will result in something (hopefully wonderful) happening, such as the display of the current weather conditions.

If you're using a table view, and you want to display more detailed information about the entry itself, you might use a Detail Disclosure button. This allows you to then use a tap on the row for something else. In the Favorites view in the iPhone application, for example, selecting the Detail Disclosure button gives you a view of the contact information; if you just tap the row, it places the call for you.

You're not limited to these kinds of indicators; you also have the option of creating your own view — you can put in any kind of control. (That's what you see in the Settings application, for example.)

5. **Create the subviews.**

Here I show you just one example (the other is the same except for the font size and text color). You get the contentView frame and base the subview on it. The inset from the left (kInset) and the width of the subview (kLabelWidth) are defined in the Constants.h file — you'll need to add them. They look like this:

```
#define kInset               10
#define kSelectLabelWidth    100
#define kDescriptLabelWidth  160
```

To hold the text, the subview you are creating is a UILabelView, which meets my needs exactly:

```
CGRect subViewFrame = cell.contentView.frame;
subViewFrame.origin.x += kInset;
subViewFrame.size.width = kInset+kSelectLabelWidth;
UILabel *selectLabel = [[UILabel alloc]
                        initWithFrame:subViewFrame];
```

You then set the label properties that you're interested in; you do it by manually writing code rather than using Interface Builder. Just set the font color and size, the highlighted font color when an item is selected; and the background color of the label (as indicated in the code that follows). Setting the background color to transparent allows me to see the bottom line of the last cell in the group.

```
selectLabel.textColor = [UIColor blackColor];
selectLabel.highlightedTextColor = [UIColor
                                    whiteColor];
selectLabel.font = [UIFont boldSystemFontOfSize:18];
selectLabel.backgroundColor = [UIColor clearColor];
[cell.contentView addSubview:selectLabel];
```

 I could have inset the view one pixel up from the bottom, made the label opaque, and given it a white (not clear) background, which would be more efficient to draw. But with such a small number of rows, making that effort really has no appreciable performance impact, and the way I've set it up here requires less code for you to go through. Feel free to do it the "right way" on your own.

After you have your label, you just set its text to one of the values you get from the dictionary created in viewDidLoad representing this row.

The trouble is, you won't get the absolute row passed to you. You get only the row within a particular section — and you need the absolute row to get the right dictionary from the array. Fortunately, one of the arguments used when this method is called is the indexPath, which contains the section and row information in a single object. To get the row or the section out of an NSIndexPath, you just have to invoke its section method (indexPath.section) or its row method (indexPath.row), either of which returns an int. This neat trick enables you to compute the offset for the row in the array you created in viewDidLoad.

So the first thing you do in the following code is compute that. If you aren't going to use the `sectionsArray` as I did, you can compute it this way (which is commented out in the code). This is also why it's so handy to have the number of rows in a section as a constant.

```
int menuOffset = (indexPath.section*kSection1Rows)+
                                    indexPath.row;
```

But if you think about it, the `menuOffset` algorithm works only if you have two sections. That's why earlier I suggest you create `section-sArray`. I did, and what's more, I added a method — `menuOffsetFor-RowAtIndexPath:` — so that I can use it again later to get the menu offset, as you'll see.

```
int menuOffset = [self menuOffsetForRowAtIndexPath:
                                    indexPath];
```

The method and its algorithm are shown in Listing 2-9:

Listing 2-9:   Computing the Menu Offset

```
- (int) menuOffsetForRowAtIndexPath:
                          (NSIndexPath *)indexPath {

  int menuOffset = indexPath.row;
  for (int sectionRow=0; sectionRow <
                    indexPath.section; ++sectionRow) {
    menuOffset += [[sectionsArray
                objectAtIndex:sectionRow] intValue];
  }
  return menuOffset;
}
```

You start by passing the row to `menuOffset`. You then increment the offset by the number of rows in each of the previous sections, which is stored in the array as an `NSNumber` (and since `NSNumber` is an object, you have to use the `intValue` method to get the number as an integer).

And then you can use that dictionary you created to assign the text to the label.

```
NSDictionary *cellText = [menuList
                    objectAtIndex:menuOffset];
selectLabel.text = [cellText objectForKey:kSelectKey];
descriptLabel.text = [cellText
                    objectForKey:kDescriptKey];
```

Finally, because you no longer need the labels you created, you release them

```
[selectLabel release];
[descriptLabel release];
```

and return the cell formatted and with the text it needs to display in that row.

```
return cell;
```

And Now . . .

You're off to a good start — and you had to use only five methods to create the table and handle user selections. You still have to create the Content views and models, but before you do that, I show you how navigation works and how to improve the user experience by saving state and allowing the user to set preferences.

Chapter 3: Navigating

In This Chapter

ᕦ **Getting back to where you once belonged**

ᕦ **Working with user preferences**

ᕦ **Getting things done with selections**

*O*nce you have set up the basics for using table views, you need to allow the user to be able to select one of the entries and navigate to it. But as you will see, there's more involved in the selection process that may meet the eye.

In the first part of this chapter I'll show you how the selection mechanism works in table views.

Next, I'll show you how that mechanism can also be used to restore the state the application was in when the user last left the application.

Finally, I show you how user preferences may come into play during selection. I'll start by showing you how preferences work, and then I'll explain how you can use those preferences when the user does make a selection.

Working with User Selections

When the user taps on a table view entry, what happens next depends on what you want your table view to do for you.

If you're using the table view to display data (as the Albums view in the iPod application does, for example), you'd want a user's tap to show the next level in the hierarchy, such as a list of songs or a detail view of an item (such as information about a song).

In your case, you're going to want your user's taps to do more for you. When the user taps the Sights entry, he gets a list of sights from which he can choose to get more information. As such, you're essentially using the table view as a table of contents, so tapping a table view entry transfers the user to the view that presents the desired information — the Car Servicing information, for example.

For the RoadTrip application, I show you how you can get table views to display data hierarchies as well as tables of content, although you have to wait for Book VI to see how to work with data hierarchies.

To move from a table view to a new Content view, first you need to create a new view controller for that view. Then you need to launch your new view controller so it creates and installs the view on the screen. But you also have to give the user a way to get back to the Main view!

Brass-tacks time: What kind of code-writing gymnastics do you have to do to get all this stuff to happen?

Actually, not that much. Table views are usually paired with *navigation bars,* which enable users to get back to preceding views. And to get a navigation bar, all you have to do is include a *navigation controller* in your application. What's more, if you wisely chose the Navigation-Based Application template at the outset of your RoadTrip project, a navigation controller was already put in place for you in the `appDelegate` created by the template. Here's the code that the template quite generously provided you with (the navigation controller is in boldface type so you can find it easier):

```
@interface RoadTripAppDelegate : NSObject
                                  <UIApplicationDelegate> {

  UIWindow                *window;
  UINavigationController *navigationController;
}

@property (nonatomic, retain) IBOutlet UIWindow *window;
@property (nonatomic, retain) IBOutlet UINavigationController
    *navigationController;
@end
```

This navigation controller is created for you in the `MainWindow.xib` file (see Figure 3-1), which you can access by double-clicking the `MainWindow. xib` file in the Groups & Files list in your Xcode project window. If you take a closer look at Figure 3-1, you can see that, when the navigation controller is selected, it points to the `RootViewController.nib` in the View window — which is to say, it's pointing to the `RootViewController` and its table view. This links together the navigation controller, the root view controller, and the view.

Not only did the Navigation-Based Application template deliver the goods in the `RoadTripAppDelegate.h` file and nib file, but it also created the code you need in the `RoadTripAppDelegate.m` file.

To get the navigation controller view to load in the window, you don't have to do anything. When you chose the Navigation-Based Application template, the following code was automatically generated for you:

```
-void)applicationDidFinishLaunching:
                        (UIApplication *)application {
  [window addSubview:[navigationController view]];
  [window makeKeyAndVisible];
}
```

When all is said and done, you have a table view with a navigation bar ready to go to work.

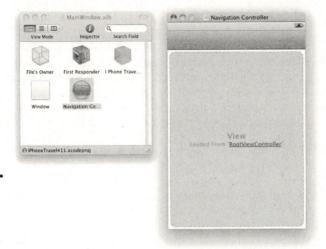

Figure 3-1:
The
navigation
controller.

Navigating the navigation controller

As the previous section explains, to give users the option of returning to a view higher up in the hierarchy (in our case, the Main view), table views are paired with navigation bars that enable a user to navigate the hierarchy. Here's what you need to know to make that work:

✦ The view below the navigation bar presents the current level of data.

✦ A navigation bar includes a title for the current view.

✦ If the current view is lower in the hierarchy than the top level, a Back button appears on the left side of the bar; the user can tap it to return to the previous level, as shown in Figure 3-2. The text in the Back button tells the user what the previous level was. In this case, it's the application's Main view, so you see the application's name — RoadTrip.

✦ A navigation bar may also have an Edit button on the right side — used to enter editing mode for the current view — or even custom buttons.

In the case of the RoadTrip application, you create a custom button that will act as an additional back button. I explain why that is needed shortly.

The navigation bar for each level is managed by a navigation controller, as mentioned in the previous section. The navigation controller maintains a stack of view controllers, one for each of the views displayed, starting with the root view controller (hence the name `RootViewController` given to the table view controller by the template). The root view controller is the very first view controller that the navigation controller pushes onto its stack when a user launches the application; it remains active until the user selects the next view to look at.

Time for a concrete example. When the user taps a row of the table view to get the map, the root view controller pushes the next view controller onto the stack. The new controller's view (the map) slides into place, and the navigation bar items are updated appropriately. When the user taps the back button in the navigation bar, the current view controller pops off the stack, the map slides off the screen, and the user finds himself back in the main (table) view.

A *stack* is a commonly used data structure that works on the principle of "last in, first out." Imagine an ideal boarding scenario for an airplane: Passengers would start being seated in the last seat in the last row, and they'd board the plane in back-to-front order until they got to the first seat in the first row, which would contain the seat for the last person to board. When the plane reached its destination, everyone would deplane (is that really a word?) in the reverse order. That last person on — the person in row one seat one — would be the first person off.

A computer stack is pretty much the same. Adding an object is called a *push* — in this case, when you tap Map row, the view controller for the Map view is pushed onto the stack. Removing an object is called a *pop* — touching the back button pops the view controller for the Heathrow view. When you pop an object off the stack, it's always the last one you pushed onto it. The controller that was there before the push is still there, and now becomes the active one. In this case, it's the root view controller.

As you know from using the built-in applications, however, when you tap a row you might find yourself not viewing some content, as you just did when you tapped the Map row, but rather at another table view. Figure 3-3 shows you what happens when you tap the Hotels row. You get another table view (which has just one entry at the moment), and tapping that entry gets you more information about the Parent's Inn. That process (for the next row tap) works the same way, and I show you how to do that in Book VI Chapter 1.

Figure 3-2:
Click the
back button
to return to
a previous
level.

Figure 3-3:
Another
table view.

Implementing the selection

At some point, you have to make sure that something actually happens when a user makes a selection. To do that, all you really need to do is implement the `tableview:didSelectRowAtIndexPath:` method to set up a response to a user tap in the Main view. This method, too, is already in the `RootViewController.m` file, courtesy of the template. You can see it all in Listing 3-1.

A lot of code in Listing 3-1 may not make sense to you. That's okay; I explain it all in detail in this chapter and the next. I include it here because it shows you the entirety of the application functionality and maintains a reference as you implement it step-by-step.

In this section, I'll be explaining the non-bolded code. This is the basic recipe you would use for handling user selection on a table view. As for the bolded code, the first set (see immediately below) has to do with saving the selection the user made in the table view. I'll explain this bit later when I show you how to save where the user is in the application in the "Saving state information step" section later in this chapter.

```
[RoadTripAppDelegate *appDelegate =
        (RoadTripAppDelegate *) [[UIApplication
                            sharedApplication] delegate];
[appDelegate.lastView replaceObjectAtIndex:0 withObject:
        [NSNumber numberWithInteger:indexPath.section]];
[appDelegate.lastView replaceObjectAtIndex:1 withObject:
            [NSNumber numberWithInteger:indexPath.row]];
```

The rest of the code in bold implements user preferences. I'll explain that bit of business in the "Using Preferences in Your Application" section later in this chapter.

Listing 3-1:   tableview:didSelectRowAtIndexPath:

```
- (void)tableView:(UITableView *)tableView
        didSelectRowAtIndexPath:(NSIndexPath *)indexPath {

[RoadTripAppDelegate *appDelegate =
        (RoadTripAppDelegate *) [[UIApplication
                            sharedApplication] delegate];
[appDelegate.lastView replaceObjectAtIndex:0 withObject:
        [NSNumber numberWithInteger:indexPath.section]];
[appDelegate.lastView replaceObjectAtIndex:1 withObject:
            [NSNumber numberWithInteger:indexPath.row]];

[tableView deselectRowAtIndexPath:indexPath
                                        animated:YES];
```

```
int menuOffset =
        [self menuOffsetForRowAtIndexPath:indexPath];
UIViewController *targetController =
      [[menuList objectAtIndex:menuOffset]
 objectForKey:kControllerKey];

if (targetController == nil) {
    BOOL realtime = !appDelegate.useStoredData;

  switch (menuOffset) {
    case 0:
      if (realtime) targetController =
            [[MapController alloc] initWithTrip:trip];
      else [self displayOfflineAlert:
            [[menuList objectAtIndex:menuOffset]
                      objectForKey:kSelectKey]];
      break;
    case 1:
      targetController =
        [[SightListController alloc] initWithTrip:trip];
      break;
    case 2:
      targetController =
            [[HotelController alloc] initWithTrip:trip];
      break;
    case 3:
      if  (realtime) targetController =
          [[WebViewController alloc] initWithTrip:trip
            tripSelector:@selector(returnWeather:)
            webControl:YES title:
            NSLocalizedString(@"Weather", @"Weather")];
      else [self displayOfflineAlert:[
            [menuList objectAtIndex:menuOffset]
                      objectForKey:kSelectKey]];
      break;
    case 4:
      targetController =
            [[WebViewController alloc] initWithTrip:trip
            tripSelector:
              @selector(returnCarServicingInformation:)
            webControl:NO title:NSLocalizedString
                (@"Car Servicing", @"Car Servicing")];
      break;
    case 5:
      targetController = [[WebViewController alloc]
  initWithTrip:trip tripSelector:
              @selector(returnCarInformation:)
            webControl:NO title:NSLocalizedString
                (@"The Car", @"Car Information")];
      break;
  }
```

(continued)

Listing 3-1 *(continued)*

```
    if (targetController) {
      [[menuList  objectAtIndex:menuOffset]
        setObject:targetController forKey:kControllerKey];
      [targetController release];
    }
  }
  if (targetController) [[self navigationController]
      pushViewController:targetController animated:YES];
}
```

Here's what all this code ends up doing for you when a user makes a selection in the Main view:

1. **Deselects the row the user selected.**

```
[tableView deselectRowAtIndexPath:indexPath
                                     animated:YES];
```

It stands to reason that if you want your app to move on to a new view, you have to deselect the row where you currently are.

2. **Computes the offset (based on section and row) into the menu array.**

```
int menuOffset = [self menuOffsetForRowAtIndexPath:
                                                indexPath];
```

You need to figure out where you want your app to land, right? I explain the menuOffsetForRowAtIndexPath:indexPath in Book V, Chapter 2.

3. **Checks to see whether the controller for that particular view has already been created.**

```
UIViewController *targetController =
                    [menuList objectAtIndex:menuOffset]
                        objectForKey:kControllerKey];
    if (targetController == nil) {
```

4. **If no controller exists, the code creates and initializes a new controller.**

I explain the mechanics of creating and initializing a new controller in Book V, Chapter 4. As you can see, you're going to use another switch statement to get to the right controller:

```
switch (menuOffset) {
```

For many of the selections, you'll always create a new controller. For example:

```
targetController = [[SightListController alloc]
    initWithTrip:trip];
```

For others you don't:

```
if (realtime) targetController =
            [MapController alloc] initWithTrip:trip];
```

```
else [self displayOfflineAlert:
            [[menuList objectAtIndex:menuOffset]
                objectForKey:kSelectKey]];
```

As I said, I explain this in the "Using Preferences in Your Application" section.

5. **If you created a new view controller, the code saves a reference to the newly created controller in the dictionary for that row.**

```
if (targetController) {
  [[menuList  objectAtIndex:menuOffset]
    setObject:targetController forKey:kControllerKey];
  [targetController release];
}
```

6. **Pushes the new or existing controller onto the stack and lets the navigation controller do the rest.**

```
if (targetController) [[self navigationController]
   pushViewController:targetController animated:YES];
```

Okay, I admit it. There's a lot of stuff in Listing 3-1 you probably haven't seen yet, but I clear it all up in Chapter 4 of this minibook. Rather than get caught up in the minutia, take some time now to look at some other issues here affecting navigation.

What other issues? Funny you should ask. "Keep the customer satisfied" is my mantra. If that means constantly refining an application design, so be it. In thinking about the RoadTrip design, two things struck me as essential if I really wanted to make this an application that focuses on the user. The first is part of Apple's Human Interface Guidelines — when it makes sense, you want the user, when he or she returns to an application, to find it in the same state as when he or she left — so it's not really something I can claim credit for. The second is something that flowed straight out of the nature of my design being able to access data even when you can't connect to the Internet.

Saving and Restoring State

When the user taps the Home button, the iPhone OS terminates your application and returns to the Home screen. The applicationWill Terminate: method is called, and your application is terminated — no ifs, ands, or buts. That means you have to save any unsaved data as well as the current state of your application if you want to restore the application to its previous state the next time the user launches it. Now, in situations like this one, you have to use common sense to decide what *state* really means. Generally, you wouldn't need to restore the application to where the user last stopped in a scrollable list, for example. For purposes of explanation, my RoadTrip app example saves the last category view that the user selected in the main table view, which corresponds to a row in a section in the table view. You might also consider saving that last view that was selected in that category.

Saving state information

Here's the sequence of events that go into saving the state:

1. **Add the new instance variable `lastView` and declare the `@property` in the `RoadTripAppDelegate.h` file.**

    This is shown in Listing 3-2. As usual, the new stuff is bold.

    As you can see, `lastView` is a mutable array. (The `NSMutableArray` business kind of gives it away.). You'll save the section as the first element in the array and the row as the second element. Because it's mutable, it'll be easier to update when the user selects a new row in a section.

2. **Add the `@synthesize` statement to the `RoadTripAppDelegate.m` file to tell the compiler to create the accessors for you.**

    The `@synthesize` statement is shown in Listing 3-3. (You guessed it — new stuff is bold.)

3. **Define the filename you'll use when saving the state information in the `Constants.h` file.**

    ```
    #define kState  @"LastState"
    ```

4. **Save the section and row that the user last tapped in the `RoadAppDelegate` object's `lastView` instance variable. This is accomplished by the first set of bolded code in the beginning of the `tableview:didSelectRowAtIndexPath:` method in the `RootViewController.m` file in Listing 3-1, and is also shown separately in Listing 3-4. You have to import `RoadTripAppDelegate.h`, as well.**

    ```
    #import "RoadTripAppDelegate.h"
    ```

    The `tableview:didSelectRowAtIndexPath:` method is called when the user taps a row in a section. As you may recall, the section and row information are in the `indexPath` argument of the `tableview:didSelectRowAtIndexPath:` method. All you have to do to save that information is to save the `indexPath.section` as the first array entry, and the `indexPath.row` as the second. (The reason I do it this way will become obvious when I show you how to write this to a file.)

5. **When the user goes back to the Main view, save that Main view location in the `viewWillAppear:` method. You need to add this method to the `RootViewController.m` file, as shown in Listing 3-5. (It's already there; all you have to do is uncomment it out.)**

The last step is to deal with the case when the user moves back to the Main view and then quits the application. To indicate that the user is at the Main view, you use –1 to represent the section and –1 to represent the row. You use minus ones in this case because, as you recall, the first section and row in a table are both 0, which requires me to represent the table (main) view itself in this clever way.

6. **Save the section and row in the `applicationWillTerminate:` method.**

   The method stub is already in the `RoadTripAppDelegate.m` file; you just have to add the code in Listing 3-6.

   In `applicationWillTerminate:`, you're saving the `lastView` instance variable (which contains the last section and row the user tapped) to the file `kState` (which is the constant you defined in Step 3 to represent the filename `LastState`).

   As you can see, reading or writing to the file system on the iPhone is pretty simple: You tell the system which directory to put the file in, specify the file's name, and then pass that information to the `writeTo File` method. Let me take you through what I just did in Step 6:

   - *Got the path to the `Documents` directory.*

     ```
     NSArray *paths = NSSearchPathForDirectoriesInDomains
             (NSDocumentDirectory, NSUserDomainMask, YES);
     NSString *documentsDirectory =[paths objectAtIndex:0];
     ```

     On the iPhone, you really don't have much choice about where the file goes. Although there's a /tmp directory, I'm going to place this file in the Documents directory because (as I explain in Book V, Chapter 2) this is part of my application's sandbox, so it's the natural home for all the app's files.

     `NSSearchPathForDirectoriesInDomains:` returns an array of directories. Because I'm interested only in the Documents directory, I use the constant `NSDocumentDirectory`, and because I'm restricted to my home directory, /sandbox, the constant `NSUserDomainMask` limits the search to that *domain*. There will be only one directory in the domain, so the one I want will be the first one returned.

   - *Created the complete path by appending the path filename to the directory.*

     ```
     NSString *filePath = [documentsDirectory
             stringByAppendingPathComponent:fileName];
     ```

     `stringByAppendingPathComponent;` precedes the filename with a path separator (/) if necessary.

   Unfortunately, this doesn't work if you're just trying to create a string representation of a URL.

- *Wrote the data to the file.*

```
[lastView writeToFile:filePath atomically:YES];
```

writeToFile: is an NSData method and does what it implies. I am actually telling the array here to write itself to a file, which is why I decided to save the location in this way in the first place. A number of other classes implement that method, including NSData, NSDate, NSNumber, NSString, and NSDictionary. You can also add this behavior to your own objects, and they could save themselves, but I don't get into that here. The atomically parameter first writes the data to an auxiliary file, and after that's successful, it's renamed to the path you've specified. This guarantees that the file won't be corrupted even if the system crashes during the write operation.

I explain a lot more about saving data in Book VI.

Listing 3-2:   Adding the Instance Variable to the Interface

```
@interface RoadTripAppDelegate : NSObject
   <UIApplicationDelegate> {

  UIWindow                  *window;
  UINavigationController    *navigationController;
  NSMutableArray            *lastView;
}

@property (nonatomic, retain) IBOutlet UIWindow *window;
@property (nonatomic, retain) IBOutlet UINavigationController
   *navigationController;
@property (nonatomic, retain) NSMutableArray *lastView;

@end
```

Listing 3-3:   Adding the @synthesize Statement to the Implementation

```
#import "RoadTripAppDelegate.h"
#import "RootViewController.h"
#import "Constants.h"

@implementation RoadTripAppDelegate

@synthesize window;
@synthesize navigationController;
@synthesize lastView;
```

Listing 3-4:   Saving indexPath in didSelectRowAtIndexPath:

```
RoadTripAppDelegate *appDelegate = (RoadTripAppDelegate *)
            [[UIApplication sharedApplication] delegate];
[appDelegate.lastView replaceObjectAtIndex:0 withObject:
            [NSNumber numberWithInteger:indexPath.section]];
[appDelegate.lastView replaceObjectAtIndex:1 withObject:
            [NSNumber numberWithInteger:indexPath.row]];
```

Listing 3-5:   Adding viewWillAppear:

```
- (void)viewWillAppear:(BOOL)animated {

  RoadTripAppDelegate *appDelegate = (RoadTripAppDelegate *)
   [[UIApplication sharedApplication] delegate];
  [appDelegate.lastView replaceObjectAtIndex:0
   withObject:[NSNumber numberWithInteger:-1]];
  [appDelegate.lastView replaceObjectAtIndex:1
   withObject:[NSNumber numberWithInteger:-1]];
}
```

Listing 3-6:   Adding applicationWillTerminate:

```
- (void)applicationWillTerminate:(UIApplication *)
                                          application {

  NSArray *paths = NSSearchPathForDirectoriesInDomains
            (NSDocumentDirectory, NSUserDomainMask, YES);
  NSString *documentsDirectory = [paths objectAtIndex:0];
  NSString *filePath = [documentsDirectory
                  stringByAppendingPathComponent:kState];
  [lastView writeToFile:filePath atomically:YES];
}
```

Restoring the state

After you've saved the state, you need to restore it the next time the application is launched. You can use my old friend `applicationDid FinishLaunching:` to carry out that task (as shown in Listing 3-7). You can find the `applicationDidFinishLaunching:` method in the `RoadTripAppDelegate.m` file. The code you need to add is in bold.

Listing 3-7:   Adding to applicationDidFinishLaunching:

```
- (void)applicationDidFinishLaunching:(UIApplication *)
                                            application {


    NSArray *paths = NSSearchPathForDirectoriesInDomains
                (NSDocumentDirectory, NSUserDomainMask, YES);
    NSString *documentsDirectory = [paths objectAtIndex:0];
    NSString *filePath = [documentsDirectory
                    stringByAppendingPathComponent:kState];
    lastView =[[NSMutableArray alloc]
                        initWithContentsOfFile:filePath];
    if (lastView == nil) {
      lastView = [[NSMutableArray arrayWithObjects:
                [NSNumber numberWithInteger:-1],
                [NSNumber numberWithInteger:-1],
                nil] retain];
    }


    [window addSubview:[navigationController view]];
    [window makeKeyAndVisible];
}
```

Reading is the mirror image of writing. You create the complete path, including the filename, just as you did when you saved the file. This time, you send the initWithContentsOfFile: message instead of writeToFile:, which allocates the lastView array and initializes it with the file. If the result is nil, there's no file, meaning that this is the first time the application is being used. In that case, you create the array with the value of section and row set to -1 and -1. (As I said in the previous section, when talking about saving state information, you use -1 -1 to indicate the Main view because 0 0 is actually the first row in the first section.)

initWithContentsOfFile: is an NSData method similar to write ToFile:. The classes that implement writeToFile: and those that implement initWithContentsOfFile: are the same.

Fortunately, restoring the current state is actually pretty straightforward, given the program architecture. The RootViewController object's view DidLoad method is called at application launch — after the first view is in place but not yet visible. At that point, you're getting ready to display the (table) view. But instead of just doing that, you see if the saved view was something other than the table view, and if it was, you take advantage of the same mechanisms that are used when the user taps a row in the table view. You invoke the didSelectRowAtIndexPath: method, which already knows how to display a particular view represented by the indexPath, that is, section and row. (Listing 3-8 shows the particulars.) You'll then save the current selection in the array.

Listing 3-8: Specifying the View to Be Displayed at Launch

```
- (void)viewDidLoad {
...

RoadTripAppDelegate *appDelegate =
(RoadTripAppDelegate *)[[UIApplication sharedApplication]
                                              delegate];
if ([((NSNumber*) [appDelegate.lastView objectAtIndex:0])
                                    intValue] != -1) {
  NSIndexPath* indexPath = [NSIndexPath indexPathForRow:
    [[appDelegate.lastView objectAtIndex:1] intValue]
    inSection:
      [[appDelegate.lastView objectAtIndex:0] intValue]];
  [self tableView:((UITableView*) self.tableView)
                    didSelectRowAtIndexPath:indexPath];
}
```

Here's what you're up to in Listing 3-8:

1. **You get the app delegate to where it's able to access the `lastView`.**

   ```
   RoadTripAppDelegate *appDelegate = (RoadTripAppDelegate
     *)[[UIApplication
                       sharedApplication] delegate];
   ```

2. **Check to see whether the last view was the Main view.**

   ```
   if ([((NSNumber*) [appDelegate.lastView
                     objectAtIndex:0]) intValue] != -1) {
   ```

3. **If the last view wasn't the Main view, create the index path using the last section and row information that was loaded into the `lastView` instance variable by `applicationDidFinishLaunching:`.**

   ```
   NSIndexPath* indexPath = [NSIndexPath indexPathForRow:
     [[appDelegate.lastView objectAtIndex:1] intValue]
     inSection:
     [[appDelegate.lastView objectAtIndex:0] intValue]];
   ```

4. **Send the `tableview:didSelectRowAtIndexPath:` message to display the right view.**

   ```
   [self tableView:((UITableView*) self.tableView)
                   didSelectRowAtIndexPath:indexPath];
   ```

The reason you created an index path was to be able to take advantage of the `didSelectRowAtIndexPath:` method to replay the last user tap in the Main view.

All this being done, the user will thank you for it. Now he or she can use the application, take a phone call, play a game, look up something on a map, and then find themselves right back where they left off when they restart the application.

Respecting User Preferences

Being able to have the user tailor an application to do things in the way they would like is an important part of creating a great user experience. The user, for example, may want to see measurements in kilometers rather than miles, or vice versa.

In this section I'll show you how to implement a user preference for whether or not to always download the latest information from the Internet when the application starts up. While this preference itself is more important in situations where data roaming is an additional charge, it does serve to illustrate how to implement any kind of preference you might want to have the user set. More importantly, it will also provide a vehicle for showing you how to cache (or save) data so you don't always have to always download it every time the user starts up the application.

Figure 3-4 shows you what I came up with for the Settings screen for the RoadTrip application.

Use Stored Data tells the application to use the last version of the data that it accessed, rather than going out on the Internet for the latest information. Although this does violate my I Want the Most Up-to-Date Information rule, it can be useful if you're on an airplane and can't access the Internet. (You can accomplish the same thing in airplane mode and by adding error checking for Internet availability, but I want to show you how to use preferences, and this is a great example. This works especially well if you're creating applications to be used globally and you don't want to subject the user to roaming changes.)

No doubt it's way cool to put user preferences in Settings. Some programmers abuse this trick, though; they make you go into Settings when it's just as easy to give the user a preference-setting capability within the application itself. You should put something in Settings only if the user changes it infrequently. In this case, stored data doesn't change often; Use Stored Data mode definitely belongs in Settings.

In the following sections, I show you how to put a toggle switch in Settings that lets you specify whether to use only stored data, and then I show you how to retrieve the setting. After that, I show you how to actually use the toggle switch setting in your code.

The Settings application uses a property list, called `Root.plist`, found in the Settings bundle inside your application. The Settings application takes what you put in the property list and builds a Settings section for your application in its list of application settings as well as the views that display and enable the user to change those settings. The next sections spell out how to put that Settings section to work for you.

Figure 3-4:
The
required
preferences.

Adding a Settings bundle to your project

For openers, you have to add a Settings bundle to your application. Here are the moves:

1. **In the Groups & Files list (at left in the Xcode project window), select the RoadTrip folder and then choose File⇨New File from the main menu, or press ⌘+N.**

    The New File dialog appears.

2. **Choose Resource under the iPhone OS heading in the left pane and then select the Settings Bundle icon, as shown in Figure 3-5.**

Figure 3-5:
Creating the
application
bundle.

3. **Click the Next button.**

4. **Choose the default name of `Settings.bundle` and then press Return (Enter) or click Finish.**

   You now see a new item called `Settings.bundle` in the `RoadTrip` folder, in the Groups & Files list.

5. **Click the triangle to expand the `Settings.bundle` subfolder.**

   You see the `Root.plist` file as well as an `en.lproj` folder. (The latter is used for localization issues.)

Setting up the property list

Property lists are widely used in iPhone applications because they provide an easy way to create structured data using named values for a number of object types.

Property lists all have a single root node, a dictionary, which means it stores items using a key-value pair, just as an `NSDictionary` does: All dictionary entries must have both a key and a value. In this dictionary, there are two keys:

✦ `StringsTable`

✦ `PreferenceSpecifiers`

The value for the first entries is a string — the name of a strings table used for localization, which I don't get into here. The second entry is an array of dictionaries — one dictionary for each preference. You probably need some time to wrap your head around that one. It'll become clearer as I take you through it.

`PreferenceSpecifiers` is where you put a toggle switch so the user can choose to use (or not use, since it's a toggle) only stored data; I refer to that choice later as *stored data mode*. Here's how it's done:

1. **In the Groups & Files list of the project window, select the triangle next to the `Settings.bundle` file to reveal the `Root.plist` file.**

2. **Double-click the `Root.plist` file to open it in a separate window.**

   Okay, you don't *really* have to do this, but I find it easier to work with this file when it's sitting in its own window.

3. **In the `Root.plist` window you just opened, click to expand all the triangles next to all the nodes, as shown in Figure 3-6.**

Figure 3-6:
Default
Root.
plist file
preferences.

4. **Under the `PreferenceSpecifiers` heading in the `Root.plist` window, move to Item 1.**

   `PreferenceSpecifiers` is an array designed to hold a set of dictionary nodes, each of which represents a single preference. For each item listed in the array, the first row under it has a key of `Type`; every property list node in the `PreferenceSpecifiers` array must have an entry with this key, which identifies what kind of entry this is. The `Type` value for the current Item 0 — `PSGroupSpecifier` — is used to indicate that a new group should be started. The value for this key actually acts like a section heading for a table view (like what you create in Book V, Chapter 2). Double-click the value next to `Title` and delete the default `Group`, as I have in Figure 3-7 (or you can put in `RoadTrip Preferences`, or be creative if you like).

5. **Seeing that Item 2 is already defined as a toggle switch, you can just modify it by changing the `Title` value from `Enabled` to `Use stored data` and the key from `enabled_preference` to `useStoredData-Preference`. This is the key you will use in your application to access the preference.**

6. **Continue your modifications by deselecting the Boolean check box next to `DefaultValue`.**

   You want the Use Stored Data preference initially to be set to Off because I expect most people will still want to go out on the Internet for the latest information, despite the high roaming charges involved.

   When you're done, the `Root.plist` window should look like Figure 3-7.

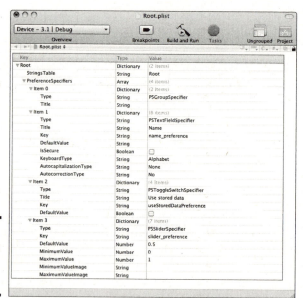

Figure 3-7:
Preferences
for
RoadTrip.

7. **Collapse the little triangles next to Items 1 and 3 (as shown in Figure 3-8) and then select those items one by one and delete them.**

   The item numbers do change as you delete them, so be careful (starting with Item 3 does make it easier). That's why you need to leave the preference item you care about open, so you can see not to delete it. Fortunately, Undo is supported here; if you make a mistake, press ⌘+Z to undo the delete.

8. **Save the property file by pressing ⌘+S.**

Figure 3-8:
Delete these
items.

Reading Settings in the Application

After you've set it up so your users can let their preferences be known in
Settings, you need to read those preferences back into the application. You
do that in the `RoadTripAppDelegate` object's `applicationDidFinish-
Launching:` method. But first, a little housekeeping — taking care of things
like new instance variables and properties and the like.

1. **Add the new instance variable `useStoredData` and declare the `@`
   property in the `RoadTripAppDelegate.h` file.**

   This is shown in Listing 3-9. (Again, the new stuff is bold.)

   Notice that the `@property` declaration is a little different than what
   you have been using so far. Up to now, all your properties have been
   declared `(nonatomic, retain)`. What's this `readonly` stuff? Because
   `useStoredData:` is not an object (it's a Boolean value), `retain` is not
   applicable. In addition, you'll enable it to be read only. If you wanted it
   to be updatable, you could make it `readwrite`.

2. **Add the `@synthesize` statement to the `RoadTripAppDelegate.m` file
   to tell the compiler to create the accessors for you.**

   This is shown in Listing 3-10. (You guessed it — new is bold.)

   You'll also have to add `kUseStoredDataPreference` to the
   `Constants.h` file;

   ```
   #define kUseStoredDataPreference
                        @"useStoredDataPreference"
   ```

Listing 3-9: Adding the Instance Variable to the Interface

```
@interface RoadTripAppDelegate : NSObject
                               <UIApplicationDelegate> {

    UIWindow                *window;
    UINavigationController  *navigationController;
    NSMutableArray          *lastView;
    BOOL                     useStoredData;
}

@property (nonatomic, retain) IBOutlet UIWindow *window;
@property (nonatomic, retain) IBOutlet UINavigationController
    *navigationController;
@property (nonatomic, retain) NSMutableArray *lastView;
@property (nonatomic, readonly) BOOL useStoredData;

@end
```

Listing 3-10: Adding the @synthesize Statement to the Implementation

```
#import "RoadTripAppDelegate.h"
#import "RootViewController.h"
#import "Constants.h"

@implementation RoadTripAppDelegate

@synthesize window;
@synthesize navigationController;
@synthesize lastView;
@synthesize useStoredData;
```

With your housekeeping done, it's time to add the necessary code to the applicationDidFinishLaunching: method. Listing 3-11 shows the code you need:

Listing 3-11: Adding to applicationDidFinishLaunching

```
- (void)applicationDidFinishLaunching:
                        (UIApplication *)application {

    if (![[NSUserDefaults standardUserDefaults]
                 objectForKey:kUseStoredDataPreference]) {
       [[NSUserDefaults standardUserDefaults]setBool:NO
                        forKey:kUseStoredDataPreference];
       useStoredData = NO;
    }
    else
```

```
useStoredData = [[NSUserDefaults standardUserDefaults]
               boolForKey:kUseStoredDataPreference];

NSArray *paths = NSSearchPathForDirectoriesInDomains
  (NSDocumentDirectory, NSUserDomainMask, YES);
NSString *documentsDirectory = [paths objectAtIndex:0];
NSString *filePath = [documentsDirectory
                      stringByAppendingPathComponent:kSt
  ate];
lastView =[[NSMutableArray alloc]  initWithContentsOfFile:f
  ilePath];
if (lastView == nil) {
  lastView = [[NSMutableArray arrayWithObjects:
              [NSNumber numberWithInteger:-1],
              [NSNumber numberWithInteger:-1],
              nil] retain];
}

[window addSubview:[navigationController view]];
[window makeKeyAndVisible];
}
```

Here's what you want all that code to do for you:

1. **Check to see whether the settings have been moved into**
    NSUserDefaults**.**

```
      if (![[NSUserDefaults standardUserDefaults]
              objectForKey:kUseStoredDataPreference]){
```

The Settings application moves the user's preferences from Settings
into NSUserDefaults only *after* the application runs for the first time.
Settings will, however, update the preferences in NSUserDefaults if
the user makes any changes.

2. **If the settings haven't been moved into NSUserDefaults yet, use the**
    default of NO (which corresponds to the default you used for the initial
    preference value).

```
      [[NSUserDefaults standardUserDefaults]setBool:NO
                      forKey:kUseStoredDataPreference];
          useStoredData = NO;
```

3. **If the settings *have* been moved into NSUserDefaults, read them in**
    and then set the useStoredData instance variable to whatever the
    user's preference is.

```
      else
        useStoredData =
                [[NSUserDefaults  standardUserDefaults]
                boolForKey:kUseStoredDataPreference];
```

Using Preferences in Your Application

Way back when, I showed you how to implement the `tableview:didSel` `ectRowAtIndexPath:` method that makes something happen when a user selects a row in the table view. (Okay, it was the "Implementing the selection" section earlier in this chapter.) And although there are other places to use stored data in your application, the `tableview:didSelectRowAtInde` `xPath:` method is one method that really needs to use it.

In Listing 3-12, the code in bold shows you what you will need to do to implement the user preference.

Listing 3-12:   tableview:didSelectRowAtIndexPath:

```
- (void)tableView:(UITableView *)tableView
        didSelectRowAtIndexPath:(NSIndexPath *)indexPath {

  [RoadTripAppDelegate *appDelegate =
          (RoadTripAppDelegate *) [[UIApplication
                            sharedApplication] delegate];
  [appDelegate.lastView replaceObjectAtIndex:0 withObject:
          [NSNumber numberWithInteger:indexPath.section]];
  [appDelegate.lastView replaceObjectAtIndex:1 withObject:
            [NSNumber numberWithInteger:indexPath.row]];

  [tableView deselectRowAtIndexPath:indexPath
                                    animated:YES];

  int menuOffset =
            [self menuOffsetForRowAtIndexPath:indexPath];
  UIViewController *targetController =
        [[menuList objectAtIndex:menuOffset]
   objectForKey:kControllerKey];

  if (targetController == nil) {
     BOOL realtime = !appDelegate.useStoredData;

     switch (menuOffset) {
       case 0:
         if (realtime) targetController =
                 [[MapController alloc] initWithTrip:trip];
         else [self displayOfflineAlert:
                 [[menuList objectAtIndex:menuOffset]
                             objectForKey:kSelectKey]];
         break;
       case 1:
         targetController =
           [[SightListController alloc] initWithTrip:trip];
         break;
       case 2:
```

```
            targetController =
                    [[HotelController alloc] initWithTrip:trip];
        break;
    case 3:
        if  (realtime) targetController =
               [[WebViewController alloc] initWithTrip:trip
                   tripSelector:@selector(returnWeather:)
                   webControl:YES title:
                   NSLocalizedString(@"Weather", @"Weather")];
        else [self displayOfflineAlert:[
                    [menuList objectAtIndex:menuOffset]
                                    objectForKey:kSelectKey]];
        break;
    case 4:
        targetController =
                [[WebViewController alloc] initWithTrip:trip
                    tripSelector:
                        @selector(returnCarServicingInformation:)
                    webControl:NO title:NSLocalizedString
                            (@"Car Servicing", @"Car Servicing")];
        break;
    case 5:
        targetController = [[WebViewController alloc]
    initWithTrip:trip tripSelector:
                    @selector(returnCarInformation:)
                    webControl:NO title:NSLocalizedString
                            (@"The Car", @"Car Information")];
        break;
    }
    if (targetController) {
        [[menuList  objectAtIndex:menuOffset]
            setObject:targetController forKey:kControllerKey];
        [targetController release];
    }
    }
    if (targetController) [[self navigationController]
        pushViewController:targetController animated:YES];
}
```

For some selections, having Internet access makes no difference. But
for other selections — Map and Weather come to mind — you've (hopefully) decided that if you're not online, you can't deliver the quality of the
information a user needs. (Face it; saved current weather conditions is an
oxymoron.) For other selections, Map for example, a network connection
is required. (Right now, no caching is available.) In that case, you send an
alert to the user (see Listing 3-13) informing him or her that the selection
is unavailable. Add the code in Listing 3-13 to RootViewController.m
and add the corresponding method declaration (see the following code) to
RootViewController.h.

```
else [self displayOfflineAlert:
        [[menuList objectAtIndex:menuOffset]
        objectForKey:kSelectKey]];
```

Listing 3-13: Displaying an Alert

```
- (void) displayOfflineAlert: (NSString*) selection {

  UIAlertView *alert = [[UIAlertView alloc]
          initWithTitle:selection
          message:@"is not available offline"
          delegate:self cancelButtonTitle: @"Thanks"
          otherButtonTitles:nil];
  [alert show];
  [alert release];
}
```

If you try to compile RoadTrip at this point, you *will* get errors. You haven't yet defined a number of classes that are used in `tableView:didSelectR owAtIndexPath:`. If you feel the need to compile the application to check syntax errors (as I do), you should only have five compiler errors, all in `tab leView:didSelectRowAtIndexPath:` as you can see in Figure 3-9.

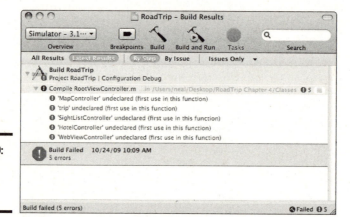

Figure 3-9: It doesn't compile quite yet.

To be able to compile the application, comment out the code shown here in bold in `tableView:didSelectRowAtIndexPath:`.

```
//    BOOL realtime = !appDelegate.useStoredData;

    switch (menuOffset) {
      case 0:
//      if (realtime) targetController = [[MapController
    alloc] initWithTrip:trip];
//      else [self displayOfflineAlert: [[menuList
    objectAtIndex:menuOffset] objectForKey:kSelectKey]];
        break;
      case 1:
```

```
//      targetController = [[SightListController alloc]
     initWithTrip:trip];
        break;
      case 2:
//      targetController = [[HotelController alloc]
     initWithTrip:trip];
        break;
      case 3:
//      if  (realtime) targetController = [[WebViewController
     alloc] initWithTrip:trip tripSelector:@
     selector(returnWeather:)
//          webControl:YES title:
             NSLocalizedString(@"Weather", @"Weather")];
//      else [self displayOfflineAlert:[[menuList
     objectAtIndex:menuOffset] objectForKey:kSelectKey]];
        break;
      case 4:
//      targetController = [[WebViewController alloc]
     initWithTrip:trip tripSelector: @selector(returnCarServici
     ngInformation:)
//          webControl:NO title:NSLocalizedString
                   (@"Car Servicing", @"Car Servicing")];
        break;
      case 5:
//      targetController = [[WebViewController alloc]
     initWithTrip:trip tripSelector: @selector(returnCarInform
     ation:)
//          webControl:NO title:NSLocalizedString
             (@"The Car", @"Car Information")];
        break;
    }
```

Chapter 4: Creating Controllers and Model Classes

In This Chapter

✔ Taking another look at model objects

✔ Taking advantage of reusable view controllers and models

✔ Accessing data on the Internet

✔ Saving and reading files

Getting the framework (no pun intended) in place for a new iPhone application is certainly a crucial part of the development process, but in the grand scheme of things, it's only the spadework that prepares the way for the really cool stuff. After all is said and done, you still need to add the content that the users will see or interact with. Content is, after all, the reason they bought this application.

The last couple of chapters have been about creating an application structure, but this chapter moves on to Content views and how to implement them. Content views display the information that the user is after when he or she is using the app.

This whole implementation thing is actually less difficult than it sounds. The real key to creating an extensible application — one where you can easily add new views — is the program architecture. When you have a table view in place, you have the structure necessary for navigation in your application. With that navigation architecture — along with the Model-View-Controller pattern I've been touting all along in this and other minibooks — the actual business of creating the views, view controllers, and the model necessary for your app turns out to be somewhat pedestrian. You do more or less the same thing over again for each new Content view. (Oh well, boring is sometimes good.)

One of the things I pay significant attention to in this chapter is the relationships that are defined in the Model-View-Controller model (MVC model, to in-the-know types like you). I want to remind you that the data and application logic about what to *do* with that data must be encapsulated in the model class(es). The views (and the view controllers) are really only conduits for displaying what the model supplies. The relationships I speak of here have to do with how a view controller for example, accesses the model to get the data needed to be displayed in a view.

To kick off the process, you first need to decide what you want the user to see whenever the user selects a particular row in the Main view of your app. He or she may see some information they are interested in — the Golden Gate Bridge for example. In this case you also need to decide where that information is going to be (physically) located. You have a number of options here. It can be 1) a program resource (kind of like a local file, which I get to later); 2) a Web page; or 3) data located on a server on the Internet.

But when the user selects a particular row what you may want to display is not (just) information, but some controls or another table view that gives you even more choices, like when you select an album in the iPod application and it gives you a list of songs you can select. The list of albums in this case is both information (what albums are available) as well as "controls" that allow you to get even more information. To ease your mind, I show you how to work with two of your three options (information and another table view) right here in this chapter. (Controls are covered in Book III.) And, oh yes, as is the case in Chapter 3 of this minibook, you also have to make some decisions about what you want to do if the user fires up your app while offline.

This RoadTrip app you're building piece by piece is going to be an application with a *lot* of functionality, so it's probably best to get some of the simpler functions out of the way first. Getting the RoadTrip app to display car model information as well as car-servicing information simply involves displaying some data in a Web view. It may be true that the Car Model Information feature gets its data from a resource, and the Car Servicing Information feature gets its data from a server on the Internet, but in all other respects, they work exactly the same. You can throw the Weather feature in here as well; it simply goes out to a Web site, but instead of launching a browser, it displays the information in your application.

Speaking of the weather, it makes a lot of sense to present that functionality first. Implementing a view that accesses a Web page — which is what the Weather feature does — is actually a superset of what you need to do to display a local resource or data from a Web server. So, if you get Weather under your belt, you'll be all set to tackle Car Model Information and Car Servicing Information.

Specifying the Content

If the user selects Weather from the Main view in the RoadTrip application, he or she comes face-to-face with an Internet site displaying weather information. (I use www.weather.com in my example, but you can use any site that you like.)

In this chapter, I show you how to code the view controller and model class it will use to get the information it needs to pass on to the view to display for each of the examples shown in Figures 4-1, and 4-2. The view controllers are the key elements here. They're the ones that get the content from the `Trip` model object — the model object you're going to in the `viewDidLoad` method of the `RootViewController` — and send it to the view to display.

When the user selects Weather from the Main view, what the user sees *does* depend on whether the device is online or in stored data mode. If the device is online, the user sees a Web page from a Web site with the weather information, as illustrated in Figure 4-2 (left). When in stored data mode, the user gets a message stating that weather data is unavailable when offline, as you can see in Figure 4-2 (right).

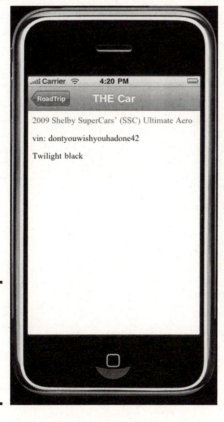

Figure 4-1:
The car information view (left) and servicing view (right).

Figure 4-2:
If you're online, you can connect to Weather (left). If you're offline, it's a different story (right).

If you're not blessed with quite a bit of object-oriented programming experience, your first inclination here would probably be to create three view controllers, one for each of the entries in the table: Weather, Car Servicing, and The Car. Although this would work, you would soon realize that all three of those controllers would be doing more or less the same thing, and all use a `UIWebView` to display the information.

In the interest of reducing the total number of classes you have to deal with, not to mention reducing typos and copy-and-paste errors, I show you how a single view controller can handle the display requirements for all three entries.

I implement this single view controller by using *selectors,* which work like function pointers in C. As a result, this chapter provides a preview of the techniques you need to employ in order to implement the asynchronous file downloads I talk about in the next minibook.

Creating the View Controller, Nib, and Model Files

Standard operating procedure for iPhone applications is to have a user tap an entry in a Main view to get to a subsequent view. For this to work, you first need to create a new view controller and then push it onto the stack. (For more on controllers and stacks as they apply to the RoadTrip application, see Chapter 3 in this minibook.) To make all that happen, you need to code all of the following: your view controller interface and implementation files, your nib files, and finally your model interface and implementation files.

Going from abstract to concrete, read on as I spell out what you need to have in place before your users can jump from one view to another in RoadTrip — say, when a user selects the The Car row in the Main view of the app and fully expects to find a new view full of information about (yep) his car. This will be the general pattern you can follow for any application that uses a table view. (For more on table views, check out Chapter 2 of this minibook.)

Adding the controller and nib file

Okay, check out how easy it is to come up with the view controller and nib files:

1. **Fire up Xcode and load your RoadTrip project.**

   You'll be building on what you've done in Chapter 1-3 of this minibook.

2. **In the RoadTrip project window, select the Classes folder, and then choose File⇨New from the main menu (or press ⌘+N) to get the New File window you see in Figure 4-3.**

3. **In the left column of the dialog, select Cocoa Touch Class under the iPhone OS heading, select the UIViewController Subclass template in the top-right pane and then click Next.**

   Be sure the With XIB for User Interface option is also selected.

   You see a new dialog asking for some more information.

4. **Enter** WebViewController.m **in the File Name field, as I did in Figure 4-4, and then click Finish.**

To make things easier to find, I keep my `WebViewController.m` and `WebViewController.h` classes in the Classes folder. And I move the `WebViewController.xib` to the Resources folder.

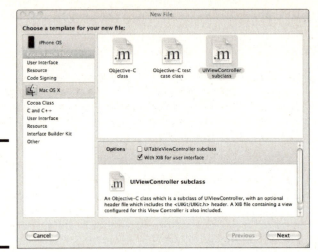

Figure 4-3:
Select the
UIView-
Controller
Subclass
template.

Figure 4-4:
Save it as
WebView-
Controller.m.

Now do it all over again (and get it out of the way) for the model classes your controllers will use. After you finish that, you're all set up to start adding code.

It would be a good idea to add a new folder in the Groups & Files list to hold all your new model classes. To do so, select the RoadTrip project icon and then choose Project➪New Group. You get a brand spanking new folder, named New Group, already selected and waiting for you to type in the name you want. To change what folder a file is in, select and then drag the file to the folder you want it to occupy. The same goes for folders as well (after all, they can go into other folders).

1. **Choose File⇨New from the main menu (or press ⌘+N) to get the New File dialog.**

Refer to Figure 4-3 if you need to see what the dialog looks like.

2. **In the leftmost column of the dialog, first select Cocoa Touch Class under the iPhone OS heading, but this time be sure to select the *Objective-C Class* template in the topmost pane. Make sure as well that the drop-down menu Subclass Of has NSObject selected and then click Next.**

You see a new dialog asking for some more information.

3. **Enter** Trip **in the File Name field and then click Finish.**

This is the main model class you'll be using.

4. **Go through steps 1-3 to create .m and .h files for** Weather, CarServicing, **and** CarInformation.

The Weather, CarServicing, and CarInformation classes are pretty straightforward — but what about this Trip thing? As you'll see, it will be the class in charge and serve to hide the other model classes — making the architecture much more flexible.

Setting up the nib file

For the RoadTrip application, you want to use a nice UIWebView to display the information for the three table view entries you are implementing in this chapter. You need to set the UIWebView up using Interface Builder, but you also need a reference to it from the WebViewController so it can pass the content from the model to the view. To do that, you need to create an *outlet* (a special kind of instance that can refer to objects in the nib) in the view controller, just as you do in Chapter 2 of Book III for the DeepThoughts application. The outlet reference will be "filled in" automatically when your application is initialized.

Here's how you should deal with this outlet business:

1. **Within Xcode, add a** webView **(**UIWebView**) outlet to the** WebViewController.h **interface file.**

You declare an outlet by using the keyword IBOutlet in the WebViewController interface file, like so

```
IBOutlet UIWebView    *webView;
```

2. **Do the File⇨Save thing to save the file.**

After it's saved — and only then — can Interface Builder find the new outlet.

3. **Use the Groups & Files list on the left in the project window to drill down to the `WebViewController.xib` file; then double-click the file to launch it in Interface Builder.**

   If the Attributes Inspector window is not open, choose Tools⇨Inspector or press Shift+⌘+1. If the View window is not visible, double-click the View icon in the `WebViewController.xib` window.

   If you can't find the `WebViewController.xib` window (you may have minimized it whether by accident, on purpose, whatever), you can get it back by choosing Window⇨WebViewController.xib or whichever nib file you're working on.

4. **Click the File's Owner icon in the `WebViewController.xib` window.**

   It should already be set to WebViewController. If not, retrace your steps to see where you may have made a mistake.

   You need to be sure that the file's owner is `WebViewController`. You can set the file's owner from the Class drop-down menu in the Identity Inspector. (If it's not visible, choose Tools⇨ Identity Inspector or press ⌘ +4.)

5. **Click in the View window and then choose UIWebView from the Class drop-down menu in the Identity Inspector.**

   The name in the `WebViewController.xib` window changes to Web View, and the title of the View window changes to Web View the next time you reopen the window after it has been closed.

6. **Back in the `WebViewController.xib` window, right-click the File's Owner icon to call up a contextual menu with a list of connections.**

   You can get the same list using the Connections tab in the Attributes Inspector. (Same drill — if it's not visible, choose Tools⇨Attributes Inspector or press ⌘ +1.)

7. **Drag from the little circle next to the `webView` outlet in the list onto the Web View window.**

   Doing so connects the `webView` outlet for `WebViewController` to the Web view.

8. **Go back to that list of connections and click the triangle next to Referencing Outlets. This time drag from the little circle next to the New Referencing Outlet list onto the Web View window.**

9. **With the cursor still in the Web View window, let go of the mouse button.**

   A pop-up menu appears (with only one term in it — delegate), looking like what you see in Figure 4-5.

10. **Choose delegate from the pop-up menu.**

    You need this later when I show you how to allow a user to go back when he or she selects a Web site link being displayed in a Web view.

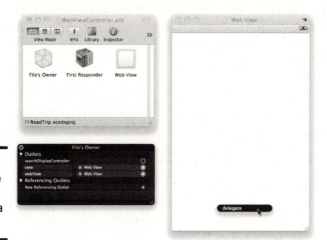

Figure 4-5:
Making the
WebView-
Controller a
delegate.

When you're done, the contextual menu should look like Figure 4-6.

Figure 4-6:
The
WebView-
Controller
connections
are all in
place.

If you think about it though, why do you need the `webView`? There's already
a pointer to the `view` object safely nestled in the view controller. There're
two reasons.

✦ **I'm lazy.** If I create a second outlet of type `UIWebView`, then every time I
access it, I don't have to cast the `UIView` into a `UIWebView`, as you can
see in the following line:

```
(UIWebView*) [self view] or (UIWebView*) self.view
```

✦ **I'm doing it for you.** It makes the code easier to follow.

At this point, you have the view controller class set up and you've arranged
for the nib loader to create a `UIWebView` object and set all the outlets for
you when the user selects Weather for the view he or she wants to see.

Yea! You're done with all the tedium! Now you can get on to the more interesting stuff.

At this point, you have the classes defined for all of the view controller and model objects. All that's left for you to do is to enter the code to make it do something — well, maybe not just *something*. How about *exactly* what you want it to do?

Getting Trippy with the Trip Model

As I point out earlier in this chapter — and numerous other times, but who's counting? — the models own and encapsulate the data and application logic. In the case of Weather, as well as The Car and Car Servicing, that means the model is the place where the knowledge of where that data is — and how to access that data — resides. It may be a Web page, a file or resource on the iPhone itself, or data that will be provided by a server on the Internet. Encapsulating that knowledge in the model allows you to change how and where the data is represented without impacting the controllers themselves. As an added bonus, you can add new controllers and views and have them access their data without having to do a lot of copy and pasting.

The model object that you'll use — at least the one that the view controllers will be aware of — is the `Trip`. It provides the interface to the View controllers that enables them to both get the data required by their views as well as inform the model object of any new information passed in by the views. (You can see how that's actually done in the next minibook). You can find that interface in Listing 4-1. Add the code in bold to `Trip.h`.

Listing 4-1:   The Trip Interface

```
@class Weather;
@class CarServicing;
@class CarInformation;

@interface Trip : NSObject   {

   NSString        *tripName;
   CarServicing    *carServicing;
   CarInformation  *carInformation;
   Weather         *weather;
}

- (id) initWithName:(NSString*) theTripName;
- (void) returnWeather:(id) theViewController;
- (void) returnCarServicingInformation:(id)
                                   theViewController;
- (void) returnCarInformation:(id) theViewController;
@end
```

The beauty of the setup here is that the view controller that's controlling the display of the Weather view only has to send the `returnWeather:` message to the `Trip` object to get the information it needs.

What may puzzle you is that the method returns a `void`, but I explain that shortly.

Before moving on, you also want to get the creation and initialization of the `Trip` object out of the way. Add the code in bold in Listing 4-2 to `Trip.m`.

Listing 4-2: Initializing the Trip Object

```
#import "Trip.h"
#import "CarInformation.h"
#import "CarServicing.h"
#import "Weather.h"
#import "WebViewController.h"


@implementation Trip

- (id) initWithName:(NSString*) theTrip {

  if ((self = [super init])) {
    tripName = theTrip;
    [theTrip retain];
    carInformation =
                [[CarInformation alloc] initWithTrip:self];
    carServicing =
                  [[CarServicing alloc] initWithTrip:self];
    weather = [[Weather alloc] init];
  }
  return self;
}

@end
```

All this method does is save the name of the trip (My trip to Graceland for example — which is specified in the `RootViewController`, as you see later on) and allocate and initialize the objects it will use — the classes you created earlier. The class you're concentrating on now is Weather, but you get to the others later in this chapter.

While Listings 4-1 and 4-2 show you what you'll do once the Trip object has been created, you'll probably notice that you haven't created it yet.

To do that, add this line of code to `viewDidLoad` in `RootViewController.m`.

```
trip = [[Trip alloc] initWithName:@"Road Trip"];
```

After creating your model object, you of course also have to import its header to be able to send it messages. Add these two lines of code to `RootViewController.m`. You also might as well add the `#import` for `WebViewController` (you'll be creating the `WebViewController` shortly) at the same time:

```
#import "Trip.h"
#import "WebViewController.h"
```

Add the new instance variable trip to `RootViewController.h`.

```
Trip            *trip;
```

You also have to make the compiler aware of the class, so add the following as well to `RootViewController.h`:

```
@class Trip;
```

This is shown in bold:

```
@class Trip;

@interface RootViewController : UITableViewController {

  NSArray         *sectionsArray;
  NSMutableArray  *menuList;
  Trip            *trip;
}

- (int) menuOffsetForRowAtIndexPath:(NSIndexPath *)indexPath;
- (void) displayOfflineAlert:(NSString*) selection;

@end
```

The compiler needs to know certain things about the classes that you're using, such as what methods you've defined and so on, and the `#import` statement in the implementation (`.m`) file generally solves that problem. But when you get into objects that point at other objects, you also need to provide that information in the interface file, which can cause a problem if there are so-called *circular dependencies*. (Sounds cool, I know, but I'm not going to get into that here; it's beyond the scope of this book.) To solve that problem, Objective-C introduces the `@class` keyword. This informs the compiler that `Trip` is a class name. At this point, in the interface file, that is enough for the compiler, but when you actually do use the class — by creating an instance of that class or sending it a message for example — you still have to do the `#import`.

You now have the `Trip` model object ready to work with. Notice that it creates and uses three other objects: `Weather`, `CarService`, and `CarInformation` (whose files you created earlier). I explain why I had you do it this way in the next section.

Now back to the real work.

Working with controllers

Okay, I spoke too fast. Before you can get back to the real work, you have to deal with one nagging question. If you're going to be relying on generic view controllers, how do they know what message to send the `Trip` to get the information they need? That feat is accomplished by the `RootViewController`, The `RootViewController` knows what the user wants to see displayed based on what entry the user selected in the `tableView:didSelectRowAtIndexPath:` method.

```
if  (realtime) targetController =
      [[WebViewController alloc] initWithTrip:trip
      tripSelector:@selector(returnWeather:)
      webControl:YES
      title:NSLocalizedString(@"Weather", @"Weather")];
else [self displayOfflineAlert:
         [[menuList objectAtIndex:menuOffset]
   objectForKey:kSelectKey]];
break;
```

When the user selects Weather in the Main view, the `RootViewController` allocates and then initializes the view controller with the data it needs — including the message it needs to send to the `Trip` object to get its data. In this case, it is its model (the `Trip`), its title (`@"Weather"`); whether or not it's a Web site (in this case `YES`). (It needs to know that in order to manage user link selections — I explain that shortly.) The last bit of data concerns what message to send the `Trip` object (in this case, `returnWeather:`). I explain the `if (realtime)` bits in Chapter 3 of this minibook, so if it isn't clear, you should review it there.

The `:@selector(returnWeather:)` part corresponds to the method you've declared in `Trip.h`.

Looking at the method declaration for `initWithTrip::::`:

```
- (id) initWithTrip:(Trip*)aTrip
                   tripSelector:(SEL)aTripSelector
                   webControl:(BOOL) ifWebControl
                   title:(NSString*) aTitle;
```

You can see that `tripSelector` is of type `SEL`. `SEL` is a *selector* that is used for a number of things in Objective-C that are beyond the scope of this book.

But it also can be used for something that you need to do, and that is act like a dynamic function pointer that, for a given name, automatically points to the implementation of the method in the class it's used with. In this case, it's returnWeather:, and it will be sent to the Trip object.

That means that the WebViewController needs to know only about the Trip object, and it can ask the Trip object to perform whatever method the selector specifies — loadWeather: when the user selects Weather or LoadCarInformation: when the user selects The Car and so on.

The @selector is a compiler directive you may not be familiar with. It tells the compiler that this is a selector.

You can also specify the selector using the NSSelectorFromString function, where the string is the name of the method. You would use this when you want to send a message whose name you may not know until runtime.

Now that you understand that the WebViewController will be initialized with the message it needs to send, based on the user selection, you can look and see how to implement that in the WebViewController.

Add the code in bold in Listing 4-3 to WebViewController.h. I also have you add the fact that the WebViewController adopts the UIWebViewDelegate protocol, which you will use when you add the ability for the user to navigate links on a Web site later in this section. You already connected the WebViewController as a Web view delegate when you worked with the nib file.

Listing 4-3:   The WebViewController Interface

```
#import <UIKit/UIKit.h>
@class Trip;

@interface WebViewController : UIViewController
                                <UIWebViewDelegate> {

    SEL                 tripSelector;
    Trip                *trip;
    IBOutlet UIWebView  *webView;
    BOOL                webControl;


}
- (id) initWithTrip:(Trip*)aTrip tripSelector:(SEL)
    aTripSelector webControl:(BOOL) ifWebControl
    title:(NSString*) aTitle;
- (void)loadWebView:(NSURLRequest*) theNSURLRequest;

@end
```

Listing 4-4 shows you how the implementation of the
`WebViewController`'s `initWithTrip::::` initializer works. Add its code
to `WebViewController.m` and its declaration to `WebViewController.h`.

Listing 4-4: The WebViewController Initializer

```
- (id) initWithTrip:(Trip*)aTrip tripSelector:(SEL)
    aTripSelector webControl:(BOOL) ifWebControl
    title:(NSString*) aTitle{
  if (self = [super initWithNibName:@"WebViewController"
                                          bundle:nil]) {
    self.title = aTitle;
    tripSelector = aTripSelector;
    trip = aTrip;
    webControl = ifWebControl;
    [trip retain];
  }
  return self;
}
```

Listing 4-4 is nothing special — just your usual run-of-the-mill initialization
method — but it's still fun to see how it gets the job done.

First, it invokes the superclass's `initWithNibName:bundle:` method:

```
if (self = [super initWithNibName:
@" WebViewController" bundle:nil]) {
```

The first thing *this* method does is invoke its superclass's initialization
method. I pass it the nib filename (the one I just created in a previous section) and `nil` as the bundle, telling it to look in the main bundle.

Note that the message to `super` precedes the initialization code added in
the method. This sequencing ensures that initialization proceeds in the
order of inheritance. Calling the superclass's `initWithNibName:bundle:`
method initializes the controller, loads and initializes the objects in the nib
file (views and controls, for example), and then sets all its outlet instance
variables and Target-Action connections for good measure. (I'll get to those
soon.)

The `init…:` methods all return a pointer to the object created — `self`,
in other words. Although that's not the case here, the reason you assign
whatever comes back from an `init…:` method to `self` is that some classes
actually return back a different class than what you created. The assignment
to `self` becomes important if your class is derived from one of those kinds
of classes. Keep in mind as well that an `init…:` method can also return `nil`
if there's a problem initializing an object. If you're creating an object where
that's a possibility, you have to take that into account. (Both of those situations are beyond the scope of this book.)

After the superclass initialization is completed, the `WebViewController` is ready to do its own initialization, including saving the `aTrip` argument to the `trip` instance variable. The only thing worth noting is that it stores the selector argument in `tripSelector`, an instance variable of type `SEL`. This is a type you may not have used before.

The place where the selector is used is in the `viewDidLoad` method. Add the code in Listing 4-5 to `WebViewController.m`.

Listing 4-5:   Adding the viewDidLoad Method

```
- (void)viewDidLoad {

  [super viewDidLoad];
  if (webControl) {
    UIBarButtonItem *backButton = [[UIBarButtonItem alloc]
      initWithTitle:@"Back" style:UIBarButtonItemStylePlain
                  target:self action:@selector(goBack:)];
    self.navigationItem.rightBarButtonItem = backButton;
    [backButton release];
  }
  [trip performSelectorOnMainThread:tripSelector
                  withObject:self waitUntilDone:NO];
}
```

This is a key part of your application framework, so take a look what is going on here in the code.

1. It checks to see whether the view is going to be displaying a Web site in the Web view. If it is, it adds a Back button to enable the user to navigate links on that site. (I explain such messy navigation details in the "Managing links in Web view Web sites" section, later in this chapter.)

2. It sends the `performSelectorOnMainThread:tripSelector withObject:self waitUntilDone:NO` message to the `Trip` object to get the data for the Web view to display.

    This message tells the `Trip` object that it is receiving the `tripSelector` message with one argument (in this case, a pointer back to itself, `self`).

`performSelectorOnMainThread:withObject:waitUntilDone` is an `NSObject` method that allows you to invoke a method in an object (in this case, `trip`). I'm not going to get into multi-threading here, but the main thread is appropriate to what you need to do. The first argument is the method you want invoked — in this case `tripSelector`, which is an instance variable that holds the selector `returnWeather:`. The argument (`withObject:`) is the pointer to the `WebViewController` — you see how that is being used shortly. The `waitUntilDone:` argument is a Boolean argument that specifies whether or not everything grinds to a halt until after the specified selector is performed on the receiver. For your purposes, NO is the right choice here.

Next look at what happens when Trip object gets the message return-Weather. Add the method in Listing 4-6 to Trip.m.

Listing 4-6:   The Trip Object's returnWeather

```
- (void) returnWeather:(id) theViewController {

  [theViewController
                loadWebView:[weather weatherRealtime]];
  }
```

All this does is send a message to the Weather model object.

Now you need to add that method to Weather.m. To do that, add Listing 4-7 to Weather.m to add the weatherRealtime method. I'll show you what this method does next.

You also need to add the method declaration to Weather.h.

```
@interface Weather : NSObject {

}
- (NSURLRequest*) weatherRealtime;

@end
```

Although it may seem pointless to have the Trip simply turn around and send a message to the Weather object, it really isn't. I explain why I am having you implement it this way in the section "What's with the Trip Model and All That Indirection?"

Listing 4-7:   The Weather Object's weatherRealtime method

```
- (NSURLRequest*) weatherRealtime {

  NSURL *url = [NSURL URLWithString:@"http://www.
    weather.com/outlook/travel/businesstraveler/local/
    UKXX0085?lswe=CarServicing,%20UNITED%20KINGDOM&lwsa=Weathe
    rLocalUndeclared&from=searchbox_typeahead"];
  if (url == NULL) NSLog( @"Data not found %@", url);

  NSURLRequest* theNSURLRequest = [NSURLRequest
    requestWithURL:url];
  return theNSURLRequest;
}
```

This method creates an `NSURLRequest` that the Web view needs to load the data. First, it creates an `NSURL` — an object that includes the utilities necessary for downloading files or other resources from Web and FTP servers. Then it takes this NSURL and creates an `NSURLRequest` from it. The `NSURLRequest` is what the `WebViewController` needs to send to the Web view in the `loadRequest:` message, which tells it to load the data associated with that particular `NSURL`.

The `NSURLRequest` class encapsulates a URL and any protocol-specific properties, all the time keeping things nicely protocol-independent. It also provides a number of other things I get around to explaining in detail in Book VI when I discuss the URL loading system — the set of classes and protocols that provide the underlying capability for an application to access the data specified by a URL. Seeing that this is the preferred way to access files both locally and on the internet, I explain the URL loading system in great detail in Book VI.

The second thing the `weatherRealtime` method does is send the `WebViewController` a `loadWebView:` message. Add Listing 4-8 to `WebController.m`.

Listing 4-8: Loading the Web View Data

```
- (void)loadWebView:(NSURLRequest*) theNSURLRequest {

  [webView loadRequest:theNSURLRequest];
}
```

The `loadRequest` message is sent to the Web view, and the Weather Web site is displayed in the window. This causes the Web view to load the data and display it in the window.

Having the `Trip` object send the `loadWebView:` message might seem a little cumbersome. It's actually a side effect of the limitations of selectors — no return type and only one argument. I examine more elegant solutions in Book VI.

Managing links in Web view Web sites

When you implemented the `WebViewController` class's `viewDidLoad` method back in Listing 4-5, I mentioned that it adds a Back button to enable the user to navigate links on that site. Why did I want you to do that?

To refresh your memory, here's another look at Listing 4-5, where you implement the Back button:

```
- (void)viewDidLoad {

  [super viewDidLoad];
```

Book V
Chapter 4

Creating Controllers
and Model Classes

```
if (webControl) {
    UIBarButtonItem *backButton = [[UIBarButtonItem alloc]
        initWithTitle:@"Back"
        style:UIBarButtonItemStylePlain
        target:self
        action:@selector(goBack:)];
    self.navigationItem.rightBarButtonItem = backButton;
    [backButton release];
}
[trip performSelectorOnMainThread:tripSelector
    withObject:self waitUntilDone:NO];
}
```

There's one interesting thing about the Weather view — or any other view that loads real Web content into your application instead of using a browser. The links are live, and from that view the user can follow those links *if you want to let them.*

I get to the if-you-want-to-let-them issue shortly, but first I need to talk about a second Back button.

Once the user is at the weather Web site, as you can see in Figure 4-7, the user might want to look at the ten-day forecast. (You can see such a link on the left in Figure 4-7, and the page display for that link on the right.)

Figure 4-7: Cruising the Web from your application (left) and even getting a forecast (right).

When the user makes use of the 10 Day link, the Web view *replaces* the content of the view, rather than *creating* a new view controller. Tapping the link doesn't change the controller in any way, so the left button won't change; you won't be able to use it to get back to a previous view — you only go back to the Main view, as the control text tells you. To solve this quandary, I created another button and labeled it Back, so the user knows he or she can use it to get back to the previous view. It's actually pretty easy to do as the following steps make clear:

1. **Create and add a Back button.**

   Okay, you already did that in Listing 4-5. The `viewDidLoad` method allocates the button and then assigns it to an instance variable that the `UINavigationController` will later use to set up the navigation bar. The `action:@selector(goBack:)` argument is the standard way to specify Target-Action — and is similar to the selector strategy you implemented in the `WebViewController`. It says that when the button is tapped, you need to send the `goBack:` message to the `target:self`, which is the `WebViewController`.

   That being said, the Apple Human Interface Guidelines say, "In addition to displaying Web content, a Web view provides elements that support navigation through open Web pages. Although you can choose to provide Web page navigation functionality, it's best to avoid creating an application that looks and behaves like a mini Web browser." In case you want to follow Apple's suggestion here, I show you how to disable links next.

2. **Add the `goBack:` method in Listing 4-9 to the `WebViewController.m` file**

Listing 4-9:   goBack: to Where You Once Belonged

```
- (IBAction)goBack:(id) sender {

  if ([webView canGoBack] == NO )
    [[self navigationController]
                        popViewControllerAnimated:YES];
  else
    [webView goBack];
}
```

The `UIWebView` actually implements much of the behavior you need here. When the user touches the Back button and `goBack:` message is sent, you first check with the Web view to see whether there's someplace to go back *to*. (It keeps a backward *and* forward list.) If there's an appropriate retreat, you send the UIWebView message (goBack:) that will reload the previous page. If not, it means that you're at the Weather content page, and you simply *pop* (remove from the stack) the WebViewController to return to the main window — the same thing the button on the left side of the navigation bar would do.

The goBack: method is part of the UIWebViewDelegate protocol.

Keeping users from going astray

Everybody knows the Internet is a tempting place. If you see a link, more often than not something goes off in your brain that says "click it." This quirk of human nature also applies to any links that might show up in the Web views of your app. If you'd prefer that your app users stick around for a bit and don't go off gallivanting around the Internet at the first opportunity, you need to disable the links. That turns out to be a two-step process:

1. **Change the webControl:(BOOL) argument to NO in initWith-
Trip:::::.**

This step keeps the Back button from showing.

2. **Implement the UIWebViewDelegate method shouldStartLoad-
WithRequest:.**

The shouldStartLoadWithRequest: method is called before a Web view begins loading content to see whether you want the load to proceed. You're only interested in doing something if the user mistakenly touched a link when he or she is in stored data mode or you really want to make Apple happy and heed its advice to disable all links. In the case of Weather, you really don't care about stored data mode, because you plan on sending an alert to the user if he or she tries to select that entry in the Main view while in stored data mode. Under other circumstances, if the Web view is stored but also has links, you want to display that view but disable the links. For example, you might want to have a link to an online manual for your car in the CarServicing view. And, because this is a generic WebViewController, you want to support that functionality, even if you know there will be some times when the user is going to resort to stored data mode.

Listing 4-10 shows the code you'd need to add in order to disable links in such a situation. Add this to WebViewController.m. You also need to import Constants.h (#import "Constants.h") because you're using the kUseStoredDataPreference. constant.

Listing 4-10: Disabling Links

```
- (BOOL)webView:(UIWebView *)webView
shouldStartLoadWithRequest:(NSURLRequest *) request
navigationType:(UIWebViewNavigationType) navigationType {

  if ((navigationType == UIWebViewNavigationTypeLinkClicked)
    && ([[NSUserDefaults standardUserDefaults] boolForKey:kUs
    eStoredDataPreference])) {
    UIAlertView *alert = [[UIAlertView alloc]
          initWithTitle:@"" message:NSLocalizedString(@"Link
    not available", @" Link not available")
          delegate:self cancelButtonTitle:NSLocalizedString(
    @"Thanks", @"Thanks") otherButtonTitles:nil];
    [alert show];
    [alert release];
    return NO;
  }
  else  return YES;
}
```

Here's the process the code uses to get the job done for you:

1. It checks to see whether the user has touched an embedded link (while in stored data mode).

   ```
   if ((navigationType ==
       UIWebViewNavigationTypeLinkClicked) &&
       ([[NSUserDefaults standardUserDefaults]
             boolForKey:kUseStoredDataPreference])) {
   ```

2. If the user is in stored data mode, it alerts him or her to the fact that the link is unavailable, and returns NO from the method.

   This informs the Web view not to load the link.

   ```
   UIAlertView *alert = [[UIAlertView alloc]
       initWithTitle:@"" message:NSLocalizedString(@"Link
       not available", @" Link not available")
       delegate:self cancelButtonTitle:NSLocalizedString(@"
       Thanks", @"Thanks") otherButtonTitles:nil];
   [alert show];
   [alert release];
   return NO;
   ```

   You create an alert here with a message telling the user that the link is not available. The Cancel button's text will be @"Thanks".

3. If the user is not in stored data mode, it returns YES to tell the Web view to load from the Internet.

If you've decided to follow Apple's suggestion and the Web view is not acting as a mini browser, you have to disable the links that are available in the content. You can do that in the shouldStartLoadWithRequest: method by coding it in the following way:

```
- (BOOL)webView:(UIWebView *) webView
  shouldStartLoadWithRequest:(NSURLRequest *) request
  navigationType:(UIWebViewNavigationType)navigationType {

  if (navigationType ==
                      UIWebViewNavigationTypeLinkClicked)
    return NO;

  else return YES;
}
```

You should add an alert to inform the user of the fact that there's no Internet gallivanting to be had here as well.

At this point, you uncomment the following lines you see in bold in `tableV iew:didSelectRowAtIndexPath:` in `RootViewController.h`, and your application will compile. You can select Weather from the Main view and find yourself at the `www.weather.com` site. After you choose a city, you can also follow the links to get more information — if you haven't disabled the links, I should add.

```
BOOL realtime = !appDelegate.useStoredData;

    switch (menuOffset) {
      case 0:
//      if (realtime) targetController = [[MapController
    alloc] initWithTrip:trip];
//      else [self displayOfflineAlert: [[menuList
    objectAtIndex:menuOffset] objectForKey:kSelectKey]];
        break;
      case 1:
//      targetController = [[SightListController alloc]
    initWithTrip:trip];
        break;
      case 2:
//      targetController = [[HotelController alloc]
    initWithTrip:trip];
        break;
      case 3:
        if  (realtime) targetController = [[WebViewController
    alloc] initWithTrip:trip
                tripSelector:@selector(returnWeather:)
                webControl:YES title:
                NSLocalizedString(@"Weather", @"Weather")];
        else [self displayOfflineAlert:[[menuList
                objectAtIndex:menuOffset]
                objectForKey:kSelectKey]];
        break;
      case 4:
//      targetController = [[WebViewController alloc]
    initWithTrip:trip tripSelector: @selector(returnCarServici
    ngInformation:)
```

```
//          webControl:NO title:NSLocalizedString
                  (@"Car Servicing", @"Car Servicing")];
      break;
   case 5:
//      targetController = [[WebViewController alloc]
   initWithTrip:trip tripSelector: @selector(returnCarServici
   ngInformation:)
//          webControl:NO title:NSLocalizedString
          (@"The Car", @"Car Information")];
      break;
   }
```

You also have to comment out the statements that allocate and initialize the `CarInformation` and `CarServicing` objects in the `Trip.m`'s init-WithName: method. Since you haven't implemented them yet the compiler whines if it sees them. The code to do that is shown in bold.

```
- (id) initWithName:(NSString*) theTrip {

  if ((self = [super init])) {
    tripName = theTrip;
//  carInformation =
              [[CarInformation alloc] initWithTrip:self];
//  carServicing =
              [[CarServicing alloc] initWithTrip:self];
    weather = [[Weather alloc] init];
  }
  return self;
}
```

You'll get a couple of compiler warnings because you haven't implemented `returnCarServicingInformation:` and `returnCarInformation:` in `Trip.m`, but you get a chance to do that in the next two sections.

Implementing CarInformation

Now that you have implemented the `WebViewController` for Weather, it's time to turn your attention to the other two views it will need to display.

In the `RootViewController`'s `didSelectRowAtIndexPath:` method you already have the code to allocate and initialize a `WebViewController` for `CarInformation` and `CarServicing`.

```
case 4:
  targetController = [[WebViewController alloc]
    initWithTrip:trip tripSelector:
    @selector(returnCarServicingInformation:)
    webControl:NO
    title:NSLocalizedString (@"Car Servicing", @"Car
                                        Servicing")];
```

```
    break;
case 5:
    targetController = [[WebViewController alloc]
      initWithTrip:trip tripSelector:
      @selector(returnCarInformation:)
      webControl:NO
      title:NSLocalizedString (@"The Car", @"Car
                                            Information")];

    break;
```

All that is left to do is implement the necessary methods in `Trip` and in `CarServicingInformation` and `CarInformation`. As you'll see, adding new functionality here is really easy. It makes things way more fun when you don't have to go out and implement two more view controllers.

You can get started by adding the selector methods in Listing 4-11 to `Trip.m`.

Listing 4-11:   The CarServicingInformation and CarInformation (Selector) Methods

```
- (void) returnCarServicingInformation:
                                    (id) theViewController {
  [theViewController
      performSelectorOnMainThread:@selector(loadWebView:)
      withObject:[carServicing
                            returnCarServicingInformation]
      waitUntilDone:NO];
}

- (void) returnCarInformation:(id) theViewController {

  [theViewController
      performSelectorOnMainThread:@selector(loadWebView:)
      withObject:[carInformation returnCarInformation]
      waitUntilDone:NO];
}
```

This should look familiar — it's the same thing you did in the `return Weather:` method earlier. (See Listing 4-6.)

From the view controller's perspective, that's all you need to do to support the Car Servicing and Car Information views. Of course you now have to add the functionality that actually returns the data

Start with `CarInformation`.

Setting up the view

In Chapter 1 of this minibook, I mention that `CarInformation` is always offline, which means it's a great way to show you how to implement static data. It hardly ever changes, so it makes sense to include it in the application itself as a resource.

The content for the `CarInformation` view is in a file I created called `CarSpecs.html`. To make it available to the application, I need to include it in the application bundle itself, although I could have downloaded it the first time the application ran. (But there's method to my madness. Including it in the bundle does give me the opportunity to show you how to handle this kind of data.)

Now, you can add it to your bundle one of two ways:

✦ Open the Project window and drag the `.html` file into the Project folder.

It's a good idea to create a new folder within your main Project folder as a snug little home for the file. (I use the Car Information folder, but you should also consider a folder called Static data where you can place all the resource-based data you'll be using.)

Or

✦ Choose Project➪Add to Project and then use the dialog that appears to navigate to and select the file you want. You can see how that process unfolds in Figure 4-8.

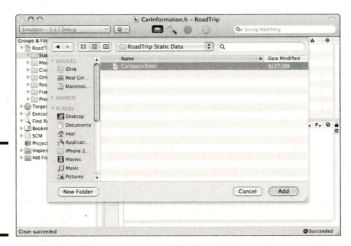

Figure 4-8:
Add
CarSpecs.
html to the
project.

The only thing at all interesting here is the fact that you're going to use some data that you've included with your application as a *resource* (which you can think about as an included file, although it doesn't live in the file system but rather is embedded in the application itself).

To start things off, you're going to have to create the CarInformation object. You already entered the code to do that in Listing 4-2 when you added the initWithName: method to Trip. Here's what that code looked like, in case you need a reminder:

```
- (id) initWithName:(NSString*) theTrip {

  if ((self = [super init])) {
    tripName = theTrip;
    carInformation =
                [[CarInformation alloc] initWithTrip:self];
    carServicing =
                [[CarServicing alloc] initWithTrip:self];
    weather = [[Weather alloc] init];
  }
  return self;
}
```

You have to enter the code in Listing 4-12 to implement the initWith Trip: method in CarInformation.m. (You also have to add the requisite #import statement to CarInformation.m.)

```
#import "Trip.h"
```

and method declaration in CarInformation.h — you know, that snippet of code that looks like the following:

```
- (id) initWithName:(NSString*) theTrip;
```

Listing 4-12:   initWithTrip:

```
- (id) initWithTrip:(Trip*) aTrip   {
  if ((self = [super init])) {
    trip = aTrip;
    [trip retain];
}
  return self;
}
```

You also have to add the new instance variable to in CarInformation.m:

```
Trip* trip;
```

As well as the @class statement:

@class Trip;

You may notice that the trip instance variable is not used. I include it because in a more complex model object, there would be some communication back to the Trip object and I put that in simply to show you how it's done. For example, when I introduce the URL loading system in Book VI, the Sights object will use it to gain access to the URL manager you'll implement.

Finally, you can add the *raison d'être* for the object's existence: accessing the CarSpecs resources you added earlier. This is the returnCarInforma tion method in Listing 4-13 you need to add to CarInformation.m, and also declare in CarInformation.h.

Listing 4-13:   The returnCarInformation Method

```
- (NSURLRequest*) returnCarInformation {

  NSString *filePath = [[NSBundle mainBundle]
    pathForResource:@"CarSpecs" ofType:@"html"];
  NSURL* carInformationData=
                    [NSURL fileURLWithPath:filePath];
  NSURLRequest* theNSURLRequest =
      [NSURLRequest requestWithURL:carInformationData];
  return theNSURLRequest;
}
```

This is the same approach you took in weatherRealtime back in Listing 4-7 — creating an NSURLRequest. This time, though, the request is pointing to a resource you've included in your application bundle.

You're using pathForResource::, which is an NSBundle method to construct the NSURL. (You use an NSBundle method when you get the application name in the RootViewController to set the title on the main window in Chapter 3 of this minibook.) Just give pathForResource:: the name and the file type. That gets packed in to the NSURLRequest and sent back to the WebViewController (via the Trip object) to load.

Pretty easy huh?

Be sure you provide the right file type; otherwise, this technique won't work.

To see what you've managed to do so far, you have to uncomment out the code in the RootViewController's tableView:didSelectRowAtInde xPath:

```
targetController = [[WebViewController alloc]
  initWithTrip:trip tripSelector:
  @selector(returnCarServicingInformation:)
  webControl:NO title:NSLocalizedString
                 (@"Car Servicing", @"Car Servicing")];
```

and the `Trip`'s `initWithTripName:`

```
carInformation =
             [[CarInformation alloc] initWithTrip:self];
```

Implementing CarServicingInformation

With the exception of how the data is accessed, `CarServicingInformation` works the same way as `CarInformation`.

Setting up the view

In Chapter 1 of this minibook, I mention that the `CarServicingInformation` data is found on a Web server, and now's the time to show you how to access that server. Additionally, I want to explain how to save that data for later use — those times when the user is in stored data mode or has no Internet access.

To start things off, you have to create the `CarServicing` object. Lucky for you, you already entered the code to do that in Listing 4-2 when you added the `initWithName:` method to `Trip`. Does the following ring a bell?

```
- (id) initWithName:(NSString*) theTrip {

  if ((self = [super init])) {
    tripName = theTrip;
    carInformation =
               [[CarInformation alloc] initWithTrip:self];
    carServicing =
               [[CarServicing alloc] initWithTrip:self];
    weather = [[Weather alloc] init];
  }
  return self;
}
```

You have to enter the code in Listing 4-14 to implement the `initWithTrip:` method in `CarServicing.m`. You also have to add the requisite `#import` statement and the method declaration in `CarServicing.h`.

Here's that tremendously complicated `#import` statement:

```
#import "Trip.h"
```

Listing 4-14:   initWithTrip:

```
- (id) initWithTrip:(Trip*) aTrip   {
  if ((self = [super init])) {
    trip = aTrip;
    [trip retain];
}
  return self;
}
```

You also have to add the new instance variable to `CarServicing.h`.

```
Trip* trip;
```

As well as the @class statement:

```
@class Trip;
```

You may notice that the trip instance variable is not used. I've included it because in a more complex model object, there would be some communication back to the `Trip` object, and I put that in simply to show you how it's done. For example, when I introduce the URL loading system in Book VI, the `Sights` object will use it to gain access to the URL manager you'll implement.

Finally, you can add the *raison d'être* for the object's existence. Add the method you see in Listing 4-15 to `CarServicing.m` and its declaration to `CarServicing.h`. Because this method also checks to see whether the user wants to use stored data, you also have to add

```
#import "RoadTripAppDelegate.h"
```

to `CarServicing.m`.

Listing 4-15:   The returnCarServicingInformation Method

```
- (NSURLRequest*) returnCarServicingInformation {

  NSURL *carServicingData = nil;
  RoadTripAppDelegate *appDelegate = (RoadTripAppDelegate *)
    [[UIApplication sharedApplication] delegate];
  BOOL realtime = !appDelegate.useStoredData;
  if (realtime) {
    carServicingData = [NSURL URLWithString:@"http://
    nealgoldstein.com/CarServicing.html"];
```

```
  [self saveCarServicingData:@"CarServicing"
withDataURL:carServicingData];
    if (!carServicingData) NSLog(@"data not there for
CarServicing");

  }
  else {
    carServicingData =
            [self getCarServicingData:@"CarServicing"];
}

  NSURLRequest* theNSURLRequest =
          [NSURLRequest requestWithURL:carServicingData];
  return theNSURLRequest;
}
```

This is the same approach you took in `weatherRealtime` and `return-CarInformation` — creating an `NSURLRequest`. This time, though, the request is for information on a Web server.

But that's not the big part. The big difference here is the following: Because you can't always count on being online — say you're driving through the mountains of Big Sur, for example — you want to be able to save the latest version of the data you have downloaded from the Internet and use that if necessary.

So how do you do that? It's all there back in Listing 4-15, which shows you the implementation of the `returnCarServicingInformation` method.

If the user is online, the method constructs the `NSURL` object that it will need to have in order to construct the `NSURLRequest`.

```
if (realtime) {
    carServicingData = [NSURL URLWithString:@"http://
    nealgoldstein.com/CarServicing.html"];
```

Then the `saveCarServicingData:` message is sent:

```
[self saveCarServicingData:@"CarServicing"
                              withDataURL:carServicingData];
```

The `saveCarServicingData:` method in Listing 4-16 downloads and saves the file containing the latest data for the car servicing. It's what will be displayed in the current view, and it'll be used later if the user specifies stored data mode. Add this method to `CarServicing.m` and its declaration to `CarServicing.h`.

Listing 4-16: Saving Car-Servicing Data

```
- (void) saveCarServicingData:(NSString*) fileName
    withDataURL:(NSURL*) url  {

  NSData *dataLoaded = [NSData dataWithContentsOfURL:url];
  if (dataLoaded == NULL)
                              NSLog( @"Data not found %@", url);
  NSArray *paths = NSSearchPathForDirectoriesInDomains
            (NSDocumentDirectory, NSUserDomainMask, YES);
  NSString *documentsDirectory = [paths objectAtIndex:0];
  NSString *filePath = [documentsDirectory
                  stringByAppendingPathComponent:fileName];
  [dataLoaded writeToFile:filePath atomically:YES];
}
```

You did the exact same thing in Chapter 3 of this minibook when you saved the current state of the application. If you need a refresher here, go back and work through that part of Chapter 3 again.

You might have noticed that I've added an NSLog message for those cases when the data can't be found. This is a placeholder for error-handling that I've left as an exercise for you.

This is definitely not the most efficient way to implement saving files for later use, but given the relatively small amount of data involved, the impact is not noticeable. In Book VI, I show you a better way to mange data.

If the user wants stored data to be used, the method returns the stored data as opposed to loading the data for its URL on the Internet. It gets the data by calling the getCarServicingData: method, which reads the data that was stored in saveCarServicingData:

```
url = [self getCarServicingData:@"CarServicing"];
```

getCarServicingData: also constructs a NSURL object that the Web view uses to load the data. So you find the path and construct the NSURL object using that path. This is shown in Listing 4-17. Add the getCarServicing Data: method (also shown in listing 4-17) to CarServicing.m and its declaration to CarServicing.h.

Listing 4-17: Getting the Saved car servicing data

```
-(NSURL*) getCarServicingData:(NSString*) fileName{

  NSArray *paths = NSSearchPathForDirectoriesInDomains
            (NSDocumentDirectory, NSUserDomainMask, YES);
  NSString *documentsDirectory = [paths objectAtIndex:0];
  NSString *filePath = [documentsDirectory
```

```
                stringByAppendingPathComponent:fileName];
    NSURL* theNSURL= [NSURL fileURLWithPath:filePath];
    if (theNSURL == NULL) NSLog (@"Data not there");
    return theNSURL;
}
```

If you're coming to this project from C++, you probably want these last two methods to be private, but there's no private construct in Objective-C. To hide them, you could have moved their declarations to the implementation file and created an Objective-C category. Here's what that would look like:

```
@interface CarServicing  ()
- (NSURL*) getCarServicingData:(NSString*) fileName;
- (void) saveCarServicingData:(NSString*) fileName
                              withDataURL:(NSURL*) url;
@end
```

You would then remove the declarations from `CarServicing.h`.

After that, the `returnCarServicingInformation` method constructs the `NSURLRequest` and returns to the `Trip` method that sent it the message.

```
NSURLRequest* theNSURLRequest = [NSURLRequest
                        requestWithURL:carServicingData];
return theNSURLRequest;
```

At this point, you need to uncomment out the following code in the `RootViewController`'s `tableView:didSelectRowAtIndexPath`:

```
targetController = [[WebViewController alloc]
    targetController = [[WebViewController alloc]
    initWithTrip:trip tripSelector:
        @selector(returnCarServicingInformation:)
     webControl:NO title:NSLocalizedString
            (@"The Car", @"Car Information")];
```

as well as the following code in the `Trip`'s `initWithTripName`;

```
carServicing =
                [[CarServicing alloc] initWithTrip:self];
```

Remember to keep the unimplemented functionality commented out in the `RootViewController`'s `tableView:didSelectRowAtIndexPath:`.

When you compile the code thus far, you can see what's shown in the first figure in Chapter 1 of this minibook. If you click or touch one of the rows, you get the kinds of content I specified (courtesy of some files I have on my Web site).

One thing I haven't shown you is all the `dealloc` methods. You can find that in the complete listing on my Web site — or maybe you should try it first yourself.

What's with the Trip Model and All That Indirection?

In Listing 4-6, you see what happens when the `Trip` object gets the `return Weather:` message — it just passes it on to the Weather object, gets the `NSURLRequest` back, and then turns around and more or less sends it back. So why all these hoops?

You have a couple of options when it comes to creating the model objects needed by the view controllers. One way is to have the view controllers create the ones they'll use. For example, the `RootViewController` would create the `CarInformation` object, and so on. That would eliminate the indirection you saw in the previous section — you know, having to go through the `Trip` object to the `CarInformation` object that does the real work.

Although that technique does work, and I've actually taken that route in past versions, I'd like you to consider a different approach that results in a more extensible program. (I explain my logic here in detail in *Objective-C For Dummies,* so if you're curious, you might want to pick up a copy of that book.)

One of the advantages of the Model-View-Controller design pattern I explain in Chapter 2 of this minibook is that it allows you to separate these three groups in your application and work on them separately. If each group has a well-defined interface, it encapsulates many of the kinds of changes that are often made so that they don't affect the other groups. This little fact is especially true of the model and view controller relationship.

If the view controllers have minimal knowledge about the model, you can change the model objects with minor impact on the view controllers.

As I mention in Chapter 2 of this minibook, what makes this possible is a well-defined interface, which you develop in the section "The Trip Model," earlier in this chapter. You create an interface between the model and the controllers by using a technique called *composition,* which is a useful way to create interfaces.

I'm a big fan of composition, because it's another way to hide what's really going on behind the curtain. It keeps the objects that use the composite object (in this case, Trip is the composite object) ignorant of the objects the composite object uses and actually makes the components ignorant of each other, allowing you to switch components in and out at will.

The `Trip` class provides the basis for such an architecture, and although I don't fully implement it here (some is done in Chapter 5 of this minibook, and the rest in Book VI), you can understand the structure and will have no trouble extending it on your own.

The class in question looks like this:

```
#import <Foundation/Foundation.h>
@class Weather;
@class CarServicing;
@class CarInformation;

@interface Trip : NSObject   {

  NSString        *tripName;
  CarServicing    *carServicing;
  CarInformation *carInformation;
  Weather         *weather;
}

- (id) initWithName:(NSString*) theTripName;
- (void) returnWeather:(id) theViewController;
- (void) returnCarServicingInformation:(id)
   theViewController;
- (void) returnCarInformation:(id) theViewController;

@end
```

Start with what happens when the `Trip` object is created. (You did that earlier in section "Getting Trippy with the Trip Model.")

```
- (id) initWithName:(NSString*) theTrip {

  if ((self = [super init])) {
    tripName = theTrip;
    carInformation =
            [[CarInformation alloc] initWithTrip:self];
    carServicing =
              [[CarServicing alloc] initWithTrip:self];
    weather = [[Weather alloc] init];
  }
  return self;
}
```

`Trip` creates the model objects, encapsulating the knowledge of what objects make up the model from the object that creates it. (In this case, `Trip` is created by the `RootViewController`.) In order to do that, you added the following line of code to the `viewDidLoad` method in `RootViewController.m`.

```
trip = [[Trip alloc] initWithName:@"Road Trip"];
```

This would hide all implementation knowledge from the view controller — it would only know about the `Trip` object and the selectors it creates.

In addition, because the `WebViewController` is generic, it is oblivious to the messages it is sending to the `Trip` object.

While trivial here, and may even appear a bit gratuitous — `Trip` just turns around and essentially resends the message — this architecture becomes important in the more complex applications you'll develop. It'll save you much grief and (make it easier) when you refactor your code to enhance and extend your app.

What's Next?

In Chapter 5 and 6 of this minibook, I cover what I consider to be a premier iPhone feature — the ability to generate customized maps in your application. I explain the map framework and show you some of the things you can do with it. As I mention, this is one of the key features of the iPhone and enables applications to provide not only context-based information (information about what is going on in the context) and functionality, but also information about the context itself.

I promise it will be fun.

Chapter 5: Finding Your Way

In This Chapter

✔ **Using the Map framework**

✔ **Specifying the location and zoom level of a map**

✔ **Annotating significant locations on the map**

✔ **Identifying the iPhone's current location**

*O*ne of the things that makes iPhone applications compelling is the ability you have as a developer to incorporate the user's location into the application functionality. And one of the more compelling ways to do that is through the use of maps.

Including the ability to display a map in RoadTrip became important as people began to realize the kinds of solutions that can be delivered on the iPhone. To many travelers, nothing brands you more as a tourist than unfolding a large paper map (except of course looking through a thick guidebook). In this chapter, I show you how to take advantage of the iPhone's built-in capability to display a map of virtually anywhere in the world, as well as determine the iPhone's location and then indicate it in the map. As I mention way back in Book I, the iPhone's awareness of your location is one of the things that enables you to develop a totally new kind of application and really differentiate an iPhone application from a desktop one.

Being able to build maps into your application is an important new feature in the iPhone 3.0 SDK and beyond, and it doesn't hurt that working with maps is one of the funnest things you can do on the iPhone because Apple makes it so easy.

In this chapter, I show you how to center your map on an area you want to display (San Francisco for example), add annotations (those cute pins in the map that display a callout to describe that location when you touch them), and even show the user's current location. (Although I don't cover it until Book VII, you can also turn the iPhone's current address into an Address Book contact.)

Building Your Map Functionality

To use maps, you have to add a few more files to your project — a `MapController.h` and `.m`, a `MapController` nib file, and model files

`Map.h` and `.m`, to be precise. (You'd already done something similar in Chapter 4 of this minibook, so if this talk of nib files and model files doesn't ring a bell, you might want to read this minibook's Chapter 4 — the figures there may prove especially helpful in jogging your memory.) You won't be using the `Map` files in this Chapter, but you will in Book VI, so you might as well create them now.

1. **In the RoadTrip Project window, select the Classes folder and then choose File⇨New from the main menu (or press ⌘+N) to call up the New File dialog.**

2. **In the left column of the dialog, select Cocoa Touch Classes under the iPhone OS heading, select the UIViewController subclass template in the top-right pane, and be sure the With XIP for User Interface check box is also selected. Then click Next.**

You see a new dialog asking for some more information.

3. **Enter MapController.m in the File Name field and then click Finish.**

4. **Choose File⇨New yet again from the main menu (or press ⌘+N) to recall the New File dialog.**

5. **In the leftmost column of the dialog, select Cocoa Touch Classes under the iPhone OS heading just like you did before, but this time select the Objective-C class template in the topmost pane, making sure that the Subclass drop-down menu has NSObject selected. Then click Next.**

You see a new dialog asking for some more information.

6. **Enter Map in the File Name field and then click Finish.**

Okay, that takes care of your `MapController.m` and .h files and your `Map.m` and .h files. One thing left to do: You have to add a new framework.

Up until now, all you've needed is the framework that more or less came supplied when you created a project. But now, you need to add a new framework to enable the Map view. (Officially it is a `MKMapView` but I'll refer to it as simply a Map view.)

1. **Click the disclosure triangle next to Targets in the Groups & Files list and then right-click on RoadTrip.**

Be sure to do this using the Targets folder, or Step 3 won't work!

2. **From the submenu that appears, select Add and then select Existing Frameworks, as I've done in Figure 5-1.**

3. **In the new window that appears (see Figure 5-2), select `MapKit.framework` and then click Add. It will go to the very bottom of your RoadTrip project files. From there, you can drag it into the Frameworks folder.**

Figure 5-1:
Adding
a new
framework.

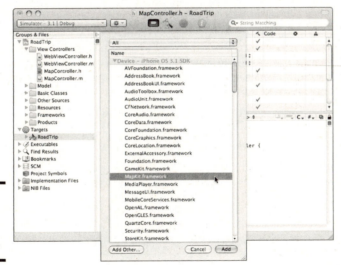

Figure 5-2:
Adding the
MapKit.
framework.

Just as in Chapter 4 of this minibook, you need to add some initialization code to get things rolling

It all starts in `RootViewController.m`.

1. **In the `RootViewController.m` file's `didSelectRowAtIndexPath:` method, create and initialize the view controller that implements the row selected by the user.**

The code is already there, so all you need to do is uncomment it out, but it doesn't hurt to review it here.

The following code allocates a `MapController` (a view controller) and then sends it the `initWithTrip:trip:` message. (I explain this process at the very end of Chapter 2 of this minibook; you might want to review that if it's been a while since you looked at it.)

```
if (realtime) targetController =
            [[MapController alloc] initWithTrip:trip];
else [self displayOfflineAlert:
                [[menuList objectAtIndex:menuOffset]
            objectForKey:kSelectKey]];
```

Notice the alert in the third line; I address this use of alerts when I talk about the Weather alert in Chapter 4 of this minibook. To use a map, your user needs to be online; that means you need to build in an alert that lets the user know whether he or she is in fact *not* online.

You also need to import the `MapController.h` and add it to the `RootViewController.m` file. Lucky for you, it's real easy. Just add the following:

```
#import "MapController.h"
```

2. **Make the `MapController` an `MKMapViewDelegate` by adding the code in bold shown in this step to the `MapView.h` file.**

   Later when you *do reverse geocoding* (getting a street address for a coordinate) you also have to become an `MKReverseGeocoderDelegate`, so you might as well do that now.

```
@interface MapController : UIViewController <
    MKMapViewDelegate, MKReverseGeocoderDelegate > {
```

3. **Declare a new instance variable in `MapController.h`.**

   By now you should know you can put it anywhere between the braces. This particular instance variable is there to connect the `MapController` to the `Trip` model.

```
Trip            *trip;
```

4. **Add the method declaration for the initialization method to `MapController.h`, being sure to add it after the } but before the @ end statement.**

```
- (id) initWithTrip: (Trip*) theTrip;
```

5. **Add the necessary `@class` and `#import` statements.**

   `#import <MapKit/MapKit.h>` gives you access to all the lovely functionality that came your way when you added the `MapKit.framework` in the last section

```
#import <MapKit/MapKit.h>
@class Trip;
```

6. **Add a `mapView` (`UIWebView`) outlet to the `MapController.h` interface file.**

```
IBOutlet MKMapView    *mapView;
```

You get a default map for free (see Figure 5-3), which is all well and good, but there's a lot more than you can do with it. For that to happen, though, you're going to need to be able to access the Map view. To do that, do the right thing and follow this step: Declare an outlet by using the keyword `IBOutlet` in the `MapController.h` interface file.

7. **Initialize the `MapController`.**

   Add the following `initWithTrip:` method to `MapController.m`

   ```
   - (id) initWithTrip: (Trip*) theTrip {

     if (self = [super initWithNibName:@"MapController"
                                       bundle:nil]) {
       trip = theTrip;
     }
     return self;
   }
   ```

   then add the `#import` statement to `MapController.m`.

   ```
   #import "Trip.h"
   ```

8. **Do the File⇨Save thing to save the file.**

   After it's saved — and only then — Interface Builder can find the new outlet.

If you were to compile and run RoadTrip now, you would be able to select Map in the Main view . . . but all you would see is a blank page. To see a map, you need to do some work in the nib file.

Setting up the nib file

For the RoadTrip application, you want to use a `MKMapView` to display the map information. To set up the `MKMapView`, you use Interface Builder. In fact, if all you did in Interface Builder was change the `UIView` to an `MKMapView`, you'd get the map you see in Figure 5-3. It doesn't get much easier than that.

This is the general approach you'll follow when you add more functionality to your application — add the new controller classes and their nib files, and new model classes to the model.

Figure 5-3:
Default Map
view — you
get a map
for free.

1. **Use the Groups & Files list on the left in the Project window to drill down to the `MapController.xib` file; then double-click the file to launch it in Interface Builder.**

   If the Attributes Inspector window is not open, choose Tools➪Inspector or press shift+⌘+1. If the View window isn't visible, double-click the View icon in the `MapController.xib` window.

   If for some reason you can't find the `MapController.xib` window (you may have minimized it whether by accident, on purpose, or whatever), you can get it back by choosing Window➪MapController.xib or whichever nib file you're working on.

2. **Select File's Owner in the `MapController.xib` window.**

   It should already be set to `MapController`. If not, retrace your steps to see where you may have made a mistake.

   You need to be sure that the File's Owner is `MapController`. You can set File's Owner from the Class drop-down menu in the Identity Inspector.

3. **Click in the View window and then choose MKMapView from the Class drop-down menu in the Identity Inspector.**

The name in the `MapController.xib` window will change to Map View, and the title of the View window will change to Map View the next time you reopen the window after it has been closed.

4. Back in the `MapController.xib` window, right-click File's Owner to call up a contextual menu with a list of connections.

You can get the same list using the Connections tab in the Attributes Inspector.

5. Drag from the little circle next to the `mapView` outlet in the list onto the Map View window.

Doing so connects the `MapController`'s `mapView` outlet to the Map view.

6. Go back to that list of connections in the File's Owner contextual menu and click the triangle next to Referencing Outlets. This time drag from the little circle next to the New Referencing Outlet list onto the Map View window.

You may recall that you did the exact same thing with the Web view in Chapter 4 of this minibook.

7. With the cursor still in the Map View window, let go of the mouse button.

A pop-up menu appears.

8. Choose Delegate from the pop-up menu.

9. Do the File⇨Save thing to save the file.

The `MapController` now has its outlet to the Map view connected, and it also will receive the delegate messages as a `MKMapViewDelegate`. I'll show you what methods you'll need to implement next.

Only after the file's saved will the changes you made be reflected in your application.

If you were to build and run your program at this point, you'd still get the default Map view you see in Figure 5-3. But you — and your users — want and deserve more than that. Figure 5-4 shows what you'd like to see on your road trip, rather than the standard Map view you get right out of the box.

Figure 5-4: San Francisco sites and where to stay.

Putting MapKit through Its Paces

You've prepared the ground for some great map functionality, but now it's time to put the code in place so that you can get some real work done. Undergirding all this effort is the `MapKit.framework` — surely one of the great features of iPhone 3.0 SDK and beyond is a new framework. MapKit enables you to bring up a simple map and also do things with your map without having to do much work at all.

The map looks like the maps in the built-in applications and creates a seamless mapping experience across multiple applications.

MKMapView

The essence of mapping on the iPhone is the `MKMapView`. It's a `UIView` subclass, and as you saw in the previous section, you can use it out of the box to create a world map. You use this class as-is to display map information and to manipulate the map contents from your application. It enables you to center the map on a given coordinate, specify the size of the area you want to display, and annotate the map with custom information.

You added the `MapKit.framework` earlier in this chapter.

When you initialize a Map view, you can specify the initial region for that map to display. You do this by setting the *region* property of the map. A region is defined by a center point and a horizontal and vertical distance, referred to as the *span*. The span defines how much of the map will be visible and also determines the zoom level. The smaller the span, the greater the zoom.

The Map view supports the standard map gestures.

✦ Scroll

✦ Pinch zoom

✦ Double-tap zoom in

✦ Two-finger–tap zoom out (You may not even have known about that one.)

You can also specify the map type — regular, satellite, or hybrid — by changing a single property.

Because `MapKit.framework` was written from scratch, it was developed with the limitations of the iPhone in mind. As a result, it optimizes performance on the iPhone by caching data as well as managing memory and seamlessly handling connectivity changes (like moving from 3g to Wi-Fi, for example).

The map data itself is Google-hosted map data, and network connectivity is required. And because `MapKit.framework` uses Google services to provide map data, using it binds you to the Google Maps/Google Earth API terms of service.

Although you shouldn't subclass the `MKMapView` class itself, you can tailor a Map view's behavior by providing a delegate object. The delegate object can be any object in your application, as long as it conforms to the `MKMapViewDelegate` protocol. (You may find out how to make the `MapController` the `MKMapView` delegate in the preceding section.)

Enhancing the map

Having this nice global map centered on the United States is kind of interesting but not very useful if you're planning to go to San Francisco. The following sections show you what you would have to do to make the map more useful.

Adding landscape mode and the current location

To start with, it would be very useful to be able to see any map in landscape mode.

Go back to your Project window in Xcode and add the following method to `MapController.m`:

```
- (BOOL)shouldAutorotateToInterfaceOrientation:
          (UIInterfaceOrientation)toInterfaceOrientation {

   return YES;
}
```

That's all you have to do to view the map in landscape mode. You can move back and forth between landscape and portrait mode and `MapKit.framework` takes care of it for you! (This is starting to be real fun.)

What about showing your location on the map? That's just as easy!

In the `MapController.m` file, uncomment out `viewDidLoad` and add the code in bold.

```
- (void)viewDidLoad {
  [super viewDidLoad];

  mapView.showsUserLocation = YES;
}
```

`showsUserLocation` is a `MKMapView` property that tells the Map view whether to show the user location. If `YES`, you get that same blue pulsing dot displayed in the built-in Map application.

If you were to compile and run the application as it stands, you'd get what you see in Figure 5-5 — a map of the USA in landscape mode with a blue dot that represents the phone's current location. (There may be a lag until the iPhone is able to determine that location, but you should see it eventually.) Of course, to see it in landscape mode, you have to turn the iPhone, or choose Hardware⇨Rotate Right (or Rotate Left) from the Simulator menu, or press ⌘+right (or left) arrow.

If you don't see the current location, you might want to check and make sure you've connected the `mapView` outlet to the Map view in the nib file — see the "Setting up the nib file" section, earlier in the chapter.

You get your current location *if you are running your app on the iPhone.* If you're running it on the Simulator, that location is Apple — beautiful, Cupertino, California, to be precise. Touching on the blue dot also displays what's called an *annotation,* and I tell you how to customize the text to display whatever you cleverly come up with — including, as you discover in the upcoming "Annotations" section, the address of the current location.

Figure 5-5: Displaying a map in landscape mode with a user location.

It's about the region

Okay, now you've got a blue dot on a map of the good ol' US of A. Cute, but still not that useful for the purposes of the app.

As I mention at the beginning of this chapter, ideally, when you get to San Francisco (or wherever), you should see a map that centers on San Francisco as opposed to the United States. To get there from here, however, is also pretty easy.

First you need to look at how you center the map.

Back in your Project window, add the following code to `MapController.m`:

```
- (void)updateRegionLatitude:(float) latitude
        longitude:(float) longitude
        latitudeDelta:(float) latitudeDelta
    longitudeDelta:(float) longitudeDelta {

  MKCoordinateRegion region;
  region.center.latitude = latitude;
  region.center.longitude = longitude;
  region.span.latitudeDelta = latitudeDelta;
  region.span.longitudeDelta = longitudeDelta;
  [mapView setRegion:region animated:NO];
}
```

Also add the declaration to the `MapController.h` file.

Setting the *region* is how you center the map and set the zoom level. You accomplish all this with the following statement:

```
[mapView setRegion:region animated:NO];
```

A region is a Map View property that specifies four things (as illustrated in Figure 5-6).

1. `region.center.latitude` specifies the latitude of the center of the map.

2. `region.center.longitude` specifies the longitude of the center of the map.

   For example, if I were to set those values as

   ```
   region.center.latitude = 37.774929;
   region.center.longitude = -122.419415;
   ```

   the center of the map would be San Francisco.

3. `region.span.latitudeDelta` specifies the north-to-south distance (in latitudinal degrees) to display on the map. One degree of latitude is approximately 111 kilometers (69 miles). A `region.span.latitudeDelta` of 0.0036 would specify a north-to-south distance on the map of about a quarter of a mile. Latitudes north of the equator have positive values, whereas latitudes south of the equator have negative values.

4. `region.span.longitudeDelta` specifies the east-to-west distance (in longitudinal degrees) to display on the map. Unfortunately, the number of miles in one degree of longitude varies based on the latitude. For example, one degree of longitude is approximately 69 miles at the equator but shrinks to 0 miles at the poles. Longitudes east of the zero meridian (by international convention, the zero or Prime Meridian passes through the Royal Observatory, Greenwich, in east London) have positive values, and longitudes west of the zero meridian have negative values.

Although the span values provide an implicit zoom value for the map, the actual region you see displayed may not equal the span you specify because the map will go to the zoom level that best fits the region that is set. This also means that even if you just change the center coordinate in the map, the zoom level may change because distances represented by a particular span may change at different latitudes and longitudes. To account for that, those smart developers at Apple included a property you can set that will change the center coordinate without changing the zoom level.

```
@property (nonatomic) CLLocationCoordinate2D centerCoordinate
```

When you change the value of this property with a new `CLLocationCoordinate2D`, the map is centered on the new coordinate, and updates span values to maintain the current zoom level.

That `CLLocationCoordinate2D` type is something you'll be using a lot, so I'd like to explain that before I take you any further.

`CLLocationCoordinate2D` type is a structure that contains a geographical coordinate using the WGS 84 reference frame (the reference coordinate system used by the Global Positioning System).

```
typedef struct {
CLLocationDegrees latitude;
CLLocationDegrees longitude;
} CLLocationCoordinate2D;
```

Here's a little explanation:

✦ `latitude` is the latitude in degrees. This is the value you set in the code you just entered (`region.center.latitude = latitude;`).

✦ `longitude` is the longitude in degrees. This is the value you set in the code you just entered (`region.center.longitude = longitude;`).

To center the map display on San Francisco, you send the `updateRegionLatitude:longitude:latitudeDelta:longitudeDelta` message (the code you just entered) when the view is loaded in the `viewDidLoad:` method. You already added some code there to display the current location, so add the code in bold to `MapController.m`.

```
- (void)viewDidLoad {

  [super viewDidLoad];
  mapView.showsUserLocation = YES;
  CLLocationCoordinate2D initialCoordinate =
                         [trip initialCoordinate];
  [self updateRegionLatitude:
              initialCoordinate.latitude
```

```
                    longitude:initialCoordinate.longitude
                    latitudeDelta:.06 longitudeDelta:.06];
    self.title = [trip mapTitle];
}
```

```
region.center.latitude = 37.774929;
region.center.longitude = -122.419415;
region.span.latitudeDelta = .06; region.span.
longitudeDelta = .06;

[mapView setRegion:region animated:YES];
```

Figure 5-6:
How regions
work.

Take a look at what adding the bold stuff does:

1. The `initialCoordinate` message is sent to the `Trip` object (remember your model from Chapter 4 in this minibook) to get the initial coordinates you want displayed. You're adding some additional functionality to the model, whose responsibility now includes specifying that location. The user may have requested that location when he or she set up the trip (I don't cover that topic in this book, leaving it as an exercise for the reader), or it may have been a default location that you decided on when you wrote the code (an airport specified in the destination, for example).

2. Your code now sets the map title by sending the `mapTitle` message to the `Trip` object — adding another model responsibility. (This gives you a chance to title the map based on whatever criteria you would like, such as the current location.)

```
- (NSString*) mapTitle{

    return @"Sites";
}
```

For all of this to work, of course, you have to add the following code to `Trip.m`. This code returns the latitude and longitude for San Francisco.

```
- (CLLocationCoordinate2D) initialCoordinate {

    CLLocationCoordinate2D startCoordinate;
    startCoordinate.latitude = 37.774929;
    startCoordinate.longitude = -122.419415;
    return startCoordinate;
}

- (NSString*) mapTitle{

    return @" map";
}
```

You of course have to include the `MapKit` in `Trip`, so add the following to `Trip.h`:

```
#import <MapKit/MapKit.h>
```

You also have to add the following to `Trip.h` (just stick it in after the braces):

```
- (CLLocationCoordinate2D) initialCoordinate;
- (NSString*)mapTitle;
```

If you compile and build your project, you should see what's shown in Figure 5-7.

You should get four compiler warnings because you haven't yet implemented the `MKReverseGeocoderDelegate` protocol. Don't worry, what you'll do in the next few sections will eliminate them.

Figure 5-7: Regions determine what you see on the map.

Dealing with failure

But what if the Internet isn't available? The Apple Human Interface Guidelines (and common sense) say that you should keep the user informed of what's going on. By virtue of the fact that you've made the `MapController` a `MKMapView` delegate, your app is in the position to send a message in the event of a load failure. Adding the following code to the `MapController.m` file makes it final:

```
- (void)mapViewDidFailLoadingMap:(MKMapView *)mapView
                       withError:(NSError *)error {

    NSLog(@"Unresolved error %@, %@", error,
                                [error userInfo]);

    UIAlertView *alert = [[UIAlertView alloc]
        initWithTitle:@"Unable to load the map"
        message:@"Check to see if you have internet access"
        delegate:self cancelButtonTitle: @"Thanks"
        otherButtonTitles:nil];
    [alert show];
    [alert release];
}
```

TIP

Testing this alert business on the Simulator doesn't always work because it does some caching. You're better off testing it on the device itself by turning on Airplane Mode.

At this point, when the user touches Map in the Main view, RoadTrip displays a map centered on San Francisco, and if you pan over to Cupertino (or wherever you are), you can see the blue dot.

Tracking location changes

You can also track changes in user location by using key-value observing, which enables you to move the map as the user changes location. I don't go into detail on key-value observing here, other than to show you the code.

First, you add the code in bold to `viewDidLoad:` in `MapController.m` to add an observer that's to be called when a certain value is changed — in this case, `userLocation`.

```
- (void)viewDidLoad {
[super viewDidLoad];
mapView.showsUserLocation = YES;
CLLocationCoordinate2D initialCoordinate =
                                        [map initialCoordi
  nate];
[self updateRegionLatitude: initialCoordinate.latitude longi
  tude:
              initialCoordinate.longitude
latitudeDelta:.06 longitudeDelta:.06];
self.title = [trip mapTitle];
  [mapView.userLocation addObserver:self forKeyPath:@"location"
                                        options:0
  context:NULL];
}
```

Adding that code causes the `observeValueForKeyPath::` message to be sent to the observer (self or the `Trip`). To implement the method in `Trip.m`, enter this method:

```
- (void)observeValueForKeyPath:(NSString *) keyPath
            ofObject:(id)object change:(NSDictionary *) change
            context:(void *) context {

NSLog (@"Location changed");
}
```

In this method, the `keyPath` field returns `mapView.userLocation.location`, which you can use to get the current location. In this example, I'm simply displaying a message on the Debugger Console, but as I said, after the user moves a certain amount, you may want to re-center the map.

Note: This isn't exactly the same location you'd get from `CLLocationManager` — it's optimized for the map, whereas `CLLocationManager` provides the raw user location.

Of course, you have to run this on the iPhone for the location to change.

Adding annotations

The `MKMapView` class supports the ability to annotate the map with custom information. There are two parts to the annotation — the annotation itself, which contains the data for the annotation, and the Annotation view that displays the data.

The annotation

An annotation plays a similar role to the dictionary you created in Chapter 2 of this minibook, where the dictionary was meant to hold the text to be displayed in the cell of a table view. Both dictionaries and annotations act as models for their corresponding view, with a view controller connecting the two.

Annotation objects are any object that conforms to the `MKAnnotation` protocol and are typically existing classes in your application's model. The job of an Annotation object is to know its location (coordinate) on the map along with the text to be displayed in the callout. The `MKAnnotation` protocol requires a class that adopts that protocol to implement the `coordinate` property. In this case, it makes sense for `Site` and `Hotel` model objects to add the responsibilities of an annotation object to their bag of tricks. After all, the `Site` and `Hotel` model objects already know what thing you want to see or what hotel you're going to stay at, respectively. It makes sense for these objects to have the coordinate and callout data as well.

Of course, the only problem is that you haven't yet created those objects. In fact, you don't create them until Book VI, where I show you how to use plists and core data to access data and store objects, respectively.

So in this case, just as an illustration, I'm going to have you add an Annotation object just to get you into the rhythm.

Here's what you need to do to make the annotations thing happen:

1. **As you did way back at the beginning of the "Building Your Map Functionality" section, go to the File⇨New File menu and create the `MapAnnotation.m` and `MapAnnotation.h` files.**

2. **Add the code in Bold to `MapAnnotation.h`.**

   ```
   #import <Foundation/Foundation.h>
   #import <MapKit/MapKit.h>


   @interface MapAnnotation : NSObject <MKAnnotation> {

     CLLocationCoordinate2D  coordinate;
     NSString                *annotationTitle;
     NSString                *annotationSubTitle;
   }
   ```

```
@property (nonatomic) CLLocationCoordinate2D
                                        coordinate;
- (id) initWithTitle:(NSString*) title
       subTitle:  (NSString*) subTitle
       coordinate:(CLLocationCoordinate2D) aCoordinate;

@end
```

3. **Add the code in bold to `MapAnnotation.m`.**

```
#import "MapAnnotation.h"

@implementation MapAnnotation
@synthesize coordinate;

- (id) initWithTitle: (NSString*) title
        subTitle:(NSString*) subTitle
        coordinate:(CLLocationCoordinate2D)
   aCoordinate {

  if ((self = [super init])) {
    coordinate = aCoordinate;
    annotationTitle = title;
    [annotationTitle retain];
    annotationSubTitle = subTitle;
    [annotationSubTitle retain];
  }
  return self;
}

-(NSString*) title {

  return annotationTitle;
}
-(NSString*) subtitle {

  return annotationSubTitle;
}

@end
```

What you did here was this:

1. **Have the `MapAnnotation` adopt the `MKAnnotation` protocol.**

   ```
   @interface MapAnnotation: NSObject <MKAnnotation>  {
   ```

2. **Add the following instance variable to the `MapAnnotation.h` file.**

   ```
   CLLocationCoordinate2D coordinate;
   ```

3. **Add the following property and method to the `MapAnnotation.h` file.**

   ```
   @property (nonatomic) CLLocationCoordinate2D
                                        coordinate;
   ```

This is a requirement if you adopt the MKAnnotation protocol and tells the MKMapView where to place the annotation.

The MKAnnotation protocol requires a coordinate property — the title method is optional.

4. **Add a synthesize statement to the MapAnnotation.m file.**

   ```
   @synthesize coordinate;
   ```

5. **Implement the MapAnnotation title and subtitle methods by adding the following to the MapAnnotation.m file:**

   ```
   -(NSString*) title {

     return annotationTitle;
   }

   -(NSString*) subtitle {

     return annotationSubTitle;
   }
   ```

6. **Next, you need to add the following to Trip.m to create the annotations.** (You're doing it here because later — after you do all that stuff in Book VI — the code you have added here will make it easier to implement the "real" annotations).

   ```
   - (NSArray*) createAnnotations {

     CLLocationCoordinate2D theCoordinate;
     theCoordinate.latitude = 37.774929;
     theCoordinate.longitude = -122.419415;
     MapAnnotation* sampleAnnotation =
             [[MapAnnotation  alloc]
                 initWithTitle: @"Sample annotation"
                 subTitle: @"pretty easy"
                 coordinate: theCoordinate];

     NSMutableArray* annotations =
             [[NSMutableArray alloc] initWithCapacity:1];
     [annotations addObject:sampleAnnotation];
     return annotations;
   }
   ```

   You can see that when I initialize the MapAnnotation object I am setting a title (@"Sample annotation") and subtitle (@"pretty easy").

Trip is creating a MapAnnotation that will initialize its coordinate property with the latitude and longitude of San Francisco, which will be used by the Map view to position the annotation.

You will also need to import `MapAnnotation`

```
#import "MapAnnotation.h"
```

and add the method declaration to the `Trip.h` file.

```
- (NSArray*) createAnnotations;
```

Finally, add the code in bold to the `viewDidLoad:` method in `MapController.m` so your code can send a message to `Trip` to create the annotations.

```
- (void)viewDidLoad {

  [super viewDidLoad];
  mapView.showsUserLocation = YES;
  CLLocationCoordinate2D initialCoordinate =
                         [trip initialCoordinate];
  [self updateRegionLatitude:initialCoordinate.latitude
    longitude:initialCoordinate.longitude
         latitudeDelta:.06 longitudeDelta:.06];
  self.title = [trip mapTitle];
  [mapView.userLocation addObserver:self
    forKeyPath:@"location"  options:0 context:NULL];
  annotations = [[NSMutableArray alloc]
                               initWithCapacity:1];
  [annotations  addObjectsFromArray:
                       [trip createAnnotations]];
}
```

The `MapController` object creates an array of annotation objects. (I'll show you how it's used next.) You'll also need to add the new annotations instance variable to `MapController.h`:

```
NSMutableArray        *annotations;
```

So far so good. `MapAnnotation` has adopted the `MKAnnotation` protocol, declared a `coordinate` property, and implemented `title` and `subtitle` methods. The `MapController` object then creates an array of these annotations (in this case one). The only thing left to do is send the array to the Map view to get the annotations displayed.

Displaying the annotations
Displaying the annotations is easy. All you have to do is add the line of code in bold to the `viewDidLoad` method in `MapController.m`.

```
- (void)viewDidLoad {

    [super viewDidLoad];
    mapView.showsUserLocation = YES;
    CLLocationCoordinate2D initialCoordinate =
                              [trip initialCoordinate];
    [self updateRegionLatitude:initialCoordinate.latitude
        longitude:initialCoordinate.longitude
              latitudeDelta:.06 longitudeDelta:.06];
    self.title = [trip mapTitle];
    [mapView.userLocation addObserver:self
        forKeyPath:@"location"  options:0 context:NULL];
    NSMutableArray* annotations = [[NSMutableArray alloc]
                                      initWithCapacity:1];
    [annotations  addObjectsFromArray:
                              [trip createAnnotations]];
    [mapView addAnnotations:annotations];
}
```

The MapController sends the addAnnotations: message to the Map view, passing it an array of objects that conform to the MKAnnotation protocol; that is, each one has a coordinate property and an optional title (and subtitle) method if you want to actually display something in the annotation callout.

The Map view places annotations on the screen by sending its delegate the mapView:viewForAnnotation: message. This message is sent for each annotation object in the array. Here you can create a custom view or return nil to use the default view. (If you don't implement this delegate method — which you won't, in this case — the default view is also used.

Creating your own Annotation views is beyond the scope of this book (although I will tell you that the most efficient way to provide the content for an Annotation view is to set its image property). Fortunately, the default Annotation view is fine for your purposes. It displays a pin in the location specified in the coordinate property of the Annotation delegate — MapAnnotation in this case, and later Sight and Hotel), and when the user touches the pin, the optional title and subtitle text will display if the title and subtitle methods are implemented in the annotation delegate.

You can also add callouts to the Annotation callout, such as a Detail Disclosure button (the one that looks like a white chevron in a blue button in a table view cell), or the Info button (like the one you see in many of the utility apps) without creating your own Annotation view. Again, another exercise for you, if you're feeling frisky.

If you compile and build your project, you can check out one of the annotations you just added in Figure 5-8.

Figure 5-8:
An
annotation.

Remember I did this here simply to show you the mechanics of how it's done. You wouldn't normally have the annotation logic in a map controller. Instead, it would be in a model object, and I show you how to do that in Book VI.

Going to the current location

Although you can pan to the user location on the map, in this case, it's kind of annoying, unless you're actually coding this at or around San Francisco. To remove at least that annoyance from your life, I want to show you how easy it is to add a button to the navigation bar to zoom you in to the current location and then back to the map region and span you're currently displaying.

1. **Add the following code to add the button in the `MapController` method `viewDidLoad`.**

You have quite a bit of code there, so this is just what to add:

```
UIBarButtonItem *locateButton =
    [[UIBarButtonItem alloc] initWithTitle: @"Locate"
    style:UIBarButtonItemStylePlain target:self
    action:@selector(goToLocation:)];
self.navigationItem.rightBarButtonItem = locateButton;
[locateButton release];
```

This may look familiar, because it's what you did to add the Back button in Chapter 4 of this minibook. When the user taps the Locate button you create here, you've specified that the `goToLocation:` message is to be sent (`action:@selector(goToLocation:)`) to the `MapController` (`target:self`).

2. **Add the `goToLocation:` method to `MapController.m`.**

```
- (IBAction)goToLocation:(id)sender {
MKUserLocation *annotation = mapView.userLocation;
CLLocation *location = annotation.location;
if (nil == location)
   return;
```

```
        CLLocationDistance distance =
                MAX(4*location.horizontalAccuracy,500);
        MKCoordinateRegion region =
            MKCoordinateRegionMakeWithDistance
                (location.coordinate, distance, distance);
    [mapView setRegion:region animated:NO];

        self.navigationItem.rightBarButtonItem.action =
                                @selector(goToTrip:);
        self.navigationItem.rightBarButtonItem.title =
                                            @"Map";
    }
```

When the user presses the Locate button, you first check to see if the location is available (it may take a few seconds after you start the application for the location to become available). If not, you simply return. (You could, of course, show an alert informing the user what is going on and try again in 10 seconds or so — I leave that up to you.)

If it's available, you compute the span for the region you'll be moving to. In this case, the code

```
        CLLocationDistance distance =
                MAX(4*location.horizontalAccuracy,1000);
```

computes the span to be four times the `horizontalAccuracy` of the device (but no less than 1,000 meters). `horizontalAccuracy` is a radius of uncertainty given the accuracy of the device; that is, the user is somewhere within that circle.

You then call the `MKCoordinateRegionMakeWithDistance` function that creates a new `MKCoordinateRegion` from the specified coordinate and distance values. `distance` and `distance` correspond to `latitudinalMeters` and `longitudinalMeters`, respectively (I'm using the same value for both arguments here).

If you didn't want to change the span, you could have simply set the Map view's `centerCoordinate` property to `userLocation`, and, as I said earlier in the "It's about the region" section, that would have centered the region at the `userLocation` coordinate without changing the span.

3. **Change the title on the button to "Map," and change the `@selector` to `(goToTrip:)`, which means that the next time the user touches the button, the `goToTrip:` message will be sent, so you'd better add the following code. This will toggle the button title back and forth depending on which view you are in:**

```
    - (IBAction) goToTrip:(id)sender {

    CLLocationCoordinate2D initialCoordinate =
                                [trip initialCoordinate];
        [self updateRegionLatitude:
                initialCoordinate.latitude longitude:
```

```
            initialCoordinate.longitude
            latitudeDelta:.06 longitudeDelta:.06];
    self.navigationItem.rightBarButtonItem.title =
                                    @"Locate";
    self.navigationItem.rightBarButtonItem.action =
                            @selector(goToLocation:);
}
```

Again add both method declarations to the `MapController.h` file.

You can see the result of touching the Locate button in Figure 5-9.

Figure 5-9:
Go to the
current
location.

Because you have the user location, you might be tempted to use that to center the map, and that would work fine, as long as you start the location-finding mechanism stuff as soon as the program launches. The problem is that, as I mention in Step 2 of the previous step list, the hardware may take a while to find the current location, and if you don't wait long enough, you get an error. You can add the code to center the map to a method that executes later, such as

```
-(void)observeValueForKeyPath:(NSString *) keyPath
  ofObject:(id)object change:(NSDictionary *) change
                        context:(void *) context {
```

which gets called as soon as the map starts getting location information. But you will see an initial view, and then a redisplay of the centered view. For aesthetic reasons then, you really need to initialize the `MapController` and `MapView` at program start — an exercise for the reader.

And There's Even More

You've covered a lot of ground in this chapter, and the map is looking pretty good. But there's another map topic you need to get under your belt: *geocoding*. I cover that bit of business in the next chapter.

Chapter 6: Geocoding and Reverse Geocoding

Geocoding allows you to take an address and turn it into a map coordinate. *Reverse geocoding* allows you to take a map coordinate (your current location, for example) and turn it into an address. In this chapter, you add both kinds of functionality to RoadTrip. You also (finally) get rid of those annoying compiler warnings.

Reverse Geocoding

Being able to see where I am on an iPhone map has some visual appeal — that dot is a real nice shade of blue — but I'm an exacting kind of guy who'd like to know *exactly* where I am in the scheme of things. I'd like to know the street address of where I'm standing, in other words. Geocoding makes that possible. (If I have the address, I can also write some code to turn the iPhone's current address into an Address Book contact — I show that to you in Book VII.)

Being able to go from a coordinate on a map to an address is called *reverse geocoding,* and thankfully the ability to do that is supplied by the `MapKit`. *Forward geocoding*, the kind of geocoding that converts an address to a coordinate, doesn't come with the `MapKit`, although many free and commercial services are available. I talk more about those options in the next section.

Keep in mind that the location may not be *completely* accurate — that whole `horizontalAccuracy` thing I talk about in Chapter 5 of this minibook does play a role here. For example, because my office is very close to my property line, my location sometimes shows up with my next-door neighbor's address.

Adding reverse geocoding to RoadTrip enables you to display the address of the current location. Just follow these steps:

1. **Import the reverse geocoder framework (conveniently named `MKReverseGeocoder`) into `MapController.h` and have `MapController` adopt the `MKReverseGeocoderDelegate` protocol.**

   That protocol should sound familiar because you should already have adopted it when you created the `MapController` back in Chapter 5 of this minibook.

   ```
   #import <MapKit/MKReverseGeocoder.h>

   @interface MapController : UIViewController
                           <MKReverseGeocoderDelegate> {
   ```

2. **Add an instance variable to hold a reference to the geocoder object.**

   ```
   MKReverseGeocoder       *reverseGeocoder;
   ```

   You use this later to release (I won't need it any more) the `MKReverseGeocoder` after you get the current address.

3. **Add the methods `reverseGeocoder:didFindPlacemark:` and `reverseGeocoder:didFailWithError:` to `MapController.m`.**

   ```
   - (void)reverseGeocoder:(MKReverseGeocoder *) geocoder
           didFindPlacemark:(MKPlacemark *) placemark {

   NSMutableString* addressString =
                                   [[NSMutableString alloc]
           initWithString: placemark.subThoroughfare];
   [addressString appendString: @" "];
   [addressString appendString:placemark.thoroughfare];
   mapView.userLocation.subtitle = placemark.locality;
   mapView.userLocation.title = addressString;
   [addressString release];
   }

   - (void)reverseGeocoder:(MKReverseGeocoder *) geocoder
     didFailWithError:(NSError *) error{

   NSLog(@"Reverse Geocoder Errored");
   }
   ```

   The `reverseGeocoder:didFindPlacemark:` message is sent to the delegate when the `MKReverseGeocoder` object successfully obtains *placemark* information for its coordinate. An `MKPlacemark` object stores placemark data for a given latitude and longitude. Placemark data includes the properties that hold the country, state, city, street address, and other information associated with the specified coordinate. The following list shows the kind of data involved here:

   - `country`: Name of country
   - `administrativeArea`: State

- `locality`: City

- `thoroughfare`: Street address

- `subThoroughfare`: Additional street-level information, such as the street number

- `postalCode`: Postal code

In this implementation, you're setting the user location annotation (`userLocation`) title (supplied by `MapKit`) to a string you create that's made up of the `subThoroughfare` and `thoroughfare` (the street address). You assign the `locality` (city) property to the subtitle.

A placemark is also an annotation and conforms to the `MKAnnotation` protocol, whose properties and methods include the placemark coordinate and other information. Because they are annotations, you can add them directly to the Map view. (For more on annotations, see Chapter 5 of this minibook.)

The `reverseGeocoder:didFailWithError:` message is sent to the delegate if the `MKReverseGeocoder` couldn't get the placemark information for the coordinate you supplied to it. The internet may not available for example. (This is a required `MKReverseGeocoderDelegate` method.)

Of course, to actually get the reverse geocoder information, you need to create an `MKReverseGeocoder` object. Make the `MapController` a delegate, send it a `start` message, and then release it when you're done with it, as follows:

1. **Allocate and start the reverse geocoder and add the `MapController` as its delegate in the `MapContoller`'s `goToLocation:` method by adding the code in bold shown here:**

```
- (IBAction)goToLocation:(id) sender{

    MKUserLocation *annotation = mapView.userLocation;
    CLLocation *location = annotation.location;
    if (nil == location)
      return;
    CLLocationDistance distance =
                MAX(4*location.horizontalAccuracy, 500);
    MKCoordinateRegion region =
                MKCoordinateRegionMakeWithDistance
            (location.coordinate, distance, distance);
    [mapView setRegion:region animated:NO];
    self.navigationItem.rightBarButtonItem.action =
                                    @selector(goToTrip:);
    self.navigationItem.rightBarButtonItem.title =
                                                @"Map";
    reverseGeocoder = [[MKReverseGeocoder alloc]
            initWithCoordinate:location.coordinate];
    reverseGeocoder.delegate = self;
    [reverseGeocoder start];
}
```

Notice how you initialize the MKReverseGeocoder with the coordinate of the current location with the following bit at the end:.

```
reverseGeocoder = [[MKReverseGeocoder alloc]
                    initWithCoordinate:location.coordinate];
```

2. **Release the MKReverseGeocoder by adding the code in bold below to goToTrip:.**

```
- (IBAction)goToTrip:(id) sender{

    [reverseGeocoder release];
    CLLocationCoordinate2D initialCoordinate =
                        [destination initialCoordinate];
    [self updateRegionLatitude:
                initialCoordinate.latitude longitude:
                initialCoordinate.longitude
                latitudeDelta:.2 longitudeDelta:.2];
    self.navigationItem.rightBarButtonItem.title =
                                        @"Locate";
    self.navigationItem.rightBarButtonItem.action =
                        @selector(goToLocation:);
}
```

You release the MKReverseGeocoder here in this method rather than in the goToLocation: method for one simple reason: Even though you start the MKReverseGeocoder in the goToLocation: method, it actually doesn't return the information in that method. It operates asynchronously; and when it either constructs the placemark or gives up, it sends the message reverseGeocoder:didFindPlacemark: or reverseGeocoder:didFailWithError:, respectively. If you're returning to the original Map view, however, you no longer care whether it succeeds or fails because you no longer need the placemark, and you release the MKReverseGeocoder.

Figure 6-1 shows the result of your adventures in reverse geocoding.

Figure 6-1:
Reverse
geocoding.

You may have noticed in the process of compiling your code to get to Figure 6-1, no pesky compiler warnings popped up onscreen. Yes, you have progressed so far that you've left the pesky things behind. Reason to celebrate.

(Forward) Geocoding

As I mention earlier in this chapter, there is reverse geocoding and there is forward geocoding, often referred to simply as geocoding proper. One of the more useful things a map can do is help you find a particular place, and this is what you do when you engage in geocoding. You take the address of something and turn it into a longitude and latitude coordinate. After you've done that, you can, say, add an annotation and drop a pin on the map at that location.

I also mention earlier that geocoding (unfortunately) is not part of `MapKit.framework`. Not to worry, though, because Google, as well as other third-party types, does provide a free service that you can use. I show you how to add such free services in a moment, but you need to start by creating a way to enter the information the service needs: the address of what you want to find and have annotated on the map. You do that by adding a toolbar to your map. (You could, of course, have added a Search bar, but adding a toolbar gives you the opportunity to add additional functionality, such as directions from your current location to the new, or any other location, or even filtering the map to show just hotels, or just sights, or both. I leave this up to you to implement, but after you get the hang of maps and of using a geocoding provider, it isn't all that difficult.)

To add the toolbar itself, add the following code to the end of the `MapController`'s `viewDidLoad` method.

```
NSMutableArray *items = [[NSMutableArray alloc]
                                    initWithCapacity:1];

UIBarButtonItem *barButton =
        [[UIBarButtonItem alloc] initWithTitle: @"Find:"
             style:UIBarButtonItemStyleBordered
             target:self
             action:@selector(find:)];
barButton.tag = 0;
barButton.width = 100;
[items addObject: barButton];
[barButton release];

UIToolbar *toolbar = [UIToolbar new];
toolbar.barStyle = UIBarStyleBlackOpaque;
[toolbar sizeToFit];
CGFloat toolbarHeight = toolbar.frame.size.height;
```

```
CGFloat navbarHeight = self.navigationController.
    navigationBar.frame.
                                        size.height;
CGRect mainViewBounds = self.view.bounds;
  [toolbar setFrame:
            CGRectMake(CGRectGetMinX(mainViewBounds),
            CGRectGetMinY(mainViewBounds) +
              CGRectGetHeight(mainViewBounds) -
            (toolbarHeight + navbarHeight),
            CGRectGetWidth(mainViewBounds),
            toolbarHeight)];
[self.view addSubview:toolbar];
      toolbar.items = items;
toolbar release];
[items release];
```

This particular bunch of code adds a toolbar to your Map view. Walking through it all, you see that the first thing you do is create an array to hold the button, similar to what you did when you created your annotations back in Chapter 5 of this minibook:

```
NSMutableArray *items = [[NSMutableArray alloc]
                            initWithCapacity:1];
```

From there, you move on to create a `UIBarButtonItem`. This is a simple bordered button with a target of `find:`. (This is the message that is sent to the `MapController` when the button is touched.)

```
UIBarButtonItem *barButton = [[UIBarButtonItem alloc]
    initWithTitle: @"Find:"
    style:UIBarButtonItemStyleBordered
    target:self action:@selector(find:)];
```

Then you give it a tag number, so you can identify it if you need to (you won't in this example) and set the width to 100 pixels.

```
barButton.tag = 0;
barButton.width = 100;
```

Next you create the toolbar itself

```
UIToolbar *toolbar = [UIToolbar new];

toolbar.barStyle = UIBarStyleBlackOpaque;
  [toolbar sizeToFit];
CGFloat toolbarHeight = toolbar.frame.size.height;
CGFloat navbarHeight =  self.navigationController.
    navigationBar.frame.
                                        size.height;

CGRect mainViewBounds = self.view.bounds;
```

```
[toolbar setFrame: CGRectMake(CGRectGetMinX(mainViewBounds),
    CGRectGetMinY(mainViewBounds) +
    CGRectGetHeight(mainViewBounds) - (toolbarHeight +
                                    navbarHeight),
    CGRectGetWidth(mainViewBounds),
    toolbarHeight)];
```

You start by getting both the toolbar and navigation bar heights, as spelled out in this section of the code:

```
CGFloat toolbarHeight = toolbar.frame.size.height;
CGFloat navbarHeight =  self.navigationController.
    navigationBar.frame.
                                        size.height;
```

You then create a View Bounds rectangle, which gives you the size of the screen.

```
CGRect mainViewBounds = self.view.bounds;
```

Okay, time to set the toolbar frame with its x coordinate equal to the left side of the screen, as follows:

```
CGRectMake(CGRectGetMinX(mainViewBounds),
```

With the x out of the way, go ahead and set its y coordinate equal to the size of the screen minus the height of the toolbar and the height of the navigation bar,

```
CGRectGetMinY(mainViewBounds) +
    CGRectGetHeight(mainViewBounds) - (toolbarHeight +
                                    navbarHeight),
```

and its width equal to the width of the screen, and its height equal to the toolbar height.

```
CGRectGetWidth(mainViewBounds),
toolbarHeight)];
```

Okay, that finishes that particular walkthrough. To put the final bow on the package, add the following bit of code: This adds the `toolbar` to the `view`, adds the `items` to the `toolbar.items`, and releases the `toolbar` and `items`.

```
 [self.view addSubview:toolbar];
toolbar.items = items;
[toolbar release];
[items release];
```

Now that you have the toolbar and the `find:` method as the target, you have to implement the `find:` method.

In this case, you create a modal view controller that allows the user to enter an address. Add the method in Listing 6-1 to `MapController.m` and the corresponding declaration to `MapController.h`.

Listing 6-1:   Implementing the find: Method

```
- (void) find:(id) sender {

FindLocationController *findLocationController =
   [[FindLocationController alloc] initWithMapController:
   self];
  UINavigationController *navigationController =
      [[UINavigationController alloc]
       initWithRootViewController: findLocationController];
  navigationController.modalTransitionStyle =
   UIModalTransitionStyleFlipHorizontal;

  [self presentModalViewController:navigationController
    animated:YES];

  [navigationController release];
  [findLocationController release];
}
```

As you can see, this code creates a new view controller and presents it as a modal view.

Of course, now you're going to have to create this new `FindLocationController` class. No rest for the weary.

Adding the FindLocationController and nib file

Putting a piece in place often requires putting yet another piece in place, and your quest to add geocoding to RoadTrip is no exception. Here's the next piece of the puzzle:

The `FindLocationController` will be responsible for creating the view that allows the user to enter the location they are looking for and then will take care of creating and initializing the `Geocoder` object that actually finds it.

1. **In the RoadTrip Project window, select the Classes folder, and then choose File⇨New from the main menu (or press ⌘+N) to get the New File dialog.**

2. **In the left column of the dialog, select Cocoa Touch Classes under the iPhone OS heading, select the UIViewController subclass template in the top-right pane, and then click Next.**

Be sure the With XIB for User Interface check box is also selected.

You see a new dialog asking for some more information.

3. **Enter** FindLocationController.m **in the File Name field and then click Finish.**

All you're really going to do in the FindLocationController view is present a Search bar and a keyboard. I'll show you how to do a plain vanilla one, but feel free to gussy it up as you'd like. You need an outlet (just as you do with all those controllers in Chapter 4 of this minibook) as well as a reference to the view from the FindLocationController. You also need to make the FindLocationController a UISearchViewDelegate so it can manage the text being entered.

The MapController will be managing the location, so the FindLocationController needs a reference to the MapController so it can pass it the text. (There are other ways that you can do this, including making the MapController a delegate of the FindLocationController, but I leave that as an exercise for you to do on your own.) You pass that reference in the initWithMapController method.

Notice you have to import the MapKit and class MapController.

1. **Start by going into FindLocationController.m and adding the necessary methods and outlets (that is, the code in bold) in Listing 6-2 (shown after the steps).**

2. **Do the File⇨Save thing to save the file.**

Only after it's saved can Interface Builder find the new outlet.

3. **Use the Groups & Files list on the left in the Project window to drill down to the FindLocationController.xib file; then double-click the file to launch it in Interface Builder.**

If the Attributes Inspector window isn't open, choose Tools⇨Inspector or press Shift+⌘+1. If the View window isn't visible, double-click the View icon in the FindLocationController.xib window.

If you can't find the FindLocationController.xib window (you may have minimized it — accidentally, on purpose, whatever) you can get it back by choosing Window⇨WebViewController.xib or whichever nib file you're working on.

4. **Select File's Owner in the FindLocationController.xib window.**

5. **It should already be set to FindLocationController. If not, retrace your steps to see where you may have made a mistake.**

You need to be sure that the File's Owner is FindLocationController. You can set the File's owner from the Class drop-down menu in the Identity Inspector.

6. **Next drag a UISearchBar from the Library window to the top of the View window, as I have in Figure 6-2.**

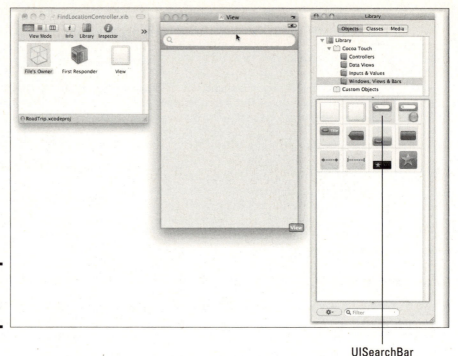

Figure 6-2:
Adding a
Search Bar.

UISearchBar

You can find `UISearchBar` in Cocoa Touch's Windows, Views & Bars folder.

7. **Back in the `FindLocationController.xib` window, right-click File's Owner to call up a contextual menu with a list of connections.**

   You can get the same list using the Connections tab in the Attributes Inspector.

8. **Drag from the little circle next to the `searchBar` outlet in the list onto the Search bar in the View window.**

   Doing so connects the `FindLocationController`'s `searchBar` outlet to the Search bar itself.

9. **Go back to that list of connections and click the triangle next to Referencing Outlets. This time drag from the little circle next to the New Referencing Outlet list onto `searchBar` in the View window.**

10. **With the cursor still in the View window, let go of the mouse button.**

    A pop-up menu appears, looking like the one in Figure 6-3.

11. **Choose delegate from the pop-up menu (OK, your choices are pretty limited; there is only the one item — delegate).**

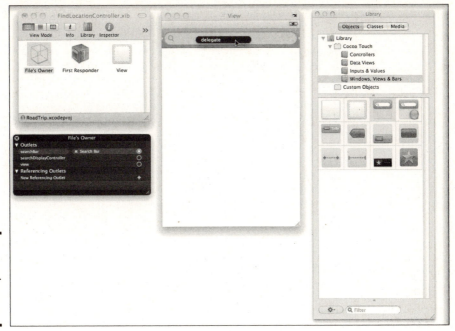

Figure 6-3:
Making the
FindLocation-
Controller a
delegate.

When you're done, the File's Owner contextual menu should look like
Figure 6-4.

Figure 6-4:
The
completed
connections.

Listing 6-2:   The FindLocationController Interface

```
#import <UIKit/UIKit.h>
#import <MapKit/MapKit.h>
@class MapController;

@interface FindLocationController : UIViewController
                            <UISearchBarDelegate> {

  MapController* mapController;
  IBOutlet    UISearchBar *searchBar;
}
```

(continued)

Listing 6-2 *(continued)*

```
- (id) initWithMapController:
                            (MapController*) mapController;


@end
```

Next stop — `FindLocationController`. Add the code in Listing 6-3 to `FindLocationController.m`.

Listing 6-3:   The FindLocationController implementation

```
#import "FindLocationController.h"
#import "MapController.h"

@implementation FindLocationController

- (id) initWithMapController:
                        (MapController*) theMapController {

  if (self = [super initWithNibName:
                    @"FindLocationController" bundle:nil]) {
    self.title = NSLocalizedString(@"Find", @"Find");
    mapController = theMapController;
  }
  return self;
}

- (void) viewDidLoad {

  searchBar.showsCancelButton = YES;
  searchBar.autocorrectionType =
                                UITextAutocorrectionTypeNo;
  [searchBar becomeFirstResponder];
}

- (void) searchBarSearchButtonClicked:
                            (UISearchBar *) theSearchBar {

  [theSearchBar resignFirstResponder];
  [mapController doFind:searchBar.text];
  [self dismissModalViewControllerAnimated:YES];
}

- (void) searchBarCancelButtonClicked:
                            (UISearchBar *)theSearchBar {

  [theSearchBar resignFirstResponder];
  [self dismissModalViewControllerAnimated:YES];
}
```

The `initWithMapController:` you see near the beginning of Listing 6-3 is nothing special. With `viewDidLoad,` you end up doing three things of interest. First, you tell the Search bar to show the Cancel button:

```
searchBar.showsCancelButton = YES;
```

Secondly, you turn off autocorrection on the keyboard (which is my own preference because autocorrection gets very annoying when the user starts searching for landmarks like Coit Tower).

```
searchBar.autocorrectionType = UITextAutocorrectionTypeNo;
```

Finally, you make the `searchBar` the first responder. What that will do is cause the keyboard to be raised when the view is displayed.

```
[searchBar becomeFirstResponder];
```

The method `searchBarSearchButtonClicked:` is a `UISearchBarDelegate` method and is called when the user taps Search on the keyboard. You'll resign as first responder, which lowers the keyboard (not really necessary since you are going to dismiss the dialog, but good form) and send a message to the `MapController` with whatever text that the user typed, and then you dismiss the `FindLocationController` and its view.

```
 [mapController doFind:searchBar.text];
self dismissModalViewControllerAnimated:YES];
```

Finally if the user taps the Cancel button, the delegate method `searchBar-CancelButtonClicked:` is invoked and you resign as first responder and dismiss the dialog.

After the user has entered the text, it's time for the `doFind:` method of the `MapController` to go to work. For that to happen, you need to enter the code in Listing 6-4 into `MapController.m` as well as a declaration in `MapController.h`.

Listing 6-4:   doFind:

```
- (void) doFind:(NSString*) newLocation {

  [mapView removeAnnotations: annotations];
  Geocoder* geocoder = [[Geocoder alloc] init];
  CLLocationCoordinate2D locationCoordinate =
                  [geocoder geocodeLocation:newLocation];
  MKCoordinateRegion initialRegion;
```

(continued)

Listing 6-4 *(continued)*

```
initialRegion.center.latitude =
                           locationCoordinate.latitude;
initialRegion.center.longitude =
                           locationCoordinate.longitude;
initialRegion.span.latitudeDelta = .06;
initialRegion.span.longitudeDelta = .06;
[mapView setRegion:initialRegion animated:NO];
MapAnnotation* findAnnotation = [[MapAnnotation alloc]
      initWithTitle: @"Found Location"
        subTitle: @"pretty easy"
        coordinate: locationCoordinate];
[annotations addObject:findAnnotation];
[mapView addAnnotations: annotations];
[findAnnotation release];
}
```

The first thing that happens with this code is that the `MapController` object sends a message to `mapView` to remove its annotations. You want your code to do that because you'll be entering a new annotation to the array for the found location. It isn't necessary, but good form nonetheless.

```
[mapView removeAnnotations: annotations];
```

Next, you allocated and initialized the `Geocoder` object and sent it a message to find the coordinate for the address or landmark the user entered.

```
Geocoder* geocoder = [[Geocoder alloc] init];
CLLocationCoordinate2D locationCoordinate = [geocoder
                          geocodeLocation:newLocation];
```

Based on the coordinate that's returned, you set up a new region for the map to move to. (You may remember this is what you did when you first displayed the map and centered it on San Francisco back in Chapter 5 of this minibook.) Here's how that worked:

```
MKCoordinateRegion initialRegion;
initialRegion.center.latitude =
                           locationCoordinate.latitude;
initialRegion.center.longitude =
                           locationCoordinate.longitude;
initialRegion.span.latitudeDelta = .06;
initialRegion.span.longitudeDelta = .06;
[mapView setRegion:initialRegion animated:NO];
```

Finally, you created a new `MapAnnotation` that marks the location you have found, added it to the annotations array, and then added the array to `mapView`.

```
MapAnnotation* findAnnotation = [[MapAnnotation alloc]
            initWithTitle: @"Found Location"
            subTitle: @"pretty easy"
            coordinate: locationCoordinate];
[annotations addObject:findAnnotation];
[mapView addAnnotations: annotations];
```

Don't forget to add the following to `MapController.m`:

```
#import "FindLocationController.h"
#import "MapAnnotation.h"
#import "Geocoder.h"
```

You can add the new location as a hotel or landmark later as you wish. You also need to add a control and some code to delete the found location when the user no longer wants it on the map.

The last step on this journey is looking at the `Geocoder` class that you need to create. To start things off,

1. **Choose File⇨New from the main menu (or press ⌘+N) to get the New File dialog.**

2. **In the leftmost column of the dialog, select Cocoa Touch Classes under the iPhone OS heading, but this time select the Objective-C Class template in the topmost pane — making sure the Subclass drop-down menu has `NSObject` selected — and then click Next.**

   You see a new dialog asking for some more information.

3. **Enter** Geocoder.m **in the File Name field and then click Finish.**

Now you need to add the code to the `Geocoder.m` and `Geocoder.h` files. You can find the interface in Listing 6-5.

Listing 6-5:   Geocoder Interface File

```
#import <Foundation/Foundation.h>
#import <CoreLocation/CoreLocation.h>

@interface Geocoder : NSObject {

  CLLocationCoordinate2D geocodedLocation;
  BOOL            accumulatingParsedCharacterData;
  BOOL            didAbortParsing;
  BOOL            parseThis;
  NSMutableArray  *currentParseBatch;
  NSMutableString *currentParsedCharacterData;
}
```

(continued)

Listing 6-5 *(continued)*

```
@property (nonatomic) CLLocationCoordinate2D
                                    geocodedLocation;
@property (nonatomic, retain) NSMutableString
                        *currentParsedCharacterData;
@property (nonatomic, retain) NSMutableArray
                                *currentParseBatch;
- (CLLocationCoordinate2D) geocodeLocation:
                            (NSString*) theLocation;
- (void)parseLocationData:(NSData *)data;

@end
```

In this interface, you can see the `geocodeLocation:` message you send from the `MapController`.

```
- (CLLocationCoordinate2D) geocodeLocation:
                            (NSString*) theLocation;
```

The rest of the code consists of a bunch of instance variables and methods used internally.

```
CLLocationCoordinate2D geocodedLocation;
BOOL            accumulatingParsedCharacterData;
BOOL            didAbortParsing;
BOOL            parseThis;
NSMutableArray  *currentParseBatch;
NSMutableString *currentParsedCharacterData;
```

Not much to linger over.

Now take a look at the code in Listing 6-6:

Listing 6-6:   Geocoder Implementation

```
#import "Geocoder.h"


@implementation Geocoder
@synthesize  geocodedLocation, currentParsedCharacterData,cur
    rentParseBatch;


- (CLLocationCoordinate2D) geocodeLocation:(NSString*)
                                        theLocation {

  NSArray *listItems =
        [theLocation componentsSeparatedByString:@" "];
  NSMutableString* geoLocate =
                        [[NSMutableString alloc] init];
```

```
    [geoLocate appendString:
                    @"http://maps.google.com/maps/geo?q="];
    int n=1;
    for (NSString* element in listItems) {
      [geoLocate appendString:element];
      if (n < [listItems count]){
        [geoLocate appendString:@"+"];
      }
      ++n;
    }
    [geoLocate appendString:@"&output=xml&oe=utf8&sensor=false
     &key=                                                    "];
    NSData* theData =[[NSData alloc] initWithContentsOfURL:
                            [NSURL URLWithString:geoLocate]];
    [self parseLocationData:theData];
    [theData release];
    [geoLocate release];
    return self.geocodedLocation;
}

- (void)parseLocationData:(NSData *)data {
    self.currentParseBatch = [NSMutableArray array];
    self.currentParsedCharacterData =
                                    [NSMutableString string];
    NSXMLParser *parser =
                  [[NSXMLParser alloc] initWithData:data];
    [parser setDelegate:self];
    parseThis = NO;
    [parser parse];
    self.currentParseBatch = nil;
    self.currentParsedCharacterData = nil;
    [parser release];
}

#pragma mark NSXMLParser delegate methods

- (void)parser:(NSXMLParser *)parser didStartElement:(NSString
   *)elementName namespaceURI:(NSString *)namespaceURI
   qualifiedName:(NSString *)qName attributes:(NSDictionary
   *)attributeDict {
    if ([elementName isEqualToString:@"coordinates"]) {
      accumulatingParsedCharacterData = YES;
      parseThis = YES;
    }
}

- (void)parser:(NSXMLParser *)parser didEndElement:(NSString
   *)elementName namespaceURI:(NSString *)namespaceURI
   qualifiedName:(NSString *)qName {
```

(continued)

Listing 6-6 *(continued)*

```objc
    if ([elementName isEqualToString:@"coordinates"]) {
      if (parseThis) {
        NSArray *listItems = [currentParsedCharacterData
                          componentsSeparatedByString:@","];
        geocodedLocation.longitude =[[listItems
                              objectAtIndex:0] doubleValue];
        geocodedLocation.latitude = [[listItems
                              objectAtIndex:1] doubleValue];
        parseThis = NO;
        accumulatingParsedCharacterData = NO; }
    }
}

- (void)parser:(NSXMLParser *)parser
    foundCharacters:(NSString *)string {

  if (accumulatingParsedCharacterData) {
    [self.currentParsedCharacterData appendString:string];
  }
}

- (void)parser:(NSXMLParser *)parser
              parseErrorOccurred:(NSError *)parseError {

  NSString *errorMessage = [parseError localizedDescription];
  UIAlertView *alertView = [[UIAlertView alloc]
        initWithTitle:NSLocalizedString(@"Geocode error",
          @"Alert displayed when parse error occurs")
        message:errorMessage delegate:nil
        cancelButtonTitle:@"OK" otherButtonTitles:nil];
  [alertView show];
  [alertView release];

}

- (void) dealloc {
  currentParsedCharacterData = nil;
  currentParseBatch = nil;
  [super dealloc];
}

@end
```

This class does two things. First, it goes out onto the Web and gets the coordinates for the address or landmark the user entered. This is accomplished by two methods

```
- (CLLocationCoordinate2D) geocodeLocation: (NSString*)
    theLocation;
- (void)parseLocationData:(NSData *)data;
```

The rest of the methods accomplish the task of parsing the XML data
retrieved in order to extract the necessary coordinates.

geocodeLocation: first takes the string and reformats it into something a
third-party geocoder like Google's can use. It takes all the words in the text,
removes the spaces, and replaces them with a single + character.

```
NSArray *listItems = [theLocation
    componentsSeparatedByString:@" "];
  NSMutableString* geoLocate = [[NSMutableString alloc]
    init];
  [geoLocate appendString:@"http://maps.google.com/maps/
    geo?q="];
  int n=1;
  for (NSString* element in listItems) {
    [geoLocate appendString:element];
    if (n < [listItems count]){
      [geoLocate appendString:@"+"];
    }
    ++n;
  }
```

Next, geocodeLocation: appends a string that tells the geocoder (say,
Google's) about the format you want the geocoded information in — as well
as some control information — and includes your API key. This key starts at
&key and is blurred out in the text because you just have to get your own —
no, you can't use mine. Google doesn't charge for it, but you do have to register; I explain how in a second:

```
[geoLocate appendString:@"&output=xml&oe=utf8&sensor=false
  &key=AQAAAAAYRMKyqUyCpJQLA4jPgwChAtPACFBRlJ3hnaJ-
  TwUtgQDIOT-8E5mmuOm_8FfglgRhB9ITCL8iKF-A"];
```

Then it simply does a "get" to the URL for the geocoded information, passing
in the formatted text string as well as the control information and API key,
and then stores what's returned in theData. (I requested the data in XML
format, but you have several alternatives, which you can specify in the control information I mention earlier.)

```
NSData* theData =[[NSData alloc]
    initWithContentsOfURL:[NSURL URLWithString:geoLocate]];
```

Finally, `geocodeLocation:` sends the `parseLocationData:` message to itself, which parses the returned XML and extracts the coordinate. There's actually a lot more there, but you can explore that on your own. Here's a road map:

✦ `parseLocationData:` allocates and initializes an `NSXMLParser` object. This class parses XML documents (including DTD declarations) in an event-driven manner. It uses several delegate methods.

✦ The first of such methods is `parser:didStartElement:namespace URI:qualifiedName:attributes:`. You override this method to see whether the current tag it's processing is `coordinates`. That's the only one you are interested in. If it's not that tag, you return `NO`. If it is that tag, you return `YES`.

✦ The parser then sends the delegate the `parser:foundCharacters:` message. This message is sent by the parser when it finds parsed character data in an element. The parser is not guaranteed to deliver all the parsed character data for an element all at once, so it's necessary to accumulate character data until the end of the element is reached.

You can also find this same strategy in Book VI, where I explain the URL Loading System and how to asynchronously download information from a server on the internet. I go into more detail about these kinds of mechanism there.

✦ After it finishes that tag, it sends the `didStartElement:namespaceUR I:qualifiedName:attributes:` message again for the next tag until it runs out of tags.

✦ For an error condition, `geocodeLocation:` sends `parseErrorOccurr ed:parseError::`.

The Goggle error codes aren't that easy to find. They're located at `http://code.google.com/apis/maps/documentation/geocoding/index.html`, along with lots of explanation of the service and process. As I mention earlier, you have to get your own API key, which you can do at `http://code.google.com/apis/maps/signup.html`.

Figure 6-5 shows you what the Google Maps Sign Up page looks like. This is obviously just a brief introduction to the Google Maps APIs. If you're going to be doing a lot with geocoding and maps, you'll have to go through the documentation yourself.

You can see the results of typing **Coit Tower San Francisco** into the ever-more complete RoadTrip app in Figure 6-6.

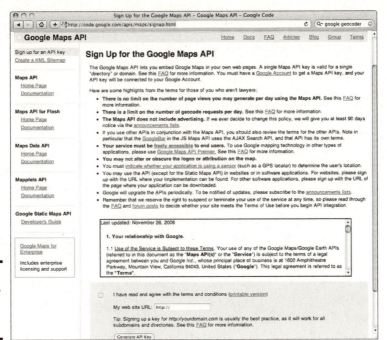

Figure 6-5:
Getting your
own API
key.

Figure 6-6:
Finding Coit
Tower.

What's Next?

You've just created a real application with quite a bit of functionality, so give yourself a pat on the back. But there's more to come.

In Book VI, I go through what you need to know about saving data. I cover plists, the URL Loading System, and core data, with a few tips and warnings thrown in for good measure.

Book VI

Storing and Accessing Data

The 5th Wave — By Rich Tennant

"Hold on, Barbara. I'm pretty sure the App Store has an iPhone application for this."

Contents at a Glance

Chapter 1: Show Me the Data

In This Chapter

✔ **Creating and using property lists**

✔ **Discovering how dictionaries work**

✔ **Updating dictionaries and property lists**

✔ **Having a property list object array) write itself to a file**

What you accomplished in Book V is all fine and dandy. You've essentially created a "wire frame" for the user experience and filled in a few of the pieces.

Although those fillings are valuable, the real meat of the RoadTrip application, besides the maps, is in the Sights and Hotels sections. But those, as opposed to car information and car servicing, are going to require some significant data. In this minibook, I show you how to deal with all that data using property lists, the URL Loading System, and Core Data.

In this chapter, you work on the Sights selection on the main screen. I show you how to create a Sights menu that uses a local image and then downloads the data about the sight from a Web server when the user selects that particular sight.

I put the data on the Web server because, if you were to offer this as a commercial app, you would want the data on the Internet so you can update it with the latest information — summer versus winter hours, for example, or letting users know that tours now start on the half hour rather than the quarter hour. You'd also want it on the Internet so you can easily add new things to play with, based on user feedback. (You can also easily add an e-mail or Twitter feature to this app, for example, although I don't have room in this book to go into that.)

In Book V, you created a generic `WebViewController`. In this chapter, you work towards creating a generic `TableViewController` that's driven by the data in a property list (also known as a *plist*).

Seeing the Sights

You will be implementing the sequence in the RoadTrip application you see documented in Figures 1-1 and 1-2.

Figure 1-1:
Tinkers to
Evers to
Chance.

Figure 1-2:
The sights
on the Map.

Pretty impressive, right? I love the way the Golden Gate Bridge gets highlighted in Figure 1-2.

To get this all to work properly, you need to do the following:

1. Create a table view to display the names of the sights as well as an image of the site, and then create the Web view to display the text that describes the sight.

2. Make a few changes in the `RootViewController` to load a `SightListController`.

3. Create a `Sight` object that "knows" what sight it is, has an image or picture of itself, holds some text describing it, and knows its location (which will also enable it to act as an annotation — you do want to be able to find it on a map don't you?). To do that, you have to create a *property list* (an iPhone data structure that I explain in detail) and then programmatically load it and use the data to create the `Sight` objects.

4. Make a few changes in `Trip` to create the `Sight` objects and load a `SightListController` (as well as implement a new annotations mechanism).

In this chapter, I show you how to do all this, although I do it in a slightly different order that will be easier for you to follow.

You start by creating part of the `SightListController`, followed by the plist. After that, you code the Sight class and then finish coding the `SightListController`.

Starting with the Table View

The way you select an application function (refer to Figure 1-1) is by selecting a row in a table view, your good friend from Book V. Although I don't go into too much detail here, I want to review how table views work.

As I think about creating yet another table view (more than two of anything qualifies for me as yet another and time to start thinking of a generic version), take a look at what the table view needs.

As I mention in Book V, Chapter 2, to get table views to work for you, you need to do the following:

1. **Supply the number of sections you want.**

   You do that with the help of the `numberOfSectionsInTableView:` method of the `UITableViewDataSource` protocol.

Book VI
Chapter 1

Show Me the Data

2. **Supply the number of rows you want in each section and specify what you want to call your section headers.**

   The `tableView:numberOfRowsInSection:` method and the `table View:titleForHeaderInSection:` method, respectively, take care of that for you. (Both are part of the `UITableViewDataSource` protocol.)

3. **Supply the text (or graphic) for each row.**

   You return that from the implementation of the `tableView:cellFor RowAtIndexPath:` method of the `UITableViewDataSource` proto-col. This message is sent for each visible row in the table view, and you return a Table View cell to display the text or graphic. This is how you get the list of sights and those nice photos you see in Figure 1-1 — more on how it actually works later.

4. **Respond to a user selection of the row.**

   You use the `tableView:didSelectRowAtIndexPath:` method of the `UITableViewDelegate`, protocol to take care of this task. In this method, you create a view controller and a new view. For example, when the user selects Golden Gate Bridge in Figure 1-1, the `tableView:did SelectRowAtIndexPath:` method is called, a `WebViewController` controller is created, and the text description of the Golden Gate Bridge is displayed in a Web view — just as the car servicing information was displayed in Book V. In this case, the "brains" behind the data will be the `Sight` object, just as the `CarServicing` object was the brains behind the car servicing information.

A `UITableView` object must have a *data source* and a *delegate*. The data source supplies the *content* for the table view, and the delegate manages the *appearance* and *behavior* of the table view. The data source adopts the `UITableViewDataSource` protocol, and the delegate adopts the `UITableViewDelegate` protocol — no surprises there. Of the preced-ing methods, only the `tableView:didSelectRowAtIndexPath:` is part of the `UITableViewDelegate`, the others are included in the `UITableViewDataSource` protocol.

Adding the controller

If you've been following along with me, note that I'll be extending what you did in Chapter 6 of Book V. You can find the application up to that point on my Web site `http://nealgoldstein.com` under Book VI Start Here.

Okay, check out how easy it is to come up with the view controller and nib files:

1. **In the RoadTrip project window, select the Classes folder, and then choose File⇨New from the main menu (or press ⌘+N) to get the New File window.**

Selecting the Classes folder first tells Xcode to place the new file in the Classes folder.

2. **In the left column of the dialog, select Cocoa Touch Classes under the iPhone OS heading, select the UIViewController subclass template in the top-right pane and then click Next.**

   Be sure the UITableViewController subclass is selected and the With XIB for User Interface is *not* selected. I show you how to create the view controller without using a nib file.

   You see a new dialog asking for some more information.

3. **Enter** SightListController.m **in the File Name field and then click Finish.**

To make things easier to find, I keep my `SightListController.m` and `.h` classes in the Classes folder.

Now do it all over again for the `Sight` model class (with the classes folder still selected).

1. **Choose File⇨New from the main menu (or press ⌘+N) to get the New File dialog.**

2. **In the leftmost column of the dialog, first select Cocoa Touch Classes under the iPhone OS heading, then select the Objective-C class template (*not* the UIViewController subclass template) in the topmost pane, make sure the Subclass drop-down menu has `NSObject` selected and then click Next.**

   You see a new dialog asking for some more information.

3. **Enter `Sight` in the File Name field and then click Finish.**

I keep my `Sight.m` and `.h` classes in the Model Classes folder.

At this point, you're all set up to start adding code.

Setting up the controller

As I mentioned when you where creating the controller file, you're going to be creating the table view without using a nib file. Although the end-result of what you are doing here is pretty sophisticated, the actual nuts-and-bolts part is really quite easy. You get it all done by using an initialization method, as follows:

1. **Add the code in bold in Listing 1-1 to `SightListController.m`.**

   You won't be using all the includes yet, but I like to get them out of the way. As you can see, all you're doing is invoking a superclass's method `initWithStyle:UITableViewStyleGrouped`. This method creates the table view and also sets the delegate. Frankly, unless you need to do something special, rolling out the `initWithStyle:UITableViewStyle Grouped:` method makes creating table views a lot less cumbersome.

2. **Add the code in bold in Listing 1-2 to `SightListController.h`.**

   The bolded stuff is simply the instance variables and the methods you'll be adding. I explain `createThumbNail:`, which takes images and sizes them for the table view, later in this chapter.

Listing 1-1:   Initialization

```
#import "SightListController.h"
#import "Trip.h"
#import "Sight.h"
#import "RoadTripAppDelegate.h"
#import "WebViewController.h"

@implementation SightListController

- (id) initWithTrip:(Trip*) theTrip {

  if (self = [super initWithStyle:UITableViewStyleGrouped]) {
    trip = theTrip;
    self.title = @"See the sights";
  }
  return self;
}

@end
```

Listing 1-2:   Setting Up the Header File

```
#import <UIKit/UIKit.h>
@class Trip;
@class Sight;

@interface SightListController : UITableViewController {

  Trip          *trip;
}

- (id) initWithTrip:(Trip*) theTrip;
- (UIImage *) createThumbNail:(Sight*) aSight;

@end
```

Creating the SightListController in the RootViewController

To get your controllers in place, the first thing you have to do is make it possible to select the Sights entry in the Main view. That means uncommenting out the `SightListController` selection in the `tableView:didSelectRowAtIndexPath:` method over in `RootViewController.m` — the stuff in bold in Listing 1-3.

Listing 1-3: **Uncommenting Out** `SightListController` **Selection**

```objc
- (void)tableView:(UITableView *)tableView
        didSelectRowAtIndexPath:(NSIndexPath *)indexPath {

  RoadTripAppDelegate *appDelegate =
              (RoadTripAppDelegate *)
              [[UIApplication sharedApplication] delegate];
  [appDelegate.lastView replaceObjectAtIndex:0 withObject:
        [NSNumber numberWithInteger:indexPath.section]];
  [appDelegate.lastView replaceObjectAtIndex:1 withObject:
        [NSNumber numberWithInteger:indexPath.row]];

  [tableView deselectRowAtIndexPath:indexPath
                                        animated:YES];

  int menuOffset =
            [self menuOffsetForRowAtIndexPath:indexPath];
  UIViewController *targetController =
            [[menuList objectAtIndex:menuOffset]
                          objectForKey:kControllerKey];

  if (targetController == nil) {
    BOOL realtime = !appDelegate.useStoredData;

    switch (menuOffset) {
      case 0:
        if (realtime) targetController =
                [[MapController alloc] initWithTrip:trip];
        else [self displayOfflineAlert:
                [[menuList objectAtIndex:menuOffset]
                            objectForKey:kSelectKey]];
        break;
      case 1:
        targetController =
          [[SightListController alloc] initWithTrip:trip];
        break;
      case 2:
//      targetController =
                [[HotelController alloc] initWithTrip:trip];
        break;
```

(continued)

Listing 1-3 *(continued)*

```
        case 3:
            if (realtime) targetController = [[WebViewController
    alloc] initWithTrip:trip tripSelector:@
    selector(returnWeather:)
                webControl:YES title:NSLocalizedString(@"Weather",
                                            @"Weather")];
            else [self displayOfflineAlert:
                [[menuList objectAtIndex:menuOffset]
                                objectForKey:kSelectKey]];
            break;
        case 4:
            targetController = [[WebViewController alloc]
    initWithTrip:trip tripSelector:@selector(returnCarServicin
    gInformation:)
                                    webControl:NO
    title:NSLocalizedString (@"Car Servicing", @"Car
    Servicing")];
            break;
        case 5:
            targetController = [[WebViewController alloc]
                initWithTrip:trip
                tripSelector:@selector(returnCarInformation:)
                webControl:NO
                title:NSLocalizedString (@"The Car", @"Car
                                        Information")];
            break;
    }
        if (targetController) {
        [[menuList   objectAtIndex:menuOffset]
    setObject:targetController forKey:kControllerKey];
        }
    }
    if (targetController) {
        [[self navigationController]
            pushViewController:targetController animated:YES];
        [targetController release];
    }
}
```

The following code allocates a `SightListController` (a view controller) and then sends it the `initWithTrip::` message. (I explain this at the very end of Book V, Chapter 2; you might want to review that if it has been a while since you looked at it.).

```
targetController =
        [[SightListController alloc] initWithTrip:trip];
```

You also need to import the `SightListController` and add it to the `RootViewController.m` file.

```
#import "SightListController.h"
```

That's all you need to do in the `RootViewController` class.

If you were to build the project as it stands now, it would compile (with a few errors you can ignore), and you'd get a table view of Sights with nothing in your list. Now that you've gotten the foundation built, it's time to go to work.

Seeing the Sights

There are a couple of things you need to do to see your (virtual) sights. You need to be able to display the sights (and their photos) in the `SightListController`, and you need to be able to have sight model objects that will provide the data not only to the controller, but to the Web view as well. Take a look at the `Sight` object that will do that.

Add the code in bold in Listing 1-4 to `Sight.h`.

Listing 1-4:   Sight.h

```
#import <MapKit/MapKit.h>
#import "WebViewController.h"
@class Trip;

@interface Sight : NSObject {

    NSString                *sightName;
    CLLocationCoordinate2D  coordinate;
    NSString                *title;
    NSString                *subtitle;
    NSString                *resource;
    NSString                *resourceType;
    NSString                *image;
    NSString                *imageType;
    Trip                    *trip;
}

@property (nonatomic, retain)    NSString *sightName;
@property (nonatomic, retain)    NSString *image;
@property (nonatomic, retain)    NSString *imageType;;
@property (nonatomic) CLLocationCoordinate2D coordinate;
- (id) initWithTrip:(Trip*) theTrip
                    sightData:(NSDictionary*) sightData;

@end
```

There are a few includes here you won't be needing until later, but I have you add them now just to get them taken care of and out of the way.

Now you have an object that can provide data for both the
`SightListController` and its Web view, and things are starting to fall
into place. Well, almost, because you'll need to figure out where the data for
each `Sight` comes from. And that's where the property lists come in.

Up to now you've gotten the data displayed in the table view by hard coding
it in your application, such as when you created the `menuList` back in Book
V, Chapter 2. Listing 1-5 shows how you did it then:

Listing 1-5:   viewDidLoad

```
- (void)viewDidLoad {
  [super viewDidLoad];
  sectionsArray = [[NSArray alloc] initWithObjects:
                     [[NSNumber alloc]initWithInt:4],
                     [[NSNumber alloc]initWithInt:2], nil];

  self.title = [[[NSBundle mainBundle] infoDictionary]
    objectForKey:@"CFBundleName"];
  menuList = [[NSMutableArray alloc] init];
  [menuList addObject:[NSMutableDictionary
     dictionaryWithObjectsAndKeys:
     NSLocalizedString(@"Map", @"Map Section"),kSelectKey,
     NSLocalizedString(@"Where you are", @"Map Explain"),
                                           kDescriptKey,
     nil, kControllerKey, nil]];
  [menuList addObject:[NSMutableDictionary
     dictionaryWithObjectsAndKeys:
     NSLocalizedString(@"Sights", @"Sights Section"),
                                           kSelectKey,
     NSLocalizedString(@"Places to see",
                 @"Places to see Explain"), kDescriptKey,
     nil, kControllerKey, nil]];
  [menuList addObject:[NSMutableDictionary
     dictionaryWithObjectsAndKeys:
     NSLocalizedString(@"Hotels", @"Hotels Section"),
                                           kSelectKey,
     NSLocalizedString(@"Places to stay",
                 @"Places to stay Explain"), kDescriptKey,
     nil, kControllerKey, nil]];
  [menuList addObject:[NSMutableDictionary
     dictionaryWithObjectsAndKeys:
     NSLocalizedString(@"Weather", @"Weather Section"),
                                           kSelectKey,
     NSLocalizedString(@"Current conditions",
                 @"Weather  Explain"), kDescriptKey,
     nil, kControllerKey, nil]];
  [menuList addObject:[NSMutableDictionary
     dictionaryWithObjectsAndKeys:
     NSLocalizedString(@"Servicing", @"Service Section"),
                                           kSelectKey,
     NSLocalizedString(@"Service records",
```

```
              @"Service records Explain"), kDescriptKey,
     nil, kControllerKey, nil]];
  [menuList addObject:[NSMutableDictionary
     dictionaryWithObjectsAndKeys:
     NSLocalizedString(@"The Car",
                 @"Car Information Section"), kSelectKey,
     NSLocalizedString(@"About the car",
                         @"About the car"), kDescriptKey,
     nil, kControllerKey, nil]];
```

Of course, doing it this way does create a problem. Although I could hard code the initial Sight data in my program, doing so doesn't give me much flexibility. This makes it really hard to update and makes the code cumbersome. In addition, although you won't be doing it here as part of the run through of the RoadTrip app, it also makes it very difficult to allow the user to enter his or her own sights.

**Book VI
Chapter 1**

Show Me the Data

Either I have to build some kind of array into my program for the sights I want to provide the user (and "waste" the CPU cycles and memory to build it every time I run the program), or I can store all of this information in a file and, based on the state I'm in (California, Colorado, whatever) or some other user preference, display the data in that file.

When that kind of data is in a file, I don't have to rebuild my program every time I add or change a sight — all I have to do is change the file, which (as you'll see) is really pretty easy. I can even allow users to add their own sights. I talk about that part of the puzzle in more detail in Chapter 3 of this minibook, but for now I concentrate on where you get the initial data.

Fortunately, Cocoa supports an easy-to-use mechanism called a *property list* (plist) to manage this kind of data.

The next section covers property lists and you will create a data source for you app's data source requirements using a plist. In Book V, you created a generic Web controller; think of using a plist in a Table view controller as a creating a generic Table view controller. The Table view controller simply displays what is in the plist.

Sight.plist Is a Plist

Property lists are used extensively by applications and other system software on Mac OS X and iPhone OS. For example, the Mac OS X Finder stores file and directory attributes in a property list, and the iPhone OS uses them for user defaults. You also get a Property List editor with Xcode, which makes property list files (or *plists* as they are referred to) easy to create and maintain in your own programs.

Figure 1-3 displays the property list I show you how to build, one that will contain the data necessary for each Sight object in the RoadTrip app.

Figure 1-3:
The Sight
property list.

When you know how to work with property lists, it's actually easy, but like
most things, getting there is half the fun.

Working with property lists

Book II has an explanation of property lists, but it never hurts to go through
it again in a new context.

Property lists are perfect for storing small amounts of data that consist
primarily of strings and numbers. What adds to their appeal is the ability to
easily read them into your program, use the data, and (although you won't
be doing it in the RoadTrip application) modify the data and then write them
back out again. That's because Cocoa provides a small set of objects that
have that behavior built right in.

The technical term for these kinds of objects is *serializable*. A serializable
object can convert itself into a stream of bytes so that it can be stored in a
file and can then reconstitute itself into the object it once was when it
is read back in — yes "beam me up, Scotty" does exist, at least on your
computer.

These objects, called *property list objects,* that you have to work with are as follows:

✦ NSData and NSMutableData

✦ NSDate

✦ NSNumber

✦ NSString and NSMutableString

✦ NSArray and NSMutableArray

✦ NSDictionary and NSMutableDictionary

As shown in the plist in Figure 1-3, the root is an array and the data for each one of the Sights is held in a dictionary. If you are a little hazy on arrays and dictionaries I will be explaining them in detail.

You'll notice a division in the preceding list. That is because there are two kinds of property list objects.

✦ **Primitives:** The term *primitives* is not a reflection on how civilized these property objects are, but it is a word used to describe the simplest kind of object. They are what they are.

✦ **Containers:** Containers can hold primitives as well as other containers.

One thing that differentiates property list object containers (NSArray, NSDictionary), besides their ability to hold other objects, is that they both have methods called writeToFile::, which write the property list to a file, and a corresponding initWithContentsOfFile:, which initializes the object with the contents of a file. So, if I create an array or dictionary and fill it chock full of objects of the property list type, all I have to do to save it to a file is tell it to go save itself — or create an array or dictionary and then tell it to initialize itself from a file.

You have already worked with arrays in Book V when you saved the current state of the object, and I'll expand on them as well as dictionaries in later sections. These containers can contain other containers as well as the primitive types. Thus, you might have an array of dictionaries (and you do), and each dictionary might contain other arrays and dictionaries, as well as the primitive types.

NSData and NSMutableData are wrappers (an object that is there mostly to turn something into an object) in which you can dump any kind of data and then have that data act as an object. You've used NSData before when you downloaded the car servicing information in Book V as well as when you used the geocoder. You haven't seen NSDate yet, and I won't be using it in the book, but for your information, it is a Cocoa class for date and time handling.

Adding a plist to Your Project

Book II covers this plists in general, but here I'll have you build a specific Sight plist:

1. **In the Groups & Files list (at the left in the Xcode project window), select Static Data (at the top of the list) and then choose File⇨New File from the main menu, or press ⌘+n.**

   The New File dialog appears.

2. **Choose Resource under the Mac OS X heading in the left pane, and then select Property List, as shown in Figure 1-4.**

Figure 1-4: Creating the plist.

3. **Click the Next button.**

   You see a new dialog asking for some more information.

4. **Enter the filename Sight.plist; then press Return (Enter) or click Finish.**

   You now see a new item called `Sight.plist` under Static Data, in the Groups & Files list shown in Figure 1-5.

   In the editor pane, you can see Xcode's Property List editor with the root entry selected. In this case, the Type has defaulted to `Dictionary`; the other option is `Array`, which is what you want, so get ready to change the root to `Array`.

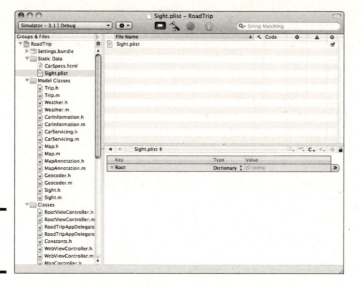

Figure 1-5:
A new plist file.

5. **In the Type pop-up menu, change the type from** `Dictionary` **to** `Array`**, as I have in Figure 1-6.**

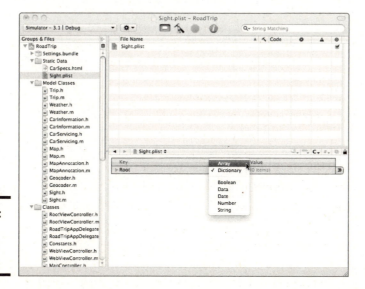

Figure 1-6:
Change the root to Array.

6. **Click the icon (the one with the three parallel lines) at the end of the entry, as shown in Figure 1-7.**

Figure 1-7:
Add an
entry.

A new entry appears, as you can see in Figure 1-8.

Item 0 is the file that holds your Sights. This is the first entry for an actual Sight itself.

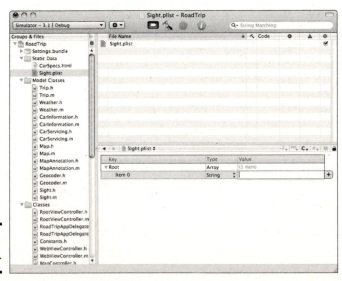

Figure 1-8:
A new entry.

7. **Select Dictionary from the Type pop-up menu, as I have in Figure 1-9.**

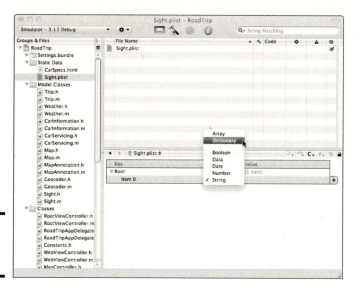

**Book VI
Chapter 1**

Show Me the Data

Figure 1-9:
Select
Dictionary.

Your new entry is made into a dictionary, as shown in Figure 1-10.

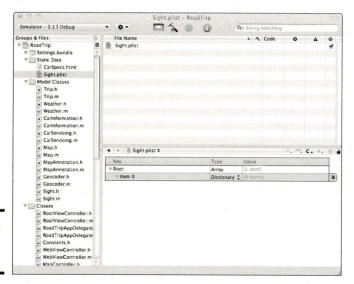

Figure 1-10:
A new
Dictionary.

8. **Click the triangle next to Item 0 and make sure it's pointing down, as shown in Figure 1-10. Then select the 3 lines icon. (Make sure the triangle is pointing down; if not, you won't see the 3 lines but you will see a +.)**

   You see a new entry under the dictionary, like the one in Figure 1-11.

These disclosure triangles work the same way as those in the Finder and the Xcode editor. The Property List editor interprets what you want to add based on the triangle. So, if the items are revealed (that is, the triangle is pointing down), it assumes you want to add a subitem. If the subitems are not revealed (that is, the triangle is pointing sideways), it assumes you want to add an item at that level. In this case, with the arrow pointing down, you will be adding a new entry — a subitem — to the dictionary. If the triangle were pointing sideways, you would be entering a new entry under the root. The icon at the end of the row also helps. If it is three lines, as you see in Figure 1-10, you're going to be creating a new subitem of the entry in that row. A +, like in Figure 1-11, tells you that you're going to be creating a new item at the same level.

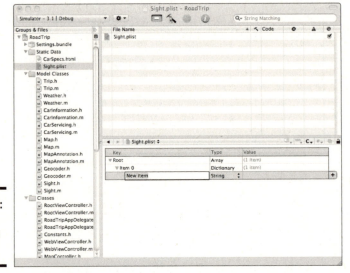

Figure 1-11:
An (new) entry in the dictionary.

9. **In the Key field, enter** `sight name` **and then double-click (or tab to) the Value field and enter** `Golden Gate Bridge`**, as shown in Figure 1-12.**

10. **Click the + icon at the end of the entry (row) you just added, and you will get a new entry. In the Key field, enter** `title` **and in the Value filed enter** `Golden Gate Bridge`**.**

    This one will be at the same level.

    It can be any of the property list objects I talk about at the beginning of this chapter, but `String`, which will already be selected, is the one you want here.

    Repeat Step 10 for the following keys and values:

Key	Value
resource	GoldenGateBridge
resource type	html
image	GGBPhoto
image type	jpg
subtitle	Don't miss it
latitude	37.818774
longitude	–122.478415

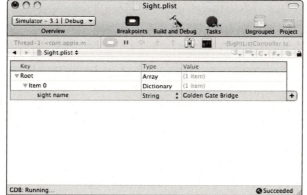

Figure 1-12:
The sight name here is Golden Gate Bridge.

11. **Click the disclosure triangle to hide the** `Dictionary` **entries, as shown in Figure 1-13.**

You want to create a parallel dictionary at this level.

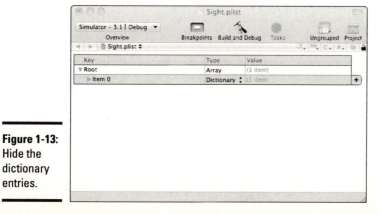

Figure 1-13:
Hide the dictionary entries.

12. **Click the + icon next to the dictionary and add another dictionary.**

As you can see, the default is `String`, as shown in Figure 1-14, so you will need to change it to `Dictionary`.

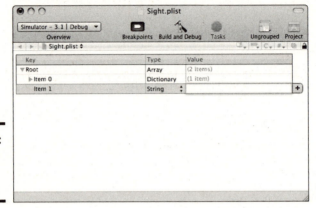

Figure 1-14:
Adding a new dictionary.

Add the following entries below to this dictionary:

Key	*Value*
sight name	Alcatraz
Title	Alcatraz
resource	Alcatraz
resource type	html
image	Alcatraz
image type	jpg
subtitle	Don't miss the boat back
latitude	37.826664
longitude	−122.423021

13. **Repeat Steps 11 and 12 to create another dictionary with the following key value pairs.**

Key	*Value*
sight name	Coit Tower
title	Coit Tower
resource	CoitTower
resource type	html

Key	Value
image	CoitTower
image type	jpg
subtitle	Great San Francisco views
latitude	37.802369
longitude	–122.405819

Make sure you spell the entries *exactly as specified* or else you won't be able to access them using the examples in this book.

When you're done, your plist should look like the one back in Figure 1-3.

If you want to be really lazy (although I don't suggest it this time), you could download the complete project from `http://nealgoldstein.com` and simply copy the plist in the same way I explain how to copy the `.png` files in the next section.

Adding images

Just as you added the `CarSpecs.html` file in Book V, Chapter 4, you do the same thing with the images you need for the `Sights` objects.

The content for the `Sight` objects are in the files (as you could tell from the plist) as GGBPhoto.jpg Alcatraz.jpg and CoitTower.jpg. (while png is the preferred format for iPhone icons, jpg or jpeg is used for photos.) To make the content available to the application, you need to include it in the application bundle itself, although you could have downloaded it the first time the application ran.

The files are included in the final code for this chapter, so first you have to download NNN from `http://nealgoldstein.com`.

Now, you can add the files to your bundle one of two ways:

✦ Open the Project window and drag the `.jpg` files into the Project folder from the NNN Project folder.

  (You should put it in the Static Data folder in your project.)

  Or

✦ Choose Project⇨Add to Project and then use the dialog that appears to navigate to and select the files you want. You can see that in Figure 1-15.

Using plists to store data

Although you won't do it here, you can also modify a plist to store data. The only restriction of note is that you can't modify a plist you've created in your bundle. You need to save it in the file system instead.

Interestingly enough, you've already done that. If you look in Book V, Chapter 3, when you saved an array, for all practical purposes, you were saving a plist. Here's what that looked like:

```
- (void)applicationDidFinishLaunching:(UIApplication *)applica-
  tion {
...
 NSArray *paths = NSSearchPathForDirectoriesInDomains
                        (NSDocumentDirectory, NSUserDomainMask,
   YES);
 NSString *documentsDirectory = [paths objectAtIndex:0];
 NSString *filePath = [documentsDirectory
                        stringByAppendingPathComponent:kSt
   ate];
 lastView =[[NSMutableArray alloc]
                                  initWithContentsOfFile:fileP
   ath];
 if (lastView == nil) {
   lastView = [[NSMutableArray arrayWithObjects:
                 [NSNumber numberWithInteger:-1],
                 [NSNumber numberWithInteger:-1],
                 nil] retain];
 }
...
- (void)tableView:(UITableView *)tableView
              didSelectRowAtIndexPath:(NSIndexPath *)index-
   Path {


 RoadTripAppDelegate *appDelegate = (RoadTripAppDelegate *)
                     [[UIApplication sharedApplication] del-
   egate];
 [appDelegate.lastView replaceObjectAtIndex:0 withObject:
                 [NSNumber numberWithInteger:indexPath.sec-
   tion]];
 [appDelegate.lastView replaceObjectAtIndex:1 withObject:
                     [NSNumber numberWithInteger:indexPath.
   row]];
...
 }
```

```
- (void)applicationWillTerminate:(UIApplication *)application {

   NSArray *paths = NSSearchPathForDirectoriesInDomains
                      (NSDocumentDirectory, NSUserDomainMask,
      YES);
   NSString *documentsDirectory = [paths objectAtIndex:0];
   NSString *filePath = [documentsDirectory
                         stringByAppendingPathComponent:kSt
      ate];
   [lastView writeToFile:filePath atomically:YES];
}
```

Figure 1-15:
Adding the
.jpg files.

At this point, you have two of the necessary components for dealing with the sights in your application: You have the data for each Sight in the plist you just created, and you have a Sight object that has an instance variable defined to hold the data.

So how do you create each Sight and get the data into it? That's another job for Trip.

Initializing the Sight Objects with plist Data

Creating a property list for your RoadTrip app data is a good start, but you also need to know how to create each of the Sight objects you need and then figure out how to initialize each object with the data from the plist. You find out how to do that stuff in this section, and, as an added bonus, I also explain a bit more about arrays and dictionaries.

You can get the `Sight` objects ball rolling with some additions to `Trip.h`. Make the following addition to the `Trip.h` files:

1. **Add an NSMutable array to hold the list of sights.**

```
NSMutableArray *sights;
```

If you're not (yet) familiar with mutable arrays, don't worry, I explain them in great detail shortly. Technically, you could use a regular array here, but I'm preparing you for the time when you'll modify this app to allow the user to add and eliminate sights.

2. **Make `sights` a property in `Trip.h`.**

```
@property (nonatomic, retain) NSMutableArray * sights;
```

If you've read my other books or earlier chapters in this book, you know that I'm not a big fan of using properties to access model information. In this case, however, I feel that it's my responsibility to show you how you can use them. So, if you don't share my anal approach to that subject, this is how you'd do it. This technique will make your list of sights available to the view controller — the one you'll code in a minute, as in the one that displays the list of sights in a table view.

Make the following additions to `Trip.m`. (This stuff is a bit more involved, unfortunately, so be prepared for a workout.)

1. **Add the following code to `Trip.m`.**

By now you should know that you can put the `# import` anywhere above the `@implementation Trip`. You need to put the `@synthesize` after the `@implementation Trip`.

```
#import "Sight.h"
...
@implementation Trip

@synthesize sights;
```

The `@ synthesize` tells the complier to generate the assessors for the sights property.

2. **Add the following code above `@implementation Trip`.**

```
@interface Trip ()
- (void) loadSights;
@end
```

Although I suggested using `loadSights` in Book V, I'm actually going to implement it here. `loadSights` is an internal method to Trip. It takes a property list and loads an array of `Sight` objects. I do want this to be a private method — accessible only to the `Trip` class. If you're coming from C++, you probably want this method to be private, but there's no private construct in Objective-C. What you need to do to hide them is make their declarations in the implementation file and create an Objective-C extension (kind of like a category). If you're unfamiliar with categories and extensions, I explain them in the next section.

Categories and extensions

One of the features of the dynamic runtime dispatch mechanism employed by Objective-C is that you can add methods to existing classes without subclassing. The Objective-C term for these new methods is *categories*. A *category* allows you to add methods to an existing class — even to one to which you do not have the source. This powerful feature allows you to extend the functionality of existing classes.

This looks a lot like class interface declaration — except the category name is listed within parentheses after the class name, and there is no superclass (or colon for that matter). Categories (unlike protocols, which I address in the next chapter) *do* have access to all the instance variables and methods of a class. And I do mean all, even ones declared `@private`, but you'll need to import the interface file for the class it extends. You can also add as many categories as you want.

You can add methods to a class by declaring them in an interface file under a category name and defining them in an implementation file under the same name. What you can't do is add more instance variables.

The methods the category adds become honestly and truly part of the class type; they aren't treated as "step methods." The methods you would add to `Trip` using a category become part of the `Trip` class and are inherited by all the class's subclasses, just like other methods. The category methods can do anything that methods defined in the class proper can do. At runtime, there's no difference.

You use a category like this to add more functionality to an existing class. For example, `UITableView.h` contains an extension to `NSIndexPath` to make it easier to represent a section and row, something you've taken advantage of every time you reference an `indexPath.row`, for example:

```
@interface NSIndexPath (UITableView)
+ (NSIndexPath *)indexPathForRow:(NSUInteger)row
    inSection:(NSUInteger)section;
@property(nonatomic,readonly) NSUInteger section;
@property(nonatomic,readonly) NSUInteger row;
@end
```

What you're doing here, however, is a bit more specialized. You're creating a *class extension.*

Class extensions are like anonymous (unnamed) categories, except that the methods they declare must be implemented in the main @implementation block for the corresponding class.

Doing it this way allows you to have a publicly declared set of methods and to then have additional methods declared privately for use solely by the class.

Class extensions allow you to declare additional methods for a class in a location other than the class @interface. This declaration is what you did when you added the following code above @implementation Trip:

```
@interface Trip ()
- (void) loadSights;
@end
```

Keep the following facts about this little snippet of code in mind:

✦ As opposed to a category, no name is given in the parentheses in the second @interface block;

✦ The implementation of the loadSights method appears within the main @implementation block for the class.

✦ The implementation of the loadSights method must appear within the @implementation for the class just like the methods/properties found in the public @interface.

If the developer doesn't have the source code or doesn't include the .m file, he or she will have no idea that the methods in an extension exist. Of course, this being Objective-C, the developer could always invoke the method if they knew about it.

But at least it makes the point — don't look behind the curtain.

Loading the Sights

To do some sight loading, add the code in bold in Listing 1-6 to the already existing initWithName: method in Trip.m. This addition invokes the method you declared in the previous section, which loads the list of sights from a property list and turns them into Sight objects — this code is starting to get exciting.

Listing 1-6:   initWithName Now Invokes loadSights

```
- (id) initWithName:(NSString*) theTrip {

  if ((self = [super init])) {
    tripName = theTrip;
```

```
    [tripName retain];
    carInformation = [[CarInformation alloc]
                                        initWithTrip:self];
    car Servicing = [[CarServicing alloc] initWithTrip:self];
    weather = [[Weather alloc] init];
    [self loadSights];
  }
  return self;
}
```

Now you see how to actually use all that data you created in the plist.

Add the code in Listing 1-7 to `Trip.m`.

Listing 1-7: Using the plist

```
- (void) loadSights {

  NSString *sightsDataPath = [[NSBundle mainBundle]
    pathForResource:@"Sight" ofType:@"plist"];
  NSArray * sightsList = [[NSArray alloc]
                  initWithContentsOfFile:sightsDataPath];
  sights = [[NSMutableArray alloc]
                  initWithCapacity:[sightsList count]];

  for (NSMutableDictionary* sightData in sightsList) {
    Sight* newSight = [[Sight alloc] initWithTrip:self
                                  sightData:sightData];
    [sights addObject:newSight];
  }
}
```

This method starts by locating the `Sights.plist` you just created in your application bundle:

```
NSString *sightsDataPath = [[NSBundle mainBundle]
  pathForResource:@"Sights" ofType:@"plist"];
```

"What bundle?" you say? Well, when you build your iPhone application, Xcode packages it as a bundle — one containing the following:

✦ The application's executable code

✦ Any resources that the app has to use (for instance, the application icon, other images, and localized content — in this case the plist, html files, and .png files)

✦ The `info.plist`, also known as the information property list, which defines key values for the application, such as bundle ID, version number, and display name

Next it loads that file into the `sightsList` array:

```
NSArray * sightsList = [[NSArray alloc]initWithContentsOfFile
    :sightsDataPath];
```

`initWithContentsOfFile:`, as I mention earlier, is a method in the array and dictionary classes:

Next you allocate an array, `sights` (the array that you made a property earlier), to hold the `Sight` objects:

```
sights = [[NSMutableArray alloc]
                        initWithCapacity:[sightsList count]];
```

Then you take each entry in the `sightsList` array and use it to create a `Sight` object and load each into the `sights` array (the one you just created — this is why you made it mutable):

```
for (NSMutableDictionary* sightData in sightsList) {
    Sight* newSight = [[Sight alloc] initWithTrip self
                                        sightData:sightData];
    [sights addObject:newSight];
}
```

You allocate a new `Sight` and initialize it with the dictionary in the plist you created for each sight and that was reconstituted when you loaded the plist into the `sightsList`. After that, you add the new `Sight` object to the `sights` array. If you aren't familiar with the `for` method, I explain it — as well as more about arrays — in the next section.

Tiptoeing through an array

Two kinds of arrays are available to you in Cocoa. The first is an `NSMutableArray`, which allows you to add objects to the area as needed — that is, the amount of memory allocated to the class is dynamically adjusted as you add more objects.

The second kind of array is an `NSArray`, which allows you to store a fixed number of objects, which are specified when you initialize the array. Because in this case you need the dynamic aspect of an `NSMutableArray`, I start my explanation there. As you remember, you used an array to save the last view in Book V, Chapter 3.

`NSMutableArray` arrays (I just call them arrays from now on when what I have to say applies to both `NSArray` and `NSMutableArray`) are ordered collections that can contain any sort of object. The collection doesn't have to be made up of the same objects. So you can have a number of `Budget` objects, for example, or `Xyz` objects mixed in — all that's fine, as long as they're all objects.

As I've said, arrays can hold only objects. But sometimes you may, for example, want to put a placeholder in a mutable array and later replace it with the "real" object. You can use an `NSNull` object for this placeholder role.

This is how you allocate and initialize the mutable array.

```
sights = [[NSMutableArray alloc]
                    initWithCapacity:[sightsList count]];
```

When you create a mutable array, you have to estimate the maximum size, which helps optimization. This is just a formality, and whatever you put here does not limit the eventual size. Here I use `[sightsList count]` — this is the number of dictionaries you created —, each of which will provide the data for a corresponding `Sight` object.

After I create a mutable array, I can start to add objects to it.

```
[sights addObject:newSight];
```

When you add an object to an Objective-C array, the object isn't copied, but rather receives a `retain` message before it's added to the array. When an array is deallocated, each element is sent a `release` message.

Technically (computer science–wise) what makes a collection an array is that you access its elements using an index, and that index can be determined at runtime. You get an individual element from an array by sending the array the `objectAtIndex:` message, which returns the array element you requested.

Depending on what you are doing with the array or how you're using it (arrays are very useful), `objectAtIndex:` will be one of the main array methods that you use.

Another method you'll use (and actually *did* use already) is `count`, which gives you the number of elements in the array — I showed you that when I explained about initializing the arrays, where it looked like this:

```
sights = [[NSMutableArray alloc]
                    initWithCapacity:[sightsList count]];
```

Objective-C 2.0 provides a language feature that allows you to enumerate over the contents of a collection. This is called *fast enumeration,* and it became available in Mac OS X 10.5 (Leopard) with version 2.0 of Objective-C. As I've mentioned, this book is based on Mac OS 10.6 — and OS 3.0 on the iPhone. (If you need to program for OS X 10.4, you need to use an `NSEnumerator`, which I don't cover in this book.) Enumeration uses the `for in` feature, which is a variation on a `for` loop.

What enumeration effectively does is sequentially march though an array, starting at the first element and returning each element for you to do "something with." The "something with" you will want to do in this case is use that element as an argument in the `initWithTrip::` message.

For example, this code marches through the array and sends the `init WithTrip::` message using each element in the array (an `NSDictionary`).

```
for (NSMutableDictionary* sightData in sightsList) {
    Sight* newSight = [[Sight alloc] initWithTrip: self
                                        sightData: sightData];
    [sights addObject:newSight];
}
```

Here's how this works:

1. Take each entry (`for`) in the array (in `sightsList`) and copy it into the variable that you've declared (`NSMutableDictionary* sight Data`).

2. Use it as an argument in the `initWithTrip:` message `initWithTrip:sightData:`.

3. Continue until you run out of entries in the array.

The identifier `sightData` can be any name you choose. `NSDictionary` is the type of the object in the array (or it can be `id`, although I won't get into that here).

To be more formal, the construct you just used is called `for in`, and it looks like

```
for ( Type aVariable in expression ) { statements }
```

or

```
Type aVariable;
for ( aVariable in expression ) { statements }
```

where you fill in what is italicized. There is one catch, however: You aren't permitted to change any of the elements during the iteration, which means you can go through the array more than once without worry.

The following section takes a more detailed look at dictionaries.

Using dictionaries

Dictionaries are the citified versions of arrays. They both pretty much do the same things, but dictionaries add a new level of sophistication.

I love dictionaries, now. But I have to admit that when I started programming with Objective-C and Cocoa, trying to get my head around the idea of dictionaries was a real challenge — not because dictionaries are hard, because they really aren't. The problem was because of what you can do with them. Not only will you use them to hold property list objects, but you can also use them to hold application objects — just as you did with the array that holds Sight objects.

Understanding a dictionary's keys and values

So, in many ways dictionaries are like the arrays you used earlier — they are a container for other objects. Dictionaries are made up of pairs of *keys* and *values.* A key-value pair within a dictionary is called an *entry.* Both the key and the value must be *objects,* so each entry consists of one *object* that is the key (usually an NSString) and a second object that is that key's value (which can be anything, but in a property list must be a property list object). Within a dictionary, the keys are unique.

You use a key to look up the corresponding value. This works like your real-world dictionary, where the word is the key, and its definition is the value. (Do you suppose that's why they're called dictionaries?)

So, for example, if you have an NSDictionary that stores the name for each Sight, you can ask that dictionary to cough up the name (value) for the site name (key).

```
self.sightName = [sightData valueForKey: @"sight name"];
```

You'll see this in action when you implement the Sight methods in the next section.

Although you can use any kind of object as a key in an NSDictionary, keys you plan on using in property list dictionaries have to be strings, and I'll stick to that here. You can also have any kind of object for a value, but again, if you're using them in a property list, they all have to be property list objects as well.

NSDictionary has a couple of basic methods you will be using:

✦ count — The count method gives you the number of entries in the dictionary.

✦ objectForKey: — The objectForKey: method gives the value for a given key.

In addition, the methods writeToFile:atomically: and initWithContentsOfFile: cause a dictionary to write a representation of itself to a file and to read itself in from a file, respectively.

If an array or dictionary contains objects that are not property list objects, you can't save and then restore them using the built-in methods for doing so.

Just as with an array, a dictionary can be *static* (NSDictionary) or *mutable* (NSMutableDictionary). NSMutableDictionary adds a couple of additional basic methods — setObjectForKey: and removeObjectForKey:, which enable you to add and remove entries, respectively.

The Sight object initializes itself with the plist dictionary

Now you can enter the code for the Sight. Add the code in bold in Listing 1-8 to Sight.m.

Listing 1-8:   Sight.m

```
#import "RoadTripAppDelegate.h"
#import "Sight.h"
#import "Trip.h"

@implementation Sight
@synthesize coordinate;
@synthesize sightName, image, imageType;

- (id) initWithTrip: (Trip*) theTrip  sightData:
    (NSDictionary*) sightData {

  if ((self = [super init])) {

    trip = theTrip;
    [trip retain];
    self.sightName =
                [sightData valueForKey: @"sight name"];
    title = [sightData valueForKey: @"title"];
    [title retain];
    subtitle = [sightData valueForKey: @"subtitle"];
    [subtitle retain];
    resource = [sightData valueForKey: @"resource"];
    [resource retain];
    resourceType =
                [sightData valueForKey: @"resource type"];
    [resourceType retain];
    if ([sightData valueForKey: @"image"]) {
      self.image = [sightData valueForKey: @"image"];
      self.imageType =
                [sightData valueForKey: @"image type"];
    }
    else {
      image = nil;
      imageType = nil;
    }
```

```
   coordinate.latitude =
      [[sightData valueForKey: @"latitude"] doubleValue];
   coordinate.longitude =
      [[sightData valueForKey: @"longitude"] doubleValue];
   }
   return self;
}

@end
```

Although in general this is just another run-of-the-mill initialization method, I want to point out a few things.

First off, `coordinate` is a property here. You do this because in Chapter 3 of this minibook you'll be making `Sight` an annotation and, as I mention in Book V, Chapter 5, having a `coordinate` property is one of the requirements for an annotation. I'll have you implement the rest of what you need to do in Chapter 3 when I show you how to display `Sight`s (and later `Hotel`s) as annotations on the map.

You use the `valueForKey:` method I explain in the previous section to get the information from the dictionary and assign it to the `Sight` instance variable.

At this point, you only have a few more things left to do before you'll be able to see the results of your efforts so far — the `SightListController` with a list of sights and thumbnail pictures of each.

Book VI
Chapter 1

Show Me the Data

Displaying the Sights in the SightListController Table View

In this home stretch, the first thing you do is implement a few of the required methods in the `SightListController`. Replace the `numberOf SectionsInTableView:` and `numberOfRowsInSection:` methods in `SightListController.m` with the methods in Listing 1-9.

Listing 1-9:   Some Table View Methods

```
- (NSInteger)numberOfSectionsInTableView:
                                (UITableView *)tableView {

    return 1;
}

- (NSInteger)tableView:(UITableView *)tableView
            numberOfRowsInSection:(NSInteger)section {

    return [trip.sights count];
}
```

That's all pretty straightforward except for the [trip.sights count] business. trip.sights is the array of Sight objects you created in Trip, and as I explain earlier, the count method tells you how many entries there are in the array.

In order to display the list of sights, you'll be doing essentially what you did in Book V to create table views — fire up the tableView:cellForRow AtIndexPath: method in order to do a little bit of formatting. Listing 1-10 shows you how that was done back then when you were dealing with the RootViewController.

Listing 1-10: Displaying a Cell

```
- (UITableViewCell *)tableView:(UITableView *)tableView
        cellForRowAtIndexPath:(NSIndexPath *)indexPath {

  UITableViewCell *cell = [tableView
      dequeueReusableCellWithIdentifier:kCellIdentifier];
  if (cell == nil) {
    cell = [[[UITableViewCell alloc] initWithStyle:UITableVie
  wCellStyleDefault
            reuseIdentifier:kCellIdentifier] autorelease];

    cell.accessoryType =
  UITableViewCellAccessoryDisclosureIndicator;

    CGRect subViewFrame = cell.contentView.frame;
    subViewFrame.origin.x += kInset;
    subViewFrame.size.width = kInset+kSelectLabelWidth;

    UILabel *selectLabel = [[UILabel alloc]
                            initWithFrame:subViewFrame];
    selectLabel.textColor = [UIColor blackColor];
    selectLabel.highlightedTextColor =
                            [UIColor whiteColor];
    selectLabel.font = [UIFont boldSystemFontOfSize:18];
    selectLabel.backgroundColor = [UIColor clearColor];
    [cell.contentView addSubview:selectLabel];

    subViewFrame.origin.x += kInset+kSelectLabelWidth;
    subViewFrame.size.width = kDescriptLabelWidth;

    UILabel *descriptLabel = [[UILabel alloc]
                            initWithFrame:subViewFrame];
    descriptLabel.textColor = [UIColor grayColor];
    descriptLabel.highlightedTextColor =
                            [UIColor whiteColor];
    descriptLabel.font = [UIFont systemFontOfSize:14];
    descriptLabel.backgroundColor = [UIColor clearColor];
    [cell.contentView addSubview:descriptLabel];
```

```
        int menuOffset =
                [self menuOffsetForRowAtIndexPath:indexPath];


        NSDictionary *cellText =
                        [menuList objectAtIndex:menuOffset];
        selectLabel.text = [cellText objectForKey:kSelectKey];
        descriptLabel.text =
                        [cellText objectForKey:kDescriptKey];
        [selectLabel release];
        [descriptLabel release];
    }
    return cell;
}
```

Book VI
Chapter 1

Show Me the Data

As you can see, the text for each cell comes from a dictionary that acts as the model for each row.

In the case of the `SightListController`, instead of a dictionary, you'll be using a `Sight` object. Add the code in Listing 1-11 to `Sight.m`.

Listing 1-11: `tableView:cellForRowAtIndexPath:`

```
- (UITableViewCell *)tableView:(UITableView *)tableView
        cellForRowAtIndexPath:(NSIndexPath *)indexPath {

    UITableViewCell *cell = [tableView
        dequeueReusableCellWithIdentifier:kCellIdentifier];
    if (cell == nil) {
      cell = [[[UITableViewCell alloc] initWithStyle:UITabl
      eViewCellStyleDefault reuseIdentifier:kCellIdentifier]
      autorelease];
    }
    cell.textLabel.text = [((Sight*)[trip.sights
                    objectAtIndex:indexPath.row]) sightName];
    cell.imageView.image = [self createThumbNail:((Sight*)
                [trip.sights objectAtIndex:indexPath.row])];
    return cell;
}
```

This listing is a mostly ordinary `tableView:cellForRowAtIndexPath:` method code. What's interesting is that you're getting the cell's text from the `Sight` object in the `trip.sights` array:

```
cell.textLabel.text = [((Sight*)[trip.sights
                    objectAtIndex:indexPath.row]) sightName];
```

Similarly, you get the cell's image from the `Sight` object, create a thumbnail from it (I explain that later), and add that to the cell:

```
cell.imageView.image = [self createThumbNail:((Sight*)
                [trip.sights objectAtIndex:indexPath.row])];
```

Even though you are using the standard default cell style in our table view . . .

```
cell = [[[UITableViewCell alloc] initWithStyle:UITableV
    iewCellStyleDefault reuseIdentifier:kCellIdentifier]
    autorelease];
```

you can easily add an image by simply assigning the image to the right cell subview. As an image expands to the right, it pushes the text in the same direction.

Because you're using the `kCellIdentifier` constant (which makes changing your mind about values at some later point much easier), you also have to import the file that declares it.

```
#import "Constants.h"
```

Later, as you will see, you'll have the `Sight` also return a `NSURLRequest`, just as you did in the model objects in Book V. The idea here is to enable a Web view to display the content — in this case, a brief description of the sight.

The difference between the `SightListController` and the `RootView Controller` implementation of `tableView:cellForRowAtIndexPath` is that the `SightListController` implementation relies on model objects created for a file (a file that you could modify at some later point) rather than the hard coded dictionary you created.

You only have one thing left to do in order to see the `SightListController` table view populated with a nice list of sights and pretty thumbnail pictures, and that is implement the `createThumbNail:` method to take the images and reduce them to a size you can display in the table view.

Drawing the Thumbs

The code for transforming images into handy thumbnails is shown in Listing 1-12:

Listing 1-12: Creating the Thumbnails

```
- (UIImage*) createThumbNail:(Sight*) aSight {

  if (aSight.image) {
    NSString *filePath = [[NSBundle mainBundle]
    pathForResource:aSight.image
                            ofType:aSight.imageType];
    UIImage* selectedImage =
        [[UIImage alloc] initWithContentsOfFile:filePath];
    CGRect rect = CGRectMake(0.0, 0.0, 36, 36);
    UIGraphicsBeginImageContext(rect.size);
    [selectedImage drawInRect:rect];
    UIImage* theScaledImage =
            UIGraphicsGetImageFromCurrentImageContext();
    UIGraphicsEndImageContext();
    return theScaledImage;
  }
  else {
    return nil;
  }
}
```

I'm not going to get too much into drawing in this book (I'm saving that for my next book, *Developing iPhone Games For Dummies*), but I do want to lay down the basic steps:

1. Make sure there is an image to create a thumbnail from:

```
if (aSight.image) {
```

2. If the image is there, then you need to grab it from the bundle:

```
NSString *filePath =
  [[NSBundle mainBundle]pathForResource:aSight.image
                        ofType:aSight.imageType];
UIImage* selectedImage =
    [[UIImage alloc] initWithContentsOfFile:filePath];
```

3. Create a rectangle that corresponds to the size you want the image to be:

```
CGRect rect = CGRectMake(0.0, 0.0, 36, 36);
```

4. Use the `UIGraphicsBeginImageContext` function to create a new image-based graphics context:

```
UIGraphicsBeginImageContext(rect.size);
```

5. After creating this context, you can draw your image contents into it:

```
[selectedImage drawInRect:rect];
```

and then use the `UIGraphicsGetImageFromCurrentImageContext` function to generate an image based on what you drew:

```
UIImage* theScaledImage =
    UIGraphicsGetImageFromCurrentImageContext();
```

6. When you're done creating images, use the
   `UIGraphicsEndImageContext` function to close the graphic context:

   ```
   UIGraphicsEndImageContext();
   ```

7. Return the new scaled image:

   ```
   return scaledImage;
   ```

Compile and Run RoadTrip

Your code should now compile and run correctly. You'll have a couple of complier warnings because you haven't implemented the `title` and `subtitle` methods of `Sight`, but you'll get to that soon. If you select Sights for the main table view, you'll see a list of sights, with an image. But if you select a row, you won't see anything because you haven't implemented its `tableView:didSelectRowAtIndexPath:` method yet.

That's what you'll need to do next.

Houston, We Have a Problem . . .

In Book V, you implemented the generic `WebViewController` that can — and did — display any kind of content that the user selected in the main table view (via the `RootViewController`), and no doubt you'd like to use it here as well.

Using `Weather` as an example, you implemented it in the following way back in Book V. (I go into more detail in the next chapter when I explain the problem you are now facing in more detail).

1. The `RootViewController`, which knows what the user wants to see displayed, sends a selector to the `WebViewController` in its `tableView:didSelectRowAtIndexPath:` method.

2. The `WebViewController` stores the selector when it initializes itself.

3. The `WebViewController` view sends a message to `Trip` perform the selector.

4. `Trip` performs the selector method, which sends a message to the `Weather` object, which returns the `NSURLRequest`.

5. `WebViewController` uses that `NSURLRequest` in its message to the Web view to load the necessary data.

The problem being . . .

The implementation of the generic `WebViewController` was predicated on `Trip` being able to identify the content object that owned the content that needed to be displayed. In the case of the content in Book V, this worked well because for any given choice of content (car information, car servicing information, or the weather) there was indeed only one possible object that was associated with a user choice. For example, if the user chose Car Information, there was only one `CarInformation` object for `Trip` to get the `NSURLRequest` from. But in the case of `Sight`, that isn't true. How, then, does `Trip` know which `Sight` object to send a message to?

What I'd like to do is include that information as a selector argument —, but the `performSelectorOnMainThread:::` method does have its limitations — the selector you want performed can't return a value and *can only take either a single argument of type `id` or no arguments at all.* Unfortunately, you are already using your single argument allowance to send a reference to the `WebViewController` that is used to send that very same `WebViewController` the `loadWebView:` message.

Fortunately, as you'll see in the next chapter, there's a good solution: making the model objects `WebViewController` delegates.

**Book VI
Chapter 1**

Show Me the Data

Chapter 2: A More Flexible Generic Controller

In This Chapter

- ✔ **Understanding the limitations of the WebViewController implementation**
- ✔ **Using delegation to encapsulate the model objects**
- ✔ **Creating your very own protocol**
- ✔ **Keeping file loading from stopping your application dead in its tracks**

As you discovered at the close of the preceding chapter, after you add multiple objects of the same type to your app mix, the techniques you've been using all along to create a generic controller just stop working. In this chapter, I show you how to accomplish what you're after by using delegation instead.

It turns out that delegation, as you probably have noticed, is used often in the framework. In fact, as you'll see, it's also used in the next chapter when I show you the preferred way to deal with downloading data — the URL loading system. This chapter, then, not only shows you how to implement a more sophisticated version of your generic `WebViewController`, and shows you how to take advantage of delegation in your own applications, but also serves to provide the background you need to have in order to make it easier for you to use the asynchronous version of the URL loading system.

Seeing How the Old School Generic Controller Worked

To refresh your memory, you implemented your generic controller by sending a selector to the `WebViewController` that the `WebViewController` would have the `Trip` object perform in order to return the `WebView Controller` an `NSURLRequest` object based on the data that the user was interested in. It would get the `NSURLRequest` from a model object — `Weather`, for example. The `WebViewController` would then pass that on to its Web view, which would then load the data.

We are going to change that. You stay with the `NSURLRequest` object, but the object that supplies the `NSURLRequest` will be asked to do it in a much different way.

Stepping through the process

Here's how the sequence went with the Old School generic controller:

1. The RootViewController sends a selector to the WebViewController.

   The RootViewController, which knows what the user wants to see displayed, sends a selector to the WebViewController in its tableVi ew:didSelectRowAtIndexPath: method. (For the rest of this section I'll be highlighting the most important things you need to pay attention to in bold).

   ```
   if  realtime) targetController =
       [WebViewController alloc] initWithTrip:trip
       tripSelector:@selector(returnWeather:)
       webControl:YES
       title:NSLocalizedString(@"Weather", @"Weather")];
   else [self displayOfflineAlert:
       [[menuList objectAtIndex:menuOffset]
                               objectForKey:kSelectKey]];
   ```

2. The WebViewController stores the selector when it initializes itself.

   Check out the bolded section in Listing 2-1.

Listing 2-1:   WebViewController Initializer

```
- (id) initWithTrip:(Trip*)aTrip tripSelector:(SEL)
  aTripSelector webControl:(BOOL) ifWebControl
  title:(NSString*) aTitle{
 if (self = [super initWithNibName:@"WebViewController"
                                        bundle:nil]) {
   self.title = aTitle;
   tripSelector = aTripSelector;
   trip = aTrip;
   webControl = ifWebControl;
   [trip retain];
  }
  return self;
}
```

3. The WebViewController sends a message to Trip to perform the selector (method).

   Again, the bolded section in Listing 2-2 shows what that looks like.

Listing 2-2: Sending the performSelectorOnMainThread::: Message

```
- (void)viewDidLoad {

  [super viewDidLoad];
  if (webControl) {
    UIBarButtonItem *backButton = [[UIBarButtonItem alloc]
      initWithTitle:@"Back" style:UIBarButtonItemStylePlain
                  target:self action:@selector(goBack:)];
    self.navigationItem.rightBarButtonItem = backButton;
    [backButton release];
  }
  [trip performSelectorOnMainThread:tripSelector
                    withObject:self waitUntilDone:NO];
}
```

4. `Trip` does what it's told and performs the selector method.

Listing 2-3 gives the details.

Listing 2-3: Trip's returnWeather

```
- (void) returnWeather:(id) theViewController {

  [theViewController
                loadWebView:[weather weatherRealtime]];
  }
```

5. The selector method sends a message to the `Weather` object, which returns the `NSURLRequest`.

Listing 2-4 has that part.

Listing 2-4: Weather's weatherRealTime Method

```
- (NSURLRequest*) weatherRealtime {

  NSURL *url = [NSURL URLWithString:@"http://www.
    weather.com/outlook/travel/businesstraveler/local/
    UKXX0085?lswe=CarServicing,%20UNITED%20KINGDOM&lwsa=Weathe
    rLocalUndeclared&from=searchbox_typeahead"];
  if (url == NULL) NSLog( @"Data not found %@", url);

  NSURLRequest* theNSURLRequest = [NSURLRequest
    requestWithURL:url];
  return theNSURLRequest;
}
```

This code simply creates an `NSURLRequest` that the Web view needs to load the data.

6. The `WebViewController` uses that `NSURLRequest` in its message to the `webView` to load the necessary data.

   Here's that message — bolded in Listing 2-5.

Listing 2-5: Loading the Web View Data

```
- (void)loadWebView:(NSURLRequest*) theNSURLRequest {

  [webView loadRequest:theNSURLRequest];
}
```

The `loadRequest` message is sent to the `webView`, and the Weather Web site is displayed.

The problem being . . .

As I said at the end of Chapter 1 of this minibook, this implementation of the `WebViewController` is predicated on `Trip` being able to identify the content object that owned the content that needed to be displayed. In the case of the content in Book V, this wasn't an issue because for any given choice of content (car information, car servicing information, or the weather) there was indeed only one possible object that was associated with a user choice. For example, if the user chose Car Information, there was only one `CarInformation` object for `Trip` to get the `NSURLRequest` from. But in the case of `Sight`, that isn't true. How does `Trip` know which `Sight` object to send a message to?

You may remember from Chapter 1 that, although I'd like to include that information as a selector argument, the `performSelectorOnMain Thread:::` method can't return a value and can only take either a single argument of type `id` or no arguments at all. Unfortunately, as you saw in Step 3 in the preceding section, you're already using your single argument allowance to send a reference to the `WebViewController` that is used to send it the `loadWebView:` message. (The bolded code in the following block is the smoking gun here.)

```
[trip performSelectorOnMainThread:tripSelector
    withObject:self waitUntilDone:NO];

- (void) returnWeather:(id) theViewController {

[theViewController loadWebView:[weather weatherRealtime]];

}
```

Although it isn't very PC to say this, there are other ways to skin a cat.

One way is to have the `SightListController` set some kind of index in `Trip` to let it know which `Sight` object in the `sights` array the user has requested information about. Although this would work, you're starting down a slippery slope of tighter coupling between the `Trip`, `SightListController`, and the `sights` array. We would, after all, like all of our objects to be as ignorant as possible of how other objects work. That makes changing things much easier.

A better alternative is to use a pattern that the framework uses when faced with a similar problem.

After all, the challenge you face here is one that is faced by the framework on a regular basis. For example, when you start up an application, the framework wants to give you the opportunity to do some application-specific initialization. But because its code was probably written before your application was a gleam in your eye, it has no idea that your application even exists.

The solution to that is to have you create an application *delegate* that implements the `ApplicationDidFinishLoading` method. At start up, the `UIApplication` object's `delegate` instance variable is assigned a reference to your app delegate object — if you have implemented it. (I show you later how the application object knows that fact.) The `UIApplication` object then sends your app delegate the `ApplicationDidFinishLoading` message.

You can use the same technique here. I show you how to make the `Weather`, `CarInformation`, `CarServicing`, and all of the `Sight` objects I've come up with so far delegates of the `WebViewController` and then change just a few things so that instead of sending the `performSelectorOnMain Thread:::` message to the `Trip` object, it sends a similar request to its delegate instead.

I start with more about delegation.

Understanding Delegation

Delegation is a pattern (I explain patterns and their importance in more detail in *iPhone Application Development For Dummies*) used extensively in the `UIKit` and `AppKit` frameworks to customize the behavior of an object without subclassing. Instead, one object (a framework object) delegates the task of implementing one of its methods to another object.

To implement a delegated method, you put the code for your application-specific behavior in a separate *(delegate)* object. When a request is made of the delegating object that it wants to give you the opportunity to respond to, the delegate's method that implements the application-specific behavior is invoked.

The methods a class delegates are defined in a *protocol*. Protocols can be *formal* or *informal*. In this case I'm going to have you use a formal one; I explain why in a second.

Naming conventions

To help you recognize a delegate method, Apple has implemented some naming conventions that it uses in the framework

✦ The name should start with the name of the class that's sending the message, but you should omit the prefix (UI for example) and make the first letter lowercase. For example, as shown below with the table view and application delegate method, respectively (in bold):

```
- (BOOL)tableView:(NSTableView *)tableView
                         shouldSelectRow:(int)row;
- (BOOL)application:(NSApplication *)sender
                  openFile:(NSString *)filename;
```

You follow the class name with a colon if there is an argument, as shown in the preceding code.

✦ If there is only one argument — say, the sender — you add a description of the method to the class name. For example

```
- (BOOL)applicationOpenUntitledFile:
                    (NSApplication *)sender;
```

Based on that, you'll name your new delegate method:

```
- (void) webViewController:
      (WebViewController *) controller
      nsurlRequestProcessMethod:(SEL)theProcessMethod;
```

As you can see, you'll still be using a selector (you can't get rid of them sometimes) but in a different way.

Using Protocols

The Objective-C language provides a way to formally declare a list of methods (including declared properties) as a protocol. Formal protocols are supported by the language and the runtime system. For example, the compiler can check for types based on protocols, and objects can report whether they conform to a protocol. That's why I have you use a formal protocol — you can never be too safe when it comes to writing code.

Declaring a protocol

You declare formal protocols with the @protocol directive. To have your WebViewController require that its delegates implement a WebView Controller:nsurlRequestProcessMethod: method, you would code the following:

```
@protocol WebViewControllerDelegate <NSObject>

- (void) webViewController:
        (WebViewController *) controller
        nsurlRequestProcessMethod:(SEL)theProcessMethod;

@end
```

Methods can be optional or required. If you don't mark a method as optional, it is assumed to be required; but you can make that designation specific via the use of the `@required` keyword.

In the `WebViewControllerDelegate` protocol I just declared, I have a required method — `WebViewController:nsurlRequestProcess Method:`

The more formal representation is

```
@protocol ProtocolName

  method declarations

@end
```

Generally, protocol declarations are in the file of the class that defines it. In this case, you will add the `WebViewControllerDelegate` protocol declaration to the `WebViewController.h` file.

Adding delegation to WebViewController

To implement delegation in `WebViewController`, start by adding the code in bold to `WebViewController.h`. You'll also have to add the code in bold that has been commented out and then delete the code in bold that has been formatted with a strikethrough in Listing 2-6.

This business about deleting the bolded stuff with strikethrough and adding the unstruck bolded stuff will be the general operating procedure for the rest of this chapter (and minibook), so I won't bore you by repeating these instructions over and over and over.

Listing 2-6:   The new WebViewController.h File

```
#import <UIKit/UIKit.h>
@class Trip;

@interface WebViewController : UIViewController
   <UIWebViewDelegate> {
```

(continued)

Listing 2-6 *(continued)*

```
// SEL                     tripSelector;
  id                       delegate;
  Trip                     *trip;
  IBOutlet UIWebView       *webView;
  BOOL                      webControl;
}
- (void)loadWebView:(NSURLRequest*) theNSURLRequest;
//- (id) initWithTrip:(Trip*)aTrip tripSelector:(SEL)
    aTripSelector webControl:(BOOL) ifWebControl
    title:(NSString*) aTitle;
- (id) initWithTrip:(Trip*)aTrip  delegate:(id) theDelegate
    webControl:(BOOL) ifWebControl title:(NSString*) aTitle;

@end

@protocol WebViewControllerDelegate <NSObject>
- (void) webViewController:(WebViewController*)
                                              controller
        nsurlRequestProcessMethod:(SEL)theProcessMethod;

@end
```

You did several things here:

1. Added the instance variable `delegate`.

   This is the object that will implement the behavior you specified in the protocol. These are generally declared to be a generic object (`id`), since the point here is that you won't know what class is implementing the delegate behavior.

2. Declared the `WebViewControllerDelegate` protocol.

3. Deleted the instance variables and method declaration you had previously used to implement the generic `WebViewController`.

Changing the way WebViewController is instantiated and initialized

With the changes you have made to `WebViewController`, you'll have to make some changes in the `RootViewController` code that allocates and initializes it.

More specifically, make the following changes to the `RootViewController`'s `tableView:didSelectRowAtIndexPath:` method, as shown in Listing 2-7.

Listing 2-7: Changes to tableView:didSelectRowAtIndexPath:

```
switch (menuOffset) {
    case 0:
      if (realtime) targetController = [[MapController
                              alloc] initWithTrip:trip];
      else [self displayOfflineAlert:
          [[menuList objectAtIndex:menuOffset]
                              objectForKey:kSelectKey]];
      break;
    case 1:
      targetController = [[SightListController alloc]
                                initWithTrip:trip];
      break;
    case 2:
  //      targetController =
              [[HotelController alloc] initWithTrip:trip];
      break;
    case 3:
//      if (realtime) targetController =
            [[WebViewController alloc] initWithTrip:trip
            tripSelector:@selector(returnWeather:)
//          webControl:YES title:
                NSLocalizedString(@"Weather", @"Weather")];
      if (realtime) targetController =
          [[WebViewController   alloc] initWithTrip:trip
          delegate:[ trip returnWeatherDelegate]
          webControl:YES title:
          NSLocalizedString(@"Weather", @"Weather")];
      else [self displayOfflineAlert:
          [[menuList objectAtIndex:menuOffset]
                              objectForKey:kSelectKey]];
      break;
    case 4:
//      targetController = [[WebViewController alloc]
          initWithTrip:trip tripSelector:@selector
          (returnCarServicingInformation:)
//          webControl:NO title: NSLocalizedString
                    (@"Car Servicing", @"Car Servicing")];
      targetController =
        [[WebViewController alloc] initWithTrip:trip
          delegate: [trip returnCarServicingDelegate]
          webControl:NO title:NSLocalizedString
                  (@"Car Servicing", @"Car Servicing")];
      break;
    case 5:
//      targetController = [[WebViewController alloc]
          initWithTrip:trip tripSelector:@selector
          (returnCarInformation:)
//          webControl:NO title:NSLocalizedString
                    (@"The Car", @"Car Information")];
```

(continued)

Listing 2-7 *(continued)*

```
        targetController = [[WebViewController alloc]
            initWithTrip:trip
            delegate: [trip returnCarInformationDelegate]
            webControl:NO title:NSLocalizedString
                    (@"The Car", @"Car Information")];
    break;
}
```

The change you made here was simply to initialize `WebViewController` with the right delegate, depending on what the user selected in the table view. You changed it from using a selector as an argument to using its delegate instead.

The only involvement now by `Trip` is to pass back the delegate for each of the selections.

Of course, you'll also need to change the initialization method in the `WebViewController`. Make the changes shown in Listing 2-8 to `WebViewController.m`.

Listing 2-8:   Implementing the New Initialization Method

```
//- (id) initWithTrip:(Trip*)aTrip tripSelector:(SEL)
    aTripSelector webControl:(BOOL) ifWebControl
    title:(NSString*) aTitle {
- (id) initWithTrip:(Trip*)aTrip  delegate:(id) theDelegate
    webControl:(BOOL) ifWebControl title:(NSString*) aTitle{

    if (self = [super initWithNibName:@"WebViewController"
    bundle:nil]) {
      self.title = aTitle;
//     tripSelector = aTripSelector;
    delegate = theDelegate;
    trip = aTrip;
    webControl = ifWebControl;
    [trip retain];
    }
    return self;
}
```

All you've done here is eliminate the `tripSelector` assignment and replace it with the `delegate` assignment instead.

You also need to make some changes in `viewDidLoad`, as shown in Listing 2-9. You'll be sending the delegate a message instead of performing the selector. Make these changes to `WebViewController.m`.

Listing 2-9:   Updating viewDidLoad

```
- (void)viewDidLoad {

  [super viewDidLoad];
  if (webControl) {
    UIBarButtonItem *backButton = [[UIBarButtonItem alloc]
                                   initWithTitle:@"Back" styl
    e:UIBarButtonItemStylePlain
                                   target:self action:@
    selector(goBack:)];
    self.navigationItem.rightBarButtonItem = backButton;
    [backButton release];
  }
  // [trip performSelectorOnMainThread:tripSelector
  withObject:self waitUntilDone:NO];
  [delegate webViewController:self
      nsurlRequestProcessMethod:@selector(loadWebView:)];
}
```

Again, this change is very straightforward. You've changed the method
so that it now simply sends a message to its delegate to construct the
NSURLRequest. You'll see in a second that this will essentially set off a
chain of events — similar in end result, but very different in execution — to
the chain of events I described at the beginning of this chapter.

One further note here.

Because the delegate method WebViewController:nsurlRequestProc
essMethod: is *required* by the WebViewControllerDelegate protocol,
you really don't have to be concerned if it's implemented. If it were optional
though, as many of the framework delegate methods are, you would need to
know whether the delegate implemented the method.

To do that, you can use the respondsToSelector: message:

```
if ([delegate respondsToSelector: @selector
      (webViewController:nsurlRequestProcessMethod:)]) {
  ... do something
}
```

respondsToSelector: is an NSObject method that tells you whether a
method has been implemented. As I said, because this particular method is
required, I don't have to determine that. However, I wanted to show you how
much information is available at runtime in Objective-C and how to implement delegation for the optional methods of formal protocols and for all
methods of informal protocols.

Adopting a protocol

Adopting a protocol is similar in some ways to declaring a superclass. In both cases, you're adding methods to your class. When you use a superclass, you're adding inherited methods; when you use a protocol, you're adding methods declared in the protocol list. A class adopts a formal protocol by listing the protocol within angle brackets after the superclass name.

```
@interface ClassName : ItsSuperclass < protocol list >
```

A class can adopt more than one protocol, and if so, names in the protocol list are separated by commas.

```
@interface Translator : NSObject < English, Italian >
```

Just as with any other class, you can add instance variables, properties, and even nonprotocol methods to a class that adopts a protocol.

In this case, the model classes will be adopting the WebViewControllerDelegate protocol.

Add the code in Listing 2-10 to the Sight.h. I show you how this works with the Sight class because it was the cause of the problems in the first place. Later, I have you apply it to the rest of the classes that will need to use it — CarInformation, CarServicing, and Weather.

Listing 2-10:   Modifying Sight.h

```
#import <MapKit/MapKit.h>
#import "WebViewController.h"
@class  Trip;
@class ServerManager;
@interface Sight : NSObject <WebViewControllerDelegate> {

    NSString                *sightName;
    CLLocationCoordinate2D   coordinate;
    NSString                *title;
    NSString                *subtitle;
    NSString                *resource;
    NSString                *resourceType;
    NSString                *image;
    NSString                *imageType;
    Trip                    *trip;
    ServerManager           *sightServerManager;
    NSMutableData           *receivedData;
    SEL                      processMethod;
    UIViewController        *viewController;
}
```

```
@property (nonatomic, retain)    NSString *sightName;
@property (nonatomic, retain)    NSString* image;
@property (nonatomic, retain)    NSString* imageType;;
@property (nonatomic) CLLocationCoordinate2D coordinate;
- (NSString*) title;
- (NSString*) subtitle;
- (id) initWithTrip: (Trip*) the Trip
                        sightData:(NSDictionary*) sightData;

@end
```

As you can see, besides adopting the `WebViewControllerDelegate` protocol, there are a few new instance variables you need to add — I explain them in the next chapter.

Now, add the code in Listing 2-11 to `Sight.m` to implement the protocol method.

Listing 2-11:   Implementing the Protocol Method

```
- (void) webViewController:
                          (WebViewController *) controller
        nsurlRequestProcessMethod:(SEL)theProcessMethod {

  viewController = controller;
  processMethod = theProcessMethod;
  RoadTripAppDelegate *appDelegate = (RoadTripAppDelegate *)
    [[UIApplication sharedApplication] delegate];
  BOOL realtime = !appDelegate.useStoredData;
  if (realtime) {
    NSString*  urlString = [[NSString alloc] initWithFormat:
    @"%@%@.%@", @"http://nealgoldstein.com/", resource,
    resourceType];
    [self downloadData: urlString];
  }
  else {
    [self get Data];
  }
}
```

Before I explain what is going on here, I want to discuss a little more about protocols.

When you adopt a protocol, you must implement all the required methods the protocol declares; otherwise, the compiler issues a warning. As you can see, the `Sight` class does define all the required methods declared in the `WebViewControllerDelegate` protocol.

Even though `Sight` implements a protocol that is declared in the `WebViewController` object, it does not automatically have access to the instance variables of the `WebViewController` object. This means that any of those instance variables that need to be accessed by delegates must be properties. This is also why the naming convention — the one that starts with a class name and passes a reference to the delegator — makes sense. This gives the delegate a consistent way to access those instance variables (and any methods it needs as well).

As you noticed, though, the file access looks very different from what you're used to. That's because I have a second problem to deal with: the issue of file loading. That's what I explain starting in the next section

Asynchronous File Loading

Previously downloading a file from a server on the Internet and making it available to the `WebViewController` and subsequently the `WebView` was not very complex. Listing 2-12 shows how you did it in `CarServicing`.

Listing 2-12:   CarServicing File Access

```
- (NSURLRequest*) returnCarServicingInformation {

  NSURL *carServicingData = nil;
  RoadTripAppDelegate *appDelegate = (RoadTripAppDelegate *)
   [[UIApplication sharedApplication] delegate];
  BOOL realtime = !appDelegate.useStoredData;
  if (realtime) {
    carServicingData = [NSURL URLWithString:@"http://
    nealgoldstein.com/CarServicing.html"];
    [self saveCarServicingData:@"CarServicing"
    withDataURL:carServicingData];
    if (!carServicingData) NSLog(@"data not there for
    CarServicing");

  }
  else {
    carServicingData = [self getCarServicingData:@"CarServic
    ing"];
  }

  NSURLRequest* theNSURLRequest =
         [NSURLRequest requestWithURL:carServicingData];
  return theNSURLRequest;
}

- (void) saveCarServicingData:(NSString*) fileName
   withDataURL:(NSURL*) url  {
```

```
NSData *dataLoaded =
                   [NSData dataWithContentsOfURL:url];
if (dataLoaded == NULL)
                       NSLog( @"Data not found %@", url);
NSArray *paths = NSSearchPathForDirectoriesInDomains
  (NSDocumentDirectory, NSUserDomainMask, YES);
NSString *documentsDirectory = [paths objectAtIndex:0];
NSString *filePath = [documentsDirectory stringByAppendingP
  athComponent:fileName];
[dataLoaded writeToFile:filePath atomically:YES];
}

-(NSURL*) getCarServicingData:(NSString*) fileName {

  NSArray *paths = NSSearchPathForDirectoriesInDomains
    (NSDocumentDirectory, NSUserDomainMask, YES);
  NSString *documentsDirectory = [paths objectAtIndex:0];
  NSString *filePath = [documentsDirectory stringByAppendingP
    athComponent:fileName];
  NSURL* theNSURL= [NSURL fileURLWithPath:filePath];
  if (theNSURL == NULL) NSLog (@"Data not there");
  return theNSURL;
}
```

I explain how this code works in Book V. Basically, you check to see whether or not you want to use real time data. If you do, you download the file

```
NSData *dataLoaded = [NSData dataWithContentsOfURL:url];
```

and then save it. You then construct the NSURLRequest, which points to the downloaded data, and then return (via Trip) the NSURLRequest to the WebViewController, which in turn passes it to its webView.

To construct the NSURLRequest, you create an NSURL — an object that includes the utilities necessary for accessing the file. This is essentially the file's location. Then you create an NSURLRequest from the NSURL. The NSURLRequest is what the WebViewController needs to send to the Web view in the loadRequest: message, which tells it to load the data associated with that NSURLRequest. Remember, at this point the file has already been downloaded and you are passing the necessary information to the WebViewController, and subsequently the Web view to access it.

The NSURLRequest class encapsulates a URL and any protocol-specific properties, in a protocol-independent manner. The NSURLRequest class is also part of the URL loading system — a set of classes and protocols that provide the underlying capability for an application to access the data specified by a URL. (No more on that for now — you get lots more on the URL loading system in the next chapter.)

At the heart of the download is the `dataWithContentsOfURL:` message that does the download of the file from the supplied URL. It's also the heart of a potential real problem.

The problem with the `dataWithContentsOfURL:` message is that while it's executing, everything else in your applications stops. It sends out the load request to the server, waits until it gets the data back, and then and only then does it return control to the main execution thread. That means for large files, or for large numbers of files, the user is blocked from doing anything until all downloads are done.

What you need to do in almost every application with any quantity of downloaded data, is the ability to download files asynchronously — or to allow other things to go on while waiting for the data.

In the next chapter, I show you how to do just that, as well as explain the URL loading system — the preferred way for your iPhone application to access data.

What I won't be able to show you, however, is what you can do to allow the user to continue using the application while files download. (Although one strategy I often use is to start any required downloads before the user needs the data — at application startup time for example). I leave that for you to explore on your own.

Chapter 3: Working the URL Loading System

In This Chapter

- ✔ Understanding the URL loading system
- ✔ Downloading data asynchronously
- ✔ Using delegation in displaying data
- ✔ Displaying the sights (as annotations) on a map

In the grand scheme of things, downloading only a small bit of data from the Internet has no impact on your app's performance, but when that begins to increase, you're going to run into trouble. That's because right now when the downloading is taking place, everything else stops. You can imagine, then, how annoyed the users will be when you start downloading lots of images and text for the sights in the RoadTrip application. Users may even have to get themselves another iPhone to keep themselves amused while waiting for the data to finish downloading.

Again, this isn't an issue in small simple apps, but it's something you must address if you're creating industrial-strength applications. By this I mean not just business applications, but anything that delivers a significant amount of content to the user.

Interestingly enough, the solution to the problem, the URL loading system, involves the use of delegation as well, as do many of the other synchronous processes you have and will use (the XML parser you used in Book V, for example).

Finally, when you *do* get the sights loaded, you're going to want to display them on the map. This chapter goes into more detail about how to do that. I also extend the map discussion from the last book and show you how to create model objects that can display themselves as annotations as well.

URL Loading System Overview

The URL loading system is a set of classes and protocols that provide the underlying capability for an application to access the data pointed to by a URL.

NSURLDownload

Although the NSURLConnection (the class you will be using) provides data to the delegate as the data is downloaded, there's also another class that's part of the URL Loading System — NSURLDownload, which writes the request data directly to disk — and I leave that for you to explore on your own. There are some significant differences between the two. For example, the NSURLConnection class provides a delegate method that allows an application to control the caching, although you won't be doing that here, while NSURLDownload downloads aren't cached.

The most commonly used classes in the URL loading system allow an application to create a request for the contents of that URL and then download it from there.

A request for the contents of a URL is represented by an NSURLRequest object — something you're already using. The NSURLRequest class encapsulates a URL and any protocol properties, in a way that is independent of the protocol itself.

An NSURLRequest contains two basic data elements of a load request: the URL to load and instructions on what to do with any cached data. It also enables you to set the timeout for a connection. In this discussion, I talk only about the data elements, but just remember that the timeout stuff is available as well, and it's something you may want to explore on your own.

Because you're already using an NSURLRequest in the current WebViewController as well as its Web View implementation (no coincidence here), all I have to do is show you how to add some additional functionality provided by the URL loading system to make the downloads *asynchronous* — in other words, going on while the user is using the application.

To do that, I show you how to use the NSURLConnection class to make the connection to the server needed by an NSURLRequest object and download the contents.

Authentication and credentials

When I first started programming on the iPhone, I was concerned about servers or Web sites that required a password to access them — how the heck do you do that? Although I don't use it in the example, this functionality is available to you in the URL loading system as well.

The URL loading system provides classes that you can use for credentials as well as providing secure credential persistence (or storage of the credentials).

Credentials can be specified to persist for a single request, for the duration of an application's launch, or permanently in the user's keychain. As I said, although you don't need to use it here, I show you an example a bit later of how to deal with servers that require a username and password.

Cookie storage

As you may be aware, cookies are often used to provide storage of data across URL requests. The URL loading system provides interfaces to create and manage cookies as well as sending and receiving cookies from Web servers.

Protocol support

If you're unfamiliar with what it means, a protocol is a convention that defines a set of rules that computers follow to communicate with each other across a network. It includes rules for connection, communication, and data transfer between two computers. The URL loading system natively supports http, https, file, and ftp protocols, and also allows you to extend the protocols that are supported for transferring data.

Using NSURLConnection — Downloading data asynchronously

`NSURLConnection` provides the most flexible method of downloading the contents of a URL, so of course you'll be using it. (Only the best for my readers.) It provides a simple interface for creating and canceling a connection, and it does that by using delegate methods to control what happens during the process.

Downloading data synchronously

As I explained, `arrayWithContents OfURL:` the method you used to download data, is a blocking call. Typically, when working with data over networks, it's best to do things asynchronously.

While this is true, `NSURLConnection` is not dogmatic in this regard. When necessary, it does provide simple and convenient support for the synchronous downloading of the contents of a URL using the class method `send SynchronousRequest:returning Response:error:`. Using this method is simple and convenient, but it has some limitations, including the following:

✔ Your application is blocked until the data has been completely downloaded, an error occurs, or the request times out.

✔ There isn't much support for authentication. If the request requires authentication in order to make the connection, valid credentials must already be available in the `NSURLCredentialStorage` or must be provided as part of the requested URL.

✔ There is no means of modifying the default behavior of response caching or accepting server redirects.

Although this may appear daunting at first, it actually isn't much more complex than the table views you've been using. In fact, all you need to do is create the connection and then implement a few delegate methods, such as

+ `connection:didReceiveResponse:`
+ `connection:didReceiveData:`
+ `connection:didFailWithError:`
+ `connectionDidFinishLoading:`

To implement asynchronous loading in the RoadTrip application, you need to create a new class: `ServerManager`.

By now you know the drill.

1. **Choose File⇨New from the main menu (or press ⌘+N) to get the New File dialog.**

2. **In the leftmost column of the dialog, first select Cocoa Touch Classes under the iPhone OS heading. Then select the Objective-C class template in the topmost pane, make sure the Subclass drop-down menu has `NSObject` selected, and then click Next.**

You see a new dialog asking for some more information.

3. **Enter ServerManager in the File Name field and then click Finish.**

You'll be using `ServerManager` as the main model class.

Start by adding the code in bold in Listing 3-1 to `ServerManager.h`.

Listing 3-1:   Working with ServerManager.h

```
@class Trip;

@interface ServerManager : NSObject
                                    <UIAlertViewDelegate> {

  NSURLConnection *currentConnection;
  id               delegate;
  NSMutableData   *rxData;
  Trip            *trip;
  SEL              sucessful;
  SEL              connectionError;
}
- (id) initWithModel:(Trip*)theModel delegate:receiver
     sucessfulSelector:(SEL)sucessfulSelector
     connectionErrorSelector:(SEL)connectionErrorSelector;
- (BOOL) get:(NSString*)urlString;
- (void) cancelConnection;
- (void) cancel;
@end
```

I'll be explaining all the instance variables and methods as I go along, but I want to start with the `get:` method that creates the `NSURLConnection` I just spoke of.

Enter the code in Listing 3-2 to `ServerManager.m`.

Listing 3-2: `get:` Makes the NSURLConnection

```
- (BOOL)get:(NSString *)urlString{

  [urlString retain];

  NSURLRequest *theRequest=[NSURLRequest
      requestWithURL:[NSURL URLWithString:urlString]
    cachePolicy:
    NSURLRequestReloadIgnoringLocalAndRemoteCacheData
      timeoutInterval:60.0];
  currentConnection=[[NSURLConnection alloc]
    initWithRequest:theRequest delegate:self];
  if (currentConnection) {
    rxData = [[NSMutableData alloc] init];
    return YES;
  }
  else {
    NSLog(@"request error ");
    [self cancel];
    return NO;
  }
}
```

Book VI
Chapter 3

Working the URL
Loading System

The `get:` method in Listing 3-2 shows you how to initiate a connection for a URL, the first step in the downloading process. This connection links you to the server or Web site you want to download data from. It begins by creating an `NSURLRequest` instance for the URL, specifying the cache access policy and timeout interval for the connection.

You'll use `NSURLRequestReloadIgnoringLocalAndRemoteCacheData`, which specifies that not only should the local cache data be ignored, but that everyone else who might have been doing any data caching (proxies and other intermediates) should ignore their caches so far as the protocol allows. You do have a few other choices:

```
NSURLRequestUseProtocolCachePolicy
NSURLRequestReloadIgnoringLocalCacheData
NSURLRequestReturnCacheDataElseLoad
NSURLRequestReturnCacheDataDontLoad
NSURLRequestReloadRevalidatingCacheData
```

I leave you to explore these on your own.

Stepping through the code in Listing 3-2, you'll note that your next task is to specify a timeout of 60 seconds. Then you create an NSURLConnection instance using the NSURLRequest and specifying the delegate.

```
currentConnection=[[NSURLConnection alloc]
    initWithRequest:theRequest delegate:self];
```

If the connection is successful, you create an instance of NSMutableData to store the data that will be provided to the delegate incrementally.

```
if (currentConnection) {
    rxData = [[NSMutableData alloc] init];
    return YES;
}
```

If NSURLConnection can't create a connection for the request, initWithRequest:delegate: returns nil, logs the errors, and cancels the connection — [self cancel].

```
else {
    NSLog(@"request error ");
    [self cancel];
    return NO;
}
```

The download starts immediately upon receiving the initWithRequest:delegate: message.

As I said, if things don't work out, you send yourself the cancel message. To set that up, enter the code in Listing 3-3 into ServerManager.m.

Listing 3-3: Adding the cancel Message

```
- (void)cancel {
  if (currentConnection) {
    [self cancelConnection];
  }
  if (rxData) {
    [rxData release];
    rxData = nil;
  }
}
```

cancel releases rxdata (the buffer you are using to hold the downloaded data) if it has been allocated and sends itself the cancelConnection message. Enter the code in Listing 3-4 to ServerManager.m to get that message set up for you.

Listing 3-4:   The cancelConnection Message

```
- (void)cancelConnection {

    [currentConnection cancel];
    [currentConnection release];
    currentConnection = nil;
}
```

All this method does is cancel and release the connection and set the instance variable to `nil;`.

You can cancel a connection any time before the delegate receives a `con nectionDidFinishLoading:` or `connection:didFailWithError:` message by sending the connection a `cancel` message.

connection:didReceiveResponse:

After the connection has been established, the delegate receives `connection:didReceiveResponse:` message. This message lets you know the server is out there and ready to roll.

You need to know that your delegate may receive the `connection:did ReceiveResponse:` message more than once for a connection. This could happen as a result of a server redirect or for a couple of other obscure reasons. This means that each time a delegate receives the `connection:didReceiveResponse:` message, it will need to reset any progress indication and discard all previously received data. To have the delegate do that, add the code in Listing 3-5 to `ServerManager.m`.

Listing 3-5:   connection:didReceiveResponse:

```
- (void)connection:(NSURLConnection *)connection didReceiveRe
    sponse:(NSURLResponse *)response {

    [rxData setLength:0];
}
```

The code simply resets the length of the received data to `0` each time it's called.

connection:didReceiveData:

When the connection is established (and you've been informed that the remote computer has made the connection via `connection:didReceive Response:`), your delegate is sent the `connection:didReceiveData:` messages as the data is received — this message is the Big Kahuna. (This whole process is similar to the XML parser process you used in Book V, Chapter 6.)

Because you may not get all the data in one fell swoop, you need to append the data as you receive it to any already received data in the NSMutableData object, rxdata, you created back in Listing 3-1.

This appending business is shown in Listing 3-6, which you should add to ServerManager.m.

Listing 3-6:   connection:didReceiveData:

```
- (void)connection:(NSURLConnection *)connection
                         didReceiveData:(NSData *)data {

    [rxData appendData:data];
}
```

You can also use the connection:didReceiveData: method to provide an indication of the connection's progress to the user.

connection:didFailWithError:

If an error crops up during the download, your delegate receives a connection:didFailWithError: message. You get an NSError object passed in as a parameter that specifies the details of the error. It also provides the URL of the request that failed in the user info dictionary using the key NSErrorFailingURLStringKey. I'll leave you to explore the innards of the NSError message on your own.

After your delegate receives a message connection:didFailWithError:, it's all over, and your delegate won't get any more messages for that connection.

Enter the code in Listing 3-7 into ServerManager.m to get this bit to work for you.

Listing 3-7:   connection:didFailWithError:

```
- (void)connection:(NSURLConnection *)connection
                     didFailWithError:(NSError *)error {
    [self cancel];
    [delegate performSelectorOnMainThread:connectionError
     withObject:error waitUntilDone:YES];

}
```

This code cancels the connection, sending itself the cancel message (which you implemented in Listing 3-4). It also performs the selector you specify when you initialize ServerManager. (You do that at the end of this section — "first things last" sometimes makes the flow easier to under-stand.) Because this is specific to a given application, and not your general implementation of the URL Loading System, I show you the business about performing the selector when I explain how `Sight` will use `ServerManager`.

connectionDidFinishLoading:

Finally, when the connection succeeds in downloading the request, your del-egate receives the `connectionDidFinishLoading:` message. — and it's all over. Your delegate will receive no further messages from the connection, and you can release the `NSURLConnection` object.

Enter the code in Listing 3-8 to `ServerManager.m` to put the icing on the cake.

Book VI Chapter 3

Working the URL Loading System

Listing 3-8:   connectionDidFinishLoading:

```
- (void)connectionDidFinishLoading:(NSURLConnection *)
                                            connection {

//RoadTripAppDelegate *appDelegate =
//                 RoadTripAppDelegate *) [[UIApplication
//                         sharedApplication] delegate];
//UIApplication* application = [UIApplication
//                                 sharedApplication];
//[appDelegate.activityIndicator stopAnimating];
//application.networkActivityIndicatorVisible = NO;
  [delegate performSelectorOnMainThread:sucessful
   withObject:rxData waitUntilDone:YES];
  [self cancelConnection];
}
```

You simply perform the selector that you specify during `ServerManager` initialization. (Not sure what "performing a selector," as in `performSelect orOnMainThread:sucessful`, might actually mean? Don't worry; I explain that — and talk about the selector you should specify in case of an error — when I explain initialization.)

Notice that some code is commented out in Listing 3-9. Here, if you've set in motion some sort of activity indicator or other kind of user feedback mecha-nism (I explain that when I explain initialization next), you comment out that code to turn it off. (I show you an example of that in the commented out code).

The use of selectors, both in the case of a successful download as well as in cases where downloads are unsuccessful, is what allows you to have several of these `ServerManager` objects working at the same time. Although it makes sense to serialize data downloads from a single site, it also may make sense to have several `ServerManager` objects that each access different sites.

This whole process mirrors a pattern used by the iPhone OS that allows you to implement asynchronous processing. You came across this when you used the XML parser in Book V, so you shouldn't be surprised to see it again.

The only thing left to do (as I have been promising to show you) is initialization. (Think of this as the icing underneath the cherry.) Enter the code in Listing 3-9 to `ServerManager.m`.

Listing 3-9: ServerManager Initialization

```
- (id) initWithModel:(Trip*)theModel  delegate:receiver
      sucessfulSelector:(SEL)sucessfulSelector
      connectionErrorSelector:(SEL)connectionErrorSelector{

  if (self = [super init]) {
    sucessful = sucessfulSelector;
    connectionError = connectionErrorSelector;
    delegate = [receiver retain];
    trip = theModel;
//  RoadTripAppDelegate *appDelegate = (RoadTripAppDelegate*)
    [[UIApplication sharedApplication] delegate];
//  UIApplication* application =
                        [UIApplication sharedApplication];
//  [appDelegate.activityIndicator startAnimating];
//  application.networkActivityIndicatorVisible = YES;
  }
  return self;
}
```

As you've seen, when you initialize a `ServerManager` instance, you need to tell it what to do in case of two scenarios — both success and failure. In the case of success, you'll perform the `sucessfulSelector`, and in the case of a failure the `connectionErrorSelector`. In the initialization method, you save these selectors for later use in `connectionDidFinishLoading:` or `connection:didFailWithError`, respectively.

Again, you'll notice some code in Listing 3-9 that's commented out:

```
RoadTripAppDelegate *appDelegate = (RoadTripAppDelegate *)
            [[UIApplication sharedApplication] delegate];
UIApplication* application = [UIApplication
                                sharedApplication];
[appDelegate.activityIndicator startAnimating];
application.networkActivityIndicatorVisible = YES;
```

This code is how you might start a progress indicator going to inform the user of what is going on. For this to work, you'd have to already had an outlet defined in the main window nib that referenced an activity indicator object that you added to the main screen in Interface Builder — I'll leave you to explore this on your own.

Alternatively, as I mentioned earlier, you might start downloads at application startup (on another thread — way, *way* out of scope for this book) and use an activity or progress indicator only when the user tries to do something that requires data you haven't yet downloaded.

One more thing

What I've been highlighting so far in this chapter with regard to dealing with downloads represents the simplest implementation of an application using `NSURLConnection`. There are some more delegate methods that provide the ability to customize the handling of server redirects, authorization requests, and caching of the response. But as I said, I don't use them here.

But one more thing I do want to explain is handling authentication challenges.

Although the server you are using for RoadTrip doesn't require a user name and password, there will probably be times when the server you want to use will in fact make that request of you. Although I have no need to implement that functionality here, Listing 3-10 shows an example of how you'd do that.

**Book VI
Chapter 3**

**Working the URL
Loading System**

Listing 3-10: connection:didReceiveAuthenticationChallenge Example

```
- (void)connection:(NSURLConnection *)connection
  didReceiveAuthenticationChallenge:
                  (NSURLAuthenticationChallenge *)challenge {

  if ([challenge previousFailureCount] != 0) {
    [connection cancel];
    UIAlertView *alert =
            [[UIAlertView alloc] initWithTitle:@"Yo!"

    message:NSLocalizedString (@" Your User Name
            and/or Password is incorrect",
                              @"No user name or password")
            delegate:self
            cancelButtonTitle:NSLocalizedString
                                  (@"Thanks", @"Thanks")
            otherButtonTitles:nil];
    [alert show];
    [alert release];
  }
  else {
    NSURLCredential *credential = [[NSURLCredential alloc]
       initWithUser:[[NSUserDefaults standardUserDefaults]
        stringForKey:kUserNamePreference]
        password:[[NSUserDefaults standardUserDefaults]
        stringForKey:kPasswordPreference]
        persistence:NSURLCredentialPersistenceNone];
```

(continued)

Listing 3-10 *(continued)*

```
    [[challenge sender] useCredential:
        credential forAuthenticationChallenge:challenge];
    [credential release];
  }
}
```

If a request requires authentication, your delegate receives a `connection` `:didReceiveAuthenticationChallenge:` message. At that point, you need to do one of the following:

+ Provide credentials to attempt to use for authentication.

+ Attempt to continue without credentials.

+ Cancel the authentication request.

In the case of Listing 3-10, the delegate has created an `NSURLCredential` object with the user name and password that are in the application's prefer-ences as well as the type of persistence to use for the credentials, and then sends the `[challenge sender]` a `useCredential:forAuthentication` `Challenge:` message:

```
NSURLCredential *credential = [[NSURLCredential alloc]
      initWithUser:[[NSUserDefaults standardUserDefaults]
          stringForKey:kUserNamePreference]
          password:[[NSUserDefaults standardUserDefaults]
          stringForKey:kPasswordPreference]
          persistence:NSURLCredentialPersistenceNone];
[[challenge sender] useCredential:
        credential forAuthenticationChallenge:challenge];
[credential release];
```

If the authentication has failed previously, it cancels the authentication chal-lenge and informs the user:

```
if ([challenge previousFailureCount] != 0) {
  [connection cancel];
  UIAlertView *alert =
    [[UIAlertView alloc] initWithTitle:@"Yo!"
      message:NSLocalizedString (@" Your User Name
      and/or Password is incorrect",
                          @"No user name or password")
      delegate:self
      cancelButtonTitle:NSLocalizedString
                          (@"Thanks", @"Thanks")
      otherButtonTitles:nil];
  [alert show];
  [alert release];
}
```

Implementing Sight *with Asynchronous Downloads*

In Chapter 2 of this minibook, you added Listing 2-12 to Sight.m so that you could make previously downloaded files from a server on the Internet available to the WebViewController and subsequently the WebView. Back then, I promised to explain some of the "stranger" code." Now that you understand the URL loading system, I can go back and do just that. If you haven't already done so, add the webViewControllerNSURLRequest:pro cessMethod: method shown in Listing 3-11 to Sight.m.

Listing 3-11: Implementing the webViewControllerNSURLRequest: processMethod: Delegate Method in Sight

```
- (void) webViewControllerNSURLRequest:(
          WebViewController *) controller
                   processMethod:(SEL)theProcessMethod {

  viewController = controller;
  processMethod = theProcessMethod;
  RoadTripAppDelegate *appDelegate =
      (RoadTripAppDelegate *)[[UIApplication
                            sharedApplication] delegate];
  BOOL realtime = !appDelegate.useStoredData;
  if (realtime) {
    NSString*  urlString = [[NSString alloc]
    initWithFormat:@"%@%@.%@", @"http://nealgoldstein.com/",
    resource,
                                    the resourceType];
    [self downloadData:urlString];
  }
  else {
    [self getData];
  }
}
```

As you recall, this is the delegate method that the WebViewController invokes in viewDidLoad:

```
[delegate webViewController:self
    nsurlRequestProcessMethod:@selector(loadWebView:)];
```

This bit of code starts the chain of events that ends with the WebViewController receiving the NSURLRequest in loadWebView: that it then passes on to its Web view.

In nsurlRequestProcessMethod::, the selector (loadWebView:) is saved in the processMethod instance variable.

```
processMethod = theProcessMethod;
```

The `downloadData:` message is then sent to `self`. Add the code in Listing 3-12 to `Sight.m` in order to get that little chore done.

Listing 3-12:   downloadData:

```
- (void)downloadData:(NSString*) urlString {

  sightServerManager = [[ServerManager alloc]
      initWithModel:trip delegate:self
      sucessfulSelector:@selector(saveData:)
      connectionErrorSelector:@selector(connectionError:)];
  [sightServerManager get:urlString];
}
```

This method allocates and initializes a `ServerManager` instance. It passes in a reference to the `Trip`, (which I don't use in this example) and two selectors. The first, `sucessfulSelector`, results in the `ServerManager` instance sending the `saveData:` message to `Sight` object when the file has been successfully downloaded. The second, `connectionErrorSelector`, results in the `ServerManager` instance sending the `Sight` object the connectionError: message if there's a connection failure.

After that's been done, the method sends the `get:` message to the `ServerManager` to get everything rolling.

Sending the right message

Now you can put things in gear by tackling the code behind the `saveData:`. message. Add what you see in Listing 3-13 to `Sight.m`.

Listing 3-13:   saveData:

```
- (void)saveData:(NSMutableData *) rxData {

  receivedData = rxData;
  [receivedData retain];
  NSArray *paths = NSSearchPathForDirectoriesInDomains(NSDocu
    mentDirectory, NSUserDomainMask, YES);
  NSString *documentsDirectory = [paths objectAtIndex:0];
  NSString *filePath = [documentsDirectory stringByAppendingP
    athComponent:sightName];
  NSURL* theFileURL = [[NSURL alloc]
    initFileURLWithPath:(NSString *)filePath];
  [receivedData writeToURL:theFileURL atomically:YES];
  NSURLRequest* theNSURLRequest = [NSURLRequest
                          requestWithURL:theFileURL];
  [viewController performSelectorOnMainThread:processMethod
          withObject:theNSURLRequest waitUntilDone:NO];
```

```
    [theFileURL release];
    [receivedData  release];
}
```

This method more or less does what `saveCarServicingData:` did in Chapter 4 of Book V.

In Book V, you get the path to the `Documents` directory.

```
NSArray *paths =
  NSSearchPathForDirectoriesInDomains(NSDocumentDirectory,
                                      NSUserDomainMask, YES);
NSString *documentsDirectory = [paths objectAtIndex:0];
NSString *filePath = [documentsDirectory
              stringByAppendingPathComponent:fileName];
```

On the iPhone, you really don't have much choice about where the file goes. Although there's a `/tmp` directory, I'm going to place this file in the `Documents` directory — because this is part of my application's sandbox (the part of the iPhone storage I can modify), so it's the natural home for all the app's files.

`NSSearchPathForDirectoriesInDomains:` returns an array of directories; because I'm only interested in the `Documents` directory, I use the constant `NSDocumentDirectory` — and because I'm restricted to my home directory/sandbox, the constant `NSUserDomainMask` limits the search to that domain. There will be only one directory in the domain, so the one I want will be the first one returned.

Continuing with the tour of Listing 3-13, you'll see that the next big step is creating the complete path by appending the path filename to the directory.

```
NSString *filePath = [documentsDirectory
              stringByAppendingPathComponent:fileName];
```

`stringByAppendingPathComponent;` precedes the filename with a path separator (`/`) if necessary.

Unfortunately, this technique doesn't work if you're just trying to create a string representation of a URL.

When you implemented the method in `saveCarServicingData:` in Book V you wrote the data to the file using :

```
 [dataLoaded writeToFile:filePath atomically:YES];
```

`writeToFile:` is an `NSData` method and does what it implies. I am actually telling the array here to write itself to a file, which is why I decided to save the location in this way in the first place.

A number of other classes can implement the `writeToFile:` method, including `NSDate`, `NSNumber`, `NSString`, and `NSDictionary`. (You can also add this behavior to your own objects, and they could save themselves — but I won't get into that here.) The `atomically` parameter first writes the data to an auxiliary file, and when that's successful, it's renamed to the path you've specified. This situation guarantees that the file won't be corrupted even if the system crashes during the write operation.

In this new implementation, things are pretty much the same, except you use

```
[receivedData writeToURL:theFileURL atomically:YES];
```

Because at present only file URLs are supported, there's no difference between this method and `writeToFile:atomically:`, except for the type of the first argument. You do this because it's the preferred method to use in the URL loading system and is likely to keep you compatible for some time in the future.

Finally `saveData:` continues to create an `NSURLRequest` and then perform the selector:

```
[viewController performSelectorOnMainThread:processMethod
            withObject:theNSURLRequest waitUntilDone:NO];
```

This final line of code completes the circle by performing the selector (which was passed in at `ServerManager` initialization in Listing 3-12 and saved in the `processMethod` instance variable) which results in the `loadWebView:` message (just as you did previously), passing in the `NSURLRequest`.

Next you need to implement the `getData` method if the user is in stored data mode. To do that, enter the code in Listing 3-14.

Listing 3-14: getData

```
- (void)getData {

    NSArray *paths = NSSearchPathForDirectoriesInDomains
    (NSDocumentDirectory, NSUserDomainMask, YES);
    NSString *documentsDirectory = [paths objectAtIndex:0];
    NSString *filePath = [documentsDirectory
                stringByAppendingPathComponent:sightName];
    NSURL* theFileURL = [[NSURL alloc]
                initFileURLWithPath:(NSString *)filePath];
    NSURLRequest* theNSURLRequest = [NSURLRequest
                            requestWithURL:theFileURL];
    [viewController performSelectorOnMainThread:processMethod
     withObject:theNSURLRequest waitUntilDone:NO];
    [theFileURL release];
}
```

`getData` is essentially the same as `saveData:`, except it does not first save the data it received from the `ServerManager` download. Instead, it uses data that was previously saved in `saveData:`.

Just like what you see in `saveData:`, `getData` creates an `NSURLRequest` and then performs the selector.

```
[viewController performSelectorOnMainThread:processMethod
            withObject:theNSURLRequest waitUntilDone:NO];
```

Now you need to take care of the `connectionError::` business. Enter the code in Listing 3-15 to `Sight.m`.

Listing 3-15:   In Case of an Error

```
- (void) connectionError:(NSError *)error {

  NSLog(@"Download NSURLConnection failed:%@ %@",
       [error localizedDescription], [[error userInfo]
                objectForKey:NSErrorFailingURLStringKey]);
  UIAlertView *alert = [[UIAlertView alloc]
        initWithTitle:@"There's been a connection failure"
        message:NSLocalizedString
          (@"Couldn't get data to display ",
          @"Couldn't get data to display")
        delegate:self
        cancelButtonTitle:NSLocalizedString
        (@"Thanks", @"Thanks") otherButtonTitles:nil];
  [alert show];
  [alert release];
}
```

This code logs the error and presents an alert to inform the user of a connection failure. Depending on your application, there might be other things you would want to do here as well.

Finally, you need to do some housekeeping. You have to import the `ServerManager`. So add

```
#import "ServerManager.h"
```

to `Sight.m`.

You'll also have to declare the methods you have added in the `Sight` interface. So add the following to `Sight.h`:

```
- (void) webViewController:(WebViewController*) controller
          nsurlRequestProcessMethod:(SEL)theProcessMethod;
- (void) downloadData:(NSString*) urlString;
- (void) saveData:(NSMutableData *) rxData;
- (void) getData;
```

Getting Trip in on the action

Because the model objects themselves are delegates, there's much less involvement in this generic controller implementation for `Trip`. `Trip`'s sole job now is to return the delegate object depending on the user's selection. However, you should be aware that a user selection no longer takes place just in `RootViewController`, but will also take place after `SightListController`.

Make the modifications to `Trip.h` you see in Listing 3-16. (Remember that you add the bold and delete the strikethrough.)

Listing 3-16:   Some Changes to Trip.h

```
#import <MapKit/MapKit.h>
#import <Foundation/Foundation.h>
#import "WebViewController.h"


@class Weather;
@class CarServicing;
@class CarInformation;

@interface Trip :NSObject   <WebViewControllerDelegate>{

  NSString       *tripName;
  CarServicing   *carServicing;
  CarInformation *carInformation;
  Weather        *weather;
  NSMutableArray *sights;

}

@property (nonatomic, retain) NSMutableArray * sights;


- (id) initWithName:(NSString*) theTripName;
//- (void) returnWeather:(id) theViewController;
//- (void) returnCarServicingInformation:(id)
    theViewController;
//- (void) returnCarInformation:(id) theViewController;
- (CLLocationCoordinate2D) initialCoordinate;
- (NSString*) mapTitle;
- (NSArray*) createAnnotations;

- (id) returnSightDelegate:(int) index;
- (id) returnWeatherDelegate;
- (id) returnCarInformationDelegate;
- (id) returnCarServicingDelegate;

@end
```

As you can see, you'll be deleting the selectors you previously used and instead creating methods that return the right delegate to the `WebViewController`.

In Listing 3-17, make the changes to `Trip.m` to implement these new methods.

Listing 3-17:   Updating Trip.m

```
- (id) returnSightDelegate:(int) index{

  return [sights objectAtIndex:index];

}
- (id) returnWeatherDelegate {

  return weather;
}

- (id) returnCarInformationDelegate {

  return carInformation;
}

- (id) returnCarServicingDelegate {

  return carServicing;
}


/*
- (void) returnWeather:(id) theViewController {

  [theViewController loadWebView:[weather
    weatherRealtime]];

}

- (void) returnCarServicingInformation:(id)
    theViewController {

  [theViewController performSelectorOnMainThread:@
    selector(loadWebView:) withObject:[carServicing
    returnCarServicingInformation] waitUntilDone:NO];
}

- (void) returnCarInformation:(id) theViewController {

  [theViewController performSelectorOnMainThread:@
    selector(loadWebView:) withObject:[carInformation
    returnCarInformation] waitUntilDone:NO];
}
*/
```

Finally, there's the last remaining method you need in the
`SightListController` — the one you did not implement in Chapter
1 of this minibook. Here's where you respond to the user selecting a particular sight (the Golden Gate Bridge, for example) by sending the `Trip`
the message for the `Sight` selector and then passing it in when you initialize the `WebViewController`. Pay particular attention to the code I have
highlighted in bold, which does that. Add all of the code in Listing 3-18 to
`SightListController.m`.

Listing 3-18: tableView:didSelectRowAtIndexPath:

```
- (void)tableView:(UITableView *)tableView
        didSelectRowAtIndexPath:(NSIndexPath *) indexPath {

  [tableView deselectRowAtIndexPath:indexPath
                                        animated:YES];
  UIViewController *targetController ;
  targetController = [[WebViewController alloc]
        initWithTrip:trip
        delegate:[trip returnSightDelegate:indexPath.row]
          webControl:YES
          title:NSLocalizedString(@"Sights", @"Sights") ];
  if (targetController) [[self navigationController] pushView
    Controller:targetController animated:YES];
  [targetController release];
}
```

Notice you've solved your problem of which `Sight` object to use, because
the `SightListController` knows what `Sight` object was chosen in its
`tableView:didSelectRowAtIndexPath:` method.

If you were to compile and build your project at this point, you'd find that
any selection in the Sights list would work just fine.

However, if you were to select something like Servicing, you would be
thrown into the debugger. That's because, to finish things up, you need to
make the changes to `CarServicing`, `CarInformation`, and `Weather` that
implement the delegate mechanism now used by the `WebViewController`
(as well as implement the way you now access data in `Sight`). Read on to
find out how to do that.

Adding Delegation and the URL Loading System to the Rest of the Model Objects

Because you've entirely changed the mechanism that results in model
objects returning the `NSURLRequest` to the `WebViewController`, you'll
have to go back and make those changes in your other model objects —

CarServicing, CarInformation, and Weather (As you've probably noticed by this point, application development is often a case of taking a step back so you can take two steps forward.)

Start with CarServicing.

Its implementation of the URL Loading System and delegation will be very similar to the Sight implementation of the URL Loading System and delegation because both download data from a server.

Start by updating the CarServicing.h file with the bolded code in Listing 3-19. (Be sure to delete the stuff in strikethrough.)

Book VI
Chapter 3

Working the URL
Loading System

Listing 3-19: CarServicing.h

```
@class Trip;
@class ServerManager;
#import "WebViewController.h"

@interface CarServicing : NSObject
                          <WebViewControllerDelegate> {

    Trip* trip;
    ServerManager       *sightServerManager;
    NSMutableData       *receivedData;
    SEL processMethod;
    UIViewController    *viewController;
}
- (id) initWithTrip:(Trip*) aTrip;
//- (NSURLRequest*) returnCarServicingInformation;
//- (void) saveCarServicingData:(NSString*) fileName
    withDataURL:(NSURL*) url;
//- (NSURL*) getCarServicingData:(NSString*) fileName;

@end
```

For all practical purposes, this is the same approach as Sight.h, although some names were changed to protect the innocent.

To be consistent with Sight, you'll make the internal methods part of a category. I explain that in Chapter 1 of this minibook, so if it isn't quite obvious, go back and review it there.

Add the code in Listing 3-20 to CarServicing.m.

Listing 3-20: CarServicing "Private" Methods

```
@interface CarServicing  ()
//- (NSURL*) getSightData:(NSString*) fileName;
- (void) downloadData:(NSString*) urlString;
- (void) saveData:(NSMutableData *) rxData;
- (void) getData;
//- (void) saveSightData: (NSString*) fileName withDataURL:
    (NSURL*) url;
@end
```

Finally, update `CarServicing.m` by adding the code in Listing 3-21.

Listing 3-21: CarServicing.m

```objc
- (void) webViewController:(WebViewController *)
        controller
        nsurlRequestProcessMethod:(SEL)theProcessMethod {

  viewController = controller;
  processMethod = theProcessMethod;
  RoadTripAppDelegate *appDelegate = (RoadTripAppDelegate *)
    [[UIApplication sharedApplication] delegate];
  BOOL realtime = !appDelegate.useStoredData;
  if (realtime) {
    NSString*  urlString = [[NSString alloc]
      initWithFormat:@"%@%@.%@",
      @"http://nealgoldstein.com/", @"CarServicing",
    @"html"];
    [self downloadData:urlString];
  }
  else {
    [self getData];
  }
}

- (void)downloadData:(NSString*) urlString {
  sightServerManager = [[ServerManager alloc]
    initWithModel:trip delegate:self
    sucessfulSelector:@selector(saveData:)
    connectionErrorSelector:@selector(connectionError:)];
  [sightServerManager get:urlString];
}

- (void)saveData:(NSMutableData *) rxData {

  receivedData= rxData;
  [receivedData retain];
  NSArray *paths = NSSearchPathForDirectoriesInDomains
            (NSDocumentDirectory, NSUserDomainMask, YES);
  NSString *documentsDirectory = [paths objectAtIndex:0];
```

```
NSString *filePath = [documentsDirectory
        stringByAppendingPathComponent:@"CarServicing"];
NSURL* theFileURL = [[NSURL alloc]
            initFileURLWithPath:(NSString *)filePath];
[receivedData writeToURL:theFileURL atomically:YES];
NSURLRequest* theNSURLRequest = [NSURLRequest
                        requestWithURL:theFileURL];
[viewController performSelectorOnMainThread:processMethod
 withObject:theNSURLRequest waitUntilDone:NO];
[theFileURL release];
[receivedData  release];
}


- (void)getData {

NSArray *paths = NSSearchPathForDirectoriesInDomains
        (NSDocumentDirectory, NSUserDomainMask, YES);
NSString *documentsDirectory = [paths objectAtIndex:0];
NSString *filePath = [documentsDirectory
        stringByAppendingPathComponent:@"CarServicing"];
NSURL* theFileURL = [[NSURL alloc]
            initFileURLWithPath:(NSString *)filePath];
NSURLRequest* theNSURLRequest = [NSURLRequest
                        requestWithURL:theFileURL];
[viewController performSelectorOnMainThread:processMethod
 withObject:theNSURLRequest waitUntilDone:NO];
[theFileURL release];
}


- (void) connectionError:(NSError *)error {

NSLog(@"Download NSURLConnection failed:%@ %@",
    [error localizedDescription], [[error userInfo]
            objectForKey:NSErrorFailingURLStringKey]);
UIAlertView *alert = [[UIAlertView alloc]
        initWithTitle:@"There's been a connection failure"
        message:NSLocalizedString
          (@"Couldn't get data to display ",
          @"Couldn't get data to display")
        delegate:self
        cancelButtonTitle:NSLocalizedString
        (@"Thanks", @"Thanks") otherButtonTitles:nil];
[alert show];
[alert release];
}
```

You also need to delete the following methods from `CarServicing.m`.

```
- (NSURLRequest*) returnCarServicingInformation {…
- (void) saveCarServicingData:(NSString*) fileName
  withDataURL:(NSURL*) url  {…
- (NSURL*) getCarServicingData:(NSString*) fileName {…
```

You need to add a new `#import` statement to `CarServicing.m` as well.

```
#import "ServerManager.h"
```

Because the code here is substantially the same as `Sight.m`, I'm not going to explain what you have done here. The only thing I want you to pay attention to is the name of the file you save in `saveData:` and load in `getData`.

So, pay attention: In the case of Sight, you're using `sightName` as the filename. The `sightName` filename is passed to the `Sight` object when it's initialized and found in the property list. In the case of `CarServicing`, you are hard coding the filename. If this were a commercial application, you would have `CarServicing` defined in the property list where you would specify some kind of filename, or create a filename using some algorithm such as hash.

Finally, you need to update both `CarInformation` and `Weather`. Make the modifications shown in Listings 3-22 and 3-23 to `CarInformation.h` and `.m`, respectively.

Listing 3-22:   CarInformation.h

```objectivec
@class Trip;
#import "WebViewController.h"


@interface CarInformation : NSObject
                           <WebViewControllerDelegate> {

    Trip* trip;
    SEL processMethod;
    UIViewController* viewController;
}
- (id) initWithTrip:(Trip*) aTrip;
// - (NSURLRequest*) returnCarInformation;

@end
```

In `CarInformation.m`, because you can reuse some of the code, you just have to change the method as needed.

Listing 3-23:   CarInformation.m

```objectivec
//- (NSURLRequest*) returnCarInformation {
- (void) webViewController:(WebViewController *)
        controller
        nsurlRequestProcessMethod:(SEL)theProcessMethod {
```

```
NSString *filePath = [[NSBundle mainBundle]
  pathForResource:@"CarSpecs" ofType:@"html"];
NSURL* carInformationData= [NSURL
  fileURLWithPath:filePath];
NSURLRequest* theNSURLRequest =
        [NSURLRequest requestWithURL:carInformationData];
// return theNSURLRequest;
  [controller performSelectorOnMainThread:theProcessMethod
    withObject:theNSURLRequest waitUntilDone:NO];
}
```

Because the data is local, there's no need to use the `ServerManager`. You're just adding the delegate and its implementation and deleting the method that created the `NSURLRequest` previously. In this particular implementation, you're deleting the `return` statement and instead sending the same `performSelectorOnMainThread:withObject:waitUntilDone` message as you did in both the `Sight` object's and `CarServicing` object's `getData` and `SaveData:` methods.

You also need to change `Weather`. Update `Weather.h` and `.m` with the code in Listings 3-24 and 3-25, respectively. You'll be making similar changes to the ones you made to `CarInformation`.

Book VI
Chapter 3

Working the URL
Loading System

Listing 3-24: Update Weather.h

```
#import "WebViewController.h"

@interface Weather : NSObject <WebViewControllerDelegate> {
}
// - (NSURLRequest*) weatherRealtime; //$$

@end
```

Listing 3-25: Update Weather.m

```
#import "Weather.h"

@implementation Weather

// - (NSURLRequest*) weatherRealtime {
- (void) webViewController:(WebViewController *)
        controller
        nsurlRequestProcessMethod:(SEL)theProcessMethod {

  NSURL *url = [NSURL URLWithString:@"http://www.
    weather.com/outlook/travel/businesstraveler/local/
    UKXX0085?lswe=CarServicing,%20UNITED%20KINGDOM&lwsa=Weathe
    rLocalUndeclared&from=searchbox_typeahead"];
```

(continued)

Listing 3-25 *(continued)*

```
if (url == NULL) NSLog( @"Data not found %@", url);
NSURLRequest* theNSURLRequest =
                    [NSURLRequest requestWithURL:url];
// return theNSURLRequest;
[controller performSelectorOnMainThread:theProcessMethod
            withObject:theNSURLRequest waitUntilDone:NO];
}

@end
```

Again, you're simply adding the delegate and its implementation and deleting the method that you'd previously used to create the NSURLRequest.

What About the Map?

In Book V, Chapter 5, I had you enter some code to display annotations. I mentioned then that while this did illustrate how to display annotations, this way of doing it was just that, an illustration.

In fact, the "right" way to do annotations is to give each model object the responsibility of displaying itself as an annotation. In this case, I'm talking about the Sight objects, and in the next chapter I show you how to do the same thing with Hotel objects.

Start with the Map object I had you create in Chapter 5 of in Book V. As you may have noticed, I never really had you do anything with it. Well, now you're going to put the Map object to work. You're going to give it a new job description: Manager of all things annotation-ish.

Add the bolded code in Listing 3-26 to Map.h.

Listing 3-26:   Map.h

```
@class Trip;

@interface Map : NSObject {

  NSMutableArray *annotations;
  Trip           *trip;
}

- (id) initWithTrip:(Trip*) theTrip;
@property (nonatomic, retain)
                      NSMutableArray * annotations;
- (void) createAnnotations;

@end
```

Aside from the (expected) initialization method, you've added an `NSMutableArray` to hold the annotation objects. You'll see how to use that shortly. You've also added a method that will be invoked when the `mapContoller` needs to get the annotations to display in the `mapView`.

You might be asking yourself why I'm telling you to add another method when you could have the `Map` create its own annotations when it's initialized. Well, you could do it that way if you knew all the annotations you'll need when the `Map` is created. But, as you'll see in Chapter 5 of this minibook, if you're going to want to add new items — like `Hotels` — while executing, you need a way to dynamically add more annotations to the map.

Now add the code in list 3-27 to `Map.m`.

Listing 3-27:   Map.m

```
#import "Map.h"
#import "Trip.h"
#import "Sight.h"

@implementation Map
@synthesize annotations;

- (id) initWithTrip:(Trip*) theTrip {

  if (self = [super init]) {
    trip = theTrip;
    annotations = [[NSMutableArray alloc]
                  initWithCapacity:[trip.sights count]];

  }
  return self;
}

- (void) createAnnotations {

  [annotations removeAllObjects];
  [annotations addObjectsFromArray:trip.sights ];

}

- (void)dealloc {

  [annotations release];
  [super dealloc];
}
@end
```

In the `initWithTrip:` method, you first create and initialize that `NSMutableArray` you declared based on the number of `Sight` objects `Trip` has created and added to the `sights` array.

```
annotations = [[NSMutableArray alloc]
                    initWithCapacity:[trip.sights count]];
```

`Map` passes this array on to the `MapController`, just like `Trip` did in Chapter 5 of Book V.

Next, you have to make some changes to `MapController` to get the annotations from `Map`.

Make the (bolded) modifications in Listing 3-28 to `MapController.m`.

Listing 3-28:   MapController.m

```
#import "Map.h"
- (id) initWithTrip:(Trip*) theTrip {

  if (self = [super initWithNibName:@"MapController"
    bundle:nil]) {
    trip = theTrip;
    map = trip.map;
    trip.mapController = self;
}
  return self;
}
- (void) refreshAnnotations {

  [mapView removeAnnotations:map.annotations];
  [map createAnnotations];
  [mapView addAnnotations:map.annotations];
}
```

Basically, all you've done here is assign an instance variable — `map` — so that `MapController` can get the annotations from `Map`. If you've been paying attention, you may wonder why I don't have the `MapController` get the `map` reference from `Trip`, since that's been my modus operandi with the model objects up till now. Why use `Map` as a `Trip` property instead?

Despite my ranting and raving, using `Map` as a `Trip` property is much easier and more convenient, and I wanted to use this opportunity to show you that. I'll leave it up to you to decide how you want to do things in your application.

You have also added a new method: `refreshAnnotations`. Although you won't actually be using this until Chapter 5 of this minibook, I have you find a home for it here.

What `refreshAnnotations` will do for you is enable you to add new annotations during execution, such as when you add a new Hotel, for example. It first removes all the annotations for the `mapView`, then has the `Map` (re)create the annotations, and then adds the annotations back to the `mapView`. (This is why you needed to add the reference to `map` to `mapController`.)

Implementing `refreshAnnotations` will require changing how you add the annotations in `viewDidLoad`. You have to modify `MapController` to get the annotations array from `Map`.

Make the modifications to `viewDidLoad` in `MapController.m` in Listing 3-29.

Listing 3-29:   Modifying viewDidLoad

```
- (void)viewDidLoad {

  [super viewDidLoad];
  mapView.showsUserLocation = YES;
  CLLocationCoordinate2D initialCoordinate =
                                [trip initialCoordinate];
  [self updateRegionLatitude:initialCoordinate.latitude
    longitude:initialCoordinate.longitude
                   latitudeDelta:.06 longitudeDelta:.06];
  self.title = [trip mapTitle];
  [mapView.userLocation addObserver:self
          forKeyPath:@"location"  options:0 context:NULL];
//annotations = [[NSMutableArray alloc]
    initWithCapacity:1];
// [annotations  addObjectsFromArray:[trip
    createAnnotations]];
// [mapView addAnnotations:annotations];
  [trip.map createAnnotations];
  [mapView addAnnotations:trip.map.annotations];

  UIBarButtonItem *locateButton =
  [[UIBarButtonItem alloc] initWithTitle:@"Locate"
          style:UIBarButtonItemStylePlain target:self
                     action:@selector(goToLocation:)];
  self.navigationItem.rightBarButtonItem = locateButton;
  [locateButton release];
  NSMutableArray *items =
             [[NSMutableArray alloc] initWithCapacity:1];
   UIBarButtonItem *barButton =
     [[UIBarButtonItem alloc] initWithTitle:@"Find:"
     style:UIBarButtonItemStyleBordered
     target:self
     action:@selector(find:)];
  barButton.tag = 0;
  barButton.width = 100;
```

(continued)

Listing 3-29 *(continued)*

```
[items addObject:barButton];
[barButton release];

UIToolbar *toolbar = [UIToolbar new];
toolbar.barStyle = UIBarStyleBlackOpaque;
[toolbar sizeToFit];
CGFloat toolbarHeight = toolbar.frame.size.height;
CGFloat navbarHeight = self.navigationController.
  navigationBar.frame.
size.height;
CGRect mainViewBounds = self.view.bounds;
[toolbar setFrame:
   CGRectMake(CGRectGetMinX(mainViewBounds),
              CGRectGetMinY(mainViewBounds) +
              CGRectGetHeight(mainViewBounds) -
              (toolbarHeight + navbarHeight),
              CGRectGetWidth(mainViewBounds),
              toolbarHeight)];
[self.view addSubview:toolbar];
[toolbar release];
toolbar.items = items;

}
```

You also need to import Map in `MapController.m`:

```
#import "Map.h"
```

and no longer release `annotations` in `dealloc`:

```
- (void)dealloc {

  //[annotations release];
  [super dealloc];
}
```

Finally, because you're doing annotations differently, you have to modify `doFind:`, which adds annotations when you find a location on the map. In this case, I'll continue to have you use the `MapAnnotation` class, to implement the annotation for the found location.

But in this case you won't be getting `Map` involved in creating the annotation, so you'll simply have the `mapView` remove the annotations and then add the new annotation to the `Map` object's `annotations` array, and then (finally) add the `annotations` back to the `mapView`.

To do that, make the modifications in Listing 3-30 to `doFind:` in `MapController.m`.

Listing 3-30: Modifications to doFind:

```
- (void) doFind:(NSString*) newLocation {

// [mapView removeAnnotations:annotations];
   [mapView removeAnnotations:map.annotations];

   Geocoder* geocoder = [[Geocoder alloc] init];
   CLLocationCoordinate2D locationCoordinate = [geocoder
     geocodeLocation:newLocation];
   MKCoordinateRegion initialRegion;
   initialRegion.center.latitude =
   locationCoordinate.latitude;
   initialRegion.center.longitude =
   locationCoordinate.longitude;
   initialRegion.span.latitudeDelta = .06;
   initialRegion.span.longitudeDelta = .06;
   [mapView setRegion:initialRegion animated:NO];
   MapAnnotation* findAnnotation = [[MapAnnotation alloc]
       initWithTitle:@"Found Location"
       subTitle:@"pretty easy"
       coordinate:locationCoordinate];
// [annotations addObject:findAnnotation];
   [map.annotations addObject:findAnnotation];

// [mapView addAnnotations:annotations];
   [mapView addAnnotations:map.annotations];
   [findAnnotation release];
}
```

You also have to make some changes to `mapController.h` to support the changes you just made. You'll need to add

```
@class Map;
Map* map;
- (void) refreshAnnotations;
```

You can delete the annotations array instance variable as well:

```
// NSMutableArray        *annotations;
```

Notice an interesting consequence of these changes.

If you had an `annotation` for a find location, it disappears if you add a new annotation (although you won't be able to see that until Chapter 5 of this minibook).

This is because you create the found location annotation in `mapController.m`, and add it to the Map's annotations array.

```
[map.annotations addObject:findAnnotation];
```

But because Map, which now owns the annotations list, doesn't know anything about the found location; if you tell it to (re)create the annotations array, it's now gone.

I'll leave it as an exercise for you to do. You need to save the found location annotation when there is one and add it to the map only when it is there.

The next thing you need to do is have Trip create and initialize the Map object and fire Trip from its job of creating the annotations array.

Make the modifications to Trip.h, as shown in Listing 3-31.

Listing 3-31:   Modifications to Trip.h

```
#import <MapKit/MapKit.h>
#import <Foundation/Foundation.h>
@class Weather;
@class CarServicing;
@class CarInformation;
@class Map;
@class MapController;

@interface Trip : NSObject   {

    NSString        *tripName;
    CarServicing    *carServicing;
    CarInformation  *carInformation;
    Weather         *weather;
    NSMutableArray  *sights;
    Map             *map;
    MapController   *mapController;

}

@property (nonatomic, retain) NSMutableArray *sights;
@property (nonatomic, retain) Map* map;
@property (nonatomic, retain) MapController
                                      *mapController;

- (id) initWithName:(NSString*) theTripName;
- (CLLocationCoordinate2D) initialCoordinate;
- (NSString*) mapTitle;
//- (NSArray*) createAnnotations;
- (id) returnSightDelegate:(int) index;
- (id) returnWeatherDelegate;
- (id) returnCarInformationDelegate;
- (id) returnCarServicingDelegate;
```

You've added the properties needed by MapController to access Map as well as allow Trip (in Chapter 5 of this minibook) to access

MapController to tell it to refresh the annotations. You've also gotten rid of the createAnnotations method. Make the modifications to the Trip.m file's initWithName: to support that, as shown in Listing 3-32.

Listing 3-32:   Trip.m initwithname:

```
- (id) initWithName:(NSString*) theTrip {

  if ((self = [super init])) {
    tripName = theTrip;
    [tripName retain];
    carInformation = [[CarInformation alloc]
   initWithTrip:self];
    carServicing = [[CarServicing alloc] initWithTrip:self];
    weather = [[Weather alloc] init];
    [self loadSights];
    map =[[Map alloc] initWithTrip:self];
  }
  return self;
}
```

In Trip.m, that also means adding

```
#import "Map.h"
#import "MapController.h"

@synthesize map;
@synthesize mapController;
```

You also need to delete createAnnotations from Trip.m:

```
- (NSArray*) createAnnotations {
```

And finally, Sight.m; you need to implement the methods that will provide the title and subtitle information for a Sight. Add the code in Listing 3-33 to Sight.m.

Listing 3-33:   Implement title and subtitle

```
- (NSString*)title{

  return title;
}
- (NSString*)subtitle{

  return subtitle;
}
```

Where Are You?

At this point, you can compile and run RoadTrip. You'll be able to select a sight and get information about it, as well as see the sights on the Map view.

You've come a long way in adding data management to your RoadTrip application — but you aren't done yet. In the next chapter, you explore Core Data and see how easy it becomes to add and manage new Hotels on your road trip (and display them on the map as well).

Chapter 4: Setting Up Core Data

In This Chapter

✔ **An introduction to Core Data**

✔ **Looking at managed objects**

✔ **The Core Data architecture**

✔ **Adding a Core Data stack**

Although property lists are definitely cool, they're far from the universal solution to data management. For example, every time you start the app you still have to build the objects (the dictionaries, arrays, and so on) that you have saved. But more importantly, the real issue is that you can save only property list *objects* in a property list. That means you can't save relationships *between* objects.

Although there are some workarounds you can try to save relationships — the code kind, not necessarily the human kind — they can be very cumbersome if you have lots of objects. Imagine if you had 50 or so states in your application, with each one having a number of cities you were planning to visit, and each one of those with a number of hotels and sights. And oh yes, what about undo and redo?

What is really needed here is *object persistence* — you want to create the object once (along with its links to other objects) and then be able to continue to use it across application launches.

Fortunately there is a great way to create object persistence on the iPhone — Core Data. It's a deep, wide, and very mature technology, used on the Mac for years, which makes the iPhone version very attractive. Core Data makes it easy to create, manage, and delete objects as well as shake to undo and redo.

In fact, Apple is heavily promoting the use of Core Data on the iPhone. For example, there used to be some sample code that showed you how to use SQLite — a relational data base built into the iPhone. Those examples are now gone, replaced by Core Data examples instead. (These examples do use SQLite as the persistent store — I explain what that means shortly.)

In this and the next chapter, I show you how to implement Core Data in RoadTrip to support adding a new hotel. I don't get into all the bells and whistles — it would take an entire book to do that. What I do is give you enough background and understanding so you'll be comfortable exploring Core Data on your own — and you'll be able to use the great sample code that Apple provides that shows you how to use Core data to do most of what you'll want to do in your application.

Core Data Basics

Think about it. You have all those great classes for views and view controllers and what have you. But what do you have for your model? You know, that thing that actually provides the content in your application?

One lousy class. That's right, one, count it, one — `NSObject`. That was until Core Data became available.

Core Data makes it easy for a developer to do two things.

✦ Create, save, and fetch objects as objects — including their connections to other objects — from a persistent store (such as a file on disk).

✦ Support undos and redos.

You do that by

1. Creating a *managed object* (data) *model* that describes the object's data and relationships to other objects.

2. Deriving your classes that are to be managed by Core Data from `NSManagedObject` instead of `NSObject`.

3. Creating a *managed object context* that manages your collection of objects — responsible for lifecycle management, validation, maintaining relationships between objects, undo/redo, and managing *the persistent store*. This mechanism is for storing your objects to disk and is pretty much handled for you.

4. Creating your objects in the more or less usual way — within the managed object context, of course — and then save them.

5. *Fetching* your saved objects, optionally using a `FetchedResultsController` to get your objects in a way that is optimized for table views.

Note that Core Data isn't restricted to document-based applications. You can, for example, create a Core Data–based application with no user interface.

Before you go any further and get your hopes up, I want to explain what Core Data is *not*.

✦ Although Core Data can use a relational database — SQLite — as one of its persistent store types, it isn't in and of itself a relational database or a relational database management system. It's about providing an infrastructure for saving objects to (and retrieving them from) storage as well as Undo and Redo support.

✦ Core Data is not an application generator — you still have to write code.

Starting with the Objects

Even though the idea of Core Data can be overwhelming at first — a lot of the documentation assumes that you are both an expert in object-oriented programming (which I am) and a data base aficionado, (which I am not), when it comes right down to it, once you wade through the mess (I personally have taken the bullet for you here) it actually makes sense.

So start at the beginning — what you need.

You want to have Core Data manage `Hotel` objects for you. You want to be able to create, save, and modify them. You'd also like to support undos and redos for the entry of new Hotel objects.

The right place to start then is with the `Hotel` class.

If you were going to create a `Hotel` class on your own, it would sort of look like Listing 4-1.

**Book VI
Chapter 4**

**Setting Up
Core Data**

Listing 4-1:   A Hotel Class

```
@class Annotation;

@interface Hotel :   NSObject   {

NSString * city;
NSString * name;
NSString * state;
NSString * street;
NSString * zip;
Annotation * annotation;
}

- (NSString *) returnCity;
- (NSString *) returnName;
- (NSString *) returnState;
- (NSString *) returnStreet;
- (NSString *) returnZip;
- (Annotation *) returnAnnotation;

@end
```

This code looks a lot like the other model objects in RoadTrip. You would also expect some kind of initialization method — but you get the picture.

You also see a reference in the Hotel interface to an Annotation class. Now, I'd gotten rid of separate annotation objects in the last chapter, and quite frankly, I would prefer to do that here as well. But after much rumination and angst I decide to add them back, only because that would enable me to show you how Core Data maintains relationships between objects.

So keep that in mind as you continue, and don't do it this way at home.

Now take a look at the Annotation class in Listing 4-2.

Listing 4-2:   An Annotation Class

```
@class Hotel;
#import <MapKit/MapKit.h>

@class Hotel;

@interface Annotation : NSObject <MKAnnotation >
{

NSString * title;
NSString * subtitle;
CLLocationCoordinate2D coordinate;
}

- (NSString *) title;
- (NSString *) subtitle;

@property (nonatomic) CLLocationCoordinate2D coordinate;

@end
```

It looks like the MapAnnotation class you declared in Book V, Chapter 5 (sans the initialization method).

As you might have guessed, though, instead of coding these objects on my own, I am going to let Core Data do it. But for Core Data to do it, it needs a description of its objects. You provide this description by creating a *managed object model* — a schema (or a diagram that represents the elements in a system using symbols) that describes the entities your application uses and the relationships between them.

Core Data uses the model to map between the managed objects in your application and the records in the database. It's important to be aware that if you change the schema in your application, Core Data won't be able to read stores you created using the previous model — you can use a migration mechanism or simply delete the application from the simulator or the phone and start over from scratch.

The managed object model is a collection of entity and property description objects that tell Core Data about the managed objects in your application. Entity description objects provide (meta) data about an entity, including its name, the name of the class that represents it in your application (this doesn't have to be the same as its name), and its attributes and relationships. Similarly, attribute and relationship (property) description objects provide information about attributes and relationships. So, with that info in hand, you're ready to go build a managed object model for `Hotels` and `Annotations` in the RoadTrip app.

Although you can create the model programmatically, I show you how to use the Xcode modeling tool (one that is quite similar to Interface Builder) to create the model graphically.

I'm going to put my model in the Resource folder, so before you start, be sure to select that folder first.

1. **Choose File➪New from the main menu (or press ⌘+N) to get the New File dialog.**

2. **In the leftmost column of the dialog, first select Resource under the iPhone OS heading, then select the Data Model template in the topmost pane as I have in Figure 4-1. Then click Next.**

   You see a new dialog asking for some more information.

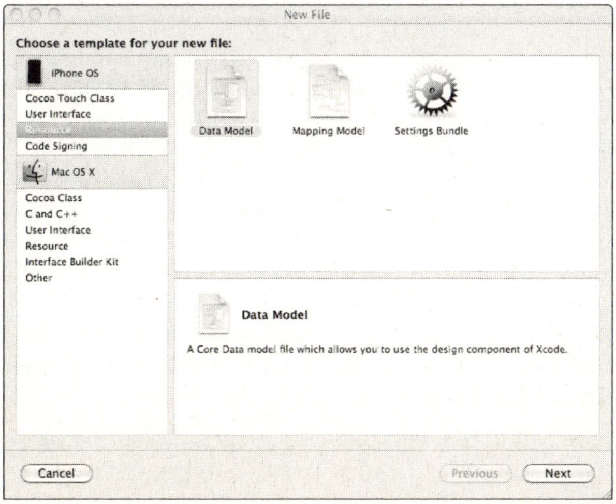

Figure 4-1:
Create a
data model.

3. **Replace** *untitled* **with** `RoadTrip` **in the Model Name field — it should read** `RoadTrip.xcdatamodel` **— and then click Next.**

4. **You see another dialog (see Figure 4-2), which will remain uncommented on because it's beyond the scope of this book, so go ahead and just click Finish.**

   You have to leave some stuff for your retirement years, right?

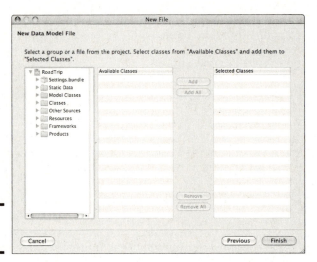

Figure 4-2: Ignore this.

You can find your managed object model `RoadTrip.xcdatamodel` in the Groups & Files list. I double-clicked it to launch it in a separate window, and if you do the same, you should see the same thing I see in Figure 4-3.

First, add an *entity*. An entity is the highest level object in a Core Data data model. Entities generally correspond to the classes traditionally used to hold data, but they can also be thought of as the objects you identify in your object-oriented programming model.

You'll have two entities when you're done — `Hotel` and `Annotation` — corresponding to the `Hotel` and `Annotation` objects you'll use in your application.

1. **With your brand-spanking-new (and empty) data model open, choose Design⊳Data Model⊳Add Entity from Xcode's main menu to add a new entity to the model.**

   You can also click the Add button (+) at the lower left of the entity pane, as I have in Figure 4-3, or right-click to use the shortcut menu within the Diagram view in the Model Editor.

   Figure 4-4 shows what you should see after doing one of those things.

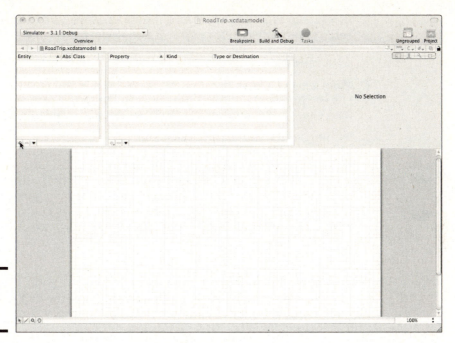

Figure 4-3:
An empty
model.

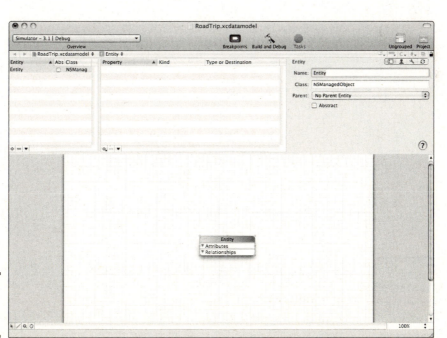

Figure 4-4:
Your first
entity.

You should see a new entry for the entity (called Entity) appear in the Entity pane at the top left of the Xcode Model Editor, and a graphical representation of the entity (a rounded rectangle) appear in the Diagram view. Now you can set the name for the new entity.

2. **Make sure you have the new entity selected in the Entity pane so that you see information about the entity in the Detail pane at the far right, then change the name of the entity to Hotel, as I have in Figure 4-5.**

Be sure not to change the class name.

The name of the entity and the name of the Objective-C class used to represent instances of the entity are not the same thing. Core Data uses the entity name to manage its data objects and so it doesn't have to be the same as its class name. In fact, you can often get away without really using any classes (although I use them in this example) other than NSManagedObject (which I explain later).

Add the Attributes

The next thing you need to do is add the attributes to the entity. These correspond to the instance variables you are used to using, which correspond to the model's data.

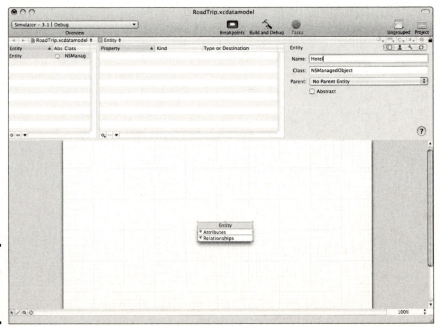

Figure 4-5:
The name of your entity is Hotel.

You start by adding the Name attribute.

1. **Make sure Hotel is selected in the Entity pane and then choose Design⇨Data Model⇨Add Attribute from Xcode's main menu.**

   You can also use the Add button (+) at the lower left of the property pane, as I have in Figure 4-6, or right-click to use the shortcut menu within the Diagram view in the Model Editor.

   You should see a new attribute (called newAttribute) appear in the Property pane in the upper-center of the window. Now you need to set its name and type.

2. **Make sure you have selected the new attribute in the Property pane; then in the Detail pane change the name of the attribute to name, as I have in Figure 4-7.**

   Next up, you need to tell Core Data what type this attribute is.

3. **Select String from the Type pop-up menu as I have in Figure 4-8.**

   You don't need to set any of the other values.

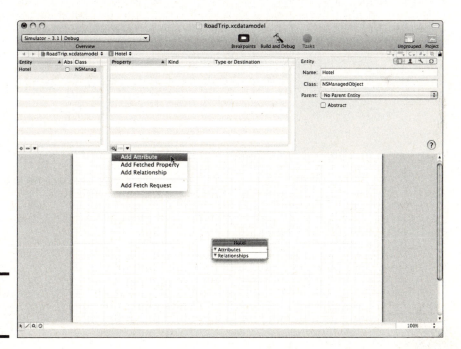

Figure 4-6:
Add an
attribute.

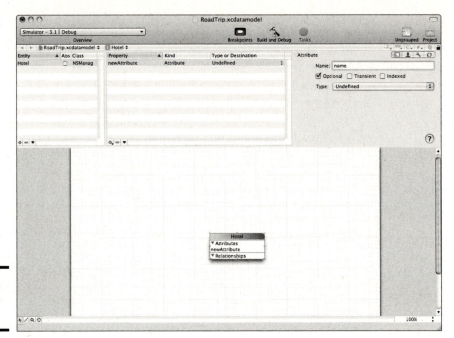

Figure 4-7:
Setting the name.

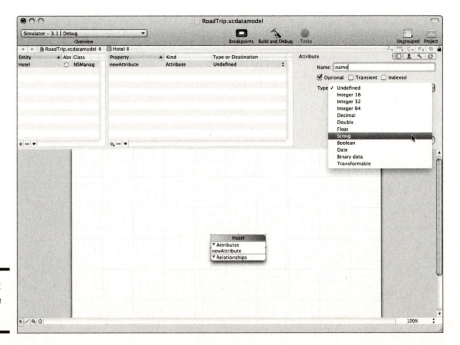

Figure 4-8:
Setting the type.

When you're done, your model should look just like mine, as shown in Figure 4-9.

Now add attributes for city, state, street, and zip code by going through Steps 1–3 for each.

When you're done, your model should look like Figure 4-10.

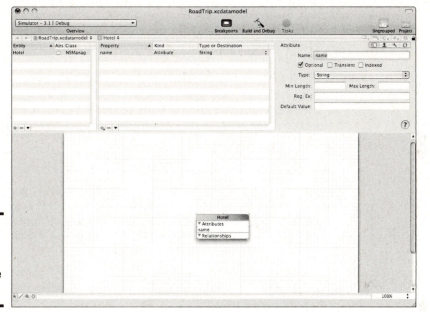

Figure 4-9:
The Hotel
entity and
with a name
attribute.

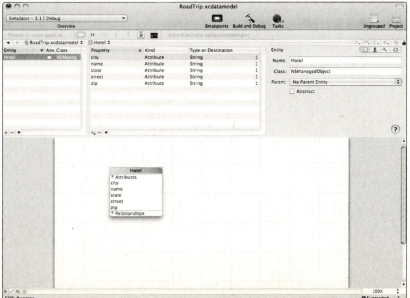

Figure 4-10:
An (almost)
complete
Hotel entity.

As I mention earlier, you need another entity as well — Annotation.

1. **Create the Annotation entity by choosing Design⇨Data Model ⇨Add Entity from Xcode's main menu to add a new entity to the model.**

    Feel free to use the Add button (+) at the lower left of the entity pane if that is more to your liking.

    You should see a new entry for the entity (called Entity) appear in the Entity pane at the top left of the Model Editor, and a graphical representation of the entity (a rounded rectangle) should appear in the Diagram view. Now you can set the name for the new entity.

2. **Make sure you have the new entity selected in the entity pane so that you see information about the entity in the detail pane at the right; then change the name of the entity to Annotation, as I have in Figure 4-11.**

    Don't change the class name.

    As you might expect, you have to add some attributes here as well.

3. **Make sure you have selected Annotation in the Entity pane; then choose Design⇨Data Model⇨Add Attribute from the Xcode main menu or use the Add button (+) at the lower left of the Property pane, as I did back in Figure 4-6, or right-click to use the shortcut menu within the Diagram view in the Model Editor.**

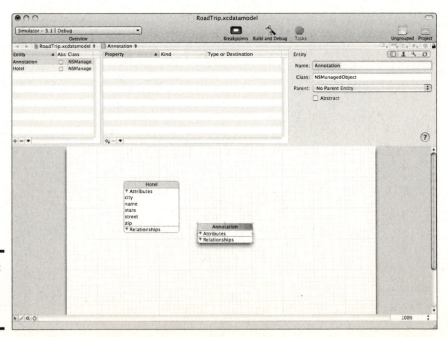

Figure 4-11: Adding the annotation entity.

You should see a new attribute (called `newAttribute`) appear in the Property pane.

It probably isn't news to you that you need to set its name and type.

4. **Make sure you've selected the new attribute in the Property pane; then in the Detail pane change the name of the attribute to latitude, as I have in Figure 4-12.**

5. **For this particular entity, choose Double from the Type pop-up menu.**

    Again, Figure 4-12 shows what that looks like.

6. **Add another attribute — longitude of type `Double`. Then add two more attributes — title and subtitle of type `String`.**

    When you're done, your model should look like Figure 4-13.

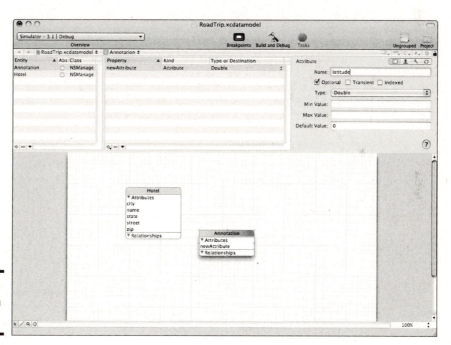

Figure 4-12:
Latitude is a
double.

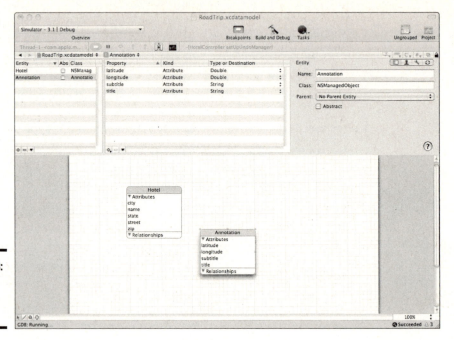

Figure 4-13:
Your two-
entity
model.

Add relationships

At this point, you may be saying to yourself, "Fine and good, I have the two entries I need, but shouldn't there be a link between `Hotel` and its `Annotation`?"

Thank you for asking. I show you how to do that now.

Now, if I had my druthers, I'd rather have set up title subtitle, latitude, and longitude as part of the Hotel entry, but doing it this way means I get to show you how to create a relation between two entities.

1. **Make sure you have selected Hotel in the Entity pane and then choose Design⇨Data Model⇨Add Relationship from the Xcode main menu.**

You can also use the Add button (+) at the lower left of the Property pane, as I have in Figure 4-14, or right-click to use the shortcut menu within the Diagram view in the Model Editor.

You should see a new relationship (called `newRelationship`) appear in the Property pane. You need to set its name and destination.

2. **Make sure you've selected `newRelationship` in the Property pane; then in the Detail pane change the name of the relationship to annotation as I have in Figure 4-15.**

Next you need to tell Core Data what the annotation's *destination* is — what it has a relationship to, in other words.

3. **Select `Annotation` from the Type pop-up menu, as I have in Figure 4-15.**

Figure 4-14:
Add a
relationship.

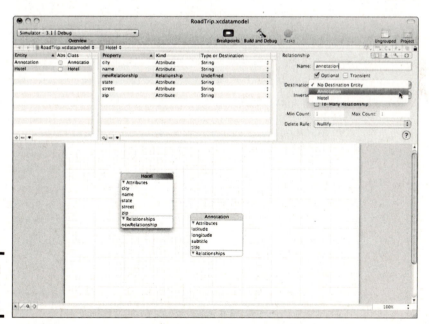

Figure 4-15:
Setting the
destination.

You don't need to set any of the other values.

When you're done, your model should look like what you see in Figure 4-16.

Figure 4-16:
The Hotel
with its
relationship
to
Annotation.

You also may want to be able to reference `Hotel` from its annotation, so let me show you how to do that as well.

1. **Make sure you've selected Annotation in the Entity pane and then choose Design⇨Data Model⇨Add Relationship from the Xcode main menu.**

As always, you can also use the Add button (+) at the lower left of the Property pane, as I did back in Figure 4-14, or right-click to use the shortcut menu within the Diagram view in the Model Editor.

You should see a new relationship (called `newRelationship`) appear in the Property pane. You need to set its name and destination — no surprise there.

2. **Make sure you have selected `newRelationship` in the Property pane; then in the Detail pane change the name of the relationship to `hotel`.**

3. **Still in the Detail pane, choose Hotel from the Destination pop-up menu.**

When you're done, it should look like Figure 4-17.

Next you want to refine the relationship a bit more. You need to create an *inverse* relationship between `Hotel` and `Annotation`. That means when Core Data loads your objects, they will point to each other.

You usually model relationships in both directions and specify the inverse relationships accordingly. Core Data uses this information to ensure consistency when a change is made to one or the other.

Make sure `Annotation` is selected in the Entity pane and then choose `Annotation` from the Detail pane's Inverse pop-up menu as I have in Figure 4-18.

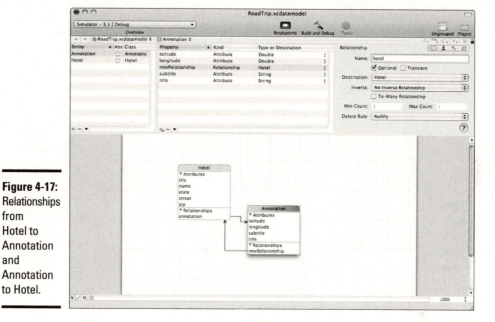

Figure 4-17:
Relationships from Hotel to Annotation and Annotation to Hotel.

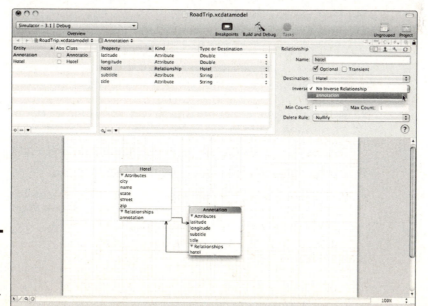

Figure 4-18:
Setting an inverse relationship.

When you're done, your data model should look like Figure 4-19.

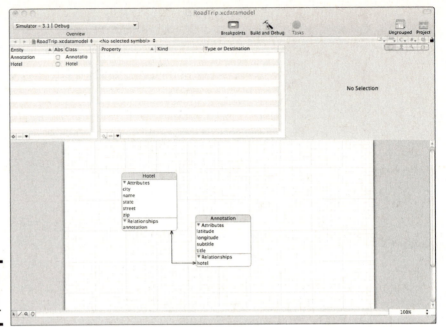

Figure 4-19:
The inverse
relationship.

Generate your classes

Of course, you still need the classes for your program. Remember, all you've done thus far is create a data model for Core Data to use to both save and get your objects. You'll still need the classes to describe them in your program.

Does that mean a lot of copy and paste? Of course not. You can now use Xcode to generate the files for your Hotel and Annotation classes.

1. **With your data model open in Xcode, select either the Hotel or the Annotation entity in the Entity pane.**

Base your selection on which item you want to create subclasses for.

2. **Choose File⇨New File from the Xcode main menu.**

3. **In the New File dialog that appears, first select Cocoa Touch Classes in the iPhone OS section on the left and then select Managed Object Class in the topmost pane, as I have in Figure 4-20.**

You'll see the screen shown in Figure 4-21.

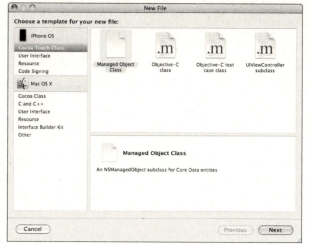

Figure 4-20:
Creating a
managed
object class.

4. **The correct location and targets should already have been selected
for you, so just click Next to accept them.**

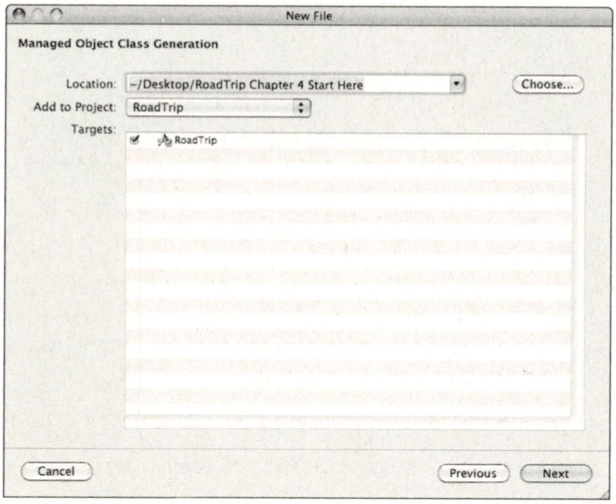

Figure 4-21:
Accept this.

You see the Managed Object Class Generation dialog shown in Figure
4-22. Make sure both Hotel and Annotation are checked. The Generate
Assessors and Generate Objective-C 2.0 Properties check boxes should
also be selected.

5. **Click Finish in the Managed Object Class Generation dialog to generate the files.**

The `Hotel` and `Annotation` class interface and implementation files are created and added to your project. Just like that.

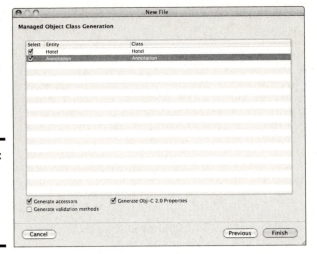

Figure 4-22:
Generating
the
Managed
Object
classes.

Listings 4-3, 4-4, 4-5, and 4-6 show the `.h` and `.m` files for `Hotel` and `Annotation`, respectively.

Listing 4-3: Generated Hotel.h Class File

```
#import <CoreData/CoreData.h>

@class Annotation;

@interface Hotel :  NSManagedObject
{
}

@property (nonatomic, retain) NSString * street;
@property (nonatomic, retain) NSString * state;
@property (nonatomic, retain) NSString * zip;
@property (nonatomic, retain) NSString * name;
@property (nonatomic, retain) NSString * city;
@property (nonatomic, retain) Annotation * annotation;

@end
```

Listing 4-4: Generated Hotel.m Class File

```
#import "Hotel.h"

#import "Annotation.h"

@implementation Hotel

@dynamic street;
@dynamic state;
@dynamic zip;
@dynamic name;
@dynamic city;
@dynamic annotation;

@end
```

Listing 4-5: Generated Annotation.h Class File

```
@class Hotel;

@interface Annotation :  NSManagedObject
{
}

@property (nonatomic, retain) NSString * title;
@property (nonatomic, retain) NSNumber * latitude;
@property (nonatomic, retain) NSNumber * longitude;
@property (nonatomic, retain) NSString * subtitle;
@property (nonatomic, retain) Hotel * hotel;

@end
```

Listing 4-6: Generated Annotation.m Class File

```
#import "Annotation.h"

#import "Hotel.h"

@implementation Annotation

@dynamic title;
@dynamic latitude;
@dynamic longitude;
@dynamic subtitle;
@dynamic hotel;

@end
```

There are a few things you should probably notice

✦ **In the interface files, all the attributes you specify in the model are represented by objects.** For example even though you specified the latitude and longitude attribute types as Double, the property values at runtime are instances of NSNumber because Core Data uses objects to represent values (shades of the property list).

✦ **In the implementation files, properties are implemented as *@dynamic*, and not the "normal" @synthesize.** Core Data generates the accessor methods at runtime. @dynamic instructs the compiler not to generate a warning if it cannot find implementations of accessor methods.

✦ **In the implementation files, there is no dealloc method.** This is because Core Data will take care of that for the *modeled properties* of the generated object. If you do add your own instance variables (and you will), you have to manage the memory for those yourself in the normal way.

✦ **The model has been updated.** The Hotel and Annotation entities are now those respective classes instead of NSManagedObject. You need to save the model file because of that.

You also have to add a few things to Annotation.h to make it work. Add the code in bold in Listing 4-7.

Listing 4-7: Modify Annotation.h Class File

```
#import <CoreData/CoreData.h>

@class Hotel;
#import <MapKit/MapKit.h>



@interface Annotation :  NSManagedObject    <MKAnnotation>
{
CLLocationCoordinate2D coordinate;
}

@property (nonatomic, retain) NSString * title;
@property (nonatomic, retain) NSNumber * latitude;
@property (nonatomic, retain) NSNumber * longitude;
@property (nonatomic, retain) NSString * subtitle;
@property (nonatomic, retain) Hotel * hotel;
@property (nonatomic) CLLocationCoordinate2D coordinate;
- (NSString *) title;
- (NSString *) subtitle;

@end
```

You've both adopted and added the required methods and properties for the MKAnnotation protocol. Although I could have simply used the title and subtitle properties as is, I want to make you more comfortable with treating the generated classes like you would any other — say, by adding methods or even by adding methods that override the generated accessors.

You also have to implement the new methods in the Annotation.m file. Add the code in bold in Listing 4-8 to that file.

Listing 4-8:   Update Annotation.m

```
#import "Annotation.h"

#import "Hotel.h"

@implementation Annotation

@dynamic title;
@dynamic latitude;
@dynamic longitude;
@dynamic subtitle;
@dynamic hotel;
@synthesize coordinate;

- (CLLocationCoordinate2D) coordinate {

  CLLocationCoordinate2D theCoordinate;
  theCoordinate.latitude = [self.latitude doubleValue];
  theCoordinate.longitude = [self.longitude doubleValue];
  return theCoordinate;
}


- (NSString *) title {
  return self.hotel.name;
}
- (NSString *) subtitle {
   return self.hotel.city;
}

@end
```

**Book VI
Chapter 4**

**Setting Up
Core Data**

You'll also notice one other thing. Instead of being derived from NSObject, Hotel, and Annotation are derived from NSManagedObject. Read on to find out why Managed slipped its way between NS and Object.

Managed objects

NSManagedObject contains the methods and properties necessary to represent any entity. It has a reference to the entity description for the entity of which it is an instance — and using the information in the entity description, information about its attributes and relationships. You can also create subclasses of NSManagedObject to implement additional behavior.

If you feel so inclined, you can think of a managed object as the object representation of a record in a table in a database. Each managed object represents the data you operate on in your application — in this case Hotel objects and their associated data — name, street address, city, state, and zip code. You can even add in reservation data and conformation number at your leisure.

NSManagedObject connects your objects to the Managed Object Context, as explained in the next section.

If you regenerate the classes, all your work will be lost. If you need to regenerate, I suggest you rename the classes, generate the new ones, and then copy and paste your additions back in.

The Managed Object Context

Now that you have your Core Data–managed object model as well as your classes, you'll want to create, save, and then restore your objects and implement undo and redo.

Luckily for you, the Core Data framework provides most of this functionality for you automatically, primarily through a managed object context (or just plain context) object. Its primary responsibility is to manage a collection of managed objects. The managed object context also allows you to use a collection of Core Data objects — collectively known as the *persistence stack* — that mediate between the objects in your application and external data stores.

You add objects and remove objects using the context. It tracks the changes you make, both to object attributes and to the relationships between objects. Because of that, the context is able to provide Undo and Redo support. It also ensures that if you change relationships between objects, the integrity of the relationship is maintained.

When you create a new managed object, you insert it into a context. You fetch existing records in the database into the context as managed objects. (I explain fetching in Chapter 5 of this minibook).

In any application, you might have multiple managed object contexts. You might want to maintain discrete sets of managed objects as well as edits to those objects; or you might want to perform a background operation by using one context while allowing the user to interact with objects in another.

When you fetch objects from a persistent store (I explain that next), you bring temporary copies into memory. You can then operate on these objects by doing things such as changing attributes and relationships and adding and deleting objects. When you're done, you save the changes you've made, and the context ensures that your objects are in a valid state. Then the changes are written to the persistent store (or stores), new records are added (for objects you created), and records are removed (for objects you deleted). But unless you actually save those changes, the persistent store remains unchanged — persistent, isn't it?

The Persistent Store Coordinator and Persistent Store

A persistent store coordinator is an instance of `NSPersistentStoreCoordinator` and manages precisely what you'd think it would manage — a collection of *persistent object stores*. A persistent object store is simply an external store (file) of persisted data. The persistent store coordinator is the object that actually maps between objects in your application and records in the database. In an iPhone application, you usually just have a single store, but in complex desktop applications there may be more than one. The persistent store coordinator manages these stores and makes them appear to the managed object contexts as a single store. If you did have multiple managed object contexts, each of these would be connected to the same coordinator.

The persistent store coordinator handles the nitty gritty of reading and writing data files. You probably won't ever directly interact with the persistent store coordinator after you've specified the location of a new external data store to be associated with your application.

The Core Data Stack

After you've created the managed object model and generated your classes and have gotten your mind around the managed object context, you still need to set up what is known as the Core Data Stack in your application. This involves creating the following:

1. The `NSManagedObjectContext`
2. The `NSManagedObjectModel`
3. The `NSPersistentStoreCoordinator`

I run through the creation of each one of these at the end of this chapter, but quite frankly, for what you'll be doing in RoadTrip, and for quite a while in your own application, you'll probably be using the boilerplate provided by Xcode.

"Coding" the stack

Way back when you created the RoadTrip project, I told you to use XCode's Project template for a navigation-based application, but to leave the Use Core Data for Storage check box deselected.

If you had selected that check box way back when, you would have found yourself with an application that had Core Data firmly integrated into your application. You'd find the Core Data stack in your application delegate, and you'd find a `RootViewController` that used Core Data as well. Although letting Xcode do it might appear to be easier, figuring out how to retrofit Core Data into an existing application is something you'll want to know how to do, and doing so will give you a better understanding of how it all works.

That being the case, you still don't want to have to type all that code in by hand, so in this section I show you how to have the best of both worlds.

To start with, I want you to create a new, throw-away project. Use the Navigation-Based Application template you see in Figure 4-23, but this time select the check box that says Use Core Data for Storage. (If you need a refresher on how to set up a project in Xcode, take another look at Book V, Chapter 1.)

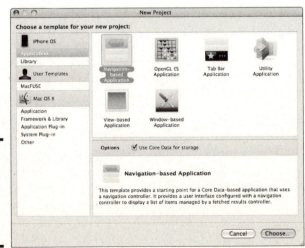

Figure 4-23: The Navigation-Based Application template.

You can name the application anything you'd like, but I use CoreData.

In this new project you just created out of thin air, you'll find that the template contains all you need to set up Core Data, and all you really need to do is copy the generated code into your RoadTrip project. Here's the blow by blow:

1. **Select the `CoreDatAppDelegate.m` file and scroll to**

```
#pragma mark -
#pragma mark Core Data stack
```

Figure 4-24 shows you where to stop.

2. **Select the code from that point, as I have in Figure 4-25, up to (but not including) the following two lines**

```
#pragma mark -
#pragma mark Memory management
```

Note that you will be including the following code as well

```
#pragma mark -
#pragma mark Application's Documents directory
```

3. **Copy all the code you've selected and paste it into `Trip.m`. (See Figure 4-26.)**

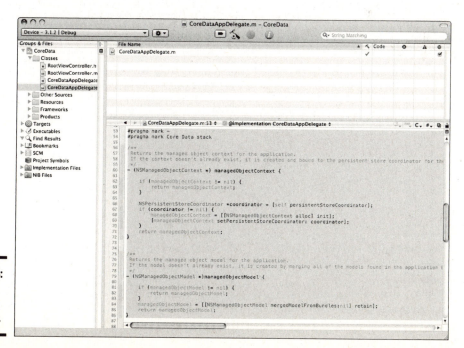

Figure 4-24:
The start
of the Core
Data Stack.

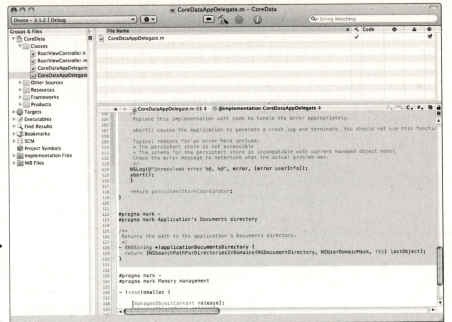

Figure 4-25:
The end of
the Core
Data Stack.

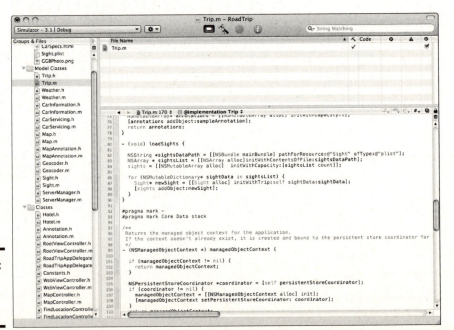

Figure 4-26:
Paste the
code into
Trip.m.

In your throw-away project, the Core Data Stack is, of course, in the application delegate. In this example, I've shown you how to have it owned by the model instead — with a little help from the Copy and Paste commands.

Adding the Core Data Framework

Okay, you have a Core Data Stack, which, admit it, didn't require much heavy lifting. Next you have to add the Core Data Framework.

Up until now, all you've needed to get by is the framework that more or less came supplied when you created a project. (Except for `MapKit` back in Book V, Chapter 5, of course, but that was the exception that proved the rule.) Now you need a new framework to enable Core Data.

1. **Click the disclosure triangle next to Targets in the Groups & Files list and then right-click RoadTrip.**

   Be sure to do this using the Targets folder, or Step 3 won't work!

2. **From the submenu that appears, choose Add and then choose Existing Frameworks.**

3. **Select CoreData Framework in the window that appears in Figure 4-27 and then click add.**

   The `CoreData.Framework` icon will appear at the bottom of the Groups & Files list.

4. **Drag the `CoreData.Framework` icon up into the Frameworks folder.**

Figure 4-27:
Adding
a new
framework.

Connecting the pieces

Clean up time. You're going to have to add some instance variables and properties and a method to the `Trip.h` file — no ifs, ands, or buts about it. Make the modifications you see bolded in Listing 4-9.

Listing 4-9: Trip.h

```
#import <MapKit/MapKit.h>
#import <Foundation/Foundation.h>
@class Weather;
@class CarServicing;
@class CarInformation;
@class Map;
@class MapController;

@interface Trip : NSObject   {

  NSString        *tripName;
  CarServicing    *carServicing;
  CarInformation *carInformation;
  Weather         *weather;
  NSMutableArray *sights;
  Map             *map;
  MapController   *mapController;

// Core Data Stack
  NSManagedObjectModel *managedObjectModel;
  NSManagedObjectContext *managedObjectContext;
  NSPersistentStoreCoordinator *persistentStoreCoordinator;

}

@property (nonatomic, retain) NSMutableArray *sights;
@property (nonatomic, retain) Map* map;
@property (nonatomic, retain) MapController *mapController;

- (NSString *)applicationDocumentsDirectory;


- (id) initWithName:(NSString*) theTripName;
- (CLLocationCoordinate2D) initialCoordinate;
- (NSString*) mapTitle;
- (id) returnSightDelegate:(int) index;
- (id) returnWeatherDelegate;
- (id) returnCarInformationDelegate;
- (id) returnCarServicingDelegate;
```

```
// Core data properties and method
@property (nonatomic, retain, readonly) NSManagedObjectModel
    *managedObjectModel;
@property (nonatomic, retain, readonly)
    NSManagedObjectContext *managedObjectContext;
@property (nonatomic, retain, readonly)
    NSPersistentStoreCoordinator *persistentStoreCoordinator;
- (NSString *)applicationDocumentsDirectory;


@end
```

Notice that the properties you just added are `readonly`.

One more thing left to do. You need to add something to the `RoadTrip_Prefix.pch` file in the Other Sources folder in Groups & Files list. (Figure 4-28 shows you the innards of the `RoadTrip_Prefix.pch` file.)

**Book VI
Chapter 4**

**Setting Up
Core Data**

Figure 4-28:
Add to the
RoadTrip_
Prefix.pch
file.

You have to add Core Data to the `RoadTrip_Prefix.pch` file to make sure it is included wherever you need it. To do so, add the code in bold in Listing 4-10 to the file.

Listing 4-10:   Modifying RoadTrip_Prefix.pch

```
#import <Availability.h>

#ifndef __IPHONE_3_0
#warning "This project uses features only available in iPhone
    SDK 3.0 and later."
#endif

#ifdef __OBJC__
    #import <Foundation/Foundation.h>
    #import <UIKit/UIKit.h>
    #import <CoreData/CoreData.h>

#endif

@end
```

You're now ready to actually use Core Data. Your project should compile and execute with no errors.

What's in the Core Data Stack

If you've been reading closely, you'll remember that I mentioned earlier that the Core Data Stack consists of:

1. The `NSManagedObjectContext`
2. The `NSPersistentStoreCoordinator`
3. The `NSManagedObjectModel`

Here's where I briefly explain the code in each of these puppies, although, as I said before, for what you'll be doing in RoadTrip, and for quite a while in your own application, you'll probably just be using the boilerplate provided by Xcode.

The Managed Object Context

Listing 4-11 shows you the code for accessing the `managedObjectContext` property. It's actually an explicit implementation of the `managedObjectContext` property getter and is invoked every time you access the property.

It returns the `NSManagedObjectContext` for the application. If the context doesn't already exist, it is created and bound to the persistent store coordinator for the application.

Listing 4-11: Creating the managedObjectContext

```
- (NSManagedObjectContext *) managedObjectContext {

    if (managedObjectContext != nil) {
        return managedObjectContext;
    }

    NSPersistentStoreCoordinator *coordinator =
                    [self persistentStoreCoordinator];
    if (coordinator != nil) {
        managedObjectContext =
                    [[NSManagedObjectContext alloc] init];
        [managedObjectContext setPersistentStoreCoordinator:
    coordinator];
    }
    return managedObjectContext;
}
```

**Book VI
Chapter 4**

**Setting Up
Core Data**

Notice that it uses (and sets) the `persistentStoreCoordinator`.

```
NSPersistentStoreCoordinator *coordinator = [self
    persistentStoreCoordinator];
    if (coordinator != nil) {
        managedObjectContext =
                    [[NSManagedObjectContext alloc] init];
        [managedObjectContext
            setPersistentStoreCoordinator: coordinator];
    }
```

The Persistent Store Coordinator

Listing 4-12 shows the code for accessing the `persistentStoreCoordi-nator` Property. It works the same way — as an explicit implementation of the `persistentStoreCoordinator` property getter and is invoked every time you access the property.

It returns the NSPersistentStoreCoordinator for the application. If the coordinator doesn't already exist, it's created, and the application's store is added to it.

Listing 4-12:   Creating the persistentStoreCoordinator

```
- (NSPersistentStoreCoordinator *)
                            persistentStoreCoordinator {

    if (persistentStoreCoordinator != nil) {
        return persistentStoreCoordinator;
    }

    NSURL *storeUrl = [NSURL fileURLWithPath:
     [[self applicationDocumentsDirectory]
     stringByAppendingPathComponent:@"CoreData.sqlite"]];

    NSError *error = nil;
    persistentStoreCoordinator =
        [[NSPersistentStoreCoordinator alloc]
        initWithManagedObjectModel:
                            [self managedObjectModel]];
    if (![persistentStoreCoordinator addPersistentStoreWit
hType:NSSQLiteStoreType configuration:nil URL:storeUrl
options:nil error:&error]) {
                                                    /*
Replace this implementation with code to handle the error
appropriately.
                                                    */
    NSLog(@"Unresolved error %@, %@", error,
                            [error userInfo]);
    abort();
    }

    return persistentStoreCoordinator;
}
```

Notice the persistent store uses SQLite as its store, although you can use others.

```
NSURL *storeUrl = [NSURL fileURLWithPath:
 [[self applicationDocumentsDirectory]
    stringByAppendingPathComponent:@"CoreData.sqlite"]];
```

Notice the error checking code:

```
if (![persistentStoreCoordinator
        addPersistentStoreWithType:NSSQLiteStoreType
        configuration:nil URL:storeUrl options:nil
                                    error:&error]) {
```

You'll see this error (in addition to when the store is not accessible) when the schema for the persistent store is incompatible with current Managed Object Model. And that happens when you change the Managed Object Model (which happens frequently during development) and either don't migrate to the new one (out of scope for this book) or delete the old one and start from scratch.

The current code uses `abort()` when that happens — causing the application to generate a crash log and terminate. Although it may be useful during development, you shouldn't do this in a shipping application. You should at least display an alert that instructs the user what has happened and/or what to do.

Notice it uses the `applicationDocumentsDirectory`.

```
NSURL *storeUrl = [NSURL fileURLWithPath:
    [[self applicationDocumentsDirectory]
    stringByAppendingPathComponent:@"CoreData.sqlite"]];
```

Listing 4-13 shows how the path to the application's `Documents` directory is returned.

Book VI
Chapter 4

Setting Up
Core Data

Listing 4-13:   Creating the applicationDocumentsDirectory

```
- (NSString *)applicationDocumentsDirectory {
    return [NSSearchPathForDirectoriesInDomains(NSDocumentDire
    ctory, NSUserDomainMask, YES) lastObject];
}
```

Also notice that the Persistent Store Coordinator uses the `managedObject-Model` property.

```
persistentStoreCoordinator =
    [[NSPersistentStoreCoordinator alloc]
    initWithManagedObjectModel: [self managedObjectModel]];
```

The Managed Object Model

Listing 4-14 shows you the code for accessing the `managedObjectModel` property. It, too, is an explicit implementation of the `managedObjectModel` property getter and is invoked every time you access the property. As you saw, it's accessed when you create the Persistent Store Coordinator.

It returns the Managed Object Model for the application. If the model doesn't already exist, it is created by merging all of the models found in the application bundle.

Listing 4-14:   Creating the managedObjectModel

```
- (NSManagedObjectModel *)managedObjectModel {

    if (managedObjectModel != nil) {
        return managedObjectModel;
    }
    managedObjectModel = [[NSManagedObjectModel
    mergedModelFromBundles:nil] retain];
    return managedObjectModel;
}
```

Putting Core Data to Work

At this point, you have what you need to start using Core Data. In the next chapter of this minibook, you do just that by using Core Data to create, manage, and save Hotel objects (which will also be used as annotations).

Chapter 5: Putting Core Data to Work

In This Chapter

✔ **Using Core Data**

✔ **Figuring out fetch requests**

✔ **Adding, saving, and loading Hotel objects with Core Data**

✔ **Supporting Undo**

When you have the infrastructure in place, as spelled out in Chapter 4 of this minibook, you still need to do one more thing to get Core Data up and running: You need to actually create the Managed Object Context in your application.

After you do that, you need to send a message to the Managed Object Context to create and delete objects as well as support iPhone's Shake feature to do undos and redos. You'll also create fetch requests to retrieve data using the Managed Object Context.

I show you how to do all of that in this chapter. But before you start, I want to explain the last major concept you need to understand to use Core Data: the fetch request.

Understanding the Fetch Request

A *fetch request* is an object that specifies what data you want, for example, "all Hotels ordered by city," or "all Hotels in Needles, California."

A fetch request has three parts:

1. The name of an entity. (You can only fetch one type of entity at a time.)

2. A predicate object that specifies conditions that objects must match.

3. An array of sort descriptor objects that specifies the order in which the objects should appear.

You send a fetch request to a Managed Object Context, which gets the objects that match your request (possibly none), adds them to the Managed Object Context, and returns them to the application. If a context already contains a managed object for an object returned from a fetch, then the existing managed object is returned in the fetch results.

The framework tries to be as efficient as possible — you get only the objects you asked for. If you follow a relationship to an object that hasn't yet been fetched, it's fetched automatically for you. If you stop using an object, by default it will be deallocated. (This is, of course, not the same as deleting it.)

Unless you really need *all* the objects of a particular entity, you can also use a predicate to limit the number of objects returned to those you're actually interested in.

In addition, your fetch request can also cache the results so that if the same data is subsequently needed, the work doesn't have to be repeated. (I explain caching later as well.)

If you're displaying objects in a table view, you can use a *fetched results controller,* NSFetchedResultsController. It, too, tries to minimize the amount of data held in memory. It efficiently manages the results returned from a Core Data fetch request to provide data for a UITableView object. You use this class to get the objects you need to create cells in such an object, as well as to determine the number of sections you need and the number of rows in each section.

Finally, as you'll soon see, a fetch request controller can monitor changes to objects and report changes to a delegate, which can then do what's necessary to update the table view accordingly (including reloading the data).

By the way, you just happen to create and use a fetched results controller later in this chapter.

Getting the Ball Rolling

To get everything up and going, you need to actually instantiate (or create) the Core Data Stack you added in the last chapter. You do that in the Trip initialization method.

Modify initWithName in Trip.m by using the bolded code in Listing 5-1.

Listing 5-1:   Modifying initWithName and Synthesizing Hotels

```
@synthesize hotels;

- (id) initWithName:(NSString*) theTrip {

  if ((self = [super init])) {

    [self managedObjectContext];
    tripName = theTrip;
    [tripName retain];
    carInformation = [[CarInformation alloc]
  initWithTrip:self];
    carServicing = [[CarServicing alloc] initWithTrip:self];
    weather = [[Weather alloc] init];
    [self loadSights];
    [self loadHotels];
    map =[[Map alloc] initWithTrip:self];
  }
  return self;
}
```

Walking through the code, you see that you create the Core Data Stack by simply making a reference to the managedObjectContext.

```
[self managedObjectContext];
```

As explained in the last chapter, that statement invokes the managed ObjectContext property's getter method which you have overridden. In that method, you create an NSManagedObjectContext (if it doesn't already exist), which in turn references the persistentStoreCoordina tor, whose property getter method you also override. In this method, you create the NSPersistentStoreCoordinator (if it doesn't exist) and reference the managedObjectModel property. You override that method, and managedObjectModel getter creates the NSManagedObjectModel if it doesn't exist.

Further down in Listing 5-1, you'll notice that you synthesize a property called hotels — you'll use this to hold an array of Hotel objects.

Finally, in the initWithName method in Trip.m, you send a message to yourself to loadHotels.

Not bad for a start. Now, enter the code in Listing 5-2 to implement load-Hotels.

Listing 5-2: loadHotels

```
-(void) loadHotels{
  NSFetchRequest *fetchRequest =
                         [[NSFetchRequest alloc] init];
  // Edit the entity name as appropriate.
  NSEntityDescription *entity = [NSEntityDescription
    entityForName:@"Hotel" inManagedObjectContext:managedObject
    Context];
  [fetchRequest setEntity:entity];

  // Set the batch size to a suitable number.
  [fetchRequest setFetchBatchSize:20];

  // Create the sort descriptors array.
  NSSortDescriptor *sortDescriptor =
                 [[NSSortDescriptor alloc]
                 initWithKey:@"city" ascending:YES];
  NSArray *sortDescriptors =
    [[NSArray alloc] initWithObjects:sortDescriptor, nil];
  [fetchRequest setSortDescriptors:sortDescriptors];

 // Execute the fetch.
 NSError *error = nil;
 NSMutableArray *mutableFetchResults =
  [[managedObjectContext executeFetchRequest:fetchRequest
                             error:&error] mutableCopy];
 if (mutableFetchResults == nil) {
    // Handle the error.
 }
 [self setHotels:mutableFetchResults];

 [fetchRequest release];
 [sortDescriptor release];
 [sortDescriptors release];
}
```

I've based this code on the templates provided in Xcode. Now I can take you through it step by step.

First you start by creating and initializing an NSFetchRequest.

```
NSFetchRequest *fetchRequest =
                         [[NSFetchRequest alloc] init];
```

You then create an NSEntityDescription object with the name of the entity (Hotel) and the Managed Object Context and bind the object to the fetch request.

```
NSEntityDescription *entity = [NSEntityDescription
    entityForName:@"Hotel" inManagedObjectContext:managedObject
    Context];
[fetchRequest setEntity:entity];
```

This takes care of the first part of a fetch request.

Next, you set the estimated batch size. Here, I tell the Managed Object Context that the most I want "fetched" is the first 20 `Hotel` objects.

```
[fetchRequest setFetchBatchSize:20];
```

You can use this feature to control the memory footprint of your application. The default value of 0 is treated as infinite. But, if you set a non-zero batch size, the collection of objects returned when the fetch is executed is broken into batches — and no more than `batchSize` objects' data will be fetched from the persistent store at a time. If you need an object that isn't in the batch, Core Data will go out and get it for you. (Okay, part 2 done.)

**Book VI
Chapter 5**

Then, you create the sort descriptor arrays and specify that you want the returned fetch to be sorted by city (`initWithKey:@"city"`) in ascending order (`ascending:YES`), add then the sort descriptor and bind it to the fetch request. This task completes the third part of the fetch request.

**Putting Core
Data to Work**

```
NSSortDescriptor *sortDescriptor =
        [[NSSortDescriptor alloc] initWithKey:@"city"
                                   ascending:YES];
NSArray *sortDescriptors =
    [[NSArray alloc] initWithObjects:sortDescriptor, nil];
fetchRequest setSortDescriptors:sortDescriptors];
```

You won't be working with a predicates here, so you finish up by executing the fetch.

```
NSError *error = nil;
NSMutableArray *mutableFetchResults =
   [[managedObjectContext executeFetchRequest:fetchRequest
                          error:&error] mutableCopy];
if (mutableFetchResults == nil) {
  // Handle the error.
}
```

Finally, you set the `hotels` property to the mutable fetch results you just created.

```
[self setHotels:mutableFetchResults];
```

And then clean up after yourself.

```
[fetchRequest release];
[sortDescriptor release];
[sortDescriptors release];
```

To finish up with all the changes you need to make to `Trip`, add the code in Listing 5-3 to `Trip.h`. You're adding the `hotels` property that you used to hold all your various `Hotel` objects and then declaring the `loadHotels` method you just coded.

Listing 5-3: Modifying Trip.h

```
#import <MapKit/MapKit.h>
#import <Foundation/Foundation.h>
@class Weather;
@class CarServicing;
@class CarInformation;
@class Map;
@class MapController;

@interface Trip : NSObject   {

    NSString                    *tripName;
    CarServicing                *carServicing;
    CarInformation              *carInformation;
    Weather                     *weather;
    NSMutableArray              *sights;
    Map                         *map;
    MapController               *mapController;
    NSMutableArray              *hotels;



    // Core Data Stack
    NSManagedObjectModel        *managedObjectModel;
    NSManagedObjectContext      *managedObjectContext;
    NSPersistentStoreCoordinator *persistentStoreCoordinator;

}

@property (nonatomic, retain) NSMutableArray *sights;
@property (nonatomic, retain) Map* map;
@property (nonatomic, retain) MapController *mapController;
 @property (nonatomic, retain) NSMutableArray * hotels;


- (id) initWithName:(NSString*) theTripName;
- (CLLocationCoordinate2D) initialCoordinate;
- (NSString*) mapTitle;
- (id) returnSightDelegate:(int) index;
- (id) returnWeatherDelegate;
- (id) returnCarInformationDelegate;
- (id) returnCarServicingDelegate;
```

```
- (void) loadHotels;
```

```
// Core data properties and method
@property (nonatomic, retain, readonly) NSManagedObjectModel
    *managedObjectModel;
@property (nonatomic, retain, readonly)
    NSManagedObjectContext *managedObjectContext;
@property (nonatomic, retain, readonly)
    NSPersistentStoreCoordinator *persistentStoreCoordinator;
- (NSString *)applicationDocumentsDirectory;
```

```
@end
```

In Chapter 3 of this minibook, you did a lot of work to make adding annotations to the map easy. Now your work will start to pay off. All you need to do to have the `Hotel` object's annotations appear on the map when you fetch them from the store is make the modifications bolded in Listing 5-4 to `createAnnotations` in `Map.m`.

Listing 5-4: Loading the Annotation Objects

```
- (void) createAnnotations {

  [annotations removeAllObjects];
  [annotations addObjectsFromArray:trip.sights ];
  for (Hotel* aHotel in trip.hotels) {
    [annotations addObject:aHotel.annotation ];
  }
}
```

This code gets the `Annotation` object referenced by a `Hotel` and adds it to the annotations array that the Map view will then use to display the annotations.

You also need to add the following to `Map.m`.

```
#import "Hotel.h"
```

Finally, you need to enable the selection of the `HotelController` in the `RootViewController`. I know, I know, I haven't even coded the `HotelController` yet, but I want to get the mundane out of the way. Add the code in Listing 5-5 to `tableView:didSelectRowAtIndexPath` in `RootViewController.m` that uncomments out the selection of the `HotelController`.

Listing 5-5:   Uncommenting Out HotelController Selection

```
- (void)tableView:(UITableView *)tableView
        didSelectRowAtIndexPath:(NSIndexPath *)indexPath {

    RoadTripAppDelegate *appDelegate =
              (RoadTripAppDelegate *)
            [[UIApplication sharedApplication] delegate];
    [appDelegate.lastView replaceObjectAtIndex:0 withObject:
            [NSNumber numberWithInteger:indexPath.section]];
    [appDelegate.lastView replaceObjectAtIndex:1 withObject:
            [NSNumber numberWithInteger:indexPath.row]];

    [tableView deselectRowAtIndexPath:indexPath
                                             animated:YES];

    int menuOffset =
              [self menuOffsetForRowAtIndexPath:indexPath];
    UIViewController *targetController =
              [[menuList objectAtIndex:menuOffset]
                            objectForKey:kControllerKey];

    if (targetController == nil) {
      BOOL realtime = !appDelegate.useStoredData;

      switch (menuOffset) {
        case 0:
          if (realtime) targetController =
                  [[MapController alloc] initWithTrip:trip];
          else [self displayOfflineAlert:
                  [[menuList objectAtIndex:menuOffset]
                                  objectForKey:kSelectKey]];
          break;
        case 1:
          targetController =
            [[SightListController alloc] initWithTrip:trip];
          break;
        case 2:
          targetController =
                [[HotelController alloc] initWithTrip:trip];
          break;
        case 3:
          if  (realtime) targetController = [[WebViewController
    alloc] initWithTrip:trip tripSelector:@
    selector(returnWeather:)
            webControl:YES title:NSLocalizedString(@"Weather",
                                            @"Weather")];
          else [self displayOfflineAlert:
                  [[menuList objectAtIndex:menuOffset]
                                  objectForKey:kSelectKey]];
          break;
        case 4:
```

```
      targetController = [[WebViewController alloc]
initWithTrip:trip tripSelector:@selector(returnCarServicing
Information:)
                            webControl:NO
title:NSLocalizedString (@"Car Servicing", @"Car
Servicing")];
      break;
    case 5:
      targetController = [[WebViewController alloc]
        initWithTrip:trip
        tripSelector:@selector(returnCarInformation:)
        webControl:NO
        title:NSLocalizedString (@"The Car", @"Car
                                    Information")];
      break;
  }
      if (targetController) {
    [[menuList   objectAtIndex:menuOffset]
  setObject:targetController forKey:kControllerKey];
    }
  }
  if (targetController) {
    [[self navigationController]
        pushViewController:targetController animated:YES];
    [targetController release];
  }
}
```

You also have to add the import to `RootViewController.m`.

```
#import "HotelController.h"
```

Adding HotelController

All that lovely coding in the preceding section got you to the point where you can select an entry in the table view that creates a `HotelController`. It's time to add the code that creates a `HotelController` when you make that selection.

This is the last piece of the puzzle you need in order to create and display `Hotel` objects.

As I explain in Chapter 4 of this minibook, if you had selected that Use Core Data for Storage check box in your Navigation-based Application template right at the beginning of your project, your `RootViewController` would have been generated with code to use Core Data. So, in the same spirit of copy and paste that you used in Chapter 4 to add the Core Data Stack, you'll add the code generated by the template to your `HotelController`.

But first you need to create the controller:

1. **In the RoadTrip project window, select the Classes folder and then choose File⇨New from the main menu (or press ⌘+N) to get the New File window.**

2. **In the left column of the dialog, select Cocoa Touch Classes under the iPhone OS heading, select the UIViewController subclass template in the top-right pane, and then click Next.**

   Be sure the `UITableViewController` subclass is selected and the With XIB for User Interface is also selected.

   You see a new dialog asking for some more information.

3. **Enter HotelController.m in the File Name field and then click Finish.**

To make things easier to find, I keep my `HotelController.m` and `.h` classes in the Classes folder. I also move the `HotelController.xib` to the Resources folder

Setting up the controller

Start with the interface file. Modify `HotelController.h` with the bolded code in Listing 5-6.

Listing 5-6:   HotelController.h

```
@class Trip;
@class Hotel;

@interface HotelController : UITableViewController
                   <NSFetchedResultsControllerDelegate> {
  NSFetchedResultsController *fetchedResultsController;
  Trip                       *trip;
  Hotel                      *hotel;
}
@property (nonatomic, retain) NSFetchedResultsController
                                *fetchedResultsController;
- (id) initWithTrip: (Trip*) aTrip;
@end
```

First of all, you have made `HotelController` an `NSFetchedResults ControllerDelegate` here. You'll see why you did that in the "Creating a fetched results controller" section, later in this chapter.

You've also declared three instance variables. One of them holds a reference to `Trip`, the second will hold a reference to a new `Hotel` object when

you do finally create one, and the third is the instance variable behind the
`fetchedResultsController` property that you also add.

Finally, you declare the `initWithTrip:` method you're going to add to
`HotelController.m`.

To implement `initWithTrip:`, add the bolded code in Listing 5-7 to
`HotelController.m`.

Listing 5-7:   initWithTrip

Book VI
Chapter 5

Putting Core
Data to Work

```
#import "HotelController.h"
#import "MapController.h"
#import "Trip.h"
#import "Hotel.h"
#import "Annotation.h"
#import "Geocoder.h"

@implementation HotelController

@synthesize fetchedResultsController;

- (id) initWithTrip: (Trip*) aTrip{
  if (self = [super initWithNibName:@"HotelController"
                                      bundle:nil]) {

    trip = aTrip;
    [trip retain];
  }
  return self;
}
```

You'll notice I had you add a number of `#import` statements. You don't
need them now, but you will need them later, so why not get that out of
the way?

Repurposing the code from the template

Working in the same spirit of copy and paste that you used in Chapter 4 of
this minibook to add the Core Data Stack, you'll add the template code to
`HotelController`. Here's how:

1. **Open the CoreData project you created in the last chapter.**

2. **Select all the code in the `RootViewController`, starting with `view-DidLoad`.**

3. **Delete all the code after `initWithTrip:` in `HotelController.m` and
   replace it with the code you copied from `RootViewController` in the
   `CoreData` project.**

Admittedly, your work isn't done yet, but this copy and paste stuff has gotten you pretty far, even if you still need to make some (minor) modifications to some of the code. You'll start with `viewDidLoad`.

You may notice some stylistic differences in the code I'm about to have you work with. That's because, as much as possible, I've retained the code that would have been generated by using a Core Data template when you first set up your project.

Modifying viewDidLoad

Make the modifications indicated in bold in Listing 5-8 to the copy of `view-DidLoad` in `HotelController.m`.

Listing 5-8:   Modifying viewDidLoad

```
- (void)viewDidLoad {
[super viewDidLoad];

// Set up the edit and add buttons.
//self.navigationItem.leftBarButtonItem =
                                     self.editButtonItem;
self.title = @"Hotels";

UIBarButtonItem *addButton = [[UIBarButtonItem alloc]
    initWithBarButtonSystemItem:UIBarButtonSystemItemAdd
  target:self action:@selector(insertNewObject)];
self.navigationItem.rightBarButtonItem = addButton;
[addButton release];
self.tableView.sectionHeaderHeight = 40.0;


NSError *error = nil;
if (![[self fetchedResultsController]
                          performFetch:&error]) {

  //Replace this implementation with code to handle the
  // error appropriately.
  SLog(@"Unresolved error %@, %@", error,
                                error userInfo]);
  abort(); //$$ not in production
  }
}
```

Looking at Listing 5-8, you see that the template code you got from your CoreData project adds an Edit button, which you won't be using, so I have you delete that. It also adds an Add button, which the user taps to add a new hotel. This Add button has the `insertNewObject` method as its target.

I also have you add a line of code to set the title of the Navigation bar to "Hotels."

The default table view is plain, and that's what you'll be using. You can, however, also have section titles, but I find the default Height value a little cramped, so I have you set it here.

```
self.tableView.sectionHeaderHeight = 40.0;
```

Creating a fetched results controller

As I mention in the opening of this chapter, if you're using a table view, a fetched results controller (`NSFetchedResultsController`) can make your life much easier. It, too, tries to minimize the amount of data held in memory by efficiently managing the results returned from a Core Data fetch request to provide data for a `UITableView` object. You use this class to get the objects you need to create cells in a `UITableView`, as well as to determine both the number of sections you need and the number of rows for each section.

You create an instance of this class by using a fetch request that specifies the entity, an array containing at least one sort ordering, and optionally a filter predicate. You can also specify a `sectionNameKeyPath` argument that the controller will use to split the results into sections, or you can pass `nil` to indicate that the controller should generate a single section. After creating an instance, you invoke `performFetch:` to actually execute the fetch.

To get all this to work for you, make the modifications in bold in Listing 5-9 to `fetchedResultsController` method in `HotelController.m`.

Listing 5-9: fetchedResultsController

```
- (NSFetchedResultsController *)fetchedResultsController {

  if (fetchedResultsController != nil) {
    return fetchedResultsController;
  }

// Create the fetch request for the entity.
  NSFetchRequest *fetchRequest =
                          [[NSFetchRequest alloc] init];
    // Edit the entity name as appropriate.
// NSEntityDescription *entity = [NSEntityDescription
   entityForName:@"Event" inManagedObjectContext:managed
   ObjectContext];
  NSEntityDescription *entity = [NSEntityDescription
       entityForName:@"Hotel"
       inManagedObjectContext:trip.managedObjectContext];
```

(continued)

Listing 5-9 *(continued)*

```
   [fetchRequest setEntity:entity];

// Set the batch size to a suitable number.
   [fetchRequest setFetchBatchSize:20];

 // Edit the sort key as appropriate.
 //NSSortDescriptor *sortDescriptor =
      [[NSSortDescriptor alloc] initWithKey:@"timestamp
 NSSortDescriptor *sortDescriptor = [[NSSortDescriptor
   alloc] initWithKey:@"city" ascending:NO];
   NSArray *sortDescriptors = [[NSArray alloc]
    initWithObjects:sortDescriptor, nil];
   [fetchRequest setSortDescriptors:sortDescriptors];


 // Edit the section name key path and cache name
// nil for section name key path means "no sections".
//NSFetchedResultsController *aFetchedResultsController =
   [[NSFetchedResultsController alloc] initWithFetchRequest
   :fetchRequest managedObjectContext:managedObjectContext
   sectionNameKeyPath:nil cacheName:@"Root"];
 NSFetchedResultsController *aFetchedResultsController =
   [[NSFetchedResultsController alloc] initWithFetchRequest:
   fetchRequest managedObjectContext:trip.managedObjectContext
   sectionNameKeyPath:@"city" cacheName:@"Root"];
   aFetchedResultsController.delegate = self;
   self.fetchedResultsController =
                                 aFetchedResultsController;
   [aFetchedResultsController release];
   [fetchRequest release];
   [sortDescriptor release];
   [sortDescriptors release];

   return fetchedResultsController;
}
```

The first thing you do to set up your very own fetched results controller is create the fetch request for the entity. For all practical purposes, this is the same thing you did in `loadHotels`, so if you aren't clear on what you've just accomplished in that regard with Listing 5-9, refer to the discussion following Listing 5-3.

What's new here is that, after you've created the fetch request, you create the fetched results controller, specify the section name key path and cache name, and then set `self` as the delegate.

```
NSFetchedResultsController *aFetchedResultsController =
    [[NSFetchedResultsController alloc] initWithFetchRequest:f
    etchRequest managedObjectContext:trip.managedObjectContext
    sectionNameKeyPath:@"city" cacheName:@"Root"];
aFetchedResultsController.delegate = self;
```

With this lovely bit of coding, you create an NSFetchedResults Controller, initializing it with the fetchRequest you just created and configured, the managedObjectContext and two other arguments — sectionNameKeyPath and cacheName.

By passing in the sectionNameKeyPath argument @"city", you're tell-ing Core Data you want to assign Hotel objects to sections in the table view based on the City key. That means that when you're done, your HotelController will display hotels by cities, as shown in Figure 5-1.

Figure 5-1: The hotel is listed under its city.

Giving a (optional) cacheName of @"Root" and a delegate — aFetched ResultsController.delegate = self;, (earlier you had the HotelController adopt the NSFetchedResultsControllerDelegate protocol) tells Core Data to cache its results so that if the same data is sub-sequently asked for again, the work doesn't have to be repeated.

Finally, you clean up by releasing the objects:

```
self.fetchedResultsController = aFetchedResultsController;
[aFetchedResultsController release];
[fetchRequest release];
[sortDescriptor release];
[sortDescriptors release];

return fetchedResultsController;
```

Adding a new hotel

Now that you have the fetched results controller set up, it will be easier to understand what you do when you actually add a hotel.

The most exciting method in the HotelController is the one that adds a new object. The insertNewObject method is the target of the Add button you added in Listing 5-8. Although I've added to this method, it is essentially the same one used in the template. In the template, you simply add a new Event object with a single attribute — a time stamp — which you initialize it with. You will be extending that to create the Hotel object and its Annotation and then add it to the managed object context.

To avoid making things more complicated than they need to be, you won't be developing the user interface in this chapter to do that. The Hotel object and its Annotation are hard coded — that will make it easier for you to follow the logic.

In Book VII, however, I'll have you add a user interface as well as show you how you'll be able to use existing contacts in your Address Book to add hotels or, alternatively, add your new hotel to your Address Book contacts.

I've indicated in bold the changes you'll need to make to the template code to add a new Hotel object and its Annotation object. I've left out or summarized most of the comments you'll see in the template code.

Make the modifications in Listing 5-10 to insertNewObject in HotelController.m.

Listing 5-10:   Adding a New Hotel

```
#pragma mark -
#pragma mark Add a new object

- (void)insertNewObject {

// Create a new instance of the entity managed by the fetched
    results controller.
```

```
//NSManagedObjectContext *context =
        [fetchedResultsController managedObjectContext];
  NSEntityDescription *entity =
      [[fetchedResultsController fetchRequest] entity];
//NSManagedObject *newManagedObject =
        [NSEntityDescription insertNewObjectForEntityFor
  Name:[entity name] inManagedObjectContext:context];
  hotel = [NSEntityDescription
      insertNewObjectForEntityForName:[entity name]
      inManagedObjectContext:trip.managedObjectContext];
// If appropriate, configure the new managed object.
// [newManagedObject setValue:[NSDate date]
   forKey:@"timeStamp"];
  [hotel setValue:@"Hotel California" forKey:@"name"];
  [hotel setValue:@"1 Dr. Carlton B. Goodlett Place"
                                    forKey:@"street"];
  [hotel setValue:@"San Francisco" forKey:@"city"];
  [hotel setValue:@"California" forKey:@"state"];
  [hotel setValue:@"94102" forKey:@"zip"];

  Annotation *annotation = [NSEntityDescription
      insertNewObjectForEntityForName:@"Annotation"
      inManagedObjectContext:trip.managedObjectContext];
  [annotation setTitle:@"Annotation"];
  [annotation setHotel:hotel];
  [hotel setAnnotation:annotation];

  Geocoder * geocoder = [[Geocoder alloc] init];
  NSString* geocodeString = [[NSString alloc ]
      initWithFormat: @" %@ %@ %@ %@",
      hotel.street, hotel.city, hotel.state, hotel.zip];
  CLLocationCoordinate2D theCoordinate =
                [geocoder geocodeLocation:geocodeString];

  hotel.annotation.latitude =
      [NSNumber numberWithDouble: theCoordinate.latitude];
  hotel.annotation.longitude =
    [NSNumber numberWithDouble: theCoordinate.longitude];
  hotel.annotation.title = hotel.name;
// Save the context.
  NSError *error = nil;
  if (![trip.managedObjectContext save:&error]) {
   // Replace this implementation with code to handle the
   // error appropriately.
  NSLog(@"Unresolved error %@, %@", error,
                                    [error userInfo]);
  abort();
  }
  [trip loadHotels];
  [trip.mapController refreshAnnotations];
}
```

Looking at Listing 5-10, you see that you start by creating a new instance of the `Hotel` entity managed by the fetched results controller. (Remember, when you set up the fetch results controller in the previous section you specified the entity you wanted was `Hotel`.)

```
NSEntityDescription *entity =
        [[fetchedResultsController fetchRequest] entity];
```

Then you create a new object using the entity name `Hotel` in the managed object context you created in `Trip`.

```
hotel = [NSEntityDescription
        insertNewObjectForEntityForName:[entity name]
        inManagedObjectContext:trip.managedObjectContext];
```

Then you set the attributes for the object. (Later you will be doing this in a dialog where the user can enter the information.)

```
[hotel setValue:@"Hotel California" forKey:@"name"];
[hotel setValue:@"1 Dr. Carlton B. Goodlett Place"
                                    forKey:@"street"];
[hotel setValue:@"San Francisco" forKey:@"city"];
[hotel setValue:@"California" forKey:@"state"];
[hotel setValue:@"94102" forKey:@"zip"];
```

Next, you need to create and configure the `Annotation`.

Creating an object doesn't automatically create the objects it has relationships to.

```
Annotation *annotation = [NSEntityDescription
        insertNewObjectForEntityForName:@"Annotation"
        inManagedObjectContext:trip.managedObjectContext];
[annotation setTitle:@"Annotation"];
[annotation setHotel:hotel];
[hotel setAnnotation:annotation];
```

Then you use your old friend the `geocoder` to get the coordinates needed for the `Annotation` as well as set them.

```
Geocoder * geocoder = [[Geocoder alloc] init];
NSString* geocodeString = [[NSString alloc ]
        initWithFormat: @" %@ %@ %@ %@",
        hotel.street, hotel.city, hotel.state, hotel.zip];
CLLocationCoordinate2D theCoordinate =
                [geocoder geocodeLocation:geocodeString];
hotel.annotation.latitude =
        [NSNumber numberWithDouble: theCoordinate.latitude];
hotel.annotation.longitude =
        [NSNumber numberWithDouble: theCoordinate.longitude];
hotel.annotation.title = hotel.name;
```

Finally, you save the context

```
NSError *error = nil;
if (![trip.managedObjectContext save:&error]) {
 // Replace this implementation with code to handle the
 // error appropriately.
NSLog(@"Unresolved error %@, %@", error,
                                    [error userInfo]);
 abort();
 }
```

and then load the new `Hotel` into the `hotels` array used by Map's `create-Annotation` method and then send a message to the `MapController` to refresh the annotations.

```
[trip loadHotels];
[trip.mapController refreshAnnotations];
```

**Book VI
Chapter 5**

**Putting Core
Data to Work**

Here's where your previous work really pays off — you already have the logic in place to dynamically add and delete annotations as needed.

Table view methods

At this point you have created the infrastructure necessary to add a hotel. Of course, this superb piece of engineering isn't worth much until you add the code to the RoadTrip app that actually displays the hotel you have added.

That's what you will do in this section.

Next you need to make some changes to the default table view methods. You'll start with `tableView:cellForRowAtIndexPath:`. Make the modifications to `HotelController.m` shown in bold in Listing 5-11.

Listing 5-11: tableView:cellForRowAtIndexPath

```
- (UITableViewCell *)tableView:(UITableView *)tableView cellF
  orRowAtIndexPath:(NSIndexPath *)indexPath {

  static NSString *CellIdentifier = @"Cell";

  UITableViewCell *cell = [tableView dequeueReusableCellWithI
    dentifier:CellIdentifier];
  if (cell == nil) {
   cell = [[[UITableViewCell alloc] initWithStyle:UITabl
   eViewCellStyleDefault reuseIdentifier:CellIdentifier]
   autorelease];
  }
// Configure the cell.
```

(continued)

Listing 5-11 *(continued)*

```
    NSManagedObject *managedObject = [fetchedResultsController
    objectAtIndexPath:indexPath];
//cell.textLabel.text =
      [[managedObject valueForKey:@"timeStamp"]
    description];
    cell.textLabel.text = [[managedObject valueForKey:@"name"]
    description];

    return cell;
}
```

Fetched results controllers are very helpful in table views because they make it easy to get the right number of sections and rows, as well as the information needed to create the cells. Here, as you can see, all you have to do is pass the fetched results controller the index path you get in this method and then it will return the object that has the data (the name of the hotel) you want to display in the cell.

```
NSManagedObject *managedObject =
  [fetchedResultsController objectAtIndexPath:indexPath];
```

You set the text in the cell to the name of the hotel.

```
cell.textLabel.text =
        [[managedObject valueForKey:@"name"] description];
```

The template code doesn't come with section heads, so you need to add the method in Listing 5-12 to `HotelController.m` to take care of the section heads we need.

Listing 5-12:   tableView:titleForHeaderInSection:

```
- (NSString *)tableView:(UITableView *)tableView titleForHead
  erInSection:(NSInteger)section {
  return [[[fetchedResultsController sections]
  objectAtIndex:section] name];
}
```

Bunches of other table view methods are available out there, but I'll leave you to explore them on your own. I do, however, come back and revisit `table View:didSelectRowAtIndexPath:` in the "Adding Delete" section, later in the chapter.

The fetched results controller's delegate

If you set a delegate for a fetched results controller, the controller registers to receive change notifications from its managed object context. (I glossed over that when I discussed caching earlier.) Any change in the managed object context to objects or section information needs to be processed and the display in the table view updated accordingly. The controller notifies the delegate when result objects change location or when sections are modified.

Listing 5-13 shows the simplest case — yes, just reloading the table view counts as change.

Listing 5-13: Reloading the Table View

```
- (void)controllerDidChangeContent:
            (NSFetchedResultsController *)controller {
    // In the simplest, most efficient, case, reload the table
    view.
    [self.tableView reloadData];
}
```

This is what you'll be using. There are also a number of other methods available that are beyond the scope of this book. You can read the comments in the generated code and see how they're implemented in the Core Data samples Apple provides.

If you don't set a delegate, the controller does not monitor changes to objects in its associated managed object context — which may be exactly what you want if there aren't going to be any changes (a read-only list, for example).

Managing memory

Finally, because you don't create the managed object context (it is created in `Trip`), you don't want to delete it either. Make the modifications shown in bold in Listing 5-14 to `dealloc` in `HotelController.m` to make sure your managed object context doesn't get tossed.

Listing 5-14: dealloc

```
- (void)dealloc {
    [fetchedResultsController release];
//  [managedObjectContext release];
    [super dealloc];
}
@end
```

You now have someplace to stay

At this point, you can compile and run the code. If you select Hotels in the main menu of your RoadTrip app, you'll be faced with the blank screen you see in Figure 5-2.

Figure 5-2:
The initial
Hotels list.

If you select the Add button (+), you'll see in Figure 5-3 that you have now successfully added a hotel.

Even cooler than that, if you go back to the Map view, you'll see (in Figure 5-4) that the hotel is now nicely displayed — with it annotation no less!

Supporting Undo

One of the great things about Core Data is that it makes it easy to support the iPhone's Shake to Undo functionality.

Now, managed objects are always associated with a Managed Object Context, which doesn't sound too surprising. But did you know that each managed object context has an Undo manager? Now that's cool. You can, for example, change a managed object's properties using an accessor method (or key-value coding, or custom key-value-observing compliant methods) and the Managed Object Context uses key-value observing to keep track of modifications to its registered objects. The place where the managed object context registers all its modification events is with its Undo manager.

Figure 5-3:
I wonder
what
checkout is
like?

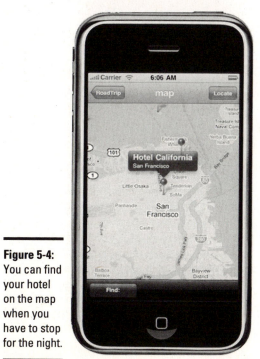

Figure 5-4:
You can find
your hotel
on the map
when you
have to stop
for the night.

To undo an operation, you simply send the context an Undo message; to redo an operation, you send the context — you guessed it — a Redo message. (You can also roll back all changes made since the last save operation by using rollback, as well as other standard Undo manager functionality, such grouping undo events. — something I won't cover here).

Supporting undo in HotelController

To begin all the undoing, the strategy here is to set up the Undo manager when you add a hotel. Make the changes marked in bold/strikeout in Listing 5-15 to the `insertNewObject` method in `HotelController.h`.

Listing 5-15:   Adding the Code to a New Object

```
#pragma mark -
#pragma mark Add a new object

- (void)insertNewObject {

// Create a new instance of the entity managed by the fetched
    results controller.
  NSEntityDescription *entity =
      [[fetchedResultsController fetchRequest] entity];
  hotel = [NSEntityDescription
      insertNewObjectForEntityForName:[entity name]
      inManagedObjectContext:trip.managedObjectContext];
  [self setUpUndoManager];
  [hotel setValue:@"Hotel California" forKey:@"name"];
  [hotel setValue:@"600 Sutter Street" forKey:@"street"];
  [hotel setValue:@"San Francisco" forKey:@"city"];
  [hotel setValue:@"California" forKey:@"state"];
  [hotel setValue:@"94108" forKey:@"zip"];

  Annotation *annotation = [NSEntityDescription
      insertNewObjectForEntityForName:@"Annotation"
      inManagedObjectContext:trip.managedObjectContext];
  [annotation setTitle:@"Annotation"];
  [annotation setHotel:hotel];
  [hotel setAnnotation:annotation];

  Geocoder * geocoder = [[Geocoder alloc] init];
  NSString* geocodeString = [[NSString alloc ]
      initWithFormat: @" %@ %@ %@ %@",
      hotel.street, hotel.city, hotel.state, hotel.zip];
  CLLocationCoordinate2D theCoordinate =
                  [geocoder geocodeLocation:geocodeString];

  hotel.annotation.latitude =
      [NSNumber numberWithDouble: theCoordinate.latitude];
  hotel.annotation.longitude =
```

```
        [NSNumber numberWithDouble: theCoordinate.longitude];
    hotel.annotation.title = hotel.name;
// Save the context.
    NSError *error = nil;
    if (![trip.managedObjectContext save:&error]) {
        // Replace this implementation with code to handle the
        // error appropriately.
        NSLog(@"Unresolved error %@, %@", error,
                                        [error userInfo]);
'Tony Bove'  abort();
    }
    [trip loadHotels];
    [trip.mapController refreshAnnotations];
}
```

The modifications spelled out in Listing 5-15 do two things for you. First, you arrange it so that you send a message to yourself to set up the Undo manager.

```
[self setUpUndoManager];
```

With that done, you then delete the code you added to save the context and refresh the annotations. That's because you don't want to save or update anything until you're quite sure what the last Undo/Redo action was. I show you later where you'll do that save and update.

Now you will have to implement two methods in `HotelController`. Start by making the changes to `HotelController.h` shown in bold in Listing 5-16.

Listing 5-16:   HotelController.h

```
@class Trip;
@class Hotel;

@interface HotelController : UITableViewController
    <NSFetchedResultsControllerDelegate> {
  NSFetchedResultsController *fetchedResultsController;
  Trip                       *trip;
  Hotel                      *hotel;
  NSUndoManager              *undoManager;
}
@property (nonatomic, retain) NSFetchedResultsController
    *fetchedResultsController;
 @property (nonatomic, retain) NSUndoManager *undoManager;
- (void)setUpUndoManager;
- (void)cleanUpUndoManager;

@end
```

Here you have declared two methods to set up (and then clean up) the Undo manager and a property to hold a reference to the Undo manager.

Next, you need to add the two methods `setUpUndoManager` and `cleanUpUndoManager` shown in Listings 5-17 and 5-18, respectively, to `TripController.m`.

Listing 5-17:   Setting Up the Undo Manager

```
- (void)setUpUndoManager {
  if (hotel.managedObjectContext.undoManager  == nil) {
    hotel.managedObjectContext.undoManager =
                                [[NSUndoManager alloc] init];
      [hotel.managedObjectContext.undoManager setActionName:
                  [NSString stringWithString:@"Add Hotel"]];

                    [hotel.managedObjectContext.undoManager
    setLevelsOfUndo:3];
      [hotel.managedObjectContext.undoManager release];
    }
  self.undoManager = hotel.managedObjectContext.undoManager ;

// Register as an observer of the hotel's context's undo
    manager.
  NSNotificationCenter *dnc =
                  [NSNotificationCenter defaultCenter];
 [dnc addObserver:self selector:@
    selector(undoManagerDidUndo:) name:NSUndoManagerDidUndoCha
    ngeNotification object:undoManager];
 [dnc addObserver:self
          selector:@selector(undoManagerDidRedo:) name:NSUnd
    oManagerDidRedoChangeNotification object:undoManager];
}
```

If the `Hotel` object's Managed Object Context doesn't already have an Undo manager, then create one and set it for the context and self.

```
if (hotel.managedObjectContext.undoManager  == nil) {
NSUndoManager *anUndoManager =
                    [[NSUndoManager alloc] init];
```

You also set what the Undo alert will display (it'll display `Add Hotel`) and the level of undo (up to 3 undos).

```
[anUndoManager setActionName:
            [NSString stringWithString:@"Add Hotel"]];
    [anUndoManager setLevelsOfUndo:3];
```

Keeping tabs on your Undo manager

The view controller needs to keep a reference to the Undo manager it creates so that it can determine whether to remove the Undo manager when editing finishes (in the case of a table view that supports editing) or when the view unloads (in our case). You also assign the newly created Undo manager to the Managed Object Context:

```
self.undoManager = anUndoManager;
    [anUndoManager release];
    hotel.managedObjectContext.undoManager = undoManager;
```

Then you register as an observer of the `Hotel` object's Managed Object Context's Undo manager. You tell the notification center to send the `undoManagerDidUndo:` message to `self` when an undo occurs and the `undoManagerDidRedo:` message when a redo occurs.

**Book VI
Chapter 5**

**Putting Core
Data to Work**

```
NSNotificationCenter *dnc =
                   [NSNotificationCenter defaultCenter];
 [dnc addObserver:self selector:@
   selector(undoManagerDidUndo:) name:NSUndoManagerDidUndoCha
   ngeNotification object:undoManager];
 [dnc addObserver:self
   selector:@selector(undoManagerDidRedo:) name:NSUndoManager
   DidRedoChangeNotification object:undoManager];
}
```

When you no longer need the Undo manager, you'll clean up after yourself. Enter the code in Listing 5-18 to `HotelController.m`.

Listing 5-18:   Cleaning Up the Undo Manager

```
- (void)cleanUpUndoManager {

// Remove self as an observer.
  [[NSNotificationCenter defaultCenter]
                                   removeObserver:self];

  if (hotel.managedObjectContext.undoManager ==
                                   undoManager) {
  hotel.managedObjectContext.undoManager = nil;
  self.undoManager = nil;
  }
}
```

You'll remove `self` as an observer and set the properties to `nil`.

You registered with the notification center to have a message sent whenever there was an undo or redo. Add the code in Listing 5-19 to `HotelController.m` to implement those methods.

Listing 5-19:   undoManagerDidUndo and undoManagerDidRedo

```
- (void)undoManagerDidUndo:(NSNotification *)
                                          notification {
  [self.tableView reloadData];
}


- (void)undoManagerDidRedo:(NSNotification *)
                                          notification {

  [self.tableView reloadData];
}
```

In both cases, you simply reload the table view to either remove (or add back) the entry.

Finally, a little housekeeping. The view controller must be first responder in order to be able to receive Shake events for undo. To do that, add the code in Listing 5-20 to `HotelController.h`.

Listing 5-20:   Setting the Correct First Responder Status

```
- (BOOL)canBecomeFirstResponder {

  return YES;
}


- (void)viewDidAppear:(BOOL)animated {

  [super viewDidAppear:animated];
  [self becomeFirstResponder];
}
```

Finally, when the view unloads and undos and redos are no longer possible, you need to save the current Managed Object Context and resign as first responder. Add the code in Listing 5-21 `HotelController.m` to send the `cleanUpUndoManager` message.

Listing 5-21:   viewWillDisappear:

```
- (void)viewWillDisappear:(BOOL)animated {
  [super viewWillDisappear:animated];
  [self cleanUpUndoManager];
  // Save the context.
  if (trip.managedObjectContext.hasChanges) {
    NSError *error = nil;
    if (![trip.managedObjectContext save:&error]) {
/*
  Replace this implementation with code to handle the error
  appropriately.
*/
      NSLog(@"Unresolved error %@, %@", error,
                                 [error userInfo]);
    abort();
    }
  }
  [trip loadHotels];
  [trip.mapController refreshAnnotations];
  [self resignFirstResponder];
}
```

**Book VI
Chapter 5**

**Putting Core
Data to
Work**

The viewWillDisappear: message is sent to the view controller, well, when the view is going to disappear. This is the place where you want to commit the changes. First, you send the cleanUpUndoManager method you implemented in Listing 5-18. Then you save the context, and then send the loadHotels and refreshAnnotations messages to ensure that the hotel will appear on the map — this is simply the code you had in insert-NewObject previously and does the same thing here. You also resign as first responder because you're ending the Undo/Redo cycle (and the view is disappearing anyway).

When you compile this code, go ahead and add a hotel using the Add button, as I have in Figure 5-5.

At this point, you can only add the hotel you hard coded in the insertNew Object method — but patience, you'll add the code and the user interface in Book VII, Chapter 1 that will allow the user to decide where he or she wants to stay.

Then either shake the device, or choose Hardware⇨Shake Gesture. You'll be given the opportunity to undo the added hotel, as shown in Figure 5-6.

If you touch Undo Add Hotel, your added hotel will be undone, as you can see in Figure 5-7.

Figure 5-5:
Adding a
hotel.

Figure 5-6:
Undo add
hotel?

Figure 5-7:
The result
of Undo Add
Hotel.

Adding Delete

After you add a Hotel, it would also be nice if you could delete it if you change your mind. Normally, you'd do that using the Edit function in the table view or a Delete button when displaying the details of the Hotel. Although you don't have either of those available yet, I still want to show you what you need to do as far as Core Data is concerned to delete an object. To do that, you'll make the `Hotel` entry in the `HotelController` selectable, and when it's selected for an entry, you will delete it.

Don't worry, I show you how to deal with delete the right way in Book VII, when I show you how to enter the hotel data in a view and interface to your Address book.

I want to point out that I won't be implementing undo for delete. I leave that as an exercise for you.

To start with, you need to modify the default `tableView:didSelectRow AtIndexPath:` method supplied in the CoreData template you pasted into your application in the previous section.

Make the modification shown in bold in Listing 5-22 to `tableView:didSelect RowAtIndexPath:` in `HotelController.m`. It was really just a stub with comments. I've omitted the comments and you can delete them if you would like.

Listing 5-22: HotelController.m

```
- (void)tableView:(UITableView *)tableView didSelectRowAtInde
    xPath:(NSIndexPath *)indexPath {
    [tableView deselectRowAtIndexPath:indexPath
                                          animated:YES];
    hotel = [[self fetchedResultsController]
                          objectAtIndexPath:indexPath];
    [trip deleteHotel:hotel];
    hotel = nil;
}
```

The first thing you do in Listing 5-22 is deselect the row, and then get the `Hotel` object you're going to delete from the `fetchedResultsCon troller` using the `indexPath` to determine which object that is. (The `fetchedResultsController` really does make things easier when you are using table view.)

```
[tableView deselectRowAtIndexPath:indexPath animated:YES];
hotel = [[self fetchedResultsController]
                          objectAtIndexPath:indexPath];
```

Then you send the `deleteHotel:` message to `Trip`, passing the `Hotel` you want to delete as an argument and setting the hotel instance variable to `nil`.

```
[trip deleteHotel:hotel];
hotel = nil;
```

Finally, you have to implement the `deleteHotel:` method. Add the code in Listing 5-23 to `Trip.m`.

Listing 5-23: deleteHotel:

```
- (void) deleteHotel:(Hotel*) theHotel {

    [hotels removeObject:theHotel];
    [managedObjectContext deleteObject:theHotel];
    // Save the context.
    NSError *error;
    if (![managedObjectContext save:&error]) {
```

```
// Replace this implementation with code to handle the error
   appropriately.

   NSLog(@"Unresolved error %@, %@", error,
                                  [error userInfo]);
   abort();
}
[self loadHotels];
if (self.mapController) [self.mapController
  refreshAnnotations];
}
```

The first thing you do is remove the `Hotel` you're deleting for the `hotels` array:

```
[hotels removeObject:theHotel];
```

Then you remove the `Hotel` from the Managed Object Context:

```
[managedObjectContext deleteObject:theHotel];
```

Then you save the Managed Object Context:

```
if (![managedObjectContext save:&error]) {

    // Replace this implementation with code to handle the
    error appropriately.

    NSLog(@"Unresolved error %@, %@", error, [error
    userInfo]);
    abort();
}
```

Again, as I mention earlier, when it comes to production code, you shouldn't simply abort when your code confronts an error.

Lastly, you reload the (remaining) hotels and then send a message to the `mapController` to refresh the annotations.

```
[self loadHotels];
  if (self.mapController) [self.mapController
                               refreshAnnotations];
```

You also have to add the following to `Trip.h`:

```
@class Hotel;
```

as well as the method declaration for `deleteHotel`:

```
- (void) deleteHotel:(Hotel*) theHotel;
```

What's Left

This chapter completes your introduction to Core Data, but there are some things you still need to add to the RoadTrip application.

For one, you'd like to be able to enter the name and address of the Hotel, instead of always having to stay at the same place. It would also be nice if you could save all that information as a contact in your Address Book. Conversely, if the information is already in your Address Book, you'd like to use that for the Hotel.

When you're on the road, you'd also like to send e-mail about where you are.

And you might like to know, at any point in time, by simply shaking your phone, how far you are from Apple Computer headquarters. (Others would like to know how far you are from a destination or sight.)

I cover all this in Book VI.

Book VII

Extending the App to the Realm of Ultracool

The 5th Wave By Rich Tennant

"Other than this little glitch with the landscape view, I really love my iPhone."

Contents at a Glance

Chapter 1: A User Interface for Adding Hotels and Using the Address Book

In This Chapter

✔ **Creating a user interface to add a hotel**

✔ **Accessing the Address Book to use exiting information**

✔ **Adding a hotel address to the Address Book**

*A*lthough the ability to add hotels that you want to stay in is obviously important (staying in the hard-coded default hotel San Francisco is a bit awkward if you're in Needles, California, for example), it's also really helpful to integrate your Address Book with your application to avoid the annoying "double" entry.

In this chapter, I show you how to create a view that allows the user to both enter a hotel as well as add that hotel to his or her Address Book. I also show you how to take a hotel already in the Address Book and add it as a hotel in the RoadTrip application.

Being able to do that becomes even more important when you realize that, even though the title of the view says "Hotels," a hotel can really be any place you're planning to stay. This includes the couch at your best friend's former girl- or boyfriend's cousin's.

Add AddHotelController

As you might expect, the first thing you need to do is add a view controller to manage the data entry view, like so:

1. **In the RoadTrip project window, select the Classes folder and then choose File⇨New from the main menu (or press ⌘+N) to get the New File window.**

2. **In the left column of the dialog, select Cocoa Touch Classes under the iPhone OS heading, select the UIViewController subclass template in the top-right pane and then click Next.**

Be sure the `UITableViewController` subclass *is not* selected and the With XIB for User Interface *is* selected.

You see a new dialog asking for some more information.

3. **Enter** AddHotelController.m **in the File Name field and then click Finish.**

To make things easier to find, I keep my `AddHotelController.m` and `.h` classes in the Classes folder. I also move the `AddHotelController.xib` to the Resources folder.

The first thing I want to have you do is create the entry screen, so start by double-clicking `AddHotelController.xib` to launch Interface Builder and start laying out the user interface. Just so you know what you're aiming for, Figure 1-1 shows what the final application is going to look like in the Simulator.

Figure 1-1:
Adding a
place to
stay.

Isn't it a beauty? Well, okay, the aesthetics do leave a bit to be desired, but I'll leave that up to you after I show you how to take care of all the plumbing you need behind it.

Adding controls to the view

The first pipes you want to lay involve adding controls to the view. Here's what you need to do:

1. **In the Resources folder (if that's where you placed it), double-click the `AddHotelController.xib` file.**

2. **Make sure the Library window is open. If it isn't, open it by choosing Tools⇨Library or pressing ⌘+Shift+L. Make sure Objects is selected in the mode selector at the top of the Library window and that Library is selected in the drop-down menu below the mode selector.**

   To refresh your memory, the Library has all the components you can use to build a user interface. These include the things you see on the iPhone screen, such as labels, buttons, and text fields; and those you need in order to create the "plumbing" to support the views (and your model), such as the view controllers.

   `AddHotelController.xib` was created by Xcode when I created `AddHotelController.m` from the template. As you can see, the file already contains a view — all I have to do here is add the static text, images, and text fields. If you drag one of these objects to the View window, it will create that object when your application is launched.

3. **Drag five Label elements from the Library window over to the View window.**

4. **Double-click each label and enter the text Name, Address, City State, and Zip as I have in Figure 1-2.**

   Labels display static text in the view. (*Static text* can't be edited by the user.)

   You may notice a rectangle around the label in Figure 1-2. I've turned on this feature so you can see the labels more clearly. (You can turn this particular feature on or off by choosing Layout⇨Show/Hide Bounds Rectangle.) This rectangle won't show onscreen when the app is running.

   Your View should look something like Figure 1-2 when you're done.

   You'll also want the labels to be right justified, which is done on the Attributes Inspector. (See Figure 1-3.) The next step shows you how.

5. **Click to select the Label text and then choose Tools⇨Attributes Inspector. (Pressing ⌘+1 is another way to call up the Attributes Inspector.) Click the Right Justified icon in the Layout section of the Inspector, as I have in Figure 1-3.**

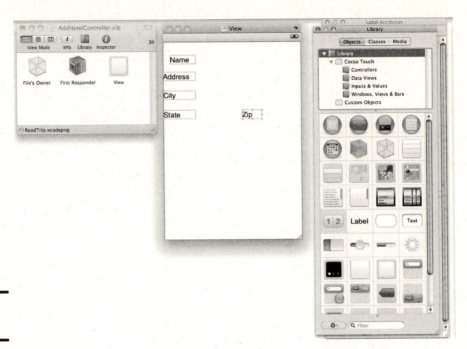

Figure 1-2:
The labels.

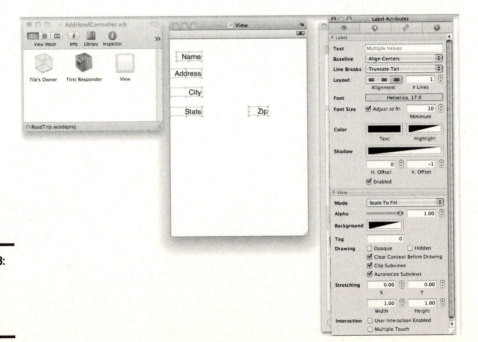

Figure 1-3:
Right
justifying
text in a
label.

6. **To add blank text fields for each label, drag in five of them from the Library window, as shown in Figure 1-4.**

   While it's not shown in any of the figures, I have Appears While Editing selected in the Clear Button drop-down menu and, I have Clear When Editing Begins deselected. These are my preferences; you should feel free to use them or experiment with your own settings.

   Finally, you need to add the buttons that will enable the user to either *get* the hotel info from his or her contacts or *save* the information he or she just entered to their contacts.

7. **Drag in two Round Rect Buttons from the Library window and add titles, as shown in Figure 1-5. (Keep the text right justified.)**

8. **Choose File⇨Save to save what you've done.**

   You can also save your work by pressing ⌘+S.

   Be sure to save your work. Forgetting to save your work has caused many developers (including yours truly) to waste prodigious amounts of time trying to figure out why something "doesn't work."

   Ready to admire your work? For that, you'll need to build and run your application.

9. **Choose File⇨Simulate Interface.**

   Admire away. (See Figure 1-6.)

Book VII Chapter 1

A User Interface for Adding Hotels and Using the Address Book

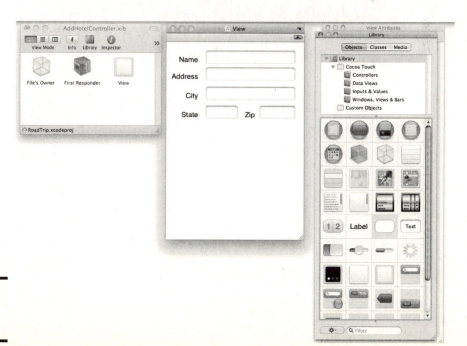

Figure 1-4:
The Text fields.

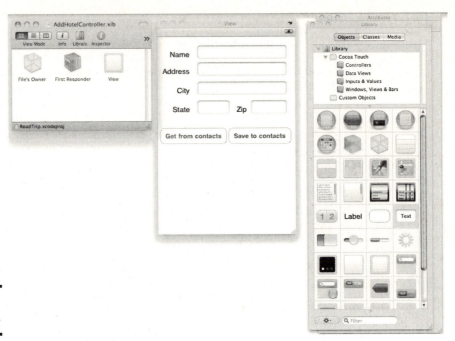

Figure 1-5:
The buttons.

Figure 1-6:
The simulated interface.

10. **Make your Xcode window the active window again.**

If you can't find it, or you minimized it, just click the Xcode icon in the Dock. The RoadTrip project should still be the active one. (You can always tell the active project by looking at the project name at the top of the Groups & Files list.)

This is the general pattern I use as I build my interface — add stuff, and then simulate it to see how it really looks.

Setting up the controller

Now that you have the view set up, you need to set up the controller so that you can

1. Get the input by first creating outlets and then connecting the outlets to Text fields in the nib file.

2. Code methods to execute when the user selects a button and connect them to the Round Rect Buttons — I just call them Buttons henceforth — in the nib file.

To refresh your memory, the view controller can refer to objects created from the nib file by using a special kind of instance variable referred to as an *outlet*. If I want (for example) to be able to access the Text Field object in my RoadTrip application, I take two steps:

1. Declare an outlet in my code by using the `IBOutlet` keyword.

2. Use Interface Builder to point the outlet to the text field I created earlier.

`IBOutlet` is a keyword that tags an instance-variable declaration so the Interface Builder application knows that a particular instance variable *is* an outlet — and can then enable the connection to it with Xcode. The fact that a connection between an object and its outlets exists is actually stored in a nib file. When the nib file is loaded, each connection is reconstituted and reestablished — thus enabling you to send messages to the object.

In my code, it turns out I need to create five outlets — one to point to each of the text fields I just set up in Interface Builder.

Then, when my application is initialized, the Text Field outlet is automatically initialized with a pointer to the text field. I can then use that outlet from within my code to get the text the user entered in the text field.

Similarly, Buttons in the nib file can be connected to methods in the view controller by using `IBAction` as a return type of the method you otherwise declare in the usual way.

**Book VII
Chapter 1**

**A User Interface
for Adding Hotels
and Using the
Address Book**

IBAction is one of those cool little techniques, like IBOutlet, that does nothing in the code but provide a way to inform Interface Builder (hence, the IB in both of them) that this method can be used as an action for Target-Action connections. All IBAction does is act as a tag for Interface Builder — identifying this method (action) as one you can connect to an object (namely, the Button) in a nib file. In this respect, this whole IBAction trick is similar to the IBOutlet. In that case, however, you were tagging instance variables, in this case, methods. Same difference.

I need to declare two methods — one to execute when the user taps the Get from Contacts button, and the other for when the user taps the Save to Contacts button.

To do that, add the bolded code in Listing 1-1 to AddHotelController.h.

Listing 1-1:   AddHotelController.h

```
@class Trip;
@class Hotel;

@interface AddHotelController : UIViewController
                                        <UITextFieldDelegate> {

    Trip                    *trip;
    Hotel                   *hotel;
    IBOutlet UITextField *street;
    IBOutlet UITextField *state;
    IBOutlet UITextField *zip;
    IBOutlet UITextField *name;
    IBOutlet UITextField *city;

}
- (id) initWithHotel:(Hotel*) theHotel
                                    trip:(Trip*) theTrip;
- (IBAction) getFromContacts:(id) sender;
- (IBAction) saveToContacts:(id) sender;

@end
```

You start by making the AddHotelController a UITextFieldDelegate — it will be handing the entry of text into the text fields. As you can see, I have had you add seven instance variables. One of them holds a reference to Trip, and the second will hold a reference to a new Hotel object when you do finally create one. The other five are the outlets I explained earlier. The outlets will automatically be initialized with a pointer to the text fields (street, state, zip, name, and city), when the application is launched and will enable you to access the text the user has entered in those fields.

I've also had you declare two new methods (and the usual initialization method), `getFromContacts:` and `saveToContacts:`, each with the keyword `IBAction` as the return type. `IBAction` is actually defined as a `void`, so if you think about it, all you've done is declare a new method with a return type of `void`.

```
- (IBAction)getFromContacts:(id)sender;
```

is the same as

```
- (void) getFromContacts:(id)sender;
```

This simply means that you've declared a method that doesn't return anything when it's sent a message.

The actual name you give the method can be anything you want, but it must have a return type of `IBAction`. Usually the action method takes one argument — typically defined as `id`, a pointer to the instance variables of an object — which is given the name `sender`. The control that triggers your action will use the `sender` argument to pass a reference to itself. So, for example, if your action method was invoked as the result of a button tap, the argument `sender` would contain a reference to the specific button that was tapped.

A word to the wise — having the `sender` argument contain a reference to the specific button that was tapped is a very handy mechanism, even if you're not going to take advantage of that in the RoadTrip application. With that reference in hand, you can access the variables of the control that was tapped.

But even though all these connects will happen automatically, it won't *automatically* happen automatically. You need to do some work back in Interface Builder first. So put aside Xcode and return to Interface Builder.

Be sure to save `AddHotelController.h` or you won't see the outlets or methods in Interface Builder.

**Book VII
Chapter 1**

A User Interface for Adding Hotels and Using the Address Book

Making the Connections in Interface Builder

In the previous section, I mentioned that if you want to be able to access the text fields (`street`, `state`, `zip`, `name`, and `city`) you've set up in RoadTrip, you had to take two steps:

1. Declare an `IBOutlet` in your code.

2. Use Interface Builder to point the outlet to the text fields you created earlier in Interface Builder.

Similarly, to execute a method in your code when the user taps a button, you also had to do two things:

1. Declare an IBAction in your code.

2. Use Interface Builder to point the event in the button you created earlier to the IBAction method in your code.

You've created the IBOutlets and the IBAction methods and now I'm going to show you how to create the connection in Interface Builder so that when the nib file is loaded, the nib loading code will create these connections automatically. With these connections established, you'll be able to get the data from your text field interface objects and receive messages from your buttons.

So, it's connection time.

1. **For your RoadTrip project, be sure to add the instance variables and methods to your code as spelled out in Steps 1 through 10 in the "Adding controls to the view" section, earlier in this chapter; then choose File⇨Save or press ⌘+S to save what you have done for each file.**

   You have to save your code; otherwise, Interface Builder won't be able to find it.

2. **In the Project window, double-click AddHotelController.xib to launch Interface Builder.**

3. **Right-click the File's Owner icon in the main nib window, as I have done in Figure 1-7, to see the list of Outlets.**

   This particular dialog can also be accessed by choosing the Connections tab in the Interface Builder Inspector.

   You also see the Receiving Actions — your IBAction labeled methods. You'll be working on that shortly.

4. **Drag from the name outlet item in the dialog onto the Name text field in the View window, as shown in Figure 1-8.**

   Interface Builder now knows that the name outlet should point to that Name text field at runtime. All is right with the world.

5. **Now drag from the File's Owner New Referencing outlet to the Name text field as well, as I have in Figure 1-9.**

   When you let go of the mouse, you'll see a pop-up menu that says delegate, as you can see in Figure 1-10.

6. **Select delegate from the pop-up menu, as I have in Figure 1-10.**

Figure 1-7:
The
AddHotel-
Controller
Outlets.

**Book VII
Chapter 1**

**A User Interface
for Adding Hotels
and Using the
Address Book**

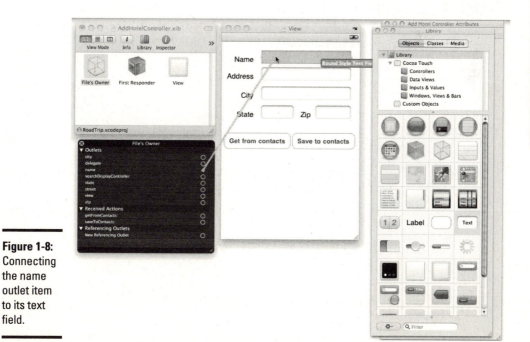

Figure 1-8:
Connecting
the name
outlet item
to its text
field.

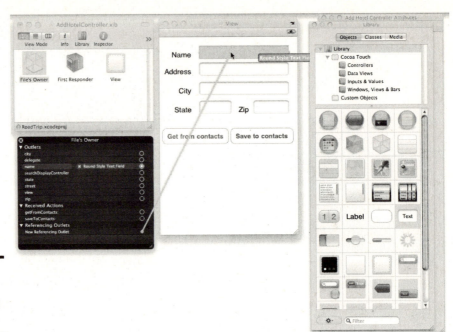

Figure 1-9:
Add a
referencing
outlet.

Figure 1-10:
Setting the
delegate.

This sets the File's Owner as the `UITextFieldDelegate`, something you'll need to do to manage the keyboard. I explain that in a later section.

When you're all done, your screen should look like mine in Figure 1-11.

7. **Repeat Steps 4–6 for the rest of the outlets.**

   `address`, `city`, `state`, and `zip`, to be precise.

   With that done, you are now ready to connect the buttons.

8. **From the same File's Owner menu, drag from `getFromContacts` under Received Actions, to the Get from Contacts button and then let go of the mouse.**

   You see a pop-up menu.

9. **Select Touch Up Inside from the pop-up menu, as I have in Figure 1-12.**

10. **Repeat Steps 8 and 9 for Save to Contacts.**

11. **Be sure to save your work.**

Figure 1-11: The first of the outlets complete.

Book VII
Chapter 1

A User Interface
for Adding Hotels
and Using the
Address Book

Figure 1-12:
Connecting
the button
to the action
method.

Adding Some Code to Actually Add Some Functionality

Making all the necessary connections Interface Builder, as spelled out in the last section, ensures that your code will compile and run (and give you a few choice warnings about unimplemented methods in the bargain), but RoadTrip really won't do anything different now as opposed to what it could do at the start of this chapter. What you *have* done, however, is gotten yourself ready to add the code to enable you to enter the hotel information.

If you're like me, you're probably impatient to actually see something work, so first add the `initWithHotel:trip:` method in Listing 1-2 to `AddHotelController.m`.

Listing 1-2: InitWithHotel:trip

```
#import "AddHotelController.h"
#import "Hotel.h"
#import "Trip.h"


@implementation AddHotelController
```

```
- (id) initWithHotel:(Hotel*) theHotel trip:(Trip*) theTrip
  {
  if (self = [super initWithNibName:@"AddHotelController"
                                        bundle:nil]) {
    hotel = theHotel;
    trip = theTrip;
  }
  return self;
}
```

This is your run-of-the-mill initialization method, and there really isn't anything left to say about it, other than you'd better not forget the #import statements, because the compiler will be happy to indirectly point out to you that they're missing. In this particular initialization method, you save a reference to the Trip (which you won't be using, but I have you do it now because as you build out the application, you're likely to need it), and you also save a reference to the Hotel object that was created and added to the Managed Object Context in the HotelController object's insert NewObject method and which you'll update based on what the user enters.

To actually display the AddHotelController, you need to add some code to HotelController. So, go ahead and add the bolded code in Listing 1-3 to the aforementioned HotelController that will create and then push the AddHotelController.

Listing 1-3: Modifying InsertNewObject

```
- (void)insertNewObject {

  NSEntityDescription *entity = [[fetchedResultsController
  fetchRequest] entity];
  hotel = [NSEntityDescription insertNewObjectForEntit
  yForName:[entity name] inManagedObjectContext:trip.
  managedObjectContext]; //$$
  [self setUpUndoManager];
  [hotel setValue:@"Hotel California" forKey:@"name"];
  [hotel setValue:@"1 Dr. Carlton B. Goodlett Place"
  forKey:@"street"];
  [hotel setValue:@"San Francisco" forKey:@"city"];
  [hotel setValue:@"California" forKey:@"state"];
  [hotel setValue:@"94102" forKey:@"zip"];

  AddHotelController *addHotelController =
    [[AddHotelController alloc] initWithHotel:hotel
                                      trip:trip];
  UINavigationController *navigationController =
    [[UINavigationController alloc] initWithRootViewController
    :addHotelController];
  navigationController.modalTransitionStyle =
                  UIModalTransitionStyleFlipHorizontal;
```

**Book VII
Chapter 1**

**A User Interface
for Adding Hotels
and Using the
Address Book**

(continued)

Listing 1-3 *(continued)*

```
//addHotelController.delegate = self;
  [self presentModalViewController:navigationController
                                          animated:YES];

  [navigationController release];
  [addHotelController release];

  Annotation *annotation = [NSEntityDescription ins
    ertNewObjectForEntityForName:@"Annotation"
    inManagedObjectContext:trip.managedObjectContext]; //$$
  [annotation setTitle:@"Annotation"];
  [annotation setHotel:hotel];
  [hotel setAnnotation:annotation];
  Geocoder * geocoder = [[Geocoder alloc] init];
  NSString* geocodeString = [[NSString alloc ]
    initWithFormat: @" %@ %@ %@ %@", hotel.street, hotel.city,
    hotel.state, hotel.zip];
  NSLog (@" finding = %@", geocodeString);
  CLLocationCoordinate2D theCoordinate = [geocoder
    geocodeLocation:geocodeString];
  hotel.annotation.latitude = [NSNumber numberWithDouble:
    theCoordinate.latitude];
  hotel.annotation.longitude =  [NSNumber numberWithDouble:
    theCoordinate.longitude];
  hotel.annotation.title = hotel.name;
}
```

Most of this code is pretty straightforward. This is the way you created view controllers in the `tableView:didSelectRowAtIndexPath:` methods in both the `SightListController` and `RootViewController` back in Books V and VI. In this case, however, you're using `presentModalView Controller`.

Modal view controllers are used in applications to allow the user to enter the information it needs. A modal view controller is not a subclass of `UIViewController`, and any view controller can be presented modally by your application. You use them when you want to show that there is a special relationship between the previous screen and the new one.

Modal controllers are used in two ways:

✦ To get information needed by the presenting controller from the user

✦ To temporarily display some content or force a change to what the user is currently doing (like the Info button you often see)

Modal view controllers are about redirecting the user's workflow temporarily in order to gather or display some information. After you have the information you need (or after you've presented the user with the appropriate information), you dismiss the modal view controller to return the application's previous state.

I chose the transition style `UIModalTransitionStyleFlipHorizontal` — where the current view does a horizontal 3D flip from right-to-left, resulting in the revealing of the new view as if it were on the back of the previous view — but you can use any transition style you like. For example, you could go for `UIModalTransitionStyleCoverVertical` (where the new view slides up from the bottom of the screen) or `UIModalTransitionStyleCrossDissolve` (where the view fades out while the new view fades in at the same time).

Dismissing the controller

When it comes time to dismiss a modal view controller, the preferred method is for the view controller that presented the modal view controller to do the dismissing. And the preferred way to do that is to use delegation.

That brings me to the commented-out line of code back in Listing 1-3:

```
//addHotelController.delegate = self;
```

I have this commented out so that you can compile and run the application to check for compiler errors and see how it works. Because I don't have the `delegate` instance variable defined, it won't compile with that line of code in there, and when I get to explaining how the view controller is dismissed a bit later in this section, I have you uncomment out that line.

For now, you can compile and run the application. Just be sure to delete any previous copies of RoadTrip on your iPhone or simulator.

You'll find that if you tap the Add button in the Hotel list, your view should flip around, showing your new data entry screen.

You can even enter data in the various text fields, but there's no way to dismiss the keyboard — tapping Return doesn't help. There's also another problem — well, actually more than one, but the one you'll notice is that there's no way to get back from this new view. (As I said, you haven't done that yet.)

You also still have to do some things to `HotelController` to make everything work, and that has to do with how you handled adding the `Hotel` object previously. So, before you do any more work on the `addHotelController`, I want you to look at what happens when it's created and pushed on to the stack.

In Chapter 5 of Book VI, you added some code to `viewWillDisappear:`. You did this because, when the view unloads, undo and redo are no longer possible; you needed to save the current Managed Object Context and resign as first responder. Listing 1-4 shows the code you added.

**Book VII
Chapter 1**

**A User Interface
for Adding Hotels
and Using the
Address Book**

Listing 1-4: viewWillDisappear:

```
- (void)viewWillDisappear:(BOOL)animated {

  [super viewWillDisappear:animated];
  [self cleanUpUndoManager];
  // Save the context.
  if (trip.managedObjectContext.hasChanges) {
    NSError *error = nil;
    if (![trip.managedObjectContext save:&error]) {
/*Replace this implementation with code to handle the
  error appropriately. */
      NSLog(@"Unresolved error %@, %@", error,
                                    [error userInfo]);
      abort();
    }
  }
  [trip loadHotels];
  [trip.mapController refreshAnnotations];

  [self resignFirstResponder];
}
```

This worked fine when the HotelController was the "last stop" in the chain. That is, after you added the hotel, the only place to go was back to the previous view controller, and if you were doing that, it meant you were done with adding a hotel, and in viewWillDisapper: you could do what you needed to based on the last user action.

When you added the AddHotelController, all this changed. The view-WillDisappear: message is now *also* sent when you're moving from the HotelController to the AddHotelController, and at that point you certainly aren't ready to do much of anything.

Having a modification essentially gum up the works of what was laid down before is not an uncommon occurrence during development — in fact, it's highly likely. (The general guideline is to count on writing any application twice.) What you did (just to demonstrate to yourself, of course) is evidence that something that works during a phase of development may not necessarily be the best long-term solution. In reality, very few projects ever go from A to B to . . . directly.

Fortunately, enhancing your code to handle this situation is easy.

All you have to do is save the new Hotel and refresh the annotations after the user has returned from the AddHotelController and entered the necessary data. To do that, you'll simply add *state information* to the HotelController — it needs to know whether it's still in the middle of adding a hotel when the view disappears, or not. If it's in the middle of adding it, don't do anything. If it's not, just do what you were doing before.

Start with adding the state information it needs — a Boolean `amEditing` — to `HotelController.h`, as shown in bold in Listing 1-5.

Listing 1-5: Adding State Information to HotelController.h

```
@class Trip;
@class Hotel;
#import "AddHotelController.h"

@interface HotelController : UITableViewController
    <NSFetchedResultsControllerDelegate,
    AddHotelControllerDelegate>{
  NSFetchedResultsController *fetchedResultsController;
  Trip                       *trip;
  Hotel                      *hotel;
  NSUndoManager              *undoManager;
  BOOL                        amEditing;
}
@property (nonatomic, retain) NSFetchedResultsController
    *fetchedResultsController;
@property (nonatomic, retain) NSUndoManager *undoManager;
- (void)setUpUndoManager;
- (void)cleanUpUndoManager;

@end
```

In `viewWillDisappear:`, check the state by adding the code in bold in Listing 1-6 to `viewWillDisappear:` in `HotelController.m`.

Listing 1-6: Checking the State

```
- (void)viewWillDisappear:(BOOL)animated {
  [super viewWillDisappear:animated];
  if (!amEditing) {
  [self cleanUpUndoManager];
  // Save the context.
  if (trip.managedObjectContext.hasChanges) {
    NSError *error = nil;
    if (![trip.managedObjectContext save:&error]) {
/* Replace this implementation with code to handle the
  error appropriately. */
    NSLog(@"Unresolved error %@, %@", error,
                                    [error userInfo]);
    abort();
    }
  }
  [trip loadHotels];
  [trip.mapController refreshAnnotations];
 [self resignFirstResponder];
  }
}
```

**Book VII
Chapter 1**

**A User Interface
for Adding Hotels
and Using the
Address Book**

Because you can never be too careful, add the code in bold in Listing 1-7 to initWithTrip: in HotelController.m to initialize the amEditing state.

Listing 1-7:   Initializing the State

```
- (id) initWithTrip: (Trip*) aTrip{
  if (self =
  [super initWithNibName:@"HotelController" bundle:nil]) {
    trip = aTrip;
    [trip retain];
    amEditing = NO;
  }
  return self;
}
```

Next, set the state to amEditing in insertNewObject in HotelController.m by adding the bolded code in Listing 1-8. That way, when the AddHotelController is presented, you'll do nothing in view-DidDisappear:.

Listing 1-8:   Setting the State to amEditing

```
- (void)insertNewObject {

  NSEntityDescription *entity = [[fetchedResultsController
  fetchRequest] entity];
  hotel = [NSEntityDescription insertNewObjectForEntit
  yForName:[entity name] inManagedObjectContext:trip.
  managedObjectContext]; //$$
  [self setUpUndoManager];
  [hotel setValue:@"Hotel California" forKey:@"name"];
  [hotel setValue:@"1 Dr. Carlton B. Goodlett Place"
  forKey:@"street"];
  [hotel setValue:@"San Francisco" forKey:@"city"];
  [hotel setValue:@"California" forKey:@"state"];
  [hotel setValue:@"94102" forKey:@"zip"];
  amEditing = YES;

  AddHotelController *addHotelController =
  [[AddHotelController alloc] initWithHotel:hotel
  trip:trip];
  UINavigationController *navigationController =
  [[UINavigationController alloc] initWithRootViewController
  :addHotelController];
  navigationController.modalTransitionStyle =
  UIModalTransitionStyleFlipHorizontal;
```

```
//addHotelController.delegate = self;
  [self presentModalViewController:navigationController
    animated:YES];
  [navigationController release];
  [addHotelController release];

  Annotation *annotation = [NSEntityDescription ins
    ertNewObjectForEntityForName:@"Annotation"
    inManagedObjectContext:trip.managedObjectContext]; //$$
  [annotation setTitle:@"Annotation"];
  [annotation setHotel:hotel];
  [hotel setAnnotation:annotation];
  Geocoder * geocoder = [[Geocoder alloc] init];
  NSString* geocodeString = [[NSString alloc ]
    initWithFormat: @" %@ %@ %@ %@", hotel.street, hotel.city,
    hotel.state, hotel.zip];
  NSLog (@" finding = %@", geocodeString);
  CLLocationCoordinate2D theCoordinate = [geocoder
    geocodeLocation:geocodeString];
  hotel.annotation.latitude = [NSNumber
    numberWithDouble:theCoordinate.latitude];
  hotel.annotation.longitude =  [NSNumber
    numberWithDouble:theCoordinate.longitude];
  hotel.annotation.title = hotel.name;
}
```

You'll set `amEditing` back to `NO` when you return for the entering data in the `AddHotelController`, but you're not there yet.

Continue on building the `AddHotelController`.

Entering and Saving the Hotel Information

I'm going to start you off with some simple stuff.

Dismissing the keyboard

To dismiss the keyboard, you need to add another method to the `AddHotelController` — `textFieldShouldReturn:`. With that method, you have to send a message to the text field to `resignFirstResponder`. When the text field receives that message, it lowers the keyboard. (I cover lowering keyboards, as well as how to scroll the view so that a text field isn't covered, in exquisite detail in my *iPhone Application Development For Dummies*; if you're dying to find out more about lowering keyboards and keeping fields uncovered, you should look at that book.)

Enter the code in Listing 1-9 to `AddHotelController`.

**Book VII
Chapter 1**

**A User Interface
for Adding Hotels
and Using the
Address Book**

Listing 1-9: Implementing textFieldShouldReturn:

```
-(BOOL)textFieldShouldReturn:(UITextField *)
                                              theTextField {

  [theTextField resignFirstResponder];
  return YES;
}
```

Now, you'll discover that, when you tap Return on the keyboard, the keyboard kindly lowers itself.

You'll also be aware of a couple of features that come with using a text field. If, after the user enters text in a text field, he or she just happens to shake the iPhone, the Undo dialog will present itself, as shown in Figure 1-13. To do this on the Simulator (which is what you see in the figure), simply choose Hardware⇨Shake Gesture and you'll see what's displayed in Figure 1-13 firsthand.

You'll also notice that pressing in a text field brings up the Select and Paste menu, as shown in Figure 1-14.

Figure 1-13:
Undo typing.

**Book VII
Chapter 1**

A User Interface
for Adding Hotels
and Using the
Address Book

Figure 1-14:
Select and
paste.

Adding Cancel and Save buttons

Now you need to add two buttons: one to save any changes, and one to
enable you to cancel any changes you've made.

To add the buttons, you need to decide how to deal with a save or a cancel.
As I indicated earlier, the preferred method is to have the controller that
presented the view controller modally become a delegate of the modal view
controller and implement a method that will dismiss it (and do whatever
else needs to be done) when the modal view controller is done doing its
thing (that is, save or cancel).

Before you do that, though, I'd like you to add the buttons. You'll do that in
the `viewDidLoad` method of the `AddHotelController`.

Add the `viewDidLoad` method to the `AddHotelController` by adding the
code in Listing 1-10 to `AddHotelController.h`.

Listing 1-10: Adding the Save and Cancel Buttons in viewDidLoad

```
- (void)viewDidLoad {

  [super viewDidLoad];
  self.navigationItem.title = @"Hotel Information";

  UIBarButtonItem *cancelButtonItem =
        [[UIBarButtonItem alloc] initWithTitle:@"Cancel"
        style:UIBarButtonItemStyleBordered target:self
        action:@selector(cancel:)];
  self.navigationItem.leftBarButtonItem =
                                        cancelButtonItem;
  [cancelButtonItem release];

  UIBarButtonItem *saveButtonItem =
        [[UIBarButtonItem alloc] initWithTitle:@"Save"
        style:UIBarButtonItemStyleDone target:self
        action:@selector(save:)];
  self.navigationItem.rightBarButtonItem = saveButtonItem;
  [saveButtonItem release];
}
```

When you created the buttons, you specified the messages that should be sent (`cancel:` and `save:`) when the user tapped a button, and to what object they should be sent (`self`).

When you specified the button style as `UIBarButtonItemStyleDone`, that resulted in the familiar blue Save button being displayed. If you compile and run RoadTrip, you'll see that trusty Save button, but don't tap either the Save or Cancel button just yet because you haven't implemented either of their action methods. In fact, you'll do that next.

Add the code in Listing 1-11 to `AddHotelController.m` to implement the `cancel:` method and the code in Listing 1-12 to the very same `AddHotelController.m` to implement the `save:` method.

Listing 1-11: The cancel: Method

```
- (IBAction)cancel:(id)sender {

  [delegate addHotelController:self didFinishWithSave:NO];
}
```

When the user taps the Cancel button, the `cancel:` message is sent to the `AddHotelController`. It then sends the `addHotelController;didFin ishWithSave:` message to its delegate (the `HotelController`). I'll show you how that is implemented after I explain the `save:` method.

Listing 1-12: The save: Method

```
- (IBAction)save:(id)sender {

  hotel.street = street.text ;
  hotel.state = state.text;
  hotel.zip = zip.text;
  hotel.name = name.text;
  hotel.city = city.text;

  [delegate addHotelController:self
                              didFinishWithSave:YES];
}
```

As you might expect, the `save:` message updates the `Hotel` object you created in the `HotelController` earlier and then also sends the `addHotel`
`Controller;didFinishWithSave:` message. The difference, as you will
notice, is that, in the case of cancel, the argument is `NO`, and in the case of
save, the argument is `YES`.

Setting up the AddHotelController delegate

Here's the deal: When it comes time to dismiss a modal view controller, the
preferred method is for the view controller that presented the modal view
controller to do the dismissing. And the preferred way to do that is delegation.

To implement that, the view controller being presented modally must define
a protocol for its delegate to implement. Stored away in this newly defined
protocol are the messages(s) that the modal view controller will send in
response to specific actions, such as taps in the Save or Cancel buttons.
The delegate needs to implement the methods and do what it needs to do to
handle either a save or a cancel, which would include — in this example —
dismissing the modal view controller.

Listing 1-13 shows the implementation of the `addHotelController:did`
`FinishWithSave:` method. Add it to `HotelController.m`.

Listing 1-13: addHotelController:didFinishWithSave

```
- (void)addHotelController:
        (AddHotelController *)controller
                          didFinishWithSave:(BOOL)save {
  amEditing = NO;
  if (save) {
    [undoManager setActionName:
             [NSString stringWithString:@"Edit Hotel"]];

    Annotation *annotation = [NSEntityDescription
        insertNewObjectForEntityForName:@"Annotation"
```

(continued)

**Book VII
Chapter 1**

A User Interface
for Adding Hotels
and Using the
Address Book

Listing 1-13 *(continued)*

```
            inManagedObjectContext:trip.managedObjectContext];

        [annotation setTitle:@"Annotation"];
        [annotation setHotel:hotel];

        [hotel setAnnotation:annotation];
        Geocoder * geocoder = [[Geocoder alloc] init];
        NSString* geocodeString = [[NSString alloc ]
        initWithFormat: @" %@ %@ %@ %@", hotel.street, hotel.city,
        hotel.state, hotel.zip];
        CLLocationCoordinate2D theCoordinate = [geocoder
        geocodeLocation:geocodeString];
        hotel.annotation.latitude = [NSNumber numberWithDouble:
        theCoordinate.latitude];
        hotel.annotation.longitude =  [NSNumber numberWithDouble:
        theCoordinate.longitude];
        hotel.annotation.title = hotel.name;

    }
    else {
      [trip.managedObjectContext deleteObject:hotel];
      hotel = nil;
      [undoManager setActionName:
            [NSString stringWithString:@"Cancel Hotel"]];
    }
    [self dismissModalViewControllerAnimated:YES];
}
```

Because you're done with adding the new hotel, you set `amEditing` to `NO`, so `viewWillDisappear:` can do its thing.

If you're going to save the result, you set an Action Name for Undo, which previously only dealt with adding a `Hotel`.

```
[undoManager setActionName:
              [NSString stringWithString:@"Edit Hotel"]];
```

The rest of the code should look familiar — really, it should. Basically, you have moved all of the code that had previously followed the creating of the `AddHotelController` in `insertNewObejct` into this new method.

Listing 1-14 shows you the code that you need to now delete (that strike-through stuff) or copy (that bold stuff) from `insertNewObject` in `HotelController.m`.

For Cancel, you delete the object you had created, set the `hotel` instance variable to `nil`, and set the Undo Manager action name.

Finally, you dismiss the modal view controller, as follows:

```
[self dismissModalViewControllerAnimated:YES];
```

Listing 1-14: Updating insertNewObject

```
- (void)insertNewObject {

   NSEntityDescription *entity = [[fetchedResultsController
   fetchRequest] entity];
   hotel = [NSEntityDescription insertNewObjectForEntit
   yForName:[entity name] inManagedObjectContext:trip.
   managedObjectContext]; //$$
   [self setUpUndoManager];
   [hotel setValue:@"Hotel California" forKey:@"name"];
   [hotel setValue:@"1 Dr. Carlton B. Goodlett Place"
   forKey:@"street"];
   [hotel setValue:@"San Francisco" forKey:@"city"];
   [hotel setValue:@"California" forKey:@"state"];
   [hotel setValue:@"94102" forKey:@"zip"];
   amEditing = YES;

   AddHotelController *addHotelController =
   [[AddHotelController alloc] initWithHotel:hotel
   trip:trip];
   UINavigationController *navigationController =
   [[UINavigationController alloc] initWithRootViewController
   :addHotelController];
   navigationController.modalTransitionStyle =
   UIModalTransitionStyleFlipHorizontal;
   addHotelController.delegate = self;
   [self presentModalViewController:navigationController
   animated:YES];
   [navigationController release];
   [addHotelController release];

   //Annotation *annotation = [NSEntityDescription
   insertNewObjectForEntityForName:@"Annotation"
   inManagedObjectContext:trip.managedObjectContext]; //$$
   //[annotation setTitle:@"Annotation"];
   //[annotation setHotel:hotel];
   // [hotel setAnnotation:annotation];
   // Geocoder * geocoder = [[Geocoder alloc] init];
   // NSString* geocodeString = [[NSString alloc ]
   initWithFormat: @" %@ %@ %@ %@", hotel.street, hotel.
   city, hotel.state, hotel.zip];
   // NSLog (@" finding = %@", geocodeString);
   // CLLocationCoordinate2D theCoordinate = [geocoder
   geocodeLocation:geocodeString];
   // hotel.annotation.latitude = [NSNumber
   numberWithDouble:theCoordinate.latitude];
   // hotel.annotation.longitude =  [NSNumber
   numberWithDouble:theCoordinate.longitude];
   /// hotel.annotation.title = hotel.name;
}
```

**Book VII
Chapter 1**

**A User Interface
for Adding Hotels
and Using the
Address Book**

You can now also uncomment out the delegate assignment, because you'll implement all of that next:

```
addHotelController.delegate = self;
```

Adding the delegation plumbing

The final step is to add all the code necessary to implement delegation

You'll start by adding the code in bold in Listing 1-15 in order to add the protocol (you'll name it `AddHotelControllerDelegate`) and other required declarations to `AddHotelController.h`.

Listing 1-15: AddHotelController.h

```
#import <UIKit/UIKit.h>
@class Trip;
@class Hotel;
@protocol AddHotelControllerDelegate;

@interface AddHotelController : UIViewController
    <UITextFieldDelegate> {

    id <AddHotelControllerDelegate> delegate;
    Trip                    *trip;
    Hotel                   *hotel;
    IBOutlet UITextField *street;
    IBOutlet UITextField *state;
    IBOutlet UITextField *zip;
    IBOutlet UITextField *name;
    IBOutlet UITextField *city;

}
- (id) initWithHotel:(Hotel*) theHotel trip:(Trip*) theTrip;
- (IBAction) getFromContacts: (id) sender;
- (IBAction) saveToContacts: (id) sender;
@property (nonatomic, assign)
            id <AddHotelControllerDelegate> delegate;

@end

@protocol AddHotelControllerDelegate
- (void)addHotelController:(AddHotelController *)controller
    didFinishWithSave:(BOOL)save;
@end
```

Both the delegate instance variable and its corresponding property may look a bit odd to you.

```
id <AddHotelControllerDelegate> delegate;
@property (nonatomic, assign)
            id <AddHotelControllerDelegate> delegate;
```

id <AddHotelControllerDelegate> tells the compiler to do type check-ing for any class assigned to this instance variable or property. The idea here is for the compiler to check to make sure that the class has adopted the AddHotelControllerDelegate protocol. This is one of the advantages of using formal protocols.

You also need to add the following @synthesize statement to AddHotelController.m.

@synthesize delegate;

Then follow up by making the changes in bold in Listing 1-16 to HotelController.h to have it adopt the protocol.

Listing 1-16:   Making Hotel Controller a Delegate

```
@class Trip;
@class Hotel;
#import "AddHotelController.h"

@interface HotelController : UITableViewController
    <NSFetchedResultsControllerDelegate,
                           AddHotelControllerDelegate> {

  NSFetchedResultsController *fetchedResultsController;
  Trip                       *trip;
  Hotel                      *hotel;
  NSUndoManager              *undoManager;
}
@property (nonatomic, retain)
    NSFetchedResultsController *fetchedResultsController;
@property (nonatomic, retain) NSUndoManager *undoManager;
- (void)setUpUndoManager;
- (void)cleanUpUndoManager;

@end
```

Using default data

You might have noticed that, when I created the hotel object in insert-NewObject, I added some default data:

```
[hotel setValue:@"Hotel California" forKey:@"name"];
[hotel setValue:@"1 Dr. Carlton B. Goodlett Place"
                             forKey:@"street"];
[hotel setValue:@"San Francisco" forKey:@"city"];
[hotel setValue:@"California" forKey:@"state"];
[hotel setValue:@"94102" forKey:@"zip"];
```

Book VII
Chapter 1

A User Interface
for Adding Hotels
and Using the
Address Book

But when you displayed the `AddHotelController` view, there was no data to be seen. That's because you never copied it from the instance variables in the `hotel` object to the text fields in the view.

Go ahead and do that now by adding the code in bold in Listing 1-17 to `viewDidLoad` in `AddHotelController.m`.

Listing 1-17:   Adding Default Data to the View

```
- (void)viewDidLoad {
    [super viewDidLoad];
  self.navigationItem.title = @"Hotel Information";

  UIBarButtonItem *cancelButtonItem = [[UIBarButtonItem
    alloc] initWithTitle:@"Cancel" style:UIBarButtonItemStyleB
    ordered target:self action:@selector(cancel:)];
  self.navigationItem.leftBarButtonItem = cancelButtonItem;
  [cancelButtonItem release];

  UIBarButtonItem *saveButtonItem = [[UIBarButtonItem alloc]
    initWithTitle:@"Save" style:UIBarButtonItemStyleDone
    target:self action:@selector(save:)];
  self.navigationItem.rightBarButtonItem = saveButtonItem;
  [saveButtonItem release];
  street.text = hotel.street;
  state.text = hotel.state;
  zip.text = hotel.zip;
  name.text = hotel.name;
  city.text = hotel.city;
```

If at this point you're thinking to yourself "I understand why you may want to have a view populated with default data under some circumstances, but this doesn't seem to be one of those times," I would have to agree with you.

The reason I'm doing it is to show you how the Undo Manager keeps track of things. I'll leave it to you, however, to implement undo in a way that is more appropriate to your own application.

As you saw in Figure 1-13 earlier, Undo works automatically when you enter some data in a text field. Now you can look what happens when you enter the data, save it, and return to the `HotelController`.

In Figure 1-15, I shook the iPhone and the Undo Edit Hotel dialog is displayed — that's because that is precisely what you set the text to say earlier in `add HotelController:didFinishWithSave:` back in Listing 1-13.

Then, if I tap Undo Edit Hotel, the display reverts back to the default — Hotel California. If I shake the device again, I get the Undo Add Hotel message, as you see in Figure 1-16.

Figure 1-15:
Undo Edit
Hotel.

Figure 1-16:
Undo Add
Hotel.

Book VII
Chapter 1

A User Interface
for Adding Hotels
and Using the
Address Book

Don't tell me what to do!

If you find autocorrecting annoying, as I do, you can shut it off programmatically.

```
- (void)viewDidLoad {

[super viewDidLoad];

self.navigationItem.title = @"Hotel Information";

UIBarButtonItem *cancelButtonItem =
        [[UIBarButtonItem alloc] initWithTitle:@"Cancel"
        style:UIBarButtonItemStyleBordered target:self
        action:@selector(cancel:)];
self.navigationItem.leftBarButtonItem =
                                    cancelButtonItem;

[cancelButtonItem release];

UIBarButtonItem *saveButtonItem =
        [[UIBarButtonItem alloc] initWithTitle:@"Save"
        style:UIBarButtonItemStyleDone target:self
                            action:@selector(save:)];
self.navigationItem.rightBarButtonItem = saveButtonItem;
[saveButtonItem release];
street.text = hotel.street;
state.text = hotel.state;
zip.text = hotel.zip;
name.text = hotel.name;
city.text = hotel.city;
name.autocorrectionType = UITextAutocorrectionTypeNo;
street.autocorrectionType = UITextAutocorrectionTypeNo;
city.autocorrectionType = UITextAutocorrectionTypeNo;
state.autocorrectionType = UITextAutocorrectionTypeNo;
zip.autocorrectionType = UITextAutocorrectionTypeNo;
}
```

You can also set all the other keyboard traits as well, including what keyboard is being used. These properties are part of the `UITextInputTraits` protocol, which defines features that are associated with keyboard input. To work correctly with the text input management system, an object must adopt this protocol. The `UITextField` and `UITextView` classes already support this protocol.

If you compile and run this code at this point, it will work, but you still get two warnings, due to the fact that you haven't implemented either of the methods you declared as `IBActions` to support the contacts buttons.

You'll do that next.

Interfacing with the Address Book Application

I started this chapter off by musing about how nice it would be to be able to add an existing contact in your Address Book to your Hotels list. Actually, doing that is easy, but in doing so you're sure to come across some concepts and record types that may seem a little alien. But no worries. Soon you'll be making your way through them like an old hand.

As you recall, you connected the Get from Contacts button to an IBAction method back in the "Setting up the controller" section, earlier in the chapter. Now, you have a chance to implement that method — and get rid of one pesky compiler warning to boot. Add the code in Listing 1-18 to AddHotelController.m.

Listing 1-18: getFromContacts:

```
#pragma mark -
#pragma mark Get from contacts

- (IBAction) getFromContacts:(id)sender {

  ABPeoplePickerNavigationController *picker =
  [[ABPeoplePickerNavigationController alloc] init];
  picker.peoplePickerDelegate = self;

  [self presentModalViewController:picker animated:YES];
  [picker release];
}
```

Entering this little bit of code results in displaying the Address Book interface that you see in Figure 1-17.

As you can see, all you really do is present a modal view controller. The one you'll be using here is one of the standard system view controllers that are part of the iPhone OS.

In most ways, presenting these standard view controllers works the same as for your custom view controllers. However, because your application doesn't have access to the views used in these controllers — surprise, surprise — all interactions with the system view controllers must take place through a delegate object.

To enable that, you'll find each system view controller defines a corresponding protocol, whose methods you implement in your delegate object. And, as with your own modal controllers, one of the most important things the delegate must do is dismiss the presented view controller by calling the dismissModalViewControllerAnimated: method of the view controller that did the presenting. In this chapter, you'll be working with the AddressBook UI controllers, which include

Book VII
Chapter 1

A User Interface
for Adding Hotels
and Using the
Address Book

+ `ABPeoplePickerNavigationController`, which prompts the user to select a person record from their Address Book

+ `ABPersonViewController`, which displays a person record to the user and optionally allows editing

+ `ABNewPersonViewController`, which prompts the user to create a new person record

+ `ABUnknownPersonViewController`, which prompts the user to complete a partial person record, and optionally allows them to add it to the Address Book

Actually, you'll *really* only be working the first and third controllers.

When you add a contact — as you will in this section — you'll work with the `ABPeoplePickerNavigationController` class. This controller allows users to browse their list of contacts and select a person, as displayed back in Figure 1-17. (You can also allow the user to browse properties, although you won't implement that here.)

Figure 1-17:
Displaying
the Address
Book
interface.

The general outline for using `ABPeoplePickerNavigationController` is as follows:

1. Create and initialize an instance of the class.

2. Set the delegate, which must adopt the `ABPeoplePickerNavigationControllerDelegate` protocol.

3. Present the People Picker as a modal view controller by using the `presentModalViewController:animated:` method.

4. The `ABPeoplePickerNavigationController` then sends a message to your delegate based upon a user's action:

You'll need to implement three separate delegate methods:

✦ `peoplePickerNavigationController:shouldContinueAfterSelectingPerson:`

✦ `peoplePickerNavigationController:shouldContinueAfterSelectingPerson:property:identifier:`

✦ `peoplePickerNavigationControllerDidCancel:`

If the user cancels, the `ABPeoplePickerNavigationController` sends the `peoplePickerNavigationControllerDidCancel:` message to your delegate, which should dismiss the controller.

If the user selects a contact, the `ABPeoplePickerNavigationController` sends the `peoplePickerNavigationController:shouldContinueAfterSelectingPerson:` message of the delegate to determine if it should allow the user to choose a specific property of the selected person. You can either return `YES` or `NO`, although in this case you will return `NO`.

If the user selects a property, the `ABPeoplePickerNavigationController` sends the `peoplePickerNavigationController:shouldContinueAfterSelectingPerson:property:identifier:` message to the delegate to determine whether it should continue. To perform the default action for the selected property (dialing a phone number, starting a new e-mail, and so on), return `YES`. Otherwise return `NO` and dismiss the picker. In this case, you'll return `NO`.

You'll start by having the `AddHotelController` adopt the `ABPeoplePickerNavigationControllerDelegate` protocol. Make the changes shown in bold in Listing 1-19 to `AddHotelController.h`.

**Book VII
Chapter 1**

**A User Interface
for Adding Hotels
and Using the
Address Book**

Listing 1-19:   Adopting the Protocol

```
@interface AddHotelController :
    UIViewController <UITextFieldDelegate,
    ABPeoplePickerNavigationControllerDelegate> {
```

There are four basic objects you need to understand in order to interact with the Address Book database:

✦ Address Books

✦ Records

✦ Single-value properties

✦ Multi-value properties

Address Books let you interact with the Address Book database and save changes to it. To use an Address Book, declare an instance of ABAddressBookRef and set it to the value returned from the function ABAddressBookCreate.

You won't declare an instance of ABAddressBookRef to access the Address Book in this section, but you will when you add a contact in the next section.

In the Address Book database, information is stored in *records*. Each record (ABRecordRef) represents a person or group. The function ABRecordGetRecordType returns kABPersonType if the record is a person, and kABGroupType if it's a group. Here, you'll be working only with persons.

Within a record, the data is stored as a collection of *properties* (similar to the Objective-C properties you're used to). The properties available for group and person objects are different, but the functions used to access them are the same. The functions ABRecordCopyValue and ABRecordSetValue get and set properties, respectively. Properties can also be removed completely, using the function ABRecordRemoveValue.

Person records are made up of both *single-value* and *multi-value properties*.

I'll explain properties in great detail in a moment.

Start by adding the code in Listing 1-20 — the key delegate method as far as you are concerned — to AddHotelController.m. That's because when the user selects a person from the Address Book, this is the message that's sent to your delegate.

Listing 1-20: peoplePickerNavigationController: shouldContinueAfterSelectingPerson:

```
- (BOOL)peoplePickerNavigationController:
 (ABPeoplePickerNavigationController *)peoplePicker
  shouldContinueAfterSelectingPerson:(ABRecordRef)person {

  name.text = (NSString*) ABRecordCopyValue(person,
                            kABPersonOrganizationProperty);
  NSString *firstName = (NSString*)
    ABRecordCopyValue(person, kABPersonFirstNameProperty);
  NSString *lastName = (NSString*)
    ABRecordCopyValue(person, kABPersonLastNameProperty);
  if (!name.text) name.text = [[NSString alloc]
         initWithFormat: @"%@ %@", firstName, lastName ];

  ABMultiValueRef multiValueRef = (NSString*)
        ABRecordCopyValue(person,kABPersonPhoneProperty);
  NSString* phoneLabel;
  NSString* iPhone=@"";
  NSString* homePhone=@"";
  for (int i=0;i <
                ABMultiValueGetCount(multiValueRef);i++) {

    phoneLabel = (NSString*) ABMultiValueCopyLabelAtIndex(mul
    tiValueRef, i);
    if([phoneLabel isEqualToString:
                    (NSString*)kABPersonPhoneIPhoneLabel])
      iPhone = (NSString*) ABMultiValueCopyValueAtIndex(multi
    ValueRef,i);
    if([phoneLabel isEqualToString:(NSString*)kABHomeLabel])
      homePhone = (NSString*) ABMultiValueCopyValueAtIndex(mu
    ltiValueRef,i);
  }

  multiValueRef = ABRecordCopyValue
                    (person, kABPersonAddressProperty);
  if (ABMultiValueGetCount(multiValueRef) > 0) {
    CFDictionaryRef dictionary = ABMultiValueCopyValueAtIndex
    (multiValueRef, 0);
    street.text = (NSString*) CFDictionaryGetValue
                        (dictionary,
    kABPersonAddressStreetKey);
    city.text = (NSString*)CFDictionaryGetValue
                    (dictionary, kABPersonAddressCityKey);
    state.text = (NSString*)CFDictionaryGetValue
                    (dictionary, kABPersonAddressStateKey);
    zip.text = (NSString*)CFDictionaryGetValue
                    dictionary, kABPersonAddressZIPKey);
    CFRelease(dictionary);
  }
  CFRelease(multiValueRef);
  [self dismissModalViewControllerAnimated:YES];
  return NO;
}
```

**Book VII
Chapter 1**

**A User Interface
for Adding Hotels
and Using the
Address Book**

As one of the arguments of `peoplePickerNavigationController:shouldContinueAfterSelectingPerson:`, you are passed the record of the person selected:

```
- (BOOL)peoplePickerNavigationController:
  (ABPeoplePickerNavigationController *)peoplePicker
  shouldContinueAfterSelectingPerson:(ABRecordRef)person {
```

As I mentioned, inside the `person` record are properties, and there are two kinds: single-value properties and multi-value properties.

Single-value properties are properties that a person can have only one of, such as first name and last name. (Okay, maybe I should say you only have one *legal* first and last name.) You'll start things off by taking care of your single-value properties, as follows:

```
name.text = (NSString*) ABRecordCopyValue
              (person, kABPersonOrganizationProperty);
```

When you're passed a person record, the way you access the single-value property — organization or name, for example — is through the `ABRecordCopyValue` function, which returns the value of a record property — in this case, `kABPersonOrganizationProperty` — as a string.

It actually returns a `CFTypeRef`, which is an untyped generic reference to any Core Foundation object. You cast it in the `ABRecordCopyValue` function to avoid compiler warnings.

I know this syntax may look weird to you, but that's because this is not iPhone specific. It comes from Core Foundation (on the Mac) which is a set of C-based programming interfaces that implement simple object models in C that encapsulate data and functions as system-managed objects and operate seamlessly with Cocoa Foundation interfaces.

`kABPersonOrganizationProperty`, and `kABPersonFirstNameProperty`, and `kABPersonLastNameProperty` are constants defined by Apple that specify which fields you're accessing. They're listed in the XCode documentation under Personal Information Properties in the `ABPerson` Reference document.

Here I have to make a few decisions. Hotels in my Address Book will have the name of the hotel in the `kABPersonOrganizationProperty`, and I'll use that for the name in my view display and the `hotel` object. But for my friend's first cousin's ex-boyfriend, there won't be one, so I'll take the first and last name properties, concatenate them, and display it as the hotel name instead. (I'll leave it to you to figure out what to do if the joker finally did find a job and his new company name is in his contact information.)

```
NSString *firstName = (NSString*)
    ABRecordCopyValue(person, kABPersonFirstNameProperty);
NSString *lastName = (NSString*)
    ABRecordCopyValue(person, kABPersonLastNameProperty);
if (!(name.text)) name.text = [[NSString alloc]
        initWithFormat: @"%@ %@", firstName, lastName ];
```

As you might expect, other properties that a person can have more than one of, such as street address and phone number, are *multi-value properties.*

Multi-value properties consist of a list of values. Each value has a text label and an identifier associated with it. There can be more than one value with the same label, but the identifier is always unique.

These properties are `ABMutableMultiValueRef`s. And just to make your life interesting, there are two types of `ABMutableMultiValueRef`s you'll have to contend with;

✦ `kABMultiStringPropertyType`, which, as you might expect, are strings.

✦ `kABMultiDictionaryPropertyType`, which, as you might expect, are dictionaries.

Although you won't be using the phone number in RoadTrip, this part of Listing 1-20 is how you would access it:

```
ABMultiValueRef multiValueRef = (NSString*)
        ABRecordCopyValue(person,kABPersonPhoneProperty);
NSString *phoneLabel;
NSString *iPhone=@"";
NSString *homePhone=@"";
for(int i=0 ;i < ABMultiValueGetCount(multiValueRef);
                                                i++) {
    phoneLabel=(NSString*)
            ABMultiValueCopyLabelAtIndex(multiValueRef,i);
    if([phoneLabel isEqualToString:
                    (NSString*)kABPersonPhoneIPhoneLabel])
        iPhone = (NSString*)
            ABMultiValueCopyValueAtIndex(multiValueRef,i);
    if([phoneLabel isEqualToString:(NSString*)kABHomeLabel])
        homePhone = (NSString*)
        ABMultiValueCopyValueAtIndex(multiValueRef,i);
}
```

Here, a person has multiple phone numbers, each of which has a text label. (In this example, I just look for iPhone and home, but you get the picture.)

Walking through this section of Listing 1-20, you see that the first thing you do is get the property using the `ABRecordCopyValue` function.

```
ABMultiValueRef multiValueRef = (NSString*)
        ABRecordCopyValue(person, kABPersonPhoneProperty);
```

In this case, the property you're getting is the Phone property (kABPerson-PhoneProperty) and is a kABMultiStringPropertyType (think string).

Because there can be zero or many phone numbers, you get the count and enumerate through the record.

```
for(int i=0; i < ABMultiValueGetCount(multiValueRef);
                                                    i++) {
```

For each entry in the record, you check to see whether it has the label of the number you're interested in, and save it if it does.

```
if([phoneLabel isEqualToString:
                    (NSString*)kABPersonPhoneIPhoneLabel])
  iPhone = (NSString*)
        ABMultiValueCopyValueAtIndex(multiValueRef,i);
if([phoneLabel isEqualToString:(NSString*)kABHomeLabel])
  homePhone = (NSString*)
        ABMultiValueCopyValueAtIndex(multiValueRef,i);
```

The first phone type — kABPersonPhoneIPhoneLabel — is listed under Phone Number Property in the ABPerson Reference, along with a bunch of others. The kABHomeLabel is under Generic Property Labels.

As I said, what makes it interesting is that there are really two kinds of mulit-value labels. The first (phone number) was a kABMultiStringProperty-Type. Street address however is a kABMultiDictionaryPropertyType.

Although street address is still an ABMultiValueRef property, it isn't a kABMultiStringPropertyType — it's, as I said, kABMultiDictionary-PropertyType instead. As such, it is a dictionary entry, which means you'll have to first get the dictionary and then get the values you're interested in.

Street addresses are represented as a multi-value of dictionaries. Each value has a label, such as home or work. Within the value, the dictionary contains keys for the different parts of a street address.

In the following section of the code you entered as part of Listing 1-20, you simply check to see whether there's an entry, and if so, you take the first street address.

```
if (ABMultiValueGetCount(multiValueRef) > 0) {
    CFDictionaryRef dictionary = ABMultiValueCopyValueAtIndex
    (multiValueRef, 0);
    street.text = (NSString*) CFDictionaryGetValue
                    (dictionary, kABPersonAddressStreetKey);
```

```
city.text = (NSString*)CFDictionaryGetValue
                (dictionary, kABPersonAddressCityKey);
state.text = (NSString*)CFDictionaryGetValue
                (dictionary, kABPersonAddressStateKey);
zip.text = (NSString*)CFDictionaryGetValue
                (dictionary, kABPersonAddressZIPKey);
CFRelease(dictionary);
}
```

You could, however, iterate through and find the one with the label you're interested in, such as home or work.

```
for(int i=0;
        i < ABMultiValueGetCount(multiValueRef); i++) {
  if ([(NSString*)
      ABMultiValueCopyLabelAtIndex(multiValueRef, i)
      isEqualToString:(NSString*)kABHomeLabel])
...
```

You could also let the user select the right address (or name field for that matter) by returning YES instead of NO in the peoplePickerNavigation Controller:shouldContinueAfterSelectingPerson: method and implementing the logic to copy the values in peoplePickershould ContinueAfterSelectingPerson:.

You also can allow the user to access groups as well, but you can explore that one on your own.

Add the code in Listing 1-21 to AddHotelController.m to add the required delegate method.

Listing 1-21: (ABPeoplePickerNavigationController *)peoplePicker shouldContinueAfterSelectingPerson:(ABRecordRef)person

```
- (BOOL)peoplePickerNavigationController:
    (ABPeoplePickerNavigationController *)peoplePicker
    shouldContinueAfterSelectingPerson:(ABRecordRef)person
    property:(ABPropertyID)property
    identifier:(ABMultiValueIdentifier)identifier{

  return NO;
}
```

This method won't be invoked because you returned NO in peoplePicker NavigationController:shouldContinueAfterSelectingPerson:, but you still need it there because it is required by the protocol.

Finally, if the user changes his or her mind and wants to cancel the Address Book lookup, add the code in Listing 1-22.

**Book VII
Chapter 1**

**A User Interface
for Adding Hotels
and Using the
Address Book**

Listing 1-22:   **Canceling the addition**

```
- (void)peoplePickerNavigationControllerDidCancel:
        (ABPeoplePickerNavigationController *)peoplePicker {

    [self dismissModalViewControllerAnimated:YES];
}
```

All you really do here is dismiss the controller.

To finish up, you also need to add some imports to
`AddHotelController.h`.

```
#import <AddressBook/AddressBook.h>
#import <AddressBookUI/AddressBookUI.h>
```

Next, you need to add the `AddressBook` and `AddressBookUI` Frameworks.

1. **Click the disclosure triangle next to Targets in the Groups & Files list
   and then right-click RoadTrip.**

   Be sure to do this using the Targets folder, or Step 3 won't work!

2. **From the menu that appears, select Add and then select Existing
   Frameworks.**

3. **Select `AddressBook.framework` and the `AddressBookUI.frame-
   work` in the window that appears and then drag them into the
   Frameworks folder.**

Adding a hotel to your Address Book

Adding a new contact to the Address Book is similar to accessing one.

You'd start by making the `AddHotelController` a
`ABNewPersonViewControllerDelegate`. You'll need to add the following
to `AddHotelController.h`.

```
@interface AddHotelController : UIViewController
        <UITextFieldDelegate,
    ABPeoplePickerNavigationControllerDelegate,
    ABNewPersonViewControllerDelegate> {
```

In this case, there is only one delegate method you'll need to implement —
the `newPersonViewController:didCompleteWithNewPerson:`
method, which is invoked when the user taps Save or Cancel. By the way,
if the user tapped Save, by the time you receive the message, the current
Address Book has been saved to the Address Book database.

At that point, it's your job to dismiss the `AbNewPersonViewController`.

Add the code in Listing 1-23 to `AddHotelController.m` to do just that.

Listing 1-23: Done with the Record

```
- (void)newPersonViewController:
  (ABNewPersonViewController *)newPersonViewController
          didCompleteWithNewPerson:(ABRecordRef)person {

  [self dismissModalViewControllerAnimated:YES];
}
```

Now they you've gotten that out of the way, you can concentrate on what you need to do to actually add the new contact. Adding a contact to the iPhone's Address Book isn't horribly complicated, but there's some work to do.

To start, you need to implement the IBAction saveToContacts: method — that's where the work will get done.

Add the code in Listing 1-24 to AddHotelController.m.

Listing 1-24: saveToContacts:

```
- (IBAction) saveToContacts:(id)sender{

  ABAddressBookRef addressBook = ABAddressBookCreate();
  ABRecordRef personRecord = ABPersonCreate();

  ABRecordSetValue(personRecord, kABPersonOrganizationPropert
   y,name.text, nil);
  ABRecordSetValue(personRecord,
               kABPersonLastNameProperty,name.text,nil);

  ABMutableMultiValueRef mutableMultiValueRef =
    ABMultiValueCreateMutable
                       (kABMultiDictionaryPropertyType);
  NSMutableDictionary *addressDictionary =
    [[NSMutableDictionary alloc] init];
  [addressDictionary setObject:street.text forKey:(NSString
   *) kABPersonAddressStreetKey];
  [addressDictionary setObject:city.text
            forKey:(NSString *)kABPersonAddressCityKey];
  [addressDictionary setObject:state.text
            forKey:(NSString *)kABPersonAddressStateKey];
  [addressDictionary setObject:zip.text
            forKey:(NSString *)kABPersonAddressZIPKey];
  ABMultiValueAddValueAndLabel(mutableMultiValueRef,
                  addressDictionary, kABWorkLabel, nil);
  ABRecordSetValue(personRecord, kABPersonAddressProperty,
                      mutableMultiValueRef, nil);
  CFRelease(mutableMultiValueRef);
  ABAddressBookAddRecord(addressBook, personRecord, nil);
  ABAddressBookSave(addressBook, nil);
```

(continued)

**Book VII
Chapter 1**

A User Interface
for Adding Hotels
and Using the
Address Book

Listing 1-24 *(continued)*

```
ABNewPersonViewController *picker =
              [[ABNewPersonViewController alloc] init];
picker.newPersonViewDelegate = self;
picker.displayedPerson = personRecord;

UINavigationController* navigationController =
  [[UINavigationController alloc] initWithRootViewController
  :picker];
[self presentModalViewController:navigationController
  animated:YES];
[picker release];
}
```

To create a new Address Book entry, start by creating a new Address Book with data from the Address Book database.

```
ABAddressBookRef addressBook = ABAddressBookCreate();
```

When you have the Address Book, you'll create the new record you want to add to it.

```
ABRecordRef personRecord = ABPersonCreate();
```

Then you'll add the data to the new record.

For single-value rewords, like name, you'll do something similar to what you did when you accessed the Address Book information back in the last section. But in this case, instead of `ABRecordCopyValue` you'll use `ABRecordSetValue`. (Kind of makes sense doesn't it?)

```
ABRecordSetValue(personRecord, kABPersonOrganizationProperty,
    name.text, nil);
ABRecordSetValue(personRecord,
    kABPersonLastNameProperty,name.text, nil);
```

This code sets the Organization and Last Name fields with the text from the Name field in the view. The last argument is a place to return any errors, but throughout this code I use `nil` — but feel free to explore that on your own.

Next in line in Listing 1-24 is adding a new address record. (I'll skip the phone number multi-value property type — but you get the drift.) To add a new address record, you create a new dictionary property type and then a new dictionary. In this case, you're creating an `ABMutableMultiValueRef` instead of the `multiValueRef` you used when you read the contact information in the previous section. It needs to be mutable because you're going to making changes to it.

```
ABMutableMultiValueRef mutableMultiValueRef =
ABMultiValueCreateMutable(kABMultiDictionaryPropertyType);
NSMutableDictionary *addressDictionary =
                    [[NSMutableDictionary alloc] init];
```

Then, you go on to add the fields you're interested in to the dictionary:

```
[addressDictionary setObject:street.text
        forKey:(NSString *) kABPersonAddressStreetKey];
  [addressDictionary setObject:city.text
            forKey:(NSString *)kABPersonAddressCityKey];
  [addressDictionary setObject:state.text
            forKey:(NSString *)kABPersonAddressStateKey];
  [addressDictionary setObject:zip.text
            forKey:(NSString *)kABPersonAddressZIPKey];
```

Then you add the value (addressDictionary) and the label (kABWork Label) to the property (mutableMultiValueRef):

```
ABMultiValueAddValueAndLabel(mutableMultiValueRef,
    addressDictionary, kABWorkLabel, nil);
```

and set it as the value of the property (kABPersonAddressProperty) in the personRecord and release the dictionary:

```
ABRecordSetValue(personRecord, kABPersonAddressProperty,
    mutableMultiValueRef,nil);
CFRelease(mutableMultiValueRef);
```

Then you add the person record to the Address Book you created and then save it, which actually updates the database:

```
ABAddressBookAddRecord(addressBook, personRecord, nil);
ABAddressBookSave(addressBook, nil);
```

Finally, you create the controller, set self as the delegate, give it the person record to display, and then modally present the controller:

```
ABNewPersonViewController *picker =
    [[ABNewPersonViewController alloc] init];
picker.newPersonViewDelegate = self;
picker.displayedPerson = personRecord;
UINavigationController* navigationController =
    [[UINavigationController alloc]
                    initWithRootViewController:picker];
self presentModalViewController:navigationController
                                    animated:YES];

[picker release];
```

**Book VII
Chapter 1**

**A User Interface
for Adding Hotels
and Using the
Address Book**

There's a lot more functionality here that I haven't coverd — updating an existing records comes to mind, as well as the ability for your application to be notified when another application makes changes to the Address Book database. I'll leave it up to you to explore that on your own.

Chapter 2: Incorporating E-Mail: Postcards from the Road

*O*ne of the great features of the handy RoadTrip app is the ability to add places you'd like to stay to the app. That's all fine and dandy, but now it's time to think about being able to tell everyone what a great time you're having while staying at all these places. It's not that I'm into Schadenfreude — but sometimes it's fun to let all your hardworking friends back home know what a great time you are having on your road trip.

One of the best ways to do that is through e-mail. Although you could take care of that by using the built-in Mail app on the iPhone, being able to do it within the app is more convenient and easier for the user, especially when adding context-specific content. In this chapter, I show you how to create a postcard-like e-mail — a *Road Card* — from directly within the RoadTrip app.

Mail on the iPhone

The standard way to interface the Message UI — and therefore use the built-in Mail app to allow a user to create, and then send, an e-mail — is to haul out the Ol' Reliable: `MFMailComposeViewController`.

The `MFMailComposeViewController` class provides a standard interface that manages the editing and sending of an e-mail. You'll use this view controller to display the standard E-mail view inside your application. You can also fill in the fields with initial values for the subject, e-mail recipients, body text, and attachments. Using the standard interface, the user can then edit the values and send the message — or change his or her mind and cancel the whole thing.

You'll want to display the Mail interface modally by using the `present ModalViewController:animated:` method. (Chapter 1 of this minibook goes more into the details of why.) Figure 2-1 shows the view that will be displayed with some of the fields already filled in.

Figure 2-1:
The new
mail
message.

The user, in fact, has the kind of control over the newly created message you would expect. As I said, he or she can edit and send or cancel the message. If he or she decides not to send it, it will remain in the Mail application's outbox. That way, the user can create e-mails even when the network is unavailable (even in airplane mode). You can see that in Figure 2-2.

Figure 2-2:
Airplane
mode on.

Although you'll be able to see the results of your work on the Simulator, you'll only be able to actually send the e-mail (or get the display you see in Figure 2-2) on the device itself.

Also, to protect the innocent, you may have noticed that real e-mail addresses are not being used. You'll have to replace them with real ones when you test your code.

The usual start to your adventure

In order to add the ability to send a "Road Card," you're going to need to add (yet another) controller.

1. **In the RoadTrip Project window, select the Classes folder in the Groups & Files list and then choose File⇨New from the main menu (or press ⌘+N) to get the New File window.**

2. **In the left column of the New File window, select Cocoa Touch Classes under the iPhone OS heading, select the `UIViewController` subclass template in the top-right pane, and then click Next.**

   Be sure the With XIB for User Interface option is not checked.

   You see a new dialog asking for some more information.

3. **Enter RoadCardController.m in the File Name field and then click Finish.**

To make things easier to find, I keep my `RoadCardController.m` and `RoadCardController.h` classes in the Classes folder.

Adding the MessageUI framework

Next you have to add the `MessageUI` framework.

At this point, you're probably pretty used to adding a new framework.

1. **Click the disclosure triangle next to Targets in the Groups & Files list and then right-click RoadTrip.**

   Be sure to do this using the Targets folder, or Step 3 won't work!

2. **From the menu that appears, choose Add and then choose Existing Frameworks.**

3. **Select MessageUI Framework in the window that appears, click Add, and then drag MessageUI into the Frameworks folder.**

Creating the Interface

The first thing you need to think about is how the user is going to get to this new functionality. There are probably a number of places you could put the gateway to the Road Card feature, but I'm going to have you add it to the main screen, right there under Weather in The Trip section. That means adding some code to the `RootViewController`.

First, you need to import `RoadCardController.h` into `RootViewController.m`.

```
#import "RoadCardController.h"
```

Next, you need to add the Road Card entry. Add the bolded code in Listing 2-1 to `viewDidLoad` in `RootViewController.m` and delete the code marked with strikethrough.

Listing 2-1:   viewDidLoad

```
- (void)viewDidLoad {

    [super viewDidLoad];
    //sectionsArray = [[NSArray alloc] initWithObjects:
                [[NSNumber alloc]initWithInt:4],
                [[NSNumber alloc]initWithInt:2], nil];
    sectionsArray = [[NSArray alloc] initWithObjects:
        [[NSNumber alloc]initWithInt:5],
        [[NSNumber alloc]initWithInt:2], nil];
    trip = [[Trip alloc] initWithName:@"Road Trip"];


    self.title = [[[NSBundle mainBundle] infoDictionary]
      objectForKey:@"CFBundleName"];
    menuList = [[NSMutableArray alloc] init];
    [menuList addObject:
      [NSMutableDictionary dictionaryWithObjectsAndKeys:
      NSLocalizedString(@"Map", @"Map Section"),kSelectKey,
      NSLocalizedString(@"Where you are", @"Map Explain"),
                                                    kDescriptKey,
        nil, kControllerKey, nil]];
    [menuList addObject:
      [NSMutableDictionary dictionaryWithObjectsAndKeys:
      NSLocalizedString(@"Sights", @"Sights Section"),
                                                    kSelectKey,
      NSLocalizedString(@"Places to see",
                  @"Places to see Explain"), kDescriptKey,
        nil, kControllerKey, nil]];
    [menuList addObject:
      [NSMutableDictionary dictionaryWithObjectsAndKeys:
```

```
        NSLocalizedString(@"Hotels", @"Hotels Section"),
                                              kSelectKey,
        NSLocalizedString(@"Places to stay",
                   @"Places to stay Explain"), kDescriptKey,
        nil, kControllerKey, nil]];
    [menuList addObject:
      [NSMutableDictionary dictionaryWithObjectsAndKeys:
      NSLocalizedString(@"Weather", @"Weather Section"),
                                              kSelectKey,
        NSLocalizedString(@"Current conditions",
                          @"Weather  Explain"), kDescriptKey,
        nil, kControllerKey, nil]];
    [menuList addObject:
      [NSMutableDictionary dictionaryWithObjectsAndKeys:
      NSLocalizedString(@"Road Card", @"Email Section"),
                                              kSelectKey,
      NSLocalizedString(@"Make 'em jealous",@"Post Card"),
                                              kDescriptKey,
      nil, kControllerKey, nil]];
    [menuList addObject:
      [NSMutableDictionary dictionaryWithObjectsAndKeys:
      NSLocalizedString(@"Servicing", @"Service Section"),
                                              kSelectKey,
        NSLocalizedString(@"Service records",
                  @"Service records Explain"), kDescriptKey,
        nil, kControllerKey, nil]];
    [menuList addObject:
      [NSMutableDictionary dictionaryWithObjectsAndKeys:
      NSLocalizedString(@"The Car",
                   @"Car Information Section"), kSelectKey,
        NSLocalizedString(@"About the car",@"About the car"),
                                              kDescriptKey,
        nil, kControllerKey, nil]];

    RoadTripAppDelegate *appDelegate =
        (RoadTripAppDelegate *)
              [[UIApplication sharedApplication] delegate];
    if ([[((NSNumber*) [appDelegate.lastView
                    objectAtIndex:0]) intValue] != -1) {
      NSIndexPath* indexPath = [NSIndexPath indexPathForRow:
          [[appDelegate.lastView objectAtIndex:1] intValue]
          inSection:[[appDelegate.lastView objectAtIndex:0]
                                              intValue]];
      [self tableView:((UITableView*) self.tableView)
                    didSelectRowAtIndexPath:indexPath];
    }
}
```

The first thing you added was a change in the number of rows in the first section — a change from 4 to 5, to be precise:

```
sectionsArray = [[NSArray alloc] initWithObjects:
  [[NSNumber alloc]initWithInt:5],
  [[NSNumber alloc]initWithInt:2], nil];
```

Then you simply inserted a new dictionary for the `RoadCardController` into the menu list, like so:

```
[menuList addObject:
   [NSMutableDictionary  dictionaryWithObjectsAndKeys:
   NSLocalizedString(@"Road Card", @"Email Section"),
                                     kSelectKey,
   NSLocalizedString(@"Make 'em jealous",@"Post Card"),
                                     kDescriptKey,
   nil, kControllerKey, nil]];
```

Pretty easy, huh? All that upfront work is now beginning to pay off. After you build and compile the project, you should see what I see in Figure 2-3.

Figure 2-3:
Adding the
Road Card
entry.

Selecting the new entry

You've added Road Card to your main screen, so you probably should write some code to do something when the Road Card is selected. That code, of course, gets added to `tableView:didSelectRowAtIndexPath:`. Make the modification to that method's `switch` statement in `RootViewController.m` as shown in bold in Listing 2-2.

Listing 2-2:   Add to the Switch in tableView:didSelectRowAtIndexPath:

```
switch (menuOffset) {
    case 0:
        if (realtime) targetController =
          [[MapController alloc] initWithTrip:trip];
        else [self displayOfflineAlert:
          [[menuList objectAtIndex:menuOffset]
                            objectForKey:kSelectKey]];
        break;
    case 1:
        targetController =
          [[SightListController alloc] initWithTrip:trip];
        break;
    case 2:
        targetController =
              [[HotelController alloc] initWithTrip:trip];
        break;
    case 3:
        if  (realtime) targetController = [[WebViewController
   alloc] initWithTrip:trip  delegate:[ trip
   returnWeatherDelegate]
            webControl:YES title:NSLocalizedString(@"Weather",
                                    @"Weather")];
        else
          [self displayOfflineAlert:
              [[menuList objectAtIndex:menuOffset]
                            objectForKey:kSelectKey]];
        break;
    case 4:
        targetController =
          [[RoadCardController alloc] initWithTrip: trip];
        break;
    //case 4:
    case 5:
        targetController =
          [[WebViewController alloc] initWithTrip:trip
   delegate:[trip returnCarServicingDelegate]
            webControl:NO title:NSLocalizedString(@"Car
   Servicing", @"Car Servicing")];
        break;
    //case 5:
    case 6:
        targetController =
          [[WebViewController alloc] initWithTrip:trip
   delegate:[trip returnCarInformationDelegate]
   webControl:NO title:NSLocalizedString(@"The Car", @"Car
   Information")];
        break;
    }
```

Reusing what you've already done in RoadTripController

I decided that the ability to send Road Cards would, most of the time, involve a sight. After all, that's what postcards from tourist places usually feature. (I know what you're thinking, but please don't go there).

That being the case, I already have some code written — the `SightList Controller` — that does a lot of what I need to do to display some sights and then do something with the selection. To take advantage of stuff I already have, I make `RoadCardController` a subclass of `SightListController`.

This also meets my criterion of trying to do as little typing (and copying and pasting) as possible.

Add the code shown in bold in Listing 2-3 to `RoadCardController.h`.

Listing 2-3:   RoadCardController.h

```
#import "SightListController.h"
#import <MessageUI/MessageUI.h>
#import <MessageUI/MFMailComposeViewController.h>
@class Sight;

//@interface RoadCardController : UIViewController {
@interface RoadCardController : SightListController
                <MFMailComposeViewControllerDelegate> {

}
- (void) displayMailCompositionInterface:(int) sightIndex;
- (void) unsupportedAlert;
- (BOOL) checkConfiguration;


@end
```

Hmm, it seems to work, as shown in Figure 2-4.

The first thing you did here (besides the requisite imports) was make the `RoadCardController` a subclass of `SightListController` and adopt the `MFMailComposeViewControllerDelegate` protocol.

```
@interface RoadCardController : SightListController
                <MFMailComposeViewControllerDelegate> {
```

I also had you add a few methods you'll be implementing. The first will actually display the controller and do all the work. The second will display an alert if the device is not configured for e-mail or it has an older version of the

OS that does not support the `MFMailComposeViewController` class (pre-iPhone OS 3.0, in other words).

Figure 2-4:
The Road
Card
interface.

Notice you didn't have to add the initializer because you inherited the one from `SightListController`. (Although I'll override it later in order to change the title.) You also don't need the `.xib` file because you're letting the inherited `SightListController` code do all the work for you. (If you're unclear on how the view got created without an `.xib` file, see Book VI, Chapter 1).

You probably can't help but notice that if you select a sight, you still get what you would have gotten if you had selected the same entry on the Sights view. (Give me a break — you haven't made the changes yet.) But so far so good.

Of course if you're an experienced object-oriented programmer, you know that the "right" way to do this is create a base class from which you derived the `SightListController` and the `RoadCardController`.

Go ahead and override the initialization method to at least get the right title. Add the code in Listing 2-4 to `RoadTripController.m`.

Listing 2-4:   Override initWithTrip:

```
- (id) initWithTrip:(Trip*) theTrip {

  if ([super initWithTrip: theTrip]) {
    self.title = @"Road Card from";
  }
  return self;
}
```

Yep. "See the sights" is now history, and "Road Card from" reigns in its place. Now it's time to add the code necessary to call the methods that will implement the Mail interface.

Creating the Mail Message

You start, as you might expect, with the `tableView:didSelectRowAt IndexPath:` method you inherit from `SightListController`. This method will give you the opportunity to do something different when the user selects a sight, and to do that, you simply override the inherited method. Add the code in Listing 2-5 to `RoadTripController.m` to do that.

Listing 2-5:   Override tableView:didSelectRowAtIndexPath:

```
- (void)tableView:(UITableView *)tableView
       didSelectRowAtIndexPath:(NSIndexPath *)indexPath {

  [tableView deselectRowAtIndexPath:indexPath
                                        animated:YES];
  if ([self checkConfiguration])
    [self displayMailCompositionInterface:indexPath.row];
  else
    [self unsupportedAlert];
}
```

As you can see, what you'll be doing when the user selects a sight is first checking to see whether `MFMailComposeViewController` is installed and mail is configured. If it is, you display the `MFMailComposeViewController`. If not, you display an alert informing the user that the e-mail is just not happening.

Go ahead and get the checking out part of the way. Add the code in Listing 2-6 to `RoadTripController.m`.

Listing 2-6:   Will It Work?

```
-(BOOL)checkConfiguration {

    Class mailClass =
            NSClassFromString(@"MFMailComposeViewController");
    if ((mailClass != nil) && ([mailClass canSendMail]))
        return YES;
    else
        return NO;
}
```

The first statement might be new to you.

```
Class mailClass =
        NSClassFromString(@"MFMailComposeViewController");
```

NSClassFromString is a Foundation function that returns the class object you have used as the argument (MFMailComposeViewController) or nil if no class by that name is currently loaded.

Without getting into too much detail, a class object is a pointer to the class data structure. In Objective-C, every object has a data structure whose first member is the isa pointer. The isa pointer, as the name suggests, points to the object's class, which is an object compiled from the class definition.

The class object has a dispatch table of pointers to the methods it implements as well as a pointer to its superclass. This isa pointer makes the dynamic aspects of Objective-C possible.

Although I haven't gotten into targeting your application for a particular OS version (and I won't — in this case I really only support iPhone OS 3.0), this shows you how to determine whether a particular feature is available on a device. Although this app can run on devices running iPhone OS 2.0 or later, the MFMailComposeViewController class is available only in iPhone OS 3.0 or later.

The one thing you *will* need to do, though, is use the canSendMail method to check whether the current device is configured to send e-mail at all. If the user's iPhone isn't able to send e-mail, you have the opportunity to notify him or her or to simply disable that feature in your app.

If MFMailComposeViewController is there and the device is configured to send e-mail, you continue; if not, you need to display an alert. The code in Listing 2-7 does that for you, so add it to RoadTripController.m.

Listing 2-7: It's Not Going to Work

```
- (void) unsupportedAlert {

  UIAlertView *alert = [[UIAlertView alloc]
    initWithTitle: @"This device does not support the
  required functionality"
    message:@"Mail is not configured or you have an older OS"
    delegate:self cancelButtonTitle:@"Thanks"
    otherButtonTitles:nil];
  [alert show];
  [alert release];
}
```

There are a number of things you could (and *should*) do here if your e-mail functionality is on the fritz, but I'll leave that to you to investigate.

Displaying the view

After you've determined that the device will work, as you saw in Listing 2-6, you send the displayMailCompositionInterface message to yourself. This is the heart of what you'll need to do. First add the code in Listing 2-8 to RoadTripController.m, and then I go through it with you step by step.

Listing 2-8: displayMailCompositionInterface

```
- (void)displayMailCompositionInterface:(int) sightIndex {
  MFMailComposeViewController *roadCard =
              [[MFMailComposeViewController alloc] init];
  roadCard.mailComposeDelegate = self;
  NSArray *toRecipients = [NSArray
      arrayWithObjects:@"neal@.com", @"neal@.com", nil];
  NSArray *ccRecipients = [NSArray
                     arrayWithObject:@"neal@.com"];
  NSArray *bccRecipients = [NSArray
                     arrayWithObject:@"neal@.com"];

  [roadCard setToRecipients:toRecipients];
  [roadCard setCcRecipients:ccRecipients];
  [roadCard setBccRecipients:bccRecipients];
  Sight* theSight = [trip.sights
                          objectAtIndex:sightIndex];
  [roadCard setSubject:[NSString stringWithFormat: @"Regards
    from %@. Wish you were there", theSight.sightName]];

  NSString *filePath = [[NSBundle mainBundle]
    pathForResource:theSight.image ofType:theSight.imageType];
  NSData *image = [NSData dataWithContentsOfFile:filePath];
  [roadCard addAttachmentData:image mimeType:@"image/jpg"
                          fileName:@"theSight.image"];
  NSString *body = [NSString stringWithFormat:
```

```
                @"Having a great time, glad I'm not there."];
    [roadCard setMessageBody:body isHTML:NO];
    [self presentModalViewController:roadCard animated:YES];
    [roadCard release];
}
```

You start by allocating and initializing the `MFMailComposeViewController` and setting the delegate. (You'll get to the delegate shortly.)

```
- (void)displayMailCompositionInterface:(int) sightIndex {
    MFMailComposeViewController *roadCard =
                [[MFMailComposeViewController alloc] init];
    roadCard.mailComposeDelegate = self;
```

You then create three arrays: one for the To recipients, one for CC recipients, and one for BCC recipients. (Only the To one is really required.) You use those arrays to set the recipients for the e-mail you're creating:

```
NSArray *toRecipients = [NSArray
        arrayWithObjects:@"neal@.com", @"neal@.com", nil];
NSArray *ccRecipients = [NSArray
                        arrayWithObject:@"neal@.com"];
NSArray *bccRecipients = [NSArray
                        arrayWithObject:@"neal@.com"];
```

Next, you set some initial values in the message. The user, of course, will be able to change those once they're displayed.

The mail composition interface itself isn't customizable, and you can't modify it. In addition, after presenting the interface, your application isn't allowed to make further changes to the e-mail content. The user may still edit the content using the interface, but programmatic changes are ignored. This means you must set the values of any of the content fields before presenting the interface.

`setToRecipients:`, for example, is a method that sets the initial recipients to include in the e-mail's To field. The argument, as you can see, is an array of NSString objects, each of which contains the e-mail address of a single recipient.

```
 [roadCard setToRecipients:toRecipients];
[roadCard setCcRecipients:ccRecipients];
[roadCard setBccRecipients:bccRecipients];
```

This method doesn't filter out duplicate e-mail addresses, so if duplicates are present, multiple copies of the e-mail message may be sent to the same address.

Next, you get the `Sight` that the user had selected in the list and then use its name to set the subject in the e-mail. (This is the same way you did it in the `SightListController`.)

```
Sight* theSight = [trip.sights objectAtIndex:sightIndex];
   [roadCard setSubject:[NSString stringWithFormat:
           @"Regards from %@. Wish you were there",
                                    theSight.sightName]];
```

`setSubject:`, as you might expect, sets the initial text for the subject line of the e-mail.

Next, you set the message body:

```
NSString *body = [NSString stringWithFormat:
           @"Having a great time, glad I'm not there."];
[roadCard setMessageBody:body isHTML:NO];
```

This part sets the initial body text of the message. The text has to be either plain text or HTML, and you tell the mail app which one you want by using the `isHTML` parameter. Even though I'm having you add simple text here, you can fancy things up using HTML. I leave it to you to be more creative.

Finally, you can add the picture by sending the `addAttachmentData:mimeType:fileName:` message:

```
NSString *filePath =
    [[NSBundle mainBundle] pathForResource:theSight.image
                               ofType:theSight.imageType];
NSData *image =
                  [NSData dataWithContentsOfFile:filePath];
[roadCard addAttachmentData:image mimeType:@"image/jpg"
                           fileName:@theSight.image];
```

As you can see, I get the right sight image from the bundle, the same way I get the images for the thumbnails, and set it in the e-mail message. `mimeType` lets the Mail program know the type of the specified data. (For example, as you see here, the MIME type for a JPEG image is `image/jpeg`.) For a list of valid MIME types, see `www.iana.org/assignments/media-types`. This parameter must not be `nil`. The filename parameter is the filename you want to associate with the data. I'm using the image name. This is the default name applied to the file when it is sent.

This method attaches the image (or images) after the message body but before the user's signature. You may attach multiple files (using different filenames), but you must do so before you display the mail composition interface. (See the Remember paragraph earlier in this section.)

You also need to import a couple of header files:

```
#import "Sight.h"
#import "Trip.h"
```

The delegate

As I mention in Chapter 1 of this minibook, delegation is the preferred way to deal with dismissing the controller (and doing whatever else needs to be done before the controller is dismissed). There's only one delegation method in the `MFMailComposeViewControllerDelegate` protocol, so you won't have trouble figuring out which one to use.

Add the code in Listing 2-9 to `RoadCardController.m`.

Listing 2-9:   Implementing the Delegate Method

```
- (void)mailComposeController: (MFMailComposeViewController*)
   controller didFinishWithResult:(MFMailComposeResult)result
   error:(NSError*)error {
 NSString* resultMessage = nil;
 switch (result)                                        {
   case MFMailComposeResultCancelled:
     resultMessage= @"Has been canceled";
     break;
   case MFMailComposeResultSaved:
     resultMessage= @"Has been saved";
     break;
   case MFMailComposeResultSent:
     resultMessage = @"Has been sent";
     break;
   case MFMailComposeResultFailed:
     resultMessage = @"Has failed";
     break;
   default:
     resultMessage = @"Was not sent";
     break;
 }
 UIAlertView *alert = [[UIAlertView alloc]
           initWithTitle:@"Your email message"
           message:resultMessage delegate:self
           cancelButtonTitle:@"Thanks"
           otherButtonTitles:nil];
 [alert show];
 [alert release];
[self dismissModalViewControllerAnimated:YES];
}
```

This message is sent to the delegate when the user has finished with the interface and is ready to dismiss it. As you've seen, your delegate object is responsible for dismissing the controller when the operation completes. You do this using the `dismissModalViewControllerAnimated:` method.

Also notice that, before you dismiss the interface, you let the user know the status of his or her request.

The result argument `MFMailComposeResult;` lets you know what happened, as you can see from the code. You use that in the `switch` statement to determine the message to place in the alert.

```
switch (result)                                                    {
    case MFMailComposeResultCancelled:
      resultMessage= @"Has been canceled";
      break;
    case MFMailComposeResultSaved:
      resultMessage= @"Has been saved";
      break;
    case MFMailComposeResultSent:
      resultMessage = @"Has been sent";
      break;
    case MFMailComposeResultFailed:
      resultMessage = @"Has failed";
      break;
    default:
      resultMessage = @"Was not sent";
      break;
  }
```

If the user taps Send, the e-mail should be queued in the user's Mail program by the time this method is called. If an error occurred while queuing the e-mail message, the error parameter contains an error object indicating the type of failure that occurred. I'll leave that as an exercise for you.

Finally, you dismiss the controller.

When you put in a real e-mail address and tap send, Figure 2-5 shows what you see.

Figure 2-5:
The
message
was sent
successfully.

More

This whole Road Card thing is something you can have a lot of fun with. You could, as you did in the earlier part of this book, also add your own photos.

Last, but not least, I want to show you a little more about core location, so gear yourself up for one final chapter. Because you're probably tired of hearing me say this by now, core location is one of the features of the iPhone that you really should consider being able to take advantage of (as you have, to some extent, with all the maps) in your app. The next (and final) chapter points you in that direction. I also take the opportunity to show you how to use the accelerometer.

Chapter 3: Are We There Yet?

In This Chapter

- ✔ **Using the Location Manager**
- ✔ **Seeing how the accelerometer really works**
- ✔ **Incorporating device movement in RoadTrip**

One summer, when I was about 8 or 9 and my brother was about 4 or 5, my father and mother decided to drive to Florida for a family vacation. We were living in Northern New Jersey at the time, and my parents packed up the car with their stuff, some toys and books for us, and off we went. (What were they thinking?) This was my very first road trip.

We had gone, oh a good 5 or 6 miles, when my brother piped up from his side of the back seat "Are we there yet?"

"No, Jay" my father replied, "we have quite a way to go."

Well, we actually got another few miles before my brother asked again "Are we there yet?"

"No," my father (still) patiently replied (although I could tell his patience was beginning to wear thin), "we have a really long way to go. A really long way to go. You are going to be in the car for a long time — a couple of days. So we aren't even close to being there yet."

Well, another few miles went by, and sure enough, from my brother's corner of the back seat came "are we there yet?"

My father at this point could see the writing on the wall and said to my brother, "No we are not! And if you ask me that one more time . . . "(Fill in the blank according to your imagination.)

Well, this kept my brother quiet for a while — a very short while. At the point he couldn't stand it anymore, out from his corner of the back seat came the immortal words "how old will I be when we get there?"

By this point in the book, it wouldn't surprise me if you could give my four-year-old brother a run for his money — over 700 pages and still counting and we're not there *yet?*

So, in this chapter, I show you how to add the last (I promise) feature to the RoadTrip app — one that lets the user know how far he is from his destination.

To do that, you need to find out a bit more about Core Location, and you also explore how to use the accelerometer because, for me at least, the right interface for this kind of question is to have the user shake his or her iPhone.

Curious how the finalized feature will look? Take a look at Figure 3-1, which shows what appears onscreen when you shake the phone. Oh, and this too, needs to be tested on your iPhone.

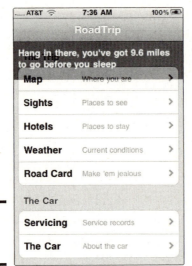

Figure 3-1:
Are we
there yet?

Adding Core Location

Core Location is an iPhone framework that enables you to determine the current location (as in where you are latitude- and longitude-wise), or heading (as in compass) of the device.

To get Core Location working for you, you start by adding Core Location to your project. To do that, you need to add the Core Location framework.

At this point, you're pretty used to adding a new framework. To refresh your memory refer to Book V, Chapter 5:

1. **Click the disclosure triangle next to Targets in the Groups & Files list and then right-click RoadTrip.**

WARNING!

Be sure to do this using the Targets folder, or Step 3 won't work!

2. **From the submenu that appears, select Add and then select Existing Frameworks.**

3. **Select `CoreLocation.framework` in the window that appears and then click Add.**

4. **Drag the newly created `CoreLocation.framework` — it's there in the Groups & Files list — into the Frameworks folder.**

This time — surprise, surprise — you won't be adding any more controllers. You'll be using what you have; not only that, you'll be working solely with the `RootViewController`.

You'll start by adding the bolded code in Listing 3-1 to `RootViewController.h`.

Listing 3-1: Updating RootViewController.h

```
@class Trip;
#import <CoreLocation/CoreLocation.h>


@interface RootViewController : UITableViewController
                                <CLLocationManagerDelegate> {

  NSArray        *sectionsArray;
  NSMutableArray *menuList;
  Trip           *trip;
  CLLocationManager       *locationManager;
  CLLocation              *currentLocation;
  CLLocation              *targetLocation;
}
@property (nonatomic retain) CLLocation *currentLocation;
- (int) menuOffsetForRowAtIndexPath:
                          (NSIndexPath *)indexPath;
- (void) displayOfflineAlert:(NSString*) selection;

@end
```

You also need to add the appropriate `@synthesize` statement to `RootViewController.m`.

```
@synthesize currentLocation;
```

Notice that you adopt the `CLLocationManagerDelegate` protocol. You've also added instance variables so that you can save the present location, specify the target location, and maintain the reference to the instance of the location manager you're about to create.

Notice that you make `currentLocation` a property. That's because, as you will see, it will be created and sent to you (as a delegate) from the location manager. That means I'll want to retain it and then release it when a new value comes along. So rather than doing all that myself, I make it a property — assigning a new `CLLocation` to that property will send a release to the `CLLocation` object there and a retain to the new one.

The `CLLocationManager` class provides a way for your application to get location and heading events. (You'll need a 3GS with a compass for the latter.)

To get the events, you create an instance of the class and set some parameters: namely the delegate (the one who gets sent the events), what you consider a significant change in location, and how accurate the location needs to be.

Start by doing all that in the `viewDidLoad` method in `RootViewController.m`. Add the bolded code in Listing 3-2.

Listing 3-2:   Setting Up the Location Manager

```
- (void)viewDidLoad {

  [super viewDidLoad];

  locationManager = [[CLLocationManager alloc] init];
  [locationManager setDesiredAccuracy:kCLLocationAccuracyB
    est];
  locationManager.distanceFilter = 10;
  [locationManager setDelegate:self];
  [locationManager startUpdatingLocation];
  targetLocation = [[CLLocation alloc]  initWithLatitude:
          (double)37.3317  longitude:(double)-122.0307];
  ...
}
```

The bolded stuff starts by creating an instance of the location manager:

```
locationManager = [[CLLocationManager alloc] init];
```

Then you set the desired accuracy:

```
[locationManager setDesiredAccuracy:kCLLocationAccuracyBest];
```

You should assign a value to this property that is appropriate for your application's needs. You can use a number of values, all of them pretty self-explanatory:

✦ kCLLocationAccuracyBest (This is the most "expensive" option in terms of time and power.)

✦ kCLLocationAccuracyNearestTenMeters

✦ kCLLocationAccuracyHundredMeters

✦ kCLLocationAccuracyKilometer

✦ kCLLocationAccuracyThreeKilometers (This option is probably good enough if you just want to know what city you're in.)

You should know that if you specify kCLLocationAccuracyBest, the initial event is delivered as quickly as possible and may not have the accuracy you want. The location manager will keep at it, though, and will deliver additional events with the accuracy you specified as the data become available.

Next you set the distance filter:

```
locationManager.distanceFilter = 10;
```

This is the minimum distance (in meters) that a device must move laterally before you get an event that notifies you that the location has changed.

Next you set the delegate:

```
[locationManager setDelegate:self];
```

As you might expect by now, that's how you'll get the location information.

Then you go and tell the location manger to get to work:

```
[locationManager startUpdatingLocation];
```

The location manager, as I said, tries to return an initial location as quickly as possible. After that, you may get more events if the distance (as specified by the distanceFilter property) changes or a more accurate location value is determined.

The user, of course, can deny an application's access to the location service data. When a user starts the app, as you see in Figure 3-2, RoadTrip asks for permission to use the current location. If the user denies the request, the CLLocationManager object reports an appropriate error to its delegate during future requests.

Finally, I hard-code the target location. That's a fancy way of saying "the place I am going to" — the one that the app will be computing the distance to.

```
targetLocation = [[CLLocation alloc]  initWithLatitude:
        (double)37.3317  longitude:(double)-122.0307];
```

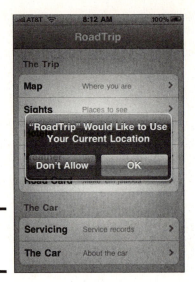

Figure 3-2:
May I
please?

Normally you'd create a view that would allow the user to decide that location for him- or herself, but in this case — because you've already gone through a similar exercise in getting user input in Chapter 1 of this minibook — I leave that part up to you.

No, those coordinates aren't for Florida — there's no need for me to return to former glories. No, that location is for Apple headquarters in Cupertino, California.

Now, although you might want to go to places like the Grand Canyon, Austin, New York, and even Graceland, there's some chance that you might get the urge to drive up to Apple headquarters and try to get a glimpse of something, anything. So I'm using those coordinates. If that road trip doesn't appeal to you, put in what you'd like, or better yet create the view that allows the user to decide.

As I said, as usual, all the action is in the delegate. There are two delegate methods you care about here. The first is `locationManager:didFailWith Error:`.

Add the code in Listing 3-3 to `RootViewController.m`.

Listing 3-3:   locationManager:didFailWithError:

```
- (void)locationManager:(CLLocationManager *)manager
               didFailWithError:(NSError *)error {

   NSLog(@"Location manager failed");
}
```

The battery life impact

Core location comes with a price and some limitations. For example, it takes a lot of power — a *lot* of power. And the more accurate the request, the more power is used. Because battery life is a constant concern for iPhone users (and thus developers), you need to balance your needs and power use.

Like many features of the iPhone, users can disable location support in the Settings application. In addition, in your app, you should turn off the location manager when you don't need it. You should match every `startUpdating Location` message with a corresponding `stopUpdatingLocation` one.

In case of an error, the `locationManager:didFailWithError:` message is sent. Although implementation of this method is optional, you should do it to create the best possible user experience.

You want to pay attention to these two situations:

+ **If the location manager can't get a location right away,** it will keep trying, but you'll get a `kCLErrorLocationUnknown` error. You might want to let the user know that this is the case if she tries to do something that requires location information.

+ **If the user denies your request to the use of the location service,** this method reports a `kCLErrorDenied` error. Upon receiving such an error, you should stop the location service.

In both cases, you need to implement this capability on your own.

The second delegate method is `locationManager:didUpdateToLocation: fromLocation:`.

Enter the code in Listing 3-4 to add this method to `RootViewController.m`.

**Book VII
Chapter 3**

Are We There Yet?

Listing 3-4:   locationManager:didUpdateToLocation:fromLocation:

```
- (void)locationManager:(CLLocationManager *)manager
   didUpdateToLocation:(CLLocation *)newLocation
         fromLocation:(CLLocation *)oldLocation {

  currentLocation = newLocation;
}
```

This message is sent to the delegate as the user moves away from the old location by the amount you specified in the `distanceFilter` earlier (or as more accurate information becomes available).

As the delegate method is called, you simply update the current location.

Now that you have the current location, you'll need to do something with it. To enable a user to request how far it is to where they are going, you could add a new choice on the main screen, just as you did with the Road Card in Chapter 1 of this minibook.

But instead I want to show you how to respond to the user shaking the iPhone (out of frustration perhaps) to see how far she is from her destination.

I can just imagine my brother doing this on our trip to Florida.

Taking the Accelerometer for a Spin

Guess what? The built-in accelerometer works pretty much the same way as the location manager — through delegation. But using it is a little different because there's only a single instance of the accelerometer, which means that only one delegate can be set for the accelerometer at a time.

The `UIAccelerometer` class lets you register to receive acceleration-related data from the hardware along the primary axes in three-dimensional space. (See Figure 3-3.)

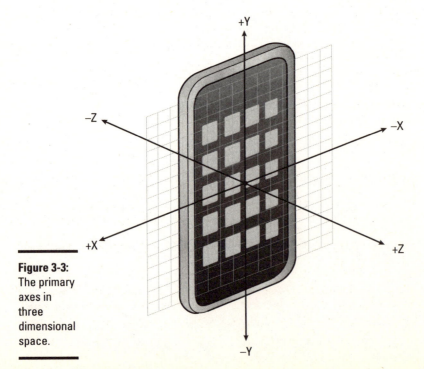

Figure 3-3: The primary axes in three dimensional space.

You can use this data to detect both the current orientation of the device (relative to the ground) and any instantaneous changes to that orientation like a shake.

To get a shake to work for you in the context of the Are We There Yet? feature, add the following instance variables and method declarations to `RootViewController.h` — the bolded stuff in Listing 3-5.

Listing 3-5:   Enhance RootViewController.h

```
#import <CoreLocation/CoreLocation.h>
@class Trip;

@interface RootViewController : UITableViewController
    CLLocationManagerDelegate, UIAccelerometerDelegate>  {

    NSArray          *sectionsArray;
    NSMutableArray *menuList;
    Trip            *trip;
    CLLocationManager       *locationManager;
    CLLocation              *currentLocation;
    CLLocation              *targetLocation;
    UIAccelerationValue      xAcceleration;
    UIAccelerationValue      yAcceleration;
    UIAccelerationValue      zAcceleration;
    BOOL                     distanceDisplayed;
    UIView                  *thereYet;
    UILabel                 *resultsDisplay;
}
@property (nonatomic retain) CLLocation *currentLocation;
- (int) menuOffsetForRowAtIndexPath:(NSIndexPath *)indexPath;
- (void) displayOfflineAlert:(NSString*) selection;
- (void) respondToShake;
- (void) hideResponse;

@end
```

Start by making `RootViewController` a `UIAccelerometerDelegate`.

```
@interface RootViewController : UITableViewController
    <CLLocationManagerDelegate, UIAccelerometerDelegate>  {
```

Then you add the instance variables you'll use in the two methods, whose declarations you have also added.

Then, access an instance of the `UIAccelerometer` class and set its parameters as I have using the bolded code in Listing 3-6. You can add this right after the core location code you just added to `viewDidLoad`.

Listing 3-6:   Accessing the Accelerometer

```objc
- (void)viewDidLoad {

  [super viewDidLoad];

  locationManager = [[CLLocationManager alloc] init];
  [locationManager setDesiredAccuracy:kCLLocationAccuracyB
    est];
  locationManager.distanceFilter = 10;

  [locationManager setDelegate:self];
  [locationManager startUpdatingLocation];
   targetLocation = [[CLLocation alloc]
      initWithLatitude:(double)37.3317
      longitude:(double)-122.0307 ];


  xAcceleration = 0.0;
  yAcceleration = 0.0;
  zAcceleration = 0.0;

  [[UIAccelerometer sharedAccelerometer]
        setUpdateInterval:(1.0 / kAccelerometerFrequency)];
   [[UIAccelerometer sharedAccelerometer]
                                        setDelegate:self];

...
}
```

First you initialize a few instance variables that you'll use next.

Notice you do not create an accelerometer object. Instead, you use the class method, as shown here:

```objc
[UIAccelerometer sharedAccelerometer]
```

You also specify the interval at which you want to receive events and set the update interval.

```objc
setUpdateInterval:(1.0 / kAccelerometerFrequency)];
```

These events are delivered to your application whether or not there has been any movement and, as you will see, it's up to you to figure out what's really happening with the device.

kAccelerometerFrequency specifies how often you want to receive updates. You need to add kAccelerometerFrequency to Constants.h.

```objc
#define kAccelerometerFrequency 25
```

This value will result in your application receiving updates every 40 milliseconds (1/25).

When specifying the update interval for acceleration events, think about how often you really need to get acceleration events. Frequency values in the 10–20 range are good enough if all you're really using the Accelerometer for is to determine the orientation of the device. For an application like RoadTrip, 25 is adequate; 30–60 is typically used for games and applications that use the accelerometers for real-time user input. Finally, 70–100 works if you need to detect high-frequency motion. The maximum frequency for accelerometer updates is based on the available hardware.

Finally, you assign the delegate.

```
[[UIAccelerometer sharedAccelerometer] setDelegate:self];
```

After you assign your delegate, you start getting updates at the frequency you specified, even if the acceleration data didn't actually change. But it's still your job, in your delegate method, to decide what's really going on with the device.

Notice I said events are delivered to your application whether or not there's been any movement. The accelerometer, at least based on the name, may not work exactly like you think it does. (That was definitely the case for me.) That's because, even if the device doesn't move, the device is still "accelerating" to the center of the Earth (if that's the planet you're on) due to the pull of gravity. That means, when my iPhone is resting flat on my desk (which keeps it from falling), the accelerometer is still passing me events that report the z axis is accelerating at approximately 1g or so, with the other axes reporting less (but still measurable) acceleration.

In fact, these are the values the accelerometer reports as my iPhone lies flat on my desk watching me work:

```
2009-12-14 08:51:38.032 RoadTrip[541:207]
                        Acceleration values at rest:
 x = -0.018112, y = -0.018112, z = -1.086731
```

The values are negative because the pull is downward.

Although this may seem like a charming interlude, knowing this will become important when I show how to actually use the data.

As one more step along the way of actually using the data, add the code in Listing 3-7 to `RootViewController.m`.

Listing 3-7: The Accelerometer Delegate Method

```
- (void) accelerometer:(UIAccelerometer*)accelerometer
    didAccelerate:(UIAcceleration*)acceleration {

  xAcceleration = (acceleration.x*kFilteringFactor) +
    (xAcceleration*(1.0-kFilteringFactor));
  yAcceleration = (acceleration.y*kFilteringFactor) +
    (yAcceleration*(1.0-kFilteringFactor));
  zAcceleration = (acceleration.z*kFilteringFactor) +
    (zAcceleration*(1.0-kFilteringFactor));
  UIAccelerationValue xFiltered =
                      acceleration.x - xAcceleration;
  UIAccelerationValue yFiltered =
                      acceleration.y - yAcceleration;
  UIAccelerationValue zFiltered =
                      acceleration.z - zAcceleration;

UIAccelerationValue intensity = sqrt
      (xFiltered * xFiltered +
       yFiltered * yFiltered +
       zFiltered * zFiltered);
  if(intensity >= kAccelerationThreshold)
    [self respondToShake];
}
```

The data you receive when your app is sent the `accelerometer:did Accelerate:` message is a `UIAcceleration` object.

The `UIAcceleration` class stores the data associated with an acceleration event. It contains the current acceleration readings along the three axes of the device (`x`, `y`, and `z` properties). Acceleration values for each axis are reported directly by the hardware as G-force values. Therefore, a value of 1.0 represents a load of about +1g along a given axis while a value of –1.0 represents –1g. And while you won't use it here, the object also has a `timestamp` property.

To figure what's really going on, you need to understand that, depending on the device orientation, some part of the reading for an axis will be simply the pull of gravity. For example, as you saw, if you lay the iPhone flat on your desk, the z value will be close to 1, and the other values will be less.

That means that if you're using the accelerometer data to detect movement, you need to first filter out the portion of the acceleration data that's caused by gravity from the portion that's caused by motion of the device. Now, if you read some of the documentation, or posts on the Internet, you'll read stuff about *low pass* and *high pass filters*. My advice to you is ignore all that stuff — your task is actually a lot simpler than that.

Start by creating a base line for the values you'll receive from each axis. For example, for the x axis, the following is done in the computation:

```
xAcceleration = (acceleration.x*kFilteringFactor) +
    (xAcceleration*(1.0 - kFilteringFactor))
```

You need to add `kFilteringFactor` to `Constants.h`.

```
#define kFilteringFactor .1
```

This generates a value that uses 10 percent (`kFilteringFactor` is equal to `.1`) of the unfiltered acceleration data — the `acceleration.x` value in the latest event which you just received in the message argument — and 90 percent of the previously filtered value `xAcceleration`, which you save after each time you receive the message.

Because acceleration data comes in regularly, this computation serves to create a base line that's pretty stable and doesn't change much in response to sudden but short-lived changes in motion. (This takes into account gravity.)

As long as nothing new is happening, the values in the acceleration events fed to you by the accelerometer will stay about the same. But when something happens, you get a sudden spike in value in one or more of the axes.

To isolate that value, you simply subtract the base line (`xAcceleration`) from the new value, which gives you the filtered value, or change.

This is the result of the computation:

```
UIAccelerationValue xFiltered =
                    acceleration.x - xAcceleration;
```

At the end of the day, what you end up with is a value that tells you the degree of acceleration along each axis above and beyond the base level.

Finally, based on *that,* you need to decide whether the change in acceleration is really significant — where "significant" here depends on what you're trying to measure.

Intensity of acceleration is measured by taking the square root of the sum of the squares of acceleration data for each of the three axes of motion.

This is computed in

```
UIAccelerationValue intensity = sqrt (xFiltered * xFiltered +
    yFiltered * yFiltered + zFiltered * zFiltered);
```

The threshold value I'm having you use is 2.0. You can play around with that value and adjust it to your liking. You'll need to add kAcceleration-Threshold to Constants.h.

```
#define kAccelerationThreshold 2.0
```

Finally, if the value is over the threshold, you send the respondToShake message.

```
if(intensity >= kAccelerationThreshold)
                                      [self respondToShake];
```

Because the UIAcceleration object has a timestamp property, you can also respond based on whether or not a certain about of time has passed (maybe or maybe not a good idea for my brother).

I'll leave it to you to think about it.

Doing something with the shake

After you've decided that the user really has meaningfully shaken the device, you need to display the miles to go in the respondToShake method.

To do that, you need to add the code in Listing 3-8 to RootViewController.m.

Listing 3-8:   **Responding to the Shake**

```
- (void) respondToShake {

  if ( distanceDisplayed) return;
  distanceDisplayed = YES;
  if (!thereYet) {
    thereYet = [[UIView alloc] initWithFrame:
                             CGRectMake (0,-100,320,70)];
    thereYet.backgroundColor = [UIColor blackColor];
    thereYet.opaque = NO;
    thereYet.alpha = .5;
    resultsDisplay = [[UILabel alloc] initWithFrame:
                             CGRectMake (10,-110,300,40)];
    resultsDisplay.numberOfLines = 2;
    resultsDisplay.font = [UIFont boldSystemFontOfSize:17];
    resultsDisplay.textColor = [UIColor whiteColor];
    resultsDisplay.opaque = YES;
    resultsDisplay.alpha = 1.0;
    resultsDisplay.backgroundColor = [UIColor clearColor];
    [self.tableView  addSubview: thereYet];
    [self.tableView  addSubview:resultsDisplay];
  }
```

```
CLLocationDistance  theDistance = [currentLocation
  getDistanceFrom: targetLocation];
resultsDisplay.text =  [[NSString alloc ]initWithFormat:
  @"Hang in there, you've got %.1f miles to go before you
  sleep", theDistance/1609.344];

[UIView beginAnimations:nil context:NULL];
  [UIView setAnimationDelay:1.0];
  [UIView setAnimationDuration:2.0];
  thereYet.frame =  CGRectMake (0,0,320,70);
  resultsDisplay.frame = CGRectMake (10,10,300,40);

  [UIView commitAnimations];
  [self performSelector:@selector(hideResponse)
   withObject:self afterDelay:5];

}
```

If you already have the distance view displayed, you don't want to redisplay it, so you check to see whether it's out there. If it is, you simply return; if not, you set the `distanceDisplayed` state variable to `YES` and continue:

```
if (distanceDisplayed) return;
distanceDisplayed = YES;
```

Next, if you haven't done so already, you create the view you want displayed.

```
if (!thereYet) {
```

Because I want to drop it down from the top, I set its origin off the screen. I do the same thing with the label that will hold the distance information.

```
thereYet = [[UIView alloc] initWithFrame:
                              CGRectMake(0,-100,320,100)];
  resultsDisplay = [[UILabel alloc] initWithFrame:
                              CGRectMake (10,-110,100,40)];
```

Then you set the background color of the view to black, but since you want it transparent you set `opaque` to `NO`, and `alpha` to `.5`. Alpha is a measure of how transparent something is — with `0` being clear and `1` being opaque. The label, on the other hand, you want opaque and the text bold so it is readable. I *do* want the background to be clear, however, so I set it to that and add both views to the Table View superview.

```
thereYet = [[UIView alloc] initWithFrame: CGRectMake (0,-
  100,320,70)];
  thereYet.backgroundColor = [UIColor blackColor];
  thereYet.opaque = NO;
  thereYet.alpha = .5;
```

```
resultsDisplay = [[UILabel alloc] initWithFrame:
CGRectMake (10,-110,300,40)];
 resultsDisplay.numberOfLines = 2;
 resultsDisplay.font = [UIFont boldSystemFontOfSize:17];
 resultsDisplay.textColor = [UIColor whiteColor];
 resultsDisplay.opaque = YES;
 resultsDisplay.alpha = 1.0;
 resultsDisplay.backgroundColor = [UIColor clearColor];
 [self.tableView  addSubview: thereYet];
 [self.tableView  addSubview:resultsDisplay];
```

Then I send the `getDistanceFrom:to` message to the `currentLocation`. This is a `CLLocation` method and returns the distance (in meters) from the receiver's coordinate to the coordinate of the specified location. I really do love this method — I only wish I had discovered it before I did the math myself.

TIP

In fact, a general philosophy to follow is to really explore what's available before you try to do anything hard yourself. That's especially true if what you want to do seems to be something that other developers need as well.

Then you set the label text accordingly:

```
CLLocationDistance   theDistance =
        [currentLocation getDistanceFrom: targetLocation];
 resultsDisplay.text =  [[NSString alloc ]initWithFormat: @"
   %.1f miles from you", theDistance/1609.344];
```

Finally, you set up and execute the animation that causes the view to drop down from the top.

I explained this in Book III, so I just show you the code here:

```
 [UIView beginAnimations:nil context:NULL];
[UIView setAnimationDelay:1.0];
[UIView setAnimationDuration:2.0];
thereYet.frame =  CGRectMake (0,0,320,70);
resultsDisplay.frame = CGRectMake (10,10,300,40);
[UIView commitAnimations];
```

An interesting thing is going on here — I have you start the animation with a delay. It's not that I'm a sadist, but this seemed like a good place to show you how to do that.

Finally, you set a time limit for how long you're going to display the view. You do that by sending a message (with a delay) to hide the views.

```
[self performSelector:@selector(hideResponse) withObject:self
   afterDelay:5];
```

performSelector:withObject:afterDelay: sends the message after a delay. Like the selectors you used in Book VI, the method should not have a significant return value and should take a single argument of type id, or no arguments. afterDelay is the minimum time before which the message is sent and, by the way, specifying a delay of 0 doesn't necessarily cause the selector to be performed immediately. The selector is still queued and then performed as soon as possible.

To slide the view back up, add the code in Listing 3-9 to RootViewController.m.

Listing 3-9: Reversing the Process

```
- (void) hideResponse {

    [UIView beginAnimations:nil context:nil];
    [UIView setAnimationDelay:1.0];
    [UIView setAnimationDuration:2.0];
    thereYet.frame =  CGRectMake (0,-100,320,70);
    resultsDisplay.frame = CGRectMake (10,-110,300,40);
    [UIView commitAnimations];
    distanceDisplayed = NO;
}
```

All you do here is reverse the process — bye-bye view.

Of course, you realize you have the accelerometer and core location busy delivering you events. If this were production code, you might want to consider turning them both off when they aren't needed, and then on again when they are.

On the other hand, especially with the location manager, there will be a lag between the time you start it and when it figures out where you are. It will be up to you to smooth out the user experience.

Yes, You're Finally There

Go out and do something interesting!

Index

Internet

Blogging For Dummies,
2nd Edition
978-0-470-23017-6

eBay For Dummies,
6th Edition
978-0-470-49741-8

Facebook For Dummies
978-0-470-26273-3

Google Blogger
For Dummies
978-0-470-40742-4

Web Marketing
For Dummies,
2nd Edition
978-0-470-37181-7

WordPress For Dummies,
2nd Edition
978-0-470-40296-2

Language & Foreign Language

French For Dummies
978-0-7645-5193-2

Italian Phrases
For Dummies
978-0-7645-7203-6

Spanish For Dummies
978-0-7645-5194-9

Spanish For Dummies,
Audio Set
978-0-470-09585-0

Macintosh

Mac OS X Snow Leopard
For Dummies
978-0-470-43543-4

Math & Science

Algebra I For Dummies,
2nd Edition
978-0-470-55964-2

Biology For Dummies
978-0-7645-5326-4

Calculus For Dummies
978-0-7645-2498-1

Chemistry For Dummies
978-0-7645-5430-8

Microsoft Office

Excel 2007 For Dummies
978-0-470-03737-9

Office 2007 All-in-One
Desk Reference
For Dummies
978-0-471-78279-7

Music

Guitar For Dummies,
2nd Edition
978-0-7645-9904-0

iPod & iTunes
For Dummies,
6th Edition
978-0-470-39062-7

Piano Exercises
For Dummies
978-0-470-38765-8

Parenting & Education

Parenting For Dummies,
2nd Edition
978-0-7645-5418-6

Type 1 Diabetes
For Dummies
978-0-470-17811-9

Pets

Cats For Dummies,
2nd Edition
978-0-7645-5275-5

Dog Training For Dummies,
2nd Edition
978-0-7645-8418-3

Puppies For Dummies,
2nd Edition
978-0-470-03717-1

Religion & Inspiration

The Bible For Dummies
978-0-7645-5296-0

Catholicism For Dummies
978-0-7645-5391-2

Women in the Bible
For Dummies
978-0-7645-8475-6

Self-Help & Relationship

Anger Management
For Dummies
978-0-470-03715-7

Overcoming Anxiety
For Dummies
978-0-7645-5447-6

Sports

Baseball For Dummies,
3rd Edition
978-0-7645-7537-2

Basketball For Dummies,
2nd Edition
978-0-7645-5248-9

Golf For Dummies,
3rd Edition
978-0-471-76871-5

Web Development

Web Design All-in-One
For Dummies
978-0-470-41796-6

Windows Vista

Windows Vista
For Dummies
978-0-471-75421-3

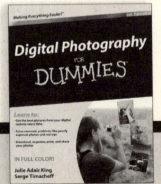

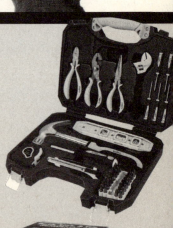

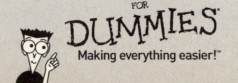

Notes

Notes